A Concise Dictionary of First Names

A Concise Dictionary of First Names

THIRD EDITION

PATRICK HANKS
and FLAVIA HODGES

OXFORD
UNIVERSITY PRESS

OXFORD

UNIVERSITY PRESS

Great Clarendon Street, Oxford OX2 6DP

Oxford University Press is a department of the University of Oxford.
It furthers the University's objective of excellence in research, scholarship,
and education by publishing worldwide in

Oxford New York

Auckland Bangkok Buenos Aires Cape Town Chennai
Dar es Salaam Delhi Hong Kong Istanbul Karachi Kolkata
Kuala Lumpur Madrid Melbourne Mexico City Mumbai Nairobi
São Paulo Shanghai Taipei Tokyo Toronto

Oxford is a registered trade mark of Oxford University Press
in the UK and in certain other countries

Published in the United States
by Oxford University Press Inc., New York

British Library Cataloguing in Publication Data

Data available

Library of Congress Cataloging in Publication Data

Data available

ISBN 0-19-866259-9

5 7 9 10 8 6 4

Typeset in Trump Mediaeval
by Alliance Phototypesetters, Pondicherry, India
Printed in Great Britain by
Clays Ltd, Bungay, Suffolk

Contents

Preface to the Third Edition

About 120 new names have been added to this third edition, many of them derived from statistical studies of names in frequent current use recorded in electronic reference sources such as telephone directories. We are grateful to Dr Kenneth Tucker of Manotick, Ottawa, Canada, for his work on the database of American personal names, which has been used in the selection of additional entries.

In addition, the appendices have been revised and expanded, and two new supplements have been added: one on Chinese names compiled by Dr Malcolm Watson, and one on Japanese names by Dr Fred Brady.

Every entry in the main text has been reviewed, and a number of improvements have been made. In particular, this revised edition takes into account work on the history of given names in the north of England by Dr George Redmonds, research based on early statistical evidence and an investigation into the influence of the godparents in name-giving. We are grateful to Dr Redmonds for his contribution to this new edition.

A significant number of names once thought to have fallen out of use around 1300 survived locally for centuries, often because of a single family, or within one family's kith and kin. Some of the most striking examples are *Alvery*, *Harold*, *Herbert*, and *Conan*. The girls' names *Olive*, *Cassandra*, and *Mildred* have a similar history, although their family connections are less obvious. Evidence is now available to show that *Amelia* and *Christabel* were in use long before the date they were once thought to have been coined.

It is clear also that many names, e.g. *Ingram*, *Otis*, *Ellis*, and *Warren*, were not necessarily transferred surnames, but survived as given names from the Norman period into the 17th century or even later. Also, there are some names which apparently go back to the Normans or even the Anglo-Saxons, such as *Oswald*, *Leonard*, and *Wilfrid*, which may actually have been revived as early as the 15th century, given new life thanks to popular church dedications.

Dr Redmonds' regional survey has also demonstrated how important it is not to categorize names too narrowly, for the widespread use in northern England of *Ninian*, *Ewan*, *Gavin*, and *Grizel*, all of them traditionally associated with Scotland, suggests that naming patterns did not respect political boundaries but reflected cross-border customs and communications. Equally, the role played by the Low Countries in the spread of the names *Herman*, *Jasper*, *Cornelius*, and *Adrian* may well have been underestimated in the past.

PWH, FMH
September 2000

Introduction

A person's given name is something very personal, but it is also a badge of cultural identity. It says something about the cultural group that he or she belongs to; in some cases even, something about the particular family which he or she comes from. Until recent years, cultural identity was closely associated with religious affiliation, but in the 20th century naming practices have become increasingly secular. Still, names such as *Aloysius*, *Ferdinand*, *Xavier*, and *Carmel* are strongly associated with the Roman Catholic Church, while *Calvin* and *Luther* are clearly Protestant. *Zipporah* is still clearly Jewish, *Siobhan* Irish, and *Rhodri* Welsh. Against this, other factors are at work. In the first place, there has been cultural seepage: *Rebecca*, *Deborah*, and *Judith* can no longer be regarded as even primarily Jewish names, nor *Alistair* and *Kenneth* as Scottish, nor *Shaun* and *Sheila* as Irish.

The process of augmenting the small stock of traditional names with new coinages has accelerated greatly since about 1960. Short forms, pet forms, nick-names, surnames, even placenames have been pressed into service. The film industry and the pop-music business have appeared, alongside hagiographies of Christian saints, as sources of names for children. This dictionary records all the traditional names of the English-speaking world—all those, in fact, which are well established or (at the very least) well on the way to becoming established.

In some cultures, for example Arabic, names are just special uses of ordinary words. In such cultures, a name can be chosen on account of its meaning, as well as on grounds of its historical or religious associations or euphony. This is not the case with English; the 'meaning' of the vast majority of English names is to be sought in languages other than modern English, often ancient languages no longer spoken and only studied by specialists. Because of this, among English speakers there can rarely be any question of choosing a name for a child on the basis of its meaning. A name is chosen either on ornamental grounds— 'because it sounds nice'—or in honour of some close relative.

There are definite vogues for given names; they come into fashion and go out again for reasons that can sometimes be recorded: for example, a name may experience a sudden increase in use after it has been used for a character in a popular book, film, or television series. More seriously (but less noticeably), a particular set of names may be associated with a religious sect or cult, which will affect the popularity of those names. In other cases, the popularity of certain names seems to ebb and flow regularly with the generations.

Biblical Names

The most widespread of all given names are those taken from names of characters in the Bible. These are borne by Jews and Christians alike all over the world: names such as *Adam* and *Eve; Benjamin, Joseph,* and *Jacob; David; Sarah, Deborah, Rebecca,* and *Ruth.* Some of these names are rare now. Among non-Jews, names such as *Reuben* and *Seth, Zillah,* and *Beulah* are associated particularly with Nonconformist sects of the 17th century and the Christian fundamentalists of the 19th. A few, especially female names such as *Abigail,* have survived or been revived in modern use, but others have once again dropped out of fashion. In general, Old Testament names are found among both Jews and Protestants, but are uncommon among Roman Catholics.

New Testament names are, of course, shared by Christians of all sects and persuasions. The most important names in the New Testament are those of the four evangelists, *Matthew, Mark, Luke,* and *John,* and the apostles, principally *Peter, James, Andrew, Thomas, Philip, Bartholomew, John, Matthew,* and *Simon. John* is trebly important: the name was borne by an apostle (the son of Zebedee), by the author of the fourth gospel, and by the forerunner of Christ, John the Baptist. The frequency of forms of *John* among early Christians ensured that it would be borne by some early saints, which further reinforced its popularity.

With the exception of Mary, the mother of Jesus, very few women play a major role in the gospels. This helps to explain why the set of conventional female Christian names is even smaller than that for males, and why *Mary* has been so enormously popular. The name *Mary* is borne by others in the New Testament—principally Mary Magdalene, a woman who 'had been healed of evil spirits and infirmities' (Luke 8), and who was identified in Christian tradition with the repentant sinner of Luke. Other important New Testament female names from the gospels are *Martha* and *Elizabeth.*

Saints' Names

A large number of names owe their importance to the fact that they were borne by early, famous, or canonized Christians, ranging from learned Church fathers (*Basil, Ambrose, Jerome, Augustine,* and *Gregory*) through innumerable martyrs (*Agatha, Agnes, Laurence, Sebastian*), mystics, ascetics, and visionaries (*Anthony, Simeon, Francis, Teresa*), founders of religious orders (*Benedict, Bernard, Dominic*), to the simple 19th-century French peasant girl (*Bernadette*), whose visions of the Virgin Mary led to the foundation of a healing shrine at Lourdes. What they all have in common is that at some time during the past two millennia a cult grew up around them. In some cases (*Christopher, George*) the legends of the cult have obscured any basis of historical fact that may once have existed.

Christian sainthood is almost the only channel by which old Roman names have been transmitted to present-day use as given names. In spite of the pervasive use of Latin during most of the Christian era, Roman names that were not borne by early saints have almost entirely dropped out of use. This is because the early Church made repeated attempts to suppress classical literature and to obliterate all memory of pagan classical history. In the Christian era, therefore, there has been almost no tradition of naming children in honour of the great figures of classical antiquity. Where a Roman name such as *Antonius*, *Claudius*, *Julius*, or *Marcus* has yielded modern derivatives, we may look with confidence for an early saint or martyr somewhere along the road.

Royal and Aristocratic Names

A name that is borne by a member of a royal family, especially a successful and much-admired monarch, invariably rapidly increases its currency among his or her subjects. Thus, the popularity of the New Testament name *Elizabeth* was greatly enhanced by the fact that it was borne by the enlightened and skilful queen of England who reigned 1558–1603. It has remained popular, partly because of that association, ever since. Its popularity increased again in the 20th century, after it became apparent in 1936 that the Princess Elizabeth would succeed to the throne.

Elizabeth, like *James* and *John*, is a biblical name, firmly rooted in the Christian tradition. However, the majority of English royal and aristocratic names, for example *William*, *Henry*, *Richard*, and *Robert*, not to mention *Charles*, have their origin in a distant, pre-Christian Germanic past. Most of these names have been transmitted to us through Norman French. With the exception of *Edward*, most names of Old English derivation, even royal names, went out of use after the Norman Conquest. *Edward* survived, mainly because King Edward the Confessor was venerated by Normans and Saxons alike. Other names derived from Old English, such as *Alfred* and *Edwin*, *Audrey* and *Elfreda*, went out of use, but were revived in the Victorian period. Many of them now once again seem somewhat old-fashioned.

A few modern English first names reflect Old Norse personal names established in England before the Norman Conquest, such as *Harold*. However, the vast majority of royal and aristocratic English names are of Norman origin.

The Normans themselves spoke French, having abandoned their Norse language and pagan culture when they established themselves in northern France in the 10th century. Even more surprisingly, they abandoned most of their traditional Norse names. Within a few decades, they adopted the Christian religion, the French language, and French names. It so happens that although the French language is mainly derived from Latin, many of its names are derived from Germanic. These are survivals of the extremely ancient names that were used in the Germanic languages once spoken in France, in particular Frankish, the vernacular of the court of Charlemagne. Thus, *William* is from *wil* meaning 'will' plus *helm* meaning 'helmet'. Germanic names normally consist of two vocabulary elements, reflecting qualities that were prized in prehistoric Germanic society: they have meanings such as 'war', 'strife', 'battle'; 'protection', 'rule', 'counsel'; 'raven', 'wolf', and 'bear'.

Many, but not all of the most common male names of Germanic origin that are used in Britain today owe their importance to having been royal names: they were borne by one or more kings of England (or, as in the case of *Robert*, Scotland). But some, such as *Gerald*, *Hugh*, and *Roger*, were borne by members of the aristocracy rather than royalty.

Rather fewer Germanic female names, such as *Alice*, *Emma*, and *Matilda*, have survived into modern English. Generally, they are no less warlike in the meaning of their components than their male counterparts. The origins of these Germanic names owe nothing to Christianity, although in some cases, for example *Bernard*, their survival does: many such names were borne by people who became Christian saints, after whom children were named in succeeding generations.

The Celtic Tradition

After Christianity and Germanic royalty, the greatest influence on the stock of names in the English-speaking world has been the Celtic tradition. Many names are now used throughout the world by people who may be only vaguely aware, if at all, of their derivation from Irish or Scottish Gaelic or from Welsh. Examples are *Brian*, *Bridget*, *Donald*, *Duncan*, *Ian*, *Kenneth*, *Kevin*, *Neil*, and *Sheila* from Irish and Scottish Gaelic, and *Gareth*, *Gladys*, *Gwendolen*, and *Trevor* from Welsh. Other Celtic names exist in an Anglicized form, but are still used mainly by people conscious of their Celtic ancestry, for example *Brendan*, *Connor*, *Cormac*, *Declan*, and *Rory* from Gaelic and *Branwen*, *Dylan*, *Dilys*, *Gwyneth*, *Olwen*, and *Wyn* from Welsh.

In Ireland, Gaelic names such as *Cathal*, *Caitlín*, *and Gráinne* have been widely revived since independence in their original form, unscrambling the garblings due to Anglicization. Increasingly now, the same is true of Scottish Gaelic names. Because of the differences in phonology and spelling, Gaelic names can look very different from English names, even when they are quite closely equivalent. For example, the Irish Gaelic form of *George* is *Seoirse*. Irish *Séamas* and Scottish *Seumas* are the Gaelic equivalents of English *James*.

A striking feature of the Gaelic naming tradition is the antiquity of its independence and folklore. *Meadhbh* (*Maeve*) recalls a 1st-century queen of Connacht, leader of the cattle raid of Cooley. The name *Deirdre* recalls the tragic story of a beautiful girl betrothed against her will to Conchobhar (*Connor*) and her elopement with her beloved Naoise, who is eventually caught and killed by Conchobhar.

In Scotland, where the Gaels settled from the 5th century onwards, particular names are sometimes associated with particular clans. So, for example, the name *Somerled* (*Somhairle* in Scottish Gaelic, Anglicized as *Sorley*) is traditionally associated with Clan Macdonald, the kindred of the Lords of the Isles. There was considerable interplay between Gaelic names and Norse names. Gaelic *Somhairle, Uisdean,* and *Raghnall (Ronald)* are from Norse, while Norse names such as *Njall* and *Brigit* are from Gaelic.

Welsh names are of similar antiquity, though there are fewer traditional names surviving in Welsh than in Gaelic. Many of the ancient names that are now in use or being revived are found in the *Mabinogi,* a medieval collection of traditional legends. These include *Branwen, Lleu, Geraint, Heilyn, Iorwerth, Rhiannon, Urien, Ynyr,* and *Pryderi.* Another group of traditional Welsh names commemorates heroes and princes who led resistance variously to the Romans (*Caradoc*), the Saxons (*Cadwaladr*), and the English (*Llewelyn, Glyndŵr*). Indeed, the most important Welsh source of names is the cycle of legends associated with the court of King Arthur, legendary defender of the Britons against the Saxon invaders. Names derived from this tradition include *Elaine, Enid, Gavin (Gawain), Guinevere, Lancelot, Merlin (Myrddin), Percival,* and *Tristan (Tristram).* The present century is witnessing not only a revival of traditional Welsh names but also an influx of new coinages. These are mainly from vocabulary elements (e.g. *Eirwen* 'snow-pure', *Glenda* 'clean-good'), but also from placenames such as *Trefor.*

The influence of literature, film, and popular culture

Works of literature have also had an influence on name choices. The names of some of Shakespeare's heroines have been used as given names, for example *Rosalind, Olivia, Portia, Perdita, Imogen, Juliet,* and *Cordelia.* However, on the whole, these have been less influential than might have been expected. Other writers have influenced particular names. Thus, *Pamela* and *Clarissa* probably owe much if not all of their popularity to Richardson; *Amelia* to Fielding; *Nicol* to Scott; *Justine* to Durrell; *Leila* to Byron and Lord Lytton; *Christabel* to Coleridge; *Maud* and *Vivien* to Tennyson; and *Pippa* to Browning. In the 19th century, the male given name *Shirley* changed sex, becoming a conventional female name after publication of Charlotte Brontë's novel *Shirley* (1849).

In the 20th century, films have had a considerable influence on the choice of names. *Tracy,* for example, underwent a great increase in popularity as a female name from the late 1950s onwards, after release of the 1956 film *High Society,* in which Grace Kelly played the character of Tracy Lord.

Not only fictional characters but also the actors who portray them can have an influence on the popularity of a name. *Greer, Cary,* and *Spencer,* for example, have been chosen as names in honour of the film stars Greer Garson, Cary Grant, and Spencer Tracy, and the popular status of *Clark* was clearly influenced by Gable, *Trevor* by Howard, *Jean* by Harlow, and *Marilyn* by Monroe.

Another characteristically 20th-century influence is that of rock and pop music: the rise of *Elvis*, *Kylie*, and *Madonna* is clearly traceable, but we can only guess how many present-day Johns and Pauls owe their name to Lennon and McCartney.

Surnames as Given Names

Throughout the English-speaking world a large number of surnames are now used as given names. Only those that have acquired conventional status are recorded here. Surnames had been sporadically used as first names for several centuries, mainly among landed families. In the 19th century this phenomenon became more frequent. In most cases it originated because of a connection between families. A bride from a rich and powerful family would christen her first-born with her own maiden surname; the conjunction of the two names would be taken as symbolic of the union between the two families. Some given names that were derived originally from surnames have become fully established as freely used first names in their own right (e.g. *Clifford*, *Dudley*, *Stanley*). In Britain such names are almost always borne by males, apart from a few conventionalized exceptions (e.g. *Shirley*, *Beverley*, *Kimberley*).

Other Sources of Given Names

There are many other sources from which a personal name may be derived. Some of them can be quite ephemeral. Since the 19th century, various types of vocabulary word have come to be used as given names: in particular, words denoting precious stones (*Beryl*, *Ruby*) and flowers (*Daisy*, *Primrose*). Sometimes a vocabulary word denoting a desirable quality for the life ahead is bestowed on a baby, as in the case of the names *Joy*, *Happy*, and *Felix*.

Occasionally, a placename will be found in use as a given name. Several of the Western Isles and other parts of Scotland have been used in this way, notably *Isla(y)* and *Iona*.

Nicknames rarely become established as personal names, but pet forms such as *Peggy* and *Bill* and short forms such as *Max* and *Kim* can take on a life of their own. Some short forms or pet forms are more commonly used than the more formal version, as in the case of *Reg*.

In the 20th century, the number of names used regularly has continued to grow apace. The use of vocabulary words as first names for women has increased, and the two categories (gemstones and flowers) have been expanded to include other precious and desirable things (*Amber*, *Jade*, *Crystal*), plants (*Bryony*, *Fern*, *Poppy*), and birds (*Kestrel*, *Teale*). Names from other countries have been enthusiastically adopted, beginning in the early years of the century with Russian names introduced via France (*Vera*, *Tanya*, *Natasha*). A couple of decades later, there was a vogue for names of Scandinavian origin (*Ingrid*, *Astrid*). Currently, certain fanciful inventions, combinations, and respellings are gaining ground, a phenomenon associated particularly with America.

Culture Variation

Black Names

In both America and Britain, the group of names typically borne by **Black** people differs noticeably from those of the White population. For example, it contains a much higher proportion of freely invented names such as *Floella*, *Laraine*, and *Latasha*. Characteristic Black names also include adopted European forms (*Antonio*, *Antoine*, *Anton*) and some surname forms that are much less common among the population as a whole (*Curtis*, *Leroy*, *Winston*).

The United States

The first European names to be established in **North America** were those brought by Puritan settlers to New England. Some of the more unusual Old Testament names remain in use, especially in rural areas, even though they are out of fashion elsewhere: for example *Jed* (*Jedidiah*), *Zeke* (*Ezekiel*), *Hephzibah*, and *Zillah*.

A characteristically American naming practice, now well established elsewhere is the adoption of a surname as a first name, not because of any family connection, but out of admiration for some famous contemporary or historical figure (e.g. *Bradford*, *Wesley*, *Winthrop*). A number of American presidents have been influential in this way, in particular *Washington* and *Lincoln*. Many first names derived from surnames are in America borne by women. A few are conventionalized in this use (*Brooke*, *Paige*), but many more are used equally for either sex, so that it is often not possible to determine the gender of a bearer from the name alone.

Another process of name creation well established in America is that of free invention. Formerly regarded as typical of the southern states, this has become more widespread. Most of the coined names are borne by women. Strategies include fanciful respelling (*Kathryn* (now the predominant form in America), *Madalynne*, *Ilayne*); the recombining of syllables from other names (*Jolene*, *Lolicia*); and elaborations with productive feminine suffixes (*-elle*, *-ette*, *-ice*, *-inda*).

Pet forms are more often used as first names in their own right in America than Britain, so that a *Pam* is not necessarily to be addressed more formally as *Pamela* nor *Bobby* as *Robert*. In the same way some informal nicknames have come to be bestowed as official first names (*Bud*, *Ginger*, *Rusty*). Terms such as *Duke*, *Earl*, *Prince*, are also regularly used as first names.

Canada

First names in **Canada** are, for the most part, shared partly with those of Britain and partly with the United States. So, for example, in Canada more surnames are used as given names than in Britain, but fewer than in the United States. The Celtic tradition is also particularly important in Canada. There are a few names that are characteristically Canadian: for example *Lorne*, *Jaime*, and *Meaghan*.

Australia and New Zealand
Australia and New Zealand share the basic stock of English first names, but also have individual characteristics of their own. Irish influence is strong in Australia, so that, for example, use of *Kelly*, *Kerry*, and *Colleen* as given names is of Australian origin. *Barry*, *Bruce*, *Charlene*, *Darlene*, *Nolene*, and *Kylie* are examples of names which have particular associations with Australia.

A few New Zealand names of Maori origin have passed into more general use, and two in particular, *Ngaio* and *Nyree*, have achieved some currency in Britain as well as New Zealand.

Acknowledgements

Many of the entries here are derived from *A Dictionary of First Names*, a much larger work published in 1990 by Oxford University Press. The present book has benefited from the comments and suggestions made by various scholars for that work, in particular Professor Tomás de Bhaldraithe of the Royal Irish Academy, Mr Ronald Black of the Department of Celtic at Edinburgh University, Professor Gwynedd Pierce, formerly of the University of Wales College of Cardiff, and Dr Joseph A. Reif of Bar-Ilan University, Israel. Mr Black checked the Gaelic forms in this book. Katherine Barber of Oxford University Press, Canada, checked the North American entries. To all these scholars we express our appreciation. For any errors that remain, we alone are responsible. We would also like to thank Sara Hawker, Ramesh Krishnamurthy, Nadia Naqib, Eva Sawers, and Della Thompson for their help in preparing the appendices for the second edition.

PWH, FMH

Symbols used in the text

♂ male name
♀ female name
◊ see also (you will find more information at the name marked)

AARON ABBIE ABE ABEL ABIGAIL ABILENE
ABNER ABRAHAM ABRAM ACACIA ACE A
DA ADAH ADAM ADDISON ADELA ADEL
AIDA ADELE ADÉLIE ADELINE ADIE ADLAI
ADRIA ADRIANNE ADRIENNE AED AEN
EAS AENGUS AERONWEN AFRICA AGATH

Aaron ♂

Biblical name, borne by the brother of
Moses, who was appointed by God to be
Moses' spokesman and became the first
High Priest of the Israelites (Exodus
4:14–16, 7:1–2). It is of uncertain origin
and meaning: most probably, like
◊**Moses**, of Egyptian rather than Hebrew
origin. The traditional derivation from
Hebrew *har-on* 'mountain of strength' is
no more than a folk etymology. The
name has been in regular use from time
immemorial as a Jewish name, and was
taken up by the Nonconformists as a
Christian name in the 17th century.

Abbie ♀

Pet form of ◊**Abigail**.
Variants: **Abbey**, **Abby**.

Abe ♂

Short form of ◊**Abraham**.

Abel ♂

Biblical name, borne by the younger son
of Adam and Eve, who was murdered for
reasons of jealousy by his brother Cain
(Genesis 4:1–8). The Hebrew form is
Hevel, ostensibly representing the
vocabulary word *hevel* 'breath',
'vapour', and so taken to imply vanity or
worthlessness. Abel is considered by the
Christian Church to have been a pre-
Christian martyr (see Matthew 23:35),
and is invoked as a saint in the litany for
the dying. Nevertheless, his name has
not been much used either before or after
its brief vogue among the Puritans.

Abigail ♀

Biblical name (meaning 'father of exaltation' in Hebrew), borne by one of King
David's wives, who had earlier been
married to Nabal (1 Samuel 25:3), and by

the mother of Absalom's captain Amasa
(2 Samuel 1:25). The name first came
into use in Britain in the 16th century,
under Puritan influence. It was a common name in literature for a lady's maid,
for example in Beaumont and Fletcher's
play *The Scornful Lady* (1616). The
biblical Abigail refers to herself as 'thy
servant' in addressing King David.
Pet forms: **Abbie**, **Abbey**, **Abby**.

Abilene ♀

U.S.: a comparatively rare name. In the
New Testament, Abilene is a region of
the Holy Land (Luke 3:1), whose name is
of uncertain origin, but may be derived
from a Hebrew word meaning 'grass'.
Several places in America have been
named from this reference, notably a
city in Kansas, which was the boyhood
home of President Dwight D. Eisenhower. Its adoption as a girl's given name
was encouraged partly by its resemblance to ◊**Abbie** and partly by the fact
that *-lene* is a productive suffix of girls'
names (as in ◊**Charlene**).

Abner ♂

Biblical name (meaning 'father of light'
in Hebrew), of a relative of King Saul,
who was in command of Saul's army
(1 Samuel 14:50; 26:5). It is not common
as a given name in England, but has
enjoyed a steady, modest popularity in
America, where it was brought in at the
time of the earliest Puritan settlements.

Abraham ♂

Biblical name, borne by the first of the
Jewish patriarchs, with whom God
made a covenant that his descendants
should possess the land of Canaan. The
Hebrew form is *Avraham*, and is of

uncertain derivation. In Genesis 17:5 it is explained as 'father of a multitude (of nations)' (Hebrew *av hamon (goyim)*). It has always been a popular Jewish given name, and was also chosen by Christians, especially by Puritans and other fundamentalists from the 16th century onwards. Various early saints of the Eastern Roman Empire also bore this name. Its currency in the United States was greatly enhanced by the fame of President Abraham Lincoln (1809–65). *Short form*: **Abe**.

Abram ♂

Biblical name, a variant of ◊**Abraham**. It was probably originally a distinct name (meaning 'high father' in Hebrew). According to Genesis 17:5, the patriarch's name was changed by divine command from *Abram* to *Abraham*. From the Middle Ages, however, if not before, it was taken to be a contracted version.

Acacia ♀

From the name of the flower, which is related to the mimosa. The plant was named by botanists in the 16th century with the Latin form *acacia* of Greek *akakia*, which had earlier been used in translations of the Bible to refer to the tree from whose wood the Arc of the Covenant was made. This word is of uncertain origin, probably a derivative of Greek *akē* 'point', 'thorn', but it has also been analysed as being from the Greek negative prefix *a-* + *kakos* 'bad', as if the flowers had the power to ward off evil influence. The given name is fairly frequent in Australia, where the acacia (usually known there as the *wattle*) is a common flower and popular national symbol. It is possible that in some cases ◊**Keisha** may be regarded as a shortened form of this name.

Ace ♂

Originally a nickname, now fairly commonly used as a given name, especially in the United States. It represents the colloquial term *ace*, referring to someone who is particularly good at some-thing. This meaning derives, via the notion of being 'number one', from the word *ace* denoting a single item (as for example the lowest (and highest) value in a suit of playing cards). This probably derives from Latin *as*, the name of a coin of low value.

Ada ♀

Of uncertain origin, not in general use before the late 18th century. It may be a Latinate variant of the biblical name ◊**Adah**. However, it has also been explained as a pet form of ◊**Adele** and ◊**Adelaide**; Germanic female names of which the first element is *adal* 'noble'. This was borne by a 7th-century abbess of Saint-Julien-des-Prés at Le Mans.

Adah ♀

Biblical name (meaning 'adornment' in Hebrew), borne by the wives of Lamech (Genesis 4:19) and of Esau (Genesis 36:2). See also ◊**Ada**.

Adam ♂

Biblical name of the first man (Genesis 2–3). It probably derives from Hebrew *adama* 'earth'; it is a common feature of creation legends that God or a god fashioned the first human beings from earth or clay and breathed life into them. The name was subsequently borne by a 7th-century Irish abbot of Fermo in Italy. It has been very popular in the English-speaking world since the 1960s. In Hebrew it is a generic term for 'man' (Genesis 5:2) and has never been considered a personal name, although *Hava* 'Eve' has enjoyed popularity as a Jewish name.

Addison ♂

Transferred use of the surname, which originated as a patronymic derived from *Addie* or *Adie*, a medieval (and occasional modern) pet form of ◊**Adam**. This is now a relatively popular given name in the United States.

Adela ♀

Latinate form of ◊**Adele**, especially popular in the late 19th century.

Adelaide ♀

Of Germanic origin (via French **Adélaïde**), from *adal* 'noble' + *heid* 'kind', 'sort'. It was borne in the 10th century by the wife of the Holy Roman Emperor Otto the Great. She became regent after his death and was revered as a saint. The given name increased in popularity in England during the 19th century, when it was borne by the wife of King William IV; she was the daughter of the ruler of the German duchy of Saxe-Meiningen. The Australian city of Adelaide was named in her honour.

Adele ♀

From French **Adèle**, an ancient name popular in medieval Europe because of the fame of a 7th-century saint, a daughter of the Frankish king Dagobert II. It is of Germanic origin, from *adal* 'noble' (a short form of a two-element name such as *Adelheid*; see ◊**Adelaide**). It was the name of William the Conqueror's youngest daughter (*c.*1062–1137), who became the wife of Stephen of Blois. However, it died out in England in the later Middle Ages. It was revived in the 19th century, being the name of a character in Johann Strauss's opera *Die Fledermaus*. Its popularity was further reinforced in the 1930s as the name of a character in the novels of Dornford Yates.

Adélie ♀

French elaboration of ◊**Adele**, now sometimes also used in the English-speaking world, with or without the accent. Adélie Land in Antarctica was named in 1840 by the French explorer Jules Dumont D'urville in honour of his wife; the Adélie penguin (*Pygoscelis adeliae*) is so named because it breeds on that coastline.

Adeline ♀

French diminutive of *Adèle* (see ◊**Adele**), used occasionally in England from the early 16th century onwards. The Latinate form **Adelina** is also found occasionally as an English name.

Adie ♂

Pet form of ◊**Adrian** or ◊**Adam**.

Adlai ♂

Biblical name, borne by a very minor character, the father of one of King David's herdsmen (1 Chronicles 27:29). It represents an Aramaic contracted form of the Hebrew name *Adaliah* 'God is just', and is one of a large crop of minor biblical names taken up by the Puritans in the 17th century. Many of them, including *Adlai*, were brought to New England by the early settlers and have survived in North America. *Adlai* is particularly associated with the American statesman and Democratic presidential candidate Adlai Stevenson (1900–65), in whose family the name was traditional: it was also borne by his grandfather (1835–1914), who was vice-president in 1893–97.

Adrian ♂

Usual English form of the Latin name *Hadriānus* 'man from Hadria'. Hadria was a town in northern Italy, which gave its name to the Adriatic Sea; it is of unknown derivation. The initial *H-* has always been very volatile. The name was borne by the Roman emperor Publius Aelius Hadrianus, during whose reign (AD 117–138) Hadrian's Wall was built across northern England. The name was later taken by several early popes, including the only English pope, Nicholas Breakspeare (Adrian IV). It was in early use among immigrants from the Low Countries, and is found in some English regions from the mid-16th century. It became particularly popular in the English-speaking world during the late 20th century.

Adrianne ♀

Modern feminine form of ◊**Adrian**, less common than ◊**Adrienne**.
Variants: **Adrianna**, **Adriana**.

Adrienne ♀

French feminine form of ◊**Adrian**, now also used in the English-speaking world.

Aed ♂

A traditional spelling of the Irish name ◊**Aodh**.

Aeneas ♂

From Latin, name of the hero of Virgil's *Aeneid*, a Trojan prince who sailed from Troy after its destruction by the Greeks and, after many adventures, settled in Latium (Italy), becoming the ancestor of the Roman people. In Scotland this name was sometimes used as a classicized form of ◊**Angus**.

Aengus ♂

Usual Irish form of ◊**Angus**.

Aeronwen ♀

Welsh: usually said to be composed of the elements *aeron* 'berries' + *(g)wen* 'white', 'fair', 'blessed', 'holy'. However, the first element may derive from the name of a shadowy Celtic goddess of battle and slaughter, known in a Latinized form as *Agrona*. The name of this goddess is probably also the second element of the placename *Aberaeron* 'rivermouth of Agrona'.

Africa ♀

Name adopted in the 20th century among American Blacks, conscious of their ancestral heritage in the continent of Africa.

Agatha ♀

Latinized version of the Greek name *Agathē*, from the feminine form of the adjective *agathos* 'good', 'honourable'. This was the name of a Christian saint popular in the Middle Ages; she was a Sicilian martyr of the 3rd century who suffered the fate of having her breasts cut off. According to the traditional iconography, she is depicted holding them on a platter. In some versions they look more like loaves, leading to the custom of blessing bread on her feast day (5 February). The name was revived in the 19th century, but has faded again since.
Pet form: **Aggie**.

Aggie ♀

Pet form of ◊**Agnes** and ◊**Agatha**.

Agnes ♀

Latinized version of the Greek name *Hagnē*, from the feminine form of the adjective *hagnos* 'pure', 'holy'. This was the name of a young Roman virgin martyred in the persecutions instigated by the Roman emperor Diocletian in AD 303. She became a very popular saint in the Middle Ages. Her name was early associated with Latin *agnus* 'lamb', leading to the consistent dropping of the initial *H*- and to her representation in art accompanied by a lamb. The colloquial form *Annes* led to some confusion with *Ann(e)* in earlier centuries. The name was revived in the 19th century, and has been especially popular in Scotland.
Pet form: **Aggie**.

Aidan ♂

Anglicized form of the ancient Gaelic name **Áedán**, a pet form of *Áed* (see ◊**Aodh**). The name was borne by various early Irish saints, notably a bishop of Ferns (d. 626), who was noted for his kindness and generosity, and the St Aidan (d. 651) who brought Christianity to the English settlers of 7th-century Northumbria, founding the monastery on the island of Lindisfarne.

Aileen ♀

Scottish variant spelling of ◊**Eileen**.

Ailie ♀

Scottish pet form of ◊**Aileen** or an Anglicized spelling of ◊**Eilidh**.

Ailish ♀

Irish Gaelic form of ◊**Alice**.

Ailsa ♀

Modern Scottish name derived from *Ailsa Craig*, name of a high rocky islet in the Clyde estuary off the Ayrshire coast, near the traditional estates of the Scottish Kennedys. This is actually from Old Norse *Alfsigesey* 'island of Alfsigr', a personal name derived from *alf* 'elf', 'supernatural being' + *sigi* 'victory'. However, use as a given name has been influenced by *Ealasaid*, the Gaelic form of ◊**Elizabeth**. Ailsa Craig is known in

Gaelic as *Allasa*, but popularly as *Creag Ealasaid*.

Aimée ♀

French: originally a vernacular nickname meaning 'beloved', from the past participle of French *aimer* 'to love' (Latin *amāre*; compare ◊**Amy**). It has been in use in French since the Middle Ages, although it has never been very common. It is now also sometimes used, with or without the accent, as a given name in the English-speaking world.
Variant: **Aimi**.

Ainsley ♂, occasionally ♀

Transferred use of the Scottish surname also spelled *Ainslie*, which is borne by a powerful family long established in the Scottish borders. It was originally a local name, taken north from either *Annesley* in Nottinghamshire or *Ansley* in Warwickshire. The former gets its name from the genitive case of the Old English name *Ān* (a short form of any of various compounds containing the word *an* 'one', 'only') + Old English *leah* 'wood', 'clearing'. The latter is from Old English *ānsetl* 'hermitage' + *lēah*.
Variant: **Ainslee**.

Aisling ♀

Irish Gaelic, pronounced '*ash*-ling': from the vocabulary word *aisling* 'dream', 'vision'. This was not in use as a personal name during the Middle Ages, but was adopted as part of the Irish revival in the 20th century.
Variants: **Aislinn**; **Ashling** (Anglicized form).

Al ♂

Short form of any of the names beginning with this syllable.

Alan ♂

Of Celtic origin and uncertain derivation (possibly a diminutive of a word meaning 'rock'). It was introduced into England by Breton followers of William the Conqueror, most notably Alan, Earl of Brittany, who was rewarded for his services with vast estates in the newly conquered kingdom. In Britain the vari-ants **Allan** and **Allen** are considerably less frequent, and generally represent transferred uses of surname forms, whereas in America all three forms of the name are approximately equally common. See also ◊**Alun**.
Short form: **Al**.

Alana ♀

Latinate feminine form of ◊**Alan**, a comparatively recent coinage.
Variants: **Alanna**, ◊**Alannah**.

Alanda ♀

Recent coinage, a feminine form of ◊**Alan** influenced by ◊**Amanda**.

Alanna ♀

Variant of ◊**Alana**.

Alannah ♀

Variant spelling of ◊**Alanna**, possibly influenced by names of Hebrew origin such as ◊**Hannah** and ◊**Susannah** and by the Anglo-Irish term of endearment *alannah* (Gaelic *a leanbh* 'O child').

Alasdair ♂

Scottish Gaelic form of ◊**Alexander**, often Anglicized as ◊**Alistair**.

Alastair ♂

Scottish variant of ◊**Alistair**; see ◊**Alasdair**.
Variant: **Alaster**.

Alban ♂

From the Latin name *Albānus*, which is of uncertain origin. It may be an ethnic name from one of the numerous places in the Roman Empire called *Alba* 'white', or it may represent a Latinized form of a British name derived from the Celtic word *alp* 'rock', 'crag'. Christian tradition has it that St Alban was the first martyr in Roman Britain, who was executed, probably in 209, at Verulamium (now known as St Albans). A Benedictine abbey was founded there and dedicated to the saint by King Offa. Derivation from *Albion*, a poetic name for Britain, is also a possibility.

Albert ♂

From an Old French name, *Albert*, of Germanic (Frankish) origin, derived

from *adal* 'noble' + *berht* 'bright', 'famous'. This was adopted by the Normans and introduced by them to England, displacing the Old English form *Æþelbeorht*. The name is popular in a variety of forms in Western Europe, and has been traditional in a number of European princely families. It was out of favour in England for centuries, however, and the revival of its popularity in the 19th century was largely in honour of Queen Victoria's consort, Prince Albert of Saxe-Coburg-Gotha.
Short forms: **Al**, **Bert**.
Pet form: **Bertie**.

Alberta ♀
Feminine form of ◊**Albert**.

Albion ♂
From the poetical name for Britain. This is often supposed to derive from Latin *albus* 'white' and to refer to the whiteness of cliffs spied from the sea, but in fact it more probably comes from the Celtic element *alp* 'rock', 'crag'. The given name has occasionally been chosen by parents in all parts of the English-speaking world who wish to commemorate their association with or affection for the British Isles.

Aldous ♂
Pronounced 'old-us'; of uncertain origin; probably a medieval short form of any of various Norman names, such as *Aldebrand*, *Aldemund*, and *Alderan*, containing the Germanic word *ald* 'old'. It was relatively common in East Anglia during the Middle Ages, but is now rare, known mainly as the given name of the novelist Aldous Huxley (1894–1963).

Alec ♂
English and Scottish short form of ◊**Alexander**, now somewhat less popular in England than ◊**Alex**.

Aled ♂
Welsh: modern coinage meaning 'child'.

Aledwen ♀
Welsh: modern coinage, feminine form of ◊**Aled** with the addition of *-wen*, a

common ending of female names in Welsh; see for example ◊**Arianwen**.

Alethea ♀
A learned coinage, not found before the 16th century. It represents the Greek word *alētheia* 'truth', and seems to have arisen as a result of the Puritan enthusiasm for using terms for abstract virtues as girls' names. See also ◊**Althea**.

Alex ♂, ♀
Short form of ◊**Alexander**, ◊**Alexandra**, and ◊**Alexis**; also commonly used as a given name in its own right.
Variant: **Alix** (♀).

Alexa ♀
Short form of ◊**Alexandra** or variant of ◊**Alexis** as a girl's name.

Alexander ♂
From the Latin form of the Greek name *Alexandros*, from *alexein* 'to defend' + *anēr* 'man', 'warrior' (genitive *andros*). The compound was probably coined originally as a title of the goddess Hera, consort of Zeus. It was also borne as a byname by the Trojan prince Paris. The name became extremely popular in the post-classical period, and was borne by several characters in the New Testament and some early Christian saints. Its use as a common given name throughout Europe, however, derives largely from the fame of Alexander the Great, King of Macedon (356–323 BC), around whom a large body of popular legend grew up in late antiquity, much of which came to be embodied in the medieval 'Alexander romances'.
Short forms: **Al**, **Alex**, **Alec**.
Pet form (chiefly Scottish): **Sandy**.

Alexandra ♀
Latinate feminine form of ◊**Alexander**. It was very little used in the English-speaking world before the 20th century, when it was brought in from Scandinavia and Eastern Europe. It owes its sudden rise in popularity in Britain at the end of the 19th century to Queen Alexandra, Danish wife of Edward VII.

Short forms: **Alex**, **Alexa**, **Sandra**.
Pet form: **Sandy** *(chiefly Scottish)*.

Alexandria ♀

Variant of ◊**Alexandra**, influenced by the name of the city in Egypt, founded by Alexander the Great in 322 BC and named in his honour. This is now a relatively common given name in the United States, where it is also found as a place name, for example in Louisiana, Minnesota, and Virginia; the last was named in 1748 after a family of local landowners whose surname was *Alexander*.

Alexia ♀

Variant of ◊**Alexis** as a girl's name.

Alexis ♀, ♂

Variant (or female derivative) of *Alexius*, the Latin spelling of Greek *Alexios*, a short form of various compound personal names derived from *alexein* 'to defend'. St Alexius was a 5th-century saint of Edessa, venerated particularly in the Orthodox Church as a 'man of God'. *Alexis* was originally a boy's name, but is now more commonly given to girls.

Alfred ♂

From an Old English name derived from *ælf* 'elf', 'supernatural being' + *ræd* 'counsel'. It was a relatively common name before the Norman Conquest of Britain, being borne most notably by Alfred the Great (849–899), King of Wessex. After the Conquest it was adopted by the Normans in a variety of more or less radically altered forms (see ◊**Avery**). In some regions the forms *Alvery* and *Avery* never fell entirely out of favour and became locally popular in the 16th century. It provides a rare example (◊**Edward** is another) of a distinctively Old English name that has spread widely on the Continent. It was strongly revived in the 19th century, along with other names of pre-Conquest historical figures, but has faded since.
Short forms: **Alf**, **Fred**.
Pet form: **Alfie**.

Alger ♂

From an Old English name derived from *ælf* 'elf', 'supernatural being' + *gār* 'spear'; it is possible that this form may also have absorbed other names with the first elements *æþel* 'noble', *ēald* 'old', and *ēalh* 'temple'. The name was not common either before or after the Norman Conquest, but was revived in the 19th century, along with other Germanic names. It is relatively common in the United States.

Algernon ♂

Of Norman French origin, originally a byname meaning 'with a moustache' (from Old French *grenon, gernon* 'moustache'). The Normans were as a rule clean-shaven, and this formed a suitable distinguishing nickname when it was applied to William de Percy, a companion of William the Conqueror. In the 15th century it was revived, with a sense of family tradition, as a byname or second given name for his descendant Henry Percy (1478–1527), and thereafter regularly used in that family. It was subsequently adopted into other families connected by marriage with the Percys, and eventually became common property.
Pet forms: **Algy**, **Algie**.

Alice ♀

Originally a variant of ◊**Adelaide**, representing an Old French spelling of a reduced form of Germanic *Adalheidis*. *Alice* and *Adelaide* were already regarded as distinct names in English during the medieval period. *Alice* enjoyed a surge of popularity in the 19th century. It was the name of the child heroine of Lewis Carroll's *Alice's Adventures in Wonderland* (1865) and *Through the Looking Glass* (1872), who was based on his child friend Alice Liddell, daughter of the Dean of Christ Church, Oxford.
Variant: **Alys**.

Alicia ♀

Modern Latinate form of ◊**Alice**.
Variants: **Alissa**, **Alyssa**.

Alick ♂
Variant of ◊Alec.

Alina ♀
Of uncertain origin. It is probably a
variant of ◊Aline, but could also be of
Arabic origin, from a word meaning
'noble' or 'illustrious'. In Scotland it
has been used as a feminine form of
◊Alistair.

Alinda ♀
In the English-speaking world this name
is of recent origin, apparently a blend of
◊Alina and ◊Linda. It is, however, also
used in German-speaking countries,
where it is derived from the ancient
Germanic personal name *Adelinde*,
from *adal* 'noble' + *lind* 'soft', 'tender'.

Aline ♀
In the Middle Ages this represented a
contracted form of ◊Adeline. In modern
use it is either a revival of this or a
respelling of ◊Aileen. In Scotland and
Ireland it has sometimes been chosen as
representing an Anglicized spelling of
the Gaelic vocabulary word *àlainn*
(Scottish), *álainn* (Irish), meaning
'lovely'.

Alison ♀
From a very common medieval name, a
Norman French diminutive of ◊Alice.
Despite its early popularity, it became
quite rare in England in the 16th century. However, it survived in Scotland,
with the result that until its revival in
England in the 20th century it had a
strongly Scottish flavour.
Variants: **Allison** (the usual North American spelling); **Alysoun** (a medieval English spelling, which has been revived in
the 20th century).
Pet forms: **Allie**, **Ally**.

Alissa ♀
Variant of ◊Alicia.

Alistair ♂
Scottish: altered spelling of **Alasdair**, the
Gaelic form of ◊Alexander. Alexander
has long been a popular name in Scotland, having been borne by three medieval kings of the country.

Variants: **Alisdair**, **Alastair**, **Alister**,
Al(l)aster.
Pet form: **Aly**.

Alix ♀
Variant of ◊Alex, used only as a feminine
name. Its formation has probably been
influenced by ◊Alice.

Alizabeth ♀
Altered spelling of ◊Elizabeth.

Allan ♂
Variant spelling of ◊Alan, used mainly in
Scotland and North America.

Allaster ♂
Scottish: variant spelling of ◊Alistair. It
is borne, for example, by a minstrel in Sir
Walter Scott's *Rob Roy* (1818), which
ensured its 19th-century popularity.

Allegra ♀
From the feminine form of the Italian
adjective *allegro* 'gay', 'jaunty' (familiar
in English as a musical tempo). It seems
to have been an original coinage when it
was given to Byron's illegitimate daughter (1817–22), but since then it has been
taken up by parents in many English-
speaking countries. It is not commonly
used as a given name in Italy.

Allen ♂
Variant spelling of ◊Alan, in Britain
generally found only as a surname, but
in North America equally common as a
given name.

Allie ♀
Pet form of ◊Alison.
Variant: ◊Ally.

Allison ♀
Variant spelling of ◊Alison.

Alma ♀
Relatively modern creation, of uncertain origin. It had a temporary vogue
following the Battle of Alma (1854),
which is named from the river in the
Crimea by which it took place; similarly
Trafalgar had occasionally been used as
a girl's name earlier in the 19th century.
Nevertheless, the historical event
seems only to have increased the

popularity of an existing, if rare, name. *Alma* is also the feminine form of the Latin adjective *almus* 'nourishing', 'kind' (compare the term *alma mater* 'fostering mother', denoting an educational establishment). The name was borne by Alma Bennett (1889–1958), American vamp of the silent screen. In Tennessee Williams's play *Summer and Smoke* (1948), a bearer of the name explains that it is 'Spanish for soul', but this seems to be no more than coincidental.

Aloha ♀
U.S.: modern name representing the Polynesian word meaning 'love' (familiar as a form of greeting and farewell in Hawaii and elsewhere in the South Pacific).

Aloysius ♂
Pronounced 'al-oo-*ish*-us'; of unknown origin, possibly a Latinized form of a Provençal version of ◊**Louis**. It was relatively common in Italy in the Middle Ages, and has subsequently enjoyed some popularity among Roman Catholics in honour of St Aloysius Gonzaga (1568–91), who was born in Lombardy.

Althea ♀
From Greek mythology. Although often considered to be a contracted form of ◊**Alethea**, it is actually a quite distinct name (Greek *Althaia*), of uncertain origin. It was borne in classical legend by the mother of Meleager, who was given a brand plucked from the fire at the instant of her son's birth, with the promise that his life would last as long as the brand did; some twenty years later she destroyed it in a fit of pique. The name was revived by the 17th-century poet Richard Lovelace, as a poetic pseudonym for his beloved.

Alton ♂
Mainly U.S.: transferred use of the English surname, which is from any of a number of places so called in England.

Alun ♂
Welsh: an ancient Welsh name, indir-

ectly related to ◊**Alan**, of which it is now generally taken to be the Welsh equivalent. It is borne in the *Mabinogi* by Alun of Dyfed, a character mentioned in passing several times. It is also a river-name and a regional name in Wales, sometimes spelled *Alyn*. *Alun* was adopted as a bardic name by John Blackwell (1797–1840) and became popular as a result of his fame.

Alva ♀
Anglicized form of the traditional Irish Gaelic name **Ailbhe**, which is derived from Old Irish *albho* 'white'. In medieval times this was a boy's name, but it has been revived mainly as a girl's name

Alvar ♂
As a medieval name this was from the Old English personal name *Ælfhere*, from *ælf* 'elf', 'supernatural being' + *here* 'army', 'warrior'. In modern use it may be a revival of this, a transferred use of the surname derived from it, or an Anglicized form of Spanish *Álvaro*, a Visigothic personal name derived from Germanic *al* 'all' + *war* 'guard'.

Alvin ♂
From an Old English personal name derived from *ælf* 'elf', 'supernatural being' + *wine* 'friend'. This was not especially common in Britain either before or after the Norman Conquest, but it is popular in the United States. The reasons for this are not entirely clear; association with ◊**Calvin** may be a factor. A more plausible (though less elevated) explanation is that this was the name given to the naughty chipmunk in a popular television cartoon series of the 1960s.
Variant: **Alwyn**.

Alys ♀
Variant spelling of ◊**Alice**.

Alyssa ♀
Variant spelling of ◊**Alissa**.

Amanda ♀
A 17th-century literary coinage from the Latin gerundive (feminine) *amanda* 'lovable', 'fit to be loved', from *amāre* 'to

love'. This is evidently modelled on ◊**Miranda**. The masculine form *Amandus*, borne by various saints from the 4th to the 7th century, seems not to have been the direct source of the feminine form. The girl's name has enjoyed considerable popularity in the mid-20th century.

Short form: **Manda**.
Pet form: ◊**Mandy**.

Amber ♀

From the vocabulary word for the gemstone *amber*, a word derived via Old French and Latin from Arabic *ambar*. This was first used as a given name at the end of the 19th century, but has become particularly popular in the past couple of decades. In part it owes its popularity to Kathleen Winsor's novel *Forever Amber* (1944).

Ambrose ♂

English form of the Late Latin name *Ambrosius*, from post-classical Greek *Ambrosios* 'immortal'. This was borne by various early saints, most notably a 4th-century bishop of Milan. The name has never been common in England, but has enjoyed considerably greater popularity in Roman Catholic Ireland, where the surname *Mac Ambrois* is Anglicized as *McCambridge*.

Amelia ♀

A blend of two medieval names: *Emilia* (which is of Latin origin: see ◊**Emily**) and the Latinized Germanic *Amalia* (a short form of various personal names containing the word *amal* 'work'). Henry Fielding is sometimes credited with having coined it for the heroine of his novel *Amelia* (1751), but forms such as *Meelia*, *Amaly* and *Aemelia* occur from the 17th century onwards.

Amos ♂

Biblical name, borne by a Hebrew prophet of the 8th century BC, whose sayings are collected in the book of the Bible that bears his name. This is of uncertain derivation, but may be connected with the Hebrew verb *amos* 'to carry'. In some traditions it is assigned the meaning 'borne by God'. The name is used among Christians as well as Jews, and was popular among the Puritans. In Britain it survived well into the 19th century, but is little used today.

Amy ♀

Anglicized form of Old French *Amee* 'beloved'. This originated in part as a vernacular nickname, in part as a form of Latin *Amāta*. The latter is ostensibly the feminine form of the past participle of *amāre* 'to love', but in fact it may have had a different, pre-Roman, origin; it was borne in classical mythology by the wife of King Latinus, whose daughter Lavinia married Aeneas and (according to the story in the *Aeneid*) became the mother of the Roman people.

Anastasia ♀

Russian: feminine form of the Greek male name *Anastasios* (a derivative of *anastasis* 'resurrection'). It has always been popular in Eastern Europe, in honour of a 4th-century saint who was martyred at Sirmium in Dalmatia. It was also used occasionally in England in the Middle Ages and as late as the 17th century. One of the daughters of the last tsar of Russia bore this name. She was murdered by the Bolsheviks in 1918, along with the rest of her family, but in 1920 a woman claiming to be the Romanov princess Anastasia came to public notice in Germany, and a film was subsequently based on this story (1956).

André ♂

French form of ◊**Andrew**.

Andrea ♀

Of disputed origin. It has been in use since the 17th century, although never common. It is now generally taken as a feminine equivalent of ◊**Andreas**, and this probably represents its actual origin. However, it was not in use in the Middle Ages, and the suggestion has also been made that it represents a coinage in English from the Greek vocabulary word *andreia* 'manliness', 'virility'.

Andreas ♂

The original New Testament Greek form of ◊**Andrew**, occasionally used in the English-speaking world as a learned variant.

Andrew ♂

English form of the Greek name *Andreas*, a short form of any of various compound names derived from *andr-* 'man', 'warrior'. In the New Testament this is the name of the first disciple to be called by Jesus. After the Resurrection, St Andrew preached in Asia Minor and Greece. He is traditionally believed to have been crucified at Patras in Achaia. He was one of the most popular saints of the Middle Ages and was adopted as the patron of Scotland, Russia, and Greece. The name has long been popular in Scotland; its popularity in England was further enhanced by its use as a British royal name for Prince Andrew (b. 1960), the Duke of York.
Short form: *Scottish* **Drew**.
Pet form: **Andy**.

Aneirin ♂

Welsh: of uncertain derivation, possibly from a word akin to Irish Gaelic *nár* 'noble', 'modest'. The original form of the name was *Neirin*; the initial *A-* was added in the 13th century. This was the name of the first known Welsh poet, who lived AD *c*.600. The 'Book of Aneirin' is a 13th-century manuscript which purports to preserve his work, including the *Gododdin*, a long work about the defeat of the Welsh by the Saxons.
Variant: **Aneurin** (a modern form).
Pet form: **Nye** (popularized as a result of the fame of the statesman Aneurin Bevan, 1897–1960).

Anéislis ♂

Traditional Irish Gaelic name, in use since the early Middle Ages, in origin a byname meaning 'careful', 'thoughtful'. It has been Anglicized as both ◊**Stanislas** and ◊**Standish**.

Angel ♀, formerly also ♂

Used occasionally in England as a boy's name from the 1400s, if not earlier, and perhaps best known as the name of Angel Clare, the chief male character in Thomas Hardy's novel *Tess of the D'Urbervilles* (1891). It is derived from the Church Latin name *Angelus*, from Greek *angelos*. This meant 'messenger' in classical Greek, but in New Testament Greek it had the specialized meaning 'messenger of God', i.e. an angel. It is now out of fashion as a boy's name in Britain, but is being increasingly bestowed as a girl's name, especially as an American Black name. It is also common as a Spanish male name. The influence of the vocabulary word *angel* is obvious, in its use as an affectionate term of address for a good (or pretty) little girl.

Angela ♀

From Church Latin, a feminine form of the boy's name *Angelus* (see ◊**Angel**). The older feminine form *Angelis* has been completely superseded by *Angela*, which increased greatly in popularity in Britain and America from the 18th century onwards.
Pet form: **Angie**.

Angelica ♀

From Church Latin, from the feminine form of the Latin adjective *angelicus* 'angelic', or simply a Latinate elaboration of ◊**Angela**.

Angelina ♀

Latinate elaboration of ◊**Angela**.

Angharad ♀

Welsh (pronounced 'ang-*kar*-ad'): composed of the Old Celtic intensive prefix *an-* + the root *cār* 'love' + the noun suffix *-ad*. This was the name of the mother of the 12th-century chronicler Giraldus Cambrensis ('Gerald the Welshman'). In the *Mabinogi*, Angharad Golden Hand at first rejects Peredur's suit, but later falls in love with him when he comes back as the unknown Mute Knight. The name has been strongly revived in Wales since the 1940s, and is well known in connection with the actress Angharad Rees (b. 1949).

Angie ♀
Pet form of ◊**Angela**.

Angus ♂
Scottish: Anglicized form of the Gaelic name **Aonghus** or **Aonghas** (pronounced '*een*-yis'), from Celtic words meaning 'one' and 'choice'. This is the name of an ancient Celtic god, and is first recorded as a personal name in Adomnan's 'Life of St Columba', where it occurs in the form *Oinogus(s)ius* as the name of a man for whom the saint prophesied a long life and a peaceful death. This is also almost certainly the name of the 8th-century Pictish king variously recorded as *Onnust* and *Hungus*.
Usual Irish form: *Aengus*.
Short form: ◊**Gus**.
Pet forms: *Angie* (Scottish, pronounced '*an*-ghee', representing Gaelic: *Angaidh*).

Anise ♀
Modern coinage, apparently from the name of the aniseed plant (Old French *anis*, from Latin and Greek). For other modern first names derived from spices, see ◊**Clove** and ◊**Juniper**. It is possible that it was influenced by the medieval first name *Annis*, a mainly Scottish vernacular form of ◊**Agnes**.

Anita ♀
Originally a Spanish pet form of *Ana*, the Spanish version of ◊**Anne**. It is now widely used in English-speaking countries with little awareness of its Spanish origin. In the 1950s it came to prominence as the name of the Swedish film actress Anita Ekberg (b. 1931).

Anitra ♀
Apparently a literary coinage by Henrik Ibsen, who used it as the name of an Eastern princess in *Peer Gynt* (1867). No Arabic original is known. It is now occasionally used as a given name, not only in Norway but also elsewhere in Scandinavia, Germany, and the English-speaking world.

Ann ♀
Variant spelling of ◊**Anne**. *Ann* was the more common of the two spellings in the 19th century, but is now losing ground to the form with final *-e*.
Pet form: **Annie**.

Anna ♀
Latinate variant of ◊**Anne**, in common use as a given name in most European languages. Among people with a classical education, it has from time to time been associated with Virgil's *Aeneid*, where it is borne by the sister of Dido, Queen of Carthage. This Phoenician name may ultimately be of Semitic origin, and thus ultimately related to the biblical *Anne*. However, the connection, if it exists, is indirect rather than direct.

Annabel ♀
Sometimes taken as an elaboration of ◊**Anna**, but more probably a dissimilated form of *Amabel*, an Old French name derived from Latin *amābilis* 'lovable'. It has been common in Scotland since the 12th century and was still in use in England in the 1600s. Its recent revival in popularity in England and elsewhere dates from the 1940s.
Variants: **Annabella** (Latinized form); **Annabelle** (Gallicized form, under the influence of ◊**Belle**).

Anne ♀
English form (via Old French, Latin, and Greek) of the Hebrew girl's name *Hanna* 'He (God) has favoured me (i.e. with a child)'. This is the name borne in the Bible by the mother of Samuel (see ◊**Hannah**), and according to non-biblical tradition also by the mother of the Virgin Mary. It is the widespread folk cult of the latter that has led to the great popularity of the name in various forms throughout Europe. The simplified form ◊**Ann** was in the 19th century very much more common, but the form with final *-e* has grown in popularity during the 20th century, partly perhaps due to the enormous popularity of L. M. Montgomery's story *Anne of Green Gables* (1908), and partly due to Princess Anne (b. 1950). See also ◊**Anna**.
Pet form: **Annie**.

Annette ♀
French pet form of ◊**Anne**, now also widely used in the English-speaking world.

Annie ♀
Pet form of ◊**Ann** or ◊**Anne**.

Anouk ♀
French: said to be a pet form of ◊**Anne**. It is famous as the adopted name of the French film actress Anouk Aimée.

Anouska ♀
French spelling of Russian **Anuska**, a pet form of ◊**Anna**.

Anthea ♀
Latinized spelling of Greek *Antheia*, a personal name derived from the feminine of the adjective *antheios* 'flowery'. This was used in the classical period as a byname of the goddess Hera at Argos, but as a modern given name it was re-invented in the 17th century by English pastoral poets such as Robert Herrick.

Anthony ♂
The usual English form of the old Roman family name *Antōnius*, which is of uncertain (probably Etruscan) origin. The spelling with -*th*- (not normally reflected in the pronunciation) represents a learned but erroneous attempt to associate it with Greek *anthos* 'flower'. In the post-classical period it was a common name, borne by various early saints, most notably a 3rd-century Egyptian hermit monk, who is regarded as the founder of Christian monasticism.
Variant: **Antony**.
Short form: **Tony**.

Antoine ♂
French form of ◊**Anthony**, now also used in the English-speaking world.

Antoinette ♀
French feminine diminutive of ◊**Antoine**, which has become very popular in the English-speaking world.
Short form: **Toinette**.

Anton ♂
German and Russian form of ◊**Anthony**, now also used in the English-speaking world.

Antonia ♀
Latin feminine form of ◊**Anthony**, unaltered since classical times, when it was a common Roman feminine family name.
Pet form: **Toni**.

Antonio ♂
Italian and Spanish form of ◊**Anthony**, from Latin *Antōnius*. It is now also used in parts of the English-speaking world.

Antony ♂
Variant spelling of ◊**Anthony**.

Antrim ♂
From the name of the region and county in Northern Ireland, in Gaelic *Aontraim*. This is probably derived from Gaelic *aon* 'one' + *treabh* 'house', and so referred originally to a single isolated dwelling that subsequently became the centre of a village and then of a town, which in turn gave its name to the county. The given name has occasionally been chosen by parents who have an association with this region.

Aodh ♂
Irish and Scottish Gaelic (pronounced '*ee*'): modern form of the Old Gaelic name *Áed*, from a vocabulary word meaning 'fire'. This was the name of the Celtic sun god and was a common personal name from the earliest times. From the later Middle Ages onwards it was commonly Anglicized as *Hugh*, and more recently as *Eugene*, but the Gaelic form is now coming back into use.

Aoibheann ♀
Traditional Irish Gaelic name (pronounced '*ee*-ven'), meaning 'beautiful'. It was a fairly common name among the ancient royal families of Ireland, and has recently been revived.
Variant: **Aoibhinn**.
Usual Anglicized form: **Eavan**.

Aoife ♀
Irish and Scottish Gaelic name, pronounced '*ee*-fya'. It is probably a

derivative of *aoibh* 'beauty' (compare ◊**Aoibheann**), but has also been associated with *Esuvia*, a Gaulish goddess. It was borne by several different heroines in ancient Irish legend, and in historical times by a daughter of King Dermot of Leinster, who married Richard de Clare, Earl of Pembroke, leader of the Anglo-Norman incursion into Ireland of 1169. *Usual Anglicized form*: **Eva**.

Aonghas ♂

The modern Scottish Gaelic form of ◊**Angus**, also spelled ◊**Aonghus**.

Aphra ♀

Of uncertain origin. It could be an altered spelling of a Late Latin name, *Afra*. This was originally an ethnic name for a woman from Africa (in Roman times meaning the area around Carthage). It was used in the post-classical period as a nickname for a dark person, and eventually became a given name, being borne, for example, by saints martyred at Brescia under the Roman emperor Hadrian and at Augsburg under Diocletian. The respelling of the name may have been prompted by Micah 1:10 'in the house of Aphrah roll thyself in the dust', where *Aphrah* is often taken as a personal name, but is in fact a place name meaning 'dust'. As a given name it has never been frequent, and is known chiefly as the name of the writer Aphra Behn (1640–89).

Apollonia ♀

Latin feminine form of the Greek masculine name *Apollonios*, an adjectival derivative of the name of the sun god, *Apollo*. This is of uncertain origin, and may be pre-Greek. St Apollonia was an elderly deaconess martyred at Alexandria under the Emperor Decius in the mid-3rd century.

April ♀

From the month (Latin *(mensis) aprīlis*, probably a derivative of *aperīre* 'to open', as the month when buds open and flowers appear). It forms a series with the more common names ◊**May** and ◊**June**, all taken from months associated with the spring, a time of new birth and growth, and may originally have been intended as an English version of the supposedly French name ◊**Avril**.

Arabella ♀

Of uncertain origin; probably an altered form of *An(n)abella* (see ◊**Annabel**). It occurs in Scotland and the North of England from the 1600s onwards.

Aranrhod ♀

Welsh: name borne in the *Mabinogi* by the mother of Dylan and Lleu Llaw Gyffes. It is apparently derived from Celtic elements meaning 'huge', 'round', or 'humped' + 'wheel'; the legendary heroine may originally have been a moon goddess. See also ◊**Arianrhod**.

Archer ♂

Transferred use of the surname, in origin an occupational name for a bowman or a maker of bows (Old French *arch(i)er*, from Latin *arc(u)ārius*, a derivative of *arcus* 'bow'. In Australia it may sometimes have been chosen as a given name in tribute to the seven Archer brothers (Charles, John, David, William, Archibald, Thomas, and Colin) who were well-known pastoralists and explorers in nineteenth-century Queensland.

Archibald ♂

Of Norman French origin, from a Germanic (Frankish) personal name derived from *ercan* 'genuine' + *bald* 'bold', 'brave'. It has long been associated with Scotland, where it is in regular use as the English equivalent of Gaelic *Gilleasbaig* (see ◊**Gillespie**).
Pet forms: **Archie**, **Archy**; **Baldie**.

Ardal ♂

Traditional Irish Gaelic name, composed of the elements *ard* 'high' (or possibly *art* 'bear') + *gal* 'valour'.
Variant: **Ardghal**.

Aretha ♀

Mainly U.S.: probably intended as a derivative of Greek *aretē* 'excellence'. It is principally associated with the name of the singer Aretha Franklin (born 1942), the 'goddess of soul'.

Ariadne ♀

From classical mythology: the name of a daughter of the Cretan king Minos. She gave the Athenian hero Theseus a ball of wool to enable him to find his way out of the Labyrinth after killing the Minotaur. He took her with him when he sailed from Crete, but abandoned her on the island of Naxos on the way back to Athens. Greek lexicographers of the Hellenistic period claimed that the name was composed of the Cretan dialect elements *ari-* (an intensive prefix) + *adnos* 'holy'. The name survived in the Christian era because of St Ariadne (d. *c.*130), an early Phrygian martyr.
Derivatives: French: **Arianne**. Italian: **Arianna**. Both these forms are now also used in the English-speaking world, along with the simplified **Ariana**.

Arianrhod ♀

Welsh: altered form of ◊**Aranrhod**, made up of modern Welsh *arian* 'silver' + *rhod* 'wheel'.

Arianwen ♀

Welsh: from *arian* 'silver' + *(g)wen*, feminine of *gwyn* 'white', 'fair', 'blessed', 'holy'. The name was borne in the 5th century by one of the daughters of Brychan, a semi-legendary Welsh chieftain.

Ariel ♂, ♀

From the biblical place name *Ariel*, said to mean 'lion of God' in Hebrew. It is mentioned in the prophecies of Ezra (8:16) and Isaiah (29:1–2). This is relatively common as a boy's name in modern Israel, but in the United States it is more frequently used as a girl's name.

Arielle ♀

Recent coinage, a distinctively female form of ◊**Ariel**, now quite common in the United States.
Variant: **Ariella**.

Arlene ♀

Modern coinage, especially common in North America. It is of unknown origin, probably a fanciful coinage based on ◊**Marlene** or ◊**Charlene**, or both. It became famous in the 1950s as the name of the American actress and beauty columnist Arlene Dahl (b. 1924).

Arlette ♀

Of ancient but uncertain origin. It is apparently a Norman French double diminutive, from Germanic *arn* 'eagle'. It was the name of the mistress of Duke Robert of Normandy in the 11th century; their son was William the Conqueror.

Arnold ♂

From an Old French name, *Arnald*, *Arnaud*, which is of Germanic (Frankish) origin, from *arn* 'eagle' + *wald* 'ruler'. It was adopted by the Normans and introduced to Britain by them. An early saint of this name, whose cult contributed to its popularity, was a musician at the court of Charlemagne. He is said to have been a Greek by birth; it is not clear when and how he acquired his Germanic name. It never entirely went out of use in England, and came back into more general favour in the 19th century, along with several other medieval Germanic names.
Short form: **Arn**.
Pet form: **Arnie**.

Art ♂

Traditional Irish Gaelic name, from a vocabulary word meaning 'bear', also 'champion'. In Irish legend Art Oenfer ('Art the lonely') is a son of Conn Cétchathach ('Conn of the Hundred Battles'), who overcomes a series of dangers and challenges in order to win his bride, Delbchaem. *Art* is also now used as a short form of ◊**Arthur**, which is of more recent origin.

Artair ♂

Scottish Gaelic form of ◊**Arthur**.

Artemas ♂

Of New Testament Greek origin, from a name representing a short form of various compound names containing that of

the goddess ◊**Artemis** (for example, *Artemidoros* 'gift of Artemis' and *Artemisthenes* 'strength of Artemis'). It is borne in the Bible by a character mentioned briefly in St Paul's letter to Titus (3:12). The name enjoyed some popularity among the Puritans in the 17th century, but fell out of use again.
Variant: **Artemus** (Latinized).

Artemis ♀

From the name of the Greek goddess of the moon and of hunting, equivalent to the Latin ◊**Diana**. It is of uncertain derivation, and may well be pre-Greek. As a given name, it is rare, but is chosen occasionally by parents in search of something distinctive. It is borne by a granddaughter of Lady Diana Cooper, perhaps as an oblique tribute to the grandmother.

Artemus ♂

Variant of ◊**Artemas**.

Arthur ♂

Of Celtic origin. King Arthur was a British king of the 5th or 6th century, about whom virtually no historical facts are known. He ruled in Britain after the collapse of the Roman Empire and before the coming of the Germanic tribes, and a vast body of legends grew up around him in the literatures of medieval Western Europe. His name is first found in the Latinized form *Artorius*; it is of obscure etymology. The spelling with *-th-* was popular among the gentry families of West Yorkshire in the late 1400s, even before Henry VII, who may have hoped to capitalize on the legend, gave the name to his son. It remained in regular use in some areas until its popularity exploded in the early 19th century, largely as a result of the fame of Arthur Wellesley (1769–1852), Duke of Wellington, the victor at the Battle of Waterloo and subsequently prime minister. Further influences were Tennyson's *Idylls of the King* (1859–85), and the widespread Victorian interest in things medieval in general and in Arthurian legend in particular.

Asa ♂

Biblical name, borne by one of the early kings of Judah, who reigned for forty years, as recorded in 1 Kings and 2 Chronicles. It was originally a byname meaning 'doctor', 'healer' in Hebrew, and is still a common Jewish name. It was first used among English-speaking Christians by the Puritans in the 17th century.

Asenath ♀

Biblical name, borne by Joseph's Egyptian wife (Genesis 41:45), who became the mother of Manasseh and Ephraim. The name is said to have meant 'she belongs to her father' in Ancient Egyptian.

Ashley ♀, ♂

Originally male, but now an increasingly popular given name for girls, this is a transferred use of the surname, which comes from any of numerous places in England named with Old English *æsc* 'ash' + *lēah* 'wood'. It is recorded as a given name in the 16th century, but its wider use was probably inspired by Anthony Ashley Cooper (1801–85), 7th Earl of Shaftesbury, a noted humanitarian who inspired much of the legislation designed to improve conditions among the working classes. It became one of the three most popular girls' names in North America in the latter half of the 20th century, with a wide variety of spellings.
Variants: **Ashlea**, **Ashleigh**, **Ashlee**, **Ashlie**, **Ashly** all (♀).

Ashling ♀

Irish: Anglicized form of ◊**Aisling**.

Ashlyn ♀

Altered form of ◊**Ashling**, or else a combination of the first syllable of the popular girl's name ◊**Ashley** with the suffix *-lyn*.
Variants: **Ashlynn**, **Ashlynne**.

Ashton ♀, ♂

Mainly U.S.: transferred use of the surname, a local name from any of the numerous places in England named

with Old English *æsc* 'ash tree' + *tūn*
'enclosure', 'settlement'. This occurs
occasionally as a boys' name in England
from the 1600s, but now it is used
mainly for girls, partly, perhaps, due to
the vogue for ◊**Ashley**.

Asia ♀

Modern name, usually chosen with
reference to the continent of Asia. The
name of this is from Greek, of uncertain
ultimate origin; it may derive from an
Assyrian element *asu* 'east'. The given
name may also sometimes be a shortened form of a name ending in these
letters, such as **Aspasia**.

Aspen ♀

Mainly U.S.: from the name of the
tree, a type of poplar with delicately
quivering leaves. The word was originally an adjective, derived from the
tree-name *asp* (Old English *æspe*), but
came to be used as a noun in the 16th
century.

Aston ♀, ♂

Generally a transferred use of the surname, a local name from any of the
numerous places in England named
with *ēast* 'east' + *tūn* 'settlement', or
occasionally *æsc* 'ash tree' + *tūn* 'settlement'. There is, however, a Middle
English personal name, *Astan(us)*
(probably a survival of Old English
Æðelstān), which may have survived in
some places in this form.

Astrid ♀

Scandinavian name, derived from Old
Norse *áss* 'god' + *fríðr* 'fair', 'beautiful'.
It has become fairly common in the
English-speaking world during the 20th
century, influenced to some extent by
Queen Astrid of the Belgians (1905–35),
who bore this name.

Auberon ♂

From an Old French name of Germanic
(Frankish) origin. There is some doubt
about its origin; it may be connected
with ◊**Aubrey** or be derived from *adal*
'noble' + *ber(n)* 'bear'.
Variant: **Oberon**.

Aubrey ♂, ♀

From a Norman French form of the
Germanic name *Alberic*, from *alb* 'elf',
'supernatural being' + *ric* 'power'. This
was the name, according to Germanic
mythology, of the king of the elves.
The native Old English form, *Ælfrīc*,
borne by a 10th-century archbishop of
Canterbury, did not long survive the
Conquest. *Aubrey* was a relatively
common given name during the Middle
Ages, but later fell out of favour. Its
occurrence since the 19th century may
in part represent a transferred use of the
surname derived from the Norman
given name, as well as a revival of the
latter. In the United States, this is
mainly used as a girl's name, perhaps
under the influence of ◊**Audrey**.

Audra ♀

Modern variant of ◊**Audrey**, used especially in the Southern United States in
forms such as **Audra Jo** and **Audra Rose**.

Audrey ♀

Much altered form of the Old English
girl's name *Æðelþryð*, derived from *æðel*
'noble' + *þryð* 'strength'. This was the
name of a 6th-century saint (normally
known by the Latinized form of her
name, *Etheldreda*), who was a particular
favourite in the Middle Ages. According
to tradition she died from a tumour of
the neck, which she bore stoically as a
divine punishment for her youthful delight in fine necklaces. The name went
into a decline at the end of the Middle
Ages, when it came to be considered
vulgar, being associated with *tawdry*,
that is, lace and other goods sold at fairs
held in her name (the word deriving
from a misdivision of *Saint Audrey*).
Shakespeare bestowed it on Touch-
stone's comic sweetheart in *As You Like
It*. In the 20th century such associations
have largely been forgotten and the
name has revived, partly due in the
1950s and 60s to the popularity of the
actress Audrey Hepburn (1929–93).

Audrina ♀

Fanciful elaboration of ◊**Audrey**, of
recent origin.

Augusta ♀

Latinate feminine form of ◊**Augustus**, which enjoyed a vogue in Britain towards the end of the 19th century.

Augustine ♂

English form of the Latin name *Augustīnus* (a derivative of ◊**Augustus**). Its most famous bearer is St Augustine of Hippo (354–430), perhaps the greatest of the Fathers of the Christian Church. He formulated the principles followed by the numerous medieval communities named after him as Austin canons, friars, and nuns. Also important in England was St Augustine of Canterbury, who brought Christianity to Kent in the 6th century. See also ◊**Austin**.

Augustus ♂

Latin name, from the adjective *augustus* 'great', 'magnificent' (from *augēre* 'to increase'). This word was adopted as a title by the Roman emperors, starting with Octavian (Caius Julius Caesar Octavianus), the adopted son of Julius Caesar, who assumed it in 27 BC and is now generally known as the Emperor Augustus. This name, together with ◊**Augusta**, was revived in England in the 18th century, but it has now again declined in popularity.
Short form: **Gus**.

Aurelia ♀

Feminine form of Latin *Aurēlius*, a family name derived from *aureus* 'golden'. The name was borne by several minor early saints, but its revival as a given name in the 17th century is probably due to its meaning rather than association with any of them.

Aurora ♀

From Latin *aurōra* 'dawn', also used in the classical period as the name of the personified goddess of the dawn. It was not used as a given name in the post-classical or medieval period, but is a reinvention of the Renaissance, and has generally been bestowed as a learned equivalent of ◊**Dawn**.

Austin ♂

Medieval vernacular form of the Latin name *Augustīnus* (see ◊**Augustine**). Both forms enjoyed some popularity in various regions of England as late as the 17th century and they are found occasionally much later, but the present-day use of this form as a given name is normally a reintroduction from its survival as a surname.
Variant: **Austen**.

Autumn ♀

Mainly U.S.: from the name of the season (Latin *autumnus*). This is now more popular as a given name than ◊**Summer**, in spite of its less sunny connotations and the fact that in American English *autumn* is felt to be a rather formal word for the season.

Ava ♀

Of uncertain origin, probably Germanic, from a short form of various female compound names containing the element *av* (of uncertain meaning). St Ava or Avia was a 9th-century abbess of Dinart in Hainault and a member of the Frankish royal family. Evidence for the existence of the name between the early Middle Ages and the mid-20th century is lacking, and it may well be a modern invention. Its popularity since the 1950s is largely due to the film actress Ava Gardner (1922–90).

Avelina ♀

Latinate form of the Norman name ◊**Evelyn**.

Avery ♂

Transferred use of the surname, which originated in the Middle Ages from a Norman French pronunciation of ◊**Alfred**.

Avis ♀

From a Norman French form of the ancient Germanic name *Aveza*, derived from a short form of one or more compound names containing the first element *av* (as in ◊**Ava**; the meaning is uncertain). The correspondence in form to the Latin word *avis* 'bird' is coincidental. The spelling **Avice** is also found.

Avon ♂

From the name of any of several rivers in England (such as the one on which Stratford-on-Avon is situated or the one that runs through Bristol, which has given its name to a modern county). All of these were originally named with a Celtic word meaning simply 'river' (Welsh *afon*, Gaelic *abhainn*). Use as a given name may in some cases have been influenced by the popularity of ◊**Evan**; a recent trend is to create new given names by varying the vowels or consonants of established ones.

Avril ♀

Although generally taken as the French form of the name of the fourth month (see ◊**April**), this has also been influenced by an Old English female personal name derived from *eofor* 'boar' + *hild* 'battle'.

Azalea ♀

Modern coinage from the name of the flowering shrub, one of the most recent of the names taken from terms denoting flora from the 19th century onwards. The shrub was named in the 18th century with the feminine form of Greek *azaleos* 'dry', because it flourishes in dry soil.

Azalia ♀

Modern coinage, an altered spelling of ◊**Azalea**, perhaps influenced by ◊**Azania** or ◊**Azaria**. *Azaliah* is also a male name (meaning 'reserved by God' in Hebrew) borne by a minor biblical character (2 Kings 22:3).

Azania ♀

Azaniah is a male name (meaning 'heard by God' in Hebrew) borne by a minor biblical character, which was occasionally used in England by Nonconformists, but this name is now bestowed chiefly with reference to the African nationalist name for South Africa, used as a symbol of resistance during the apartheid era.

Azaria ♀

From the male biblical name *Azariah* (meaning 'helped by God' in Hebrew). This was in occasional use in England from the 17th century onwards, probably in honour of the biblical prophet who recalled King Asa to a proper observance of religion (2 Chronicles 15:1–8). The name is borne by a number of other minor characters in the Bible, all of them male. However, the *-a* ending ensures that it is used as a girl's name in the modern English-speaking world.

Azelia ♀

Modern coinage, apparently a variant of ◊**Azalia**, possibly influenced by Greek *azēlos* 'not jealous'.

Babs ♀

Informal pet form of ◊**Barbara**.

Bailey ♀, ♂

Transferred use of the surname, which has various origins. Most commonly it was an occupational name for a bailiff or administrative official; in other cases it was a local name for someone who lived near a bailey, i.e. a city fortification; in others it may be a local name from *Bailey* in Lancashire, which gets its name from Old English *bēg* 'berry' + *lēah* 'wood', 'clearing'. In the United States this is now more common as a girl's name than a boy's name.
Variants: **Bailie**, **Baily**, **Bailee**, **Baileigh**; **Baylie**, **Baylee**, **Bayleigh**.

Baldie ♂

Scottish pet form of ◊**Archibald**.

Baldwin ♂

From an Old French name of Germanic (Frankish) origin, derived from *bald* 'bold', 'brave' + *wine* 'friend'. This was adopted by the Normans and introduced by them to Britain. In the Middle Ages it was a comparatively common name, which gave rise to a surname. It was borne by the Norman crusader Baldwin of Boulogne, who in 1100 was elected first king of Jerusalem, and by four further crusader kings of Jerusalem. It continued to be used by some families in England into the 17th century, but in modern times it normally represents a transferred use of the surname rather than a direct revival of the Norman given name.

Balthasar ♂

Name ascribed in medieval Christian tradition to one of the three wise men of the Orient who brought gifts to the infant Jesus. The name is a variant of that of the biblical king *Belshazzar* and means 'Baal protect the king'. It has never been a common given name in the English-speaking world.
Variant: **Balthazar**.

Baptist ♂

English form of Church Latin *baptista*, Greek *baptistēs* (a derivative of *baptein* 'to dip'), the epithet of the most popular of the numerous saints called ◊**John**. As an English name it is used mainly in the United States by members of evangelical sects.

Barbara ♀

From Latin, meaning 'foreign woman' (a feminine form of *barbarus* 'foreign', from Greek, referring originally to the unintelligible chatter of foreigners, which sounded to the Greek ear like no more than *bar-bar*). St Barbara has always been one of the most popular saints in the calendar, although there is some doubt whether she ever actually existed. According to legend, she was imprisoned in a tower and later murdered by her father, who was then struck down by a bolt of lightning. Accordingly, she is the patron of architects, stonemasons, and fortifications, and of firework makers, artillerymen, and gunpowder magazines.
Variant: **Barbra** (a modern contracted spelling, as in the case of the singer, actress, film director Barbra Streisand, b. 1942).
Short form: **Barb** (mainly North American, informal).
Pet forms: **Barbie**, **Babs**.

Barclay ♂

Transferred use of the Scottish surname, which was taken to Scotland in the 12th century by Walter de *Berchelai*, who became chamberlain of Scotland in 1165. His descendants became one of the most powerful families in Scotland. The surname is from *Berkeley* in Gloucestershire, which is named with Old English *beorc* 'birch tree' + *lēah* 'wood', 'clearing'.

Barnabas ♂

From the New Testament, where *Barnabas* represents a Greek form of an Aramaic name meaning 'son of consolation'. St Barnabas was a Jewish Cypriot, one of the earliest Christian missionaries, who sold his property and gave the proceeds to the Church. He worked with St Paul until about 48 AD.

Barnaby ♂

Variant of ◊**Barnabas**, from a medieval vernacular form.

Barney ♂

Pet form of ◊**Barnaby** or its learned equivalent ◊**Barnabas**.
Variant: **Barny**.

Baron ♂

From the title of nobility, along the lines of ◊**Earl** and ◊**Duke**. The title arose in the Norman feudal system and seems to be of Germanic origin, derived from Old English *beorn* 'young warrior' or a related continental Germanic form. In part the given name, and in particular the variant **Barron**, may represent the surname derived from the title.

Barrett ♂

Transferred use of the surname, which is of obscure origin. It is probably a nickname from Middle English *baret* 'dispute', 'argument'. The transferred use as a given name is recent.

Barry ♂

Anglicized form of the Irish Gaelic name **Barra** (Old Irish *Bairre*), a short form of *Fionnb(h)arr* (see ◊**Finbar**). In the 20th century this name has become very popular throughout the English-speaking world, particularly in Australia.
Pet forms: **Baz**, **Bazza** (Australian informal).

Bart ♂

Short form of ◊**Barton** and ◊**Bartholomew**.

Bartholomew ♂

Of New Testament origin, the name of an apostle mentioned in all the synoptic gospels (Matthew, Mark, and Luke) and in the Acts of the Apostles. It is an Aramaic formation meaning 'son of Talmai', and has been assumed by many scholars to be a byname of the apostle ◊**Nathaniel**. *Talmai* is a Hebrew name, said to mean 'abounding in furrows' (Numbers 13:22).
Short form: **Bart**; **Bartle**, **Bartin** (formerly in frequent use).

Barton ♂

Transferred use of the surname, originally a local name from any of the numerous places in England so called from Old English *bere* 'barley' + *tūn* 'enclosure', 'settlement'.
Short form: **Bart**.

Basil ♂

From the Greek name *Basileios* 'royal' (a derivative of *basileus* 'king'). This name was borne by St Basil the Great (*c*. 330–379), bishop of Caesarea, a theologian regarded as one of the Fathers of the Eastern Church. It was also the name of several early saints martyred in the East.

Baxter ♂

Transferred use of the surname, which originated in the Middle Ages as an occupational name for a baker, Old English *bæcestre*. The *-estre* suffix was originally feminine, but by the Middle English period the gender difference had been lost; *Baxter* was merely a regional variant of *Baker*.

Bay ♂, ♀

As a male name this is generally a short form of ◊**Bailey**, although it is sometimes used as an independent first name. As a female name it is likely to be, at least in part, a transferred use from the various plants known as *bay* (Old French *baie*, Latin *bāca*, earlier *bacca*, 'berry'). These are similar to the laurels (see ◊**Laurel**) and the leaves of several species are used as flavouring agents (compare ◊**Juniper** and ◊**Cinnamon**).

Baylie ♀
Mainly U.S.: variant spelling of ◊**Bailey**.
Variants: **Baylee**, **Bayleigh**.

Baz ♂
Mainly Australian: informal pet form of ◊**Barry**.
Variant: **Bazza**.

Bea ♀
Short form of ◊**Beatrice** or ◊**Beatrix**.

Beatrice ♀
Italian and French form of ◊**Beatrix**, occasionally used in England during the Middle Ages, and strongly revived in the 19th century. It is most famous as the name of Dante's beloved.
Short forms: **Bea**, **Bee**.
Pet forms: **Beat(t)ie**.

Beatrix ♀
From a Late Latin personal name, which was borne by a saint martyred in Rome, together with Saints Faustinus and Simplicius, in the early 4th century. The original form of the name was probably *Viātrix*, a feminine version of *Viātor* 'voyager (through life)', which was a favourite name among early Christians. This was then altered by association with Latin *Beātus* 'blessed' (*Via-* and *Bea-* sometimes being pronounced the same in Late Latin). See also ◊**Beatrice**.
Short forms: **Bea**, **Bee**.
Pet forms: **Beat(t)ie**.

Beau ♂
Recent coinage as a given name, originally a nickname meaning 'handsome', as borne by the Regency dandy Beau Brummell (1778–1840), the dandy who was for a time a friend of the Prince Regent. The word was also used in the 19th century with the meaning 'admirer' or 'sweetheart'. Its adoption as a given name seems to have been due to

the hero of P. C. Wren's novel *Beau Geste* (1924) or to the character of Beau Wilks in Margaret Mitchell's *Gone with the Wind* (1936), which was made into an exceptionally popular film in 1939.

Becca ♀
Modern shortened form of ◊**Rebecca**.

Beck ♀
Modern informal short form of ◊**Rebecca**.

Becky ♀
Pet form of ◊**Rebecca**. It was especially popular in the 18th and 19th centuries.

Bee ♀
Variant spelling of ◊**Bea**.

Beige ♀
U.S.: modern coinage, apparently from the colour. This comes from French, and referred originally to undyed woollen cloth; its further derivation is unknown. Its use as a given name may have been influenced in part by the semantically similar ◊**Fawn** and the phonetically similar ◊**Paige**.

Béibhinn ♀
Traditional Irish Gaelic name, pronounced '*bay*-vin', meaning 'white lady' or 'fair lady'. It is sometimes Anglicized as **Bevin**.

Belinda ♀
Of uncertain origin. It was used by Sir John Vanbrugh for a character in his comedy *The Provok'd Wife* (1697), was taken up by Alexander Pope in *The Rape of the Lock* (1712), and has enjoyed a steady popularity ever since. It is not certain where Vanbrugh got the name from. The notion that it is Germanic (with a second element *lind* 'soft', 'tender', 'weak') is not well founded. In Italian literature it is the name ascribed to the wife of Orlando, vassal of Charlemagne, but this use is not supported in Germanic sources. The name may be an Italian coinage from *bella* 'beautiful' (see ◊**Bella**) + the feminine name suffix *-inda* (compare, for example, ◊**Lucinda**).

Bella ♀

Shortened form of *Isabella*, the Italian version of ◊**Isabel**, but also associated with the Italian adjective *bella*, feminine of *bello* 'handsome', 'beautiful' (Late Latin *bellus*).

Belle ♀

Variant of ◊**Bella**, reflecting the French feminine adjective *belle* 'beautiful'.

Ben ♂

Short form of ◊**Benjamin**, or less commonly of ◊**Benedict** or ◊**Bennett**.
Pet forms: **Benny, Bennie**.

Benedict ♂

From Church Latin *Benedictus* 'blessed'. This was the name of the saint (c.480–c.550) who composed the Benedictine rule of Christian monastic life that is still followed in essence by all Western orders. He was born near Spoleto in Umbria, central Italy. After studying in Rome, he went to live as a hermit at Subiaco, and later organized groups of followers and imitators into monastic cells. In c.529 he moved to Monte Cassino, where he founded the great monastery that is still the centre of the Benedictine order. His rule is simple, restrained, and practical. The name is used mainly by Roman Catholics. See also ◊**Bennett**.

Benjamin ♂

Biblical name, borne by the youngest of the twelve sons of Jacob. His mother Rachel died in giving birth to him, and in her last moments she named him *Benoni*, meaning 'son of my sorrow'. His father, however, did not wish him to bear such an ill-omened name, and renamed him *Benyamin* (Genesis 35.16–18; 42:4). This means either 'son of the right hand' or more likely 'son of the south' (Hebrew *yamin* can also mean 'south'), since Benjamin was the only child of Jacob born in Canaan and not in Mesopotamia to the north. Another tradition is that the second element of the name is a variant of the Hebrew plural noun *yamim*, which means 'days' but is used idiomatically to mean 'year' or 'years'. The name would then mean 'son of (my) old age' and refer to the fact that Benjamin was Jacob's youngest child. In the Middle Ages the name was often given to sons whose mothers had died in childbirth. Today it has no such unfortunate associations, but is still mainly a Jewish name.
Short form: **Ben**.
Pet forms: **Benny, Bennie, Benji(e)**.

Bennett ♂

The normal medieval vernacular form of ◊**Benedict**, borne by women as well as men in the past. Now sometimes used as an antiquarian revival, but more often a transferred use of the surname derived from the medieval given name.
Variants: **Benett, Bennet, Benet**.

Benson ♂

Transferred use of the surname, which originated in part as a patronymic from *Ben(n)*, a short form of ◊**Benedict**, and in part as a local name from *Benson* (formerly *Bensington*) in Oxfordshire.

Bentley ♂

Transferred use of the surname, which originated as a local name from any of the dozen or so places in England so called from Old English *beonet* 'bent grass' + *lēah* 'wood', 'clearing'.

Berenice ♀

From the Greek personal name *Berenikē*, which seems to have originated in the royal house of Macedon. It is almost certainly a Macedonian dialectal form of the Greek name *Pherenikē* 'victory bringer'. It was introduced to the Egyptian royal house by the widow of one of Alexander the Great's officers, who married Ptolemy I. It was also borne by an early Christian woman mentioned in Acts 25, for which reason it was felt to be acceptable by the Puritans in the 17th century. It has now fallen out of fashion again. See also ◊**Bernice**.

Bernadette ♀

French feminine diminutive of ◊**Bernard**. Its use in Britain and Ireland is almost exclusively confined to Roman Catholics, who take it in honour of St Bernadette Soubirous (1844–79), a French peasant girl who had visions of the Virgin Mary and uncovered a spring near Lourdes where miraculous cures are still sought.

Variant: **Bernardette**.

Bernard ♂

From an Old French name of Germanic (Frankish) origin, derived from *ber(n)* 'bear' + *hard* 'hardy', 'brave', 'strong'. This was the name of three famous medieval churchmen: St Bernard of Menthon (923–1008), founder of a hospice on each of the Alpine passes named after him; the monastic reformer St Bernard of Clairvaux (1090–1153); and the scholastic philosopher Bernard of Chartres. It was adopted by the Normans and introduced by them to England. A native Old English form, *Beornheard*, was superseded by the Norman form.

Pet form: **Bernie**.

Bernice ♀

Contracted form of ◊**Berenice**. This is the form that is used in the Authorized Version of the Bible, and it is now fairly popular in the English-speaking world.

Pet form: **Binnie**.

Berry ♀

From the vocabulary word (Old English *berie*). This is one of the less common of the names referring to flowers, fruit, and vegetation introduced as given names in the 20th century.

Bert ♂

Short form of any of the various names containing this syllable as a first or second element, for example ◊**Albert** and ◊**Bertram**. See also ◊**Burt**.

Pet form: **Bertie**.

Bertha ♀

Latinized version of a Continental Germanic name, a short form of various compound women's personal names derived from *berht* 'famous' (akin to Modern English *bright*). It probably existed in England before the Conquest, and was certainly reinforced by Norman use, but fell out of use in the 15th century. It was reintroduced into the English-speaking world from Germany in the 19th century, but has once again gone out of fashion.

Bertram ♂

From an Old French name of Germanic (Frankish) origin, from *berht* 'bright', 'famous' + *hramn* 'raven'. Ravens were traditional symbols of wisdom in Germanic mythology; Odin was regularly accompanied by ravens called Hugin and Munin. This name was adopted by the Normans and introduced by them to Britain. See also ◊**Bertrand**.

Short form: **Bert**.

Bertrand ♂

Medieval French variant of ◊**Bertram**, imported to Britain by the Normans. In modern times it has been made famous by the English philosopher Bertrand Russell (1872–1970).

Beryl ♀

One of several women's names that are taken from gemstones and which came into fashion at the end of the 19th century. Beryl is a pale green semiprecious stone (of which emerald is a variety). Other colours are also found. The word is from Greek, and is ultimately of Indian origin.

Bess ♀

Short form of ◊**Elizabeth**, in common use in the days of Queen Elizabeth I, who was known as 'Good Queen Bess'.

Pet forms: **Bessie**, **Bessy**.

Bet ♀

Short form of ◊**Elizabeth**.

Beth ♀

Short form of ◊**Elizabeth**, not used before the 19th century, when it became popular in America and elsewhere after publication of Louisa M. Alcott's novel *Little Women* (1868), in which Beth March is one of the four sisters who are the central characters.

Bethan ♀

Originally a Welsh pet form of ◊**Beth**, now also popular elsewhere in the English-speaking world.

Bethany ♀

Of New Testament origin. In the New Testament it is a place name, that of the village just outside Jerusalem where Jesus stayed during Holy Week, before going on to Jerusalem and crucifixion (Matthew 21:17; Mark 11:1; Luke 19:29; John 12:1). Its Hebrew name may mean 'house of figs' (*beth te'ena* or *beth te'enim*). The given name is favoured mainly by Roman Catholics, being bestowed in honour of Mary of Bethany, sister of Martha and Lazarus. She is sometimes identified with Mary Magdalene (see ◊**Madeleine**), although the grounds for this identification are very poor.

Betsy ♀

Pet form of ◊**Elizabeth**, a blend of *Betty* (see ◊**Bet**) and *Bessie* (see ◊**Bess**).

Bette ♀

Variant of ◊**Betty**, associated particularly with the film actress Bette Davis (1908–89), born Ruth Elizabeth Davis.

Bettina ♀

Latinate elaboration of ◊**Betty**.

Betty ♀

Pet form of ◊**Elizabeth**, dating from the 18th century. In the 17th century it is also found occasionally as a pet form of ◊**Beatrice**.
Variant: ◊**Bette**.

Beulah ♀

Biblical name, pronounced '*byoo*-la': from the name (meaning 'married' in Hebrew) applied to the land of Israel by the prophet Isaiah (Isaiah 62:4). 'The land of Beulah' has sometimes been taken as a reference to heaven. It was taken up as a given name in England at the time of the Reformation and was used among the Puritans in the 17th century. It was borne by the American actress Beulah Bondi (1899–1981), and was immortalized by Mae West's

instruction to her maidservant: 'Beulah, peel me a grape.'

Beverley ♀, also ♂

Transferred use of the surname, which is from a place in Humberside named with Old English *beofor* 'beaver' + *lēac* 'stream'. The spelling **Beverly** is now used more or less exclusively for girls, and is the usual form of the girl's name in America. It is not clear why it should have become such a popular girl's name. Association with Beverly Hills in Los Angeles, the district where many film stars live, may have been a factor.
Variant: **Beverly**.

Bevin ♀

Anglicized form of the Gaelic name ◊**Béibhinn**.

Bianca ♀

Italian: from *bianca* 'white' (i.e. 'pure', but see also ◊**Blanche**). The name was used by Shakespeare for characters in two of his plays set in an Italian context: the mild-mannered sister of Katharina, the 'shrew' in *The Taming of the Shrew*, and a courtesan in *Othello*. It came to prominence in the 1970s as the name of Bianca Jagger, the Nicaraguan fashion model, peace worker, and diplomat, who was for a time married to the rock singer Mick Jagger.

Biddy ♀

Of Anglo-Irish origin: pet form of ◊**Bride** or ◊**Bridget**. It was formerly quite common, but is now seldom used outside Ireland, partly perhaps because the informal expression 'an old biddy' in English has come to denote a tiresome old woman.

Bijou ♀

From French *bijou* 'jewel', also used as a pet name. The French vocabulary word derives from Breton *bizou* 'ring'.

Bill ♂

Altered short form of ◊**William**, not used before the 19th century. The reason for the change in the initial consonant is not clear, but it conforms to the pattern regularly found when English words beginning with *w-* are borrowed into Gaelic. The nickname 'King Billy' for William of Orange is an early example from Ireland which may have influenced English usage.

Pet forms: **Billy**, ◊**Billie**.

Billie ♀, ♂
Variant of *Billy* (see ◊**Bill**), now mainly used for girls, and sometimes bestowed at baptism as a female equivalent of ◊**William**.

Binnie ♀
Pet form of ◊**Bernice**, associated particularly with the actress and singer Binnie Hale (1899–1984).

Blain ♂
Anglicized form of the Gaelic personal name *Bláán*, originally a byname representing a diminutive form of *blá* 'yellow'. This was the name of an early Celtic saint who lived in the 6th century.

Variants: **Blaine**, **Blane**.

Blair ♂, ♀
Transferred use of the Scottish surname, in origin a local name from any of various places named with Gaelic *blàr* 'plain', 'field'. In North America it is now widely used as a girl's name.

Variant: **Blaire**.

Blaise ♂
French: the name (Latin *Blasius*, probably from *blaesus* 'lisping') of a saint popular throughout Europe in the Middle Ages but almost forgotten today. He was a bishop of Sebaste in Armenia, and was martyred in the early years of the 4th century; these bare facts were elaborated in a great number of legends that reached Europe from the East at the time of the Crusades. He was supposedly endowed with miraculous healing power, and while imprisoned and awaiting torture and execution he miraculously saved a boy from choking to death. He is the patron of sufferers from sore throats.

Blake ♂
Transferred use of the surname, which has two quite distinct etymologies. It is both from Old English *blæc* 'black' and from Old English *blāc* 'pale', 'white'; it was thus originally a nickname given to someone with hair or skin that was either remarkably dark or remarkably light. It is now quite popular as a boy's name.

Blanche ♀
Originally a nickname for a blonde, from *blanche*, feminine of Old French *blanc* 'white' (of Germanic origin). It came to be associated with the notion of whiteness as indicating purity, and was introduced into England as a given name by the Normans. A pale complexion combined with light hair has long been an ideal of beauty in Europe (compare Modern English *fair*, which at first meant 'beautiful' and then, from the 16th century, 'light in colouring').

Blane ♂
Variant spelling of ◊**Blain**.

Bláthnat ♀
Traditional Irish Gaelic name, pronounced '*blah*-nat', from a diminutive of *blath* 'flower'. This was the name of a queen of West Munster, who fell in love with Cú Chulainn, who abducted her, killing her husband Cú Roí. She was, however, killed by Cú Roí's minstrel, who seized her and leapt off a cliff to the rocks below.

Blodwedd ♀
Welsh: name borne by a character in the *Mabinogi*. She was conjured up out of flowers as a bride for Lleu Llaw Gyffes, and was originally called *Blodeuedd*, a derivative of *blawd* 'flowers'. After she had treacherously had her husband killed she was transformed into an owl, and her name was changed to *Blodeuwedd* 'flower face', an allusion to the markings round the eyes of the owl.

Blodwen ♀
Welsh traditional name, derived from *blawd* 'flowers' + *(g)wen* 'white', feminine of *gwyn* 'white', 'fair', 'blessed', 'holy'. The name was relatively

common in the Middle Ages and has recently been revived.

Blossom ♀

19th-century coinage, from the vocabulary word for flowers on a fruit tree or ornamental tree (Old English *blōstm*), used as an affectionate pet name for a young girl.

Bly ♂

Transferred use of the surname, in origin an Anglicized form of Irish Gaelic *Ó Blighe* 'descendant of Blighe', a personal name probably derived from Old Norse *Blígr* (from *blígja* 'to gaze').

Blythe ♀

Modern coinage, apparently an altered spelling of the vocabulary word *blithe* 'carefree', 'cheerful' (Old English *blīðe* 'kind', 'pleasant', 'joyous'). In part it may represent a transferred use of the surname with this spelling, derived from the vocabulary word during the Middle Ages.

Boaz ♂

Biblical Hebrew name of uncertain origin, said by some to be from a word meaning 'swiftness'. In the Bible it is borne by a distant kinsman of Ruth, who treats her generously and eventually marries her. The given name was in occasional use in England in the 17th and 18th centuries but is now very rare. It is sometimes used in Jewish families.

Bob ♂

Altered short form of ◊**Robert**, a later development than the common medieval forms *Hob*, *Dob*, and *Nob*, all of which, unlike *Bob*, have given rise to English surnames.
Pet forms. **Bobby**, ◊**Bobbie**.

Bobbie ♀, ♂

Variant of *Bobby* (see ◊**Bob**), now mainly used as a girl's name, in part as a pet form of ◊**Roberta**.
Variant: **Bobbi**.

Bond ♂

Transferred use of the surname, originally denoting a medieval farmer who was a smallholder or peasant farmer. The word (Middle English *bonde*) is of Germanic origin and seems to have referred to a tenant farmer 'bound' to an overlord and owing him rent or service.

Bonita ♀

Coined in the United States in the 1940s from the feminine form of Spanish *bonito* 'pretty'. This is not used as a given name in Spanish-speaking countries. *Bonita* looks like the feminine form of a medieval Latin male name, *Bonītus* (from *bonus* 'good'), which was borne by an Italian saint of the 6th century and a Provençal saint of the 7th. However, no medieval record of the feminine form in use as a given name is known.
Pet form: ◊**Bonnie**.

Bonnie ♀

Chiefly North American: originally an affectionate nickname from the Scottish word *bonnie* 'fine', 'attractive', 'pretty'. However, it is not—or at any rate has not been until recently—used as a given name in Scotland. Its popularity may be attributed to the character of Scarlett O'Hara's infant daughter Bonnie in the film *Gone With the Wind* (1939), based on Margaret Mitchell's novel of the same name. (Bonnie's name was really Eugenie Victoria, but she had 'eyes as blue as the bonnie blue flag'.) A famous American bearer was Bonnie Parker, accomplice of the bank robber Clyde Barrow; their life together was the subject of the film *Bonnie and Clyde* (1967). The name has enjoyed a vogue in the second part of the 20th century, and has also been used as a pet form of ◊**Bonita**.

Booker ♂

Transferred use of the surname, in origin an occupational name for either a scribe or binder of books (a derivative of Middle English *boke* 'book', Old English *bōc*), or else a bleacher of cloth (a derivative of Middle English *bouken* 'to steep in lye', Middle Dutch *būken*).

Boone ♂

Transferred use of the surname, in origin a nickname from Old French *bon* 'good' (Latin *bonus*). Use as a given name may have been inspired by the legendary U.S. frontiersman Daniel Boone (1734–1820).

Booth ♂

Transferred use of the surname, originally given to someone who lived in a small hut or bothy, the typical dwelling of a cowherd or shepherd (Middle English *bōth(e)*, of Scandinavian origin). Use as a given name may have originated in honour of William Booth (1829–1912), founder of the Salvation Army.

Boris ♂

Russian: from the Tartar nickname *Bogoris* 'small'. Later, however, it was taken to be a shortened form of the Russian name *Borislav*, from *bor* 'battle' + *slav* 'glory'. The name was borne in the 9th century by a ruler of Bulgaria who converted his kingdom to Christianity and gave shelter to disciples of Saints Cyril and Methodius when they were expelled from Moravia. The name was also borne by a 10th-century Russian saint, son of Prince Vladimir of Kiev and brother of St Gleb. It is as a result of his influence that *Boris* is one of the very few non-classical names that the Orthodox Church allows to be taken as baptismal name (although the saint himself bore the baptismal name *Romanus*).

Boyd ♂

Transferred use of the common Irish and Scottish surname, which is of uncertain derivation. It may originally have represented a local name from the island of Bute in the Firth of Clyde, known in Gaelic as *Bod* (genitive case *Bóid*). The first known bearer of the surname is Robertus *de Boyd*, recorded in Scotland in the early 13th century. More recently the surname has been associated with the Gaelic vocabulary word *buidhe* yellow, referring to a hair colour, but this is an unlikely derivation as the *d* was lost from the pronunciation of that word

at an early stage (it is the origin of the surname *Bowie*).

Brad ♂

Mainly North American: short form of ◊**Bradford** and ◊**Bradley**.

Braden ♂

Mainly U.S.: transferred use of the Irish surname, Gaelic Ó *Bradáin* 'descendant of Bradán'. The latter is a personal name meaning 'salmon'.

Bradford ♂

Mainly U.S.: transferred use of the surname, in origin a local name from any of the numerous places in England so called from Old English *brād* 'broad' + *ford* 'ford'. The surname was borne most famously by William Bradford (1590–1657), leader of the Pilgrim Fathers from 1621 and governor of Plymouth Colony for some 30 years. It was also the name of another William Bradford (1722–91), a printer who played an important part in the American Revolution.

Bradley ♂

Mainly North American: transferred use of the surname, in origin a local name from any of the numerous places in England so called from Old English *brād* 'broad' + *lēah* 'wood', 'clearing'. The most famous American bearer of this surname was General Omar N. Bradley (1893–1981).

Brady ♂, ♀

Mainly North American: transferred use of the surname, which is of Irish origin, from Gaelic Ó *Brádaigh* 'descendant of Brádach'. *Brádach* is an old Irish byname of uncertain origin, possibly a contracted form of *brághadach* 'large-chested', from *brágha* 'chest'.

Brandon ♂

Mainly North American: transferred use of the surname, in origin a local name from any of various places so called, most of which get their name from Old English *brōm* 'broom', 'gorse' + *dūn* 'hill'. In some cases it may be an altered form of ◊**Brendan**. There has perhaps also been some influence from the

surname of the Italian American actor
Marlon Brando (b. 1924).

Brandy ♀
Mainly U.S.: ostensibly from the
vocabulary word for the type of liquor
(earlier known as *brandy wine* or
brand(e)wine, from Dutch *brandewijn*
'distilled wine'), but probably invented
as a feminine form of ◊**Brandon**.
Variants: **Brandie**, **Brandi**.

Brant ♂
Mainly U.S.: probably a variant of the
rather more common ◊**Brent**. The English surname *Brant* is a relatively in-
frequent variant of *Brand*, derived from
the Old Norse personal name *Brandr*,
meaning 'sword' (compare ◊**Brenda**).

Branton ♂
Mainly U.S.: variant of ◊**Brandon** or
transferred use of the surname *Branton*.
This is a local name from places in
Northumbria and West Yorkshire so
named from Old English *brōm* 'broom',
'gorse' + *tūn* 'enclosure', 'settlement'.

Branwen ♀
Welsh traditional name, apparently
from *brân* 'raven' + *(g)wen*, feminine of
gwyn 'white', 'fair', 'blessed', 'holy', but
more probably a variant of ◊**Bronwen**.
The story of Branwen, daughter of Llŷr,
forms the second chapter or 'branch' of
the *Mabinogi*: it tells of her beauty and
of the conflict on her account between
her brother Bran, King of the 'Island of
the Mighty' (i.e. Britain), and her husband Matholwch, King of Ireland.
Variant: **Brangwen**.

Braxton ♂
Transferred use of the surname, in origin
a local name from an unidentified place.
The place name seems to be composed of
the genitive case of the Old English
personal name *Bracc* + Old English *tūn*
'enclosure', 'settlement'. Use as a given
name has apparently been influenced by
the popularity of names such as ◊**Brant**
and ◊**Branton**, and the adoption as given
names of similar sounding surnames
such as ◊**Caxton** and ◊**Paxton**.

Breanna ♀
Mainly U.S.: variant spelling of
◊**Brianna**.
Variant: **Breanne**.

Breda ♀
Irish: Anglicized form of Gaelic *Bríd* (see
◊**Bride**, ◊**Bridget**).
Variant: **Breeda**.

Bree ♀
Anglicized form of the Irish Gaelic name
Bríghe, a variant of *Brighid* (see
◊**Bridget**).

Brenda ♀
A very popular name, of uncertain derivation. Until the 20th century it was
confined mainly to Scotland and Ireland.
It is probably of Scandinavian rather
than Celtic origin, however: a short
form of any of the various compound
names derived from Old Norse *brand*
'sword'. Its popularity in Gaelic-
speaking countries has no doubt been
influenced by its similarity to ◊**Brendan**.

Brendan ♂
Irish: from the old Irish personal name
Bréanainn, derived from a Celtic word
meaning 'prince'. This was the name of
two 6th-century Irish saints, Brendan
the Voyager and Brendan of Birr. According to Irish legend, the former was
the first European to set foot on North
American soil. The modern Irish Gaelic
form **Breandán** and the Anglicized
Brendan are based on the medieval Latin
form *Brendanus*.

Brenna ♀
Mainly U.S.: modern coinage, apparently created as a feminine form of
◊**Brennan**, but perhaps also influenced
by ◊**Brianna**.

Brennan ♀
Mainly U.S.: transferred use of the Irish
surname, Gaelic *Ó Braonáin* 'descendant of Braonán'. The latter is a personal
name derived from a diminutive of
braon 'moisture', 'drop'. It may also
be taken as a contracted form of
◊**Brendan**.

Brent ♂

Transferred use of the surname, which is derived from any of several places in Devon and Somerset which are on or near prominent hills, and were named with a Celtic or Old English term for a hill. The given name has enjoyed considerable popularity in Britain and the United States in the 1970s and 1980s, and may have been influenced by ◊Brett, which has experienced a similar vogue, starting somewhat earlier.

Brenton ♂

Mainly U.S.: transferred use of the surname, in origin a local name from a place near Exminster in Devon, so called from Old English *Brȳningtūn* 'settlement associated with Brȳni'. The latter is a personal name derived from *bryne* 'fire', 'flame'. The modern given name may also be a variant of ◊Branton.

Brett ♂

Transferred use of the surname, which originated in the Middle Ages as an ethnic name for one of the Bretons who arrived in England in the wake of the Norman Conquest. As a surname it is most common in East Anglia, where Breton settlement was particularly concentrated. As a given name, it has enjoyed something of a vogue in the latter half of the 20th century.

Brewster ♂

Mainly U.S.: transferred use of the surname, in origin an occupational name for a brewer, Middle English *brēowestre*. The *-estre* suffix was originally feminine, but by the Middle English period this grammatical distinction had been lost (compare ◊Baxter).

Brian ♂

Originally Irish: perhaps from an Old Celtic word meaning 'high' or 'noble'. The name has been perennially popular in Ireland, in particular on account of the fame of Brian Boru (Gaelic *Brian Bóroimhe*), a warrior of the 10th century who eventually became high king of Ireland. In the Middle Ages it was relatively common in East Anglia, where it

was introduced by Breton settlers, and in northern England, where it was introduced by Scandinavians from Ireland. It was quite popular in Yorkshire in the early 16th century, largely because it had long been a family name among the Stapletons, who had Irish connections. They first used it after Sir Gilbert Stapleton married Agnes, the daughter of the great northern baron Sir Brian fitzAlan. In Gaelic Scotland it was at first borne exclusively by members of certain professional families of Irish origin.

Brianna ♀

A female equivalent of ◊Brian, found occasionally in England from the 16th century onwards.
Variant: **Brianne**. *See also* ◊Breanna.

Briar ♀

20th-century coinage from the vocabulary word *briar* or *brier* (Old English *brær*), denoting a thorny bush of wild roses ('sweet briar') or brambles.

Brice ♂

The name of a saint who was a disciple and successor of St Martin of Tours. His name is found in the Latinized forms *Bri(c)tius* and *Bricius* and is probably of Gaulish origin, possibly derived from a word meaning 'speckled' (compare Welsh *brych*).

Bride ♀

Irish: Anglicized form of *Bríd*, the modern Gaelic contracted form of *Brighid* (see ◊Bridget).
Pet form: **Bridie**.

Bridget ♀

Anglicized form of the Gaelic name *Brighid* (pronounced 'breed'). This was the name of an ancient Celtic goddess, which in Gaulish would have been *Brigindos*, meaning 'the exalted one'. St Brigid of Kildare (c.450–c.525) is one of the patron saints of Ireland. Very few facts are known about her life. She founded a religious house for women at Kildare, and is said to have been buried at Downpatrick, where St Patrick and St

Columba were also buried. Many of the stories of miracles told about St Brigid seem to be Christianized versions of pagan legends concerning the goddess. The popularity of the name was further reinforced throughout Europe, especially in Scandinavia in the form **Birgit**, as the name of the patron saint of Sweden (1304–73). She was a noblewoman of Irish stock who, after the death of her husband, founded an order of nuns, the Bridgettines. Later she went to Rome and attempted to introduce religious reforms there.
Variants: **Brigid**, **Brigit**, ◊**Brigitte**, **Bride**, **Breda**.
Pet forms: ◊**Biddy**, **Bridie**.

Brie ♀
Variant spelling of ◊**Bree**, altered in form to coincide with the name of a district in northern France (so called from Late Latin *bracia* 'marshland') famous for its production of a variety of soft cheese. This is now a relatively common first name in Australia.

Brigham ♂
Mainly U.S.: name adopted in honour of the early Mormon leader, Brigham Young (1801–77). It was originally a surname, a local name from places in Cumbria and North Yorkshire so called from Old English *brycg* 'bridge' + *hām* 'homestead', 'settlement'. It is not known why the Mormon leader received this given name; he was the son of John and Abigail Young of Whitingham, Vermont.

Brighton ♂
Transferred use of the surname, in origin a local name from Breighton on the River Derwent, so called from Old English *brycg* 'bridge' + *tūn* 'enclosure', 'settlement'. The surname is unlikely to derive from Brighton in Sussex, as this was known as *Brighthelmestone* 'settlement of Brighthelm' until the end of the 18th century, but in some cases the first name may have been given with reference to it—or in the hope that the child so named should turn out to have a bright personality or intellect.

Brigitte ♀
French form of ◊**Bridget**, associated particularly with the French film star of the 1950s Brigitte Bardot (b. 1934 as Camille Javal).

Brina ♀
In part a reduced form of names such as ◊**Sabrina**; in part an Anglicized form of the Jewish name **Brayne** (from Yiddish **Brayndel**, an affectionate diminutive form of *broyn* 'brown'); in part a variant of ◊**Brianna**.

Briony ♀
Variant spelling of ◊**Bryony**.

Britt ♀
Swedish: contracted form of *Birgit*, the Swedish version of ◊**Bridget**, made famous in the English-speaking world by the Swedish actress Britt Ekland (b. 1924; her surname was originally Eklund).

Brittany ♀
Mainly North American: modern coinage, taken from the traditionally Celtic-speaking region of north-west France, known in medieval Latin as *Britannia*, because it was settled by refugees from Cornwall and Devon following the establishment of the Anglo-Saxon kingdom of Wessex. Its adoption as a given name has also been influenced by ◊**Britt**, of which it is sometimes regarded as the full form. In recent years it has rapidly established itself as a very popular name in North America: in one 1989 survey it was the most commonly used of all girls' names in the United States.

Brock ♂
Transferred use of the surname, in origin a nickname for someone resembling a badger (Middle English *broc(k)*, Old English *brocc*, of Celtic origin).

Broderick ♂
Transferred use of the surname, which is a derivative of the Welsh personal name ◊**Rhydderch**.

Brontë ♀
Transferred use of the surname borne by the literary sisters Charlotte (1816–55),

Emily (1818–48), and Anne (1820–49). The spelling Brontë (influenced by Greek *brontē* 'thunder') was adopted by their father Patrick in place of the form *Prunty*. *Prunty* is an Irish surname (Gaelic *Ó Proinntigh*) indicating descent from a bearer of the personal name *Proinnteach* 'Bestower' (originally a by-name for a generous person). Use as a given name seems to have been inspired by the character in the film *The Green Card*.

Brónach ♀
Traditional Irish Gaelic name, meaning 'sorrowful'.

Bronwen ♀
Welsh: from *bron* 'breast' + *(g)wen*, feminine of *gwyn* 'white', 'fair', 'blessed', 'holy'.

Brooke ♀
Mainly U.S.: transferred use of the surname, originally a local name for someone who lived near a brook or stream (Old English *bróc*). It has been borne by two American film actresses: Brooke Adams (b. 1949) and Brooke Shields (b. 1965).

Bruce ♂
Transferred use of the Scottish surname, now used as a given name throughout the English-speaking world, but in recent years particularly popular in Australia. The surname was originally a Norman baronial name, but a precise identification of the place from which it was derived has not been made (there are a large number of possible candidates). The Bruces were an influential Norman family in Scottish affairs in the early Middle Ages; its most famous member was Robert 'the Bruce' (1274–1329), who is said to have drawn inspiration after his defeat at Methven from the perseverance of a spider in repeatedly climbing up again after being knocked down. He ruled Scotland as King Robert I from 1306 to 1329.

Bruno ♂
From the Germanic word *brun* 'brown'.

This was in use as a name in many of the ruling families of Germany during the Middle Ages. It was borne by a 10th-century saint, son of the Emperor Henry the Fowler, and by the Saxon duke who gave his name to Brunswick (German *Braunschweig*, i.e. 'Bruno's settlement'). Its use in the English-speaking world, which dates from the end of the 19th century, may have been partly influenced by Lewis Carroll's *Sylvie and Bruno* (1889), but more probably it was first used by settlers of German ancestry in the United States.

Brutus ♂
From an old Roman family name, borne most notably by the statesman Marcus Junius Brutus, who was one of the assassins of Julius Caesar. It is therefore sometimes taken as symbolic of resistance to tyranny. It was originally a byname meaning 'dull' or 'stupid', and is still only occasionally used as a first name because of its association with the English vocabulary word 'brute'. Junius Brutus Booth (1796–1852), father of the actor Edwin Thomas Booth and Lincoln's assassin John Wilkes Booth, was explicitly named in admiration for the Roman who struck a blow for freedom in conspiring against an elected official who had become a tyrant.

Bryan ♂
Variant of ◊**Brian**, influenced by the usual spelling of the associated surname.

Bryant ♂
Transferred use of the surname, which is derived from the given name ◊**Brian**. The final *-t* seems to have arisen as a result of a mishearing by English speakers of the devoicing of the *-n* in Gaelic, reinforced by association with names such as ◊**Constant**.

Bryce ♂, sometimes ♀
Mainly North American: variant of ◊**Brice**, now fairly commonly used as a given name, originating as a transferred use of the Scottish surname derived from the medieval given name.

Bryn ♂

Welsh: 20th-century coinage from the Welsh topographical term *bryn* 'hill', in part as a short form of ◊**Brynmor**. See also ◊**Brynn**.

Brynmor ♂

Welsh: 20th-century coinage from the name of a place in Gwynedd, named with *bryn* 'hill' + *mawr* 'large'.

Brynn ♂, ♀

Variant spelling of ◊**Bryn**. In the United States this is now used predominantly as a girl's name, perhaps by association with names such as ◊**Lynn**.

Bryony ♀

From the name of the plant (Greek *bryonia*). This is one of the names coined in the 20th century from vocabulary words denoting flowers. *Variant*: **Briony**.

Bryson ♂

Mainly U.S.: transferred use of the surname, which has a double origin. In part it represents a patronymic derived from the given name ◊**Brice** or ◊**Bryce**, in part it is an Anglicized form of the Irish Gaelic surname *Ó Briosáin*, an altered form of *Ó Muirgheasáin* 'descendant of Muirgheasán'. The latter is a personal name perhaps derived from *muir* 'sea' + *gus* 'vigour' + the diminutive suffix *-an*. The Ó Muirgheasáins were hereditary poets (and keepers of the relics of St Columba) in Donegal and Scotland.

Buck ♂

Mainly U.S.: from the nickname *Buck*, denoting a robust and spirited young man, from the vocabulary word for a male deer (Old English *bucc*) or a he-goat (Old English *bucca*).

Bud ♂

Mainly U.S.: originally a short form of the nickname or vocabulary word *buddy* 'friend', which may be an alteration, perhaps a nursery form, of *brother* or else derived from the Scottish Gaelic vocative case *a bhodaich* 'old man'. *Variant*: **Buddy**.

Buffy ♀

Informal pet form of ◊**Elizabeth**, based on a child's unsuccessful attempts to pronounce the name.

Bunty ♀

Nickname and occasional baptismal name, relatively popular in the early 20th century, but of uncertain derivation. It seems most likely that it derives from what was originally a dialectal pet name for a lamb, from the verb to *bunt* 'to butt gently'.

Burgess ♂

Transferred use of the surname, in origin a status name from the Old French word *burgeis* 'freeman of a borough' (a derivative of *burg* 'town', of Germanic origin).

Burnett ♂, ♀

Transferred use of the surname (from an Old French diminutive of *brun* 'brown'), in origin a nickname referring to brown colouring of hair, complexion, or clothing. As a female first name it may have been chosen in some cases with reference to the plant *Sanguisorba minor*, known as *burnet*, whose leaves are used for salad (compare ◊**Sorrel** and ◊**Fennel**). *Variant*: **Burnet**.

Burt ♂

Mainly U.S.: of various origins. In the case of the film actor Burt Lancaster (b. 1913) it is a short form of ◊**Burton**, but it has also been used as a variant spelling of ◊**Bert**. The pianist and composer Burt Bacharach (b. 1928) was the son of a Bert Bacharach, and his given name is presumably simply a variation of his father's.

Burton ♂

Transferred use of the surname, in origin a local name from any of the numerous places in England so called. In most cases the place name is derived from Old English *burh* 'fortress', 'fortified place' + *tūn* 'enclosure', 'settlement'.

Buster ♂

Mainly U.S.: originally a nickname from the slang term of address *buster* 'smasher', 'breaker', a derivative of the verb *bust* (altered form of *burst*). It was the nickname of the silent movie comedian Joseph Francis 'Buster' Keaton (1895–1966).

Buxton ♂

Transferred use of the surname, in origin a local name from a place in Derbyshire noted for its thermal springs. In the Middle Ages this place was known as *Buchestanes* or *Bucstones*, i.e. 'bowing stones', and was probably named from logan stones (boulders so poised that they rocked at a touch) in the vicinity.

Use as a given name seems to have been influenced by the popularity of names such as ◊**Buck** and ◊**Bud**, and the adoption of given names of similar sounding surnames such as ◊**Caxton** and ◊**Paxton**.

Byron ♂

Transferred use of the surname, first bestowed as a given name in honour of the poet Lord Byron (George Gordon, 6th Baron Byron, 1784–1824). The surname derives from the Old English phrase *æt ðæm bȳrum* 'at the byres or cattlesheds', and denoted someone who lived there because it was his job to look after cattle.

CADE CADELL CADOGAN CAESAR CAHAN
CAILE CAILEIGH CAITLÍN CAITRÍN CALE CA
LE CALEIGH CALICO CALISTA CALLY CALU
M CALVIN CAMEO CAMERON CAMILLA CA
M BELL CANDACE CANDICE CANDIDA CA
NDICE CANNA CAPRICE CAOIMHE C

Cade ♂

Transferred use of the surname, which originated as a nickname from a word denoting something round and lumpish. It is one of several given names that owe their origin to their use for a character in Margaret Mitchell's novel *Gone with the Wind* (1936).

Cadell ♂

Welsh traditional name, derived from *cad* 'battle' + the diminutive suffix *-ell*.

Cadogan ♂

Anglicized form of the Old Welsh personal name *Cadwgan* or *Cadwgawn*, derived from *cad* 'battle' + *gwogawn* 'glory', 'distinction', or 'honour'. The name was borne by several Welsh princes in the early Middle Ages, and is mentioned as the name of two characters in the *Mabinogi*. It was revived in the 19th century, perhaps in part as a transferred use of the surname derived from it.

Caesar ♂

Mainly U.S.: Anglicized form of Italian *Cesare* or French *César*, or a direct adoption of the Roman imperial family name *Caesar*, of uncertain meaning. It has been connected with Latin *caesaries* 'head of hair', but this is no more than folk etymology; the name may be of Etruscan origin. Its most notable bearer was Gaius Julius Caesar (?102–144 BC) and it also formed part of the full name of his relative Augustus (Gaius Julius Caesar Octavianus Augustus). Subsequently it was used as an imperial title and eventually became a vocabulary word for an emperor (leading to German *Kaiser* and Russian *tsar*).

Cahan ♂

Irish: see ◊**Kane**.

Caile ♂

Variant spelling of ◊**Cale**.

Caileigh ♀

See ◊**Kayley**.

Caitlín ♀

Irish Gaelic form of ◊**Katherine**, pronounced 'kat-*leen*'. It is being increasingly widely used in the English-speaking world, generally without the accent and with the pronunciation '*kate*-lin'.

Caitrín ♀

Irish Gaelic form of ◊**Katherine**.

Cale ♂

Mainly U.S.: of uncertain origin; perhaps a short form of ◊**Caleb** or a transferred use of a surname.
Variants: **Caile**, **Cayle**, **Kale**, **Kail(e)**, **Kayle**.

Caleb ♂

Biblical name, borne by an early Israelite, one of only two of those who set out with Moses from Egypt to live long enough to enter the promised land (Numbers 26:65). The name, which is apparently derived from the word for 'dog' in Hebrew, is said in some traditions to symbolize his devotion to God. It was popular among the Puritans and was introduced by them to America, where it is still in use.

Caleigh ♀

See ◊**Kayley**.

Calico ♀

Apparently from the name of the cotton fabric, originally so called because it was imported from the Indian port of Calicut (now Kozhikode) in Kerala. It may have come to be adopted as a first name by association with ◊**Dimity**.

Calista ♀
From the Late Latin name *Calixta*, feminine form of *Calixtus* (from Latin *calix* 'cup', adopted by Christians with specific reference to the cup containing the wine of the Christian sacrament). The male name was borne by three popes, including a 3rd-century saint (d. 222); it never enjoyed great popularity in England, but it became common in Bohemia, especially among members of a Hussite sect calling themselves Calixtines, who believed that wine as well as bread should be given to the laity in the Eucharist. In modern times this name is borne by the actress Calista Flockhart, star of the TV show Ally McBeal. There is also an apparent association with Greek *kallista* (feminine form) 'fairest', 'most beautiful'.

Cally ♀
Mainly U.S. It probably originated as a variant of ◊**Kelly**, since none of the women's names beginning with the syllable *Cal-* (e.g. *Calliope* and *Calista*) has ever been common.
Variant: **Callie**.

Calum ♂
Scottish Gaelic form of the Late Latin personal name *Columba* 'dove'. This was popular among early Christians because the dove was a symbol of gentleness, purity, peace, and the Holy Spirit. St Columba was one of the most influential of all the early Celtic saints. He was born in Donegal in 521 into a noble family, and was trained for the priesthood from early in life. He founded monastery schools at Durrow, Derry, and Kells, and then, in 563, sailed with twelve companions to Scotland, to convert the people there to Christianity. He established a monastery on the island of Iona, and from there converted the Pictish and Irish inhabitants of Scotland. He died in 597 and was buried at

Downpatrick. The usual Irish form of his name is **Colm**.

Calvin ♂
Especially North American: from the French surname, used as a given name among Nonconformists in honour of the French Protestant theologian Jean Calvin (1509–64). The surname meant originally 'little bald one', from a diminutive of *calve*, a Norman and Picard form of French *chauve* 'bald'. (The theologian was born in Noyon, Picardy.)

Cameo ♀
Apparently a transferred use of the vocabulary word (Italian *cammeo*, which is probably of Oriental origin) referring to the relief carving of a layered mineral carried out in such a way as to result in foreground and background of contrasting colours, and by extension to anything else—including a baby—that is small but perfectly formed.

Cameron ♂, ♀
Transferred use of the Scottish surname, which is borne by one of the great Highland clans. Their name is popularly derived from an ancestor with a crooked nose (Gaelic *cam sròn*). There were also Camerons in the Lowlands, apparently the result of an assimilation to this name of a Norman baronial name derived from *Cambernon* in Normandy. It is common in North America and in the United States is well established as a girl's name.

Camilla ♀
Feminine form of the old Roman family name *Camillus*, of obscure and presumably non-Roman origin. According to tradition, recorded by the Roman poet Virgil, Camilla was the name of a warrior maiden, Queen of the Volscians, who fought in the army of Aeneas (*Aeneid* 7:803–17).

Campbell ♂
Transferred use of the Scottish surname, borne by one of the great Highland clans, whose head is the Duke of Argyll. The

name is derived from an ancestor with a crooked mouth (Gaelic *cam beul*).

Candace ♀

The hereditary name of a long line of queens of Ethiopia. One of them is mentioned in the Bible, when the apostle Philip baptizes 'a man of Ethiopia, an eunuch of great authority under Candace queen of the Ethiopians, who had the charge of all her treasure' (Acts 8:27).

Candice ♀

Apparently a respelling of ◊**Candace**, perhaps influenced by ◊**Clarice** or by a folk etymology deriving the name from Late Latin *canditia* 'whiteness'. The name is best known as that of the American actress Candice Bergen (b. 1946).

Candida ♀

From Late Latin, meaning 'white'. The colour was associated in Christian imagery with purity and salvation (see Revelation 3:4 'thou hast a few names even in Sardis which have not defiled their garments; and they shall walk with me in white: for they are worthy'). This was the name of several early saints, including a woman supposedly cured by St Peter himself.

Candy ♀

Especially North American: from an affectionate nickname derived from the vocabulary word *candy* 'confectionery'. The word *candy* is from French *sucre candi* 'candied sugar', i.e. sugar boiled to make a crystalline sweet. The French word is derived from Arabic *qandi*, which is in turn of Indian origin. *Candy* is also found as a short form of ◊**Candice**.

Canice ♂

Irish: from the Latinized form, *Canicius*, of the traditional Gaelic personal name *Cainneach*, originally a byname meaning 'handsome'. This name was borne by a large number of early saints, of whom the most important is the 6th-century founder of the town of Kilkenny (Gaelic *Cill Chainnigh*).

Canna ♀

Apparently from the name of a genus of plants that have attractive, brightly coloured flowers and are widely cultivated in parts of the world with a warm climate. This is now relatively well established as a first name in Australia. The botanical name represents Latin *canna* 'reed'.

Caprice ♀

From the vocabulary word referring to a whim or something whimsical. The word came into English via French from Italian *capriccio*, which originally referred to a sensation of horror making the hair stand on end (from Italian *capo* 'head' + *riccio* 'hedgehog'); its later meaning derives from association with the stubbornness of the goat (Italian *capra*).

Caoimhe ♀

Irish Gaelic name, pronounced '*kee*-va', from a vocabulary word meaning 'gentleness', 'loveliness', or 'grace'.

Cara ♀

20th-century coinage, from the Italian term of endearment *cara* 'beloved' or the Irish Gaelic vocabulary word *cara* 'friend'.

Caradoc ♂

Welsh, pronounced 'ka-*rad*-ok': respelling of *Caradog*, an ancient Celtic name apparently derived from the root *cār* 'love'. A form of this name was borne by the British chieftain recorded under the Latinized version *Caractacus*, son of Cunobelinos. He rebelled against Roman rule in the 1st century AD, and although the rebellion was swiftly put down he is recorded by the Roman historian Tacitus as having impressed the Emperor Claudius by his proud bearing in captivity.

Careen ♀

Of recent origin and uncertain derivation. Its first appearance seems to have been in Margaret Mitchell's novel *Gone with the Wind* (1936), where it is borne by one of the sisters of Scarlett O'Hara.

The name may represent a combination of ◊**Cara** with the diminutive suffix *-een* (of Irish origin, as in ◊**Maureen**), or it may be an altered form of ◊**Corinne** or ◊**Carina**.

Carey ♀
Variant spelling of ◊**Cary**, used mainly as a girl's name, under the influence of ◊**Carrie**.

Carina ♀
Late 19th-century coinage, apparently representing a Latinate elaboration of the feminine adjective *cara* 'beloved'; in part it may also have been inspired by ◊**Karin**.

Carissa ♀
Apparently a simplified spelling of ◊**Charissa**, or an elaborated form of ◊**Carys**.

Carl ♂
From an old-fashioned German spelling variant of *Karl*, the German version of ◊**Charles**. It is now increasingly used in the English-speaking world, and for some reason is particularly popular in Wales.

Carla ♀
Feminine form of ◊**Carl**.

Carlotta ♀
Italian form of ◊**Charlotte**, occasionally used in the English-speaking world.

Carlton ♂
Transferred use of the surname, a local name from any of various places (in Beds., Cambs., Co. Durham, Leics., Lincs., Northants, Notts., Suffolk, and Yorks.) named with Old English *carl* '(free) peasant' + *tūn* 'settlement', i.e. 'settlement of the free peasants'. This is the same name as ◊**Charlton**, *Ch-* representing the southern (Anglo-Saxon) pronunciation, while *C-* represents the northern (Anglo-Scandinavian) version.

Carly ♀
Pet form or variant of ◊**Carla**.
Variant: **Carlie**.

Carlyle ♂
Transferred use of the surname, in origin a local name from *Carlisle* in Cumbria. The first syllable of the place name represents the British element *ker* 'fort'; the second derives from the Romano-British name of the settlement *Luguvalium*. The surname is now common in Northern Ireland as well as in northern England and Scotland. Use as a given name may also have originated as an elaborated form of ◊**Carl**.

Carmel ♀
Of early Christian origin, referring to 'Our Lady of Carmel', a title of the Virgin Mary. *Carmel* is the name (meaning 'garden' or 'orchard' in Hebrew) of a mountain in the Holy Land near modern Haifa, which was populated from very early Christian times by hermits. They were later organized into the Carmelite order of monks. The name is used mainly by Roman Catholics.
Variant: **Carmela**.

Carmen ♀
Spanish form of ◊**Carmel**, altered by folk etymology to the form of the Latin word *carmen* 'song'. It is now sometimes found as a given name in the English-speaking world, in spite of, or perhaps because of, its association with the tragic romantic heroine of Bizet's opera *Carmen* (1875), based on a short story by Prosper Mérimée.

Carol ♀, originally ♂
Anglicized form of *Carolus* (see ◊**Charles**), or of its feminine derivative **Carola**. It has never been common as a boy's name, and has become even less so since its growth in popularity as a girl's name. This seems to be of relatively recent origin (not being found much before the end of the 19th century). It probably originated as a short form of ◊**Caroline**.

Carole ♀
French form of ◊**Carol**, formerly quite commonly used in the English-speaking world. In the 1930s it was associated particularly with the film star Carole

Lombard (1908–42). Now that *Carol* is used almost exclusively for girls, the form *Carole* has become rather less frequent.

Caroline ♀
From the French form of Latin or Italian **Carolina**, a feminine derivative of *Carolus* (see ◊**Charles**). This name was used by certain gentry families from the 17th century onwards, no doubt in honour of the Stuart kings named *Charles*.
Short forms: **Caro**; ◊**Carrie**.

Carolyn ♀
Altered form of ◊**Caroline**.

Carrie ♀
Pet form of ◊**Caroline** or occasionally of other girls' names beginning with the syllable *Car-*.

Carson ♂
Transferred use of the mainly Scottish surname, which is of uncertain derivation. The first known bearer is a certain Robert *de Carsan* (or *de Acarson*), recorded in 1276; the 'de' suggests derivation from a place name, but no suitable place has been identified. Among Protestants in Northern Ireland, it is sometimes bestowed in honour of Edward Carson (1854–1935), the Dublin barrister and politician who was a violent opponent of Home Rule for Ireland. In America the popularity of the name may have been affected by the legendary Missouri frontiersman Kit Carson (1809–68).

Carter ♂
Transferred use of the surname, which originated as an occupational name for someone who transported goods in a cart.

Cary ♂, sometimes ♀
Transferred use of the surname, which comes from one of the places in Devon or Somerset so called from an old Celtic river name. *Cary* became popular as a given name in the middle of the 20th century, due to the fame of the film actor Cary Grant (1904–89), who was born in Bristol and made his first theatrical

appearances under his original name of Archie Leach.
Variant: ◊**Carey**.

Caryl ♀, occasionally ♂
Of uncertain origin, probably a variant of ◊**Carol**.

Carys ♀
Welsh: modern coinage, from *câr* 'love' + the ending *-ys*, derived by analogy with names such as ◊**Gladys**.

Casey ♂, ♀
Especially North American: bestowed originally in honour of the American engine driver and folk hero 'Casey' Jones (1863–1900), who saved the lives of passengers on the 'Cannonball Express' at the expense of his own. He was baptized Johnathan Luther Jones in Cayce, Kentucky, and acquired his nickname from his birthplace. As a girl's name it is a variant of ◊**Cassie**.
Variant: **Casy**.

Caspar ♂
Dutch form of ◊**Jasper**, also found as an occasional variant in English. According to legend, this was the name of one of the three Magi or 'wise men' who brought gifts to the infant Christ. The magi are not named in the Bible, but early Christian tradition assigned them the names *Caspar*, *Balthasar*, and *Melchior*.
Variant: **Casper**.

Cass ♀
Medieval and modern short form of ◊**Cassandra**.

Cassandra ♀
From Greek legend. Cassandra was a Trojan princess blessed with the gift of prophecy but cursed with the fate that nobody would ever believe her. She was brought back to Greece as a captive concubine by Agamemnon, but met her death at the hands of his jealous wife Clytemnestra. Although it was never generally popular, this name was in occasional use from the Middle Ages until the 18th century, and has recently been revived by parents looking to the

pages of classical mythology for distinctive names.

Cassia ♀
Feminine form of ◊**Cassius** or ◊**Cassian**. It may also in part represent an adoption of the name of the spice (see ◊**Kezia**).

Cassian ♂
From Latin *Cassiānus*, an elaboration of ◊**Cassius**. This name was borne by several early saints, most notably one martyred at Tangier in 298.

Cassidy ♀, ♂
Especially North American: from the Irish Gaelic surname *Ó Caiside*. Its use as a girl's name may be due to the *-y* ending, coupled with the fact that it could be taken as an expanded form of ◊**Cass**.

Cassie ♀
Pet form of ◊**Cass**.
Variant: **Cassy**.

Cassius ♂
From an old Roman family name, borne most notably by the senator Gaius Cassius Longinus who led the conspiracy to assassinate Julius Caesar. The Latin name is of uncertain derivation, possibly connected with *cassus* 'empty', 'hollow'. Like other famous names from Roman history, such as ◊**Caesar** and *Pompey*, this name was commonly bestowed on slaves by their owners, and at one time it was fairly common among Blacks in the United States. Because of these associations it was repudiated by the boxer Cassius Clay (b. 1942), who changed his name to Muhammed Ali.

Casy ♂, ♀
Variant spelling of ◊**Casey**.

Cath ♀
Short form of ◊**Catherine** and *Catharine*.

Cathal ♂
Irish Gaelic name, pronounced '*ko*-hal'. It is derived from the Old Celtic words *cath* 'battle' + *val* 'rule'. It was borne by a 7th-century saint who served as head of the monastic school at Lismore, Co.

Waterford, before being appointed bishop of Taranto in south Italy.
Variant: **Cal** (in Ulster).

Catherine ♀
Variant spelling of ◊**Katherine**. This form of the name is also used in France.
Variant: **Catharine** (English only).
Short form: **Cath**.
Pet form: **Cathy**.

Cathleen ♀
Variant spelling of ◊**Kathleen**.

Cathy ♀
Pet form of ◊**Catherine** and *Catharine*.

Catrin ♀
Welsh form of ◊**Katherine**.

Catrina ♀
Simplified spelling of ◊**Catriona**.

Catriona ♀
Anglicized form of the Gaelic names **Ca(i)trìona** (Scottish) and **Caitríona** (Irish), which are themselves forms of ◊**Katherine**. As the accents show, it is stressed on the second *i*. The name is now also used elsewhere in the English-speaking world, although it is still especially popular among people of Scottish ancestry. It attracted wider attention as the title of Robert Louis Stevenson's novel *Catriona* (1893), sequel to *Kidnapped*.

Caxton ♂
Transferred use of the surname, in origin a local name from a place in Cambridgeshire. The place name derives from the genitive case of the Old Norse byname *Kakkr* (apparently a derivative of *kokkr* 'lump') + Old English *tūn* 'enclosure', 'settlement'. The surname is well known, as it was borne by William Caxton (?1422–91) who established the first printing press in England, but the reason for its recent adoption as a given name is not clear.

Cayle ♂
Variant spelling of ◊**Cale**.

Cayleigh ♀
See ◊**Kayley**.

Ceallach ♂, ♀

Traditional Irish Gaelic name, pronounced '*kell*-ach', said to mean 'bright-
headed'. See ◊**Kelly**.

Cecil ♂

Transferred use of the surname of a great
noble family, which rose to prominence
in England during the 16th century. The
Cecils were of Welsh origin, and their
surname represents an Anglicized form
of the Welsh given name *Seissylt*, apparently a Brittonic or Old Welsh form of
the Latin name *Sextilius*, from *Sextus*
'sixth'. In the Middle Ages *Cecil* was
occasionally used as an English form of
Latin *Caecilius* (an old Roman family
name derived from the byname *Caecus*
'blind'), borne by a minor saint of the 3rd
century, a friend of St Cyprian.

Cecilia ♀

From the Latin name *Caecilia*, feminine
of *Caecilius* (see ◊**Cecil**). This was a good
deal more common than the masculine
form, largely due to the fame of the 2nd-
or 3rd-century virgin martyr whose
name is still mentioned daily in the
Roman Catholic Canon of the Mass. She
is regarded as the patron saint of music
and has inspired works such as Purcell's
'Ode on St Cecilia's Day', although
the reasons for this association are not
clear.

Cecily ♀

From the medieval vernacular form of
◊**Cecilia**.
Variant: **Cicely**.
Pet forms: **Sessy**, **Sissy**.

Cedric ♂

Coined by Sir Walter Scott for the character Cedric of Rotherwood in *Ivanhoe*
(1819). It seems to be an altered form of
Cerdic, the name of the traditional
founder of the kingdom of Wessex.
Cerdic was a Saxon (Scott's novel also
has a Saxon setting), and his name is
presumably of Germanic origin, but the
formation is not clear. The name has
acquired something of a 'sissy' image,
partly on account of Cedric Errol
Fauntleroy, the long-haired, velvet-

suited boy hero of Frances Hodgson
Burnett's *Little Lord Fauntleroy* (1886).
A well-known bearer was the film actor
Sir Cedric Hardwicke (1893–1964).

Ceinwen ♀

Welsh traditional name, pronounced
'*kayn*-wen', from *cain* 'fair', 'lovely' +
(g)wen 'white', 'blessed', 'holy'. It was
borne by a 5th-century saint, daughter of
the chieftain Brychan, about whom
little is known.

Céleste ♀

French, now also quite common in the
English-speaking world (usually without the accent): from Latin *Caelestis*
'heavenly', a popular name among early
Christians.

Celia ♀

From Latin *Caelia*, feminine form of the
old Roman family name *Caelius* (of
uncertain origin, probably a derivative of
caelum 'heaven'). The name was not
used in the Middle Ages, but was introduced to the English-speaking world as
the name of a character in Shakespeare's
As You Like It. It was popularized in the
1940s by the actress Celia Johnson
(1908–82). This name is sometimes
taken as a short form of ◊**Cecilia**.

Ceri ♀, ♂

Welsh (pronounced '*kerry*'): of uncertain
origin. As a girl's name it is probably a
short form of ◊**Ceridwen**.

Ceridwen ♀

Welsh (pronounced 'ke-*rid*-wen'): name
in Celtic mythology of the goddess of
poetic inspiration. This is apparently
derived from *cerdd* 'poetry' + *(g)wen*
feminine of *gwyn* 'white', 'fair',
'blessed', 'holy'. It is said to have been
the name of the mother of the legendary
6th-century Welsh hero Taliesin, but it
is not clear whether in fact it represents
a personal name or whether Taliesin is
to be regarded as the son of the goddess of
poetry.

Cerise ♀

Modern coinage, apparently from
French *cerise* 'cherry' (see ◊**Cherry**) or

the English word for the colour (which is borrowed from the French term). However, it may be simply a combination of elements, e.g. from ◊**Ceri** and ◊**Louise**.

Chad ♂
Modern spelling of the Old English name *Ceadda*, the name of a 7th-century saint who was Archbishop of York. His name is of uncertain derivation.

Chadwick ♂
Mainly U.S.: transferred use of the surname, in origin a local name from any of the various places in England named as the 'dairy farm (Old English *wīc*) of Ceadda (see ◊**Chad**) or Ceadel'. In modern use, this name is sometimes taken, wrongly, as a full form of *Chad*.

Chalice ♀
Although coinciding in form with the name of the ecclesiastical vessel (via Old French from Latin *calix* 'cup') which features in many versions of the legend of the Holy Grail, this apparently originated as a first name from the combination of syllables found in other popular female names, such as ◊**Charlotte** and ◊**Alice**.

Chance ♂
Mainly U.S.: transferred use of the surname, in origin a nickname for an inveterate gambler, or perhaps for someone who had survived an accident by a remarkable piece of luck, from Anglo-Norman *chea(u)nce* '(good) fortune'.

Chandler ♂
Transferred use of the surname, which originated as an occupational name for someone who made and sold candles (an agent noun from Old French *chandele* 'candle'). The extended sense 'retail dealer' arose in the 16th century.

Chanel ♀
Mainly U.S.: transferred use of the French surname *Chanel*, borne most notably by Gabrielle 'Coco' Chanel (1883–1971), who founded a famous Parisian fashion house.
Variant: **Chanelle**.

Chantal ♀
French name now sometimes used in the English-speaking world. It was originally bestowed as a given name in honour of St Jeanne-Françoise Frémiot (1572–1641), a woman of great piety who in 1592 married the Baron de Chantal (whose title denoted a place in Saône-et-Loire). After her husband's death she adopted a strict religious life under the instruction of St Francis of Sales, and in 1610 founded an order of nuns, the Visitandines, devoted at first to charitable works, later (after official intervention by the clergy) to teaching and devotion to the Sacred Heart of Jesus.

Chantel ♀
Altered spelling of ◊**Chantal**.
Variants: **Chantelle**, **Shantell**.

Chapman ♂
Transferred use of the surname, which originated in the Middle Ages as an occupational name for a merchant or pedlar, from Old English *cēapmann* (a compound of *cēapan* 'to buy', 'sell', 'trade' + *mann* 'man').

Charis ♀
From Greek *kharis* 'grace'. This was a key word in early Christian thought, but was not used as a name in the early centuries after Christ or in the Middle Ages. As a given name it is a 17th-century innovation, probably chosen to express the Christian concept of charity. In later use it may sometimes have been selected as a classical reference to the three Graces (Greek *kharites*).

Charisma ♀
Modern name, from the vocabulary word denoting personal magnetism or charm (from Greek *charisma* 'blessing', referring originally to the spiritual gifts conferred by the Holy Spirit on the Christian apostles). It may be chosen by parents in the hope that the child will have this quality, or it may simply represent an elaboration of ◊**Charis**.

Charissa ♀

Apparently a recent elaboration of
◊**Charis**, perhaps as a result of blending
with ◊**Clarissa**.

Charity ♀

From the vocabulary word, denoting
originally the Christian's love for his
fellow man (Latin *caritās*, from *carus*
'dear'). In spite of St Paul's words 'and
now abideth faith, hope, charity, these
three; but the greatest of these is
charity' (1 Corinthians 13:13), *Charity* is
now rarely used as a given name in
comparison with the shorter ◊**Faith** and
◊**Hope**.

Charlene ♀

Chiefly Australian and North American: 20th-century coinage, from
◊**Charles** + the feminine name-suffix
-ene. It may have been influenced by the
older but much rarer French name
Charline, a feminine diminutive of
◊**Charles**.

Charles ♂

From a Germanic word, *karl*, meaning
'free man', akin to Old English *ceorl*
'man'. The name, Latin form *Carolus*,
owed its popularity in medieval Europe
to the Frankish leader Charlemagne
(?742–814), who in 800 established
himself as Holy Roman Emperor. His
name (Latin *Carolus Magnus*) means
'Charles the Great'. *Carolus*—or *Karl*,
the German form—was a common
name among Frankish leaders, including Charlemagne's grandfather Charles
Martel (688–741). *Charles* is the French
form . The name occurs occasionally in
medieval Britain as *Karolus* or *Carolus*;
it had a certain vogue in West Yorkshire
from the 1400s, particularly among
gentry families. The form *Charles* was
introduced to Britain by Mary Queen of
Scots (1542–87), who had been brought
up in France. She chose the names
Charles James for her son (1566–1625),
who became King James VI of Scotland
and, from 1603, James I of England. His
son and grandson both reigned as King
Charles, and the name thus became

established in the 17th century both in
the Stuart royal house and among
English and Scottish supporters of the
Stuart monarchy. In the 18th century it
was to some extent favoured, along
with ◊**James**, by Jacobites, supporters of
the exiled Stuarts, opposed to the Han-
overian monarchy, especially in the
Highlands of Scotland. In the 19th
century the popularity of the name
was further enhanced by romanti-
cization of the story of 'Bonnie
Prince Charlie', leader of the 1745
rebellion.
Pet form: **Charlie**.

Charlie ♂, ♀

Pet form of ◊**Charles**, also of ◊**Charlotte**.

Charlotte ♀

French feminine diminutive of
◊**Charles**, used in England since the 17th
century, but most popular in the 18th
and 19th centuries, in part due to the
influence of firstly Queen Charlotte
(1744–1818), wife of George III, and
secondly the novelist Charlotte Brontë
(1816–55).
Pet forms: **Lottie**, **Tottie**, **Charlie**.

Charlton ♂

Transferred use of the surname, used as a
given name largely as a result of the
fame of the film actor Charlton Heston
(b. 1924 as John Charles Carter; *Charlton* was his mother's maiden name). The
surname was originally a local name
from any of numerous places, mainly in
southern England, named in Old English
as the 'settlement of the free peasants',
Old English *ceorlatun* (compare ◊**Carl-
ton**). The first element of the place name
is ultimately connected with the name
◊**Charles**.

Charmaine ♀

Possibly a variant of ◊**Charmian**, influenced by names such as ◊**Germaine**, but
more probably an invented name based
on the vocabulary word *charm* + *-aine* as
in ◊**Lorraine**. It is not found before 1920,
but enjoyed some popularity in the
1960s due to The Bachelors' hit song of
this name.

Charmian ♀

From the Late Greek name *Kharmion* (a diminutive of *kharma* 'delight'). The name was used by Shakespeare in *Antony and Cleopatra* for one of the attendants of the Egyptian queen; he took it from Sir Thomas North's translation of Plutarch's *Parallel Lives*.

Chas ♂

Short form of ◊**Charles**, originally from a written abbreviation.

Chase ♂

Especially U.S.: transferred use of the surname, which originated in the Middle Ages as a nickname for a huntsman, from Anglo-Norman *chase* 'chase', 'hunt'.

Chasity ♀

Mainly U.S.: a simplified form of ◊**Chastity** or a blend of that name with ◊**Charity**.

Chastity ♀

Mainly U.S.: from the vocabulary word, which is from Late Latin *castitās*, a derivative of *castus*, 'pure', 'undefiled'. This name became known when it was given by the singer and actress Cher Bono to her daughter.

Chauncey ♂

U.S. coinage from a well-known New England surname. It was first chosen as a given name in honour of the Harvard College president Charles Chauncy (1592–1672), the New England clergyman Charles Chauncy (1705–87), or the naval officer Isaac Chauncey (1772–1840). These three men were descended from a single family; the surname is found in England in the Middle Ages, and probably has a Norman baronial origin, but is now extinct in Britain.
Variant: **Chauncy**.

Chaz ♂

Pet form of ◊**Charles**, derived in part from the use of **Chas** as a written abbreviation for that name.

Chelle ♀

Informal short form of ◊**Michelle**. See also ◊**Shell**.

Chelsea ♀

A 20th-century coinage enjoying a certain vogue. Ostensibly it is from the district of south-west London, which became known as the hub of the Swinging Sixties. (It was named in Old English as the 'chalk landing place', *cealc hȳð*). It is also the name of several places in North America, the earliest of which, in Maryland, was named in 1739. It is the name of the daughter of President Clinton. Another influence on the coinage may have been the given name ◊**Kelsey**.
Variants: **Chelsey**, **Chelsie**.

Cherelle ♀

Apparently a respelling of ◊**Cheryl**, influenced by the popular name ending *-elle* (originally a French feminine diminutive suffix).

Cherene ♀

Chiefly U.S.: modern coinage, a combination of *Cher-* (compare the many names following) with the feminine ending *-ene*.

Cherida ♀

Modern coinage, a blend of ◊**Cheryl** and ◊**Phillida**. It may also have been influenced by the Spanish vocabulary word *querida* 'darling' (compare French ◊**Cherie**).

Chérie ♀

Modern coinage from the French vocabulary word *chérie* 'darling'.
Variant: **Cheri**.

Cherish ♀

Modern coinage, apparently an alteration of ◊**Cheryth** to match the vocabulary word *cherish* 'to treasure', 'care for' (borrowed in the Middle Ages from Old French *cherir*, a derivative of *cher* 'dear').

Cherry ♀

19th-century coinage, probably taken from the vocabulary word denoting the fruit (Middle English *cheri(e)*, from Old

French *cherise*). However, in some cases it is also derived from a transferred use of the surname *Cherry* (to which the naturalist and pioneer photographer Cherry Kearton (1871–1940) owed his name). Dickens used *Cherry* as a pet form of ◊**Charity**: in *Martin Chuzzlewit* (1844) Mr Pecksniff's daughters Charity and Mercy are known as Cherry and Merry. In modern usage it is perhaps in some cases an Anglicization of French ◊**Chérie**.

Cheryl ♀
Not found before the 1920s, and not common until the 1940s, but increasingly popular since, being borne, for example, by the American actress Cheryl Ladd (b. 1951). It appears to be a blend of ◊**Cherry** and ◊**Beryl**.

Cheryth ♀
Evidently a blend of ◊**Cherry** with ◊**Gwyneth**, influenced by the biblical placename *Cherith*. The brook Cherith was a dry riverbed in which the prophet Elijah took refuge from the wrath of Ahab and Jezebel (1 Kings 17:3–5).

Chester ♂
Transferred use of the surname, in origin a local name from the city of *Chester*, so called from an Old English form of Latin *castra* 'legionary camp'. Use as a given name has become quite common in the 20th century.

Chevonne ♀
Anglicized spelling of ◊**Siobhán**.

Chiara ♀
Italian form of ◊**Clara**, pronounced 'kee-*ah*-ra': now also occasionally used in the English-speaking world. The name has always been particularly popular in Italy and has been borne by several Italian saints, notably Clare of Assisi (*c.*1193–1253), an associate of Francis of Assisi and founder of the order of nuns known as the Poor Clares. See also ◊**Ciara**.

Chloe ♀
Pronounced 'khloh-ee': from the Late Greek name *Khloē*, originally used in the classical period as an epithet of the

fertility goddess Demeter. It may be indirectly connected with ◊**Chloris**. A person of this name receives a fleeting mention in the New Testament (1 Corinthians 1:11), but its use as a given name in the English-speaking world almost certainly derives from this reference, leading to its adoption in the 17th century among the Puritans. It has fared better since than many of the minor biblical names taken up at that time.

Chloris ♀
From Greek mythology. *Khlōris* was a minor goddess of vegetation; her name derives from Greek *khlōros* 'green'. It was used by the Roman poet Horace for one of his loves (see also ◊**Lalage**), and was taken up by Augustan poets of the 17th and 18th centuries.

Chorine ♀
Apparently an altered form of ◊**Corinne**, coinciding with the vocabulary word formerly used to refer to a female dancer in music hall and variety shows (a French formation, from *chor-* 'dance' + the feminine diminutive suffix *-ine*).

Chris ♂, ♀
Short form of ◊**Christopher**, and of ◊**Christine** and the group of related girls' names.

Chriselda ♀
Elaboration of ◊**Chris**, apparently on the model of ◊**Griselda**.

Chrissie ♀
Pet form of ◊**Christine** and the group of related girls' names. It is especially common in Scotland.
Variant: **Chrissy**.

Christa ♀
Latinate short form of ◊**Christine** and ◊**Christina**. It seems to have originated in Germany, but is now also well established in the English-speaking world.

Christabel ♀
Medieval coinage from the name of *Christ* combined with the productive

suffix -bel 'beauty' (see ◊Belle). This name is recorded in Yorkshire from the mid 1400s onwards. Its popularity was enhanced by its use for the heroine of a poem (1816) by Samuel Taylor Coleridge (1772–1834). The name was borne by the pioneer suffragette Christabel Pankhurst (1880–1958), in whose honour it is now sometimes bestowed.
Variants: **Christabelle**, **Christabella**.

Christelle ♀
Altered form of ◊Christine, derived by replacement of the feminine diminutive suffix -ine with the equally feminine suffix -elle. The name is now also used in the English-speaking world, where its popularity has been enhanced by its resemblance to ◊Crystal, of which it may in some cases be a variant.

Christene ♀
Variant of ◊Christine, influenced by the productive feminine name suffix -ene.
Variant: **Christeen**.

Christian ♂, ♀
From Latin *Christiānus* 'follower of Christ', in use as a given name during the Middle Ages, and sporadically ever since. In the Middle Ages it was more commonly a girl's name than a boy's. The name of *Christ* (Greek *Khristos*) is a translation of the Hebrew term *Messiah* 'anointed'.

Christiana ♀
Medieval learned feminine form of ◊Christian. As a recent revival it represents an elaborated form of ◊Christina. It is also sometimes spelled **Christianna**, under the influence of the name ◊Anna.

Christie ♀, ♂
Pet form of ◊Christine or, particularly in Scotland and Ireland, of ◊Christopher.
Variant: **Christy**.

Christina ♀
Simplified form of Latin *Christiāna*, feminine of *Christiānus* (see ◊Christian), or a Latinized form of Middle English *Christin* 'Christian' (Old English *christen*, from Latin).

Christine ♀
French form of ◊Christina, not much used in Britain until the end of the 19th century. Until fairly recently it was principally associated with Scotland, but now it is very popular in all parts of the English-speaking world.
Short form: **Chris**.
Pet forms: **Chrissie**, **Chrissy**, **Christie**, **Christy**, ◊**Kirstie**.

Christmas ♂
From the festival celebrating the birth of Christ (so called from *Christ* (see ◊Christian) + *mass* festival). It is sometimes given to a boy born on Christmas Day. See also ◊Noël and ◊Natalie.

Christopher ♂
From the Greek name *Khristophoros*, from *Khristos* 'Christ' + *pherein* 'to bear'. This was popular among early Christians, conscious of the fact that they were metaphorically bearing Christ in their hearts. A later, over-literal interpretation of the name gave rise to the legend of a saint who actually bore the Christ-child over a stream; he is regarded as the patron of travellers. In England the name was uncommon in the Middle Ages, but became very popular in the 16th century, especially in parts of the North.
Short form: **Chris**.
Pet forms: **Kit**. *Scottish, Irish*: **Christie**, **Christy**.

Christy ♂, ♀
Variant spelling of ◊Christie.

Chrystal ♀
Rare variant spelling of ◊Crystal, apparently influenced by Greek *khrysos* 'gold'.
Variant: **Chrystalla** (Latinate).

Chuck ♂
North American: now usually taken as a pet form of ◊Charles. It was originally a nickname, from an English term of endearment (as in Shakespeare's phrase 'dearest chuck'), probably from Middle English *chukken* 'to cluck'.
Pet form: **Chuckie**.

Cian ♂

Irish: traditional Gaelic name, pronounced '*kee*-an', derived from the Irish vocabulary word meaning 'ancient'. It was borne by a son-in-law of Brian Boru, who played a leading role in the battle of Clontarf (1014).
Anglicized forms: **Kean(e)**.

Ciara ♀

Irish, pronounced '*kee*-a-ra': modern coinage, created as a feminine form of ◊**Ciarán**.

Ciarán ♂

Irish Gaelic name, pronounced '*kee*-a-rawn' and often Anglicized as ◊**Kieran**. It was originally a byname, a diminutive form of *ciar* 'black'. It was borne by two Irish saints, a hermit of the 5th century and the founder of the monastery at Clonmacnoise (d. 547).

Cicely ♀

Variant of ◊**Cecily**. This was a common form of the name in the Middle Ages, and was well known between the wars as the name of the British actress and singer Cicely Courtneidge.
Pet form: ◊**Sissy**.

Cilla ♀

Pet form of ◊**Priscilla**, associated chiefly with the Liverpudlian singer and TV personality Cilla Black, whose real name is Priscilla White.

Cillian ♂

Irish Gaelic name often Anglicized as ◊**Killian**. It was originally a byname representing a diminutive form of Gaelic *ceallach* 'strife', or possibly derived from Gaelic *ceall* 'monastery', 'church' (see ◊**Kelly**), and was borne by various early Irish saints, including the 7th-century author of a life of St Bridget and missionaries to Artois and Franconia.

Cindy ♀

Pet form of ◊**Cynthia** or, less often, of ◊**Lucinda**, now very commonly used as a given name in its own right, especially in North America. It has sometimes been taken as a short form of the name of the fairy-tale heroine *Cinderella*, which is in fact unrelated (being from French *Cendrillon*, a derivative of *cendre* 'cinders').

Cinnamon ♀

Modern name, from the term for the spice (Greek *kinnamon*, of Semitic origin), in part perhaps referring to its warm brown colour. Use as a first name may have been influenced by other names which coincide in form with the names of spices, although they partly have other origins; see for example ◊**Cassia** and ◊**Fennel**.

Claiborne ♂

Transferred use of the surname of a major American family. William Claiborne (*c*.1587–*c*.1677), the second son of Edmund Cliburne of Cliburn in Westmorland (now Cumbria), was a founding colonist in Virginia. His descendant William Charles Claiborne (1775–1817) was the first governor of Louisiana.

Claire ♀

French form of ◊**Clara**. It was introduced to Britain by the Normans, but subsequently abandoned. This spelling was revived in the 19th century as a variant of ◊**Clare**.
Variant: **Clair**.

Clancy ♂

Mainly U.S.: transferred use of the Irish surname, Gaelic *Mac Fhlannchaidh* 'son of Flannchadh'. The latter is an ancient Irish personal name, probably composed of elements meaning 'red warrior'.
Variant: **Clancey**.

Clara ♀

Post-classical Latin name, from the feminine form of the adjective *clārus* 'famous'. In the modern English-speaking world it represents a re-Latinization of the regular English form ◊**Clare**. It was made famous in the 1920s by the silent film actress Clara Bow (1905–65), known as 'the It girl' (because, whatever 'it' was, she had it).

Clare ♀

The normal English vernacular form of
◊**Clara** during the Middle Ages and
since.

Clarence ♂

In use from the mid-19th century, but
now rare. It was first used in honour of
the popular elder son of Edward VII,
who was created Duke of Clarence in
1890, but died in 1892. His title (*Dux
Clarentiae* in Latin) originated with a
son of Edward III, who in the 14th
century was married to the heiress of
Clare in Suffolk (which is so called from
a Celtic river name and has no connection with the given name ◊**Clare**). The
title has been held by various British
royal princes at different periods in
history. In the United States the name
was borne most notably by the American defence lawyer Clarence Darrow
(1857–1938), played in various films by
Orson Welles, Spencer Tracey, and
Henry Fonda.

Clarette ♀

Rare elaborated form of ◊**Clare**, with the
French feminine diminutive suffix *-ette*.
The formation may have been influenced by the wine *claret* (Medieval Latin
(vīnum) clārātum 'clarified wine').

Clarice ♀

Medieval English and French form of the
Latin name *Claritia*. This may have
meant 'fame' (an abstract derivative of
clārus 'famous'), but as a given name it
may have been no more than an arbitrary
elaboration of ◊**Clara**. It was borne by a
character who features in some versions
of the medieval romances of Roland and
the other paladins of Charlemagne.

Clarinda ♀

Elaboration of ◊**Clara** with the suffix -
inda (as in ◊**Belinda** and ◊**Lucinda**).
Clarinda first appears in Spenser's *Faerie
Queene* (1596). The formation was
influenced by *Clorinda*, which occurs in
Torquato Tasso's *Gerusalemme
Liberata* (1580). This is itself an arbitrary
elaboration of ◊**Chloris**. Robert Burns
(1759–96) wrote four poems *To Clarinda*.

Clarissa ♀

Latinate form of ◊**Clarice** occasionally
found in medieval documents. It was
revived by Samuel Richardson as the
name of the central character in his
novel *Clarissa* (1748).

Clark ♂

Transferred use of the surname, which
originated as an occupational name
denoting a clerk (Latin *clēricus*), in the
Middle Ages a man in minor holy orders
who earned his living by his ability to
read and write). Since the 1930s, when it
was associated particularly with the
film star Clark Gable (1901–60), it has
been widely used as a given name,
especially in North America.
Variant: **Clarke**.

Clarrie ♂, ♀

Pet form of ◊**Clarence**, also of ◊**Clara** and
various similar women's names.

Claud ♂

Anglicized spelling of ◊**Claude**.

Claude ♂

French: from the Latin name *Claudius*,
an old Roman family name derived from
the byname *Claudus* 'lame'. It was
borne by various early saints, but its
popularity in France is largely due to the
fame of the 7th-century St Claude of
Besançon. In France, *Claude* also occasionally occurs as a girl's name.

Claudette ♀

French: feminine diminutive form of
◊**Claude**, now also occasionally used in
the English-speaking world. It gained
considerable prominence in the 1930s
as the name of the French film star
Claudette Colbert (1903–96), a Hollywood favourite for many years. Her
original name was Lily Claudette
Chauchoin.

Claudia ♀

From the Latin female name, a feminine
form of *Claudius* (see ◊**Claude**). The
name is mentioned in one of St Paul's
letters to Timothy (2, 4:21 'Eubulus
greeteth thee, and Pudens, and Linus,
and Claudia, and all the brethren'), as a

result of which it was taken up in the 16th century.

Claudine ♀
French: feminine diminutive form of ◊**Claude**. It was made popular at the beginning of the 20th century as the name of the heroine of a series of novels by the French writer Colette (1873–1954), and is now also occasionally used in the English-speaking world.

Claus ♂
German form of ◊**Nicholas**, representing a shortened form of *Niclaus* or *Niklaus*. In America this name tends to be associated with the figure of *Santa Claus* (originally *Sankt Niklaus*), which inhibits serious use of it.

Clay ♂
Either a shortened form of ◊**Clayton** or a transferred use of the surname *Clay*, a local name for someone who lived on a patch of land whose soil was predominantly clay (Old English *clæg*).

Clayton ♂
Especially U.S.: transferred use of the surname, originally a local name from any of the several places in England (for example, in Lancs., Staffs., Sussex, and W. Yorks.) named with Old English *clæg* 'clay' + *tūn* 'enclosure', 'settlement'.

Cledwyn ♂
Welsh traditional name, apparently derived from *caled* 'hard', 'rough' + *(g)wyn* 'white', 'fair', 'blessed', 'holy'.

Clem ♂, ♀
Short form of the boy's name ◊**Clement** and of girls' names such as ◊**Clemence**. *Pet form*: **Clemmie** (♀).

Clematis ♀
From the name of the flower (so named in the 16th century from Greek *klēmatis* 'climbing plant'), perhaps under the influence of names such as ◊**Clemence**, with the ending *-is* found in names such as ◊**Phyllis**.

Clemence ♀
Medieval French and English form of Latin *Clēmentia*, a derivative of *Clēm-*

ens (see ◊**Clement**) or an abstract noun meaning 'mercy'. It has never been particularly common, but is still occasionally used.

Clemency ♀
Rare variant of ◊**Clemence** or a direct use of the abstract noun, on the model of ◊**Charity**, ◊**Faith**, ◊**Mercy**, etc.

Clement ♂
From the Late Latin name *Clēmens* (genitive *Clēmentis*) meaning 'merciful'. This was borne by several early saints, notably the fourth pope and the early Christian theologian Clement of Alexandria (Titus Flavius Clemens, AD ?150–?215).

Clementine ♀
Feminine form of ◊**Clement**, created with the French feminine diminutive suffix *-ine*. The name was first used in the 19th century, and for a time it was very popular. It is now largely associated with the popular song with this title. The Latinate form **Clementina** is also found.

Clemmie ♀, ♂
Pet form of ◊**Clem**, borne more often by girls than by boys.

Cleo ♀
Short form of ◊**Cleopatra**. See also ◊**Clio**.

Cleopatra ♀
From the Greek name *Kleopatra*, derived from *kleos* 'glory' + *patēr* 'father'. This was borne by a large number of women in the Ptolemaic royal family of Egypt. The most famous (?69–30 BC) was the lover of Mark Antony, and has always figured largely in both literature and the popular imagination as a model of a passionate woman of unsurpassed beauty, who 'gave all for love' and in the process destroyed the man she loved. She had previously been the mistress of Julius Caesar.

Cliff ♂
Short form of ◊**Clifford**, now also sometimes of ◊**Clifton**. It is commonly used as a given name, especially since the

advent in the 1950s of the pop singer Cliff Richard (real name Harry Webb). It has sometimes also been associated with ◊**Clive**.

Clifford ♂

Transferred use of the surname, recorded as a given name from the 17th century. There are several places (e.g. in Gloucestershire, Herefordshire, and Yorkshire) so named, from Old English *clif* 'cliff', 'slope', 'riverbank' + *ford* 'ford'.

Clifton ♂

Transferred use of the surname, a local name from any of the numerous places named with Old English *clif* 'cliff', 'slope', 'riverbank' + *tūn* 'enclosure', 'settlement'. Use of this as a given name is more recent than that of ◊**Clifford**. It may in some cases have been adopted as an expanded form of ◊**Cliff**.

Clint ♂

Short form of ◊**Clinton**, made famous by the actor Clint Eastwood (b. 1930).

Clinton ♂

Mainly North American: transferred use of the English surname, a local name from *Glympton* in Oxfordshire or *Glinton* in Northants. It was originally used as a given name in America in honour of the Clinton family, whose members included the statesman George Clinton (1739–1812), governor of New York, and his nephew De Witt Clinton (1769–1828), who was responsible for overseeing the construction of the Erie Canal. It was also borne by Sir Henry Clinton (1735–95), British commander-in-chief in America during the Revolution.

Clio ♀

From Greek *Kleio*, the name borne in classical mythology both by one of the nymphs and by one of the Muses. It is probably ultimately connected with the word *kleos* 'glory'; compare ◊**Cleopatra**. The name is now sometimes used as a variant of ◊**Cleo**.

Cliona ♀

Anglicized form of the traditional Irish Gaelic name *Clíodhna*, which is of unknown origin. In Irish legend, Clíodhna was one of three beautiful daughters of the poet Libra; she eloped with Ciabhán, a prince of Ulster, but was drowned by a great wave shortly afterwards, while he was away hunting.

Clitus ♂

Mainly U.S.: Latinized form of Greek *Kleitos*, the name of one of Alexander the Great's generals. This name is probably ultimately connected with *Kleio* (see ◊**Clio**).

Clive ♂

Transferred use of the surname, in origin a local name from any of the various places (in e.g. Cheshire, Shropshire) so called from Old English *clif* 'cliff', 'slope'. As a given name it seems to have been originally chosen in honour of 'Clive of India' (Robert Clive, created Baron Clive of Plassey in 1760).

Clodagh ♀

Irish: of recent origin. It is the name of a river in Tipperary, and seems to have been arbitrarily transferred to use as a given name. There may be some association in the minds of givers with the Latin name *Clōdia* (borne by the mistress of the Roman poet Catullus), a variant of ◊**Claudia**.

Clove ♀

From the name of the spice (via Old French from Latin *clāvus* 'nail', referring to the shape of the dried flower buds. In part it may also represent a short form of ◊**Clover**.

Clover ♀

Modern coinage taken from word denoting the plant (Old English *clāfre*).

Clyde ♂

Mainly North American: from the name of river in south-west Scotland that runs through Glasgow, perhaps by way of a surname derived from the river name, although for many Scottish emigrants it was the point of departure from Scotland. The given name gained some currency, especially in the American

South. The bank robber Clyde Barrow became something of a cult figure after the film *Bonnie and Clyde* (1967), in which he was played by Warren Beatty.

Cody ♂, ♀

Mainly U.S. and Australian: transferred use of the Irish surname, an Anglicized form of Gaelic *Ó Cuidighthigh* 'descendant of Cuidightheach' (originally a byname for a helpful person) or of *Mac Óda* 'son of Óda' (a personal name of uncertain origin). Use as a given name has been at least in part inspired by William Frederick Cody (1846–1917), better known as 'Buffalo Bill', the showman of the Wild West.
Variants: **Codi**, **Codie**, **Codee** all (♀).

Colbert ♂

Transferred use of the surname, derived from an Old French given name of Germanic (Frankish) origin, from *col* (of uncertain meaning) + *berht* 'bright', 'famous'. This was introduced to Britain by the Normans. It survived long enough to give rise to the surname, but its use as a given name died out soon after.

Colby ♂

Mainly U.S.: transferred use of the surname, in origin a local name from places in Norfolk and Cumbria, so called from the Old Norse personal name *Koli* (a byname for a swarthy person, from *kol* 'charcoal') + Old Norse *býr* 'settlement'. Use as a given name seems to have been influenced by the 1980s television serial *The Colbys*, a spinoff from *Dynasty*.

Cole ♂

Transferred use of the surname, itself derived from a medieval given name of uncertain origin. It may represent a survival into Middle English of the Old English byname *Cola* 'swarthy', 'coal-black', from *col* 'charcoal'. As a given name, it is associated with the songwriter Cole Porter (1893–1964).

Coleman ♂

Variant of ◊**Colman**. In part it also represents a transferred use of the sur-name, which derives in most cases from the Gaelic personal name *Colmán*, but in others may be an occupational term for a charcoal burner.

Colette ♀

French feminine diminutive form of the medieval name *Col(le)*, a short form of ◊**Nicholas**. It was given particular currency from the 1920s onwards by the fame of the French novelist Colette (1873–1954).

Colin ♂

Diminutive form of the medieval name *Col(le)*, a short form of ◊**Nicholas**. In Scotland it has been used as an Anglicized form of the Gaelic name *Cailean*, particularly favoured among the Campbells and the MacKenzies. *Cailean* relates to St Columba (see ◊**Calum**) as *Crisdean* does to Christ and *Moirean* to Mary.

Coll ♂

From a medieval short form of ◊**Nicholas**. Its use as a modern given name in part represents a transferred use of the surname derived from the given name in the Middle Ages. In Scotland it has been used as an Anglicized form of the Gaelic name *Colla*, perhaps from an Old Celtic root meaning 'high'.

Colleen ♀

Mainly North American and Australian: from the Anglo-Irish vocabulary word *colleen* 'girl', 'wench' (Gaelic *cailín*). It became established as a name in the inter-War years in North America, and was associated with the star of the silent screen Colleen Moore (1901–88), whose original name was Kathleen Morrison. It is not used as a given name in Ireland. It is sometimes taken as a feminine of ◊**Colin** or a variant of ◊**Colette**.

Collette ♀

Variant spelling of ◊**Colette**.

Colm ♂

Irish Gaelic form of Latin *Columba*; see ◊**Calum**.
Variant: **Colum**.

Colman ♂

Irish: Anglicized form of the Gaelic name **Colmán**, from Late Latin *Columbānus*, a derivative of *Columba* (see ◊**Calum**). The name was borne by a large number of early Irish saints, including Colman of Armagh, a 5th-century disciple of St Patrick. See also ◊**Coleman**.

Colton ♂

Mainly U.S.: transferred use of the surname, in origin a local name from any of various places in England so called. The place name is of varied origin: in most cases it derives from the Old English personal name *Cola*, a byname for a swarthy person (from *col* 'charcoal') + Old English *tūn* 'enclosure', 'settlement', and so is a doublet of ◊**Colby**.

Columbine ♀

From Italian *Colombina*, a diminutive of *Colomba* 'dove'. In the tradition of the *commedia dell'arte* this is the name of Harlequin's sweetheart. The modern name, however, was coined independently as one of the many girls' names taken in the 19th century from vocabulary words denoting flowers. The columbine gets its name from the fact that its petals are supposed to resemble five doves clustered together.

Comhghall ♂

Irish Gaelic name, pronounced '*cow-all*', meaning 'fellow hostage'. This was borne by several early Irish saints, including the 6th-century founder of the great monastery at Bangor. The name is Anglicized as **Cowall**.

Conall ♂

Irish and Scottish Gaelic traditional name, composed of Old Celtic words meaning 'wolf' and 'strong'. This name was borne by many early chieftains and warriors of Ireland, including the Ulster hero Conall Cearnach, one of the two sons of Niall of the Nine Hostages. (The other was Eoghan.) Conall gave his name to *Tirconell*, otherwise known as Donegal.

Conan ♂

Irish and English: Anglicized form of the Celtic name **Conán**. For the most part this is of Irish Gaelic origin, a pet form of *cú* 'hound' or 'wolf'. However, it was in use in Yorkshire, especially among the Askes and the Bartons, from the 12th to the 16th centuries. In this case, the name was derived from Conan, Earl of Richmond (*d.* 1171), and is of Breton origin. In Irish legend, Conán was a foul-mouthed and abusive member of the Fianna, the band of followers of the legendary hero Finn mac Cumhaill (Finn McCool). After undergoing many trials and tribulations, Conán is awarded the 'fourteen best women in the Land of Promise' as compensation for his troubles. In historical times, the name was borne by a 7th-century saint, bishop of the Isle of Man. Sir Arthur Conan Doyle (1859–1930), creator of Sherlock Holmes, was born in Edinburgh, of Irish stock. The science-fiction creation Conan the Destroyer owes more to the villain of legend than to the bishop or the writer.

Conley ♂

Irish: Anglicized form of the Gaelic name **Conlaodh**, which is probably from *connla* 'pure', 'chaste', 'sensible' + the personal name ◊**Aodh**. St Conlaodh or Conláed, a contemporary of St Brighid (see ◊**Bridget**), was the first bishop of Kildare.

Conn ♂

Irish Gaelic name meaning 'chief'. It is now also used as a short form of ◊**Connor** and of various non-Irish names beginning with the syllable *Con-*.

Connie ♀

Pet form of ◊**Constance**.

Connor ♂

Irish: Anglicized form of the Gaelic name **Conchobhar**, which probably meant 'lover of hounds'. Conchobhar is a legendary king of Ulster who lived at the time of Christ.

Conrad ♂

The usual English spelling of *Konrad*, a Germanic personal name derived from *kuon* 'bold' + *rad* 'counsel'. It was used occasionally in Britain in the Middle Ages in honour of a 10th-century bishop of Constance, but modern use in the English-speaking world is a reimportation from Germany dating mainly from the 19th century.

Constance ♀

Medieval form of the Late Latin name *Constantia*, which is either a feminine derivative of *Constans* (see ◊**Constant**), or an abstract noun meaning 'constancy'. This was a popular name among the Normans, and was borne by, amongst others, the formidable Constance of Sicily (1158–98), wife of the Emperor Henry VI.
Pet form: **Connie**.

Constant ♂

Medieval form of the Late Latin name *Constans* 'steadfast' (genitive *Constantis*). This was not a common name in the Middle Ages, but was used particularly in the Maude family. The vernacular variant *Costin* is also found. The name was taken up more widely among Christians from the 17th century onwards, partly because of its transparent meaning and partly as expressing a determination to follow the exhortations of St Peter: 'Be sober, be vigilant; because your adversary the devil, as a roaring lion, walketh about, seeking whom he may devour; whom resist stedfast [*constant*] in the faith.' (1 Peter 5:8–9).

Constantine ♂

From the Late Latin name *Constantīnus*, a derivative of *Constans*; see ◊**Constant**. In early modern English the names *Constant* and *Constantine* were not always clearly distinguished. The Roman emperor Constantine the Great (?288–337) is specially honoured in the Christian Church as the first Christian emperor. The name was also borne by three kings of medieval Scotland, where

it represents an Anglicized form of the Gaelic name ◊**Conn**.

Cora ♀

Name apparently coined by James Fenimore Cooper for one of the characters in *The Last of the Mohicans* (1826). It could represent a Latinized form of Greek *Korē* 'maiden'. In classical mythology this was a euphemistic name of the goddess of the underworld, Persephone, and would not have been a well-omened name to take.

Coral ♀

Late 19th-century coinage. This is one of the group of girls' names taken from the vocabulary of gemstones. Coral is a pink calcareous material found in warm seas; it actually consists of the skeletons of millions of tiny sea creatures. The word is from Late Latin *corallium* and is probably ultimately of Semitic origin.

Coralie ♀

Apparently an elaboration of ◊**Cora** or ◊**Coral** on the model of ◊**Rosalie**.

Corbin ♂

Mainly U.S.: of uncertain derivation, perhaps a short form of the rare given name ◊**Corbinian**, or a transferred use of the surname, in origin a nickname from a diminutive form of Anglo-Norman *corb* 'crow'.

Corbinian ♂

The name of a Frankish saint (?670–770) who evangelized Bavaria from a base at Freising, near Munich. His name was presumably originally Frankish, but in the form in which it has been handed down it appears to be an adjectival derivative of Latin *corvus* 'crow', 'raven', which had a Late Latin variant *corbus*. This may represent a translation of the Germanic personal name *Hraban*.

Cordelia ♀

Name used by Shakespeare for King Lear's one virtuous daughter. It is not clear where he got it from; it does not seem to have a genuine Celtic origin. It may be a fanciful elaboration of Latin *cor* 'heart' (genitive *cordis*).

Cordula ♀

Apparently a Late Latin diminutive form of *cor* 'heart' (genitive *cordis*). A saint of this name was, according to legend, one of Ursula's eleven thousand companions.

Coretta ♀

Elaborated form of ◊**Cora**, with the addition of the productive feminine suffix *-etta* (originally an Italian diminutive form). This is the name of the widow of the American civil rights campaigner Martin Luther King.

Corey ♂

Mainly North American, especially common as a Black name. The reasons for its popularity are not clear. It may well be a transferred use of the English surname *Corey*, which is derived from the Old Norse personal name *Kori*. *Variants*: **Cory**, **Corie**.

Corin ♂

From Latin *Quirīnus*, the name of an ancient Roman divinity partly associated with the legendary figure of Romulus. It is of uncertain origin, probably connected with the Sabine word *quiris* or *curis* 'spear'. In the early Christian period the name was borne by several saints martyred for the faith. The name is occasionally also used in the English-speaking world (where it is often regarded as a male equivalent of ◊**Corinna**), notably by the actor Corin Redgrave (b. 1939).

Corinna ♀

From the Greek name *Korinna* (probably a derivative of *Korē*; compare ◊**Cora**), borne by a Boeotian poetess of uncertain date, whose works survive in fragmentary form. The name was also used by the Roman poet Ovid for the woman addressed in his love poetry.

Corinne ♀

French form of ◊**Corinna**, also used in the English-speaking world.

Cormac ♂

Irish Gaelic traditional name, of uncertain origin. It has been a very popular name in Ireland from the earliest times. Cormac Ó Cuilleannáin, a 10th-century king and bishop, was the author of a dictionary of the Irish language.

Cornelia ♀

From the Latin feminine form of the old Roman family name ◊**Cornelius**. It was borne in the 2nd century BC by the mother of the revolutionary reformers Tiberius and Gaius Sempronius Gracchus, and is still occasionally bestowed in her honour.

Cornelius ♂

From an old Roman family name, *Cornēlius*, which is of uncertain origin, possibly a derivative of Latin *cornu* 'horn'. This was the name of a 3rd-century pope who is venerated as a saint. The name was particularly popular in the Low Countries, and immigrants contributed to its frequency in the north of England from the 1400s.

Cornell ♂

Medieval vernacular form of ◊**Cornelius**. In modern use it normally represents a transferred use of the surname, which has multiple origins.

Cory ♂

Variant spelling of ◊**Corey**.

Cosima ♀

Feminine form of ◊**Cosmo**, occasionally used in the English-speaking world. The name was borne by Cosima Wagner (1837–1930), daughter of Franz Liszt and devoted wife of Richard Wagner.

Cosmo ♂

Italian form (also found as **Cosimo**) of the Greek name *Kosmas* (a short form of various names containing the word *kosmos* 'order', 'beauty'). This was borne by a Christian saint martyred, together with his brother Damian, at Aegea in Cilicia in the early 4th century. It was first brought to Britain in the 18th century by the Scottish dukes of Gordon, who had connections with the ducal house of Tuscany. The name was traditional in that family, having been borne most famously by Cosimo de'

Medici (1389–1464), its founder and one of the chief patrons of the Italian Renaissance.

Coty ♂

Mainly U.S.: transferred use of the rare surname, apparently in origin a local name from a diminutive form of French *côte* 'riverbank'. Use as a given name has probably been influenced by its resemblance to ◊**Cody**.

Courtney ♂, ♀

Mainly North American: transferred use of the surname, originally a Norman baronial name from any of various places in Northern France called *Courtenay* 'domain of Curtius'. However, from an early period it was wrongly taken as a nickname derived from Old French *court nez* 'short nose'.

Cowal ♂

Anglicized form of Irish ◊**Comhghall**.

Coy ♂

Mainly U.S.: of uncertain origin. It is hardly likely to be from the modern English vocabulary word, which has both feminine and pejorative connotations. It probably represents a transferred use of the surname *Coy* or perhaps *McCoy*, a variant of *McKay*, meaning 'son of Aodh' (see ◊**Aidan**).

Craig ♂

From a nickname from the Gaelic word *creag* 'rock', or in some cases a transferred use of the Scottish surname derived as a local name from this word. The given name is now fashionable throughout the English-speaking world, and is chosen by many people who have no connection with Scotland.

Creighton ♂

Pronounced '*krai*-ton': transferred use of the Scottish surname, in origin a local name from *Crichton* in Midlothian, so called from Gaelic *crìoch* 'border', 'boundary' + Middle English *tune* 'settlement' (Old English *tūn*).

Cressa ♀

Modern name, apparently originating as a contracted short form of ◊**Cressida**.

Cressida ♀

From a medieval legend, told by Chaucer and Shakespeare among others, set in ancient Troy. Cressida is a Trojan princess, daughter of Calchas, a priest who has defected to the Greeks. When she is restored to her father, she jilts her Trojan lover Troilus in favour of the Greek Diomedes. The story is not found in classical sources. Chaucer used the name in the form *Criseyde*, getting it from Boccaccio's *Criseida*. This in turn is ultimately based on Greek *Khryseis* (a derivative of *khrysos* 'gold'), the name of a Trojan girl who is mentioned briefly as a prisoner of the Greeks at the beginning of Homer's *Iliad*. Chaucer's version of the name was Latinized by Shakespeare as *Cressida*. In spite of the unhappy associations of the story, the name has enjoyed some popularity in the 20th century.

Crichton ♂

Variant of ◊**Creighton**.

Crispin ♂

From Latin *Crispīnus*, a derivative of the old Roman family name *Crispus* 'curly (-headed)'. St Crispin was martyred with his brother Crispinian in *c*.285, and the pair were popular saints in the Middle Ages.

Cristina ♀

Italian, Spanish, and Portuguese form of ◊**Christina**, sometimes also used in the English-speaking world.

Crystal ♀

19th-century coinage. This is one of the group of names taken from or suggestive of gemstones. The word *crystal*, denoting high-quality cut glass, is derived from Greek *krystallos* 'ice'. As a boy's name, *Crystal* originated as a Scottish pet form of ◊**Christopher**, but it is rarely used today.
Variant: **Krystle**.

Curt ♂

Originally an Anglicized spelling of the German name *Kurt* (contracted form of

Konrad; see ◊**Conrad**), but now also used as a short form of ◊**Curtis**.

Curtis ♂
Transferred use of the surname, which originated in the Middle Ages as a nickname for someone who was 'courteous' (Old French *curteis*). At an early date, however, it came to be associated with Middle English *curt* 'short' + *hose* 'leggings'; compare ◊**Courtney**.

Cushla ♀
From the Irish term of endearment *cushla macree*, Gaelic *cuisle mo croidhe* 'beat of my heart'. The word is not normally used as a given name in Ireland.

Cuthbert ♂
From an Old English personal name derived from *cūð* 'known' + *beorht* 'bright', 'famous'. This was borne by two pre-Conquest English saints: a 7th-century bishop of Lindisfarne and an 8th-century archbishop of Canterbury who corresponded with St Boniface. The name has been in continuous use in the northern counties of England from the 13th century. *Cuddy* is a traditional vernacular pet form.

Cy ♂
Short form of ◊**Cyrus**.

Cynthia ♀
From Greek *Kynthia*, an epithet applied to the goddess Artemis, who was supposed to have been born on Mount *Kynthos* on the island of Delos. The mountain name is of pre-Greek origin. *Cynthia* was later used by the Roman poet Propertius as the name of the woman to whom he addressed his love poetry. The English given name was not used in the Middle Ages, but dates from the classical revival of the 17th and 18th centuries.

Cyprian ♂
From the Late Latin family name *Cypriānus* 'native of Cyprus', borne by one of the leading figures in the history of the Western Church. A 3rd-century bishop of Carthage, he wrote widely on theological themes and did much to further the unity of the Church.

Cyril ♂
From the post-classical Greek name *Kyrillos*, a derivative of *kyrios* 'lord'. It was borne by several early saints, most notably the theologians Cyril of Alexandria and Cyril of Jerusalem. It was also the name of one of the Greek evangelists who brought Christianity to the Slavic-speaking regions of Eastern Europe; in order to provide written translations of the gospels for their converts, they devised the alphabet still known as Cyrillic. In Yorkshire, this was a favourite name of the Arthington family, but in their case it started out as *Searle*, a personal name of Germanic origin introduced to Britain by the Normans.

Cyrille ♂, ♀
French form of ◊**Cyril**, now also occasionally used in the English-speaking world, sometimes as an elaborated spelling variant and sometimes as a feminine form.

Cyrus ♂
Mainly U.S.: from the Greek form (*Kyros*) of the name of several kings of Persia, most notably Cyrus the Great (d. 529 BC). The origin of the name is not known, but in the early Christian period it was associated with Greek *kyrios* 'lord', and borne by various saints, including an Egyptian martyr and a bishop of Carthage.
Short form: **Cy**.

DAFFODIL DAFYDD DAGMAR DAHLIA DA
I DAISY DALE DALEY DALIA DALLAS DALTO
N DALY DALYA DAMARIS DAMASK DAMH
NAIT DAMIAN DAMON DAN DANA DAN
E DANIEL DANIELA DANIELLE DANNY DAP
HNE DARBY DARCY DARELL DAREN DARIA

Daffodil ♀

One of the rarer flower names, which perhaps originated as an expanded version of ◊**Daffy**. The flower got its name in the 14th century from a run-together form of Dutch *de affodil* 'the asphodel'.

Dafydd ♂

Welsh form of ◊**David**, pronounced '*dav-ith*'; see also ◊**Dewi**. This form of the name was in widespread use during the Middle Ages. Later it was largely replaced by the English form *David*, but from the late 19th century it has come into its own again.

Dagmar ♀

Scandinavian: reworking of the Slavonic name *Dragomira* (from *dorog* 'dear' + *meri* 'great', 'famous'), the name of a Czech princess (d. 1212), who became queen of Denmark under the official name Margarethe. By folk etymology, her Czech name was reinterpreted as Old Danish *dag* 'day' + *mār* 'maid'.

Dahlia ♀

From the name of the flower, which was so called in the 19th century in honour of the pioneering Swedish botanist Anders Dahl (1751–89). His surname is from a Swedish word related to English ◊**Dale**.

Dai ♂

Welsh, pronounced '*dye*': now used as a Welsh pet form of ◊**David**, but originally of distinct origin, probably from an Old Celtic word *dei* 'to shine'.

Daisy ♀

From the word denoting the flower, Old English *dægesēage* 'day's eye', so called because it uncovers the yellow disc of its centre in the morning and closes its petals over it again at the end of the day. The name was used early on as a punning pet form of ◊**Margaret**, by association with French *Marguerite*, which is both a version of that name and the word for the flower. It was not widespread until taken up at the end of the 19th century as part of the general vogue for flower names.

Dale ♂, ♀

Transferred use of the surname, originally a local name for someone who lived in a *dale* or valley. It is now fairly commonly used as a given name, especially in North America, along with other monosyllabic surnames of topographical origin (see for example ◊**Dell** and ◊**Hale**).

Daley ♂

From the Irish surname, the Gaelic form of which is *Ó Dálaigh* 'descendant of Dálach'. The latter is a personal name derived from *dál* 'assembly', 'gathering'.
Variant: **Daly**.

Dalia ♀

In part a simplified spelling of ◊**Dahlia**, in part a Jewish name derived from Modern Hebrew *dalia* 'flowering branch'.
Variant: **Daliah** (associated especially with the Israeli film actress Daliah Lavi, b. 1940).

Dallas ♂

Mainly U.S.: transferred use of the surname, adopted in honour of George Mifflin Dallas, Vice-President 1845–49, after whom the city in Texas is named. The surname is of Scottish origin, derived from the village of Dallas in Morayshire, named in Gaelic as *Dalfhas* 'meadow stance', i.e. a meadow traditionally used as a night's resting place by cattle droves.

Dalton ♂

Mainly North American: transferred use of the surname, in origin a local name from any of various places named in Old English as 'the settlement in the valley', from *dæl* 'valley' + *tūn* 'enclosure', 'settlement'.

Daly ♂

Variant spelling of ◊**Daley**.

Dalya ♀

Variant spelling of ◊**Dalia**, influenced by Russian names such as *Katya* and *Tanya*.

Damaris ♀

New Testament: name of a woman mentioned as being converted to Christianity by St Paul (Acts 17:34). Its origin is not clear, but it is probably Greek, perhaps a late form of *Damalis* 'calf'. It was taken up in the 16th century, along with the names of other characters fleetingly mentioned in the New Testament, and has been occasionally used ever since.

Damask ♀

Apparently from the name of the fabric, which is decorated with patterning of contrasting texture but the same colour. This is so called because it was originally imported from Damascus in Syria. Use as a first name may have been inspired by association with names such as ◊**Dimity** and ◊**Calico**. It may also in part have been adopted with reference to the distinctive dusky pink colour of the damask rose (*Rosa damascena*).

Damhnait ♀

Irish Gaelic name, pronounced '*dav*-nit', a feminine diminutive, meaning 'fawn', from *damh* 'stag'. A 6th-century saint of this name founded a convent in Co. Monaghan. It is sometimes Anglicized as **Davnat**. See also ◊**Dymphna**.

Damian ♂

From Greek *Damianos*, the name of the brother of Cosmas (see ◊**Cosmo**). The two brothers were martyred together at Aegea in Cilicia in the early 4th century. The origin of the name is not certain, but it is probably akin to ◊**Damon**.

Damon ♂

From a classical Greek name, a derivative of *damān* 'to tame', 'to subdue' (often a euphemism for 'kill'). This was made famous in antiquity by the story of Damon and Pythias. In the early 4th century BC Pythias was condemned to death by Dionysius, ruler of Syracuse. His friend Damon offered to stand surety for him, and took his place in the condemned cell while Pythias put his affairs in order. When Pythias duly returned to be executed, rather than absconding and leaving his friend to his fate, Dionysius was so impressed by the trust and friendship of the two young men that he pardoned both of them. The name was not used in the early centuries of the Christian era or during the Middle Ages. Its modern use dates from the 1930s and is due at least in part to the fame of the American short-story writer Damon Runyon (1884–1946). It is sometimes taken as a variant of ◊**Damian**.

Dan ♂

In modern use this is taken as a short form of ◊**Daniel**, but it is also an independent biblical name, meaning 'he judged' in Hebrew, borne by one of Jacob's twelve sons (Genesis 30:6). *Pet form*: **Danny**.

Dana ♂, ♀

Mainly North American: of unknown origin, perhaps a transferred use of a surname that is fairly common in the United States. This may be of Irish origin, although the surname is not known in Ireland. *Dana* or *Ana* was the name of an ancient Irish fertility goddess, and this was also used in medieval times as a girl's name. It is not clear whether there is any connection between this ancient Irish name and the modern given name. Modern use as a boy's given name began in honour of Richard Henry Dana (1815–82), author of *Two Years before the Mast*. A lawyer by profession as well as a writer and traveller, he supported the rights of fugitive slaves before and during the Civil War. The popularity of the given name was increased by the fame of the film star Dana Andrews (1909–92). *Dana* is now sometimes also used as a feminine form of ◊**Dan** or ◊**Daniel**.

Dane ♂

Transferred use of the surname, in origin a local name representing a dialect variant of ◊**Dean** that was common in south-east England, rather than an ethnic name for someone from Denmark. The latter sense may be behind the given name in some cases.

Daniel ♂

Biblical name (meaning 'God is my judge' in Hebrew), borne by the prophet whose story is told in the Book of Daniel. He was an Israelite slave of the Assyrian king Nebuchadnezzar, who obtained great favour through his skill in interpreting dreams and the 'writing on the wall' at the feast held by Nebuchadnezzar's son Belshazzar. His enemies managed to get him cast into a lions' den, but he was saved by God. This was a favourite tale in the Middle Ages, often represented in miracle plays.

Daniela ♀

Latinate feminine form of ◊**Daniel**, occasionally used in the English-speaking world.

Danielle ♀

French feminine form of ◊**Daniel**, occasionally used also in the English-speaking world.

Danny ♂

Pet form of ◊**Dan**.

Daphne ♀

Name borne in Greek mythology by a nymph who was changed into a laurel by her father, a river god, to enable her to escape the attentions of Apollo. The name means 'laurel' in Greek. According to the myth the nymph gave her name to the shrub, but in fact of course it was the other way about: her name was taken from the vocabulary word (which is probably of pre-Greek origin). The name came into use in England at the end of the 19th century, when it was adopted as part of the vogue for flower names at that time.

Darby ♂

Transferred use of the surname, in origin a local name from the city of *Derby* or the district of West Derby near Liverpool. These are so called from Old Norse *diur* 'deer' + *býr* 'settlement'. In Ireland this name has been used as an Anglicized form of Gaelic *Diarmaid* (see ◊**Dermot**).

Darcy ♂, ♀

Transferred use of the English and Irish surname, originally a Norman baronial name (*d'Arcy*) borne by a family who came from *Arcy* in northern France. The surname was well established in north central England from the Middle Ages onwards, and various gentry families used it as a first name from the late 1500s. It has always had a somewhat aristocratic flavour, which has enhanced its popularity as a given name. It is the surname of the hero of Jane Austen's novel *Pride and Prejudice* (1813). Use as a girl's name has been enhanced by the British ballerina Darcey Bussell (born 1969).
Variant: **Darcey**.

Darell ♂

Especially U.S.: variant spelling of ◊**Darrell**.

Daren ♂

Variant spelling of ◊**Darren**.

Daria ♀

Of classical Greek origin: feminine form of the much rarer male name ◊**Darius**. St Daria (d. 283) was a Greek woman married to an Egyptian Christian called Chrysanthus; they both lived at Rome and were martyred under the joint emperors Numerian and Carinus.

Darien ♂

Mainly U.S.: of uncertain origin, perhaps a cross between ◊**Darren** and ◊**Darius**. Its identity in form with a region of Panama and Colombia seems to be merely coincidental.

Darin ♂

Mainly U.S.: variant of ◊**Darren**, associated with the singer Bobby Darin (1936–73), who was originally called Walden Robert Cassotto. He chose the name that he made famous from the list of surnames in a telephone directory.

Variant: **Darrin**.

Darina ♀

Anglicized form of the Irish Gaelic name **Dáirine**, meaning 'fertile', a feminine diminutive of *Dáire* (see ◊**Darragh**).

Darius ♂

Especially U.S.: from Greek *Dareios*, originally a transliterated version of the name of various ancient Persian kings. The original form of the name is said to have been *Darayavahush*, from *daraya(miy)* 'possess' or 'maintain' + *vahu* 'well', 'good'. An obscure saint of this name was martyred at Nicaea with three companions at an uncertain date.

Darlene ♀

Especially Australian and North American: modern coinage, an alteration of the affectionate term of address *Darling*, by fusion with the suffix *-lene*, found as an ending in other girls' names.

Variant: **Darleen**.

Darnell ♂

Mainly U.S.: of uncertain derivation. It may represent a transferred use of a surname, or it may be a variant of ◊**Darrell**, influenced by the plant name *darnel*.

Darragh ♂

Irish and Scottish name, of Gaelic origin. It is popularly associated with the Scottish Gaelic vocabulary word *darach* 'oak' (Irish *dair*, genitive *darach*). As an Irish name it also functions as an Anglicized form of the Gaelic name **Dáire**, from a vocabulary word meaning 'fertile'. This was the name of an ancient Irish fertility god associated with a bull cult. The Brown Bull of Cooley (subject of the legendary cattle raid) was originally owned by a certain Dáire mac Fiachna.

Darrell ♂

Especially North American: transferred use of the surname, originally a Norman baronial name (*d'Airelle*) borne by a family who came from *Airelle* in Calvados. It was first used as a given name towards the end of the 19th century, and has enjoyed a considerable vogue in the latter part of the 20th century.

Variants: **Darrel**, **Darell**.

Darren ♂

20th-century coinage, of uncertain derivation. It may be a transferred use of a surname (itself of obscure origin). It seems to have been first borne by the American actor Darren McGavin (b. 1922). It came to public notice as the name of a character in the popular American television comedy series *Bewitched*, made in the 1960s.

Variant: **Daren**.

Darrene ♀

Feminine form of ◊**Darren**, formed by fusion with the productive feminine suffix *-ene*.

Darryl ♂, occasionally ♀

Variant of ◊**Darrell**. Like its variant **Daryl**, it is occasionally borne by women, no doubt by analogy with names such as ◊**Cheryl**. A recent influence on the girl's name is the actress Daryl Hannah.

Darwin ♂

Transferred use of the surname, which in turn probably derives from the Old English personal name *Dēorwine*, composed of the elements *dēor* 'dear', 'beloved' + *wine* 'friend'. Use as a given name seems to have originated in honour of Charles Darwin (1809–82), founder of the theory of evolution.

Dassah ♀
Jewish: shortened form of ◊**Hadassah**, as a result of erroneous association of the first syllable with the Hebrew definite article *ha*.

Dave ♂
Informal short form of ◊**David**.

David ♂
Biblical name, borne by the greatest of all the kings of Israel, whose history is recounted with great vividness in the first and second books of Samuel and elsewhere. As a boy he killed the giant Philistine Goliath with his slingshot. As king of Judah, and later of all Israel, he expanded the power of the Israelites and established the security of their kingdom. He was also noted as a poet, many of the Psalms being attributed to him. The Hebrew derivation of the name is uncertain; it is said by some to represent a nursery word meaning 'darling'. It is a very popular Jewish name, but is almost equally common among Gentiles in the English-speaking world. It is particularly common in Wales and Scotland, having been borne by the patron saint of Wales (see ◊**Dewi**) and by two medieval kings of Scotland.
Short form: **Dave**.
Pet forms: Scottish: **Davy, Davey, Davie**.
Welsh: ◊**Dai**.

Davina ♀
Latinate feminine form of ◊**David**. The name seems to have originated in Scotland, and is occasionally elaborated to **Davinia**, on the model of ◊**Lavinia**.

Davis ♂
Mainly U.S.: transferred use of the surname, in origin a patronymic from the given name ◊**Davy**. Use as a given name is often in honour of Jefferson Davis (1808–89), President of the Confederate States during the Civil War.
Variant: **Davies**.

Davy ♂
Pet form of ◊**David**.
Variants: **Davey, Davie**.

Dawn ♀
From the vocabulary word for daybreak, originally bestowed as a given name in the 1920s, no doubt because of the connotations of freshness and purity of this time of day. It may have originated as a translation of ◊**Aurora**. Twin girls are sometimes given the names *Dawn* and ◊**Eve**, although the latter name does not in fact have anything to do with the time of day. The name is also associated with the actress Dawn Addams (b. 1930).

Dawson ♂
Transferred use of the surname, in origin a patronymic from *Daw*, a Middle English pet form of ◊**David**.

Dean ♂
Transferred use of the surname, which has a double origin. In part it is a local name for someone who lived in a valley (Middle English *dene*, Old English *denu*), in part an occupational name for someone who served as a dean, i.e. ecclesiastical supervisor (Latin *decanus*). The given name also sometimes represents Italian *Dino* (short form of names such as *Bernardino*), as in the case of the American actor and singer Dean Martin (1917–95).
Variants: **Deane, Dene**.

Deanna ♀
Variant of ◊**Diana**, coined in 1936 by the film star and singer Deanna Durbin (b. 1921), whose original given names were *Edna May*. It is now sometimes used as a feminine form of ◊**Dean**.

Deborah ♀
Biblical name (meaning 'bee' in Hebrew), borne by the nurse of Rebecca (Genesis 35:8) and by a woman judge and prophet (Judges 4–5), who led the Israelites to victory over the Canaanites. It has always been popular as a Jewish name, and was taken up among Christians by the Puritans in the 17th century, in part because the bee was a

symbol of industriousness. It has steadily increased in popularity ever since. Among other famous bearers is the actress Deborah Kerr (b. 1921).
Variants: **Debora**, **Debra**.
Short form: **Deb**.
Pet forms: **Debbie**, **Debbi**, **Debi**, **Debs**.

Declan ♂

Irish: Anglicized form of Gaelic *Deaglán*, of uncertain derivation. It was borne by a 5th-century disciple of St Colman, who became a bishop in the district of Ardmore, Co. Waterford. In recent years the name has been strongly revived in Ireland.

Dee ♀, ♂

Pet form of any of the given names beginning with the letter *D-* (compare ◊**Kay**), in particular ◊**Dorothy**. It is also used as an independent name, and may in some cases be associated with the River Dee (compare ◊**Clyde**).

Deforest ♂

Mainly U.S.: transferred use of the surname, apparently adopted in honour of John DeForest (1826–1906), the author of several novels, mostly set during the American Civil War, which enjoyed great popularity at the end of the 19th century.
Variant: **Deforrest**.

Deiniol ♂

Welsh, pronounced '*day*-nyol': usually regarded as the Welsh form of ◊**Daniel**, but the name is ancient in Wales and possibly a Celtic origin should be sought. It was borne by a 6th-century Welsh saint.

Deirdre ♀

Name borne in Celtic legend by a tragic heroine, sometimes referred to as 'Deirdre of the Sorrows'. The story goes that she was betrothed to Conchobhar, King of Ulster, but instead eloped with her beloved Naoise. Eventually, however, the jilted king murdered Naoise and his brothers, and Deirdre herself died of a broken heart. She is sometimes taken as symbolic of the fate of Ireland

under English rule, but this has not stopped her name's being used by English parents with no Celtic blood in them. It became popular in Ireland and elsewhere in the Edwardian era, following retellings of the legend by both the poet W. B. Yeats (1907) and the playwright J. M. Synge (1910). The name itself is of uncertain derivation; the earliest Celtic forms are very variable.

Del ♂

British colloquial pet form of ◊**Derek**, with alteration of the exposed -*r* of the short form to -*l* (compare ◊**Sal** and ◊**Tel**).

Delia ♀

From a classical Greek epithet of the goddess Artemis, referring to her birth on the island of *Delos* (compare ◊**Cynthia**). It was taken up by the pastoral poets of the 17th century, and has been moderately popular ever since.

Delice ♀

Anglicized or Frenchified form of ◊**Delicia**.

Delicia ♀

Feminine form of the Late Latin name *Delicius*, a derivative of *deliciae* 'delight'. Use as a given name seems to be a modern phenomenon; it is not found in the Middle Ages.

Delilah ♀

Biblical name (of uncertain origin), borne by Samson's mistress, who wheedled him into revealing that the secret of his strength was in his hair, and then cut it off while he was asleep and betrayed him to the Philistines (Judges 16:4–20). Although the biblical Delilah was deceitful and treacherous, the name was taken up enthusiastically by the Puritans in the 17th century, perhaps because she was also beautiful and clever. The name fell out of use in the 18th century, but has been occasionally revived as an exotic name.
Variant: **Delila**.

Dell ♂
Transferred use of the surname, originally a local name for someone who lived in a *dell* or hollow.

Della ♀
Name which first appeared in the 1870s and has continued to grow steadily in popularity ever since. Its derivation is not clear; if it is not simply an arbitrary creation, it may be an altered form of ◊**Delia** or ◊**Delilah**, or a short form of ◊**Adela**. In modern use it is sometimes taken as a feminine form of ◊**Dell**.

Delores ♀
Variant of ◊**Dolores**, quite common in the United States.
Variant: **Deloris**.

Delphine ♀
French: from Latin *Delphīna* 'woman from Delphi'. The Blessed Delphina (1283–1358) was a Provençal nun, who was probably named in honour of the 4th-century St Delphinus of Bordeaux. In modern times the name may sometimes be chosen for its association with the *delphinium* flower.

Delwyn ♀
Welsh: modern name composed of the words *del* 'pretty', 'neat' + *(g)wyn* 'white', 'fair', 'blessed', 'holy'.

Delyth ♀
Welsh: modern name composed of the vocabulary word *del* 'pretty', 'neat' + the ending *-yth*, formed on the analogy of names such as ◊**Gwenyth**.

Demelza ♀
Modern Cornish name, which has no history as a Celtic personal name but is derived from a place name in the parish of St Columb Major. The given name began to be used in the 1950s and was given a boost by the serialization on British television of the 'Poldark' novels by Winston Graham, in which it is the name of the heroine.

Den ♂
Short form of ◊**Dennis**.
Pet form: **Denny**.

Dena ♀
Modern coinage, representing either a respelling of ◊**Dina**, or else a form created as a feminine version of ◊**Dean**.

Dene ♂
Variant spelling of ◊**Dean**.

Denice ♀
Altered form of ◊**Denise**.

Denis ♂
Variant spelling of ◊**Dennis**. This is the usual French form of the name.

Denise ♀
Feminine form of ◊**Denis**. See also ◊**Dionysia**.

Dennis ♂
Vernacular English form, based on French *Denis*, of the Greek name *Dionysios*, Late Latin *Dionisius*, which was borne by several early Christian saints, including St Denis, a 3rd-century evangelist who converted the Gauls and became a patron saint of Paris. It was on his account that the name was popular in France and was adopted by the Normans. In classical times, the name was an adjective denoting a devotee of the god *Dionysos*, a relatively late introduction to the classical pantheon; his orgiastic cult seems to have originated in Persia or elsewhere in Asia.
Variant: **Denis**.
Short form: **Den**.
Pet form: **Denny**.

Denton ♂
Transferred use of the surname, originally a local name from any of the numerous places named in Old English as 'the settlement in the valley', from *denu* 'valley' + *tūn* 'enclosure', 'settlement'.

Denzil ♂
From the Cornish surname, the original spelling of which was *Denzell*, a local name from a place in Cornwall. It came to be used as a given name in the Hollis family in the 16th century, when the Hollis family and the Denzell family became connected by marriage,

and spread from there into more general use.

Deon ♂
Variant spelling of ◊**Dion**.

Deonne ♀
Feminine form of ◊**Deon**.

Derek ♂
From a Low German form of *Theodoric* (see ◊**Terry**), introduced to Britain during the Middle Ages by Flemish weavers.
Variants: **Dereck**, **Der(r)ick**.
Pet form: **Del**.

Dermot ♂
Irish: Anglicized form of the Gaelic name *Diarmaid*, earlier *Diarm(u)it*. The derivation is uncertain; it has been suggested that it is composed of the words *dí* 'without' + *airmit* 'injunction' or *airmait* 'envy'.

Derrick ♂
Variant spelling of ◊**Derek**. This is the usual American spelling of the given name, but in Britain it is more common as a surname than as a given name.

Derrin ♂
Of uncertain origin, perhaps an elaboration of ◊**Derry** influenced by ◊**Darren**.

Derry ♂
Of uncertain origin, perhaps a cross between ◊**Derek** and ◊**Terry**.

Dervila ♀
Irish: Anglicized form of the Gaelic name **Deirbhile** (pronounced 'djair-veel-a'), from *der* 'daughter' + *file* 'poet'. This was the name of an Irish saint who founded a convent at Fallmore, Co. Mayo, in the 6th century. It has absorbed the ancient Irish name **Dearbháil** 'daughter of Fál', Fál being a poetic name for Ireland. The latter is more correctly Anglicized as **Derval**.
Variant: **Dervla**.

Deryn ♂
Of uncertain origin, perhaps an altered form of ◊**Derrin**, or a shortened form of Welsh *aderyn* 'bird' (which is occasionally used as a female first name).

Desdemona ♀
Name occasionally chosen by parents in search of an unusual name, who are no doubt attracted by the sweet nature and innocence of Shakespeare's character and not deterred by her tragic fate. She was murdered by her husband Othello in an ill-founded jealous rage, and her name is in fact particularly appropriate to her destiny, as it probably represents a Latinized form of Greek *dysdaimōn* 'ill-starred'.

Desirée ♀
French (now also used in the English-speaking world, usually without the accent): from Latin *Desiderāta* 'desired'. This name was given by early Christians to a longed-for child, but the French form is now often taken as suggesting that the bearer will grow up into a desirable woman.

Desmond ♂
Of Irish origin: from the Gaelic by-name *Deas-Mhumhan* '(man from) south Munster'.
Short form: **Des**.

Destiny ♀
Mainly U.S.: from the vocabulary word denoting the power of fate (Old French *destinee*, from Late Latin *destināta*). This has recently become established as a given name, with variant spellings such as **Destinie**, **Destiney**, and **Destinee**.

Devereux ♂
Especially U.S.: transferred use of a surname, which was originally a Norman baronial name derived (with fused preposition *de*) from *Evreux* in Eure. It was the family name of the 16th-century earls of Essex: Robert Devereux, the 2nd earl, was a favourite of Queen Elizabeth I, later disgraced and executed for treason.

Devin ♂
Mainly U.S.: transferred use of the Irish surname, Gaelic *Ó Damháin* 'descendant of Damhán'. The latter is a byname meaning 'fawn' (see ◊**Dymphna**).

Devon ♀, ♂
Mainly North American: from the name of the English county, either directly or as a transferred use of the surname. It derives from a British tribal name, said to mean 'worshippers of the god Dumnōnos'.
Variant: **Devonne** (♀).

Dewey ♂
Mainly U.S.: of uncertain origin, perhaps a respelling of ◊**Dewi**.
Variant: **Dewy**.

Dewi ♂
A Welsh form (earlier *Dewydd*) of ◊**David**, traditionally associated with the patron saint of Wales. This form of the given name was little used during the Middle Ages, but during the 20th century it has become quite common in Wales, though rare elsewhere. St Dewi was born in South Wales in the 5th century and became the first bishop of Menevia, the tiny cathedral city now known as St Davids.

Dewy ♂
Mainly U.S.: variant spelling of ◊**Dewey**.

Dexter ♂
Mainly U.S.: transferred use of the surname. Although this is now a male given name, the word that gave rise to the surname originally denoted a female dyer, from Old English *dēag* 'dye' + *-estre*, feminine ending of agent nouns. However, the distinction of gender was already lost in Middle English. The name coincides in form with Latin *dexter* 'right-handed', 'auspicious', and may sometimes have been chosen because of this.
Short form: **Dex**.
Pet form: **Dexy**.

Dextra ♀
Modern name, apparently coined as a feminine equivalent of ◊**Dexter**. It represents the feminine form of Latin *dexter* 'right-handed', 'auspicious'.

Dharma ♀
From the Sanskrit word (meaning 'decree' or 'custom') used in Hinduism and Buddhism to refer to the body of central tenets of the belief system. It has achieved limited use as a first name in the English-speaking world as a result of increasing popular interest in Eastern spirituality; compare ◊**Karma**, ◊**Nirvana**, and ◊**Samsara**.

Di ♀
Short form of ◊**Diana** and ◊**Diane**.

Diahann ♀
Elaborated variant of ◊**Diane**, associated particularly with the American actress Diahann Carol (b. 1935).

Diamond ♀
One of the most recent of the girls' names adopted from the vocabulary of gemstones, this enjoys some currency in the United States.

Diana ♀
Name borne in Roman mythology by the goddess of the moon and of hunting, equivalent to the Greek Artemis. In mythology she is characterized as both beautiful and chaste. Her name is of ancient and uncertain derivation. It probably contains a first element that is also found in the name of the Greek god *Dionysos* (see ◊**Dennis**) and the Latin name of the supreme god *Jupiter*. It was adopted in Britain during the Tudor period as a learned name, a borrowing from Latin influenced by the French form ◊**Diane**. Although it was much used by Elizabethan poets celebrating the virgin goddess and alluding to the virgin queen, it was not particularly popular as a given name until the end of the 19th century. In earlier centuries some clergymen were reluctant to baptize girls with this pagan name, mindful of the riots against St Paul stirred up by worshippers of Diana of the Ephesians (Acts 19:24–41). In the late 20th century, its popularity received a boost because of its association with the late Diana, Princess of Wales (1961-97), who was renowned for her beauty, glamour, and compassion.
Short form: **Di**.

Diane ♀

French form of ◊**Diana**, now also used in the English-speaking world. It was especially popular among the Renaissance aristocracy, who loved hunting and were therefore proud to name their daughters after the classical goddess of the chase.
Variants: **Dianne** (by association with ◊**Anne**); **Dyan** (U.S.).
Short form: **Di**.

Diandrea ♀

Modern coinage, apparently a blend of ◊**Diana** and ◊**Andrea**.

Diarmaid ♂

Irish and Scottish Gaelic name normally Anglicized as **Dermot**. In Irish legend, Diarmaid was the lover of Gráinne, who had been promised to the ageing hero Finn mac Cumhaill, leader of the Fianna. The lovers eloped, but were pursued for sixteen years by Finn; according to one version of the story, Diarmaid was eventually killed by a wild boar and Gráinne died of grief. The derivation of the name is uncertain; it has been suggested that it may be from the phrase *dí airmait* 'without envy'.
Variant: **Diarmait**.

Dick ♂

Short form of ◊**Richard**. The alteration of the initial consonant is supposed to result from the difficulty that English speakers in the Middle Ages had in pronouncing the trilled Norman *R-*.

Dickie ♂

Pet form of ◊**Dick**, with the originally Scottish and northern English diminutive suffix *-ie*. This has more or less completely replaced the medieval diminutive *Dickon*, with the Old French suffix *-on*.

Digby ♂

Transferred use of the surname, in origin a local name from a place in Lincolnshire, so called from Old Norse *díki* 'ditch' + *býr* 'settlement'.

Dillon ♂

Variant spelling of ◊**Dylan**, based on an English surname of different origin. The surname *Dillon* or *Dyllon* derives in part from a now extinct Norman French personal name of Germanic origin; in part it is a local name from *Dilwyn* in Hereford.

Dilly ♀

Pet form of ◊**Dilys** and ◊**Dilwen**, now sometimes used as an independent given name.

Dilwen ♀

Welsh: modern name, from *Dil-* (see ◊**Dilys**) + *(g)wen*, feminine form of *gwyn* 'white', 'fair', 'blessed', 'holy'.

Dilys ♀

Welsh: of modern origin, from the vocabulary word *dilys* 'genuine', 'steadfast', 'true'.

Dimity ♀

Apparently from the name of the light cotton fabric, which came into English from Italian in the 15th century and is derived from the Greek prefix *di-* 'two', 'double' + Greek *mitos* 'warp thread'. However, since it is found primarily as an Irish name, it may have originated as a feminine equivalent of ◊**Dermot** (Gaelic *Diarmaid*, earlier *Diarm(u)it*).

Dina ♀

In part a variant spelling of ◊**Dinah**, with which it often shares the same pronunciation. In part, however, it derives from the Italian name *Dina*, a short form of diminutives such as *Bernardina*.

Dinah ♀

Biblical name (a feminine form derived from Hebrew *din* 'judgement'), borne by a daughter of Jacob. She was raped by Shechem but avenged by her brothers Simeon and Levi (Genesis 34). In modern times it is generally taken as a variant of the much more common ◊**Diana**.

Dion ♂

French: from Latin *Dio* (genitive *Diōnis*), a short form of the various names of Greek origin containing as their first element *Dio-* 'Zeus'. Examples include *Diodoros* 'gift of Zeus' and *Diogenēs* 'born of Zeus'. It is also used in the English-speaking world, especially as a Black name.

Dionne ♀
Feminine form of ◊**Dion**.

Dionysia ♀
Latin form of ◊**Denise**; see ◊**Dennis**. The Latin form *Dionysia* was in use in northern England until the 17th century; the pet form **Dye** is the source of the surname *Dyson*.

Dionysius ♂
Latin form of ◊**Dennis**.

Dirk ♂
Flemish and Dutch form of ◊**Derek**. Its use in the English-speaking world since the 1960s is largely due to the fame of the actor Dirk Bogarde (b. 1921; originally Derek Niven van den Bogaerde). He is of Dutch descent, although he was actually born in Scotland. The manly image of the name has been reinforced by its coincidence in form with the Scottish vocabulary word *dirk* 'dagger' (from Gaelic *durc*).

Dittany ♀
From the name of a plant (Greek *diktamnon*, from Mount *Dikte* in Crete where it grew in profusion) famed in classical times for its medicinal qualities.

Diva ♀
Apparently from the vocabulary word denoting a female opera singer or other highly admired woman. The word came into English from Italian in the 19th century and literally means 'goddess' (from the feminine form of Latin *dīvus* 'divine').

Dixie ♀
Mainly U.S.: name chosen as symbolic of the American South. The nickname is of uncertain origin. It is said to be from the ten-dollar bills printed in New Orleans, named in the Cajun dialect from French *dix* 'ten'.

Dodie ♀
Pet form of ◊**Dorothy**, derived from a

child's unsuccessful attempts to pronounce the name.

Dolly ♀, in Scotland occasionally ♂
Originally (from the 16th century onwards) a pet form of ◊**Dorothy**; now also a pet form of ◊**Dolores**. It is also found as an independent given name (taken as being from the vocabulary word *doll*, which was in fact derived in the 17th century from the pet name for *Dorothy*). In Gaelic areas of Scotland it is found as a pet form of the boy's name ◊**Donald**.

Dolores ♀
Spanish: from *Maria de los Dolores* 'Mary of the Sorrows', a reference to the Seven Sorrows of the Virgin Mary. The feast of Our Lady's Dolours was established in 1423. The name is now also borne in the English-speaking world, mainly by Roman Catholics. In part, it was popularized by the film star Dolores Del Rio (1905–83), born in Mexico as Dolores Asunsolo.
Variants: **Delores**, **Deloris**.
Pet forms: **Lola**, **Lolita**, **Dolly**.

Dominic ♂
From the Late Latin name *Dominicus*, a derivative of *dominus* 'lord'. It is used mainly by Roman Catholics, in honour of St Dominic (1170–1221), founder of the Dominican order of monks.
Variant: **Dominick** (an old spelling, still in occasional use).

Dominique ♀
Feminine form of ◊**Dominic**, from a French form that is used as both a girl's and a boy's name.

Don ♂
Short form of ◊**Donald**. It is also a variant of the Irish name ◊**Donn**.
Pet forms: **Donny**, **Donnie**.

Donagh ♂
Irish: Anglicized form of the Gaelic name **Donnchadh**; see ◊**Duncan**.

Donal ♂
Irish: Anglicized form of the Gaelic name **Dónal**, earlier **Domhnall**, from

Old Celtic *dubno* 'world' + *val* 'rule'. This was very popular in ancient Ireland, being borne by five High Kings of Ireland and three saints. The spelling **Donall** is also found.

Donald ♂

Scottish: Anglicized form of the Gaelic name *Domhnall*, from Old Celtic *dubno* 'world' + *val* 'rule'. The final *-d* of the Anglicized form derives partly from misinterpretation by English speakers of the Gaelic pronunciation, and partly from association with Germanic-origin names such as ◊**Ronald**. This name is strongly associated with clan Macdonald, the clan of the medieval Lords of the Isles. *Donald* is now also quite commonly used by families with no Scottish connections.

Short form: **Don**.

Pet forms: **Donny**, **Donnie**; **Dolly** (in Gaelic Scotland).

Donall ♂

Variant spelling of ◊**Donal**.

Donn ♂

Irish: ancient Gaelic byname meaning either 'brown' or 'king', in use from the earliest times until the 19th century. In Irish mythology this is the name of the king of the underworld.

Donna ♀

Of recent origin (not found before the 1920s). It is derived from the Italian vocabulary word *donna* 'lady' (compare ◊**Madonna**), but it is now also used as a feminine form of ◊**Donald**.

Donnchadh ♂

Gaelic form of ◊**Duncan**.

Donnell ♂

Transferred use of the Scottish and Irish surname, derived in the Middle Ages from the given name ◊**Donald**.

Donny ♂

Pet form of ◊**Donald**.

Variant: **Donnie**.

Donovan ♂

Transferred use of the Irish surname, Gaelic *Ó Donndubháin* 'descendant of

Donndubhán'. The latter is a personal name from *donn* 'brown' + *dubh* 'black', 'dark' + the diminutive suffix *-án*. Its use as a given name dates from the early 1900s. The folk-rock singer Donovan may have had some influence on its increase in popularity in the 1960s.

Dora ♀

19th-century coinage, representing a short form of ◊**Isidora**, ◊**Theodora**, ◊**Dorothy**, and any other name containing the Greek word *dōron* 'gift'. Wordsworth's daughter (b. 1804), christened Dorothy, was always known in adult life as Dora. The name's popularity was enhanced by the character of Dora Spenlow in Dickens's novel *David Copperfield* (1850).

Dorcas ♀

From Greek *dorkas* 'doe', 'gazelle'. It was not used as a personal name by the ancient Greeks, but is offered in the Bible as an interpretation of the Aramaic name ◊**Tabitha** (Acts 9:36), and was taken up by the early Christians. It was much used among the Puritans in the 16th century, and has remained in occasional use ever since.

Dorean ♀

Irish: Anglicized form of the Gaelic name **Dáireann** or **Doirind**, which is of uncertain origin. Gaelic *der Fhinn* 'daughter of Finn' has been suggested. It has been revived as a given name in the 20th century. It is probably the source of the English name ◊**Doreen**, which is one of its Anglicized forms; others are **Dorren** and **Derinn**.

Doreen ♀

Anglicization of the Irish name ◊**Dorean**. It may also be a derivative of ◊**Dora** with the addition of the productive suffix *-een*, representing an Irish pet form.

Variants: **Dorene**, **Dorine**.

Doria ♀

Of uncertain origin, probably a backformation from ◊**Dorian** or else an elaboration of ◊**Dora** on the model of the numerous women's given names ending in -*ia*.

Dorian ♂

Early 20th-century coinage, apparently invented by Oscar Wilde, as no evidence has been found of its existence before he used it for the central character in *The Portrait of Dorian Gray* (1891). Dorian Gray is a dissolute rake who retains unblemished youthful good looks; in the attic of his home is a portrait which does his ageing for him, gradually acquiring all the outward marks of his depravity. This macabre background has not deterred parents from occasionally bestowing the name on their children. Wilde probably took the name from Late Latin *Dōriānus*, from Greek *Dōrieus*, member of the Greek-speaking people who settled in the Peloponnese in pre-classical times. *Dorian* would thus be a masculine version of ◊**Doris**. It may have been selected occasionally by admirers of ancient Sparta and its militaristic institutions, since the Spartans were of Dorian stock.
Variant: **Dorien**.

Dorinda ♀

Artificial elaboration of ◊**Dora**, with the suffix -*inda* (as for example ◊**Clarinda**). The name was coined in the 18th century, and has undergone a modest revival of interest in the 20th.

Doris ♀

From the classical Greek ethnic name meaning 'Dorian woman'. The Dorians were one of the tribes of Greece; their name was traditionally derived from an ancestor, *Dōros* (son of Hellen, who gave his name to the Hellenes), but it is more likely that Doros (whose name could be from *dōron* 'gift') was invented to account for a tribal name of obscure origin. In Greek mythology, Doris was a minor goddess of the sea, the consort of Nereus and the mother of his daughters, the Nereids or sea-nymphs, who numbered fifty (in some versions, more). The name was especially popular from about 1880 to about 1930, and was borne by the

American film star Doris Day (b. 1924 as Doris Kappelhoff), among others.

Dorothea ♀

Latinate form of a post-classical Greek name, from *dōron* 'gift' + *theos* 'god' (the same elements as in ◊**Theodora**, but in reverse order). The masculine form *Dōrotheus* was borne by several early Christian saints, the feminine only by two minor ones, but only the girl's name has survived. In modern use in the English-speaking world it represents either a 19th-century Latinization of ◊**Dorothy** or a learned reborrowing.

Dorothy ♀

Usual English form of ◊**Dorothea**. The name was not used in the Middle Ages, but was taken up in the 16th century and became common thereafter. It was borne by the American film star Dorothy Lamour (1914–1996), born Dorothy Kaumeyer.
Short form: **Dot**.
Pet forms: **Dottie**, **Dotty**, **Dodie**, **Dolly**.

Doug ♂

Short form of ◊**Douglas**.

Dougal ♂

Scottish: Anglicized form of the Gaelic name *Dubhghall* or *Dùghall*, from *dubh* 'black', 'dark' + *gall* 'stranger'. This was a byname applied to Danes, in contrast to the fairer Norwegians and Icelanders (see ◊**Fingal**).
Variants: **Dugal(d)**.
Pet form: **Dougie**.

Douglas ♂

Transferred use of the surname borne by one of the most powerful families in Scotland, the earls of Douglas and of Angus, also notorious in earlier times as Border reivers. Their surname is derived from the place in the Southern Uplands of Scotland where they had their stronghold, named with the Gaelic words *dubh* 'black' + *glas* 'stream'.
Short form: **Doug**.

Dove ♀

Modern name, from the vocabulary word denoting the bird (Middle English *douve*, from Old Norse *dōfa*), noted as a symbol of peace and gentleness.

Drake ♀

Transferred use of the surname, which is derived in part from the Old English byname *Draca* 'Snake', 'Dragon' (which survived into the Middle Ages as a given name), and in part from Middle English *drake* 'male duck' (imported from Middle Low German) used as a nickname. Use as a given name is likely to have originated in honour of the English explorer Sir Francis Drake (?1540–96).

Dreda ♀

Shortened form of ◊**Etheldreda**, quite commonly used as an independent given name in the 19th century, when the longer form was also in fashion. It has survived slightly better than the four-syllable original, but is nevertheless now rare.

Drew ♂

Scottish short form of ◊**Andrew**, often used as an independent name in Scotland, and in recent years increasingly popular elsewhere in the English-speaking world.

Drusilla ♀

From a Late Latin name, a feminine diminutive of the old Roman family name *Dr(a)usus*, which was first taken by a certain Livius, who had killed in single combat a Gaul of this name and, according to a custom of the time, took his victim's name as a cognomen. Of the several women in the Roman imperial family who were called Livia Drusilla, the most notorious was Caligula's sister and mistress. The name is borne in the Bible by a Jewish woman, wife of the Roman citizen Felix, who was converted to Christianity by St Paul (Acts 24:24). In England it was taken up as a given name in the 17th century as a result of the biblical mention.

Drystan ♂

Welsh variant of ◊**Tristan**. Drystan son of Tallwch is fleetingly mentioned in the *Mabinogi* as one of the members of King Arthur's council of advisers.

Duald ♂

Irish: Anglicized form of the Gaelic name **Dubhaltach** (pronounced '*doo*-al-tah'), which probably means 'black-haired' (Gaelic *dubh-fholtach*). The Anglicized form **Dualta** is also found.

Duane ♂

Irish: Anglicized form of the Gaelic name *Dubhán* (pronounced '*doo*-vain'). This was originally a byname, a diminutive of Gaelic *dubh* 'dark', 'black'. In modern use it may be derived from the surname *Ó Dubháin* 'descendant of Dubhán'. Its popularity in the mid-1950s was influenced by the guitarist Duane Eddy.
Variants: **Dwane**, **Dwayne**.

Dudley ♂

Transferred use of the surname of a noble family, who came originally from Dudley in the West Midlands, named in Old English as the 'wood or clearing of Dudda'. Their most famous member was Robert Dudley, Earl of Leicester (?1532–88), who came closer than any other man to marrying Queen Elizabeth I. This given name is much less common in North America than in England.
Short form: **Dud**.

Duff ♂

Scottish: from the Gaelic nickname *dubh* 'black', i.e. 'dark-haired one'. In modern use it is in part a transferred use of the surname *Duff*, derived from the nickname.

Dugald ♂

Anglicized form of the Gaelic name **Dubhghall** (see ◊**Dougal**). The final -*d* is due to a mishearing of the Gaelic form, in which the final -*ll* sounds like -*ld* to English ears.

Duke ♂

In modern use this normally represents a coinage parallel to ◊**Earl** and ◊**King**, but it has been used as a short form of ◊**Marmaduke** from at least the early

1600s. It is especially popular in the United States.

Dulcie ♀

Learned re-creation in the 19th century of the medieval name *Dowse*, Late Latin *Dulcia*, a derivative of *dulcis* 'sweet'.

Duncan ♂

Scottish: Anglicized form of the Gaelic name *Donnchadh*, from *donn* 'brown' + *chadh* 'chief' or 'noble'. This was the name of a 7th-century Scottish saint (abbot of Iona), a 10th-century Irish saint (abbot of Clonmacnoise), and two medieval kings of Scotland. The final *n* in the Anglicized form seems to be the result of confusion with the Gaelic word *ceann* 'head', due to the Latinized form *Duncanus*. In Ireland, *Donnchadh* is now often spelled *Donncha*; it was formerly sometimes Anglicized as ◊**Dennis**.

Dunstan ♂

From an Old English personal name derived from *dun* 'dark' + *stān* 'stone', borne most notably by a 10th-century saint who was archbishop of Canterbury. The name is now used mainly by Roman Catholics.

Dustin ♂

Transferred use of the surname, which is of uncertain origin, probably a Norman form of the Old Norse personal name *Þórsteinn*, composed of elements meaning 'Thor's stone'. It is now used fairly regularly as a given name, largely as a result of the fame of the film actor Dustin Hoffman (b. 1937), who is said to have been named in honour of the less well-known silent film actor Dustin Farman (1870–1929).

Dusty ♂, ♀

Apparently a pet form, or in some cases a feminine form, of ◊**Dustin**. As a girl's name it was made familiar in the 1960s by the singer Dusty Springfield.

Dwane ♂

Variant spelling of ◊**Duane**.
Variant: **Dwayne**.

Dwight ♂

Transferred use of the surname, which probably comes from the medieval English female name *Diot*, a pet form of *Dionysia* (see ◊**Dennis**). It is especially common in North America, where its increase in popularity since the Second World War is mainly a result of the fame of the American general and president Dwight D. Eisenhower (1890–1969). He was named in honour of the New England philosopher Timothy Dwight (1752–1817) and his brother Theodore Dwight (1764–1846).

Dwyer ♂

From the Irish surname *O Duibhuidhir* 'descendant of *Duibhuidhir*', a personal name composed of the elements *dubh* 'dark', 'black' + *odhar* 'sallow', 'tawny' (or possibly *eidhir* 'sense', 'wisdom').

Dyan ♀

Modern variant spelling of ◊**Diane**, especially popular in the United States.

Dylan ♂

Welsh: of uncertain origin, probably connected with a Celtic word meaning 'sea'. In the *Mabinogi* it is the name of the miraculously born son of Arianrhod, who became a minor divinity of the sea. In the second half of the 20th century the name has become fairly popular outside Wales as a result of the fame of the Welsh poet Dylan Thomas (1914–53) and the American singer Bob Dylan (b. 1941), who changed his surname from Zimmerman as a tribute to the poet.

Dylanne ♀

Feminine form of ◊**Dylan**, a modern coinage based on the pattern of French names.

Dymphna ♀

This is the name of a medieval Flemish saint about whom little is known beyond the fact that she is regarded as the protector of lunatics and epileptics. According to legend, she was an Irish girl who had been abused by her father and killed by him when she opposed his wishes. Her relics are preserved at

Gheel, near Antwerp in Belgium, where an important mental hospital of medieval foundation still bears her name. Her name has been identified, rightly or wrongly, with Irish ◊**Damhnait**.
Variant: **Dympna**.

EAMON EARL EARLA EARNEST EARNESTIN
E EAVAN EBENEZER EBONY ECHO ED EDAN
EDDIE EDEN EDGAR EDIE EDITH EDMOND
EDMUND EDNA EDOM EDSEL EDWARD ED
WIN EDWINA EFFIE EGAN EGBERT EGLANTI
NE EIDOWEN EILEEN EILIDH EILIS EIRA EIR

Eamon ♂

Irish name, pronounced '*ay*-mon', the Gaelic form of ◊**Edmund**. The normal Gaelic spellings are *Éamon(n)* or *Éaman(n)*. Éamon de Valera (1882–1973) was president of Ireland 1959–73. The name was popularized throughout Britain in the 1950s due to the fame of the broadcaster Eamon Andrews (1922–87).

Earl ♂

North American: from the rank of the peerage, originally a nickname parallel to ◊**Duke**, ◊**King**, etc. The title was used in England in Norman times as an equivalent of the French *comte* 'count'; it is from Old English *eorl* 'warrior', 'nobleman', 'prince'. In some cases the given name may have been taken from the surname *Earl*, which was originally either a nickname or a term denoting someone who worked in the household of an earl.
Variants: **Earle**, **Erle**.

Earla ♀

Mainly U.S.: coined as a feminine form of *Earl*.
Elaborated forms: **Earlina**, **Earline**, **Earlene**, **Earleen**.

Earnest ♂

Mainly North American variant spelling of ◊**Ernest**.

Earnestine ♀

Especially U.S.: variant spelling of ◊**Ernestine**.

Eavan ♀

Anglicized form of the Gaelic name ◊**Aoibheann**.

Ebenezer ♂

Biblical term, originally a place name (meaning 'stone of help' in Hebrew). This was the site of the battle where the Israelites were defeated by the Philistines (1 Samuel 4:1). After they took their revenge, Samuel set up a memorial stone bearing this name (1 Samuel 7:12). It was taken up as a given name by the Puritans in the 17th century, possibly after being misread in the Bible as a personal name, or else because of its favourable etymological connotations. It now has unfavourable connotations because of the miserly character of Ebenezer Scrooge in Charles Dickens's *A Christmas Carol* (1843).

Ebony ♀

From the name of the deeply black wood (Late Latin *ebenius*, from Greek *ebenos*, ultimately of Egyptian origin). This name has been adopted recently (since the 1970s) by Blacks as a symbol of pride in their colour.

Echo ♀

In modern use, probably directly from the vocabulary word (Greek *ēkhō*, which reached English via Latin). In classical mythology, this was the name of a nymph who pined away with love for Narcissus until nothing remained except her disembodied voice. Although the Greek word purports to be derived from the name of the nymph, in fact the word is of Indo-European origin, and so the truth seems to be that the nymph was invented to explain the word.

Ed ♂

Short form of the various boys' names with the first syllable *Ed-*, especially ◊**Edward**.

Edan ♂

Scottish and Irish: variant of ◊**Aidan**. St
Edan was an Irish disciple of St David of
Wales who later became bishop of Ferns.

Eddie ♂

Pet form of ◊**Ed**.

Eden ♀, ♂

This name is found as a pet form of
◊**Edith** in Yorkshire from the 15th
century onwards, but in present-day use
it is mainly U.S., referring to the biblical
'Garden of Eden', so named from
Hebrew '*ēden* 'place of pleasure'. As a
boy's name it may also represent a
variant of ◊**Edan** or a transferred use of a
surname, itself derived in the Middle
Ages from a given name *Edun* or *Edon*.
This is of Old English origin, from *ēad*
'prosperity', 'riches' + *hūn* 'bear cub'.

Edgar ♂

From an Old English personal name
derived from *ēad* 'prosperity', 'riches' +
gār 'spear'. This was the name of an
English king and saint, Edgar the
Peaceful (d. 975), and of Edgar Atheling
(?1060–?1125), the young prince who
was chosen by the English to succeed
Harold as king in 1066, but who was
supplanted by the Normans.

Edie ♀

Pet form of ◊**Edith**.

Edith ♀

From an Old English female personal
name derived from *ēad* 'prosperity',
'riches' + *gȳð* 'strife'. This was borne by a
daughter (961–984) of Edgar the Peaceful
(she was named in accordance with
the common Old English practice of
repeating name elements within a
family). She spent her short life in a
convent, and is regarded as a saint.
Pet form: **Edie**.

Edmond ♂

French form of ◊**Edmund**, also occasionally used in the English-speaking
world.

Edmund ♂

From an Old English personal name

derived from *ēad* 'prosperity', 'riches' +
mund 'protector'. It was borne by
several early royal and saintly figures,
including a 9th-century king of East
Anglia killed by invading Danes, allegedly for his adherence to Christianity.
In the 16th and 17th centuries, there was
a good deal of interchange between
Edmund and *Edward*.

Edna ♀

In Ireland this has been used as an
Anglicized form of ◊**Eithne**. The name
occurs in the apocryphal Book of
Tobit, where it is the name of the
mother of Sarah and stepmother of
Tobias. This is said to be from
Hebrew '*ednah* 'pleasure', 'delight',
and if so it is connected with the name of
the Garden of ◊**Eden**. The earliest
known uses of the given name in
England are in the 17th century, when it
was probably imported from Ireland,
although the spelling *Ednah* supports
the idea that it was taken from the
Bible.

Edom ♂

Biblical name (meaning 'red' in Hebrew), which was the byname of Esau. It
was given to him because he sold his
birthright for a bowl of red lentil soup.
This was frequently used as a given
name in medieval Scotland, where it
was taken to represent a variant of
◊**Adam**. It is occasionally bestowed in
modern times by parents with Scottish
connections.

Edsel ♂

In Germanic mythology this name is a
variant of *Etzel*, apparently derived from
adal 'noble', or else from the nickname
Atta 'father'. In modern times its best-
known bearer was Edsel Ford, son of
Henry Ford, founder of the Ford Motor
Corporation. The family was partly of
Dutch or Flemish descent, but the
reason for the choice of given name is
not known. *Edzell* is the name of a castle
in Tayside in Scotland, but it is not clear
whether this was a factor in the choice of
the given name.

Edward ♂

From an Old English personal name derived from *ēad* 'prosperity', 'riches' + *weard* 'guard'. This has been one of the most successful of all Old English names, surviving from before the Conquest to the present day, and even being exported into other European languages. It was the name of three Anglo-Saxon kings and has been borne by eight kings of England since the Norman Conquest. It is also the name of the youngest son of Queen Elizabeth II. The most influential early bearer was King Edward the Confessor (?1002–66; ruled 1042–66). In a troubled period of English history, he contrived to rule fairly and (for a time at any rate) firmly. But in the latter part of his reign he paid more attention to his religion than to his kingdom. He died childless, and his death sparked off conflicting claims to his throne, which were resolved by the victory of William the Conqueror at the Battle of Hastings. His memory was honoured by Normans and English alike, for his fairness and his piety. Edward's mother was Norman; he had spent part of his youth in Normandy; and William claimed to have been nominated by Edward as his successor. Edward was canonized in the 12th century, and came to be venerated throughout Europe as a model of a Christian king.
Short forms: **Ed**, **Ned**, **Ted**.
Pet form: **Eddie**.

Edwin ♂

From an Old English personal name derived from *ēad* 'prosperity', 'riches' + *wine* 'friend'. It was borne by a 7th-century king of Northumbria, who was converted to Christianity by St Paulinus and was killed in battle against pagan forces, a combination of circumstances which led to his being venerated as a martyr. It occurs occasionally from the mid-16th century, but in modern use it is largely the result of a 19th-century revival.

Edwina ♀

19th-century coinage, representing a Latinate feminine form of ◊**Edwin** or, in at least one case, of ◊**Edward**. Edwina Ashley, a descendant of Lord Shaftesbury who became the wife of Earl Mountbatten, was so named in honour of Edward VII; the king had originally wished her to be called *Edwardina*.

Effie ♀

Pet form of ◊**Euphemia**, now as rarely used as the full form, but popular in the 19th century.

Egan ♂

Irish: Anglicized form of the Gaelic name **Aogán**, earlier *Aodhagán*, a double diminutive of ◊**Aodh**. In some cases it may be a transferred use of the surname, which has the same origin.

Egbert ♂

From an Old English personal name derived from *ecg* 'edge (of a sword)' + *beorht* 'bright', 'famous'. It was borne by two English saints of the 8th century and by a 9th-century king of Wessex. It survived for a while after the Conquest, but fell out of use by the 14th century. It was briefly revived in the 19th century, but is now again completely out of fashion.

Eglantine ♀

Flower name, used as a nickname by Chaucer, and occasionally as a given name in the 18th and 19th centuries, but not at present in use. It is from an alternative name for the sweetbrier, derived in the 14th century from Old French *aiglent*, ultimately a derivative of Latin *acus* 'needle', referring to the prickly stem of the plant.

Eiddwen ♀

Welsh, pronounced 'aithe-wen': modern coinage, apparently derived from *eiddun* 'desirous', 'fond', with the feminine names suffix *(g)wen*, from *gwyn* 'white', 'fair', 'blessed', 'holy'.

Eileen ♀

Anglicized form of the Irish Gaelic name spelt **Eibhlín**, **Eilín**, or **Aibhilín**. This is derived from Norman French *Aveline*, a derivative of ◊**Ava**. *bh* is normally

pronounced as 'v' in Gaelic, but is sometimes silent, whence the Anglicized form. This name became extremely popular in many parts of the English-speaking world in the early part of the 20th century.
Variant: **Aileen** (esp. Scottish).

Eilidh ♀
Scottish Gaelic name, pronounced '*ay*-lee', a comparatively recent coinage on the basis of English *Ellie*.
Variant: **Ailie** (an Anglicized spelling).

Eilis ♀
Gaelic form of ◊**Elizabeth**.

Eira ♀
Welsh: modern coinage from the vocabulary word *eira* 'snow'.

Eireen ♀
Of recent origin, a respelling of ◊**Irene** under the influence of ◊**Eileen**.

Eirlys ♀
Welsh: modern coinage from the vocabulary word for the snowdrop.

Eirwen ♀
Welsh: modern coinage, from *eira* 'snow' + *(g)wen*, feminine form of *gwyn* 'white', 'fair', 'blessed', 'holy'.

Eithne ♀
Irish Gaelic: traditional name, pronounced '*ee*-na', apparently from the vocabulary word *eithne* 'kernel', which was used as a term of praise in bardic poetry. The name has been Anglicized variously as ◊**Edna**, ◊**Ena**, **Et(h)na**, and **Ethenia**. St Ethenia was a daughter of King Laoghaire and one of St Patrick's first converts, together with her sister Fidelma.

Elaine ♀
Originally an Old French form of ◊**Helen**, but now generally regarded as an independent name. The Greek and Latin forms of the name had a long vowel in the second syllable, which produced this form (as opposed to ◊**Ellen**) in Old French. In Arthurian legend, Elaine is the name of one of the women who fell in love with Lancelot. The name occurs

in this form in the 15th-century English *Morte D'Arthur* of Thomas Malory. In the 19th century it was popularized in one of Tennyson's *Idylls of the King* (1859). Most of the characters in Arthurian legend have names that are Celtic in origin, although subjected to heavy French influence, and it has therefore been suggested that *Elaine* may actually be derived from a Welsh word meaning 'hind' or 'fawn'.

Eldon ♂
Transferred use of the surname, in origin a local name from a place in Co. Durham, so called from the Old English male personal name *Ella* + Old English *dūn* 'hill'.

Eleanor ♀
From an Old French respelling of the Old Provençal name *Alienor*. This has sometimes been taken as a derivative of ◊**Helen**, but it is more probably of Germanic derivation (the first element being *ali* 'other', 'foreign'; the second is obscure). The name was introduced to England by Eleanor of Aquitaine (1122–1204), who came from south-west France to be the wife of King Henry II. It was also borne by Eleanor of Provence, the wife of Henry III, and Eleanor of Castile, wife of Edward I.
Variants: **Ellenor**, **Elinor**.

Elen ♀
Welsh form of ◊**Helen**. It is identical with the Welsh vocabulary word *elen* 'nymph', but this is unlikely to be the origin. It is found in Welsh texts from an early period as an equivalent of *Helen*, for example as the name of the mother of Constantine, finder of the True Cross.
Variant: **Elin**.

Elena ♀
Italian and Spanish form of ◊**Helen**, now sometimes also used in the English-speaking world.

Eleonora ♀
Italian form of ◊**Eleanor**, now sometimes also used in the English-speaking world.

Eleri ♀

Welsh: ancient name of uncertain origin. It was borne in the 5th century by a daughter of the semi-legendary chieftain Brychan. *Eleri* is also a Welsh river name, and here it is probably derived from *alar* 'surfeit'. It is not clear whether there is a connection between the personal name and the river name.

Elfreda ♀

19th-century revival of a Latinized form of the Old English female personal name *Ælfþryð*, from *ælf* 'elf', 'supernatural being' + *þryð* 'strength'. This form may also have absorbed the Old English name *Æðelþryð*, which was originally distinct (see ◊**Audrey**).
Short form: **Freda**.

Eli ♂

Biblical name, from a Hebrew word meaning 'height'. This was borne by the priest and judge who brought up the future prophet Samuel (1 Samuel 4). It was especially popular among Puritans in the 17th century.

Elias ♂

Biblical name, from the Greek form (used in the New Testament) of the name of the prophet ◊**Elijah**. See also ◊**Ellis**.

Elijah ♂

Biblical name (meaning 'Yahweh is God' in Hebrew), borne by an Israelite prophet whose exploits are recounted in the First and Second Book of Kings. Elijah's victory over the prophets of Baal on Mount Carmel played an important part in maintaining the Jewish religion, recognizing just one God. This story, and other stories in which he figures, including his conflicts with Ahab's queen, Jezebel, and his prophecies of doom, are among the most vivid in the Bible. For some reason it has not been much used as a given name by Christians, although it is found among the early Puritan settlers in New England. More recently, it has been adopted among Black Muslims.

Elin ♀

Welsh: variant of ◊**Elen**.

Elinor ♀

Variant spelling of ◊**Eleanor**.

Eliot ♂

Variant spelling of ◊**Elliot**.
Variant: **Eliott**.

Elisabeth ♀

The spelling of ◊**Elizabeth** used in the Authorized Version of the New Testament, and in most modern European languages. This was the name of the mother of John the Baptist (Luke 1:60). Etymologically, the name means 'God is my oath', and is therefore identical with *Elisheba*, the name of the wife of Aaron according to the genealogy at Exodus 6:23. The final element seems to have been altered by association with Hebrew *shabbāth* 'Sabbath'.

Élise ♀

French: short form of ◊**Elisabeth**. The name was introduced into the English-speaking world (where it is often written without the accent) in the late 19th century.

Elita ♀

Modern coinage, apparently derived from the vocabulary word *élite*, denoting a select group of people, with the addition of the Latinate suffix *-a*. The word came into English from French in the 18th century; it derives from the past participle of *élire* 'to choose' (Latin *ēligere*). Use as a given name seems to reflect a desire on the part of the parents that their daughter should achieve success in life or be a member of an élite.

Eliza ♀

Short form of ◊**Elizabeth**, first used in the 16th century, and popular in the 18th and 19th centuries. It was used by George Bernard Shaw for the main female character, Eliza Dolittle, in his play *Pygmalion* (1913), which was the basis for the musical and film *My Fair Lady*.

Elizabeth ♀

The usual spelling of ◊**Elisabeth** in English. It was first made popular by being borne by Queen Elizabeth I of England (1533–1603). In the 20th century it became extremely fashionable, partly because it was the name of Elizabeth Bowes-Lyon (b. 1900), who in 1936 became Queen Elizabeth as the wife of King George VI; even more influentially, it is the name of her daughter Queen Elizabeth II (b. 1926).
Variant: **Elisabeth**. See also ◊**Elspeth** and ◊**Isabel**.
Short forms: **Eliza, Elsa, Liza, Lisa, Liz; Beth, Bet, Bess; Lisbet.**
Pet forms: **Elsie, Bessie, Bessy, Betty, Betsy, Tetty, Libby, Lizzie, Lizzy, Buffy.**

Ella ♀

Of Germanic origin, introduced to Britain by the Normans. It was originally a short form of any of various compound names containing *ali* 'other', 'foreign' (compare ◊**Eleanor**). It is now often taken to be a variant or pet form of ◊**Ellen**.

Ellen ♀

Originally a variant of ◊**Helen**, although now no longer associated with that name. Initial *H*- tended to be added and dropped rather capriciously, leading to many doublets (compare for example ◊**Esther** and *Hester*).
Pet form: ◊**Nell**.

Ellenor ♀

Variant spelling of ◊**Eleanor**, the result of blending with ◊**Ellen**.

Ellie ♀

Pet form of any of the numerous girls' names beginning with the syllable *El-*, in particular ◊**Eleanor**.

Elliot ♂

Transferred use of the surname, itself derived from a medieval (Norman French) masculine given name. This was a diminutive of *Elie*, the Old French version of ◊**Elias**.
Variants: **Elliott, Eliot(t)**.

Ellis ♂

From a medieval vernacular form of

◊**Elias**, in use as a given name in northern England from the 14th century onwards. In modern use it is often a transferred use of the surname derived from this name. In Wales it is now often taken as an Anglicized form of the Old Welsh name *Elisud*, a derivative of *elus* 'kind', 'benevolent'.

Elmer ♂

Transferred use of the surname, itself derived from an Old English personal name derived from *æðel* 'noble' + *mær* 'famous'. This has been used as a given name in the United States since the 19th century, in honour of the brothers Ebenezer and Jonathan Elmer, leading activists in the American Revolution. It is also found in Canada.

Elroy ♂

Variant of ◊**Leroy**. The initial syllable seems to be the result of simple transposition of the first two letters; it may also have been influenced by the Spanish definite article *el*.

Elsa ♀

Shortened form of ◊**Elisabeth** or ◊**Elizabeth**. The name was borne by the English-born film actress Elsa Lanchester (1902–86). Elsa Belton was a character in Angela Thirkell's once widely read *Barsetshire Chronicles*. The name is now also associated with the lioness named Elsa featured in the book *Born Free*, by Joy Adamson, which was made into a film.

Elsdon ♂

Mainly U.S.: transferred use of the surname, in origin a local name from a place in Northumbria. The place name is recorded in the 13th century in the forms *Eledene, Hellesden, Elisden*, and *Ellesden*; it is probably named as 'Elli's valley' (Old English *denu*).

Elsie ♀

Scottish simplified form of *Elspie*, a pet form of ◊**Elspeth**. This came to be used as an independent name, and in the early 20th century proved more popular than *Elspeth*.

Elspeth ♀
Scottish contracted form of ◊**Elizabeth**.

Elton ♂
Transferred use of the surname, in origin a local name from any of numerous places in England so called (mostly from the Old English masculine personal name *Ella* + Old English *tūn* 'enclosure', 'settlement'). In England it is largely associated with the singer-songwriter Elton John; born Reginald Dwight, he adopted the given name by which he is famous in honour of the saxophonist Elton Dean.

Eluned ♀
Welsh: apparently a revival of the older Welsh name **Luned**, or **Lunet**. *Lunete* is the form of the name used by the French writer Chrétien de Troyes. Compare ◊**Lynette**.

Elvira ♀
Spanish name of Germanic (Visigothic) origin, very common in the Middle Ages and enjoying a minor revival today. The original form and meaning of the elements of which it is composed are uncertain (probably *ali* 'other', 'foreign' + *wēr* 'true'). The name was not used in the English-speaking world until the 19th century, when it was made familiar as the name of the long-suffering wife of Don Juan, both in Mozart's opera *Don Giovanni* (1789) and Byron's satirical epic poem *Don Juan* (1819–24). It is the name of the heroine of the Swedish film *Elvira Madigan* (1967), directed by Bo Widerberg, a romantic tragedy about a pair of lovers who would rather die than be separated.

Elvis ♂
Of obscure derivation, made famous by the American rock singer Elvis Presley (1935–77). It may be a transferred use of a surname, or it may have been made up, but it was certainly not chosen for the singer in anticipation of a career in show business, for his father's name was Vernon Elvis Presley. A shadowy Irish St Elvis, of the 6th century, is also known as *Elwyn*, *Elwin*, *Elian*, and *Allan*.

Elwyn ♂
Welsh and Irish: of uncertain origin. In the modern Welsh name the influence of the word *(g)wyn* 'white', 'fair', 'blessed', 'holy' is apparent (see ◊**Delwyn**). However, this is also one of the forms used for the name of a 6th-century Irish saint; it may be no more than a variant of ◊**Alan**.

Elyse ♀
Altered spelling of ◊**Élise**.

Emanuel ♂
See ◊**Emmanuel**.

Emer ♀
Irish Gaelic: Anglicized form of Irish Gaelic **Eimer** or **Émer**: a traditional name of uncertain derivation. This was the name of Cú Chulainn's beloved, a woman of many talents who was blessed with the gifts of beauty, voice, sweet speech, needlework, wisdom, and chastity. It has been revived as a given name in the 20th century. It is familiar in Scotland in the spelling *Eimhir* through the 'Poems to Eimhir' of Sorley MacLean (b. 1911).

Emerald ♀
From the name of the gemstone, representing a vernacular form of ◊**Esmeralda**.

Emery ♂
Transferred use of the surname, derived in the Middle Ages from a personal name introduced to England by the Normans. This was originally composed of the Germanic elements *amal* 'bravery', 'vigour' + *rīc* 'power', but soon assumed a variety of forms such as *Amauri* and *Emauri*.

Emily ♀
From a medieval form of the Latin name *Aemilia*, the feminine version of the old Roman family name *Aemilius* (probably from *aemulus* 'rival'). It was not common in the Middle Ages, but was revived in the 19th century and is very popular today. Its best-known 19th century bearer was probably the novelist and poet Emily Brontë (1818–48).

Emlyn ♂
Welsh: of uncertain origin, possibly
from Latin *Aemiliānus* (a derivative of
the old Roman family name *Aemilius*;
see ◊**Emily**). On the other hand, it may
have a Celtic origin; there are Breton and
Irish saints recorded as *Aemilianus*,
which may be a Latinized form of a lost
Celtic name.

Emma ♀
Old French name, of Germanic (Frankish) origin, originally a short form of
compound names such as ◊**Ermintrude**,
containing the word *erm(en)*, *irm(en)*
'entire'. It was adopted by the Normans
and introduced by them to Britain, but
its popularity in medieval England was
greatly enhanced by the fact that it had
been borne by the mother of Edward the
Confessor, herself a Norman.

Emmanuel ♂
Biblical name (meaning 'God is with
us' in Hebrew) used for the promised
Messiah, as prophesied by Isaiah (7:14;
referred to in Matthew 1:23). The
Authorized Version of the Bible uses the
Hebrew form *Immanuel* in the Old
Testament, *Emmanuel* in the New.
Variant: **Emanuel**.

Emmarald ♀
Variant of ◊**Emerald**, influenced by the
given name ◊**Emma**.

Emmeline ♀
Old French name of Germanic (Frankish) origin, introduced to Britain by the
Normans. In origin it seems to have
been a derivative of ◊**Emma**, but when it
was revived in the 19th century there
was some confusion with ◊**Emily**. A
famous bearer was the suffragette
Emmeline Pankhurst (1858–1928),
mother of Christabel and Sylvia.

Emmet ♂
Transferred use of the surname, itself
derived from the medieval female given
name *Emmet*, a diminutive form of
◊**Emma**. It may sometimes be used by
parents with Irish connections, in honour of the rebel Robert Emmet (1778–

1803), who led a disastrous attempt at
rebellion against the English.
Variant: **Emmett**

Emmy ♀
Pet form of ◊**Emma**, ◊**Emily**, and related
names. It is sometimes found in the
southern United States in combinations
such as **Emmy Jane** and **Emmy Sue**.

Emrys ♂
Welsh form of ◊**Ambrose**, very common
in families of Welsh origin in the 20th
century.

Emyr ♂
Welsh, pronounced '*em*-ear': originally a
byname meaning 'ruler, king, lord'. The
name was borne by a 6th-century Breton
saint who settled in Cornwall.

Ena ♀
One of several Anglicized forms of the
Gaelic name ◊**Eithne**. In the case of
Queen Victoria's granddaughter Princess Ena (Victoria Eugénie Julia Ena,
1887–1969) it had a different origin: it
was a misreading by the minister who
baptized her of a handwritten note of the
originally intended name ◊**Eva**. In
England, the name is remembered principally as that of the fearsome Ena
Sharples in the television soap opera
Coronation Street.

Enfys ♀
Welsh: modern name, taken from the
vocabulary word meaning 'rainbow'.

Enid ♀
Celtic name of uncertain derivation,
borne by a virtuous character in the
Arthurian romances, the long-suffering
wife of Geraint. The name was revived
in the second half of the 19th century,
following Tennyson's *Idylls of the King*
(1859), which contains the story of Geraint and Enid, in which Enid recovers
her husband's trust by patience and
loyalty after he has suspected her,
wrongly, of infidelity.

Enoch ♂
Biblical name (possibly meaning 'experienced' in Hebrew), borne by the son

81

ERNA

of Cain (Genesis 4:16–22) and father of
Methuselah (Genesis 5:18–24). The latter is said to have lived for 365 years. The
apocryphal 'Books of Enoch' are attributed to him.

Enola ♀
20th-century coinage of uncertain derivation. One theory is that it originated
as a reversal in spelling of the word
alone, but this may be no more than
coincidental.

Enos ♂
Biblical name (meaning 'mankind' in
Hebrew), borne by a son of Seth and
grandson of Adam (Genesis 4:26), who
allegedly lived for 905 years.

Eóghan ♂
Traditional Gaelic name, pronounced
'*yew*-en' or '*yo*-wen'; supposedly derived
from *iúr* 'yew' and meaning 'born of
yew'. In Irish legend, this was the name
of one of the two sons of Niall of the
Nine Hostages (the other was Conall);
he gave his name to County Tyrone (Tír
Eoghain).
Anglicized forms: **Ewan**, **Euan**, **Owen**,
Eugene.

Eoin ♂
Irish Gaelic form of ◊**John**.

Ephraim ♂
Biblical name, pronounced '*ee*-frame';
borne by one of the sons of Joseph and
hence one of the tribes of Israel. The
name probably means 'fruitful' in Hebrew; it is so explained in the Bible
(Genesis 41:52 'and the name of the
second called he Ephraim: For God hath
caused me to be fruitful in the land of my
affliction'). This was used by the Puritans in the 16th century, and was used
more widely in the 18th and 19th centuries. It is still a common Jewish given
name.

Erasmus ♂
Latinized form of Greek *Erasmos*, a
derivative of *erān* 'to love'. St Erasmus
(d. 303) was a bishop of Formiae in
Campania, martyred under Diocletian;
he is numbered among the Fourteen

Holy Helpers and is a patron of sailors.
This is a fairly rare given name in the
English-speaking world. It is sometimes
bestowed in honour of the great Dutch
humanist scholar and teacher Erasmus
Rotterodamus (?1466–1536).

Eric ♂
Of Old Norse origin, from *ei* 'ever',
'always' (or *einn* 'one', 'alone') + *ríkr*
'ruler'. It was introduced into Britain by
Scandinavian settlers before the
Norman Conquest. As a modern
given name, it was revived in the mid-
19th century and has remained in use
since.

Erica ♀
Latinate feminine form of ◊**Eric**,
coined towards the end of the 18th
century. It has also been reinforced by
the fact that *erica* is the Latin word for
'heather'.

Erin ♀
From Irish Gaelic *Éirinn*, dative case of
Éire 'Ireland'. *Erin* has been used as a
poetic name for Ireland for centuries,
and in recent years this has become a
popular given name, especially in North
America, even among people with no
Irish ancestry.

Erla ♂
Variant spelling of ◊**Earla**.

Erle ♀
Variant spelling of ◊**Earl**.

Ermintrude ♀
Of Germanic origin, adopted from Old
French by the Normans and introduced
by them to Britain. It is derived from
erm(en), *irm(en)* 'entire' + *traut* 'beloved'. It did not survive long into the
Middle Ages, but was occasionally revived in the 18th and 19th centuries. It is
now completely out of fashion.

Ern ♂
Short form of ◊**Ernest**.
Pet form: **Ernie**.

Erna ♀
Simplified version of *Ernesta*, created as
a feminine form of ◊**Ernest**.

Ernan ♂

Irish: Anglicized form of the Gaelic name *Earnán*, possibly a derivative of *iarn* 'iron'. St Earnán is the patron saint of Tory Island.

Ernest ♂

Of Germanic origin, derived from the Old High German vocabulary word *eornost* 'serious business', 'battle to the death'. The name was introduced into England in the 18th century by followers of the Elector of Hanover, who became George I of England. A variant spelling, **Earnest**, has arisen by association with the modern English adjective *earnest*, which is, however, only distantly connected with the name.
Short form: **Ern**.
Pet form: **Ernie**.

Ernestine ♀

Elaborated feminine form of ◊**Ernest**, created in the 19th century.

Errol ♂

Transferred use of the Scottish surname, which derives from a place name. It has been made famous by the film actor Errol Flynn (1909–59), noted for his 'swashbuckling' roles. He was born in Australia, but spent most of his career in Hollywood. It is now very popular as a Black name, influenced by such figures as the jazz pianist Erroll Garner.
Variant: **Erroll**.

Erskine ♂

Transferred use of the Scottish surname, which derives from the name of a place near Glasgow. The surname has also been taken to Ireland by Scottish settlers, and was first brought to public attention as a given name by the half-Irish writer and political activist Erskine Childers (1870–1922).

Esmeralda ♀

From the Spanish vocabulary word *esmeralda* 'emerald'. Its occasional modern use as a given name dates from Victor Hugo's *Notre Dame de Paris* (1831), in which it is the nickname of the gypsy girl loved by the hunchback

Quasimodo; she was given the name because she wore an amulet containing an artificial emerald.
Variant: **Esmerelda**.

Esmond ♂

From an Old English personal name derived from *ēast* 'grace', 'beauty' + *mund* 'protection'. A Norman French form is found, reflecting a Continental Germanic original. However, it was not used in Britain as a given name between the 14th century and the late 19th century, when it was revived.

Esta ♀

Latinate respelling of ◊**Esther**.

Estelle ♀

Old French name meaning 'star' (Latin ◊**Stella**), comparatively rarely used during the Middle Ages. It was revived in the 19th century, together with the Latinate form **Estella**, which was used by Dickens for the ward of Miss Havisham in *Great Expectations* (1861).

Esther ♀

Biblical name, borne in the Bible by a Jewish captive who became the wife of the Persian king Ahasuerus. According to the book of the Bible that bears her name, she managed, by her perception and persuasion, to save large numbers of the Jews from the evil machinations of the royal counsellor Haman. Her Hebrew name was *Hadassah* 'myrtle', and the form *Esther* is said to be a Persian translation of this, although others derive it from Persian *stara* 'star'. It may also be a Hebrew form of the name of the Persian goddess *Ishtar*.

Esyllt ♀

Welsh: traditional name, probably meaning 'of fair aspect'. It is the Welsh form of ◊**Isolde**.

Étaín ♀

Traditional Irish Gaelic name, sometimes identified as that of the ancient Celtic sun goddess, said to be derived from *ét* 'jealousy'.

Ethan ♂

Biblical name (meaning 'firmness' or 'long-lived' in Hebrew) of an obscure figure, Ethan the Ezrahite, mentioned as a wise man whom Solomon surpassed in wisdom (1 Kings 4:31). The name was sparingly used even among the Puritans, but became famous in the United States since it was borne by Ethan Allen (1738–89), leader of the 'Green Mountain Boys', a group of Vermont patriots who fought in the American Revolution.

Ethel ♀

19th-century revival of an Old English name, a short form of various female personal names containing *ethel* 'noble' as a first element, for example ◊**Etheldreda**. The name enjoyed great popularity for a period at the beginning of the 20th century. It is at present out of fashion.

Etheldreda ♀

Latinized form of the Old English female personal name *Æðelþryð* (see ◊**Audrey**). It was taken up as a given name in the 19th century, but is now rare.

Ethna ♀

Irish: Anglicized form of ◊**Eithne**.
Variant: **Etna**.

Etta ♀

Short form of the various names such as *Rosetta* and *Henrietta* ending in this element, originally an Italian feminine diminutive suffix.

Euan ♂

Scottish: Anglicized form of Gaelic ◊**Eóghan**.

Eudora ♀

Ostensibly a Greek name, from *eu* 'well', 'good' + a derivative of *dōron* 'gift'. However, there is no saint of this name, and it is more probably a 19th-century learned coinage, made up of elements which are common in other given names.

Eugene ♂

From the Old French form of the Greek name *Eugenios* (from *eugenēs* 'well-born', 'noble'). This name was borne by various early saints, notably a 5th-century bishop of Carthage, a 7th-century bishop of Toledo, and four popes. It is sometimes used as an Anglicized form of Irish ◊**Eóghan**.
Short form: **Gene**.

Eugenia ♀

Feminine form of Greek *Eugenios* or Latin *Eugenius*; see ◊**Eugene**.

Eugénie ♀

French form of ◊**Eugenia**. The name was introduced to England as the name of the Empress Eugénie (Eugenia María de Montijo de Guzmán, 1826–1920), wife of Napoleon III, and has since been occasionally used (sometimes without the accent) in the English-speaking world.

Euna ♀

Scottish: Anglicized form of the Gaelic name *Ùna* (see ◊**Úna**).

Eunan ♂

Irish and Scottish: Anglicized form of the Gaelic name *Ádhamhnán*, traditionally said to be a diminutive form of *Ádhamh*, the Gaelic version of ◊**Adam**. However, it is more likely to be a diminutive of *adomnae* 'great fear', i.e. 'little horror'. The name was borne by a 7th-century saint, abbot of Iona and biographer of St Columba.

Eunice ♀

From a Late Greek name, derived from *eu* 'well', 'good' + *nikē* 'victory'. This is mentioned in the New Testament as the name of the mother of Timothy, who introduced him to Christianity (2 Timothy 1:5). This reference led to the name being taken up by the Puritans in the 16th century.

Euphemia ♀

Latin form of a Late Greek name derived from *eu* 'well', 'good' + *phēnai* 'to speak'. This was the name of various early saints, notably a virgin martyr said to have been burnt at the stake at Chalcedon in 307. It had a limited popularity in some regions in the 16th and 17th centuries and returned to favour in the

Victorian period, especially in the pet form ◊**Effie**.

Eustace ♂

From the Old French form of the Late Greek names *Eustakhios* and *Eustathios*. These were evidently of separate origin, the former derived from *eu* 'well', 'good' + *stakhys* 'grapes', the latter from *eu* + *stēnai* 'to stand'. However, the tradition is very confused. The name was introduced in this form to Britain by the Normans, among whom it was popular as a result of the fame of St Eustace, who was said to have been converted to Christianity by the vision of a crucifix between the antlers of the stag he was hunting.

Eva ♀

Latinate form of ◊**Eve**, now very popular in its own right. It is also found as an Anglicization of the Gaelic name ◊**Aoife**.

Evadne ♀

From a Greek personal name derived from *eu* 'well', 'good' + another element, of uncertain meaning. The name was borne by a minor figure in classical legend, who threw herself on to the funeral pyre of her husband, and was therefore regarded as an example of wifely piety. The modern spelling and pronunciation are the result of transmission through Latin sources. The name has never been common. It is associated with the character of Dr Evadne Hinge in the British comedy television series *Hinge and Bracket*.

Evan ♂

As a Welsh name this represents an Anglicized form of *Iefan*, a later development of ◊**Ieuan**. As a Scottish name it is a variant of ◊**Euan**.

Evander ♂

Classical name used in the Scottish Highlands as an Anglicized form of Gaelic *Ìomhair* (see ◊**Ivor**). In classical legend, *Evander* is the name of an Arcadian hero who founded a city in Italy where Rome was later built. It is a

Latin form of Greek *Euandros*, derived from *eu* 'good' + *anēr* 'man' (genitive *andros*).

Evangeline ♀

Fanciful name derived from Latin *evangelium* 'gospel' (Greek *euangelion*, from *eu* 'good' + *angelma* 'tidings') + the suffix *-ine* (in origin a French feminine diminutive). *Evangeline* is the title of a narrative poem (1848) by the American poet Henry Wadsworth Longfellow, in which the central character is called Evangeline Bellefontaine.

Eve ♀

English vernacular form of the name borne in the Bible by the first woman, created from one of Adam's ribs (Genesis 2: 22). It derives, via Latin *Ēva*, from Hebrew *Havva*, which is considered to be a variant of the vocabulary word *hayya* 'living' or 'animal'. Adam gave names to all the animals (Genesis 2: 19–20) and then to his wife, who was 'the mother of all living' (Genesis 3:20). *Pet form*: Evie.

Evelina ♀

Latinate form of the girl's name ◊**Evelyn**, or combination of ◊**Eve** with the suffix *-lina*.

Evelyn ♂, ♀

Modern use of this as both a boy's and a girl's name derives from a transferred use of an English surname, from the Norman female name *Aveline*, an elaborated form of ◊**Ava**. It is also found as a variant Anglicization of Irish *Éibhleann* (see ◊**Evlin**).
Variants: **Evelyne**, **Eveline** (♀).

Everard ♂

From an Old English personal name derived from *eofor* 'boar' + *heard* 'hardy', 'brave', 'strong'. This was reinforced at the time of the Norman Conquest by a Continental Germanic form introduced to Britain by the Normans. The modern given name may be a transferred use of the surname, but it was in regular use in the Digby family of Rutland from the 15th to the 17th centuries, probably as a survival of the Norman name. It alternated in this family with ◊**Kenelm**.

Everett ♂

Transferred use of the surname, a variant of ◊**Everard**.

Evette ♀

Altered form of ◊**Yvette**, influenced by ◊**Eve**.

Evie ♀

Pet form of ◊**Eve** or ◊**Eva**, occasionally also of ◊**Evelyn** as a girl's name.

Evlin ♀

Anglicized form of the Irish Gaelic name **Éibhleann**, said to be a derivative of the Old Irish vocabulary word *óiph* 'radiance', 'beauty', and sometimes found in the form **Éibhliu**. It is sometimes confused with *Eibhlín*, the Gaelic form of ◊**Evelyn**.

Evonne ♀

Altered form of ◊**Yvonne**, influenced by ◊**Eve**.

Ewan ♂

The usual Anglicized form in Scotland and Northern Ireland of Gaelic **Eóghan** (see ◊**Euan**). It is also found in northern England from the 14th century onwards. *Variant*: **Ewen**.

Ewart ♂

Transferred use of the Scottish surname, probably first used as a given name in honour of the Victorian statesman William Ewart Gladstone (1809–98). The surname has several possible origins: it may represent a Norman form of ◊**Edward**, an occupational name for a ewe-herd, or a local name from a place in Northumbria.

Ezekiel ♂

Biblical name, pronounced 'ez-*ee*-kee-el': meaning 'God strengthens' in Hebrew. This was borne by one of the major prophets. The book of the Bible that bears his name is known for its vision of a field of dry bones, which Ezekiel prophesies will live again (chapter 37). His prophecies were addressed to the Jews in Babylonian exile, after Nebuchadnezzar had seized Jerusalem in 597 BC.
Short form: **Zeke**.

Ezra ♂

Biblical name (meaning 'help' in Hebrew), borne by an Old Testament prophet, author of the book of the Bible that bears his name. This was one of the Old Testament names taken up by the Puritans in the 17th century.

FABIA FABIAN FABIOLA FAE FAIRFAX FAIT
H FANCY FANNY FAY FAYE FELICE FELICIA F
ELICITY FELIX FENELLA FENICIA FENN FEN
NE FENTON FERDINAND FERGAL FERGUS
FEIN FERRIS FFION FIACHRA FIDELMA FIES
TA FE FIFI FILLAN FINBAR FINELLA FINGA

Fabia ♀

Latin feminine form of the old Roman family name *Fabius*, said to be a derivative of *faba* 'bean'.

Fabian ♂

From the Late Latin name *Fabiānus*, a derivative of the old Roman family name *Fabius* (see ◊**Fabia**). It was borne by an early pope (236–250), who was martyred under the Emperor Decius. The name was introduced into Britain by the Normans and occurs occasionally in the 16th and 17th centuries, but it has never been much used in the English-speaking world.

Fabiola ♀

Late Latin feminine diminutive form of the old Roman family name *Fabius* (see ◊**Fabia**). St Fabiola (d. *c*.400) was a Roman widow who founded the first Western hospital, originally a hostel to accommodate the flood of pilgrims who flocked to Rome, in which she tended the sick as well as accommodating the healthy.

Fae ♀

Variant spelling of ◊**Fay**.

Fairfax ♂

Transferred use of the surname, recorded from the early 17th century. It was originally a nickname for someone with beautiful long hair (Old English *fæger* 'lovely' + *feax* 'hair', 'tresses'). The surname is that of a prominent English family: the 3rd Baron Fairfax was the leader of the Roundhead army during the Civil War, and the 6th Baron Fairfax was a notable early colonist in Virginia.

Faith ♀

From the abstract noun denoting the quality of believing and trusting in God. The name began to be used in the 16th century, and was very popular among the Puritans of the 17th.

Fancy ♀

From the vocabulary word referring to the quality of imagination (in origin it is a contracted form of *fantasy*) or to an unusual idea (compare ◊**Caprice**). It may also in part have been taken from the corresponding adjective as a reference to a dainty baby girl.

Fanny ♀

Pet form of ◊**Frances**, very popular in the 18th and 19th centuries, but now much rarer.

Fay ♀

Late 19th century coinage, from the archaic word *fay* 'fairy'. It was to some extent influenced by the revival of interest in Arthurian legend, in which Morgan le Fay is King Arthur's half-sister, a mysterious sorceress who both attempts to destroy Arthur and tends his wounds in Avalon after his last battle. She is sometimes identified with the 'Lady of the Lake'. Between the wars the name came to prominence as that of the British actress Fay Compton (1894–1979).
Variants: ◊**Faye**, **Fae**.

Faye ♀

Variant of ◊**Fay**, associated particularly with the American actress Faye Dunaway (b. 1941).

Felice ♀

Italian form (pronounced 'fe-*lee*-tchay') or French form (pronounced 'fe-*leess*') of ◊**Felicia**.

Felicia ♀
Latinate feminine form of ◊**Felix**, of medieval origin.

Felicity ♀
From the abstract noun denoting luck or good fortune (via Old French from Latin *felicitās*; compare ◊**Felix**). The English vocabulary word was first used as a given name in the 17th century. It also represents the English form of the Late Latin personal name *Felicitas*, which was borne by several early saints, notably a slave who was martyred in 203 together with her mistress Perpetua and several other companions.
Pet form: **Flick**.

Felix ♂
Latin name meaning 'lucky', which has from time to time been popular as a given name in Britain and elsewhere because of its auspicious omen. It was in use as a byname in Latin, being applied for example to the dictator Sulla (138–178 BC). It was very popular among the early Christians, being borne by a large number of early saints.

Fenella ♀
Scottish and Irish: Anglicized form of the Gaelic name ◊**Fionnuala**.
Variants: **Finella**, **Fi(o)nola**.

Fenicia ♀
Of uncertain origin, probably just an alteration of ◊**Felicia**. It could also represent an Anglicized form of Latin *Phoenicia* 'Phoenician woman', although there does not seem to be a saint of that name, as is normally the case for names derived from Latin.

Fenn ♂
Mainly U.S.: transferred use of the surname, in origin a local name for someone who lived in a low-lying marshy area, from Old English *fenn* 'marsh', 'fen'. It is also found as a short form of ◊**Fenton**.

Fennel ♀
From the name of the plant (Latin *faeniculum*, a diminutive of *faenum* 'hay'), whose seeds are used as a spice.

This probably came to be used as a first name because of its resemblance to a short form of ◊**Fenella**.

Fenton ♂
Transferred use of the surname, in origin a local name from any of the various places (for example, in Cumbria, Lincs., Northumbria, Notts., Staffs., and W. Yorks.) so called from Old English *fenn* 'marsh', 'fen' + *tūn* 'enclosure', 'settlement'.

Ferdinand ♂
From a Spanish name, originally *Ferdinando* (now *Hernán*), which is of Germanic (Visigothic) origin, derived from *farð* 'journey' (or possibly an altered form of *frið* 'peace') + *nand* 'ready', 'prepared'. This was a traditional name in the royal families of Spain from an early date. It appeared in Britain in the 16th century, having been introduced by Roman Catholic supporters of Queen Mary I, who married Philip II of Spain in 1554.
Pet form: **Ferdi**.

Fergal ♂
Irish: Anglicized form of the Gaelic name *Fearghal*, derived from *fear* 'man' + *gal* 'valour'. This was the name of an 8th-century king of Ireland, Fearghal mac Mácldúin, famous for his murderous exploits.

Fergus ♂
Scottish and Irish: Anglicized form of the Gaelic name *Fearghas*, derived from *fear* 'man' + *gus* 'vigour'. This was the name of a shadowy hero in Irish mythology, also of the grandfather of St Columba. It is still used mainly in Scotland and Ireland and by those who remain conscious of their Gaelic ancestry.
Pet form: **Fergie**.

Fern ♀
From the vocabulary word denoting the plant (Old English *fearn*). Use of this word as a given name is of comparatively recent origin: it is one of several words denoting flowers and plants that have been pressed into service during the past

hundred years. Its popularity is steadily increasing.

Ferris ♂
Irish: Anglicized spelling of the vocative case, *Phiarais*, of *Piaras*, a Gaelic form of ◊**Peter**. Compare ◊**Hamish** for a similar derivation from a vocative.

Ffion ♀
Welsh form of ◊**Fiona**. The spelling *ff-* is used in Welsh to represent the sound *f* rather than the *v* indicated by a single *f-*.

Fiachra ♂
Traditional Irish Gaelic name derived from *fiach* 'hunt' + *rí* 'king'. This was the name in Irish legend of one of the children of Lir, who were turned into swans by their stepmother. In historical times, it was borne by an Irish saint and missionary in France (died 670 at Meaux). An inn was named after him, which in turn gave its name to the *fiacre*, a type of horse-drawn four-wheeled hackney cab.

Fidelma ♀
Latinized form of the traditional Irish Gaelic name **Feidhelm**, the origin of which is unknown. In Irish legend it is borne by a daughter of Conchobhar mac Nessa, a female warrior renowned for her beauty. It was also the name of one of St Patrick's first converts, a daughter of King Laoghaire and sister of St Eithne.

Fiesta ♀
From the vocabulary word (borrowed from Spanish, from Latin *(dies) festa*) referring to a carnival or celebration. It seems to have been chosen as a first name because of its happy association, or perhaps to commemorate the rejoicing over the birth of a baby.

Fife ♂
Transferred use of the Scottish surname, which originated in the Middle Ages as a local name for someone from the Kingdom (now region) of Fife. In Gaelic legend this is said to get its name from the legendary Pictish hero *Fib*, one of the seven sons of Cruithne.
Variant: **Fyfe**.

Fifi ♀
French nursery form of ◊**Joséphine**. In the English-speaking world it now has definite connotations of frivolity.

Fillan ♂
Scottish: Anglicized form of the Gaelic name **Faolán**, which means 'wolf'. St Fillan was an early medieval missionary to Scotland.

Finbar ♂
Irish: Anglicized form of the Gaelic name **Fionnb(h)arr**, derived from *fionn* 'white', 'fair' + *barr* 'head'. This was the name of at least three early Irish saints, one of whom became the first bishop of Cork in the 6th century. He is the subject of many legends, for example that he crossed the Irish Sea on horseback. The pet form of his name is **Bairre** (see ◊**Barry**), and the Isle of Barra in the Hebrides is said to be named after him.

Finella ♀
Anglicized form in Scotland of the Gaelic name ◊**Fionnuala**; see also ◊**Fenella**.

Fingal ♂
Scottish: Anglicized form of the Gaelic name *Fionnghall*, derived from *fionn* 'white', 'fair' + *gall* 'stranger'. It was originally a byname applied to Norse settlers (compare ◊**Dougal**), and was used by James Macpherson (1736–96), author of the Ossianic poems, to render the name of the Gaelic hero Fionn mac Cumhaill (see ◊**Finn**).
Variant: **Fingall**.

Finlay ♂
Scottish: Anglicized form of the Gaelic name *Fionnlagh*, derived from *fionn* 'white', 'fair' + *laogh* 'warrior' or 'calf'.
Variant: **Finley**.

Finn ♂
Irish: traditional Gaelic name meaning 'white', 'fair' (the modern Gaelic form is **Fionn**). The legendary hero Finn Mac-Cool (Finn mac Cumhaill in Irish) was noted for his wisdom and fairness. He was leader of the Fenians or *Fianna*, a

band of warriors about whom many stories are told. There may be a basis of fact behind the legends, in that Finn may be identified with an Irish leader who defended Ireland against Norse raiders.

Finnian ♂
Irish: Anglicized form of Gaelic *Finnén*, a derivative of Old Irish *finn* 'white', 'fair'. This name was borne by two 6th-century Irish bishops.
Variant: **Finian**.

Finola ♀
Irish and Scottish: Anglicized form of ◊**Fionnuala**.

Fintan ♂
Anglicized form of the traditional Irish Gaelic name **Fiontan**, a derivative of *finn* 'white', 'fair' + *tine* 'fire'. This name was borne by numerous early Irish saints.

Fiona ♀
Scottish: Latinate derivative of the Gaelic word *fionn* 'white', 'fair'. It was first used by James Macpherson (1736–96), author of the Ossianic poems, which were supposedly translations from ancient Gaelic. It was subsequently used as a pen-name by William Sharp (1855–1905), who produced many romantic works under the name of Fiona Macleod. It has since become popular throughout the English-speaking world.

Fionnuala ♀
Irish Gaelic name, pronounced 'fyun-noo-a-la': the modern form of *Fionn-guala*, a traditional name derived from *fionn* 'white', 'fair' + *guala* 'shoulder'. In Ireland it is Anglicized as **Finuala** or **Fi(o)nola**, and in Scotland as **Fenella** or **Finella**.
Short form: **Nuala**.

Fionola ♀
One of several Anglicized forms of the Gaelic name ◊**Fionnuala**. See also ◊**Fenella** and ◊**Finola**.

Flair ♀
Modern name, apparently from the vocabulary word denoting a particular talent for something. The word came

into English from French in the 19th century and is a derivative of *flairer* 'to smell out', 'discern'. Use as a given name seems to reflect a desire on the part of the parents that their daughter should exhibit such talent in life; there may also be some influence from the similar sounding ◊**Fleur**.

Flann ♂
Irish Gaelic: from a nickname meaning 'red' or 'ruddy'. It is a traditional name, borne by several early Irish heroes, and was at one time also used as a girl's name.

Flannan ♂
Irish: Anglicized form of the Gaelic name *Flannán*, originally a diminutive of Gaelic *flann* 'red', 'ruddy'. St Flannan is the patron of the diocese of Killaloe in Co. Clare, and this is still a popular given name in that area.

Flavia ♀
Feminine form of the old Roman family name *Flāvius* (from *flāvus* 'yellow (-haired)'). This was the name of at least five minor early saints.

Fletcher ♂
Transferred use of the surname, in origin an occupational name for a maker of arrows, from Old French *flech(i)er*, an agent derivative of *fleche* (of Germanic origin). An early bearer of this as a given name was Fletcher Christian, leader of the mutiny on the *Bounty* in 1789.

Fleur ♀
From an Old French name meaning 'flower', occasionally used in the Middle Ages. Modern use, however, seems to derive mainly from the character of this name in John Galsworthy's *The Forsyte Saga* (1922).

Flick ♀
Informal pet form based on ◊**Felicity**.

Flinders ♂
Transferred use of the surname, which represents an altered form of *Flanders*, and originally denoted someone who came to England from that region. Its

occasional use as a given name is probably in honour of the explorer Matthew Flinders (1774–1814). Flinders Petrie (1853–1942) was a famous British archaeologist.

Flint ♂

For the most part from the vocabulary word denoting a type of particularly hard rock (Old English *flint*), chosen as representing qualities of strength, endurance, and determination. In some cases it may represent a transferred use of the surname, which was originally given to someone who lived by a notable outcrop of this rock.

Flo ♀

Short form of ◊**Florence** and ◊**Flora**, common in the early part of the 20th century, but now widely considered somewhat old-fashioned.

Floella ♀

Recent coinage, in Britain especially popular as a Black name. It is evidently a compound of ◊**Flo** and ◊**Ella**.

Flora ♀

Name borne in Roman mythology by the goddess of flowers and the spring (a derivative of Latin *flōs* 'flower', genitive *flōris*). It is also the feminine form of the old Roman family name *Flōrus*, likewise derived from *flōs*. *Flora* was little used in England before the 18th century, when it was imported from Scotland. In 1746 Flora Macdonald (1722–90), daughter of Ranald Macdonald of Milton in South Uist, helped Bonnie Prince Charlie to escape from there to the Island of Skye, disguised as a woman, after his defeat at Culloden. In fact, *Flora* was merely an Anglicized form of her Gaelic name, *Fionnaghal*, a variant of *Fionnghuala* (see ◊**Fenella**). However, her fame made the name *Flora* popular in the Highlands and elsewhere.
Short form: **Flo**.
Pet form: Scottish: **Florrie** *(Gaelic Flòraidh)*.

Florence ♀, formerly also ♂

Medieval form of the Latin masculine name *Florentius* (a derivative of *florens* blossoming, flourishing) and its feminine form *Florentia*. In the Middle Ages the name was commonly borne by men (as, for example, the historian Florence of Worcester), but it is now exclusively a girl's name. This was revived in the second half of the 19th century, being given in honour of Florence Nightingale (1820–1910), the founder of modern nursing, who organized a group of nurses to serve in the Crimean War. She herself received the name because she was born in the Italian city of Florence (Latin *Florentia*, Italian *Firenze*).
Short form: **Flo**.
Pet form: **Flossie**.

Florida ♀

From the name of the U.S. state, originally so named in Spanish because of its lush vegetation (from Latin *flōridus* 'flowery'). It may also in part have originated as an elaboration of ◊**Flora** or more modern form of ◊**Florence**.

Florrie ♀

Scottish pet form of ◊**Flora**, now little used except in the Highlands.

Flossie ♀

Pet form from a contraction of ◊**Florence**, common in the 19th century, but no longer much used. The popularity of the name was perhaps enhanced by association with the soft downy material known as *floss*.

Flower ♀

From the vocabulary word (from Old French; compare ◊**Fleur**), which is also sometimes used as a term of endearment.

Floyd ♂

Transferred use of the Welsh surname, in origin a variant of ◊**Lloyd**. This form of the name results from an attempt to represent the sound of the Welsh initial *Ll-* using traditional English pronunciation and orthography. In the 20th century it has been particularly common in the southern United States.

Forbes ♂

Transferred use of the Scottish surname, in origin a local name from the lands of Forbes in Aberdeenshire. These are named from the Gaelic word *forba* 'field', 'district' + the locative suffix *-ais*. In Scotland this name was traditionally pronounced in two syllables, but a monosyllabic pronunciation is now the norm.

Ford ♂

Transferred use of the common surname, in origin a local name for someone who lived near a place where a river could be crossed by wading through it (Old English *ford*).

Forrest ♂

Transferred use of the surname, in origin a local name for someone who lived in or by an enclosed wood, Old French *forest*.
Variant: **Forest**. *Compare* ◊**Deforest**.

Foster ♂

Transferred use of the surname, an occupational name with at least four possible derivations: from Middle English *foster* 'foster parent', *for(e)ster* 'forester', *fors(e)ter* 'shearer', or *fu(y)ster* 'saddle-tree maker'.

Fox ♂

Generally a transferred use of the surname, which derives as a nickname from the animal (Old English *fox*). This may originally have been given to a cunning person, or to someone with red hair, or for some other anecdotal reason. Use as a given name may have originated in honour of George Fox (1624–91), founder of the Quaker movement. In Ireland it has also been used as English translation of the Gaelic nickname *sionnach* 'fox'. As a Jewish name it has been used as an Anglicized form of the Yiddish nickname *fiksl* 'fox'.

Fran ♀, ♂

Short form of ◊**Frances**, or less commonly of ◊**Francis**.

France ♂, ♀

Mainly U.S.: short form of ◊**Francis** or ◊**Frances** or bestowed with reference to the country.

Francene ♀

Variant spelling of ◊**Francine**.
Variant: **Franceen**.

Frances ♀

Feminine form of ◊**Francis**. In the 16th century the two spellings were used indiscriminately for both sexes, the distinction in spelling not being established until the 17th century.
Short form: **Fran**.
Pet form: **Fanny**.

Francesca ♀

Italian form of ◊**Frances**. Originally a vocabulary word meaning 'French', it was bestowed from the 13th century onwards in honour of St Francis of Assisi. It has also been used independently as an English name. Its most famous bearer was Francesca di Rimini, daughter of Giovanni da Polenta, Count of Ravenna. A legendary beauty, she was betrothed by her father to the misshapen Giovanni Malatesta, Lord of Rimini, in return for military support. Malatesta's good-looking younger brother, Paolo, acted as his proxy in the betrothal, but Francesca and he fell in love. They were discovered, and put to death by Malatesta in 1289. Their tragedy is enshrined in the Fifth Canto of Dante's *Inferno*, as well as in several other works of literature and in a symphonic fantasy by Tchaikovsky.

Francine ♀

From a French diminutive pet form of *Françoise*, the French form of ◊**Frances**.
Variants: **Francene**, **Franceen**.

Francis ♂

English form of Italian *Francesco*, originally a vocabulary word meaning 'French' or 'Frenchman' (Late Latin *Franciscus*; compare ◊**Frank**). This was a nickname given to St Francis of Assisi (1181–1226) because of his wealthy father's business connections with France. His baptismal name was

Giovanni, the Italian form of *John*. He
had a pleasant, ordinary life as a child
and young man, but after two serious
illnesses, a period of military service,
and a year as a prisoner of war in Perugia,
he turned from the world and devoted
himself to caring for the poor and sick.
He was joined by groups of disciples,
calling themselves 'minor friars' (*friari
minores*). The main features of the
Franciscan rule are humility, poverty,
and love for all living creatures. The
given name occurs occasionally in England as early as 1300, and more frequently from the early 16th century,
when there was a surge of admiration
for, and imitation of, Italian Renaissance
culture.
Short forms: ◊**Frank**, **Fran**, **France**.

Frank ♂
Of Germanic origin. The name referred
originally to a member of the tribe of the
Franks, who are said to have got the
name from a characteristic type of
spear that they used. When the
Franks migrated into Gaul in the 4th
century, the country received its
modern name of France (Late Latin
Francia) and the tribal term Frank came
to mean 'Frenchman'. The name is now
quite often taken as a short form of
◊**Francis**.

Frankie ♂,♀
Pet form of ◊**Frank**, also sometimes of
◊**Frances**, ◊**Francesca**, or ◊**Francine**. As a
girl's name, it is perhaps most familiar as
the name of the heroine of *The Ballad of
Frankie and Johnny*.

Franklin ♂
Transferred use of the surname, derived
from Middle English *frankeleyn* 'freeman', denoting a member of a class of
men who were not of noble birth but
who were nevertheless freeholders. The
vocabulary word is derived from Old
French *franc*, meaning both 'free' and
'Frankish'. The connection between
freemen and Franks is reflected in the
Late Latin term *francālia*, originally
denoting lands held by Franks, which

came to mean lands not subject to taxes.
The given name is now quite common,
especially in the United States, where it
is often bestowed in honour of the
statesman and scientist Benjamin
Franklin (1706–90). A more recent
influence was President Franklin D.
Roosevelt (1882–1945).

Fraser ♂
Scottish: transferred use of the surname
of a leading Scottish family. The surname is of Norman origin, but its exact
derivation is uncertain. The earliest
forms recorded are *de Frisselle* and *de
Fresel(iere)*, but it was altered, possibly
by association with Old French *fraise*
'strawberry'.
Variants: **Frazer**, **Frazier**.

Fred ♂
Short form of ◊**Frederick** or, occasion-
ally, of ◊**Alfred**.
Pet forms: **Freddie**, **Freddy**.

Freda ♀
Short form of various names such as
◊**Elfreda** and ◊**Winifred**, also occasion-
ally of ◊**Frederica**.
Pet form: **Freddie**.

Freddie ♂,♀
Pet form of ◊**Fred** and ◊**Freda**.
Variant: **Freddy** mostly (♂).

Frederica ♀
Latinate feminine form of ◊**Frederick**.
Short forms: **Freda**.

Frederick ♂
From an Old French name of Germanic
origin, from *fred*, *frid* 'peace' + *rīc*
'power', 'ruler'. It was adopted by the
Normans and introduced into Britain by
them, but did not survive long. Modern
use in Britain dates from the 17th century, and it became more frequent in the
18th among followers of the Elector of
Hanover, who in 1714 became George I
of England. It was reinforced by the
vogue for Germanic names in Victorian
times.
Variants: **Frederic**, **Fredric**.
Short form: **Fred**.
Pet forms: **Freddy**, **Freddie**.

Freya ♀

Scottish: of Old Norse origin. *Freya* or *Fröja* was the goddess of love in Scandinavian mythology, and her name is most probably derived from a word related to Old High German *frouwa* 'lady', 'mistress' (German *Frau*). The name has for long been a traditional one in Shetland, and it is still used in Scotland. A notable modern bearer was the explorer and writer Freya Stark.

Frost ♂

Transferred use of the surname, in origin a nickname for someone of an icy or unbending disposition or who had white hair or a white beard. (Old English *frost* is a derivative of *frēosan* 'to freeze'.) As a first name it may have been given to a child born during an exceptionally cold spell, or in honour of the American poet Robert Frost (1874–1963).

Fry ♂

Transferred use of the surname, in origin denoting either a free person rather than a serf (from Old English *frīg* 'free', a byform of *frēo*) or else a small person (from Old Norse *frió* 'seed'). Elizabeth Fry (1780–1845) was a celebrated Quaker prison reformer, noted for her compassion.

Fulk ♂

Of Germanic origin, introduced to Britain by the Normans. The name originally represented a short form of various compound names containing the word *volk* 'people, tribe' (compare modern English *folk*). It has gradually died out of general use, but is still used in certain families, in particular the Grevilles. Fulke Greville, 1st Baron Brooke, was a leading figure at the court of Elizabeth I. See also ◊**Greville**.
Variant: **Fulke**.

Fulton ♂

Transferred use of the Scottish surname, which seems to have been originally a local name from a lost place in Ayrshire. Robert Fulton (1765–1815) was the American engineer who designed the first commercially successful steamboat.

Fulvia ♀

From the feminine form of the old Roman family name *Fulvius*, a derivative of Latin *fulvus* 'dusky', 'tawny' (ultimately akin to *flāvus*; compare ◊**Flavia**). The name does not seem to have been much used among early Christians, and there are no saints Fulvia or Fulvius. In classical times its most famous bearer was the wife of Mark Antony, who opposed Octavian by force on her husband's behalf while he was in Egypt.

Fyfe ♂

Scottish: variant spelling of ◊**Fife**.

GABRIEL GABRIELA GABRIELLE GAE GAENO
R GAIA GAIL GALA GALE GALEN GAMALIEL
GARDNER GARETH GARFIELD GARNER GA
RRET GARRET GARRICK GARRISON GARRY
GARTH GARY GAVIN GAY GAYLE GAYLORD
GAYNOR GAZ GEARÓID GED GEMMA GEN

Gabriel ♂

Biblical name (meaning 'man of God' in Hebrew), borne by one of the archangels. Gabriel appeared to Daniel in the Old Testament (Daniel 8:16; 9:21), and in the New Testament to Zacharias (Luke 1:19; 26:27) and, most famously, to Mary to announce the impending birth of Christ (Luke 1:2). *Gabriel* has occasionally been used as a given name in the English-speaking world, mainly as a result of Continental European influence.

Gabriela ♀

Latinate feminine form of ◊**Gabriel**.

Gabrielle ♀

French feminine form of ◊**Gabriel**.

Gae ♀

From the English vocabulary word *gay* in its original meaning 'blithe' or 'cheerful'. This came to be used as a given name in the early 20th century because of its well-omened meaning, but fell out of favour again in the 1960s, when the vocabulary word acquired the meaning 'homosexual'; only the spelling *Gae* is still in use for the name.

Gaenor ♀

Welsh: apparently a form of ◊**Gaynor** adapted to Welsh orthography. It also may have been influenced by the name of the saint commemorated at *Llangeinwyr* in Glamorgan, known popularly as *Llangeinor*. Her name is derived from Welsh *cain* 'beautiful' + *(g)wyry(f)* 'maiden'.

Gaia ♀

From the name (a derivative of Greek *gē* 'earth') borne in classical mythology by the primeval goddess of the earth, who gave birth to Ouranos 'sky' and had children by him: Okeanos 'sea', Kronos 'time', and the Titans. It has become fairly commonly used as a modern first name since the popularization of James Lovelock's conception of the whole earthly ecosystem as a living self-regulating entity under this name.

Gail ♀

Shortened form of ◊**Abigail**. It is now very common as an independent given name, but was not found before the middle of the 20th century.
Variants: **Gale**, **Gayle**.

Gala ♀

Of Russian origin, a short form of **Galina**, which is said to be from the Greek name *Galēnē* 'calm', although it may actually be a vernacular form of ◊**Helen**.

Gale ♀

Variant spelling of ◊**Gail**.

Galen ♂

From the name of the Graeco-Roman medical writer Claudius *Galēnus* (AD ?130–?200). His name represents a Latinized form of a Greek name derived from *galēnē* 'calm'.

Gamaliel ♂

Biblical name, apparently meaning 'benefit of God' in Hebrew, occurring in both the Old and the New Testaments. In the Old Testament it is the name of the prince of the tribe of Manasseh at the time of the Exodus (Numbers 1:10); in the New Testament it is born by a wise Pharisee (Acts 5:34) and a teacher of St Paul (Acts 22:3), who may be the same person. It was used as an English first name by Puritans in the 17th century; in more recent times it is associated with the U.S. president Warren Gamaliel Harding (1865–1923).

Gardner ♂
Transferred use of the surname, in origin an occupational name for someone responsible for the maintenance of the grounds of a manor house or abbey (a derivative of Middle English *gardin*, from Norman French, of Germanic origin).

Gareth ♂
Apparently of Celtic origin, but uncertain derivation. It first occurs in Malory's *Morte D'Arthur* as the name of the lover of Eluned, and seems to have been heavily altered from its original form, whatever that may have been (possibly the same as ◊**Geraint**). It is now very popular in Wales. ◊**Gary**, which is actually an independent name, is often taken to be a pet form of it.

Garfield ♂
Transferred use of the surname, in origin a local name for someone who lived near a triangular field, from Old English *gār* 'triangular piece of land' + *feld* 'open country'.

Garner ♂
Transferred use of the surname, in origin an occupational name for someone responsible for supervising the stores kept in a granary (Old French *gernier*, from Latin *grānārium*, a derivative of *grānum* 'grain', 'corn').

Garnet ♂
Transferred use of the surname, in origin probably an occupational name for a grower or seller of pomegranates (from a metathesized form of Old French *(pome) grenate*, Latin *pomum grānātum* 'fruit full of seeds'). The name of the red-coloured precious stone derives from the same source, in reference to the fruit's bright red colour, and use as a modern first name may have been inspired by the adoption of other terms denoting gemstones used as female names. It may also

in part reflect the fame of the British field marshal Sir Garnet Wolseley (1833–1913).
Variant: **Garnett**.

Garret ♂
Transferred use of the surname, which is derived from the given names ◊**Gerald** and ◊**Gerard**. In Ireland it often represents a direct Anglicization of *Gearóid*, the Gaelic form of ◊**Gerald**, and is the name of the former taoiseach, Garret Fitzgerald (b. 1926).
Variant: **Garrett**.

Garrick ♂
Mainly U.S.: transferred use of the surname, in some cases perhaps adopted in honour of the English actor-manager David Garrick (1717–79). He was of Huguenot descent, the grandson of a certain David *de la Garrique*. This is a Languedoc place name, from *garrigue*, denoting a stretch of open limestone country.

Garrison ♂
Mainly U.S.: transferred use of the surname, originally a local name from *Garriston* in North Yorkshire or else a patronymic for the son of someone called ◊**Garret**. William Lloyd Garrison (1805–79) was a prominent American anti-slavery campaigner: the given name may originally have been bestowed in honour of him. It is now sometimes given to the sons of fathers who are called ◊**Gary** or ◊**Garry**.

Garry ♂
Variant spelling of ◊**Gary**, influenced by ◊**Barry**.

Garth ♂
Transferred use of a surname, but often taken to be a contracted form of ◊**Gareth**. As a surname it originated in the north of England, as a local name for someone who lived near an enclosure of some sort (Old Norse *garðr*). In modern times its popularity has been influenced by the virile superhero of this name, the main character in a long-running strip cartoon in the *Daily Mirror* newspaper.

Gary ♂

Transferred use of a surname, which is probably derived from a Norman personal name of Continental Germanic origin, a short form of any of the various compound names with *gar* 'spear' as a first element. One bearer of this surname was the American industrialist Elbert Henry Gary (1846–1927), who gave his name to the steel town of Gary, Indiana (chartered in 1906). In this town was born the theatrical agent Nan Collins, who suggested *Gary* as a stage name for her client Frank J. Cooper, who thus became Gary Cooper (1901–61). His film career caused the name to become enormously popular from the 1930s to the present day. Its popularity has been maintained by the cricketer Gary Sobers (b. 1936; in his case it is in fact a pet form of *Garfield*) and the pop singer Gary Glitter (real name Paul Gadd). It is now often taken as a pet form of ◊**Gareth**.

Variant: **Garry**.
Pet form: **Gaz** (informal).

Gavin ♂

Of Celtic origin, but uncertain ultimate derivation; it first appears in French sources as *Gauvain*. The name is borne in the Arthurian romances by one of the knights of the Round Table (more familiar in English versions as Sir Gawain). It was still in use in the north of England as late as the early 18th century and never died out in Scotland, whence it has been reintroduced in the past couple of decades. It is now widely popular in England, Wales, and elsewhere in the English-speaking world.

Gay ♀, ♂

Now obsolete variant of ◊**Gae**. It was generally a girl's name, but has also been borne by men, in Ireland as a pet form of ◊**Gabriel**.

Gayle ♀

Variant spelling of ◊**Gail**. Its popularity has no doubt been increased by the fame of the American film actress Gayle Hunnicutt (b. 1942).

Gaylord ♂

Transferred use of a surname, which is a form, altered by folk etymology, of the Old French nickname *Gaillard* 'dandy'. In the past it may have been chosen as a given name because parents liked the idea of their son's living as a fine lord, but it now seems likely to suffer the same fate as ◊**Gay**.

Gaynor ♀

Medieval form of the name of Arthur's queen, *Guinevere*, recently undergoing a strong revival in popularity.

Gaz ♂

Informal pet form of ◊**Gary**.
Variant: **Gazza**.

Gearóid ♂

Irish Gaelic form of ◊**Gerald**.

Ged ♂

Short form of ◊**Gerald** or ◊**Gerard**.

Gemma ♀

From a medieval Italian nickname meaning 'gem', 'jewel'. It has been chosen in modern times mainly because of its transparent etymology. Among Roman Catholics it is sometimes chosen in honour of St Gemma Galgani (1878–1903), who was the subject of many extraordinary signs of grace, such as ecstasies and the appearance of the stigmata.
Variant: **Jemma**.

Gene ♂, ♀

Short form of ◊**Eugene**, now quite commonly used as a boy's given name, especially in North America. It has been made familiar by film actors such as Gene Autry, Gene Hackman, Gene Kelly, and Gene Wilder. It is also occasionally used as a girl's name, in which case it represents a respelling of ◊**Jean**.

Genette ♀

Variant spelling of ◊**Jeannette**.

Geneva ♀

Of recent origin and uncertain derivation: possibly a variant of ◊**Jennifer**. In form it coincides with the name of the city in Switzerland (compare ◊**Florence** and ◊**Venetia**). It may alternatively have been intended as a short form of ◊**Geneviève**.

Geneviève ♀

The name of the patron saint of Paris, a 5th-century Gallo-Roman nun who encouraged the people of Paris in the face of the occupation of the city by the Franks and threatened attacks by the Huns. Her name is probably derived from Celtic words meaning 'people, tribe' and 'woman', but if so it has been heavily altered during its transmission through French sources. The name was introduced to Britain from France in the 19th century and is now in steady use, often without the accent.

Geoff ♂

Short form of ◊**Geoffrey**. See also ◊**Jeff**.

Geoffrey ♂

Of Germanic (Frankish and Lombard) origin, introduced to Britain by the Normans. It was in regular use among the counts of Anjou, ancestors of the English royal house of Plantagenet, who were descended from Geoffrey Plantagenet, Count of Anjou (1113–51). It was a particularly popular name in England and France in the later Middle Ages; notable bearers in England include the poet Geoffrey Chaucer (c.1340–1400) and in Wales the chronicler Geoffrey of Monmouth (d. 1155). The original form and meaning of the elements of which the name is composed are disputed. According to one theory, the name is merely a variant of ◊**Godfrey**; others derive the first part from the Germanic word *gawia* 'territory', *walah* 'stranger', or *gisil* 'pledge'. Medieval forms can be found to support all these theories, and it is possible that several names have fallen together, or that the name was subjected to reanalysis by folk etymology at an early date.
Variant: ◊**Jeffrey**.

Geordie ♂

Pet form of ◊**George**, still used in Scotland and the north of England. It is from

this name that the generic term *Geordie* for a Tynesider derives.

George ♂

Via Old French and Latin, from Greek *Georgios* (a derivative of *geōrgos* 'farmer', from *gē* 'earth' + *ergein* 'to work'). This was the name of several early saints, including the shadowy figure who is now the patron of England (as well as of Germany and Portugal). Gibbon identified him with a Cappadocian leader of this name, but this cannot be right. If the saint existed at all, he was perhaps martyred in Palestine in the persecutions of Christians instigated by the Emperor Diocletian at the beginning of the 4th century. The popular legend in which the hero slays a dragon is a medieval Italian invention. He was for a long time a more important saint in the Orthodox Church than in the West, and the name was not much used in England during the Middle Ages, even after St George came to be regarded as the patron of England in the 14th century. Its use increased from the 1400s, and by 1500 it was regularly among the most popular male names. This popularity was reinforced when George I came to the throne in 1714, bringing this name with him from Germany. It has been one of the most popular English boys' names ever since.
Pet forms: **Georgie**, **Geordie**.

Georgene ♀

Altered form of ◊**Georgine**, by association with the productive suffix *-ene*.

Georgette ♀

French feminine diminutive of *Georges*, the French form of ◊**George**, now also used in the English-speaking world. The crêpe material so called derives its name from that of an early 20th-century French dressmaker, Mme Georgette de la Plante.

Georgia ♀

Latinate feminine form of ◊**George**. It was borne by a 5th-century saint who became a recluse near Clermont in the Auvergne.

Georgiana ♀

Elaborated Latinate form of ◊**Georgia** or ◊**Georgina**.

Georgie ♀, ♂

Occasionally used as a pet form of ◊**George**, but more commonly as a girl's name, a pet form of ◊**Georgia** or ◊**Georgina**.

Georgina ♀

Latinate feminine derivative of ◊**George**. This feminine form originated in Scotland in the 18th century, when *George* itself became common among anti-Jacobites.

Georgine ♀

French form of ◊**Georgina**, now also used in the English-speaking world.

Geraint ♂

Welsh, pronounced '*gher*-aynt': of uncertain origin, derived from a British name that first appears in a Greek inscription in the form *Gerontios*, possibly influenced by the Greek vocabulary word *gerōn* 'old man' (genitive *gerontos*). The story of Geraint (or *Gereint*), son of Erbin of Cornwall, is told in the *Mabinogi*. Geraint is one of the knights of Arthur's Round Table. He wins the love of Enid at a tournament, and marries her. He is infatuated with her to the point of neglecting all else, but comes to suspect her, wrongly, of infidelity. By her submissiveness and loyalty, she regains his trust. The story of Geraint and Enid was used by Tennyson in the *Idylls of the King* (1859). In recent years the name has become extremely popular in Wales.

Gerald ♂

From an Old French name of Germanic (Frankish) origin, derived from *gār*, *gēr* 'spear' + *wald* 'rule'. It was adopted by the Normans and introduced by them to Britain, where it soon became confused with ◊**Gerard**. It died out in England at the end of the 13th century. However, it continued in Ireland, where it had been brought in the 12th century at the time of Strongbow's invasion. It was revived in England in the 19th century, along with several other long-extinct names of Norman, Old English, and Celtic origin, and is now more common than *Gerard*, which survived all along as an English 'gentry' name.

Variant: **Jerrold**.
Short form: **Ged**.
Pet forms: **Gerry**, **Jerry**.

Geraldine ♀

Feminine derivative of ◊**Gerald**, invented in the 16th century by the English poet the Earl of Surrey, in a poem praising Lady Fitzgerald. It remained very little used until the 18th century, when it suddenly increased in popularity.

Pet form: **Gerry**.

Gerard ♂

Old French name of Germanic (Frankish) origin, introduced to Britain by the Normans. It is derived from *gār*, *gēr* 'spear' + *hard* 'brave', 'hardy', 'strong'. In the later Middle Ages this was a much more common name than ◊**Gerald**, with which it was sometimes confused. Nowadays it is less common, surviving mainly among Roman Catholics, in honour of the many saints of this name.

Variants: **Gerrard**, **Jerrard**.
Short form: **Ged**.
Pet forms: **Gerry**, **Jerry**.

Germaine ♀, ♂

Feminine form of the rarer French boy's name **Germain** (Late Latin *Germānus* 'brother'; the original reference may have been to the concept of Christian brotherhood). Germaine Cousin (*c.*1579–1601) was a Provençal saint, the daughter of a poor farmer. Her canonization in 1867 gave an additional impulse to the use of the name in Europe and the English-speaking world. This form of the name is now also used as a boy's name in the United States; see also ◊**Jermaine**.

Gerrard ♂

Variant spelling of ◊**Gerard**, in part from the surname derived from the given name in the Middle Ages.

Gerry ♂, ♀
Pet form of ◊**Gerald**, ◊**Gerard**, or
◊**Geraldine**; it is also sometimes used as
a girl's name. See also ◊**Jerry**.

Gertrude ♀
From a Germanic female personal name,
derived from *gār*, *gēr* 'spear' + *þrūþ*
'strength'. The name is not found in
England immediately after the Conquest, but only in the later Middle
English period. It may have been introduced by migrants from the Low Countries who came to England in
connection with the cloth trade, and
was certainly in consistent use in some
areas throughout the 16th and 17th
centuries, although it was not
generally popular until the 19th century,
when many medieval names were
revived. It has now fallen from favour
again.
Short form: **Gert**.
Pet form: **Gertie**.

Gervaise ♂
Norman name of unknown origin. It has
been suggested that it might be Germanic, with *gēr* 'spear' as the first
element; if so, the second element is
unknown. The given name is
bestowed in honour of a certain St
Gervasius, whose remains, together
with those of Protasius, were discovered
in Milan in the year 386. Nothing is
known about their lives, but St Ambrose, who had ordered the search for
their remains, declared that they were
martyrs, and a cult soon grew up.
Given these circumstances, we might
expect their names to be Greek or Latin,
but if they are, the origins are unknown.
The name is in use mainly among
Roman Catholics. *Protasius* has not
survived as a given name. See also
◊**Jarvis**.
Variant: **Gervase**.

Ghislain ♀
Of recent origin, or at any rate a recent
introduction to the English-speaking
world. It is evidently a revival of the Old
French oblique case of ◊**Giselle**, in a
spelling that suggests Low German,
Dutch, or Flemish influence.
Variant: **Ghislaine**.

Gib ♂
Medieval and modern short form of
◊**Gilbert**.
Variant: **Gibb**.

Gideon ♂
Biblical name (meaning 'he who cuts
down' in Hebrew), borne by an Israelite
leader appointed to deliver his people
from the Midianites (Judges 6:14). He did
this by getting his army to creep up on
them with their torches hidden in
pitchers. The name was popular among
the 17th-century Puritans, and is still
occasionally used in the United States.

Gigi ♀
French pet form of ◊**Giselle**, made
famous in the English-speaking world
by Lerner and Loewe's immensely
popular musical *Gigi* (1958), starring
Leslie Caron in the title role.

Gilbert ♂
Old French name of Germanic (Frankish) origin, derived from *gisil* 'pledge' +
berht 'bright', 'famous'. It was adopted
by the Normans and introduced by them
to Britain. This was the name of the
founder of the only native British religious order (abolished at the Dissolution
of the Monasteries), St Gilbert of Sem-
pringham (?1083–1189), in whose honour it is still sometimes bestowed,
especially among Roman Catholics. It
gained a wider currency in the 19th
century.
Short form: **Gib**.

Giles ♂
Much altered English vernacular form of
the Late Latin name *Aegidius*, from
Greek *Aigidios* (a derivative of *aigidion*
'kid', 'young goat'), via Old French *Gide*.
The name was very popular in the
Middle Ages, as the result of the fame of
the 8th-century St Giles. According to
tradition, he was an Athenian citizen
who fled to Provence because he could
not cope with the fame and adulation

caused by his power to work miracles, in particular by healing the lame and crippled.

Variant: **Gyles**.

Gill ♀
Short form of ◊**Gillian**, rather less frequent than ◊**Jill**.

Gillaine ♀
Modern name, representing an altered form of ◊**Gillian** inspired by the several women's names ending in *-aine*, such as ◊**Lorraine**. The name ◊**Ghislain** may also have been an influence.

Gillespie ♂
Scottish: Anglicized form of Gaelic *Gille Easbaig* 'bishop's servant'. Gille Easbaig Cambeul ('wry-mouth') was the founder of Clan Campbell.

Gillian ♀
Variant of ◊**Julian**, from which it was differentiated in spelling only in the 17th century.

Variant: **Jillian**.
Short forms: Gill, Jill.
Pet form: Gilly.

Gilly ♀
Pet form of ◊**Gill**. There may have been some influence from the name of the *gillyflower* (earlier *gilofre*, *girofle*, from Late Greek *karyophyllon*).

Gilroy ♂
Transferred use of the Irish and Scottish surname, perhaps influenced to some extent by ◊**Elroy** and ◊**Leroy**. The surname is of Gaelic origin, from *an giolla ruadh*, 'the red-haired lad'.

Gina ♀
Shortened form of ◊**Georgina**. As an Italian name it also represents a short form of *Giorgina* or *Luigina*, and was made famous by the actress Gina Lollobrigida (b. 1927).

Ginger ♂, ♀
Originally a nickname for someone with red hair, occasionally used as a given name in the 20th century. As a girl's name it sometimes also represents a pet form of ◊**Virginia**, as in the case of the film star Ginger Rogers, born in 1911 as Virginia McMath.

Ginny ♀
Pet form of ◊**Virginia**.

Giselle ♀
French name of Frankish origin, from the Germanic word *gisil* 'pledge'. It was a common practice in medieval Europe to leave children as pledges for an alliance, to be brought up at a foreign court, and the name may be derived as a byname from this practice. This was the name by which the wife of Duke Rollo of Normandy (*c*.860–*c*.930) was known. On her account the name enjoyed considerable popularity in France from an early period. Use of the name in English-speaking countries is much more recent, and is due mainly to the ballet *Giselle* (first performed in 1841).

Pet form: ◊**Gigi**.

Gladstone ♂
Transferred use of the Scottish surname, in origin a local name from *Gledstanes* in Biggar, so called from Old English *glæd* 'kite' + *stān* 'rock' (the final *-s* is a later addition). As a given name it has sometimes been bestowed in honour of the Victorian Liberal statesman William Ewart Gladstone (1809–98). It is now favoured by West Indians: the Warwickshire and England fast bowler Gladstone Small is of West Indian parentage.

Gladwin ♂
Transferred use of the surname, itself from a medieval given name derived from Old English *glæd* 'bright' + *wine* 'friend'.

Gladys ♀
From the Welsh name *Gwladus*, which is of uncertain derivation. It has been quite widely used outside Wales in the 20th century.

Glen ♂
From the Gaelic word *gleann* 'valley', in some cases perhaps representing a transferred use of the surname derived from this word. In recent years it has been used far beyond Scotland as a given

name. There has been some confusion
with the Welsh name ◊**Glyn**, which has
the same meaning.
Variant: **Glenn**.

Glenda ♀
Welsh: modern coinage, composed of
the vocabulary words *glân* 'clean',
'pure', 'holy' + *da* 'good'. It is associated
particularly with the actress and politician Glenda Jackson (born 1937).

Glenn ♂, ♀
Variant spelling of ◊**Glen**, borne as a
girl's name by the American actress
Glenn Close.

Glenna ♀
Modern coinage, invented as a female
form of ◊**Glen**.

Glenys ♀
Welsh: modern coinage from *glân* 'pure',
'holy' + the ending *-ys* by analogy with
names such as ◊**Dilys** and ◊**Gladys**.

Gloria ♀
From the Latin word meaning 'glory',
not used as a given name before the 20th
century, but now very popular. It first
occurs as the name of a character in
George Bernard Shaw's play *You Never
Can Tell* (1898).

Glory ♀
Anglicized form of ◊**Gloria**, now occasionally used as a given name.

Glyn ♂
Welsh: from the Welsh place name
element *glyn* 'valley'. This has been
adopted as a given name in the 20th
century, as the result of a desire to
bestow on Welsh children specifically
Welsh names.
Variant: **Glynn**.

Glyndwr ♂
Welsh, pronounced '*glin*-doo-er': adopted in the 20th century in honour of the
medieval Welsh patriot Owain Glyndŵr
(*c.*1359–1416; known in English as
Owen Glendower). In his case it was a
byname referring to the fact that he
came from a place named with Welsh
glyn 'valley' + *dŵr* 'water'.

Glynis ♀
Altered form of ◊**Glenys**.

Glynn ♂
Welsh: variant spelling of ◊**Glyn**.

Gobbán ♂
Traditional Irish Gaelic name, from
gobha 'smith'. In Irish legend Gobbán
was a master craftsman who could
fashion a sword or spear with just three
blows of his hammer.

Gobnat ♀
Traditional Irish Gaelic name, feminine
of ◊**Gobbán**. St Gobnat was the found-
ress of the monastery at Ballyvourney,
Co. Cork, at a place where she encoun-
tered nine white deer.

Goddard ♂
English: from the Old English personal
name *Godeheard*, composed of the
elements *god* 'god' + *heard* 'hardy',
'brave'. In modern use it is probably a
transferred use of the surname derived
from this in the Middle Ages, rather
than a revival.

Godfrey ♂
From the Old French name *Godefroy*,
which is of Germanic (Frankish) origin,
from *god* 'god' (or *gōd* 'good') + *fred*, *frid*
'peace'. This was adopted by the Nor-
mans, and introduced by them to Britain. It was a very popular name in the
Middle Ages, and was borne by, among
others, a Norman saint (*c.*1066–1115)
who became bishop of Amiens. There
has been considerable confusion with
◊**Geoffrey**.

Godwin ♂
From the Old English personal name
Godwine, derived from *god* 'god' + *wine*
'friend'. This was borne in the 11th
century by the Earl of Wessex, the most
important man in England after the
king. He was an influential adviser to
successive kings of England, and father
of the King Harold who was defeated at
Hastings in 1066. The personal name
continued in use after the Norman
Conquest long enough to give rise to a
surname. Modern use as a given name is

probably a transferred use of the surname, rather than a revival of the Old English name.

Goldie ♀

From a nickname for a blonde, a girl with golden hair, as in the case of the actress Goldie Hawn (b. 1945).

Gomer ♂

Biblical name (meaning 'complete' in Hebrew), borne by a son of Japheth and grandson of Noah. It was taken up by the Puritans, and is still in occasional use in the United States. *Gomer* is also an English surname, and the given name may also be a transferred use of this. It is derived from an Old English personal name derived from *gōd* 'good' + *mær* 'famous'.

Goodwin ♂

Transferred use of the surname, which is derived from the Old English personal name *Gōdwine*, from *gōd* 'good' + *wine* 'friend'. There has been considerable confusion with ◊**Godwin**.

Gordon ♂

Transferred use of the Scottish surname, which is derived from a place name. It is a matter of dispute whether it referred originally to the Gordon in Berwickshire or to a similarly named place in Normandy. As a given name it seems to have been taken up in honour of Charles George Gordon (1833–85), the British general who died at Khartoum.

Goronwy ♂

Welsh: of uncertain derivation, borne in the *Mabinogi* by Goronwy the Staunch, Lord of Penllyn. He became the lover of the flower-maiden Blodeuedd and murdered her husband Lleu Llaw Gyffes, but Lleu was later restored to life and definitively dispatched Goronwy.

Grace ♀

From the abstract noun (via Old French, from Latin *grātia*), this name occurs occasionally in the 15th century, and by the 1540s was among the most popular girls' names in some parishes. It has always been particularly popular in

Scotland and northern England (borne, for example, by Grace Darling, the lighthouse keeper's daughter whose heroism in 1838, saving sailors in a storm, caught the popular imagination). In more recent times it was famous as the name of the actress Grace Kelly (1928–82), who became Princess Grace of Monaco. In Ireland it is used as an Anglicized form of ◊**Gráinne**.

Gracie ♀

Pet form of ◊**Grace**. It was made famous by the Lancashire singer and comedienne Gracie Fields (1898–1979), whose original name was Grace Stansfield.

Grafton ♂

Transferred use of the surname, in origin a local name from any of several places named with the Old English elements *grāf* 'grove' + *tūn* 'enclosure', 'settlement'. In the United States it seems to have been adopted as a given name in honour of the third Duke of Grafton, Augustus Henry Fitzroy, who served as British Prime Minister 1767–70 and who favoured conciliation with the American colonies.

Graham ♂

Transferred use of a Scottish surname, in origin a local name from *Grantham* in Lincolnshire. This is recorded in Domesday Book not only in its current form but also as *Grandham*, *Granham*, and *Graham*; it was apparently named as the 'gravelly place', from Old English *grand* 'gravel' + *hām* 'homestead'. The surname was taken to Scotland in the 12th century by Sir William de Graham, founder of a famous clan. The earls of Montrose were among his descendants. *Variants*: **Grahame**, **Graeme**.

Gráinne ♀

Irish Gaelic name, pronounced 'gronnya'. It is of uncertain origin, possibly connected with *grán* 'grain', as the name of an ancient corn goddess. In Irish legend Gráinne was the daughter of King Cormac; she was beloved by the hero Finn, but eloped with Finn's nephew Diarmait. Finn pursued them over great

distances, and eventually brought about
the death of Diarmait, after which
Gráinne killed herself. Gráinne Uí
Mháille, known in English as Grace
O'Malley, was a semi-legendary com-
mander of war galleys on the Mayo coast
in the late 16th century, 'for forty years
the stay of all rebellions in the west'.
The name is sometimes Anglicized as
◊**Grace**.

Grania ♀
Latinized form of the Irish Gaelic name
◊**Gráinne**.
Variant: **Granya**.

Grant ♂
Transferred use of the surname, very
common in Scotland, where it is the
name of a famous clan. It is derived from
a nickname meaning 'large' (Anglo-
Norman *grand*). In the United States the
name is sometimes bestowed in
honour of the Civil War general and
18th president, Ulysses S. Grant
(1822–85).

Granville ♂
From one of the Norman baronial names
that subsequently became aristocratic
English surnames and are now used
intermittently as boy's given names.
This one derives from any of several
places in Normandy named with Old
French *grand* 'large' + *ville* 'settlement'.

Granya ♀
Variant spelling of ◊**Grania**, influenced
by Russian names such as ◊**Sonya** and
◊**Tanya**.

Gray ♂
See ◊**Grey**.

Grayson ♂
Transferred use of the surname, in origin
a patronymic for someone who was the
son of a steward (Middle English *greyve*,
from Old Norse *greifi*).

Greer ♀
Transferred use of the Scottish surname,
which originated in the Middle Ages
from a contracted form of ◊**Gregor**. It has
become known as a girl's name in the

English-speaking world through the
fame of the actress Greer Garson
(b. 1908), whose mother's maiden name
it was.
Variant: **Grier**.

Greg ♂
Short form of ◊**Gregory** and ◊**Gregor**.
Variant: **Gregg**.

Gregor ♂
Scottish form of ◊**Gregory**. In part it
represents an Anglicized form of Gaelic
Griogair, which gave rise to the Highland surname *MacGregor*.

Gregory ♂
Via Latin *Gregorius* from the post-
classical Greek name *Gregōrios* 'watchful' (a derivative of *gregōrein* 'to watch',
'be vigilant'). The name was a very
popular one among the early Christians,
who were mindful of the injunction 'be
sober, be vigilant' (1 Peter 5:8). It was
borne by a number of early saints. The
most important, in honour of whom the
name was often bestowed from medieval times onwards, were Gregory of
Nazianzen (c. 329–90), Gregory of Nyssa
(d. c. 395), Gregory of Tours (538–94), and
Pope Gregory the Great (c. 540–604). A
famous bearer of the name in modern
times is the film star Gregory Peck (b.
1916). The name has traditionally been
popular in Scotland, where it is often
found in the form *Gregor*.
Short forms: **Greg(g)**.

Greta ♀
Short form of *Margareta*, a Latinate form
of ◊**Margaret**. It became fairly popular in
the English-speaking world as a result of
the fame of the Swedish-born film actress Greta Garbo (1905–92; b. Greta
Louisa Gustafsson).

Greville ♂
Transferred use of the surname, which is
a Norman baronial name from *Gréville*
in La Manche. The Greville family were
earls of Warwick, and held Warwick
Castle from the time of Queen Elizabeth
I, who granted it to her favourite Fulke
Greville (1554–1628).

Grey ♂

Transferred use of the surname, in origin a nickname for someone with grey hair or a grey beard (from Old English *græg*). In Scotland and Ireland it has also been used as a translation of various Gaelic surnames derived from *riabhach* 'brindled', 'grey', such as *Mac Riabhaich*. *Variant*: **Gray** (the usual U.S. form of the vocabulary word).

Grier ♀

Variant spelling of ◊**Greer**.

Griff ♂

Welsh: informal short form of ◊**Griffith**.

Griffin ♂

Welsh: from a medieval Latinized form, *Griffinus*, of ◊**Griffith**.

Griffith ♂

Welsh: Anglicized form of *Gruffudd* or *Griffudd*, Old Welsh *Grip(p)iud*. The second element of this means 'lord, prince'; the first is of uncertain origin. Gruffydd ap Llewellyn (d. 1063) was one of the most able rulers of Wales in the Middle Ages, scoring some notable victories over the English until he was eventually defeated by King Harold in 1063.
Short form: **Griff**.

Griselda ♀

Of uncertain origin, possibly from a Germanic name derived from *gris* 'grey' + *hild* 'battle'. It became popular in the Middle Ages with reference to the tale of 'patient Griselda' (told by Boccaccio and Chaucer), who was taken as a model of the patient, long-suffering wife.

Grizel ♀

Medieval vernacular form of ◊**Griselda**, used particularly in Scotland, and in the north of England at least as late as the 18th century. The name has now died out, no doubt in part because of its similarity to the vocabulary word *grizzle* meaning 'to grumble or whine'.

Grover ♂

Transferred use of the surname, in origin a local name for someone who lived near a grove of trees (Old English *grāf*). Use as a given name is partly due to the U.S. president (Stephen) Grover Cleveland (1837–1908).

Guaire ♂

Traditional Irish Gaelic name, of uncertain origin. It is said to be from a word meaning 'noble' or 'proud'.

Guinevere ♀

From the Old French form of the Welsh name *Gwenhwyfar*, from *gwen* 'white', 'fair', 'blessed', 'holy' + *hwyfar* 'smooth', 'soft'. It is famous as the name of King Arthur's wife, who in most versions of the Arthurian legends is unfaithful to him, having fallen in love with Sir Lancelot. See also ◊**Gaynor** and ◊**Jennifer**.

Gus ♂

Short form of ◊**Augustus** or ◊**Angus**. In the case of Gus the Theatre Cat, a character in T.S. Eliot's *Old Possum's Book of Practical Cats* (1939), it is a short form of *Asparagus*!
Pet form: **Gussie**.

Guy ♂

From an Old French name, of Germanic (Frankish) origin, originally a short form of a compound name starting with *witu* 'wood' or *wīt* 'wide'. This was adopted by the Normans and introduced by them to England. In Old French initial *w*- regularly became *gu*-. The usual Norman forms of the name were *Gy* or *Guido*. In medieval Latin the same name is found as *Wido*. It was a popular name among the Normans, enhanced no doubt by the romance of Guy of Warwick, recounting the exploits of a folk hero of the Crusades.

Gwen ♀

Welsh: short form of ◊**Gwendolen** or ◊**Gwenllian**, or an independent name from Welsh *gwen*, the feminine form of *gwyn* 'white', 'fair', 'blessed', 'holy' (see ◊**Gwyn**). It was borne by a 5th-century saint, aunt of St David and mother of the minor saints Cybi and Cadfan.

Gwenda ♀

Welsh: of modern origin, composed of the vocabulary words *gwen* 'white', 'fair', 'blessed', 'holy' (see ◊**Gwen**) + *da* 'good'.

Gwendolen ♀

Welsh: from *gwen* 'white', 'fair', 'blessed', 'holy' (see ◊**Gwyn**) + *dolen* 'ring', 'bow'. According to Geoffrey of Monmouth, this was the name of the wife of a mythical Welsh king Locrine, who abandoned her for a German princess called Estrildis. Gwendolen in revenge had Estrildis and her daughter Sabrina drowned in the River Severn. The name is borne by one of the principal characters in Oscar Wilde's play *The Importance of Being Earnest* (first performed in 1895).
Variants: **Gwendolin**, **Gwendolyn**; **Gwendoline** (formed under the influence of ◊**Caroline** and other girls' names ending in *-ine*).

Gwenllian ♀

Welsh traditional name, derived from *gwen* 'white', 'fair', 'blessed', 'holy' (see ◊**Gwyn**) + *lliant* 'flood', 'flow' (probably in the transferred sense 'foamy' or 'white', referring to a pale complexion).

Gwenyth ♀

Welsh: variant of ◊**Gwyneth**. It may alternatively be based on Welsh *gwenith* 'wheat', a word used in poetry to mean 'the favourite' or 'the pick of the bunch'.

Gwilym ♂

Welsh form of ◊**William**, in use since the Middle Ages.

Gwyn ♂

Welsh: originally a byname from Welsh *gwyn* 'white', 'fair', 'blessed', 'holy'. See also ◊**Wyn**.

Gwynedd ♂

Welsh name, pronounced 'goo-*in*-eth': taken from a region of medieval North Wales (now resurrected as the name of a new composite county in Wales).

Gwyneth ♀

Welsh: altered form of ◊**Gwynedd**, used as a girl's name. Its popularity from the late 19th century, at first in Wales and then more widely in the English-speaking world, seems to have been due originally to the influence of the popular novelist Annie Harriet Hughes (1852–1910), who adopted the pen-name Gwyneth Vaughan.

Gwynfor ♂

Welsh: coined in the 20th century from *gwyn* 'white', 'fair', 'blessed', 'holy' + the mutated form of *mawr* 'great', 'large' (found in this form in a number of place names).

Gyles ♂

Variant spelling of ◊**Giles**.

Gypsy ♀

From the vocabulary word for a Romani or traveller. The word derives from *Egyptian*, as in the Middle Ages the Romanis were believed to have come to Europe from Egypt; in fact they dispersed from an original home in north India. This name may sometimes be chosen by parents who hope that their daughter will exhibit a free spirit. The American dancer Gypsy Rose Lee may have been an influence, although in her case the name was a nickname.

HADASSAH HAIDEE HAILEY HAL HALE HA
LEY HALL HAMILTON HAMISH HANK HA
NNAH HANNIBAL HAPPY HARDING HAR
DY HARLAN HARLEY HAROLD HARPER HA
RRIET HARRIETTE HARRISON HARRY HAR
TLEY HARVARD HARVEY HATTIE HAWK H

Hadassah ♀

Hebrew form of *Esther*, which is the
Persian form of the name. See Esther 2:7.
This form is now sometimes chosen as a
modern Jewish given name.
Short form: **Dassah**.

Haidee ♀

As the name of a character in Byron's
poem *Don Juan* (1819–24), this may have
been intended to be connected with the
classical Greek adjective *aidoios* 'modest'. In modern use it is taken as a
variant of ◊**Heidi**.

Hailey ♀

Variant spelling of ◊**Hayley**.
Variant: **Hailee**.

Hal ♂

Short form of ◊**Harry**, of medieval origin.
It was used by Shakespeare in *King
Henry IV* as the name of the king's son,
the future Henry V. Similar substitution
of *-l* for *-r* has occurred in derivatives of
Terry (*Tel*), *Derek* (*Del*), and in girls'
names such as *Sally* (from *Sarah*).

Hale ♂

Transferred use of the surname, in origin
a local name for someone living in a
nook or recess (Old English *halh*).

Haley ♀

Variant spelling of ◊**Hayley**.
Variant: **Haleigh**.

Hall ♂

Transferred use of the surname, which
originated as a local name for someone,
usually a servant or retainer, who lived
at a manor house (Old English *heall*).

Hamilton ♂

Mainly North American: transferred use
of the Scottish surname. This was
brought to Scotland in or before the 13th
century from a village (now deserted)
called *Hamilton* or *Hameldune*, near
Barkby in Leicestershire (named with
Old English *hamel* 'blunt', 'flat-topped'
+ *dūn* 'hill'). It is the surname of an
enormously widespread and influential
family, who acquired many titles, including the dukedom of Hamilton. The
town near Glasgow so called is named
after the family, not vice versa. Use as a
given name seems to have begun in the
United States in honour of Alexander
Hamilton (?1757–1804), who was Secretary of the Treasury under George
Washington and did much to establish
the political and financial system on
which the industrial growth and prosperity of the United States came to be
founded. He was killed in a duel with the
irascible Aaron Burr.

Hamish ♂

Scottish: Anglicized spelling of the
vocative case, *Sheumais*, of the Gaelic
version of ◊**James**. It is now sometimes
chosen by families with no Scottish
connections.

Hank ♂

Originally a medieval back-formation
from *Hankin*, which is composed of *Han*
(a short form of *Jehan* ◊**John**) + the
Middle English diminutive suffix *-kin*.
However, the suffix was mistaken for
the Anglo-Norman diminutive *-in*,
hence the form *Hank*. *Hank* is now
sometimes used as an independent
given name in North America, where it
is usually taken as a pet form of ◊**Henry**.
It has more or less died out in Britain.

Hannah ♀
Biblical name, borne by the mother of the prophet Samuel (1 Samuel 1:2), Hebrew *Hanna*. It is derived from a Hebrew word meaning 'He (i.e. God) has favoured me (i.e. with a child)'. See also ◊**Anne**. This form of the name was taken up as a given name by the Puritans in the 16th and 17th centuries.

Hannibal ♂
Name of the Carthaginian general Hannibal Barca (247–182 BC), who led an army from Spain across the Alps and into Italy to attack the Romans. He was eventually defeated by Scipio at the battle of Zama, but not until he had shaken the Roman republic to its core. His name is composed of the Phoenician element *hann* 'grace', 'favour' + the name of the god *Baal* 'lord'. It has recently been made famous by the character of the cannibalistic maniac Hannibal Lecter, created by Thomas Harris in the novels *Red Dragon* (1981) and its sequels *Silence of the Lambs* (1988) and *Hannibal* (1999).

Happy ♀
From the vocabulary word (originally meaning 'prosperous', a derivative of *hap* 'chance', 'good luck', of Old Norse origin), occasionally used in the 20th century for the sake of the good omen of its meaning; compare ◊**Merry** and ◊**Gay**.

Harding ♂
Especially U.S.: transferred use of the surname, which is derived from a medieval English given name. The Old English form was *Hearding*, a derivative (originally patronymic in form) of *Heard* 'hardy', 'brave', 'strong', a byname or short form of the various compound personal names containing this element. Use as a given name may have been influenced by the U.S. president Warren Gamaliel Harding (1865–1923).

Hardy ♂
Especially U.S.: transferred use of the surname, in origin a nickname for a brave or stouthearted man (from Middle English, Old French *hardi*, of Germanic origin). It may in part also be used as a pet form of ◊**Harding**.

Harlan ♂
Especially U.S.: transferred use of the surname, in origin a local name from any of various places in England called *Harland*, from Old English *hār* 'grey' or *hara* 'hare' + *land* 'cleared land'. Use as a given name honours the American judge John Marshall Harlan (1833–1911), a conservative Republican who was nevertheless a pioneering supporter of civil rights in the Supreme Court. He was a descendant of the Quaker George Harland from Durham, England, who emigrated to Delaware in 1687, and became governor there in 1695. *Variant*: **Harland**.

Harley ♂
Especially U.S.: transferred use of the surname, in origin a local name from places in Shropshire and West Yorkshire, so called from Old English *hær* 'rock', 'heap of stones', or *hara* 'hare' + *lēah* 'wood', 'clearing'. Among bikers it has been used with the Harley Davidson motorcycle in mind.

Harold ♂
From an Old English personal name derived from *here* 'army' + *weald* 'ruler', reinforced before the Norman Conquest by the related Scandinavian form *Haraldr*, introduced by Norse settlers. The name was not common in the later Middle Ages, probably because it was associated with the unfortunate King Harold, killed at the Battle of Hastings in 1066. It was used in some parts of Nottinghamshire in the 16th and 17th centuries, and revived more generally in the 19th century, along with a number of other Old English names.

Harper ♂, ♀
Mainly U.S.: transferred use of the surname, in origin an occupational name for someone who played the harp. As a girl's name it has been borne in particular by the southern American writer Harper Lee, author of *To Kill a Mockingbird* (1960).

Harriet ♀

Anglicized form of French *Henriette*, a feminine diminutive of ◊**Henry** (French *Henri*) coined in the 17th century. It was quite common in England in the 18th and early 19th centuries.
Pet form: **Hattie**.

Harriette ♀

Variant of ◊**Harriet**, probably coined to look more feminine, but it could be a reconstructed form, blending ◊**Harriet** with its source *Henriette*.

Harrison ♂

Especially U.S.: transferred use of the surname, which originated as a patronymic meaning 'son of Harry'. Use as a given name may have been influenced by the U.S. presidents William Henry Harrison (1773–1841) and his grandson Benjamin Harrison (1833–1901). A more recent influence is the actor Harrison Ford (b. 1942).

Harry ♂

Pet form of ◊**Henry**. This was the usual English form of ◊**Henry** in the Middle Ages and later. It was used by Shakespeare, for example, as the familiar name of the mature King Henry V (compare ◊**Hal**).

Hartley ♂

Transferred use of the surname, in origin a local name from any of the numerous places so called. Most (for example, those in Berkshire, Dorset, Hampshire, and Kent) are so called from Old English *heorot* 'hart', 'male deer' + *lēah* 'wood', 'clearing'. One in Northumbria is from *heorot* + *hlāw* 'hill', and one in Cumbria is probably from *haraŏ* 'wood' + *clā* 'claw', i.e. river-fork.

Harvard ♂

Mainly U.S.: transferred use of the surname, which is from an Old Norse personal name derived from *herr* 'army' + *varþr* 'guardian' (akin to Old English *Hereweard*). Use as a given name has no doubt been influenced by Harvard College in Cambridge, Massachusetts. This takes its name from John Harvard (1607–38), who emigrated from London in 1637 and left half his wealth and the whole of his library to support the newly founded college.

Harvey ♂

Transferred use of the surname, which is derived from a Breton personal name composed of *haer* 'battle' + *vy* 'worthy'. It was introduced to Britain by Bretons who settled in East Anglia and elsewhere in the wake of the Norman Conquest.
Short forms: **Harv(e)**.

Hattie ♀

Pet form of ◊**Harriet**.

Hawk ♂

From the term denoting the bird of prey (Middle English *hauk*, from Old English *hafoc*), or a transferred use of the surname derived from this word.
Variant: **Hawke**.

Hawkin ♂

Transferred use of the surname, in origin a medieval diminutive form of ◊**Hal**.

Haydn ♂

From the surname of the composer, adopted in his honour particularly by the music-loving Welsh. Josef Haydn (1732–1809) was court composer and kapellmeister to the powerful Count Nicholas Esterhazy, and spent most of his working life at the Esterhazy palace near Vienna. His surname is a respelling of the nickname *Heiden* 'heathen' (Middle High German *heiden*, Old High German *heidano*).
Variants: **Hayden**, **Haydon**.

Hayley ♀

Transferred use of the surname, which derives from a place name, probably *Hailey* in Oxfordshire, which was originally named from Old English *hēg* 'hay' + *lēah* 'clearing'. Use as a given name began in the 1960s, inspired perhaps by the actress Hayley Mills (b. 1946), daughter of Sir John Mills and Mary Hayley Bell. It has enjoyed great popularity since then.

Variants: **Haylee, Hailey, Hailee, Haley, Haleigh**.

Hazel ♀

From the vocabulary word denoting the tree (Old English *hæsel*), or its light reddish-brown nuts. This is one of the most successful of the names coined in the 19th century from words denoting plants. The fact that it also denotes an eye colour may have been a factor in its continuing popularity.

Heath ♂

Transferred use of the surname, in origin a local name for someone who lived on a patch of heathland (Old English *hæð*).

Heather ♀

From the vocabulary word denoting the hardy, brightly coloured plant (Middle English *hather*; the spelling was altered in the 18th century as a result of folk etymological association with *heath*). The name was first used in the late 19th century; it has been particularly popular since about 1950.

Heaven ♀

From the vocabulary word denoting the sky or the abode of God (Old English *heofon*), a place of eternal happiness.

Hebe ♀

Pronounced '*hee*-bee': from a Greek name, a feminine form of the adjective *hēbos* 'young'. This was borne in Greek mythology by a minor goddess who was a personification of youth. She was a daughter of Zeus and the wife of Hephaistos; it was her duty to act as cup-bearer to the gods. The name was taken up in England in the late 19th century, but it has fallen out of fashion again.

Heber ♂

Irish: Anglicized form of the Gaelic name *Éibhear* (pronounced '*ay*-ver'). This was borne in Irish legend by the son of Míl, leader of the Gaelic race that first conquered Ireland. *Hever* is also a biblical name (meaning 'enclave' in Hebrew), borne by various minor characters in the Bible.

Hector ♂

Name borne in classical legend by the Trojan champion who was killed by the Greek Achilles. His name (Greek *Hektōr*) is probably an agent derivative of Greek *ekhein* 'to restrain'. It was never popular in England, but there are occasional examples from the Middle Ages. In Scotland it was used as a classicized form of the Gaelic personal name *Eachann*, which is composed of the elements *each* 'horse' + *donn* 'brown'.

Heddwyn ♂

Welsh, pronounced '*heth*-win': modern coinage, from *hedd* 'peace' + *(g)wyn* 'white', 'fair', 'blessed', 'holy'. Use as a given name was popularized by the fame of the poet Ellis Humphrey Evans, who posthumously won the bardic chair at the National Eisteddfod in 1917, having been killed in the First World War; his bardic name was *Hedd Wyn*.

Hedley ♂

Transferred use of the surname, in origin a local name from one of several places in Durham and Northumbria so called from Old English *hæþ* 'heather' + *lēah* 'wood', 'clearing'.

Heidi ♀

Swiss pet form of *Adelheid*, the German form of ◊**Adelaide**. The name is now also popular in the English-speaking world, largely due to Johanna Spyri's children's classic *Heidi* (1881).

Heilyn ♂

Welsh traditional name, pronounced '*hay*-lin': originally an occupational byname for a steward or wine-pourer, composed of the stem of the verb *heilio* 'to prepare', 'wait on' + the diminutive suffix -*yn*. The name is borne in the *Mabinogi* by two characters: Heilyn the son of Gwynn the Old, and Heilyn the Red, son of Cadwgawn.

Heledd ♀

Welsh traditional name, pronounced '*hell*-eth': of uncertain derivation. It was borne by a semi-legendary princess of the 7th century, in whose name a lament for her brother's death was composed in the 9th century.

Helen ♀

English vernacular form of the name (Greek *Hēlēnē*) borne in classical legend by the famous beauty, wife of Menelaus, whose seizure by the Trojan prince Paris sparked off the Trojan War. Her name is of uncertain origin; it may be connected with a word meaning 'ray' or 'sunbeam'; compare Greek *hēlios* 'sun'. It has sometimes been taken as connected with the Greek word meaning 'Greek', *Hellēn*, but this is doubtful speculation. In the early Christian period the name was borne by the mother of the Emperor Constantine, who is now usually known by the Latin version of her name, *Helena*. She is credited with having found the True Cross in Jerusalem. She was born in about 248, probably in Bithynia. However, in medieval England it was thought that she had been born in Britain, which greatly increased the popularity of the name there.

Helena ♀

Latinate form of ◊**Helen**.

Helga ♀

From an Old Norse woman's personal name, a derivative of the adjective *heilagr* 'prosperous', 'successful' (from *heill* 'hale', 'hearty', 'happy'). It was introduced to England before the Conquest, but did not survive long. It has been reintroduced to the English-speaking world in the 20th century from Scandinavia and Germany. See also ◊**Olga**.

Henrietta ♀

Latinate form of French *Henriette*, a feminine diminutive of *Henri*, the French form of ◊**Henry**. Henrietta Maria (1609–69) was the wife of King Charles I, the daughter of Henry IV of France, in whose honour the name was sometimes chosen by gentry families in the 17th century. It enjoyed a revival in the late 19th century. See also ◊**Harriet**.
Pet forms: **Hennie**, **Hettie**, **Hattie**.

Henry ♂

A perennially popular given name, of Continental Germanic origin, from *haim* 'home' + *rīc* 'power', 'ruler'. It was an Old French name, adopted by the Normans and introduced by them to Britain. It has been borne by eight kings of England. Not until the 17th century did the form *Henry* (as opposed to ◊**Harry**) become the standard vernacular form, mainly due to the influence of the Latin form *Henricus* and French *Henri*.
Pet forms: ◊**Hal**, ◊**Hank**, ◊**Harry**.

Hephzibah ♀

Biblical name (meaning 'my delight is in her' (i.e. a new-born daughter)), borne by the wife of Hezekiah, King of Judah; she was the mother of Manasseh (2 Kings 21). It is also used in the prophecies of Isaiah as an allusive name for the land of Israel (compare ◊**Beulah**).
Variant: **Hepzibah**.

Herbert ♂

From an Old French name of Germanic (Frankish) origin, introduced to Britain by the Normans. It is derived from *heri*, *hari* 'army' + *berht* 'bright', 'famous'. An Old English form, *Herebeorht*, existed in England before the Conquest, but was superseded by the Norman form, which gave rise to an important surname. The family in question were earls of Pembroke in the 16th and 17th centuries; they included the poet George Herbert. By the end of the Middle Ages *Herbert* was little used, although it remained a favourite with some families, notably the Saint Quintins of East Yorkshire. Its greater frequency in Britain from the 19th century onwards is due partly to the trend for the revival of medieval names of Germanic origin and partly to the trend for the transferred use of surnames.
Short form: **Herb**.
Pet form: **Herbie**.

Herman ♂

English form of *Hermann*, from a Germanic personal name derived from *heri*, *hari* 'army' + *man* 'man'. The name was in use among the Normans and was borne by many immigrants from the Low Countries in the 15th century. Perhaps because of that it continued in occasional use well into the 1700s. It was revived more generally in Britain in the 19th century, when it also became common in America, most probably as a result of the influence of German immigrants.

Hermia ♀

Latinate derivative of the name of the Greek god *Hermes* (compare ◊**Hermione**). This was used by Shakespeare for the name of a character in *A Midsummer Night's Dream* (1595).

Hermione ♀

Name borne in classical mythology by a daughter of Helen and Menelaus, who grew up to marry her cousin Orestes. It is evidently a derivative of *Hermes*, name of the messenger god, but the formation is not clear. The name was used by Shakespeare for one of the main characters in *A Winter's Tale*, and is still occasionally used in the 20th century.

Hesketh ♂

Transferred use of the surname, in origin a local name from any of the various places in northern England named with Old Norse *hestr* 'horse' + *skeiðr* 'racecourse'. Horse racing and horse fighting were favourite sports among the Scandinavian settlers in England.

Hester ♀

Variant of ◊**Esther**, of medieval origin. For a long while the two forms were interchangeable, the addition or dropping of *h-* being commonplace in a whole range of words, but now they are generally regarded as two distinct names.

Hettie ♀

Pet form of ◊**Henrietta** and occasionally also of ◊**Hester**.

Hewie ♂

Scottish and N. English: variant spelling of ◊**Hughie**.

Hilary ♀, ♂

From the medieval form of the (post-classical) Latin masculine name *Hilarius* (a derivative of *hilaris* 'cheerful') and its feminine form *Hilaria*. From the Middle Ages onwards, the name was borne principally by men (in honour of the 4th-century theologian St Hilarius of Poitiers). Now, however, it is more commonly given to girls.
Variant: **Hillary** (♀; the usual U.S. spelling).

Hilda ♀

Of Germanic origin, a Latinized short form of any of several girls' names derived from *hild* 'battle'. Many of these are found in both Continental Germanic and Old English forms. St Hilda (614–80) was a Northumbrian princess who founded the abbey at Whitby and became its abbess. *Hilda* was a popular name in England both before and after the Norman Conquest. Its popularity waned in Tudor times, but it never quite died out, and was strongly revived in the 19th century.
Variant: **Hylda**.

Hill ♂

Transferred use of the surname, in origin a local name for someone who lived on or near a hill (Old English *hyll*). As a first name it may in part represent a short form of ◊**Hilton**.

Hillary ♀

Variant spelling of ◊**Hilary**, found mainly in North America.

Hilly ♀

Pet form of ◊**Hilary** or ◊**Hillary**.

Hilton ♂

Transferred use of the surname, in origin a local name from any of the many places named with the Old English elements *hyll* 'hill' + *tūn* 'enclosure', 'settlement'. As a first name it is sometimes chosen because of its association with the chain of luxury hotels founded by Conrad Hilton (1887–1979).

Hiram ♂

Biblical name, borne by a king of Tyre who is repeatedly mentioned in the

Bible (2 Samuel 2:11; 1 Kings 5; 9:11; 10:11; 1 Chronicles 14:1; 2 Chronicles 2:11) as supplying wood, craftsmen, and money to enable David and Solomon to construct various buildings. It was also the name of a craftsman of Tyre who worked in brass for Solomon (1 Kings 7:13). The name is presumably of Semitic origin, but is probably a Phoenician name; if it is Hebrew, it may be a shortened form of *Ahiram* 'brother of the exalted'. In England, the name was taken up by the Puritans in the 17th century, but soon dropped out of use again. It is still used in the United States.

Hobart ♂

Transferred use of the surname, itself representing a variant of the given name ◊**Hubert**. In some cases the given name may derive from the city in Tasmania, named from Robert Hobart, 4th Earl of Buckingham, who was Secretary of State for War and the Colonies at the time (1804) when it was founded.

Holly ♀

From the vocabulary word denoting the evergreen shrub or tree (Middle English *holi(n)*, Old English *holegn*). The name was first used at the beginning of the 20th century, and has been particularly popular since about 1960. It is bestowed especially on girls born around Christmas, when sprigs of holly are traditionally taken indoors to decorate rooms.
Variant: **Hollie**.

Homer ♂

English form of the name of the Greek epic poet *Homēros*, now regularly used as a given name in the United States (compare ◊**Virgil**). Many theories have been put forward to explain the origin of the name of the poet, but none is conclusive. It is identical in form with the Greek vocabulary word *homēros* 'hostage'.

Honesty ♀

From the vocabulary denoting the quality (via Old French, from Latin *honestās*,

connected with *honor* 'honour'). It was rare as a name until the 20th century, but at least one example from the 17th century is recorded. Modern use may have also been influenced by the fact that there is a flower named with this word.

Honey ♀

From the vocabulary word (Old English *huneg*). Honey was used throughout the Middle Ages in place of sugar (which was only introduced from the New World in the 16th century), and the word has long been used as a term of endearment. Modern use as a given name was prompted by a character in Margaret Mitchell's novel *Gone with the Wind* (1936), made into a film in 1939.

Honor ♀

Variant spelling of ◊**Honour**; the dominant spelling of both the vocabulary word and the given name in the United States today. This spelling of the name is also found in Britain, as in the case of the actress Honor Blackman (b. 1926).

Honora ♀

Latinate elaboration of ◊**Honor**, used mainly in Ireland.

Honour ♀

From the vocabulary word denoting the quality (via Old French, from Latin *honor*). The name was popular with the Puritans in the 17th century and has survived quietly to the present day.
Variant: **Honor**.

Hope ♀

From the vocabulary word (Old English *hopa*) denoting the quality, in particular the Christian quality of expectation in the resurrection and in eternal life. The name was created by the Puritans and has been one of their most successful coinages.

Hopkin ♂

Transferred use of the surname, now found mainly in Wales. It is derived from a medieval given name, a pet form (with the diminutive suffix -*kin*) of *Hob*, a short form of ◊**Robert** that probably had its origin through English mishearing of the Norman pronunciation of *R*-.

Horace ♂

From the old Roman family name ◊**Horatius**. The name was once widely used among admirers of the Roman poet Horace (Quintus Horatius Flaccus), but it is at present out of fashion. See also ◊**Horatio**.

Horatia ♀

Feminine form of Latin ◊**Horatius**. It has never been common in the English-speaking world, but was borne, for example, by the daughter of Horatio Nelson.

Horatio ♂

Variant of ◊**Horace**, influenced by the Latin form ◊**Horatius** and the Italian form *Orazio*. It is chiefly known as having been borne by Admiral Horatio Nelson (1758–1805), victor of many sea battles with the French during the Napoleonic Wars, culminating in the Battle of Trafalgar, in which he was killed.

Horatius ♂

An old Roman family name, which is of obscure, possibly Etruscan, origin. Its most famous bearer was the Roman poet Quintus Horatius Flaccus (65–8 BC), generally known in English as ◊**Horace**. From the mid-19th century, the name has occasionally been used by English speakers in its original Latin form. This probably owes more to the *Lays of Ancient Rome* (1842) by Thomas Babbington Macaulay than to the poet Horace. Macaulay relates, in verse that was once enormously popular, the exploit of an early Roman hero, recounting 'How Horatius kept the bridge'.

Hortense ♀

French form of Latin *Hortensia*, the feminine version of the old Roman family name *Hortensius*. This is of uncertain origin, but may be derived from Latin *hortus* 'garden'. The given name began to be used in the English-speaking world in the 19th century, but is not common today.

Howard ♂

Transferred use of the surname of an English noble family. The surname has a large number of possible origins, but in the case of the noble family early forms often have the spelling *Haward*, and so it is probably from a Scandinavian personal name derived from *hā* 'high' + *ward* 'guardian'. (The traditional derivation from the Old English name *Hereweard* 'army guardian' is untenable.) It is now a widespread and popular given name.

Howell ♂

Anglicized form of the Welsh name ◊**Hywel**, or a transferred use of the surname derived from that name.

Hubert ♂

Old French name of Germanic (Frankish) origin, derived from *hug* 'heart', 'mind', 'spirit' + *berht* 'bright', 'famous'. It was popular among the Normans, who introduced it to Britain, where it was later reinforced by settlers from the Low Countries. An 8th-century St Hubert succeeded St Lambert as bishop of Maastricht and is regarded as the patron of hunters, since, like St Eustace, he is supposed to have seen a vision of Christ crucified between the antlers of a stag.

Hugh ♂

From an Old French name, *Hugues*, *Hugo*, of Germanic (Frankish) origin, derived from *hug* 'heart', 'mind', 'spirit'. It was originally a short form of various compound names containing this element. This was borne by the aristocracy of medieval France, adopted by the Normans, and introduced by them to Britain.

Hughie ♂

Pet form of ◊**Hugh**.
Variant: **Hewie**.

Hugo ♂

Latinized form of *Hugh*, used throughout the Middle Ages in official documents, and occasionally revived as a modern given name.

Hulda ♀

Biblical name (meaning 'weasel' in Hebrew), borne by a prophetess who foretold to Josiah the destruction of Jerusalem (2 Kings 22).
Variant: **Huldah**.

Humbert ♂

From an Old French name of Germanic (Frankish) origin, derived from *hun* 'bear-cub', 'warrior' + *berht* 'bright', 'famous'. It was adopted by the Normans and introduced by them to Britain. However, it was not common in Britain in the Middle Ages, and has always had a Continental flavour. It was used by Vladimir Nabokov for the name of the demented pederast, Humbert Humbert, who is the narrator in his novel *Lolita* (1955). This has no doubt contributed to its demise as a given name in the English-speaking world.

Humphrey ♂

From a Norman name, *Hunfrid*, of Germanic origin, derived from *hun* 'bear-cub', 'warrior' + *fred, frid* 'peace'. The Norman form absorbed the native Old English form, *Hunfrith*, which existed in England before the Conquest. The spelling with -*ph*- reflects classicizing influence. It has always enjoyed a modest popularity in England. Perhaps its best known bearer was the youngest son of King Henry IV, the Duke of Gloucester (1391–1447), known as 'Duke Humphrey'. He was noted as a patron of literature, and founded what became the Bodleian Library at Oxford. In modern times, probably the most famous bearer has been the film star Humphrey Bogart (1899–1957).
Variants: **Humphry, Humfr(e)y**.

Hunter ♂

Transferred use of the surname, in origin an occupational name. The term was used not only of hunters on horseback of game such as stags and wild boars, which was in the Middle Ages a pursuit restricted to the ranks of the nobility, but also of much humbler bird catchers and poachers seeking food.

Huw ♂

Welsh form of ◊**Hugh**, now sometimes also used in other parts of the English-speaking world.

Huxley ♂

Transferred use of the surname, in origin a local name from a place in Cheshire which is apparently so called from the genitive case of the Old English personal name *Hucc* + Old English *lēah* 'wood', 'clearing'. Use as a given name originated in honour of the English biologist Thomas Huxley (1825–95), a leading supporter of the evolutionary theories of Charles Darwin.

Hyacinth ♀

English form of the name (Greek *Hyakinthos*) borne in classical mythology by a beautiful youth who was accidentally killed by Apollo and from whose blood sprang a flower bearing his name (not the modern hyacinth, but a type of dark lily). The name was later borne by various early saints, principally one martyred in the 3rd century with his brother Protus. This encouraged its use as a male name in Christian Europe, including, occasionally, Britain. However, in Britain at the end of the 19th century there was a vogue for coining new girls' names from vocabulary words denoting plants and flowers (e.g. ◊**Daisy**, ◊**Ivy**). *Hyacinth* accordingly came to be regarded exclusively as a girl's name. It has never been common.

Hyam ♂

Jewish: from the Hebrew word *hayyim* 'life'. This is sometimes added to the existing given name of a seriously ill person during prayers for his recovery.

Hylda ♀

Variant spelling of ◊**Hilda**.

Hywel ♂

Welsh traditional name, pronounced '*how*-el', originally a byname from a vocabulary word meaning 'eminent, conspicuous'. This name was common in the Middle Ages and lies behind the Anglicized surname *Howell*. In the 20th century it has been revived and now enjoys great popularity.

Variants: **Hywell**; **Howell** (Anglicized).

IAIN IAN IDA IDRIS IDWAL IEUAN IFOR IG
NATIUS IKE ILLTUD ILONA IMOGEN INA I
NA NA INDIA INÉS INGA INGRAM INGRI
D IGO INNES IOLE IOLO IOMHAR IONA I
ONE IORWERTH IRA IRENE IRIS IRMA IRVI
N VINE IRVING IRWIN ISA ISAAC ISABEL I

Iain ♂

Distinctively Scottish variant of ◊Ian.
Iain is the normal Gaelic spelling.

Ian ♂

Scottish form of ◊John, now also extensively used in the wider English-
speaking world.

Ida ♀

Originally a Norman name, of Germanic origin, derived from *īd* 'work'.
This died out during the later Middle
Ages. It was revived in the 19th century,
influenced by its use in Tennyson's *The
Princess* (1847) for the central character,
who devotes herself to the cause of
women's rights and women's education
in a thoroughly Victorian way. The
name is also associated with Mount Ida
in Crete, which was connected in classical times with the worship of Zeus,
king of the gods, who was supposed to
have been brought up in a cave on the
mountainside. In the 1930s it became
famous as the name of the film star Ida
Lupino (1914–96).

Idris ♂

Welsh traditional name, derived from
iud 'lord' + *rīs* 'ardent', 'impulsive'. It
was common in the Middle Ages and
earlier, and has been strongly revived
since the late 19th century.

Idwal ♂

Welsh traditional name, derived from
iud 'lord', 'master' + *(g)wal* 'wall', 'ram-
part'.

Ieuan ♂

Pronounced '*yai*-yan': the original
Welsh form of ◊John, from Latin
Johannes. Later forms are **Iefan** and **Ifan**.

Ifor ♂

Welsh: traditional name of uncertain
derivation. It has sometimes been Anglicized as ◊Ivor, but there is in origin no
connection between the two names.

Ignatius ♂

Late Latin name, derived from the old
Roman family name *Egnatius* (of uncertain origin, possibly Etruscan). This
was altered in the early Christian period
by association with Latin *ignis* 'fire'. It
was borne by various early saints, and
more recently by St Ignatius Loyola
(1491–1556), who founded the Society of
Jesus (Jesuits). In the modern English-
speaking world it is used mainly if not
exclusively by Roman Catholics.

Ike ♂

English: pet form of ◊Isaac. However, it
was made famous in the 20th century as
the nickname of the American general
and president Dwight D. Eisenhower
(1890–1969). In this case, of course, it
was based on his surname.

Illtud ♂

Welsh traditional name, derived from *il,
el* 'multitude' + *tud* 'land', 'people'. This
was borne by a famous Welsh saint (d.
*c.*505) who founded the abbey of Llant-
wit (originally *Llan-Illtut* 'church of
Illtud').
Variant: **Illtyd** (a modern spelling).

Ilona ♀

Hungarian form of ◊Helen, now also
sometimes used in the English-speaking
world.

Imogen ♀

The name owes its existence to a character in Shakespeare's *Cymbeline*

(1609), but in earlier accounts of the events on which the play is based this character is named as *Innogen*. The modern form of the name is thus due to a misreading of these sources by Shakespeare, or of the play's text by his printer. The name *Innogen* is of Celtic origin, from Gaelic *inghean* 'girl', 'maiden'.

Ina ♀

Short form of any of the various girls' names ending in these two syllables (representing a Latinate feminine suffix), for example *Christina* and *Georgina*. See also ◊**Ena**.

Inanna ♀

From the name of a Sumerian goddess, queen of heaven and earth. Her name is of uncertain derivation, but it seems to lie behind the name *Anna* borne by the sister of Dido, Queen of Carthage, in Virgil's Aeneid; this a quite different name from the one of Hebrew origin that gave rise to the traditional European given name ◊**Anna**.

India ♀

From the name of the subcontinent, used as the name of a character in Margaret Mitchell's novel *Gone with the Wind* (1936). In the case of India Hicks, Lord Mountbatten's granddaughter, the name was chosen because of her family's association with the subcontinent.

Inés ♀

Spanish form of ◊**Agnes**. The name is now also used, usually without the accent, in the English-speaking world.

Inga ♀

Respelled version of the German and Scandinavian name *Inge*, a short form of ◊**Ingrid** or any of various other names (for example *Ingeborg*) based on the name of the old Germanic fertility god *Ing*.

Ingram ♂

Transferred use of the surname, which is derived from a medieval given name. This was originally a contracted form of the Norman name *Engelram*, composed of the ethnic name *Engel* 'Angle' (or *Ing*, name of the Old Norse fertility god) + *hramn* 'raven'. *Engelram* never went completely out of use as a given name in the north of England.

Ingrid ♀

From an Old Norse female personal name composed of the name of the fertility god *Ing* + *fríðr* 'fair', 'beautiful'. It was introduced into the English-speaking world from Scandinavia in the 20th century and became very popular, largely because of the fame of the Swedish film actress Ingrid Bergman (1915–82).

Inigo ♂

From the medieval Spanish given name *Íñigo*, a vernacular derivative of ◊**Ignatius**, apparently the result of crossing with a name recorded in the Middle Ages as *Ennecus*. This is of uncertain, possibly Basque, origin. *Íñigo* is now rarely used as a given name in Spain. In the English-speaking world it is mainly associated with the architect and stage designer Inigo Jones (1573–1652). The name had previously been borne by his father, a London clothmaker, who may well have received it at around the time of Queen Mary's marriage to Philip of Spain, when Spanish ways and Spanish names were fashionable, especially among devout Roman Catholics. The architect passed it on to his son, but later occurrences are rare.

Innes ♂, ♀

Scottish: Anglicized form based on the pronunciation of the Gaelic name *Aonghas* (see ◊**Angus**). It is also a surname, and use as a girl's name is in part the result of a regular trend (see for example ◊**Lesley**), but it may also have been influenced by adoption in the English-speaking world of the Spanish name ◊**Inés**.

Iole ♀

Pronounced 'eye-*oh*-lee': name borne in classical mythology by a daughter of Eurytus of Oechalia, Herakles' infatuation with her led to his murder by his wife Deianeira. It represents the classical Greek vocabulary word meaning 'violet', and may in part have been chosen as a learned response to the 19th-century vogue for given names derived from words denoting flowers and plants.

Iolo ♂
Welsh: pet form of ◊**Iorwerth**.

Íomhar ♂
Scottish Gaelic form of ◊**Ivor**.

Iona ♀
From the name of the tiny sacred island in the Hebrides, off the west coast of Mull. In 563 St Columba came from Ireland to found a monastery here. It became the most important centre of Christianity in northern Britain, from which missionaries went out all over Scotland and northern England, and from which the monastery at Lindisfarne was founded. The name of the island is said to be the result of a misreading of Latin *Ioua*, representing its Gaelic name *Ì*, from Old Norse *ey* 'island'.

Ione ♀
Pronounced 'eye-*oh*-nee': 19th-century coinage, apparently with reference to the glories of Ionian Greece in the 5th century BC. No such name exists in classical Greek.

Iorwerth ♂
Welsh traditional name, pronounced '*yor*-werth'; derived from *iōr* 'lord' + a mutated form of *berth* 'handsome'. It is borne in the *Mabinogi* by the jealous brother of Madawg, son of Maredudd. *Iorwerth* came to be regarded as a Welsh form of ◊**Edward**, but it has no actual connection with that name.
Variant: **Yorath**.
Pet form: **Iolo**.

Ira ♂
Biblical name (meaning 'watchful' in Hebrew), borne by a character mentioned very briefly in the Bible, one of the chief officers of King David (2 Samuel 20:26). It was taken up by the Puritans in the 17th century, and is still occasionally used, mainly in the United States.

Irene ♀
Name (from Greek *eirēnē* 'peace') borne in Greek mythology by a minor goddess who personified peace, and by a Byzantine empress (752–803). The name was taken up in the English-speaking world at the end of the 19th century, and became popular in the 20th, partly as a result of being used as the name of a character in John Galsworthy's *The Forsyte Saga* (1922). It was formerly pronounced in three syllables, as in Greek, but is now thoroughly naturalized as an English name and usually pronounced as two syllables.

Iris ♀
Name (from Greek *iris* 'rainbow') borne in Greek mythology by a minor goddess, one of the messengers of the gods, who was so named because the rainbow was thought to be a sign from the gods to men. In English her name was used in the 16th century to denote both the flower and the coloured part of the eye, on account of their varied colours. In modern English use the name is often taken as being from the word for the flower, but it is also in use in Germany, where there is no such pattern of flower names.

Irma ♀
German: pet form of various girls' names of Germanic origin beginning with the element *irm(en)*, *erm(en)* 'whole', 'entire', for example *Irmgard* and *Irmtraud*. It was introduced to the English-speaking world at the end of the 19th century.

Irvin ♂
Mainly U.S.: variant of ◊**Irvine** or ◊**Irving**.

Irvine ♂
Mainly North American: transferred use of the Scottish surname, in origin a local name from a place in the former county of Ayrshire. The place name is probably derived from a Celtic river name, akin to Welsh *ir*, *yr* 'green', 'fresh' + *afon* 'water'.

119

ISIDORE

Irving ♂

Transferred use of the Scottish surname, in origin a local name from a place in the former county of Dumfriesshire, which has the same origin as ◊**Irvine**. In the case of the songwriter Irving Berlin (1888–1989), the name was adopted: he was of Jewish origin, and was originally called Israel Baline. This is now a common given name, especially in North America. Among Jewish bearers, it is generally taken as an English equivalent of ◊**Israel**.

Irwin ♂

Transferred use of the surname, which is derived from the medieval given name *Erwin*, from Old English *eofor* 'boar' + *wine* 'friend'. There has also been some confusion with ◊**Irving**.

Isa ♀

Originally a short form of ◊**Isabel** and related names (the mining centre of Mount Isa in Queensland, Australia, was named by the prospector John Campbell Miles after his sister Isabella), but now more commonly used as an independent first name, pronounced '*eye*-za'.

Isaac ♂

Biblical name, borne by the son of Abraham, who was nearly sacrificed by his father according to a command of God which was changed at the last moment. A ram, caught in a nearby thicket, was sacrificed instead (Genesis 22:1–13). Isaac lived on to marry Rebecca and become the father of Esau and Jacob. The derivation of the name is not certain; it has traditionally been connected with the Hebrew verb meaning 'to laugh'. It was borne by both Christians and Jews in the Middle Ages and was taken up by the Puritans in the 16th century. It is more common as a Jewish name.
Pet form: ◊**Ike**.

Isabel ♀

Originally a Spanish version of ◊**Elizabeth**, which was coined by deletion of the first syllable and alteration of the final consonant sound to one that

can normally end a word in Spanish. The name was imported into France in the early Middle Ages, and thence into England. It was a royal name, and its popularity may have been enhanced by the fact that it was borne by a queen of England Isabella (1296–1358), daughter of Philip IV of France—even though she led a turbulent life and eventually had her husband, Edward II, murdered.
Variants: **Isobel**, **Isbel**.
Pet forms: **Izzy**, **Izzie**.

Isabella ♀

Latinate form of ◊**Isabel**, which became popular in England in the 18th century.

Isabelle ♀

French form of ◊**Isabel**, occasionally used in the English-speaking world.

Isadora ♀

Variant spelling of ◊**Isidora**, borne for example by the American dancer Isadora Duncan (1878–1927).

Isaiah ♂

Biblical name (meaning 'God is salvation' in Hebrew), borne by the most important of the major prophets. Rather surprisingly perhaps, the name has never been common in the English-speaking world, although it was occasionally used among the Puritans in the 17th century. It is well established as a Jewish name.

Isbel ♀

Scottish contracted form of ◊**Isabel** and ◊**Isobel**.

Iseult ♀

French form of ◊**Isolde**.

Isidora ♀

Feminine form of ◊**Isidore**. This name was little used in the Middle Ages, but has recently become modestly popular.
Pet forms: **Izzy**, **Izzie**.

Isidore ♂

English form (via Old French and Latin) of the Greek name *Isidōros*, composed of the name of the goddess *Isis* (of Egyptian origin) + Greek *dōron* 'gift'. In spite of its pagan connotations the name was a common one among early Christians, and was borne for example by the great encyclopedist St Isidore of Seville (*c*.560–636). By the late Middle Ages, however, it had come to be considered a typically Jewish name (although originally adopted as a Christianized version of ◊**Isaiah**).

Pet forms: **Izzy**, **Izzie**.

Isla ♀

Scottish, pronounced 'ai-la': 20th-century coinage, from *Islay*, name of an island in the Hebrides pronounced thus.

Islwyn ♂

Welsh: taken from the name of a mountain in the county of Gwent, named with Welsh *is* 'below' + *llwyn* 'grove'.

Isobel ♀

Variant spelling of ◊**Isabel**, found mainly in Scotland.

Isolde ♀

The name of the tragic mistress of Tristan in the Arthurian romances. There are several versions of the story. The main features are that the beautiful Isolde, an Irish princess, is betrothed to the aged King Mark of Cornwall. However, through accidentally drinking a magic potion, she and the young Cornish knight Tristan fall in love, with tragic consequences. The story has exercised a powerful hold on the European imagination. The name was relatively common in Britain in the Middle Ages, but is much rarer today. The Welsh form **Esyllt** probably originally meant 'of fair aspect'.

Variant: **Isolda**.

Israel ♂

Biblical name: originally the byname (meaning 'he who strives with God' in Hebrew) given to Jacob after he had wrestled with an angel: 'Thy name shall be called no more Jacob, but Israel: for as a prince hast thou power with God and with men, and hast prevailed' (Genesis 32:28). The name was later applied to his descendants, the Children of Israel, and was chosen as the name of the modern Jewish state. The given name was used by the Puritans in the 16th century, but is now once again almost exclusively a Jewish name.

Ita ♀

Irish: Anglicized form of the Gaelic name **Íde** (pronounced '*ee*-da', of uncertain origin (possibly connected with Old Irish *ítu* 'thirst'). This name was borne by a 6th-century saint who founded a convent in Limerick.

Ivan ♂

Russian form of ◊**John**, sometimes used in the English-speaking world in the 20th century. In Northern Ireland it is sometimes found as a variant of ◊**Ewan**.

Ivo ♂

Form of ◊**Yves** used in Germany and occasionally in the English-speaking world. It represents the nominative case of the Latinized form of the name.

Ivon ♂

Variant of ◊**Ivo**, derived from the oblique case of the name.

Ivor ♂

Of Scandinavian origin, from an Old Norse personal name derived from *ýr* 'yew', 'bow' + *herr* 'army'. In the 1920s and 30s it came to prominence as the name of the songwriter and actor Ivor Novello (1893–1951).

Variant: Scottish Gaelic: **Íomhar**.

Ivy ♀

From the vocabulary word denoting the plant (Old English *īfig*). This given name was adopted at the end of the 19th century together with a large number of other words denoting flowers and plants pressed into service as girls' names. It is currently somewhat out of fashion.

Izzy ♀, ♂

Pet form of ◊**Isabel**, ◊**Isidora**, and, as a boy's name, ◊**Isidore**.

Variant: **Izzie**.

JABEZ JACINTA JACK JACKIE JACKLYN JACK
SON JACKY JACLYN JACOB JACQUELINE JA
CQUELYN JACQUETTA JACQUI JADE JAGO J
AIME JAIMIE JAKE JAMES JAMESINA JAME
SON JAMIE JAMIESON JAN JANCIS JANE JA
NELLE JANET JANETTE JANEY JANICE JANIE

Jabez ♂

Biblical name, said to mean 'sorrowful' in Hebrew: 'and his mother called his name Jabez, saying Because I bare him with sorrow' (I Chronicles 4:9). It is now out of fashion, but it was popular among the Puritans in the 17th century, as the mention of Jabez in the Bible lent support to the Protestant work ethic. Jabez was 'more honourable than his brethren'; he called on the Lord for protection and wealth, and the Lord duly obliged.

Jacinta ♀

Spanish name, equivalent of ◊Hyacinth.

Jack ♂

Originally a pet form of ◊John, but now well established as a given name in its own right. It is derived from Middle English *Jankin*, later altered to *Jackin*, from *Jan* (a contracted form of *Jehan* 'John') + the diminutive suffix *-kin*. This led to the back-formation *Jack*, as if the name had contained the Old French diminutive suffix *-in*. It is sometimes also used as an informal pet form of ◊James, perhaps influenced by the French form *Jacques*. See also ◊Jock and ◊Jake.

Jackie ♂, ♀

Originally a boy's name, a pet form of ◊Jack, but now also used as a girl's name, a pet form of ◊Jacqueline.
Variant: **Jacky**.

Jacklyn ♀

Variant spelling of ◊Jaclyn, influenced by ◊Jack.

Jackson ♂

Transferred use of the surname, meaning originally 'son of Jack' and in modern times sometimes bestowed with precisely this meaning. In the United States it has also been used in honour of President Andrew Jackson (1767–1845) and the Confederate general Thomas 'Stonewall' Jackson (1824–63).

Jacky ♂, ♀

Variant spelling of ◊Jackie.

Jaclyn ♀

Simplified spelling of ◊Jacquelyn.

Jacob ♂

English form of the biblical Hebrew name *Yaakov*. This was borne by perhaps the most important of all the patriarchs in the Book of Genesis. Jacob was the father of twelve sons, who gave their names to the twelve tribes of Israel. He was the son of Isaac and Rebecca. According to the story in Genesis, he was the cunning younger twin, who persuaded his fractionally older brother Esau to part with his right to his inheritance in exchange for a bowl of soup ('a mess of pottage'). Later, he tricked his blind and dying father into blessing him in place of Esau. The derivation of the name has been much discussed. It is traditionally explained as being derived from Hebrew *akev* 'heel' and to have meant 'heel grabber', because when Jacob was born 'his hand took hold of Esau's heel' (Genesis 25:26). This is interpreted later in the Bible as 'supplanter'; Esau himself remarks, 'Is he not rightly named Jacob? for he has supplanted me these two times' (Genesis 27:36). As a given name, *Jacob* is especially common as a Jewish name, although it was also used by the Puritans from the 16th century onwards. Compare ◊James.

Jacqueline ♀

Feminine diminutive form of *Jacques*, the French version of ◊James. In the 1960s it became very popular in the United States and elsewhere, influenced in part by the fame and stylish image of Jacqueline Bouvier Kennedy Onassis, whose family is of French extraction. *Pet forms*: Jackie, Jacky, Jacqui (all now very common).

Jacquelyn ♀

Respelled form of ◊Jacqueline, influenced by the productive suffix *-lyn* (see ◊Lynn).
Variants: Jac(k)lyn.

Jacquetta ♀

Respelling (influenced by ◊Jacqueline) of the Italian name *Giachetta*, a feminine diminutive of *Giac(om)o*, the Italian version of ◊James.

Jacqui ♀

Pet form of ◊Jacqueline, once a modish spelling of what was normally written *Jackie*, but now well established.

Jade ♀

From the name of the precious stone, a word that reached English from Spanish *(piedra de) ijada*, which literally means '(stone of the) bowels'. It was so called because it was believed to have the magical power of providing protection against disorders of the intestines. The vogue for this word as a given name developed later than that for other gemstone names, possibly because it sounds the same as the vocabulary word denoting a broken-down old horse or a nagging woman. Its popular appeal received a considerable boost in the early 1970s when the daughter of the English rock singer Mick Jagger was so named.

Jago ♂

Cornish form of ◊James. It has increased in popularity recently, perhaps as a transferred use of the surname *Jago*, which itself derives from the Cornish given name.

Jaime ♂, ♀

This is the Spanish form of ◊James, but in the United States and Canada it has in recent years come to be used also as a girl's name, apparently a respelling of the girl's name ◊Jamie.

Jaimie ♀

Variant spelling of the girl's name ◊Jamie.
Variant: Jaimee.

Jake ♂

Variant of ◊Jack, of Middle English origin, which has now come back into fashion as an independent given name. It is also sometimes used as a short form of ◊Jacob.

James ♂

English form of the name borne in the New Testament by two of Christ's disciples, James son of Zebedee and James son of Alphaeus. This form comes from Late Latin *Iacomus*, a variant of *Iacobus*, Latin form of Greek *Iakobos*. This is the same name as Old Testament ◊Jacob (Hebrew *Yaakov*). For many centuries now it has been thought of in the English-speaking world and elsewhere as a distinct name. In Britain, *James* is a royal name that from the beginning of the 15th century onwards has been associated particularly with the Scottish house of Stewart: James I of Scotland (1394–1437; ruled 1424–37) was a patron of the arts and a noted poet, as well as an energetic ruler. King James VI of Scotland (1566–1625; reigned 1567–1625) succeeded to the throne of England in 1603. His grandson, James II of England (1633–1701; reigned 1685–8) was a Roman Catholic, deposed in 1688 in favour of his Protestant daughter Mary and her husband William of Orange. From then on he, his son (also called James), and his grandson Charles ('Bonnie Prince Charlie') made various unsuccessful attempts to recover the English throne. Their supporters were known as Jacobites (from Latin *Iacobus*), and the name James became for a while particularly associated with

123

JANET

Roman Catholicism on the one hand, and Highland opposition to the English government on the other.
Short form: **Jim**.
Pet forms: **Jamey, Jamie, Jimmy, Jimmie**.

Jamesina ♀
Latinate feminine elaboration of ◊**James**, at one time regularly used in Scotland, but now obsolete.

Jameson ♂
Transferred use of the surname, in origin a patronymic meaning 'son of James'.

Jamie ♂, ♀
Originally a male pet form of ◊**James** and still so used, especially in Scotland and Northumberland. In North America it is now widely used as a girl's name, a feminine equivalent of *James*.
Variants: **Jamey; Jamee, Jami** (♀) only.

Jamieson ♂
Transferred use of the Northern English and Scottish surname, in origin a patronymic meaning 'son of Jamie'.
Variant: **Jamieson**.

Jan ♂, ♀
As a boy's name this represents a revival of Middle English *Jan*, a byform of ◊**John**, or an adoption of the common European form with this spelling. As a girl's name it is a short form of names such as ◊**Janet** and ◊**Janice**.

Jancis ♀
Modern blend of ◊**Jan** and ◊**Frances**, first used in the novel *Precious Bane* (1924) by Mary Webb, for the character of Jancis Beguildy, daughter of Felix and Hephzibah.

Jane ♀
Originally a feminine form of ◊**John**, from the Old French form *Je(h)anne*. Since the 17th century it has proved the most popular of the feminine forms of *John*, ahead of ◊**Joan** and ◊**Jean**. It now also commonly occurs as the second element in combinations such as *Sarah-Jane*. In Britain it is still one of the most frequent of all girls' names, but in the

United States it barely scraped into the top three hundred names bestowed on baby girls in 1989. It is not a royal name, but was borne by the tragic Lady Jane Grey (1537–54), who was unwillingly proclaimed queen in 1553, deposed nine days later, and executed the following year. Seventy years earlier, the name had come into prominence as that of Jane Shore, mistress of King Edward IV and subsequently of Thomas Grey, 1st Marquess of Dorset, Lady Jane's grandfather. Jane Shore's tribulations in 1483 at the hands of Richard III, Edward's brother and successor, became the subject of popular ballads and plays, which may well have increased the currency of the name in the 16th century. A 19th-century influence was its use as the name of the central character in Charlotte Brontë's novel *Jane Eyre* (1847). In the 20th century it has been used intermittently since the 1940s as the name of a cheerful and scantily clad beauty whose adventures are chronicled in a strip cartoon in the *Daily Mirror*, and in the 1940s was borne by the statuesque American film star Jane Russell (b. 1921).
Variant: **Jayne**. See also ◊**Jean**, ◊**Joan**, and ◊**Joanna**.
Pet forms: **Janey, Janie, Jaynie**.

Janelle ♀
Modern elaborated form of ◊**Jane**, with the feminine ending *-elle* abstracted from names such as ◊**Danielle**. In the United States in 1989 this form was far more commonly bestowed than the simple *Jane*.
Variant: **Janella** (a Latinate form; for the ending, compare ◊**Prunella**).

Janet ♀
Originally a diminutive of ◊**Jane**, already in common use in the Middle English period. It remained in use in Scotland and in some parts of England well into the 17th century and was revived at the end of the 19th century to much more widespread use, while still retaining its popularity in Scotland.
Short form: ◊**Jan**.

Janette ♀

Either an elaborated version of ◊Janet, emphasizing the feminine form of the suffix, or a simplified form of ◊Jeannette.

Janey ♀

Pet form of ◊Jane.
Variants: **Janie**, **Jaynie**.

Janice ♀

Derivative of ◊Jane, with the addition of the suffix *-ice*, abstracted from girls' names such as ◊Candice and ◊Bernice. It seems to have been first used as the name of the heroine of the novel *Janice Meredith* by Paul Leicester Ford, published in 1899.
Variant: **Janis**.
Short form: **Jan**.

Janie ♀

Variant spelling of ◊Janey.

Janine ♀

Simplified form of ◊Jeannine.

Janis ♀

Variant spelling of ◊Janice, made popular in the 1960s and 70s by the American rock singer Janis Joplin (1943–70).

Janna ♀

Latinate elaboration of the girl's name ◊Jan.

Jared ♂

Biblical name (probably meaning 'descent' in Hebrew), borne by a descendant of Adam (Genesis 5:15). According to the Book of Genesis, he became the father of Enoch at the age of 162, and lived for a further eight hundred years. This name was occasionally used by the Puritans. It was briefly revived in the 1960s, for reasons that are not clear.

Jarlath ♂

Irish: Anglicized form of the Gaelic name **Iarlaithe**, derived from *ior* (an element of uncertain meaning) + *flaith* 'prince', 'leader'. St Jarlath was a 5th-century saint, the patron of the diocese of Tuam in Co. Galway. *Jarlath* is still a popular given name in that area.

Jarrett ♂

Transferred use of the surname, in origin a variant of ◊Garrett. The popularity of the given name may also have been influenced by ◊Jared.

Jarvis ♂

Transferred use of the surname, which is from a Middle English form of the Norman given name ◊Gervaise. Modern use may in part represent an antiquarian revival of the medieval given name.

Jaslyn ♀

Modern coinage, apparently a combination of the first syllable of ◊Jasmine with the common suffix *-lyn*.

Jasmine ♀

From the vocabulary word denoting the climbing plant with its delicate, fragrant flowers (from Old French, ultimately from Persian *yasmin*).
Variants: **Jasmin**, ◊Yasmin.

Jason ♂

English form of the name (Greek *Iasōn*) borne in classical mythology by a hero, leader of the Argonauts, who sailed to Colchis in search of the Golden Fleece, enduring many hardships and adventures. The sorceress Medea fell in love with him and helped him to obtain the Fleece; they escaped together and should have lived happily ever after. However, Jason fell in love with another woman and deserted Medea. Medea took her revenge by killing her rival, but Jason himself survived to be killed in old age by one of the rotting timbers of his ship, the *Argo*, falling on his head. The classical Greek name *Iasōn* probably derives from the Greek vocabulary word *iasthai* 'to heal'. In New Testament Greek, the name probably represents a classicized form of ◊Joshua. It was borne by an early Christian in Thessalonica, at whose house St Paul stayed (Acts 17:5–9; Romans 16:21). Probably for this reason, it enjoyed some popularity among the Puritans in the 16th and 17th centuries. In the mid-20th century it enjoyed a sudden burst of popularity, although it was also the subject of some rather surprising hostility. A 20th-century influence has been the film actor Jason Robards (b. 1920); his father, also a film actor, was likewise called Jason Robards. A more recent influence is the Australian actor Jason Donovan. The name has been used for various characters in films and television series.

Jasper ♂

The usual English form of the name assigned in Christian folklore to one of the three Magi or 'wise men', who brought gifts to the infant Christ at his birth (Matthew 2:1). The name does not appear in the Bible, and is first found in medieval tradition. It seems to be ultimately of Persian origin, from a word meaning 'treasurer'. There is probably no connection with the English vocabulary word *jasper* denoting a gemstone, which is of Semitic origin. The name was introduced into England from the Low Countries in the Middle Ages and although it never became popular continued to be widely used in parts of the north.

Javan ♂

Biblical name, borne by a son of Japheth (Genesis 10:2). It seems to be derived from a Hebrew word meaning 'wine'. Use as a modern given name has probably been influenced by names such as ◊Jeavon.

Jay ♂, ♀

Pet form of any of the given names beginning with the letter J- (compare ◊Dee and ◊Kay); now also used as an independent given name.

Jayden ♂

Modern coinage, apparently an elaboration of ◊Jay by way of a blend with *Hayden* (see ◊Haydn).

Jayne ♀

Elaborated spelling of ◊Jane.

Jaynia ♀

Modern coinage, an elaboration of ◊Jayne.

Jaynie ♀

Variant spelling of ◊Janey.

Jazz ♂

Mostly a nickname for the bearer of any given name beginning with J-, but sometimes used as an independent given name and in part associated with the vocabulary word referring to lively or enthusiastic activity. This word came into English from Black slang of the southern United States in the early 20th century, and is of unknown origin. (There have been innumerable speculations.)

Jean ♀

Like ◊Jane and ◊Joan, a medieval variant of Old French *Je(h)anne*. Towards the end of the Middle Ages this form became largely confined to Scotland. In the 20th century it has been more widely used in the English-speaking world, but still retains a Scottish flavour.

Jeana ♀

Latinate elaboration of ◊Jean, common especially in the United States.

Jeane ♀

Variant spelling of ◊Jean, common especially in the United States.

Jeanette ♀

Variant spelling of ◊Jeannette, in the 1920s and 30s associated particularly with the singer and film star Jeanette MacDonald (1902–65).

Jeanie ♀

Pet form of ◊Jean.

Jeanine ♀

Variant spelling of ◊Jeannine.

Jeannette ♀

French diminutive form of *Jeanne*, feminine form of *Jean* 'John', now also commonly used in the English-speaking world.

Jeannie ♀

Variant spelling of ◊Jeanie.

Jeannine ♀

French diminutive form of *Jeanne*,

feminine form of *Jean* 'John', now also sometimes used in the English-speaking world.

Jeavon ♂
Transferred use of the surname, originally a nickname from Anglo-Norman French *jovene* 'young' (Latin *iuvenis*). Use as a given name has probably been influenced by its similarity in sound to ◊**Evan**.
Variant: **Jevon**.

Jed ♂
Mainly U.S.: now generally used as an independent given name, this was originally a short form of the biblical name **Jedidiah**. This means 'beloved of God' in Hebrew, and was used as an alternative name of King Solomon (2 Samuel 12:25). It was a favourite with the Puritans, who considered themselves, too, to be loved by God, but the full form fell out of favour along with other rare or unwieldy Old Testament names. See also ◊**Ged**.

Jeff ♂
Short form of ◊**Jeffrey**, now also used as an independent given name, especially in North America.

Jefferson ♂
Transferred use of the surname, originally a patronymic meaning 'son of Jeffrey'. The given name is still sometimes so used. In the United States it has often been bestowed in honour of the statesman Thomas Jefferson (1743–1826), principal author of the Declaration of Independence, who became the third president of the Union. He is also remembered as a scientist, architect, and writer.

Jeffrey ♂
Variant spelling of ◊**Geoffrey**, common in the Middle Ages (as reflected in surnames such as *Jefferson*). This is the usual spelling of the name in North America and is now becoming more common in Britain.
Variant: **Jeffery**.
Short form: **Jeff**.

Jem ♂
From a medieval vernacular form of ◊**James**. In modern use, however, it is often used as a short form of ◊**Jeremy**.

Jemima ♀
Biblical name (meaning 'dove' or 'bright as day' in Hebrew), borne by the eldest of the daughters of Job, born to him towards the end of his life when his prosperity had been restored (Job 42:14). The name is recorded from the early 1700s in England, and became common in the first part of the 19th century. It has continued steadily in modern use since then.

Jemma ♀
Variant spelling of ◊**Gemma**.

Jenessa ♀
Recent coinage, a blend of ◊**Jennifer** and ◊**Vanessa**.

Jenkin ♂
Transferred use of the surname, which is derived from the medieval given name *Jankin*. This was a pet form of the boy's name ◊**Jan**, with the diminutive suffix -*kin*. The modern given name is popular in Wales, where the surnames *Jenkin* and *Jenkins* are common.

Jenna ♀
Fanciful alteration of ◊**Jenny**, with the Latinate feminine ending -*a*.

Jenni ♀
Variant spelling of ◊**Jenny**, now commonly used for the sake of variety or stylishness (-*i* as an ending of girls' names being in vogue; compare ◊**Jacqui** and ◊**Toni**).

Jennifer ♀
Of Celtic (Arthurian) origin. This represents a Cornish form of the name of King Arthur's unfaithful ◊**Guinevere**. At the beginning of the 20th century, the name was merely a Cornish curiosity, but since then it has become enormously popular all over the English-speaking world, partly due to the influence of the film star Jennifer Jones (b. 1919 as Phyllis Isley). Another factor in its rise

was probably Bernard Shaw's use of it for the character of Jennifer Dubedat in *The Doctor's Dilemma* (1905). See also ◊**Gaynor**.

Jenny ♀
Now universally taken as a short form of ◊**Jennifer**. In fact, this name existed during the Middle Ages as a pet form of ◊**Jean**.
Variants: **Jenni**, **Jenna**.

Jeremiah ♂
Biblical name (meaning 'appointed by God' in Hebrew), borne by a Hebrew prophet of the 7th–6th centuries BC, whose story, prophecies of judgement, and lamentations are recorded in the book of the Bible that bears his name. The Book of Lamentations is also attributed to him; it bewails the destruction of Jerusalem and the temple by the Babylonians in 587 BC. Despite the gloomy subject-matter of these texts, the name enjoyed some popularity among Puritans and Christian fundamentalists, partly perhaps because Jeremiah also preached reconciliation with God after his wrath was assuaged.

Jeremy ♂
Anglicized form, used in the Authorized Version of the New Testament (Matthew 2:17, 27:9), of the biblical name ◊**Jeremiah**.
Short form: **Jem**
Pet form: **Jerry**.

Jermaine ♂
Variant spelling of ◊**Germaine**, now quite common as a boy's name in the United States.

Jerome ♂
English and French (**Jérôme**) vernacular form of the Greek name *Hieronymos*, derived from *hieros* 'holy' + *onoma* 'name'. St Jerome (*c.*342–420) was a citizen of the Eastern Roman Empire, who bore the Greek names Eusebios Hieronymos Sophronios; he was chiefly responsible for the translation into Latin of the Bible, the Vulgate. He also wrote many works of commentary and expos-

ition on the Bible, and is regarded as one of the Doctors of the Church. The Greek form of the name was used occasionally in England; it is recorded in Nottinghamshire, for example, in the late 16th century. Both *Jerome* and *Jeronimus* are found in Yorkshire and elsewhere from that date onwards.
Pet form: **Jerry**.

Jerrard ♂
Rare variant of ◊**Gerard**.

Jerrold ♂
Rare variant of ◊**Gerald**, probably a transferred use of the surname derived from the given name in the Middle Ages.

Jerry ♂, ♀
As a boy's name this is a pet form of ◊**Jeremy** or ◊**Gerald**, or occasionally of ◊**Gerard** and ◊**Jerome**. As a girl's name it is a variant of ◊**Gerry**.

Jervaise ♂
Variant spelling of ◊**Gervaise**.

Jess ♀, ♂
Usually a girl's name, a short form of ◊**Jessie** or ◊**Jessica**. As a boy's name, it is a short form of ◊**Jesse**.

Jessamine ♀
From an archaic variant of the flower name ◊**Jasmine**, possibly chosen as a first name because of association with ◊**Jessica**.

Jesse ♂
Biblical name (meaning 'gift' in Hebrew), borne by the father of King David (1 Samuel 16), from whose line (according to the New Testament) Jesus was ultimately descended. It was popular among the Puritans, and is still used fairly frequently in the United States, more rarely in Britain.
Variant or short form: **Jess**.

Jessica ♀
Apparently of Shakespearian origin. This was the name of the daughter of Shylock in *The Merchant of Venice* (1596). Shakespeare's source has not been established, but he presumably intended it to pass as a typically Jewish

name. It may be from a biblical name that appeared, in the translations available in Shakespeare's day, as *Jesca* (Genesis 11:29; *Iscah* in the Authorized Version). This occurs in a somewhat obscure genealogical passage; Iscah appears to have been Abraham's niece.
Short form: **Jess**.

Jessie ♀
Pet form of ◊**Jessica**, also recorded in Scotland from an early date as a pet form of ◊**Jean**, although the derivation is not clear. The Gaelic form is *Teasag*. It is now quite often used in Scotland and elsewhere as a given name in its own right.
Short form: **Jess**.

Jethro ♂
Biblical name, borne by the father of Moses's wife Zipporah (Exodus 3:1; 4:18). It seems to be a variant of the Hebrew name *Ithra*, said to mean 'excellence', which is found at 2 Samuel 17:25. It was popular among the Puritans, but then fell out of general use. It was borne by the agricultural reformer Jethro Tull (1674–1741). In 1968 a 'progressive rock' group in Britain adopted the name Jethro Tull, and shortly afterwards the given name *Jethro* enjoyed a revival of popularity.

Jetta ♀
Comparatively recent coinage, a Latinate derivative of the vocabulary word denoting the mineral *jet*. This word is derived from Old French *jaiet*, from Latin *(lapis) gagātēs* 'stone from Gagai'. The latter was a city in Lycia, Asia Minor.

Jevon ♂
Variant spelling of ◊**Jeavon**.

Jewel ♀
A recent adoption of the vocabulary word meaning 'gemstone' (from Old French *jouel*, diminutive of *jou* 'plaything', 'delight', Latin *iocus*). The given name may derive from its use as a term of affection, or may have been suggested by the vogue in the 19th century for

creating given names from words denoting particular gemstones, e.g. ◊**Beryl**, ◊**Ruby**.

Jill ♀
Short form (respelled) of ◊**Gillian**, now often used as a given name in its own right. It was already used as a prototypical girl's name in the phrase 'Jack and Jill' in the 15th century.

Jillian ♀
Variant spelling of ◊**Gillian**.

Jim ♂
Short form of ◊**James**, already common in the Middle Ages.
Pet forms: **Jimmy**, **Jimmie**.

Jo ♀, ♂
Usually a girl's name, a short form of ◊**Joanna**, ◊**Joanne**, ◊**Jody**, or ◊**Josephine**, sometimes used in combination with other names, for example *Nancy Jo* and *Jo Anne* (see ◊**Joanne**). Occasionally it is a boy's name, a variant of ◊**Joe**.

Joachim ♂
Biblical name, probably from the Hebrew name *Johoiachin*, meaning 'established by God'. This was borne by a king of Judah who was defeated by Nebuchadnezzar and carried off into Babylonian exile (2 Kings 24). His father's name was *Jehoiakim*, and there has clearly been some confusion between the two forms in the derivation of the modern name. The reason for its great popularity in Christian Europe is that in medieval tradition it was the name commonly ascribed to the father of the Virgin Mary. He is not named at all in the Bible, but with the growth of the cult of Mary many legends grew up about her early life, and her parents came to be venerated as saints under the names Joachim and Anne.

Joan ♀
Contracted form of Old French *Jo (-h)anne*, from Latin *Io(h)anna* (see ◊**Joanna**). In England this was the usual feminine form of ◊**John** from the Middle English period onwards, but in the 16th and 17th centuries it was largely

superseded by ◊Jane. It was strongly revived in the first part of the 20th century, partly under the influence of George Bernard Shaw's play *St Joan* (1923), based on the life of Joan of Arc (1412–31). Claiming to be guided by the voices of the saints, she persuaded the French dauphin to defy the occupying English forces and have himself crowned, and she led the French army that raised the siege of Orleans in 1429. The following year she was captured by the Burgundians and sold to the English, and a year later she was burned at the stake for witchcraft at the age of 18 or 19. Her story has captured the imagination of many writers, and she is variously portrayed as a national and political hero, a model of apolitical straightforwardness and honesty, and a religious heroine. She was canonized in 1920.
Pet forms: **Joanie**, **Joni**.

Joanna ♀

From the Latin form, *Io(h)anna*, of Greek *Iōanna*, the feminine equivalent of *Iōannēs* (see ◊**John**). In the New Testament, this name is borne by a woman who was one of Jesus's followers (Luke 8:3; 24:10). She was the wife of the steward of the household of King Herod Antipas. The name was regularly used throughout the Middle Ages in most parts of Europe as a feminine equivalent of ◊**John**, but in England it has only been in common use as a vernacular given name since the 19th century.
Short form: **Jo**.

Joanne ♀

From Old French *Jo(h)anne*, and so a doublet of ◊**Joan**. This too was revived as a given name in its own right in the first half of the 20th century. It has to some extent been influenced by the independently formed combination *Jo Anne*.
Short form: **Jo**.

Job ♂

Biblical name, pronounced rhyming with 'robe'. It is borne in the Bible by the hero of the Book of Job, a man of exemplary patience, whose faith was

severely tested by God's apparently motiveless maltreatment of him. His name, appropriately enough, means 'persecuted' in Hebrew. His story was a favourite one in the Middle Ages and frequently formed the subject of miracle plays. The name was used among Puritans and Christian fundamentalists, but is currently out of favour.

Joby ♀

Fairly well established modern name of uncertain origin. It may represent a pet form of the unusual name **Jobina** (coined as a feminine form of ◊**Job**), but more likely it is a variation on ◊**Jody**.
Variant: **Jobey**.

Jocasta ♀

Name borne in classical legend by the mother of Oedipus, King of Thebes. As the result of a series of misunderstandings, she also became his wife and the mother of his children. The derivation of her name is not known. In spite of its tragic associations, the name has enjoyed a certain vogue in recent years.

Jocelyn ♀, ♂

Now normally a girl's name, but in earlier times more often given to boys. It represents a transferred use of the English surname, which in turn is derived from an Old French masculine personal name introduced to Britain by the Normans in the form *Joscelin*. This was originally a derivative, *Gautzelin*, of the name of a Germanic tribe, the *Gauts*. The spelling of the first syllable was altered because the name was taken as a double diminutive (with the Old French suffixes *-el* and *-in*) of *Josce* (see ◊**Joyce**).
Variant: **Josceline** (♀).
Short form: **Joss**.

Jock ♂

Scottish: variant of ◊**Jack**, sometimes used as an archetypal nickname for a Scotsman.
Pet forms: **Jockie**, **Jockey**.

Jodene ♀

Recent fanciful coinage, formed from ◊**Jody** plus the productive suffix *-ene*.

Jody ♀, ♂

Of uncertain origin. It may have originated as a pet form of ◊**Judith** and ◊**Jude**, but if so the reason for the change in the vowel is not clear. Alternatively, it may be a playful elaboration of ◊**Jo** or ◊**Joe**. *Variants*: **Jodie** (associated particularly with the actress Jodie Foster, b. 1962 as Alicia Christian Foster); **Jodi**.

Joe ♂

Short form of ◊**Joseph**.
Variant: **Jo**.
Pet form: **Joey**.

Joel ♂

Biblical name, composed of two different Hebrew elements, *Yah(weh)* and *El*, both of which mean 'God'; the implication of the name is that the Hebrew God, *Yahweh*, is the only true god. This is a common name in the Bible, being borne by, among others, one of King David's 'mighty men' (1 Chronicles 11:38), and a minor prophet who lived in the 8th century BC. The name has been perennially popular as a Jewish name; it was also taken up by the Puritans and other Christian fundamentalists. It is still used in North America. In Britain, however, it is not at all common.

Joelle ♀

Borrowing of the fashionable French name *Joëlle*, a feminine form of ◊**Joel**. Its selection as a given name may also have been influenced by the fact that it can be taken as a combination of ◊**Jo** and the productive suffix *-elle* (originally a French feminine diminutive ending).

Joely ♀

Modern name, apparently a pet form of ◊**Jolene**, influenced in spelling by the boy's name ◊**Joel**. It may also represent a respelling of an Anglicized pronunciation of ◊**Jolie**.

Joey ♂

Pet form of ◊**Joe**.

Johanna ♀

Latinate feminine form of *Johannes* (see ◊**John**), a variant of ◊**Joanna**.

John ♂

English form of Latin *Io(h)annes*, New Testament Greek *Iōannēs*, a contracted form of the Hebrew name *Johanan* 'God is gracious' (the name of several different characters in the Old Testament, including one of King David's 'mighty men'). *John* is the spelling used in the Authorized Version of the New Testament. The name is of great importance in early Christianity: it was borne by John the Baptist (the precursor of Christ himself, who baptized sinners in the River Jordan), by one of Christ's disciples (John the Apostle, a fisherman, brother of James), and by the author of the fourth gospel (John the Evangelist, identified in Christian tradition with the apostle, but more probably a Greek-speaking Jewish Christian living over half a century later). The name was also borne by many saints and by twenty-three popes, including John XXIII (Giuseppe Roncalli, 1881–1963), whose popularity was yet another factor influencing people to choose this given name. It was also a royal name, being borne by eight Byzantine emperors and by kings of Hungary, Poland, Portugal, France, and elsewhere. In its various forms in different languages, it has been the most perennially popular of all Christian names.
Pet forms: **Johnny**, **Johnnie**, ◊**Jack**, ◊**Hank**.

Johnathan ♂

Respelled form of ◊**Jonathan**, as if a combination of ◊**John** and ◊**Nathan**.

Johnny ♂, ♀

Pet form of ◊**John**. In the United States it is occasionally also used as a girl's name.
Variant: **Johnnie**.

Jolene ♀

Recent coinage, combining the short form ◊**Jo** with the productive suffix *-lene*, extracted from names such as ◊**Marlene**. It seems to have originated in the United States in the 1940s. It was made famous by a hit song with this title, recorded by Dolly Parton in 1979.

Jolie ♀

From the French nickname or term of endearment *jolie* 'pretty one'. This is the feminine form of the adjective *joli*, which originally meant 'gay' or 'festive' and may derive from Old Norse *jōl* 'Yule'.

Jolyon ♂

Medieval variant spelling of ◊**Julian**. Its occasional use in modern Britain derives from the name of a character in John Galsworthy's sequence of novels *The Forsyte Saga* (1922), which was serialized on television in the late 1960s.

Jon ♂

Simplified spelling of ◊**John** or short form of ◊**Jonathan**.

Jonah ♂

Biblical name (meaning 'dove' in Hebrew), borne by a prophet whose adventures are the subject of one of the shorter books of the Bible. God appeared to Jonah and ordered him to go and preach in Nineveh. When Jonah disobeyed, God caused a storm to threaten the ship in which Jonah was travelling. His shipmates, realizing that Jonah was the cause of their peril, threw him overboard, whereupon the storm subsided. A 'great fish' swallowed Jonah and delivered him, willy-nilly, to the coasts of Nineveh. This story was immensely popular in the Middle Ages, and a favourite subject of miracle plays.

Jonas ♂

Variant of ◊**Jonah**, from the New Testament Greek form of the name. Both *Jonah* and *Jonas* were used by the Puritans, the latter from the 1560s at least.

Jonathan ♂

Biblical name, meaning 'God has given', composed of the same elements as those of ◊**Matthew**, but in reverse order. This is the name of several characters in the Bible, most notably a son of King Saul, who was a devoted friend and supporter of the young David, even when David and Saul were themselves at loggerheads (1 Samuel 31; 2 Samuel 1:19–26). The name is often taken as symbolic of steadfast friendship and loyalty.
Variants: **Jonathon**, **Johnathan**.
Short form: **Jon**.

Joni ♀

Modern respelling of *Joanie*, pet form of ◊**Joan**. It is particularly associated with the Canadian folk singer Joni Mitchell (b. 1943 as Roberta Joan Anderson).

Jonina ♀

Name coined recently as a feminine form of ◊**John**, preserving the connection more clearly than ◊**Jane**, ◊**Jean**, and ◊**Joan**, each of which has acquired a distinctive status of its own.

Jonquil ♀

From the name of the flower, which was taken into English from French *jonquille* (a diminutive of Spanish *junco*, Latin *juncus* 'reed'). This is one of the latest and rarest of the flower names, which enjoyed a brief vogue during the 1940s and 1950s.

Jools ♂, ♀

Respelling of the English pet name ◊**Jules**, clearly indicating the difference in pronunciation from the French name of the same form.

Jordan ♂, ♀

Originally a name given to a child of either sex baptized in holy water that was, purportedly at least, brought from the River Jordan, whose Hebrew name, *ha-yarden*, means 'flowing down'. It was in this river that Christ was baptized by John the Baptist, and medieval pilgrims to the Holy Land usually tried to bring back a flask of its water with them. The modern given name is either a revival of this, or else a transferred use of the surname that was derived from the medieval given name.
Variants: **Jorden**, **Jordin**, **Jordon**, **Jordyn** (all mainly U.S.).

Jory ♀

Pet form of ◊**Marjorie**.

Jos ♂, ♀
Short form of ◊**Joseph**, ◊**Josiah**, or
◊**Jocelyn**.

Josceline ♀
Variant of ◊**Jocelyn** as a girl's name.

Joseph ♂
English form of the biblical Hebrew
name *Yosef*, meaning '(God) shall add
(another son)'. This was borne by the
favourite son of Jacob, whose brothers
became jealous of him and sold him into
slavery (Genesis 37). He was taken to
Egypt, where he rose to become chief
steward to Pharaoh, and was eventually
reconciled to his brothers when they
came to buy corn during a seven-year
famine (Genesis 43–7). In the New Testament *Joseph* is the name of the husband of the Virgin Mary. It is also borne
by a rich Jew, Joseph of Arimathea
(Matthew 27:57; Mark 15:43; Luke
23:50; John 19:38), who took Jesus down
from the Cross, wrapped him in a
shroud, and buried him in a rock tomb.
According to medieval legend, Joseph of
Arimathea brought the Holy Grail to
Britain. The name was uncommon in
Britain in the Middle Ages but was
revived by the Puritans, and achieved
popularity in the 18th century.
Short forms: **Joe**, **Jo**.

Josephine ♀
From French *Joséphine*, a feminine
equivalent of ◊**Joseph** formed with the
diminutive suffix *-ine*. It is now widely
used in the English-speaking world.
Short form: **Jo**.
Pet form: **Josie**.

Josette ♀
Modern French pet form of *Joséphine*,
sometimes also used in the English-
speaking world in the 20th century.

Josh ♂
Short form of ◊**Joshua**.

Joshua ♂
Biblical name (meaning 'God is salvation' in Hebrew), borne by the Israelite
leader who took command of the children of Israel after the death of Moses

and led them, after many battles, to take
possession of the promised land. The
name is especially common as a Jewish
name, and has also been favoured by
Nonconformist Christians.

Josiah ♂
Biblical name (meaning 'God heals' in
Hebrew), borne by a king of Judah,
whose story is recounted in 2 Kings 22–
23. This was fairly frequently used as a
given name in the English-speaking
world, especially among Dissenters,
from the 18th to the early 20th century.
The spelling **Josias** was also in use
among Puritans from the 16th century.
The most famous English bearer is the
potter Josiah Wedgwood (1730–95). In
North America this was a recurrent
name in the Quincy family of Massachusetts; the best-known Josiah Quincy
(1744–75) was a pre-Revolutionary patriot, who died at the age of thirty-one
while returning from arguing the cause
of the American colonists in London.

Josie ♀
Pet form of ◊**Josephine**, now widely used
as an independent given name.

Joss ♂, ♀
Short form of ◊**Jocelyn**, occasionally
used as an independent given name. In
part it may also be a revival of a medieval
boy's name (see ◊**Joyce**).

Joy ♀
From the vocabulary word (Old French
joie, Late Latin *gaudia*). Being 'joyful in
the Lord' was a duty that the Puritans
took seriously, so the name became
popular in the 17th century under their
influence. In modern times, it is generally bestowed with reference to the
parents' joy in their new-born child, or
with the intention of wishing her a
happy life.

Joyce ♀, formerly ♂
Apparently from the Norman male
name *Josce* (Middle English *Josse*),
which in turn is from *Jodocus*, a Latinized form of a Breton name, *Iodoc*,
meaning 'lord', borne by a 7th-century

Breton saint. The name was in use in England among Breton followers of William the Conqueror. However, although this was fairly common as a male given name in the Middle Ages, it had virtually died out by the 14th century. There is evidence of its use as a girl's name from the 16th century onwards in parishes with strong Puritan links, which suggests that it may have been associated with the vocabulary word *joy*; see ◊**Joy**. It was strongly revived in the 19th century under the influence of popular fiction. It is borne by characters in Mrs Henry Wood's *East Lynne* (1861) and Edna Lyall's *In the Golden Days* (1885). Modern use may well have been influenced also by the common Irish surname derived from the medieval Norman male name. See also ◊**Joss**.

Judah ♂
Biblical name (said to mean 'praised' in Hebrew), borne by the fourth son of Jacob (Genesis 29:35), who gave his name to one of the twelve tribes of Israel and to one of its two kingdoms.

Judd ♂
Medieval pet form of ◊**Jordan**, now restored to use as a given name from the derived surname.

Jude ♂
Short form of *Judas*, itself a Greek form of ◊**Judah**. This form is occasionally used in the New Testament and elsewhere to distinguish the apostle Jude (Judas Thaddaeus), to whom one of the Epistles in the New Testament is attributed, from the traitor Judas Iscariot. The name is also borne by the central character in Thomas Hardy's gloomy novel *Jude the Obscure* (1895). More recently it received some support from the Lennon and McCartney song 'Hey Jude' (1968).

Judge ♂
Generally, no doubt, a transferred use of the surname, rather than a coinage with direct reference to the legal officer (Old French *juge*, from Latin *iudex*). As a

Jewish name it represents a translation of the Hebrew name **Dayan**, which denotes a rabbinic judge.

Judith ♀
Biblical name, meaning 'Jewess' or 'woman from Judea', borne by a Jewish heroine whose story is recorded in the Book of Judith in the Apocrypha. Judith is portrayed as a beautiful widow who delivers her people from the invading Assyrians by gaining the confidence of their commander, Holofernes, and cutting off his head while he is asleep; without their commander, the Assyrians are duly routed. The name is also borne by one of the Hittite wives of Esau (Genesis 26:34). This has been a perennially popular Jewish name. In the English-speaking world it was taken up by the Puritans in the 16th century, and has enjoyed great popularity in the 20th century. It was in occasional use among Gentiles before this: for example, it was borne by a niece of William the Conqueror.
Pet forms: **Judy**, **Judi**, **Judie**.

Judy ♀
Pet form of ◊**Judith**, recorded from the 17th century. This was the name adopted by the singer and film star Judy Garland (1922–69, original name Frances Gumm).
Variants: **Judi**, **Judie**.

Jules ♂, now sometimes also ♀
French form of ◊**Julius**. It is a very common given name in France and is occasionally used in the English-speaking world, where it is also fairly common as an informal pet form of ◊**Julian** and ◊**Julie**.

Julia ♀
Feminine form of the old Roman family name ◊**Julius**. A woman called Julia is mentioned in Paul's Epistle to the Romans (Romans 16:15), and the name was borne by numerous early saints. Its frequency increased with the vogue for classical names in the 18th century, and it continues to enjoy considerable popularity, although the recent

introduction of ◊**Julie** to the English-speaking world has reduced this somewhat.

Julian ♂, occasionally ♀

From the common Late Latin name *Juliānus*, a derivative of ◊**Julius**. In classical times *Juliānus* was a name borne not only by various minor early saints, but also by the Roman emperor Julian 'the Apostate', who attempted to return the Roman Empire from institutionalized Christianity to paganism. For many centuries the English name *Julian* was borne by women as well as men, for example by the Blessed Julian of Norwich (*c*.1342–after 1413). The differentiation in form between *Julian* and ◊**Gillian** did not develop until the 16th century. *Julian* is still occasionally used as a girl's name.

Variant: ◊**Jolyon** (♂).

Juliana ♀

Latin feminine form of *Juliānus* (see ◊**Julian**), which was revived in England in the 18th century and has been used occasionally ever since.

Julianne ♀

Modern combination of the given names ◊**Julie** and ◊**Anne**, perhaps sometimes intended as a form of ◊**Juliana**.

Julie ♀

French form of ◊**Julia**. This was imported to the English-speaking world in the 1920s, and for some reason has become enormously popular. Its popularity was increased in the 1960s by the fame of the actresses Julie Harris (b. 1925), Julie Andrews (b. 1935 as Julia Wells), and Julie Christie (b. 1940).

Juliet ♀

Anglicized form of French *Juliette* or Italian *Giulietta*, diminutive forms of ◊**Julia**. The name is most famous as that of the 'star-crossed' heroine of Shakespeare's tragedy *Romeo and Juliet*.

Julitta ♀

Of uncertain origin, probably a Late Latin form of ◊**Judith**, influenced by ◊**Julia**. This was the name borne by the mother of the infant saint Quiricus; she was martyred with him at Tarsus in 304.

Julius ♂

Roman family name, of obscure derivation, borne most notably by Gaius Julius Caesar (?102–44 BC). It was in use among the early Christians, and was the name of an early and influential pope (337–52), as well as of a later pope (1443–1513) who attempted to combat the corruption of the Renaissance papacy.

June ♀

The most successful and enduring of the names coined in the early 20th century from the names of months of the year (compare ◊**April** and ◊**May**).

Juniper ♀

From the name of the plant (derived in the Middle Ages from Late Latin *iunipērus*, of uncertain origin). The term is also used in the Authorized Version of the Old Testament as a translation of Hebrew *rothem*, a substantial desert shrub whose wood was used in the building of the temple of Solomon. This is not a particularly common given name; there may have been some influence from ◊**Jennifer** (the surname *Juniper* is in part derived from *Jennifer*).

Justin ♂

English form of the Latin name *Justīnus*, a derivative of ◊**Justus**. The name was borne by various early saints, notably a 2nd-century Christian apologist and a (possibly spurious) boy martyr of the 3rd century. As an English name, *Justin* has enjoyed considerable popularity in the second part of the 20th century.

Justina ♀

Feminine form of ◊**Justin**, from Latin *Justīna*. This was the name of an early virgin martyr executed at Padua under Diocletian.

Justine ♀

Feminine form of ◊**Justin**, from a French version of ◊**Justina**. Its popularity in Britain since the 1960s was partly due to the influence of Lawrence Durrell's novel of this name.

Justus ♂
Latin name meaning 'just' or 'fair'. Because of its transparently well-omened meaning, it has been used occasionally as a given name in several countries, including Germany and the Netherlands.

KAILEY KALE KALEY KANE KARA KAREN KA
RIN KARL KARMA KATARINA KATE KATELY
N KATERINA KATH KATHA KATHARINE K
ATHERINE KATHERYN KATHLEEN KATHR
YN KATHY KATIE KATLYN KATRINA KATRI
NE KAT KATYA KAY KAYE KAYLA KAYLEY K

Kailey ♀

Variant spelling of ◊**Kayley**.
Variants: **Kaily**, **Kailee**, **Kaileigh**.

Kale ♂

Mainly North American: of uncertain origin, perhaps an Anglicized form of the Irish Gaelic name ◊**Cathal**. It may have been invented as a masculine equivalent of the currently popular ◊**Kayley** and its variants.

Kaley ♀

Variant spelling of ◊**Kayley**.
Variants: **Kalie**, **Kalee**, **Kaleigh**.

Kane ♂

Irish: Anglicized form of the traditional Gaelic name *Cathán*, meaning 'little battler', a derivative of *cath* 'battle'.

Kara ♀

Variant spelling of ◊**Cara**.

Karen ♀

Danish form of ◊**Katherine**, first introduced to the English-speaking world by Scandinavian settlers in America. It has been used in Britain only since the 1950s, but has become very popular.

Karin ♀

Swedish form of ◊**Katherine**, found as a less common variant of ◊**Karen** in America and Britain.

Karl ♂

German and Scandinavian form of ◊**Charles**. See also ◊**Carl**.

Karma ♀

From the Sanskrit word (meaning 'action' or 'effect') used in Hinduism and Buddhism to refer to the principle by which a person's actions in this world determine the fate that awaits him or her after death. In English the word is sometimes used more loosely to refer to the processes of destiny, and it has sometimes been chosen as a given name with reference to this idea.

Katarina ♀

Swedish form of ◊**Katherine**, also occasionally used in the English-speaking world.

Kate ♀

Short form of ◊**Katherine** (or any of its variant spellings), reflecting the French pronunciation with -*t*- for -*th*-, which was also usual in medieval England. This short form has been continuously popular since the Middle Ages. It was used by Shakespeare for two important characters: the daughter of the King of France who is wooed and won by King Henry V, and the 'shrew' in *The Taming of the Shrew*.

Katelyn ♀

Elaboration of ◊**Kate** with the suffix -*lyn* (see ◊**Lynn**), or a respelling of ◊**Caitlín**.

Katerina ♀

Russian popular form of ◊**Katherine**, also occasionally used in the English-speaking world.

Kath ♀

Modern short form of ◊**Katherine** and its variants.

Katha ♀

Altered form of ◊**Kathy** or elaborated form of ◊**Kath**, with the Latinate feminine suffix -*a*.

Katharine ♀

Variant of ◊**Katherine**, associated by folk etymology with Greek *katharos* 'pure'.

This is the preferred spelling in Germany and North America: it is the one used, for example, in the name of the film star Katharine Hepburn (b. 1909).

Katherine ♀
English form of the name of a saint martyred at Alexandria in 307. The story has it that she was condemned to be broken on the wheel for her Christian belief. However, the wheel miraculously fell apart, so she was beheaded instead. There were many elaborations on this story, which was one of the most popular in early Christian mythology, and she has been the object of a vast popular cult. The earliest sources that mention her are in Greek and give the name in the form *Aikaterinē*. The name is of unknown etymology; the suggestion that it may be derived from *Hēcatē*, the pagan goddess of magic and enchantment, is not convincing. From an early date, it was associated with the Greek adjective *katharos* 'pure'. This led to spellings with -*th*- and to a change in the middle vowel (see ◊**Katharine**). Several later saints also bore the name, including the mystic St Katherine of Siena (1347–80) who both led a contemplative life and played a role in the affairs of state of her day. *Katherine* is also a royal name: in England it was borne by the formidable and popular Katherine of Aragon (1485–1536), first wife of Henry VIII, as well as by the wives of Henry V and Charles II.
Variants: **Katharine**, **Catherine**, **Catharine**, **Kath(e)ryn**, **Cathryn**.
Short forms: ◊**Kate**, **Kath**, **Cath**.
Pet forms: **Kathy**, **Cathy**, **Katy**, **Katie**, **Kit(ty)**.

Katheryn ♀
Altered spelling of ◊**Katherine**, influenced by the productive name suffix -*yn*.

Kathleen ♀
Of Irish origin: traditional Anglicized form of Gaelic ◊**Caitlín**.
Variant: **Cathleen**.

Kathryn ♀
Simplified form of ◊**Katheryn**, now the most common version of ◊**Katherine** in the United States.

Kathy ♀
Pet form of ◊**Katherine** and its variants.

Katie ♀
Variant spelling of ◊**Katy**.

Katlyn ♀
Variant of ◊**Katelyn**.

Katrina ♀
Variant spelling of ◊**Catrina**.

Katrine ♀
German and Danish contracted form of *Katharine*, now also occasionally used in the English-speaking world.

Katy ♀
Pet form of ◊**Katherine** and its many variants.

Katya ♀
Russian pet form of *Yekaterina* 'Katherine', now sometimes used as a given name in the English-speaking world.

Kay ♀, ♂
Pet form of any of the various names beginning with the letter *K*- (compare ◊**Dee** and ◊**Jay**), most notably ◊**Katherine** and its many variants. As a boy's name it may also in part represent the name of the Arthurian knight Sir Kay, although he is not a particularly attractive character. His name is probably a Celticized form of Latin *Gaius*, an ancient Roman given name of uncertain derivation. As a girl's name it was famous as that of the actress Kay Kendall (1926–59; original name Justine McCarthy).

Kaye ♀
Variant spelling of ◊**Kay** as a girl's name.

Kayla ♀
Altered form of ◊**Kayley**, a recent coinage now enjoying a considerable vogue in North America.
Variant: **Kaylah**.

Kayley ♀
Of recent origin and uncertain derivation, occurring in a remarkably large

number of different spellings. It is
probably a transferred use of the Irish
surname *Kayley*, an Anglicized form of
Gaelic *Ó Caollaidhe* 'descendant of
Caollaidhe'. The latter is an ancient
(male) personal name derived from *caol*
'slender'. Its adoption as a modern
given name has probably also been
influenced by the popularity of ◊**Keeley**,
◊**Kelly**, and ◊**Kylie**, not to mention
◊**Cally**.
Variants: **Kayly**, **Kayli(e)**, **Kaylee**,
Kayleigh, **Kail(e)y**, **Kailee**, **Kaileigh**, **Kaley**,
Kalie, **Kalee**, **Kaleigh**; **Cayleigh**, **Caileigh**,
Caleigh.

Kaz ♀
Mainly Australian: informal pet form of
◊**Karen**.

Kean ♂
Irish: Anglicized form of the Gaelic
name ◊**Cian**.
Variant: **Keane**.

Keanu ♂
Hawaiian name meaning 'cool breeze
blowing down from the mountains',
recently made popular by the film actor
Keanu Reeves (b. 1965).

Keegan ♂
Transferred use of the Irish surname, an
Anglicized form of Gaelic *Mac Aodha-
gáin*, a patronymic from the personal
name *Aodhagán*, double diminutive of
Aodh (see ◊**Aidan**).

Keeley ♀
Of recent origin and uncertain etymol-
ogy, possibly an alteration of ◊**Keelin** to
fit in with the pattern of girls' names
ending in *-(e)y* or *-ie*. The Irish surname
Keeley is a variant of ◊**Kayley**.
Variants: **Keely**, **Keelie**, **Keeleigh**,
◊**Keighley**.

Keelin ♀
Irish: Anglicized form of the Gaelic
name *Caoilfhionn*, derived from *caol*
'slender' + *fionn* 'white'.

Keenan ♂
Transferred used of the Irish surname,
Gaelic *Ó Cianáin* 'descendant of

Cianán'. The latter is a personal name
representing a diminutive of ◊**Cian**.

Keeva ♀
Irish: Anglicized form of the Gaelic
name ◊**Caoimhe**.

Keighley ♀
Fanciful respelling of ◊**Keeley**, inspired
by the Yorkshire town of *Keighley*,
which is, however, pronounced '*keeth*-
lee'.

Keir ♂
Transferred use of the Scottish surname,
pronounced 'keer', in origin a variant of
◊**Kerr**. The name has sometimes been
chosen in honour of the trade unionist
and first Labour MP, James Keir Hardie
(1856–1915), whose mother's maiden
name was Keir.

Keisha ♀
U.S., pronounced '*kay*-sha': modern
coinage of uncertain origin. It is mainly
used by Blacks and may derive from a
West African language. One suggested
meaning is 'favourite daughter', from
nkisa.

Keith ♂
Transferred use of a Scottish surname,
originally a local name derived from
lands so called in East Lothian, probably
from a Celtic (Brythonic) word meaning
'wood'. The principal family bearing this
surname were hereditary Earls Maris-
chal of Scotland from 1455 to 1715. This
is one of a number of Scottish aristocratic surnames that have become well
established since the 19th century as
boys' names throughout the English-
speaking world, not just in Scotland.
Others include ◊**Bruce**, ◊**Douglas**, and
◊**Graham**.

Kelan ♂
Irish, pronounced '*kee*-lan': Anglicized
form of Gaelic *Caolán*, originally a
byname representing a diminutive form
of *caol* 'slender'.

Kellen ♂
Of uncertain derivation, perhaps an
altered form of ◊**Kelan**, or from the

Scottish surname *McKellen* (Gaelic *Mac Ailein* 'son of Alan' or *Mac Cailein* 'son of Colin').

Kelly ♀, ♂
Originally an Anglicized form of the ancient Irish Gaelic male name *Ceallach*, a traditional name of disputed origin. It is said to mean 'bright-headed', or possibly also 'strife', but could equally well be from *ceall*, genitive plural of *cill* 'monastery', 'church'. It is now very widely used as a girl's name, especially in Australia, but also elsewhere in the English-speaking world. This is a transferred use of the surname *Ó Ceallaigh* 'descendant of Ceallach').
Variants: **Kelley**, **Kellie** (♀).

Kelsey ♂, ♀
Transferred use of the surname, which is from an Old English masculine personal name *Cēolsige*, derived from *cēol* 'ship' + *sige* 'victory'. Its use as a girl's name may have been influenced by names such as ◊**Elsie**.
Variant: **Kelsie**.

Kelvin ♂
Modern given name, first used in the 1920s and increasing in popularity from the 1950s onwards. It is taken from the name of the Scottish river which runs through Glasgow into the Clyde (compare ◊**Clyde**). Its choice as a given name may also have been influenced by names such as ◊**Kevin** and ◊**Melvin** and the fame of the scientist Lord Kelvin (1824–1907).

Kemp ♂
Transferred use of the surname, which originated in the Middle Ages as an occupational name or nickname from Middle English *kempe* 'athlete', 'wrestler' (from Old English *kempa* 'warrior', 'champion').

Ken ♂
Short form of ◊**Kenneth**, or occasionally of various other boys' names with this first syllable.

Kenda ♀
Modern name, apparently a shortened

form of ◊**Kendall**. It has perhaps been created by analogy with the pair of names ◊**Linda** and ◊**Lindall**.

Kendall ♂, ♀
Transferred use of the surname, which is at least in part a local name, either from *Kendal* in Cumbria (formerly the county town of Westmorland), so named because it stands in the valley of the river *Kent*, or from *Kendale* in Driffield, Humberside, where the first element is Old Norse *keld* 'spring'. The surname may in some cases be derived from the Welsh personal name *Cynddelw*, which is of uncertain origin, perhaps from an Old Celtic word meaning 'high', 'exalted' + *delw* 'image', 'effigy'.
Variants: **Kendal**, **Kendel(l)**, **Kendle**.

Kendra ♀
Recently coined name, probably as a feminine form of ◊**Kendrick**, currently enjoying a vogue in North America.

Kendrick ♂
In modern use a transferred use of the surname, the origins of which are complex. The source in many cases is the Old Welsh personal name *Cynwrig*. This is of uncertain derivation: it may be composed of elements meaning 'high', 'exalted' + 'hill' or 'summit'. The Scottish surname *Ken(d)rick* is a shortened form of *MacKen(d)rick* (Gaelic *Mac Eanraig* 'son of Henry'); Scottish bearers are descended from a certain Henry MacNaughton, and the (Mac)Ken(d)ricks are a sept of Clan MacNaughton. As an English surname, *Ken(d)rick* is derived, at least in part, from the Middle English given name *Cenric*, in which two Old English personal names have fallen together: *Cēnrīc* (from *cēne* 'keen' + *rīc* 'power') and *Cyneric* (from *cyne* 'royal' + *rīc* 'power'). *Cenric* survived as a Christian name into the 17th century.
Variant: **Kenrick**.

Kenelm ♂
From an Old English personal name derived from *cēne* 'keen', 'bold' + *helm* 'helmet', 'protection'. The name was

popular in England during the Middle Ages, when a shadowy 9th-century Mercian prince of this name was widely revered as a saint and martyr, although his death seems to have been rather the result of personal and political motives. It has remained in occasional use ever since, especially in the Digby family, where it tended to alternate with ◊**Everard**. The most famous Sir Kenelm Digby (1603–65) was noted as a writer, scientist, adventurer, diplomat, and lover.

Kennard ♂

Transferred use of a surname, derived from a Middle English personal name in which several earlier names have fallen together. The first element is either *cēne* 'keen' or *cyne* 'royal'; the second is either *weard* 'guardian' or *heard* 'hardy', 'brave', 'strong'.

Kennedy ♂, ♀

Anglicized form of Irish Gaelic *Cinnéidigh*, a traditional name derived from *ceann* 'head' + *éidigh* 'ugly'. In recent years it has sometimes been used as a given name in the English-speaking world in honour of the assassinated American president John F. Kennedy (1917–63) and his brother Robert (1925–68). Use as a girl's name is well established, although not frequent.

Kenneth ♂

Scottish: Anglicized form of two different Gaelic names, *Cinaed* and *Cainnech*. The former seems to have been originally a personal name meaning 'born of fire' and was the Gaelic name of Kenneth mac Alpin (d. 858), first king of the united Picts and Scots. The latter is a byname meaning 'handsome', and survives today in Scotland as the common Gaelic name *Coinneach* (compare ◊**Mackenzie**). In the 20th century *Kenneth* has enjoyed great popularity as a given name well beyond the boundaries of Scotland.

Short form: **Ken**.
Pet form: **Kenny**.

Kenrick ♂

Simplified spelling of ◊**Kendrick**.

Kent ♂

Transferred use of the surname, in origin a local name from the English county. This is probably named with a Celtic word meaning 'border'. Use as a given name is of recent origin, but it is now quite popular. It may in part be seen as a short form of ◊**Kenton**.

Kenton ♂

Transferred use of the surname, in origin a local name from any of various places so called. The one in Devon gets its name from the British river name *Kenn* + Old English *tūn* 'enclosure', 'settlement'; the one in north-west London is from the Old English personal name *Cēna* 'keen' + *tūn*; the one in Northumberland is from Old English *cyne-* 'royal' + *tūn*; and that in Staffordshire is probably from the personal name *Cēna* 'keen' or *Cyna* 'royal' + *tūn*.

Kenzie ♀

Modern name, a reduced form of ◊**Mackenzie**. It may in part have been influenced by ◊**Kezia**.

Keren ♀

Shortened form of the Biblical name *Keren-happuch*, borne by the third of Job's daughters (Job 42:14). The name meant 'horn of eye-paint' in Hebrew.

Kerena ♀

Latinate elaboration of ◊**Keren**

Kermit ♂

Of Irish and Manx origin, from the Gaelic surname form *Mac Dhiarmaid* 'son of Diarmad' (see ◊**Dermot**). The name was borne by a son of the American president Theodore Roosevelt, and more recently by a frog puppet on Jim Henson's *Muppet Show*.

Kerr ♂

Transferred use of the surname, which is a northern English local name for someone who lived by a patch of wet ground overgrown with brushwood (Old Norse *kjarr*).

Kerry ♀, ♂

Of recent, Australian, origin, probably from the name of the Irish county. It is now becoming relatively common in Britain as well as Australia, especially as a girl's name.
Variants: **Kerrie**, **Kerri**, **Keri** all (♀). See also ◊**Ceri**.

Kester ♂

Medieval Scottish form of ◊**Christopher**, occasionally revived as a modern given name.

Kestrel ♀

One of the rarer girls' names derived from vocabulary words denoting birds that have come into use in the 20th century. The word itself derives from Old French *cresserelle*, apparently a derivative of *cressele* 'rattle'.

Keturah ♀

Biblical name (meaning 'incense' in Hebrew), borne by the wife Abraham married after Sarah's death (Genesis 25:1). The name is occasionally chosen in the English-speaking world by parents in search of an unusual name.

Kevin ♂

Of Irish origin: Anglicized form of the Gaelic name *Caoimhín*, originally a byname representing a diminutive of *caomh* 'comely', 'beloved'. This was the name of a 7th-century saint who is one of the patrons of Dublin.

Kezia ♀

Biblical name, borne by one of Job's daughters, born to him towards the end of his life, after his prosperity had been restored (Job 42:14). It represents the Hebrew word for the cassia tree (the English name of which is derived, via Latin and Greek, from Hebrew or a related Semitic source).
Variant: **Keziah**.
Pet forms: **Kizzie**, **Kizzy**.

Kia ♀

Modern name of uncertain origin, possibly an arbitrary coinage. In Australia and New Zealand it may have been inspired by the Maori phrase *kia ora* 'be well', which is used as a greeting or to wish someone good luck.

Kiera ♀

Recently coined feminine form of ◊**Kieran**; see also ◊**Ciara**.

Kieran ♂

Irish: Anglicized form of Gaelic ◊**Ciarán**.
Variants: **Kyran**; **Kieron** (borne, for example, by the Irish actor Kieron Moore, b. 1925).

Killian ♂

Irish: Anglicized form of Gaelic ◊**Cillian**. This name was borne by various early Irish saints, including the 7th-century author of a 'Life of St Bridget', and missionaries to Artois and Franconia.
Variant: **Kilian**.

Kilroy ♂

Transferred use of the surname, which is in origin a variant of ◊**Gilroy**.

Kim ♀, ♂

Originally a short form of ◊**Kimberley**, now established as an independent given name. The hero of Rudyard Kipling's novel *Kim* (1901) bore the name as a short form of *Kimball* (a surname used as a given name). In recent years, as a girl's name it has been borne by a number of well-known people, including the film stars Kim Novak (b. 1933) and Kim Bassinger (b. 1953).

Kimberley ♀, ♂

The immediate source of the given name is the town in South Africa, the scene of fighting during the Boer War, which brought it to public notice at the end of the 19th century. The town was named after a certain Lord Kimberley, whose ancestors derived their surname from one of the places in England called Kimberley. The first part of the place name derives from various Old English personal names; the second (from Old English *lēah*) means 'wood' or 'clearing'.
Variants: **Kimberly** (the more common North American spelling), **Kimberli(e)**, **Kimberlee**, **Kimberleigh** all ♀.

King ♂

From the vocabulary word for a male monarch, bestowed, especially in America, with a hint of the notion that the bearer would have kingly qualities; compare ◊**Duke** and ◊**Earl**. In some cases it may be a transferred use of the surname (originally a nickname or an occupational name given to someone who was employed in a royal household). Its frequency has increased recently as a Black name, no doubt partly in honour of the civil rights leader Martin Luther King (1929–68).

Kingsley ♂, ♀

Transferred use of the surname, originally a local name derived from various places (in Cheshire, Hampshire, Staffordshire) named in Old English as *Cyningeslēah* 'king's wood'. It is not clear what was the initial impulse towards its use as a given name; the usual pattern in such cases is for a mother's maiden name to be chosen as a given name, but in this case the choice may have been made in honour of the author Charles Kingsley (1819–75).
Variants: **Kingsly**, **Kingslie**.

Kirk ♂

Transferred use of the surname, originally a northern English and Scottish local name for someone who lived near a church (from Old Norse *kirkja*). Recent use has probably been influenced to some extent by the film actor Kirk Douglas, born in 1916 as Issur Danielovich Demsky.

Kirsten ♀

Danish and Norwegian form of ◊**Christine**, now well established also in the English-speaking world.

Kirstie ♀

Scottish pet form of ◊**Kirstin**, now used as an independent given name throughout the English-speaking world.

Kirstin ♀

Scottish vernacular form of ◊**Christine**, now also used outside Scotland.

Kirsty ♀

Variant spelling of ◊**Kirstie**.

Kit ♂, ♀

Pet form of ◊**Christopher**; also of ◊**Katherine** and its variants.

Kitty ♀

Pet form of ◊**Katherine**.

Kizzie ♀

Pet form of ◊**Kezia**.
Variant: **Kizzy**.

Kris ♀, ♂

Short form of ◊**Kristina**, ◊**Kristene**, ◊**Kristen**, or any other name beginning with this syllable.

Krista ♀

Variant spelling of ◊**Christa**.

Kristeen ♀

Fanciful respelling of ◊**Christine**.
Variants: **Kristene**, **Kristine**.

Kristen ♂

Danish form of ◊**Christian**.

Kristene ♀

Fanciful respelling of ◊**Christine**.

Kristie ♀

Variant of the girl's name ◊**Christie**, under the influence of the Scottish form ◊**Kirstie**.

Kristina ♀

Swedish and Czech form of ◊**Christina**.

Kristine ♀

Variant spelling of ◊**Christine**, under the influence of ◊**Kristina**.

Kristy ♀

Variant spelling of ◊**Kristie**.

Kyla ♀

Recently coined name, created as a feminine form of ◊**Kyle** or else a variant of ◊**Kylie**.

Kyle ♂, ♀

Scottish: from a topographic term denoting a narrow strait or channel, from Gaelic *caol* 'narrow'. In part it is a transferred use of the surname, a local name from the region in Ayrshire named with this word.

Kylie ♀
Of Australian origin, said to represent an Aboriginal term for the boomerang. However, it seems more likely that the name is an invention, influenced by ◊**Kyle** and ◊**Kelly**. It is extremely popular in Australia and, in part due to the Australian actress Kylie Minogue (b. 1968), it has also acquired some currency in Britain and elsewhere.
Variants: **Kylcy**, **Kylee**, **Kyleigh**.

Kylin ♀
Apparently an elaboration of ◊**Kyla** or

◊**Kylie**, perhaps by association with ◊**Keelin**. The fact that it is pronounced much the same as a Chinese word denoting a mythological creature resembling the unicorn is presumably no more than coincidence.

Kyra ♀
Either from medieval Greek *kyra* 'lady' (classical Greek *kyria*) or a variant spelling of *Cyra*, a feminine form of ◊**Cyrus**. In other cases it is a name formed as a feminine equivalent of ◊**Kyran**.

Kyran ♂
Variant spelling of ◊**Kieran**.

LACEY LACHLAN LAETITIA LAILA LALAGE L
AMBERT LAMONT LANA LANCE LANCELO
T LANDON LANE LANI LANIE LANNA LAOI
SE LARA LARAINE LARCH LARISSA LARK LA
RR LASSARINA LATASHA LATISHA LAURA
LAUREL LAURELLE LAUREN LAURENCE LAU

Lacey ♀, ♂

Transferred use of the surname, originally a Norman baronial name from *Lassy*, Calvados. The Lacey family was powerful in Ireland during the early Middle Ages.
Variant: **Lacy**.

Lachlan ♂

Scottish (Gaelic *Lachlann*, earlier *Lochlann*): said to refer originally to a migrant from Norway, the 'land of the lochs'. It is normally used only in families that have some connection with the Highlands of Scotland.

Laetitia ♀

Pronounced 'le-*tish*-a': Latin word meaning joy, occasionally used as a given name in the English-speaking world.

Laila ♀

Variant spelling of ◊**Leila**.

Lalage ♀

Classical name, pronounced '*lal*-a-dgee' or '*lal*-a-ghee'. It was used by Horace in his *Odes* as the name of his beloved of the moment. This was a literary pseudonym derived from Greek *lalagein* 'to chatter' or 'babble'. It has enjoyed a modest popularity among classically educated parents since the 19th century. It is the name of the narrator in E. Arnot Robertson's *Ordinary Families* (1933) and it also occurs in John Fowles's *The French Lieutenant's Woman* (1969).
Pet forms: **Lally**, **Lallie**.

Lambert ♂

Transferred use of the surname, which is from an Old French given name of Germanic origin, from *land* 'land', 'territory'

+ *beorht* 'famous'. This was introduced to Britain by the Normans, but its frequency in Britain in later centuries owed something to immigrants from the Low Countries, and it continued in occasional use into the 18th century at least. St Lambert of Maastricht was a 7th-century saint who aided St Willibrord in his evangelical work.

Lamont ♂

Mainly U.S.: transferred use of the Irish and Scottish surname, derived from the medieval given name *Lagman*, from Old Norse *Logmaðr*, from *log* 'law' + *maðr* 'man'. The final *t* of the surname is not etymological, but in the medieval period *d* and *t* were added or dropped capriciously at the ends of words after *n* (for the reverse process, compare ◊**Rosalyn**).

Lana ♀

Especially North American: of uncertain origin. If not simply an invention, it may have been devised as a feminine equivalent of ◊**Alan** (of which it is an anagram), or a shortened form of ◊**Alana**. It seems to have been first used by the film actress Lana Turner (b. 1920), whose original name was *Julia*.

Lance ♂

Old French form of the Germanic personal name *Lanzo*, a short form of various compound names with the first element *land* 'land', 'territory' (compare ◊**Lambert**), but associated from an early date with Old French *lance*, 'lance' (the weapon, from Latin *lancea*). The modern use as a given name most probably arose as a transferred use of the surname derived from the medieval given name, although it is also commonly taken as a short form of ◊**Lancelot**.

Lancelot ♂

The name borne by one of King Arthur's best and most valued knights, who eventually betrayed his trust by becoming the lover of Queen Guinevere. The name is of uncertain origin. It is probably, like other Arthurian names, of Celtic derivation, but has been heavily distorted by mediation through French sources.

Landon ♂

Mainly U.S.: transferred use of the surname, in origin a local name from any of various places in England called *Langdon*, from Old English *lang* 'long' + *dūn* 'hill'.

Lane ♂, occasionally ♀

Mainly U.S.: apparently a transferred use of the surname, in origin a local name for someone who lived in or by a lane (Old English *lane*, originally denoting a narrow pathway between hedges or banks).

Lani ♀

U.S., pronounced 'lah-nee': modern coinage from the Polynesian word meaning 'sky', 'heaven', which is commonly used in Hawaii in compound names such as **Leilani** 'flower of heaven'.

Lanie ♀

Recent coinage, apparently originally a pet form of ◊**Elaine**, pronounced 'lay-nee', this is now fairly common in the United States as an independent first name.

Lanna ♀

Shortened form of ◊**Alanna**.

Laoise ♀

Irish Gaelic name, pronounced 'lee-sha', of uncertain origin. It may be identical with the old Gaelic name *Luigsech* 'radiance', a derivative of *Lug*, name of the goddess of light.

Lara ♀

Russian short form of ◊**Larissa**, introduced in the early 20th century to the English-speaking world. Here it became popular in particular as the name of one of the principal characters in Boris Pasternak's novel *Dr Zhivago* (1957), which was made into a popular Hollywood film in 1965. The name is associated with a musical theme, 'Lara's theme', from the film score by Maurice Jarre.

Laraine ♀

Mainly U.S., especially as a Black name: of uncertain origin, perhaps a variant spelling of ◊**Lorraine** or derived from the French phrase *la reine* 'the queen'. Compare ◊**Raine**.
Variants: **Lareine**, **Lareina**.

Larch ♀

Mainly U.S.: from the name of the tree (adopted in the 16th century from German *larche*, ultimately from Latin *larix*).

Larissa ♀

Of uncertain origin. It is the name of a Greek martyr venerated in the Eastern Church, and may perhaps be derived from the ancient Thessalian town of Larissa.

Lark ♀

Mainly North American and Australian: from the name of the bird (Old English *lāwerce*). This is one of a small set of girl's names derived from vocabulary words denoting birds, which achieved some currency in the mid-20th century. The lark is traditionally associated with early rising and cheerfulness, and is noted for its sweet song.

Larry ♂

Pet form of ◊**Laurence** or ◊**Lawrence**.

Lassarina ♂

Irish: Anglicized form of the Gaelic name *Lasairíona*, derived from *lasair* 'flame' + *fíon* 'wine'.

Latasha ♀

Mainly U.S., especially as a Black name: a recent coinage, blending ◊**Latisha** and ◊**Natasha**.

Latisha ♀

Mainly U.S., especially as a Black name: a recent coinage, probably a respelling of ◊**Laetitia**.

Laura ♀

Feminine form of the Late Latin male name *Laurus* 'Laurel'. St Laura was a 9th-century Spanish nun who met her death in a cauldron of molten lead. Laura is also the name of the woman addressed in the love poetry of the Italian poet Petrarch (Francesco Petrarca, 1304–74), and it owes much of its subsequent popularity to this. There have been various speculations about her identity, but it has not been established with any certainty. He first met her in 1327 while living in Avignon, and she died of the plague in 1348. The current popularity of the given name in the English-speaking world dates from the 19th century, when it was probably imported from Italy.

Laurel ♀

19th-century adoption of the vocabulary word for the tree (Middle English *lorel*, a dissimilated form of Old French *lorer*), probably influenced by ◊**Laura**. It may have been taken as a pet form of the latter.

Laurelle ♀

Elaborated form of ◊**Laurel**.

Lauren ♀

Apparently modelled on ◊**Laurence**, this was first used, or at any rate first brought to public attention, by the film actress Lauren Bacall (born Betty Jean Perske in 1924), famous for her partnership with Humphrey Bogart. They appeared together in several films, especially *To Have and Have Not* (1943) and *The Big Sleep* (1946). See also ◊**Loren**.

Laurence ♂

From a French form of Latin *Laurentius* 'man from Laurentum'. *Laurentum* was a town in Latium, which may have got its name from Latin *laurus* 'laurel', although it is more probably of pre-Roman origin. The given name was popular in the Middle Ages, under the influence of a 3rd-century saint who was one of the seven deacons of Rome. He was martyred in 258. The legend is that, having been required to hand over the

Church's treasures to the civil authorities, he assembled the poor and sick and presented them. For this act of Christian defiance, he was roasted to death on a gridiron. In England the name is also associated with St Laurence of Canterbury (d. 619). A more recent influence has been the actor Sir Laurence Olivier (1907–89). See also ◊**Lawrence**.
Pet form: **Larry**.

Lauretta ♀

Italian diminutive form of ◊**Laura**, also sometimes used in the English-speaking world.

Laurie ♀, ♂

Pet form of ◊**Laura**, ◊**Laurel**, and ◊**Laurence**.

Lavender ♀

From the vocabulary word denoting the herb with sweet-smelling flowers (Old French *lavendre*, from Late Latin *lavendula*).

Lavinia ♀

Name, according to Roman mythology, of the wife of Aeneas, and thus the mother of the Roman people. Legend had it that she gave her name to the Latin town of *Lavinium*, but in fact she was almost certainly invented to explain the place name, which is of pre-Roman origin. She was said to be the daughter of King Latinus, who was similarly invented to account for the name of *Latium*.

Lawrence ♂

Anglicized spelling of ◊**Laurence**. This is the usual spelling of the surname, and is now becoming increasingly common as a given name, especially in North America.
Pet form: **Larry**.

Lawson ♂

Transferred use of the surname, in origin a patronymic from *Law*, a Middle English pet form of ◊**Laurence**. In Australia it has been fairly regularly used as a given name in honour of the explorer William Lawson (1774–1850) and the writer Henry Lawson (1867–1922).

Layla ♀
Variant of ◊**Leila**.

Laz ♂
Modern informal pet form of ◊**Larry** (compare *Baz* from *Barry* and *Gaz* from *Gary*).

Lea ♀
Variant spelling of ◊**Leah** or ◊**Lia**, or possibly sometimes a shortened form of ◊**Azalea**. It is sometimes a variant of the girl's name ◊**Lee**, from an alternative form of the surname, pronounced as a single syllable.

Leaf ♂
From the vocabulary word for the part of a plant (Old English *lēaf*). This was one of the names taken from the world of nature in the 1960s under 'hippy' influence, and it has not been enduringly popular. Choice as a given name may have been influenced by the Scandinavian name *Leif*, from Old Norse *Leifr*, meaning 'heir'.

Leah ♀
Biblical name (meaning 'languid' in Hebrew), borne by the elder sister of Rachel (Genesis 29:23). Jacob served her father Laban for seven years in return for the hand of Rachel, but was deceived into marrying Leah first. He was then given Rachel as well, but had to labour seven more years afterwards. The name is mainly Jewish, although it also enjoyed some popularity among the Puritans in the 16th century.

Leander ♂
Latin form of the Greek name *Leandros*, derived from *leōn* 'lion' + *anēr* 'man' (genitive *andros*). In Greek legend, Leander swam across the Hellespont every night to visit his beloved Hero and back again every morning; he was eventually drowned during a storm. In Christian times, the name was borne by a 6th-century saint, the brother of Sts Fulgentius, Isidore, and Florentina. He was a leading ecclesiastical figure of his day, a friend of Gregory the Great, and became archbishop of Seville. In modern times, the name has occasionally been used as an elaboration of the boy's name ◊**Lee**.

Leanne ♀
Modern combination of ◊**Lee** and ◊**Anne**, or else a respelling of ◊**Liane**.
Variant: **Leanna**.

Leary ♂
Irish: Anglicized form of the Gaelic name **Laoghaire**, which is said to mean 'calf herd'. This was borne by several early Irish saints, princes, and kings, including the High King of Ireland at the time of St Patrick (5th century). It is found as a surname, also in the form *O'Leary*, and modern use as a given name may be due to transferred use of the surname.

Leda ♀
Name borne in classical mythology by a queen of Sparta, who was ravished by Zeus in the shape of a swan. She gave birth to two eggs which, when hatched, revealed the two sets of twins: Castor and Pollux, and Helen and Hermione.

Lee ♂, ♀
Transferred use of the surname, in origin a local name from any of numerous places so called from Old English *lēah* 'wood', 'clearing'. It is especially popular now in the United States, where it is sometimes chosen in honour of the great Confederate general Robert E. Lee (1807–70). It is also popular in Canada.

Leesa ♀
Respelled version of ◊**Lisa**, influenced by ◊**Lee**.

Leigh ♂, ♀
Variant of ◊**Lee**, from an alternative spelling of the surname. Use as a girl's name may have been influenced by the British actress Vivien Leigh (1913–67), born Vivien Hartly.

Leighton ♂
Transferred use of the surname, in origin a local name from any of several places named with Old English *lēac* 'leek' +

tūn 'enclosure', 'settlement', for example Leighton Buzzard in Bedfordshire.

Leila ♀

Of Arabic origin, now fairly common in the English-speaking world, having been used as a name for an oriental beauty by both Byron, in *The Giaour* (1813) and *Don Juan* (1819–24), and by Lord Lytton for the heroine of his novel *Leila* (1838). In Arabic it means 'night', apparently alluding to a dark complexion.
Variants: **Laila**, **Layla**, **Lila**.

Leland ♂

Mainly U.S.: transferred use of the surname, in origin a local name for someone who lived by a patch of fallow land, from Middle English *lay*, *ley* 'fallow' + *land* 'land'. The surname is well established in the United States. It was borne by the humorous writer Charles Leland (1824–1903), author of *The Breitmann Ballads*, and it is also the name of a city in Mississippi.

Len ♂

Short form of ◊**Leonard**, also of ◊**Lionel**.
Pet form: **Lenny**.

Lena ♀

Abstracted from various names ending in these syllables, such as *Helena* and *Magdalena*. In America it is famous as the name of the singer Lena Horne (1917–91).

Lenda ♀

20th-century coinage, an arbitrary alteration of ◊**Linda**.

Lennan ♂

Anglicized form of the Irish Gaelic name **Leannán** 'darling', 'sweetheart', a word also used to denote a fairy lover. This was a common given name in medieval times, especially in Co. Clare, though its revival no doubt has also something to do with the transparent meaning of the vocabulary word.

Lennard ♂

Variant spelling of ◊**Leonard**, perhaps in part a transferred use of the surname, which was derived from the given name in the Middle Ages.

Lennox ♂

Transferred use of the Scottish surname, which is also the name of an earldom. It originated as a local name from a district north of Glasgow formerly known as *The Levenach*. This was the first name of the British composer Sir Lennox Berkeley (1903–89).

Lenny ♂

Pet form of ◊**Len**.
Variant: **Lennie**.

Lenora ♀

Originally a contracted form of ◊**Leonora**, although sometimes chosen as an expanded version of ◊**Lena**.

Leo ♂

From a Late Latin personal name, meaning 'lion', which was borne by a large number of early Christian saints, most notably Pope Leo the Great (?390–461).
Variant: **Leon** (taken from the oblique case).

Leona ♀

Latinate feminine form of ◊**Leo**.

Leonard ♂

From an Old French personal name of Germanic origin, derived from *leon* 'lion' + *hard* 'hardy', 'brave', 'strong'. This was the name of a 5th-century Frankish saint, the patron of peasants and horses. Although it was introduced into Britain by the Normans, *Leonard* was an uncommon name during the Middle Ages. It was revived in some areas towards the end of the 1400s, and in the 19th century became very popular.
Variant: **Lennard**.
Short form: **Len**.
Pet forms: **Lenny**, **Lennie**.

Léonie ♀

French: from Latin *Leonia*, feminine form of *Leonius*, derived from *leo* 'lion'. It is now also widely used (normally without the accent) in the English-speaking world.

Leonora ♀
Shortened form of ◊**Eleonora**.

Leopold ♂
From an Old French name of Germanic (Frankish) origin, from *liut* 'people' + *bold* 'bold', 'brave'. The first element was altered by association with Latin *leo* 'lion'. A name of this origin may have been introduced into Britain by the Normans, but if so it did not survive long. It was reintroduced from the Continent towards the end of the 19th century in honour of Leopold, King of the Belgians (1790–1865), the uncle of Queen Victoria, to whom he was an influential adviser in her youth: she named one of her sons after him.

Leroy ♂
Now considered a typically Black American given name, but formerly also extensively borne by White Americans. It is from a French nickname meaning 'the king', but it is not entirely clear why this particular form should have become such a popular given name in English.

Les ♂
Short form of ◊**Leslie**.

Lesley ♀, ♂
Variant of ◊**Leslie**, now the usual form as a girl's name in Britain. Its first recorded use as such is in a poem by Robert Burns.

Leslie ♂, ♀
Transferred use of the Scottish surname derived from the lands of *Lesslyn* in Aberdeenshire (a place name perhaps named in Gaelic as *leas cuilinn* 'garden of hollies'). Surnames and clan names have been used as given names more readily and from an earlier date in Scotland than elsewhere, and this is the name of an ancient family, who in the 14th and 15th centuries were close associates of the Scottish royal house of Stewart and who have held the earldom of Rothes since 1457. The British film actor Leslie Howard (1890–1943), who was of Hungarian origin, had a considerable influence on the popularity of the name, especially in the United States, where he appeared in *Gone with the Wind* (1939). A famous female bearer is the French film actress Leslie Caron (b. 1930).
Short form: **Les** (♂).

Lester ♂
Transferred use of the surname, in origin a local name from the city of *Leicester*. The place name is recorded in the 10th century as *Ligora cæster*, representing a British name of obscure origin + the Old English term *cæster* 'Roman fort'.

Leticia ♀
Simplified spelling of ◊**Laetitia**.

Lettice ♀
From the medieval vernacular form of the Latin name ◊**Laetitia**. It was popular among the Victorians, but is now out of fashion.
Pet forms: **Letty**, **Lettie**.

Levi ♂
Biblical name (meaning 'associated' in Hebrew), given by Jacob's wife Leah to her third son as an expression of her hope, 'Now this time will my husband be joined unto me, because I have born him three sons: therefore was his name called Levi' (Genesis 29:34). The Levites (a Jewish priestly caste) are descended from Levi. In the New Testament, Levi is a byname of the apostle and evangelist Matthew. In modern times the name is mainly Jewish.

Levon ♂
U.S.: of unknown origin; possibly an unexplained variant of ◊**Levi**.

Lewie ♂
Respelling of ◊**Louis**, or a pet form of ◊**Lewis**.

Lewis ♂
Common English form, since the Middle Ages, of the French name ◊**Louis**. In modern use it is also in part a transferred use of the surname derived from this given name.
Pet form: **Lewie**.

Lex ♂
Shortened form of ◊**Alex**.

Lexine ♀
Elaboration of ◊**Lexy** with the addition of the feminine diminutive suffix *-ine*.

Lexy ♀
Pet form of ◊**Alexandra**, particularly common in Scotland.

Lia ♀
Italian: of uncertain derivation, probably a short form of *Rosalia* (see ◊**Rosalie**).

Liadan ♀
Anglicized form of the Irish Gaelic name **Líadan**, probably a derivative of *liath* 'grey'. In Irish legend, Líadan forsook her lover Cuirithir in order to enter a nunnery; both of them died of grief.

Liam ♂
Irish: short form of *Uilliam*, Gaelic form of ◊**William**. It is now generally used as an independent given name.

Liane ♀
Of uncertain origin, probably a short form of French *Éliane*, from Latin *Aeliāna*, the name of an early martyr at Amasea in Pontus. *Aeliānus* was an old Roman family name, perhaps a hypercorrected form of *Ēliānus* or *Hēliānus*, from Greek *hēlios*.
Variant: **Lianne**.

Libby ♀
Pet form of ◊**Elizabeth**, based originally on a child's mispronunciation.

Liberty ♀
From the vocabulary word meaning 'freedom', chosen as a given name by parents for whom this is an important value. The word came into English via Old French from Latin *lībertās*, a derivative of *līber* 'free'.

Lila ♀
Variant spelling of ◊**Leila**.

Lilac ♀
From the vocabulary word denoting the shrub with large sprays of heavily scented purple or white flowers. The word is from French, which derived it via Spanish from Arabic *līlak*, from Persian *nīlak* 'bluish', a derivative of *nīl* 'blue'.

Lilian ♀
Of uncertain origin, first recorded in the late 16th century, and probably derived from a nursery form of ◊**Elizabeth**. It is now sometimes regarded as a derivative of the flower name ◊**Lily**, but this was not used as a given name in England until the 19th century.
Variant: **Lillian**.

Lilith ♀
The name borne, according to medieval tradition, by a wife of Adam prior to Eve. She is said to have been turned into an ugly demon for refusing to obey him. *Lilith* occurs in the Bible as a vocabulary word meaning 'night monster' or 'screech owl' (Isaiah 34:14), and in Jewish folklore is the name of an ugly demon. In spite of its unpleasant connotations, it has occasionally been used as a given name in the 20th century, perhaps in part being taken as an elaborated form of ◊**Lily**.

Lily ♀
From the vocabulary word for the flower (via Old French, from Latin *lilium*), regarded in Christian imagery as a symbol of purity.
Variant: **Lillie** (borne, for example, by the actress Lillie Langtry (1853–1929), friend of King Edward VII).

Lincoln ♂
Transferred use of the surname, in origin a local name from the name of the city of Lincoln. This is found in the 7th century as *Lindum colonia*, probably from an Old Welsh word meaning 'lake' (compare modern Welsh *llyn*) + the Latin defining term *colonia* 'colony', 'settlement'. As a given name it has sometimes been bestowed in honour of Abraham Lincoln (1809–65), 16th president of the United States, who led the Union to victory in the Civil War and enforced the emancipation of slaves.

Linda ♀
Of relatively recent origin and uncertain etymology. It is first recorded in the 19th century. It may be a shortened form of

◊**Belinda**, an adoption of Spanish *linda* 'pretty', or a Latinate derivative of any various other Germanic female names ending in -*lind* meaning 'weak', 'tender', 'soft'. It has become very popular in the 20th century.
Pet forms: **Lindie**, **Lindy**.

Lindall ♀
Transferred use of the surname, in origin a local name from *Lindal* in Lancashire. The place name is derived from Old English *līn* 'flax' + *dæl* 'valley'. Use as a given name seems to have originated as an elaborated form of ◊**Linda**.
Variants: **Lindal**, **Lindell**.

Linden ♀
Ostensibly from the vocabulary word denoting the lime tree (originally the adjectival form, derived from Old English *linde*). However, the given name is of recent, probably 20th-century, origin and it is more likely that this is simply an elaboration of ◊**Linda**, along the lines of ◊**Lauren** from ◊**Laura**.

Lindie ♀
Pet form of ◊**Linda**.

Lindon ♂
Variant spelling of ◊**Lyndon**.

Lindsay ♀, ♂
Transferred use of the Scottish surname, originally borne by Sir Walter de Lindesay, one of the retainers of King David I of Scotland (1084–1153), who took the name to Scotland from Lindsey in Lincolnshire. This place was named in Old English as the 'wetland (Old English *ey*) belonging to Lincoln'. It was at first used as a boy's name, and this is still the case in Scotland, but elsewhere it is now nearly always used for girls.
Variants: **Lindsey**, **Lins(e)y**, **Lynsey**, **Linzi**.

Lindy ♀
Pet form of ◊**Linda**.

Linford ♂
Transferred use of the surname, a local name from any of various places, most of which are named with Old English *līn*

'flax' or *lind* 'lime tree' + *ford* 'ford'. In the case of Great and Little Linford in Berkshire, the first element is Old English *hlyn* 'maple'. As a given name it is associated in particular with the British athlete Linford Christie.

Linnet ♀
Simplified spelling of ◊**Linnette**, strongly influenced in popularity by the vocabulary word for the small bird (Old French *linotte*, a derivative of *lin* 'flax', on the seeds of which it feeds).

Linnette ♀
Variant spelling of ◊**Lynette**.

Linsey ♀
Simplified spelling of *Lindsey* (see ◊**Lindsay**).
Variant: **Linsy**.

Linton ♂
Transferred use of the surname, originally a local name from any of numerous places in England so called. Most get the name from Old English *līn* 'flax', 'cotton' or *lind* 'lime tree' + *tūn* 'enclosure', 'settlement'.

Linus ♂
Latin form of the Greek name *Linos*, which is of uncertain origin. In Greek mythology, Linus is a famous musician who taught music to Hercules; it is also the name of an infant son of Apollo who was exposed to die on a mountainside in Argos. The name may have been invented to explain the obscure refrain, '*ailinon*', of the so-called 'Linus song', traditionally sung at harvest time in Argos. In the Christian era, *Linus* was the name of the second pope, St Peter's successor, who was martyred in *c.*76. He has been tentatively identified with the Linus to whom Paul sends greetings in 2 Timothy 4:21. Nowadays, the given name is associated with a character in the popular *Peanuts* strip cartoon series, a little boy inseparable from his security blanket.

Linzi ♀
Fanciful respelling of ◊**Lindsay**.

Liona ♀
Altered form of ◊**Leona**, influenced by
◊**Lionel**.

Lionel ♂
From a medieval diminutive of the Old
French name *Léon* (see ◊**Leo**) or the
Middle English nickname *Lion*.

Lis ♀
Variant spelling of ◊**Liz**. See also ◊**Lys**.

Lisa ♀
Variant of ◊**Liza**, influenced by French
Lise and German *Liese*.

Lisbet ♀
Pet form of ◊**Elizabeth**.

Lisette ♀
French diminutive form of *Lise*, which
is itself a shortened form of ◊**Elisabeth**.

Lisha ♀
Modern coinage, a shortened and respelled form of names such as ◊**Delicia**
and ◊**Felicia**, on the model of *Trisha*
from ◊**Patricia**.

Lissa ♀
Short form of ◊**Melissa**. See also ◊**Lyssa**.

Livia ♀
In modern use often taken as a short
form of ◊**Olivia**, but originally a distinct
name, a feminine form of the Roman
family name *Livius*. This is of uncertain
derivation, perhaps connected with
lividus 'bluish'.

Liz ♀
The most common of all the various
short forms of ◊**Elizabeth**.

Liza ♀
Shortened form of ◊**Eliza**.
Variant: **Lisa**.

Lizzie ♀
Pet form of ◊**Liz**, with the diminutive
suffix *-ie*.
Variant: **Lizzy**.

Lleu ♂
Welsh: traditional name, the pronunciation of which is difficult for English
speakers; an approximation is 'hlae'. It

means 'bright, shining', and is akin to
the name of the Celtic god known in Old
Irish as *Lugh*, Gaulish *Lugus*. This name
was borne in the *Mabinogi* by Lleu Llaw
Gyffes 'Lleu Skilful Hand', the son of
Aranrhod. It has been revived in modern
times.

Llew ♂
Welsh: traditional name meaning 'lion'.
It is also used as a short form of
◊**Llewelyn**.

Llewelyn ♂
Very popular traditional Welsh name: an
altered form (influenced by the vocabulary word *llew* 'lion') of *Llywelyn*, an
ancient name of uncertain derivation. It
probably goes back to the Old Celtic
name *Lugobelinos*, the first element of
which is *Lugu-* (the name of a god; see
◊**Lleu**); the second is a name-forming
element found also in names such as
Cunobelinus (*Cymbeline*). In historical
times the name was borne in particular
by Llewelyn ap Iorwerth (1173–1240)
and his grandson Llewelyn ap Gruffydd
(d. 1282), Welsh princes who for a time
united their countrymen in North Wales
and led opposition to the power of the
Norman barons in South Wales and the
Marches.

Lloyd ♂
Transferred use of the Welsh surname,
originally a nickname meaning 'grey
(-haired)' (Welsh *llwyd*). See also ◊**Floyd**.

Logan ♂
Transferred use of the Scottish surname,
in origin a local name from a place so
called in Ayrshire.

Lois ♀
New Testament: name, of unknown
origin, borne by the grandmother of the
Timothy to whom St Paul wrote two
epistles (see 2 Timothy 1:5). Both
Timothy and his mother Eunice bore
common Greek names, but *Lois* remains unexplained.

Lola ♀
Spanish pet form (originally a nursery
form) of ◊**Dolores**, now established as an

independent given name in the English-speaking world. It owes some of its popularity to the fame of Lola Montez (1818–1861), stage name adopted by Marie Gilbert, an Irish dancer and courtesan who had affairs with Liszt, Dumas, and others. From 1846–8 she so captivated the elderly Ludwig I of Bavaria that she became the virtual ruler of the country, precipitating riots, a constitutional crisis, and the abdication of the king. She arrived in New York in 1851, and spent the last years of her life working to help prostitutes.

Lolicia ♀
Mainly U.S.: elaborated form of ◊**Lola**, with the addition of a suffix derived from names such as ◊**Delicia**.

Lolita ♀
Spanish diminutive form of ◊**Lola**. This was once quite common as a given name in its own right in America, with its large Hispanic population, but has since been overshadowed by its association with Vladimir Nabokov's novel *Lolita* (1955). The Lolita of the title is the pubescent object of the narrator's desires, and the name is now used as a generic term for any under-age sex kitten.

Lonnie ♂
Of uncertain origin, possibly an Anglicized or pet form of the Spanish name *Alonso* or a variant of ◊**Lenny**. It is chiefly associated in Britain with the skiffle singer Lonnie Donegan, famous in the 1950s and 1960s.

Lora ♀
German form of ◊**Laura**, occasionally also used in the English-speaking world.

Lorcan ♂
Irish: Anglicized form of the Gaelic name *Lorcán*, from a diminutive of Gaelic *lorc* 'fierce'. This was borne by St Lorcán Ó Tuathail (1128–80), archbishop of Dublin, known in English as Laurence O'Toole.

Loreen ♀
Elaboration of ◊**Lora**, with the addition of the suffix *-een* (originally an Irish diminutive, Gaelic *-ín*).
Variant: **Lorene**.

Lorelle ♀
Elaboration of ◊**Lora**, with the addition of the suffix *-elle* (originally a French feminine diminutive).

Loren ♀, occasionally ♂
Variant spelling of ◊**Lauren**.

Lorena ♀
Latinate elaboration of the girl's name ◊**Loren**.

Lorene ♀
Variant spelling of ◊**Loreen**.

Loreto ♀
Religious name borne by Roman Catholics, referring to the town in central Italy to which in the 13th century the Holy House of the Virgin is supposed to have been miraculously transported from Nazareth by angels.

Loretta ♀
Variant of ◊**Lauretta**, normally borne by Roman Catholics, among whom it is associated with ◊**Loreto**.

Lori ♀
Pet form of ◊**Lorraine** or variant of ◊**Laurie**.

Lorin ♂
Mainly U.S.: variant spelling of the boy's name ◊**Loren**.
Variant: **Lorrin**.

Lorinda ♀
Elaboration of ◊**Lora**, with the addition of the productive feminine suffix *-inda* (compare ◊**Belinda**, ◊**Clarinda**, and ◊**Lucinda**).

Lorna ♀
Invented by R. D. Blackmore for the heroine of his novel *Lorna Doone* (1869), child captive of the outlawed Doones on Exmoor, who is eventually discovered to be in reality Lady Lorna Dugal, daughter of the Earl of Dugal. Blackmore seems to have derived the name from the Scottish place name *Lorn(e)* (Gaelic *Latharna*), a

territory in Argyll. The given name is now popular in Scotland.

Lorne ♂
Mainly Canadian: of uncertain derivation, but most probably taken from the name of territory of *Lorne* in Argyll (and thus representing a masculine form of ◊**Lorna**). One of the earliest bearers was the Canadian actor Lorne Greene (b. 1915), and the given name is now also fairly common in Scotland.

Lorraine ♀
Transferred use of the surname, in origin denoting a migrant from the province of *Lorraine* in eastern France. This derives its name from Latin *Lotharingia* 'territory of the people of Lothar'. The latter is a Germanic personal name derived from *hlud* 'fame' + *heri, hari* 'army'. *Lorraine* began to be used as a girl's name in Scotland in the 19th century, and has recently become enormously popular, for reasons which are not clear.
Variants: **Loraine**, **Lorane**.

Lorri ♀
Variant spelling of ◊**Lori**.

Lorrin ♂
Mainly U.S.: variant spelling of the boy's name ◊**Loren**.

Lottie ♀
Pet form of ◊**Charlotte**. It was a common girl's name in the 19th century, but is much less used at the present time.
Variant: **Lotty**.

Lou ♂, ♀
Short form of ◊**Louis** or, less commonly, ◊**Louise**.

Louella ♀
Modern coinage from the first syllable of ◊**Louise** + the productive suffix *-ella* (an Italian or Latinate feminine diminutive; compare ◊**Ella**). It is particularly associated with the Hollywood gossip columnist Louella Parsons (1880–1972).
Variant: **Luella**.

Louie ♂
Variant spelling of ◊**Lewie**.

Louis ♂
An extremely common French name, of Germanic (Frankish) origin, from *hlud* 'fame' + *wīg* 'warrior'. It was very common in French royal and noble families. Louis I (778–840) was the son of Charlemagne, who ruled both as King of France and Holy Roman Emperor. Altogether, the name was borne by sixteen kings of France up to the French Revolution, in which Louis XVI perished. Louis XIV, 'the Sun King' (1638–1715), reigned for seventy-two years (1643–1715), presiding in the middle part of his reign over a period of unparalleled French power and prosperity. In modern times *Louis* is also found in the English-speaking world (usually pronounced '*loo-ee*'). In Britain the Anglicized form ◊**Lewis** is rather more common, whereas in America the reverse is true.
Short form: **Lou**.

Louisa ♀
Latinate feminine form of ◊**Louis**, commonly used as an English given name since the 18th century.

Louise ♀
French feminine form of ◊**Louis**, introduced to England in the 17th century.
Short form: **Lou**.

Lourdes ♀
Religious name borne by Roman Catholics, referring to the place in southern France where a shrine was established after a young peasant girl, Bernadette Soubirous, had visions of the Virgin Mary and uncovered a healing spring in 1858. In recent times, Lourdes has become a major centre for pilgrimage, especially by people suffering from various illnesses or physical handicaps.

Lovell ♂
Transferred use of the surname, which originated in the Middle Ages from the Old (Norman) French nickname *Louvel* 'wolf-cub', a diminutive of *lou* 'wolf'.

Lowell ♂
Mainly U.S.: transferred use of the surname of a well-known New England

family, whose members included the poet Robert Lowell (1917–77). The surname is a variant of ◊**Lovell**.

Loyal ♂

Mainly U.S.: name derived from the modern English adjective (from Old French *leial*, from Latin *legalis* 'legal').

Luana ♀

First used in King Vidor's 1932 film *The Bird of Paradise* as the name of a Polynesian maiden, and taken up since. It is apparently an arbitrary combination of the syllables *Lu-* and *-ana*.
Variants: **Luanna**, **Luanne**.

Lucas ♂

In part a learned form of ◊**Luke**, in part a transferred use of the surname derived from it in the Middle Ages. The Latin form *Lucas* was often used in the Middle Ages in written documents in place of the spoken vernacular form *Luke*, hence the common surname. It is also the spelling preferred in the Authorized Version of the New Testament, which has had some influence on its selection as a given name.

Lucetta ♀

Fanciful elaboration of ◊**Lucia** or ◊**Lucy**, formed with the productive suffix *-etta*, originally an Italian feminine diminutive suffix. The name is found in Shakespeare, where it is borne by Julia's waiting woman in *Two Gentlemen of Verona*, but it is not much used in Italy and was unusual in England before the 19th century.

Lucia ♀

Feminine form of the old Roman given name *Lucius*, which is probably a derivative of Latin *lux* 'light'. The girl's name is common in Italy and elsewhere, and is found as a learned, Latinate doublet of *Lucy* in England. St Lucia of Syracuse, who was martyred in 304, was a very popular saint in the Middle Ages; she is often represented in medieval art as blinded and with her eyes on a platter, but the tradition that she had her eyes put out is probably based on nothing

more than the association between light and eyes.

Lucilla ♀

Latin pet form of ◊**Lucia**, with the diminutive feminine suffix *-illa*. This name was borne by various minor early saints, including one martyred at Rome in *c*.258.

Lucille ♀

French form of ◊**Lucilla**, used also in the English-speaking world, especially in the southern United States. A well-known bearer of the name was the American comedy actress Lucille Ball (1910–89).

Lucinda ♀

Derivative of ◊**Lucia**, with the addition of the productive suffix *-inda*. The formation is first found in Cervantes's *Don Quixote* (1605), but was not much in use in the 17th century except as a literary name. It enjoyed considerable popularity in England in the 18th century, and has been in use ever since.

Lucretia ♀

Feminine form of the Roman family name *Lucretius*, which is of unknown derivation. In Roman legend, this is the name of a Roman maiden of the 5th century BC who killed herself after being raped by the King of Rome; the resulting scandal led to the end of the monarchy. It was also borne by a Spanish martyr who perished under Diocletian, but is now chiefly remembered as the name of Lucrezia Borgia (1480–1519), regarded in legend as a demon poisoner who had incestuous relations with her father, Pope Alexander VI, and her brother Cesare. Although these allegations cannot now be disproved, history records her, after her marriage in 1501 to Alfonso d'Este, Duke of Ferrara, as being in reality a beautiful, intelligent, and fair-minded woman, and a generous patron of the arts.

Lucy ♀

From Old French *Lucie*, the vernacular form of ◊**Lucia**. It is sometimes assumed that *Lucy* is a pet form of ◊**Lucinda**, but there is no etymological justification for this assumption. It was in fairly widespread use in the Middle Ages, and increased greatly in popularity in the 18th century.

Ludmila ♀

Russian and Czech: from a Slavonic personal name derived from *lud* 'people', 'tribe' (a borrowing from Germanic *liut*) + *mil* 'grace', 'favour'. St Ludmila (d. 921) was a duchess of Bohemia and grandmother of St Wenceslas; she was murdered on the orders of her mother-in-law and came to be regarded as a martyr.
Variant: **Ludmilla** (in the English-speaking world).

Ludovic ♂

From Latin *Ludovicus*, the form used in medieval documents to represent the Germanic name *Hludwig* (see ◊**Louis**). In the west of Scotland it came to be used as an Anglicized form of the Gaelic name *Maol Dòmhnaich*, pronounced 'meel *dauv*-nach' and meaning 'devotee of the Lord', probably because both contain the same succession of consonants: *l-d-v-c(h)*.
Short form: **Ludo**.

Luella ♀

Variant spelling of ◊**Louella**.

Luke ♂

Middle English vernacular form of ◊**Lucas**, Latin form of the post-classical Greek name *Loukas* 'man from Lucania'. This owes its perennial popularity throughout Christian Europe to the fact that, from the 2nd century onwards, the third gospel in the New Testament has been ascribed to the Lucas or Luke mentioned at various places in Acts and in the Epistles. Little is known about him beyond the facts that he was a doctor, a Gentile, and a friend and convert of St Paul.

Lulu ♀

Pet form, originally a reduplicated nursery form, of *Luise*, the German form of ◊**Louise**. It is now also used in the English-speaking world, both as a pet form of *Louise* and as an independent given name.

Luther ♂

Mainly North American: from the German surname, which is from a Germanic personal name derived from *liut* 'people' + *heri*, *hari* 'army'. It is commonly bestowed among evangelical Protestants, in honour of the ecclesiastical reformer and theologian Martin Luther (1483–1546). In recent times it has also been bestowed in honour of the assassinated civil rights leader Martin Luther King (1929–68).

Lyall ♂

Transferred use of the Scottish surname, which is probably derived from the Old Norse personal name *Liulfr*, of which the first element is obscure. The second is clearly Old Norse *úlfr* 'wolf'. See also ◊**Lyle**.

Lydia ♀

Of Greek origin, meaning 'woman from Lydia', an area of Asia Minor. The name is borne in the Bible by a woman of Thyatira who was converted by St Paul and who entertained him in her house (Acts 16:14–15, 40). It has enjoyed steady popularity in the English-speaking world since the 16th century.

Lyle ♂

Transferred use of the mainly Scottish surname, in origin a local name for someone who came 'from the island' (Anglo-Norman *de l'isle*). (The island in question would in many cases have been an area of higher, dry ground in a marsh or fen, rather than in a sea or river.) There may have been some confusion with ◊**Lyall**.

Lyn ♀

Variant spelling of ◊**Lynn**.

Lynda ♀

Variant spelling of ◊**Linda**.

Lyndon ♂

Transferred use of the surname, in origin a local name from a place in the former

county of Rutland (now part of Leicestershire), so called from Old English *lind* 'lime tree' + *dūn* 'hill'. In the United States, use as a given name has been influenced by the American president Lyndon Baines Johnson (1908–73).
Variant: **Lindon**.

Lynette ♀
In modern use a derivative of ◊**Lynn**, formed with the French feminine diminutive suffix *-ette*. However, this is not the origin for the name as used in Tennyson's *Idylls of the King* (1859–85), through which it first came to public attention. There, it represents an altered form of some Celtic original; compare Welsh ◊**Eluned**.
Variants: **Lynnette**, **Lin(n)ette**, **Linnet**.

Lynn ♀
Of uncertain origin: possibly an altered short form of ◊**Linda**, or a derivative of the French name *Line*, which originated as a short form of various girls' names ending in this syllable, for example *Caroline*. The element *-lyn(n)* has been a productive suffix of English girls' names since at least the middle of the 20th century. *Lynn* itself has enjoyed considerable popularity in recent times.

Lynsey ♀
Variant spelling of ◊**Lindsay**.

Lyra ♀
Modern coinage, apparently from Latin *lyra* 'lyre'; choice as a given name evokes images of gentle music and harmony.

Lys ♀
Variant spelling of ◊**Liz**, apparently inspired by medieval French *(fleur de) lys* 'lily'.

Lysette ♀
Variant spelling of ◊**Lisette**.

Lyssa ♀
Short form of ◊**Alyssa**. In form it coincides with the name, in Greek mythology, of the personification of madness or frenzy. See also ◊**Lissa**.

MAB MABEL MABELLE MABLE MACK MACK
ENZI MAY MADDIE MADDISON MADD
Y MADELINE MADELEINE MADELINE MA
DELYN MADGE MADISON MADLYN MAD
OLIN MADONNA MAE MAEVE MAGDALE
N MAGGIE MAGNUS MAIDIE MAIR MAIRE

Mab ♀

Short form of ◊**Mabel**. See also ◊**Maeve**.

Mabel ♀

Originally a nickname from the Old
French vocabulary word *amabel*, *am-
able* 'lovely' (akin to modern English
amiable 'friendly', 'good-humoured').
The initial vowel began to be lost as
early as the 12th century (the same
woman is referred to as both *Mabilia* and
Amabilia in a document of 1185), but a
short vowel in the resulting first syllable
was standard, giving a rhyme with
babble, until the 19th century, when
people began to pronounce the name to
rhyme with *table*.

Mabelle ♀

Elaborated form of ◊**Mabel**, under the
influence of the French phrase *ma belle*
'my beautiful one'.

Mable ♀

Variant spelling of ◊**Mabel**.

Mack ♂

Originally a common nickname for
bearers of any of the Scottish and Irish
patronymic surnames beginning with
Mac or *Mc*, this is now sometimes used
as an independent first name, especially
in the U.S.

Mackenzie ♂, ♀

Mainly North American: transferred use
of the Scottish surname, which is from
Gaelic *Mac Coinnich*, a patronymic
from *Coinneach* 'comely'. The *z* of the
surname represents the medieval letter
yogh, which was pronounced as a 'y'
glide. In North America this is more
commonly used for girls than boys.
Variants: **Makenzie**, **Makensie** (♀).

Macy ♂, ♀

Transferred use of the surname, in origin
a Norman baronial name from any of the
places in northern France called *Massey*
(Latin *Macciācum*, a derivative of the
Gallo-Roman personal name *Maccius*).
The famous New York department
store, Macy's, was founded in 1858 by
R.H. Macy. Use as a first name has been
influenced by the rhyming ◊**Stacey**,
◊**Tracy**, ◊**Lacey**, and ◊**Pacey**. It has
recently achieved prominence as a
result of the fame of the female pop
singer Macy Gray (real name *Natalie
McIntyre*), who adopted as a stage name
the name of a childhood neighbour.
Variant: **Macey**.

Maddie ♀

Variant spelling of ◊**Maddy**.

Maddison ♂, ♀

Variant spelling of ◊**Madison**.

Maddy ♀

Pet form of ◊**Madeleine** and its variants.
In the United States it is also used as a
pet form of the modern girl's name
◊**Madison**.
Variant: **Maddie**.

Madelaine ♀

Variant spelling of ◊**Madeleine**.

Madeleine ♀

The French form of the byname of a
character in the New Testament, Mary
Magdalene 'Mary of Magdala'. Magdala
was a village on Lake Galilee, a few
miles north of Tiberias. The woman
'which had been healed of evil spirits
and infirmities' (Luke 8:2) was given this
name in the Bible to distinguish her
from other bearers of the very common

name ◊**Mary**. It was widely accepted in Christian folk belief that she was the same person as the repentant sinner who washed Christ's feet with her tears in the previous chapter (Luke 7), but there is no support in the text for this identification.
Variants: **Madelaine, Madeline, Mad(e)lyn, Madoline**; ◊**Magdalen**.
Pet forms: **Maddy, Maddie**.

Madeline ♀
Variant of ◊**Madeleine**, common especially in Ireland.

Madelyn ♀
Variant of ◊**Madeleine**, influenced by the productive name suffix *-lyn* (see ◊**Lynn**).

Madge ♀
Pet form of ◊**Margaret**, a palatalized version of *Mag(g)* (see ◊**Maggie**).

Madison ♀, ♂
Mainly U.S.: transferred use of the surname, in origin a metronymic from the medieval woman's given name *Madde*, a pet form of ◊**Madeleine** (see ◊**Maddy**) or ◊**Maud**. Use as a given name seems to have been influenced by the statesman James Madison (1751–1836), who was president during the War of 1812 and took part in drafting the U.S. constitution and Bill of Rights. It is currently enjoying something of a vogue as a girl's name.
Variant: **Maddison**.
Pet forms: **Maddy, Maddie** (♀).

Madlyn ♀
Contracted spelling of ◊**Madelyn**.

Madoline ♀
Variant of *Madeline* (see ◊**Madeleine**).

Madonna ♀
From an Italian title of the Virgin Mary (literally 'my lady'), applied to countless Renaissance paintings of a beautiful young woman (with and without an infant), representing the mother of Christ. Its use as a given name is a fairly recent phenomenon, arising among Americans of Italian descent. In the 1980s, the name became particularly

well known as a result of the fame of the American pop star Madonna Ciccone (b. 1958).

Mae ♀
Variant spelling of ◊**May**, possibly influenced by ◊**Maeve**. It has been most notably borne by the American film actress Mae West (b. 1892), whose prominent bust led to her name being given, by members of the RAF, to a type of inflatable life jacket used in the Second World War. This spelling is now no longer much used.

Maeve ♀
Irish: Anglicized form of Gaelic **Meadhbh** (earlier *Medb*), an ancient name meaning 'intoxicating', 'she who makes drunk'. It is borne by the Queen of Connacht in the Irish epic *Táin Bó Cuailnge*. In this, Meadhbh leads a raid on Ulster in order to seize the Brown Bull of Cooley, but she is repulsed single-handed by the hero Cú Chulainn. Shakespeare's Queen Mab, 'the fairy's midwife' (*Romeo and Juliet* I. iv. 53), owes her name, if nothing else, to the legendary Queen of Connacht.
Variants: **Mave, Meave**.

Magdalen ♀
Older English form of ◊**Madeleine**, usually pronounced '*maud*-lin'. This was the usual form of the given name in the Middle Ages.

Maggie ♀
Pet form of ◊**Margaret**. In the Middle Ages the short form *Mag(g)* was common, as a result of the early loss in pronunciation of the English preconsonantal *r*. This is not now used as a given name, but has given rise to the surname *Maggs*.

Magnus ♂
Originally a Latin byname meaning 'great', this was first extracted from the name of *Charlemagne* (recorded in Latin chronicles as *Carolus Magnus* 'Charles the Great') and used as a given name by the Scandinavians. It was borne by seven medieval kings of Norway, including

Magnus I (1024–47), known as Magnus the Good, and Magnus VI (1238–80), known as Magnus the Law Mender. There are several early Scandinavian saints called Magnus, including an earl of Orkney (d. 1116), to whom Kirkwall cathedral is dedicated. The name was imported to Scotland and Ireland during the Middle Ages.

Maidie ♀
From a pet form of the vocabulary word *maid* 'young woman' (Old English *mæg(den)*), originally used as an affectionate nickname.

Mair ♀
Welsh form of ◊**Mary**, derived from Latin *Maria* via Old Welsh *Meir*. See also ◊**Mari**.

Máire ♀
Irish Gaelic form of ◊**Mary**.

Mairéad ♀
Irish Gaelic form of ◊**Margaret**, pronounced '*my*-raid' (in Munster) or '*ma-raid*' (in Connacht). The name is also used in Scotland, where it is spelled **Mairead** or **Maighread**.

Mairenn ♀
Irish: traditional Gaelic name, said to be derived from *muir* 'sea' + *fhionn* 'fair'. *Variant*: **Muireann**.

Màiri ♀
Scottish Gaelic form of ◊**Mary**.

Maisie ♀
Scottish: pet form derived from *Mairead*, the Gaelic form of ◊**Margaret**, with the Scottish and northern English diminutive suffix *-ie*.

Makenzie ♀
Simplified spelling of the girl's name ◊**Mackenzie**. *Variant*: **Makensie**.

Malachy ♂
Traditional name in Ireland, representing an adaptation of more than one medieval Gaelic name to a biblical name. St Malachy (1095–1148), born Máel Maedhog (see ◊**Madoc**) Ó Morgair,

was a famous bishop of Armagh, who did much to promote greater contact between the Church in Ireland and the papacy in Rome. His biography was written by St Bernard of Clairvaux. Earlier, *Malachy* had been used as a name of an Irish king who defeated the Norse invaders. His Gaelic baptismal name was *Maoileachlainn* 'devotee of St Seachnall or Secundinus', but in medieval sources this has already been altered to coincide with that of the biblical prophet **Malachi**. Malachi was the last of the twelve minor prophets of the Old Testament; he foretold the coming of Christ and his name means, appropriately, 'my messenger' in Hebrew.

Malcolm ♂
Anglicized form of the medieval Gaelic name *Mael Coluim* 'devotee of St Columba'. Columba, whose name means 'dove' in Latin, was a 6th-century monk of Irish origin who played a leading part in the conversion to Christianity of Scotland and northern England; see also ◊**Calum** and ◊**Colm**. He has always been one of the most popular saints in Scotland, but in the Middle Ages it was felt to be presumptuous to give the names of saints directly to children; instead their blessing was invoked by prefixing the name with *mael* 'devotee of' or *gille* 'servant of'.

Malerie ♀
Modern coinage, apparently a respelling of ◊**Mallory** influenced by ◊**Valerie**.

Mallory ♂, ♀
Especially North American: transferred use of the surname, which originated as a Norman French nickname for an unfortunate person, from Old French *malheure* 'unhappy' or 'unlucky'. This is now well established as a girl's name in North America. *Variant*: **Mallery**.

Malvina ♀
Semi-fictional name, based on Gaelic *mala mhìn* 'smooth brow', invented by James Macpherson (1736–96), the Scottish antiquarian poet who published

works allegedly translated from the ancient Gaelic bard Ossian. The name became popular in Scandinavia because of the admiration of the Emperor Napoleon for the Ossianic poems: he was godfather to several of the children of his marshal Jean Baptiste Bernadotte (who ruled Norway and Sweden (1818–44) as Karl XIV Johan) and imposed his own taste in naming practices on them, hence the frequency of Ossianic given names in Scandinavia. *Las Malvinas* is the Argentinian name for the Falkland Islands, but it has no connection with the Ossianic name, being derived from the name of the French seaport St Malo.

Mamie ♀

Short form of ◊**Margaret** or ◊**Mary**, originating as a nursery form. It has occasionally been used as an independent given name, especially in America, where it was the name by which the wife of President Eisenhower was usually known.

Manda ♀

Shortened form of ◊**Amanda**.

Mandy ♀, ♂

Pet form of ◊**Amanda**, now sometimes used as an independent given name.

Manfred ♂

From an old Germanic personal name, usually said to be from *man* 'man' + *fred*, *frid* 'peace'. However, it is more likely that the first element was *magin* 'strength' (the usual Norman form being *Mainfred*) or *manag* 'much'. This name was in use among the Normans, who introduced it to Britain. However, it did not become part of the common stock of English given names, and was reintroduced from Germany in the 19th century. It was a traditional name among the Hohenstaufens, and was borne by the last Hohenstaufen king of Sicily (1258–66), who died in battle against papal forces at Benevento. The name was also used by Byron for the central character in his poetic drama *Manfred* (1817), a brooding outcast, tormented by incestuous love for his half-sister.

Manley ♂

Transferred use of the surname, which in most cases originated as a local name from places in Devon and Cheshire, named in Old English as 'the common wood or clearing', from *(ge)mæn* 'common', 'shared' + *lēah* 'wood', 'clearing'. Its choice as a first name may well have been influenced by association with the vocabulary word *manly* and the hope that the qualities denoted by the adjective would be attributes of the bearer. The vocabulary word may also lie behind some cases of the surname, as a nickname for a 'manly' person.

Manny ♂

Pet form of ◊**Emmanuel**, found mainly as a Jewish name.

Mara ♀

Of biblical origin, from Hebrew *Mara* 'bitter', a name referred to by Naomi when she went back to Bethlehem because of the famine in the land of Moab and the deaths of her husband and two sons: 'call me not Naomi, call me Mara: for the Almighty hath dealt very bitterly with me' (Ruth 1:20).

Marc ♂

French form of ◊**Mark**, now also quite popular in the English-speaking world. It was given some currency in England in the 1960s by the pop singer Marc Bolan.

Marcel ♂

French: from the Latin name *Marcellus*, originally a diminutive of ◊**Marcus**. The name has always been popular in France as it was borne by a 3rd-century missionary to Gaul, martyred at Bourges with his companion Anastasius. It is now occasionally also used in the English-speaking world.

Marcella ♀

Feminine form of *Marcellus*; see ◊**Marcel**. St Marcella was a Roman noblewoman of the late 4th century who lodged St Jerome for three years.

March ♂

Transferred use of the surname. This has two origins: 1. local name for someone who lived on the border between two territories, especially in the Marches between England and Wales or England and Scotland (from Norman French *march* 'boundary', of Germanic origin); 2. nickname for someone with some association with the month of March (Old French *march(e)*, Latin *(mensis) Martius*, a derivative of *Mars*; cf. ◊**Martin**). In part this name may also have been adopted as a first name by association with the female names ◊**April**, ◊**May**, and ◊**June**, bearing in mind that Mars, the roman god of war, after whom the month is named, is male.

Marcia ♀

Often used as a feminine equivalent of ◊**Mark**, but in fact a feminine form of *Marcius*, itself a derivative of ◊**Marcus**. One St Marcia is commemorated in a group with Felix, Luciolus, Fortunatus, and others; another with Zenais, Cyria, and Valeria; and a third with Ariston, Crescentian, Eutychian, Urban, Vitalis, Justus, Felicissimus, Felix, and Symphorosa. None is individually very famous.

Variant: **Marsha**.

Pet forms: **Marcie**, **Marcy**, **Marci** (mainly North American).

Marcus ♂

The original Latin form of ◊**Mark**, of unknown derivation; it may possibly be connected with *Mars*, the name of the Roman god of war, or the adjective *mas* 'male', 'virile' (genitive *maris*). This was one of the very small number of Roman given names of the classical period. There were only about a dozen of these in general use, with perhaps another dozen confined to particular families. *Marcus* has been in use in the English-speaking world since the 16th century if not earlier; in the 20th century it enjoyed a considerable increase in popularity. As an American Black name it is sometimes bestowed in honour of the Black Consciousness leader Marcus Garvey (1887–1940).

Marea ♀

Altered spelling of ◊**Maria**.

Mared ♀

Welsh form of ◊**Margaret**, a simplified form of *Marged*.

Maretta ♀

Scottish: Anglicized form of *Mairead*, the Gaelic version of ◊**Margaret**. See also ◊**Marietta**.

Marga ♀

Short form of ◊**Margaret** or any of the large number of related names beginning with these two syllables.

Margaret ♀

An extremely common medieval given name, derived via Old French *Marguerite* and Latin *Margarīta* from Greek *Margarītēs*, from *margaron* 'pearl', a word ultimately of Hebrew origin. The name was always understood to mean 'pearl' throughout the Middle Ages. The first St Margaret was martyred at Antioch in Pisidia during the persecution instigated by the Emperor Diocletian in the early 4th century. However, there is some doubt about her name, as the same saint is venerated in the Orthodox Church as ◊**Marina**. There were several other saintly bearers of the name, including St Margaret of Scotland (d. 1093), wife of King Malcolm Canmore and daughter of Edmund Ironside of England. It was also the name of the wife of Henry VI of England, Margaret of Anjou (1430–82), and of Margaret Tudor (1489–1541), sister of Henry VIII, who married James IV of Scotland and ruled as regent there after his death. See also ◊**Margery**, ◊**Marjorie**.

Short forms: **Meg**, **Peg**, **Madge**, **Marge**.

Pet forms: ◊**Maggie**, **Meggie**, ◊**Peggy**, **Margie**, ◊**May**. See also ◊**Daisy**.

Margery ♀

The usual medieval vernacular form of ◊**Margaret** (now also commonly spelled ◊**Marjorie**). This form of the name is preserved in the nursery rhyme 'Seesaw, Margery Daw'.

Margie ♀
Pet form of ◊**Margaret**, from the informal short form *Marge*.
Variants: **Marjie**, **Marjy**, **Marji**.

Margot ♀
French pet form of ◊**Marguerite**, now used as an independent given name. In England it is still usually pronounced in the French way, but in Eastern Europe the final consonant is sounded, and this has had some influence in America.

Marguerite ♀
French form of ◊**Margaret**, also used in the English-speaking world, where its use has been reinforced by the fact that the name was adopted in the 19th century for a garden flower, a large cultivated variety of daisy. *Margaret* was earlier used in English as a dialect word denoting the ox-eye daisy, and the French equivalent was borrowed into English just in time to catch the vogue for deriving girls' names from vocabulary words denoting flowers. See also ◊**Daisy**.

Mari ♀
Welsh form of ◊**Mary**; see also ◊**Mair**.

Maria ♀
Latin form of ◊**Mary**. In the English-speaking world it is a learned revival dating from the 18th century, pronounced both 'ma-*ree*-a' and, more traditionally, 'ma-*rye*-a'. The Latin name *Maria* arose as a back-formation from the early Christian girl's name *Mariam*. This was taken as a Latin accusative case. In fact, however, it is an indeclinable Aramaic alternative form of the Hebrew name ◊**Miriam**.

Mariah ♀
Elaborated spelling of ◊**Maria**, influenced by the many girls' names of Hebrew origin ending in -*a* plus an optional final *h*.

Mariamne ♀
The form of ◊**Miriam** used by the Jewish historian Flavius Josephus, writing in Latin in the 1st century BC, as the name of the wife of King Herod. On the basis of this evidence, it has been thought by some to be closer to the original form of the name actually borne by the Virgin Mary, and has therefore been bestowed in her honour.

Marian ♀
Originally a medieval variant spelling of ◊**Marion**. However, in the 18th century, when combined names began to come into fashion, it was sometimes understood as a combination of ◊**Mary** and ◊**Ann**.

Marianne ♀
Extended spelling of ◊**Marian**, reinforcing the association of the second element with ◊**Ann(e)**. It also represents a French assimilated form of ◊**Mariamne**. *Marianne* is the name used for the symbolic figure of the French Republic.

Marie ♀
French form of ◊**Maria**. When first introduced to England in the Middle Ages, it was Anglicized in pronunciation and respelled ◊**Mary**. This French form was reintroduced into the English-speaking world as a separate name in the 19th century, and is still pronounced more or less in the French manner, although sometimes with the stress on the first syllable.

Mariella ♀
Italian diminutive form of ◊**Maria**, now sometimes used as an independent given name in the English-speaking world.

Marietta ♀
Italian diminutive form of ◊**Maria**, now quite often used as a given name in the English-speaking world. In Gaelic Scotland *Mar(i)etta* is quite commonly used as an Anglicized form of *Mairead*, the Gaelic form of ◊**Margaret**.

Marigold ♀
One of the older of the group of names that were adopted from words for flowers in the late 19th and early 20th centuries. The Old English name of the flower was *golde*, presumably from *gold*

(the precious metal), in reference to its colour. At some time before the 14th century the flower became associated with the Virgin Mary, and its name was extended accordingly to *marigold*.

Marilee ♀
Modern coinage, a combination of ◊**Mary** and ◊**Lee**.

Marilene ♀
Modern coinage, a combination of the name ◊**Mary** with the productive suffix *-lene*, or else a variant of ◊**Marilyn**.

Marilla ♀
Apparently an arbitrary elaboration of ◊**Maria**, with the syllable *-illa* derived from names such as ◊**Priscilla**.

Marilyn ♀
20th-century elaboration of ◊**Mary**, with the addition of the productive suffix *-lyn* (see ◊**Lynn**). A major influence on the popularity of the name was the film star Marilyn Monroe (1926–62), originally named Norma-Jean Baker.
Variants: **Marilynn**, **Marylyn(n)**, ◊**Marilene**.

Marina ♀
From a Late Latin name, a feminine form of the family name *Marīnus*. This was in fact a derivative of *Marius*, a traditional name of uncertain derivation, but even during the early centuries AD it was widely assumed to be identical with the Latin adjective *marīnus* 'of the sea'. The early saints of this name are all of very doubtful historical authenticity.

Marion ♀
Originally a medieval French diminutive form of ◊**Marie**, introduced to Britain in the Middle Ages, and now completely Anglicized in pronunciation.

Marisa ♀
20th-century elaboration of ◊**Maria**, with the suffix *-isa* abstracted from such names as *Lisa* and *Louisa*.

Marissa ♀
Variant of ◊**Marisa**, with the suffix

-issa, abstracted from names such as *Clarissa*.

Marius ♂
Latin name occasionally used in English and other languages. It is of uncertain origin: it may be connected with *Mars*, the name of the god of war, or perhaps *mas*, *maris* 'virile'. The Italian, Spanish, and Portuguese equivalent **Mario** is extremely popular, being taken as the masculine form of ◊**Maria** and therefore associated with the cult of the Virgin Mary.

Marjie ♀
Variant spelling of ◊**Margie**.
Variants: **Marjy**, **Marji**.

Marjorie ♀
The usual modern spelling of ◊**Margery**. It seems to have arisen as the result of folk etymological association of the name with that of the herb *marjoram* (compare ◊**Rosemary**). This word is of uncertain origin; its Middle English and Old French form was *majorane*, without the first *-r-*.
Variant: **Marjory**.

Mark ♂
From the Latin name ◊**Marcus**, borne by the Evangelist, author of the second gospel in the New Testament, and by several other early and medieval saints. In Arthurian legend, King *Mark* is the aged ruler of Cornwall to whom Isolde is brought as a bride by Tristan; his name was presumably of Celtic origin, perhaps derived from the element *march* 'horse'. This was not a particularly common name in the Middle Ages.

Marlene ♀
Contracted form of Latin *Maria Magdalene* (see ◊**Madeleine**). The name is of German origin, but is now also widely used in the English-speaking world, normally in a pronunciation with two syllables (compare ◊**Arlene** and ◊**Charlene**). Probably the first, and certainly the most famous, bearer of the name was the film star Marlene Dietrich (1901–92), who was christened Maria

Magdalena von Losch. The name was further popularized in the 1940s by the wartime German song 'Lili Marlene', which was immensely popular among both German and British troops in North Africa.

Marlon ♂

Name apparently first brought to public attention by the American actor Marlon Brando (b. 1924). The name was borne also by his father. It is of uncertain origin, possibly derived from ◊**Marc** with the addition of the French diminutive suffix -*lon* (originally a combination of two separate suffixes, -*el* and -*on*). The actor's family is partly of French extraction.

Marmaduke ♂

Of uncertain derivation. It is generally held to be an Anglicized form of the Old Irish name *Mael-Maedóc* 'devotee of Maedóc'. The name *Maedóc* was borne by various early Irish saints, most notably a 6th-century abbot of Clonmore and a 7th-century bishop of Ferns. Mael-Maedóc Ó Morgair (1095–1148) was a reformer of the Church in Ireland and a friend of Bernard of Clairvaux. However, the modern Gaelic form (from *c.*1200) is *Maol-Maodhóg* (pronounced 'mulmay-og'), so that the name would have had to have been borrowed into English before this loss of the *d*. Marmaduke has never been common except in a small area of North Yorkshire.
Short form: ◊**Duke**.

Marna ♀

Swedish vernacular form of ◊**Marina**, now occasionally also used in the English-speaking world.
Pet form: **Marnie** (well established as an independent given name in North America).

Marquis ♂

Mainly U.S.: taken from the vocabulary word denoting the rank of nobility (compare ◊**Earl**, ◊**Prince**, ◊**King**). This derives from Old French *marchis*, i.e. 'lord of the marches (border districts)'. The spelling was later influenced by the

Provençal and Spanish equivalents. Use as a given name may also have been influenced by the Scottish surname *McMarquis*, Gaelic *Mac Marcuis*, a patronymic from ◊**Marcus**.

Marsh ♂

Transferred use of the surname, in origin a local name for someone who lived on a patch of marshy ground, from Middle English *mersche* (Old English *mersc*). It is also used as an informal short form of ◊**Marshall**, and possibly also as a masculine equivalent of ◊**Marsha**, by backformation.

Marsha ♀

Phonetic spelling of ◊**Marcia**, associated particularly with the American film star Marsha Hunt (b. 1917).

Marshall ♂

Transferred use of the surname, derived from a Norman French occupational term that originally denoted someone who looked after horses, ultimately from Germanic *marah* 'horse' + *scalc* 'servant'. By the time it became fixed as a surname it had the meaning 'shoeing smith'; later it came to denote an official whose duties were to a large extent ceremonial. The surname is pronounced the same as the Latin name *Martial* (from Latin *Mars*, genitive *Martis*; compare ◊**Martin**). This may have contributed something to its use as a given name.

Martha ♀

New Testament name, of Aramaic rather than Hebrew origin, meaning 'lady'. It was borne by the sister of Lazarus and Mary of Bethany (John 11:1). According to Luke 10:38, when Jesus visited the house of Mary and Martha, Mary sat at his feet, listening to him, while Martha 'was cumbered about much serving', so that she complained to Jesus, 'Lord, dost thou not care that my sister hath left me to serve alone?' For this reason, the name *Martha* has always been associated with hard domestic work, as opposed to the contemplative life.

Marti ♀

Short form of ◊**Martina** or ◊**Martine**. Its best-known bearer in Britain is the English comedienne Marti Caine (b. 1945). *Variants*: **Martie**, **Marty**.

Martin ♂

English form of the Latin name *Martīnus*. This was probably originally derived from *Mars* (genitive *Martis*), the name of the Roman god of war (and earlier of fertility). *Martin* became very popular in the Middle Ages, especially on the Continent, as a result of the fame of St Martin of Tours. He was born the son of a Roman officer in Upper Pannonia (an outpost of the Roman Empire, now part of Hungary), and although he became a leading figure in the 4th-century Church, he is chiefly remembered now for having divided his cloak in two and given half to a beggar. The name was also borne by five popes, including one who defended Roman Catholic dogma against Eastern Orthodox theology. He died after suffering imprisonment and privations in Naxos and public humiliation in Constantinople, and was promptly acclaimed a martyr by supporters of the Roman Church. Among Protestants, the name is sometimes bestowed in honour of the German theologian Martin Luther (1483–1546); *Martin* was used as a symbolic name for the Protestant Church in satires by both Dryden and Swift. A further influence may be its use as the given name of the civil-rights leader Martin Luther King (1929–68).
Variant: **Martyn**.
Pet form: **Marty**.

Martina ♀

Feminine form of the Latin name *Martīnus* (see ◊**Martin**). It was in use from an early period, being borne by a notorious poisoner mentioned by the historian Tacitus. The 3rd-century saint of the same name is of doubtful authenticity. Modern use of the name in the English-speaking world seems to be the result of German or Eastern European influence, as in the case of the

tennis player Martina Navratilova (b. 1956), who was born in Czechoslovakia.

Martine ♀

French form of ◊**Martina**, also used in the English-speaking world.

Marty ♂, ♀

Short form of ◊**Martin** or of ◊**Martina** and ◊**Martine**. It has sometimes been used as an independent boy's name in the latter part of the 20th century, being associated particularly with the comedian Marty Feldman (1933–83), the 1960s pop singer Marty Wilde (b. 1938 as Reginald Smith), and the country-and-western singer Marty Robbins (b. 1926).

Martyn ♂

Variant spelling of ◊**Martin**.

Marvin ♂

Medieval variant of ◊**Mervyn**, resulting from the regular Middle English change of *-er-* to *-ar-*. Modern use may represent a transferred use of the surname derived from this in the Middle Ages. It is very popular in the United States, where it is associated in particular with the American singer Marvin Gaye (1939–84).

Mary ♀

Originally a Middle English Anglicized form of French ◊**Marie**, from Latin ◊**Maria**. This is a New Testament form of ◊**Miriam**, which St Jerome derives from elements meaning 'drop of the sea' (Latin *stilla maris*, later altered by folk etymology to *stella maris* 'star of the sea'). *Mary* was the name of the Virgin Mary, mother of Jesus Christ, who has been the subject of a cult from earliest times. Consequently, the name was extremely common among early Christians, several saints among them, and by the Middle Ages was well established in every country in Europe at every level of society. It has been enduringly popular ever since. In the New Testament, *Mary* is also the name of several other women: Mary Magdalene (see ◊**Madeleine**); Mary the sister of Martha, who sat at Jesus's feet while Martha served (Luke 10:38–42; John 11:1–46; 12:1–9) and who came to be taken in Christian tradition as symbolizing the value of a contemplative life; the mother of St Mark (Colossians 4:10); and a Roman matron mentioned by St Paul (Romans 16:6).

Marylyn ♀
Variant spelling of ◊**Marilyn**.
Variant: **Marylynn**.

Mason ♂
Especially U.S.: transferred use of the surname, which originated in the early Middle Ages as an occupational name for a worker in stone, Old French *maçon* (of Germanic origin, connected with Old English *macian* 'to make').

Masterman ♂
Transferred use of the surname, which originated in Scotland as a term denoting a retainer or servant: the 'man' of the 'master'. This was used in particular for the eldest sons of barons and the uncles of lords. As a given name it is principally known from the central character of Captain Frederick Marryat's novel *Masterman Ready* (1841).

Mathew ♂
Variant spelling of ◊**Matthew**.

Mathias ♂
Variant spelling of ◊**Matthias**.

Matilda ♀
Latinized form of a Germanic personal name derived from *maht*, *meht* 'might' + *hild* 'battle'. This was the name of an early German queen (895–968), wife of Henry the Fowler, who was noted for her piety and generosity. It was also the name of the wife of William the Conqueror and of the daughter of Henry I of England (see ◊**Maud**). The name was introduced into England by the Normans, and this Latinized form is the one that normally occurs in medieval records, while the vernacular form *Maud* was the one in everyday use. *Matilda* was revived in England as a learned form in the 18th century.
Variant: **Mathilda**.
Short form: **Tilda**.
Pet forms: **Mattie**, **Matty**; **Tilly**, **Tillie**.

Matt ♂
Short form of ◊**Matthew**.

Matthew ♂
English form of the name of the Christian evangelist, author of the first gospel in the New Testament. His name is a form of the Hebrew name *Mattathia*, meaning 'gift of God', which is fairly common in the Old Testament, being rendered in the Authorized Version in a number of different forms: *Mattan(i)ah*, *Mattatha(h)*, *Mattithiah*, *Mattathias*, and so on. In the Authorized Version, the evangelist is regularly referred to as *Matthew*, while the apostle chosen to replace Judas Iscariot is distinguished as ◊**Matthias**. A related name from the same Hebrew roots, but reversed, is ◊**Jonathan**.
Variant: **Mathew**.
Short form: **Matt**.
Pet forms: **Mattie**, **Matty**.

Matthias ♂
New Testament Greek form of the Hebrew name *Mattathia* (see ◊**Matthew**), or rather of an Aramaic derivative. The Latin form of the name is *Matthaeus*. In English the form *Matthias* is used in the Authorized Version of the New Testament to distinguish the disciple who was chosen after the treachery of Judas to make up the twelve (Acts 1:23–26) from the evangelist *Matthew*. However, this distinction is not observed in other languages, where *Matthias* (or a version of it) is often a learned doublet existing alongside a vernacular derivative.
Variant: **Mathias**.

Mattie ♂, ♀
Pet form of ◊**Matthew** or ◊**Matilda**.
Variant: **Matty**.

Maud ♀
Medieval vernacular form of ◊**Matilda**. This form was characteristically Low German (i.e. including medieval Dutch and Flemish). The wife of William the Conqueror, who bore this name, was the daughter of Baldwin, Count of Flanders. In Flemish and Dutch the letter *-t-* was

generally lost when it occurred between vowels, giving forms such as *Ma(h)auld*. *Maud* or *Matilda* was also the name of the daughter (1102–67) of Henry I of England; she was married early in life to the Holy Roman Emperor Henry V, and later disputed the throne of England with her cousin Stephen. In 1128 she married Geoffrey, Count of Anjou. A medieval chronicler commented, 'she was a good woman, but she had little bliss with him'. The name *Maud* became quite common in England in the 19th century, when its popularity was influenced in part by Tennyson's poem *Maud*, published in 1855.

Maude ♀
Variant of ◊**Maud**, the usual spelling of the name in North America.

Maura ♀
Of Celtic origin. St Maura was a 5th-century martyr, of whom very little is known; her companion is variously named as *Britta* (of Celtic origin) and *Baya* (of Latin origin). In Ireland *Maura* is now commonly regarded as a form of ◊**Mary** (see also ◊**Moira** and ◊**Maureen**).

Maureen ♀
Anglicized form of Irish Gaelic *Máirín*, a pet form of *Máire*. Among other influences, the name was popularized by the film actress Maureen O'Hara (b. 1920). See also ◊**Moreen**.
Variants: **Maurene**, **Maurine**.
Short form: **Mo**.

Maurice ♂
From the Late Latin name *Mauricius*, a derivative of *Maurus* (a byname meaning 'Moor', i.e. 'dark', 'swarthy'), borne by, among others, an early Byzantine emperor (*c*.539–602). It was introduced to Britain by the Normans, and was popular in the Middle English period, but was not widely adopted by the nobility, and became rare in the 17th century. It is now sometimes believed in Britain and America to be a mainly French name, perhaps because of the enormous popular influence of the French singer and film actor Maurice

Chevalier (1888–1972), who, in his public image at least, was the very epitome of Gallic charm. See also ◊**Morris**.
Short form: **Mo**.

Mave ♀
Variant spelling of ◊**Maeve**, also sometimes used as an informal short form of ◊**Mavis**.

Mavis ♀
Not found before the last decade of the 19th century. It is one of the small class of girls' names taken from vocabulary words denoting birds. *Mavis* is another word for the song-thrush, first attested in Chaucer. It is from Old French, and probably ultimately of Breton origin.

Max ♂
Short form of ◊**Maximilian** and, perhaps now more commonly in the English-speaking world, of ◊**Maxwell**. It is also used as an independent given name.

Maxie ♂, ♀
Pet form of ◊**Max**, now more commonly used as a girl's name in its own right.

Maximilian ♂
From the Latin name *Maximiliānus* (a diminutive of *Maximus* 'greatest'). This was borne by a 3rd-century saint numbered among the 'Fourteen Holy Helpers'. Although already existing, the name was reanalysed in the 15th century by the Emperor Friedrich III, who bestowed it on his first-born son (1459–1519), as a blend of the names *Maximus* and *Aemiliānus*, intending thereby to pay homage to the two classical Roman generals Q. Fabius Maximus 'Cunctator' and P. Cornelius Scipio Aemilianus. The name became traditional in the Habsburg family in Austria-Hungary and also in the royal house of Bavaria. It was borne by an ill-fated Austrian archduke (1832–67) who was set up as emperor of Mexico but later overthrown and shot.

Maxine ♀
Modern coinage, first recorded around 1930. It is a derivative of ◊**Max** by addition of the feminine ending *-ine*.

Maxwell ♂

Transferred use of the Scottish surname, in origin a local name from a minor place on the River Tweed, named as 'the stream (Old English *well(a)*) of Mack'. The latter is a form of ◊**Magnus**. Maxwell was the middle name of the newspaper tycoon William Maxwell Aitken, Lord Beaverbrook (1879–1964), who was born in Canada, and it has been used as a given name among his descendants. It is now also frequently taken as an expansion of ◊**Max**.

May ♀

Pet form of both ◊**Margaret** and ◊**Mary**. The popularity of this name, which was at its height in the early 20th century, has been reinforced by the fact that it fits into the series of month names with ◊**April** and ◊**June**, and also belongs to the group of flower names, being another word for the hawthorn, whose white flowers blossom in May. It has been out of fashion for a time.

Maya ♀

Latinate version of ◊**May** or a respelled form of the name of the Roman goddess *Māia*, influenced by the common English name *May*. The goddess Maia was one of the Pleiades, the daughters of Atlas and Pleione; she was the mother by Jupiter of Mercury. Her name seems to be derived from the root *māi-* 'great', seen also in Latin *māior* 'larger'. In the case of the American writer Maya Angelou (b. 1929), *Maya* is a nickname which she acquired in early childhood as a result of her younger brother's referring to her as 'mya sista'.

Maybelle ♀

Altered form of ◊**Mabel**, influenced by the independent names ◊**May** and ◊**Belle**.

Maynard ♂

Transferred use of the surname, which is derived from a Norman French given name of Germanic origin, from *magin* 'strength' + *hard* 'hardy', 'brave', 'strong'.

Meagan ♀

Recent variant spelling of ◊**Megan**.
Variant: **Meaghan**.

Meave ♀

Variant of ◊**Maeve**.

Meg ♀

Short form of ◊**Margaret**, an alteration of the obsolete short form *Mag(g)* (as in ◊**Maggie**). Until recently *Meg* was a characteristically Scottish pet form, but it is now used more widely. Its popularity no doubt owes something to Meg March, one of the four sisters who are the main characters in Louisa M. Alcott's novel *Little Women* (1855).

Megan ♀

Welsh pet form of ◊**Meg**, nowadays generally used as an independent first name both within and beyond Wales, but nevertheless retaining a strong Welsh flavour.
Variants: **Meghan**, **Meag(h)an** (pseudo-Irish spellings much used in Australia and Canada).

Meggie ♀

Pet form of ◊**Meg** or of ◊**Megan**, as in the case of the central character of Colleen McCullough's novel *The Thorn Birds* (1977).

Meghan ♀

Recent variant spelling of ◊**Megan**.

Mehetabel ♀

Biblical name (meaning 'God makes happy' in Hebrew), borne by a character, 'the daughter of Matred, the daughter of Mezahab', who is mentioned in passing in a genealogy (Genesis 36:39). The name achieved some currency among the Puritans in the 17th century. Nowadays, however, it is chiefly associated with the companion (a cat) of Archy, the cockroach in the poems of Don Marquis (1927).
Variant: **Mehitabel**.

Meical ♂

Welsh form of ◊**Michael**.
Short form: **Meic**.

Meilyr ♂

Welsh, pronounced 'may-leer': traditional name derived from an Old Celtic name, *Maglorīx*, derived from *maglos* 'chief' + *rīx* 'ruler'.

Meinwen ♀

Welsh, pronounced 'mayn-wen': modern coinage composed of the elements *main* 'slender' + *(g)wen*, feminine form of *gwyn* 'white', 'fair', 'blessed', 'holy'.

Meirion ♂

Welsh: traditional name, derived in the sub-Roman period from Latin *Mariānus* (a derivative of *Marius*; see ◊**Maria**).

Mel ♂, ♀

Short form of ◊**Melvin** or ◊**Melville**, or, in the case of the girl's name, of ◊**Melanie** or the several other girls' names beginning with this syllable. It is also found independently as an Irish boy's name, having been borne by a medieval saint who founded the monastery at Ardagh.

Melanie ♀

From an Old French form of Latin *Melania*, a derivative of the feminine form, *melaina*, of the Greek adjective *melas* 'black', 'dark'. This was the name of two Roman saints of the 5th century, a grandmother and granddaughter. St Melania the Younger was a member of a rich patrician family. She led an austere and devout Christian life and, on inheriting her father's wealth, she emancipated her slaves, sold her property, and gave the proceeds to the poor. She also established several contemplative houses, including one on the Mount of Olives, to which she eventually retired. The name *Melanie* was introduced to England from France in the Middle Ages, but died out again. It has been reintroduced and has become popular in the late 20th century.
Variants: **Melany**, ◊**Melony**.

Melchior ♂

From the name assigned by medieval tradition to one of the three Magi. It is said to be of Persian origin, composed of the elements *melk* 'king' + *quart* 'city'.

Melinda ♀

Modern coinage, derived from the first syllable of names such as ◊**Melanie** and ◊**Melissa**, with the addition of the productive suffix *-inda* (as in ◊**Lucinda**).

Melissa ♀

From the Greek word *melissa* 'bee'. It is the name of the good witch who releases Rogero from the power of the bad witch Alcina in Ariosto's narrative poem *Orlando Furioso* (1532). The name has recently increased considerably in popularity, together with other girls' names sharing the same first syllable.
Variant: **Melitta** (from an ancient Greek dialectal variant of the same word).

Melody ♀

Modern transferred use of the vocabulary word (Greek *melōdia* 'singing of songs', from *melos* 'song' + *aeidein* 'to sing'), chosen partly because of its pleasant associations and partly under the influence of other girls' names with the same first syllable.

Melony ♀

Variant of ◊**Melanie**, perhaps influenced by ◊**Melody**.
Variants: **Mellony**, **Mel(l)oney**.

Melville ♂

Mainly North American: transferred use of the Scottish surname, which originated as a Norman baronial name borne by the lords of a place in northern France called *Malleville* 'bad settlement', i.e. settlement on infertile land. The name was taken to Scotland as early as the 12th century and became an important surname there; use as a given name seems also to have originated in Scotland.

Melvin ♂

Very popular modern name of uncertain origin, probably a variant of the less common ◊**Melville**. The variant **Melvyn** is associated particularly with the film star Melvyn Douglas (1901–81).

Mercedes ♀

Spanish name associated with the cult of the Virgin Mary, from the liturgical title *Maria de las Mercedes* (literally, 'Mary of Mercies'; in English, 'Our Lady of Ransom'). Latin *mercēdes* (plural) originally meant 'wages' or 'ransom'. In Christian theology, Christ's sacrifice is regarded as a 'ransom for the sins of mankind', hence an 'act of ransom' was seen as identical with an 'act of mercy'. There are feasts in the Roman Catholic calendar on 10 August and 24 September to commemorate the Virgin under this name. As a given name, this is now occasionally used in England, and more commonly in the United States, but normally only by Roman Catholics. It is associated with the American film actress Mercedes McCambridge (b. 1918). A more materialistic association with the high-class German brand of car so named may also be having an influence on the continued use of the name in this increasingly secular age.

Mercer ♂

Transferred use of the surname, in origin an occupational name for a trader (Old French *mercier*, from Late Latin *mercārius*, a derivative of *merx* 'merchandise'). Use as a given name in the United States may have originated in honour of General Hugh Mercer, killed at the battle of Princeton in 1777. It may sometimes also have been chosen as a kind of male equivalent of ◊**Mercy**.

Mercia ♀

Latinate elaboration of ◊**Mercy**, coinciding in form with the name of the Anglo-Saxon kingdom of Mercia, which dominated England during the 8th century under its king, Offa.

Mercy ♀

From the vocabulary word denoting the quality of magnanimity, and in particular God's forgiveness of sinners, a quality much prized in Christian tradition. The word is derived from Latin *mercēs*, which originally meant 'wage' or 'reward' (see ◊**Mercedes**). The name was much favoured by the Puritans; Mercy is the companion of Christiana in the second part of John Bunyan's *Pilgrim's Progress* (1684). Subsequently, it fell out of use as a given name. In modern use, this is often an Anglicized form of *Mercedes*.

Meredith ♂, ♀

From the Old Welsh personal name *Maredudd*, later *Meredudd*. This is of uncertain origin; the second element is Welsh *iudd* 'lord'. In recent years the name has sometimes been given to girls, presumably being thought of as the formal form of ◊**Merry**.

Merfyn ♂

Welsh: traditional name derived from Old Welsh *mer*, probably meaning 'marrow' + *myn* 'eminent'. This name was borne by a shadowy 9th-century Welsh king.

Meriel ♀

Northern English form of the Scottish name ◊**Muriel**. It is recorded frequently in Yorkshire from the 15th century onwards.

Merle ♀, ♂

Probably a contracted form of ◊**Meriel**, but also associated with the small class of girls' names derived from birds, since it is identical in form with Old French *merle* 'blackbird' (Latin *merula*). The name came to public notice in the 1930s with the actress Merle Oberon (1911–79); she was born Estelle Merle O'Brien Thompson. In Britain this is still normally a girl's name; in the United States it is more commonly given to boys.

Merlin ♂

Usual English form of the Welsh name *Myrddin*. The name is most famous as that of the legendary magician who guides the destiny of King Arthur. It is apparently composed of Old Celtic elements meaning 'sea' and 'hill' or 'fort', but it has been distorted by mediation through Old French sources, which associated the second element with the diminutive suffix -*lin*.

Variant: **Merlyn** (occasionally given to girls, as if containing the productive suffix of girls' names *-lyn*).

Merrill ♂
Transferred use of the surname, which was derived in the Middle Ages from the girl's name ◊**Meriel** or ◊**Muriel**.

Merrily ♀
Mainly U.S.: apparently a respelling of ◊**Marilee**, reshaped to coincide with the adverb derived from the adjective *merry*.

Merrilyn ♀
Recent coinage, a blend of ◊**Marilyn** and ◊**Merry**.

Merry ♀
Apparently an assimilated form of ◊**Mercy**. In Dickens's novel *Martin Chuzzlewit* (1844), Mr Pecksniff's daughters ◊**Charity** and *Mercy* are known as *Cherry* and *Merry*. Nowadays the name is usually bestowed because of its association with the adjective denoting a cheerful and jolly temperament (compare ◊**Happy**). In the accent of Canada and the central and northern United States there is no difference in pronunciation between *Merry* and *Mary*.

Merton ♂
Transferred use of the surname, in origin a local name from any of several places named in Old English as *mere tūn* 'settlement by the lake'. Use as a given name may have been influenced by its similarity in sound to the traditional given name ◊**Martin**.

Mervyn ♂
Anglicized form of Welsh ◊**Merfyn**, now widely popular both in and beyond Wales.
Variant: **Mervin**.
Short form: **Merv**.

Meryl ♀
Recent coinage, owing its current popularity to the fame of the American actress Meryl Streep (b. Mary Louise Streep in 1949). It has also been influenced in part by the ending *-yl* in names such as ◊**Cheryl**.

Meurig ♂
Welsh form of ◊**Maurice**, pronounced '*may*-rig'. It is derived from Latin *Mauricius* via Old Welsh *Mouric*.

Mia ♀
Danish and Swedish pet form of ◊**Maria**. It is now also used in the English-speaking world, largely as a result of the fame of the actress Mia Farrow (b. 1945).

Micah ♂
Biblical name (meaning 'who is like Yahweh?' in Hebrew, and thus a doublet of ◊**Michael**). This was the name of a prophet, author of the book of the Bible that bears his name, and which dates from the late 8th century BC.

Michael ♂
English form of a common biblical name (meaning 'who is like God?') borne by one of the archangels, who is also regarded as a saint of the Catholic Church. In the Middle Ages, Michael was regarded as captain of the heavenly host (see Revelation 12:7–9), symbol of the Church Militant, and patron of soldiers. He was often depicted bearing a flaming sword. The name is also borne by a Persian prince and ally of Belshazzar mentioned in the Book of Daniel. See also ◊**Michal**.
Short forms: **Mike**, **Mick**.
Pet form: **Micky**.

Michaela ♀
Latinate feminine form of ◊**Michael**.

Michal ♀
Biblical name (meaning 'brook' in Hebrew) borne by a daughter of Saul who married King David. It is probably through confusion with this name that ◊**Michael** has occasionally been used as a girl's name in the English-speaking world.

Michelle ♀
French feminine form of *Michel*, the French form of ◊**Michael**. This name is now also used extensively in the English-speaking world (partly influenced by a Beatles song with this name as its title).
Short forms: **Chelle**, ◊**Shell**.

Mick ♂

Short form of ◊**Michael**; now common as a generic, and often derogatory, term for a Catholic Irishman.
Pet form: **Micky**. See also ◊**Mikki**.

Mickenzie ♀

Altered form of ◊**Mackenzie**, influenced by the name ◊**Mick**.

Mignonette ♀

Pronounced 'mee-nyon-*et*': probably a direct use of the French nickname *mignonette* 'little darling', a feminine diminutive of *mignon* 'sweet', 'cute', 'dainty'. Alternatively, it may belong to the class of names derived from vocabulary words denoting flowers (the word in English is used for various species of *Reseda*).

Mihangel ♂

Older Welsh form of ◊**Michael**, representing a contraction of the phrase 'Michael the Archangel'.

Mike ♂

Usual short form of ◊**Michael**. It is also used as an independent given name, particularly in the United States.
Pet form: **Mikey**.

Mikki ♀

Feminine variant of *Micky* (see ◊**Mick**) or pet form of ◊**Michaela**, now sometimes used as an independent given name.
Variants: **Micki**, **Mickie**, **Mickey**.

Mildred ♀

From an Old English female personal name *Mildþrýð*, derived from *mild* gentle + *þrýð* 'strength'. This was the name of a 7th-century abbess, who had a less famous but equally saintly elder sister called *Mildburh* and a younger sister called *Mildgýð*; all were daughters of a certain Queen Ermenburh. Their names illustrate clearly the Old English pattern of combining and recombining the same small group of name elements within a single family. This name was in use, at least in Yorkshire, in the 17th century; it enjoyed a strong revival throughout England in the 19th century.

Miles ♂

Of Norman origin but uncertain derivation. Unlike most Norman names, it is, as far as can be ascertained, not derived from any known Old French or Germanic name element. It may be a greatly altered pet form of ◊**Michael**, which came to be associated with the Latin word *miles* 'soldier' because of the military attributes of the archangel Michael. However, the usual Latin form of the name in the Middle Ages was *Milo*. There is a common Slavonic name element *mil* 'grace', 'favour', with which it may possibly have some connection. The name has been modestly popular in England ever since the Norman Conquest. See also ◊**Milo** and ◊**Myles**.

Milla ♀

Shortened form of ◊**Camilla**.

Millenna ♀

Name chosen for some of the babies born at the turn of the millennium (from Latin *mille* 'thousand' + *annus* 'year'), in 2000. It may also have been influenced by the Czech name *Milena*, a short form of various compound Slavonic names containing the element *mil* 'grace', 'favour' (cf. ◊**Miles**).

Miller ♂

Transferred use of the surname, in origin an occupational name for someone who ran a mill, grinding grain into flour. This is from Middle English *mille*, *milne*, from Old English *mylen*.

Millicent ♀

From an Old French name, *Melisende*, of Germanic (Frankish) origin, from *amal* 'labour' + *swinth* 'strength'. This was the name of a daughter of Charlemagne. It was adopted by the Normans and introduced by them to Britain.

Millie ♀

Pet form of ◊**Millicent**, and also, less commonly, of names such as ◊**Mildred** and ◊**Camilla**.

Milo ♂

Latinized form of ◊**Miles**, regularly used in documents of the Middle Ages, and revived as a given name in the 19th century.

Milton ♂

Transferred use of the surname, in origin a local name from the numerous places so called, a large number of which get their name from Old English *mylentūn* 'settlement with a mill'. Others were originally named as 'the middle settlement (of three)', from Old English *middel* 'middle' + *tūn* 'settlement'. The surname is most famous as that of the poet John Milton (1608–74), and the given name is sometimes bestowed in his honour.
Short form: **Milt**.

Mimi ♀

Italian pet form of ◊**Maria**, originally a nursery name. The heroine of Puccini's opera *La Bohème* (1896) announces 'They call me Mimi', and since that time the name has occasionally been used in the English-speaking world.

Mimosa ♀

From the word denoting the pink and white flowering plant, which was named in the 17th century, probably as a derivative of Latin *mīmus* 'mime', 'mimic'; the idea is that it mimics an animal in its sensitivity to touch.

Minnie ♀

Pet form of ◊**Wilhelmina**, at its peak of popularity in the latter half of the 19th century, when several names were introduced into Britain from Germany in the wake of Queen Victoria's consort, Prince Albert of Saxe-Coburg-Gotha, whom she married in 1840. It has now largely fallen out of use, partly because German names in general became unacceptable in Britain during the First World War, partly perhaps also because of association with cartoon characters such as Minnie Mouse (in Walt Disney's animations) and Minnie the Minx (in the *Beano* 'children's comic').

Mirabelle ♀

French: from Latin *mīrābilis* 'wondrous', 'lovely' (a derivative of *mīrāri* 'to

wonder at', 'admire'; compare ◊**Miranda**). The same name is found in Italian in the form **Mirabella**. Both the French and Italian forms were quite common in the later Middle Ages. The form *Mirabel* is found occasionally in France and England as a boy's name. By the 16th century, both forms were rare.
Variant: **Mirabella** (a Latinate form).

Miranda ♀

Invented by Shakespeare for the heroine of *The Tempest* (1611). It represents the feminine form of the Latin gerundive *mīrandus* 'admirable', 'lovely', from *mīrāri* 'to wonder at', 'admire'; compare ◊**Amanda** for a similar formation.

Mireille ♀

French: apparently first used, in the Provençal form **Mireio**, as the title of a verse romance by the poet Frédéric Mistral (1830–1914). The name is probably a derivative of Provençal *mirar* 'to admire' (compare ◊**Miranda**). The poet himself declared it to be a form of ◊**Miriam**, but this was apparently in order to overcome the objections of a priest to baptizing his god-daughter with a non-liturgical name. The name is now occasionally also used in the English-speaking world.

Miriam ♀

Biblical name: the Old Testament form of the Hebrew name *Maryam* (see ◊**Mary**). Of uncertain ultimate origin, this is first recorded as being borne by the elder sister of Moses (Exodus 15:20). Since the names of both Moses and his brother Aaron are probably of Egyptian origin, it is possible that this female name is too. It was enthusiastically taken up as a given name by the Israelites, and is still found mainly, but by no means exclusively, as a Jewish name.

Missy ♀

Modern coinage from a pet form of the vocabulary word *miss*, applied to a young girl (compare ◊**Maidie**). It is common as a pet name and form of address in the southern United States.

The vocabulary word *miss* originated in Middle English as a short form of *mistress*.

Misty ♀
Modern coinage, apparently from the vocabulary word.

Mitchell ♂
Transferred use of the surname, itself derived from a common medieval form of ◊**Michael**, representing an Anglicized pronunciation of the French name *Michel*, introduced to Britain by the Normans.
Short form: **Mitch**.

Mo ♀, ♂
Short form of ◊**Maureen** and, less commonly, of ◊**Maurice**.

Moira ♀
Anglicized form of Irish Gaelic *Máire*, (a form of ◊**Mary**). This is now a popular name in its own right throughout the English-speaking world.
Variant: **Moyra**.

Moirrey ♀
Manx form of ◊**Mary**. Compare Irish *Muire*, which is used to refer to the Virgin Mary, not as an everyday first name.

Molly ♀
Long-established pet form of ◊**Mary**, representing an altered version of the earlier pet form *Mally*. The name is chiefly associated with Ireland, although it is not known to be Gaelic. It is at present somewhat out of fashion.

Mona ♀
Anglicized form of the Gaelic name *Muadhnait*, a feminine diminutive of *muadh* 'noble'. It is no longer restricted to people with Irish connections, and has sometimes been taken as connected with Greek *monos* 'single', 'only'.

Monica ♀
Of uncertain ultimate origin. This was the name of the mother of St Augustine, as transmitted to us by her famous son. She was a citizen of Carthage, so her name may well be of Phoenician origin,

but in the early Middle Ages it was taken to be a derivative of Latin *monēre* 'to warn', 'counsel', or 'advise', since it was as a result of her guidance that her son was converted to Christianity.

Monroe ♂
Transferred use of the Scottish surname, usually spelled *Munro*. The ancestors of the Scottish Munros are said to have originally come from Ireland, apparently from a settlement by the River Roe in County Derry; their name is therefore supposed to be derived from Gaelic *bun Rotha* 'mouth of the Roe'. In the United States the popularity of the given name may have been influenced by the fame of James Monroe (1758–1831), fifth president of the United States and propounder (in 1823) of the Monroe Doctrine, asserting that European powers should not seek to colonize in North or South America and that the United States would not intervene in European affairs. A more recent influence could have been the film star Marilyn Monroe (1926–62), whose original name was Norma-Jean Baker; however, the name is not normally bestowed on girls, so the influence of her adopted surname does not appear to have been significant.
Variants: **Monro**, **Munro(e)**.

Montague ♂
Transferred use of the surname, originally a Norman baronial name borne by the lords of Montaigu in La Manche. (The place name is from Old French *mont* 'hill' (Latin *mons*, genitive *montis*) + *aigu* pointed (Latin *acūtus*). A certain Drogo of Montaigu is known to have accompanied William the Conqueror in his invasion of England in 1066, and *Montague* thus became established as an aristocratic British family name.

Montgomery ♂
Transferred use of the surname, originally a Norman baronial name from various places in Calvados. The place name is derived from Old French *mont*

'hill' + the Germanic personal name *Gomeric* 'power of man'. It has never been common as a given name, although it was given additional currency by the actor Montgomery Clift (1920–66), and during and after the Second World War by the British field marshal, Bernard Montgomery (1887–1976).

Montmorency ♂

Transferred use of the surname, originally a Norman baronial name from a place in Seine-et-Oise. The place name is derived from Old French *mont* 'hill' + the Gallo-Roman personal name *Maurentius*. The given name enjoyed a brief vogue in the 19th century, but is now regarded as affected and so hardly ever used.

Monty ♂

Short form of ◊**Montague** or of the much rarer ◊**Montgomery** and ◊**Montmorency**. It is now sometimes found as an independent given name. As a Jewish name, it was originally used as an approximate English equivalent of ◊**Moses**.

Mór ♀

Scottish and Irish Gaelic: from the vocabulary word *mór* 'large', 'great'. This was the commonest of all girls' names in late medieval Ireland, and has continued in frequent use in both Scotland and Ireland to the present day. *Pet forms*: ◊**Morag**, ◊**Moreen**.

Morag ♀

Scottish: Anglicized spelling of Gaelic *Mórag*, a pet form of ◊**Mór**. In the 20th century this name has become hugely popular in its own right in Scotland, and is also used elsewhere in the English-speaking world.

Moray ♂

Scottish: variant of ◊**Murray**, and the more usual spelling of the place name from which the surname is derived.

Moreen ♀

Irish: Anglicized form of Gaelic *Móirín*, a pet form of ◊**Mór**. It has now been to a large extent confused with ◊**Maureen**.

Morgan ♂, ♀

Welsh: traditional boy's name derived from Old Welsh *Morcant*. The first element is of uncertain derivation, the second represents the Old Celtic element *cant* 'circle', 'completion'. In recent years it has occasionally been used outside Wales as a girl's name, perhaps with conscious reference to King Arthur's jealous stepsister Morgan le Fay.

Morley ♂

Transferred use of the surname, in origin a local name from any of the numerous places named with Old English *mōr* 'moor', 'marsh' + *lēah* 'wood', 'clearing'.

Morna ♀

Irish and Scottish: variant of ◊**Myrna**. This is the name borne by Fingal's mother in the Ossianic poems of James Macpherson (compare ◊**Malvina**).

Morris ♂

Variant of ◊**Maurice**. The spelling *Morris* was quite common as a given name in the Middle Ages, but it fell out of use and was readopted in modern times, in part from the surname earlier derived from the given name.

Mortimer ♂

Transferred use of the surname, in origin a Norman baronial name borne by the lords of *Mortemer* in Normandy. The place name meant 'dead sea' in Old French, and probably referred to a stagnant marsh. It was not used as a given name until the 19th century.

Morton ♂

Transferred use of the surname, in origin a local name from any of the numerous places so called from Old English *mōr-tūn* 'settlement by or on a moor'. It is also widely used as a Jewish name, having been adopted as an approximate English equivalent of ◊**Moses**. *Short form*: **Mort**.

Morven ♀

This was the name of Fingal's kingdom in the Ossianic poems of James Macpherson. In reality it is a district in north Argyll, on the west coast of Scotland,

properly *Morvern*, known in Gaelic as *a'
Mhorbhairne* 'the big gap'. *Morven*
could alternatively be held to represent
Gaelic *mór bheinn* 'big peak'.

Morwenna ♀

Cornish and Welsh: from an Old Celtic
personal name derived from an element
akin to Welsh *morwyn* 'maiden'. It was
borne by a somewhat obscure Cornish
saint of the 5th century; churches in her
honour have named several places in
Cornwall. The name was revived in
Wales in the mid-20th century as a
result of nationalistic sentiment.

Moses ♂

Biblical name, the English form of the
name of the patriarch (**Moshe** in Hebrew) who led the Israelites out of Egypt
(Exodus 4). His name is thought to be of
Egyptian origin, most probably from the
same root as that found in the second
element of names such as *Tutmosis* and
Rameses, where it means 'born of (a
certain god)'. Various Hebrew etymologies have been proposed, beginning with
the biblical 'saved (from the water)'
(Exodus 2:10), but none is convincing. It
is now mainly a Jewish name, although
until the mid-20th century it also enjoyed considerable popularity among
Christians in England, especially among
Puritans and Nonconformists.

Moss ♂

Transferred use of the surname derived
from the usual medieval vernacular
form of ◊**Moses**, or a revival of this form.
In Wales it has in recent years also been
used as a short form of ◊**Mostyn**.

Mostyn ♂

Welsh: from the name of a place in
Clwyd, on the Dee estuary. The place in
fact derives its name from Old English
rather than Welsh elements: it appears
in Domesday Book as *Mostone*, from
Old English *mos* 'moss' + *tūn* 'enclosure', 'settlement'.

Moya ♀

Modern name of uncertain origin; it may
be derived from ◊**Moyra**.

Moyra ♀

Variant spelling of ◊**Moira**.

Muir ♂

Transferred use of the Scottish surname,
in origin a local name representing a
Scottish dialect variant of *moor* 'rough
grazing'.

Muireall ♀

Scottish Gaelic traditional name, pronounced '*moor*-all', apparently from Old
Celtic words meaning 'sea' + 'bright'. It
is often Anglicized as ◊**Muriel**.

Muireann ♀

Irish Gaelic traditional name, pronounced '*mwir*-an', apparently from
muir 'sea' + *fionn* 'white', 'fair'. The
spelling **Muirinn** is also used, and there
has been considerable confusion with
◊**Maureen** and ◊**Moreen**.

Muiris ♂

Irish form of ◊**Maurice**. In part it also
represents a contracted form of the
Gaelic name *Muirgheas*, which is probably derived from *muir* 'sea' + *gus* 'vigour'.

Muirne ♀

Irish Gaelic traditional name, pronounced '*moor*-nya', originally a byname meaning 'beloved'.
Anglicized forms: **Myrna**, **Morna**.

Mungo ♂

Scottish and northern English: of uncertain derivation. It is recorded as the
byname of St Kentigern, the 6th-century
apostle of south-west Scotland and
north-west England. Having been
glossed in Latin by his biographer as
carissimus amicus 'dearest friend', the
name (in its Brythonic form *Munghu*)
came to represent later Welsh *fy nghi*
'my dog', i.e. 'my pet'.
Variant: **Munga** (Scottish Gaelic).

Munroe ♂

Variant spelling of ◊**Monroe**.
Variant: **Munro**.

Murchadh ♂

Traditional Gaelic name, pronounced
'*moor*-ha', derived from *muir* 'sea' +

cadh 'battle'. It was borne by many medieval kings and princes.
Anglicized form: ◊**Murrough**.

Murdo ♂

Scottish: Anglicized spelling of the traditional Gaelic name *Muireadhach*, meaning 'lord', but said to be a derivative of *muir* 'sea'.
Variant: **Murdoch**.

Murgatroyd ♂

Transferred use of the Yorkshire surname, in origin a local name from an unidentified place named as 'the clearing (Yorkshire dialect *royd*) belonging to (a certain) Margaret'.

Muriel ♀

Of Celtic origin; see ◊**Muireall**. Forms of the name are found in Breton as well as in Scottish and Irish Gaelic, and in the Middle Ages it was in use even in the heart of England, having been introduced from various sources; the surname *Merrill* is derived from it. See also ◊**Meriel**.

Murray ♂

Transferred use of the Scottish surname, in origin a local name from the region now called *Moray*.
Variant: **Moray**.

Murrough ♂

Anglicized form of Gaelic ◊**Murchadh**.

Myfanwy ♀

Welsh: name composed of the Welsh affectionate prefix *my-* + *banwy*, a variant form of *banw*, akin to *benyw* or *menyw* 'woman'. Its popularity dates only from relatively recent times, when specifically Welsh names have been sought as tokens of Welsh national identity.

Myles ♂

Variant spelling of ◊**Miles**.

Myra ♀

Invented in the 17th century by the poet Fulke Greville (1554–1628). It is impossible to guess what models he had consciously or unconsciously in mind, but it has been variously conjectured that the name is an anagram of ◊**Mary**; that it is a simplified spelling of Latin *myrrha* 'myrrh', 'unguent'; and that it is connected with Latin *mīrāri* 'to admire' or 'wonder at' (see ◊**Miranda**).

Myriam ♀

Variant spelling of ◊**Miriam**. This is the usual spelling of the name in France.

Myrna ♀

Irish: Anglicized form of Gaelic ◊**Muirne**, now also used elsewhere in the English-speaking world. It is associated with the film star Myrna Loy (1905–93).
Variant: **Morna**.

Myron ♂

From a classical Greek name, derived from Greek *myron* 'myrrh'. The name was borne by a famous sculptor of the 5th century BC. It was taken up with particular enthusiasm by the early Christians because they associated it with the gift of myrrh made by the three kings to the infant Christ, and because of the association of myrrh (as an embalming spice) with death and eternal life. The name was borne by various early saints, notably a 3rd-century martyr of Cyzicus and a 4th-century bishop of Crete. Their cult is greater in the Eastern Church than the Western.

Myrtle ♀

From the vocabulary word denoting the plant (Old French *myrtille*, Late Latin *myrtilla*, a diminutive of classical Latin *myrta*). This is one of the group of plant names that became popular as girls' names in the late 19th century.

NADIA NADINE NAHUM NAN NANCY NA
NDA NANETTE NAOISE NAOMH NAOMI
NARELLE NAT NATALIE NATALYA NATAS
HA NATHALIE NATHAN NATHANIEL NEA
L NED NEIL NELL NELSON NENA NERIDA N
ERISSA NEROLI NERYS NESSA NESTA NESTO

Nadia ♀

French and English spelling of Russian
Nadya (a pet form of *Nadezhda* 'hope').
This name has enjoyed a considerable
vogue in the English-speaking world in
the 20th century.

Nadine ♀

French elaboration of ◊**Nadia**. Many
names of Russian origin became established in France and elsewhere in the
early 20th century as a result of the
popularity of the Ballet Russe, established in Paris by Diaghilev in 1909.

Nahum ♂

Biblical name (meaning 'comforter' in
Hebrew), borne by a prophet of the 7th
century BC. He was the author of the
book of the Bible that bears his name, in
which he prophesies the downfall of
Nineveh, which fell in 612 BC. This is a
well-established Jewish name, which
was also popular among 17th-century
Puritans in England. It was borne by the
minor Restoration dramatist Nahum
Tate (1652–1715), who rewrote Shakespeare's *King Lear* with a happy ending.

Nan ♀

Originally a pet form of ◊**Ann** (for the
initial *N-*, compare ◊**Ned**). It is now also
widely used as a short form of ◊**Nancy**.

Nancy ♀

Of uncertain origin. From the 18th century it is clearly used as a pet form of
◊**Ann** (see ◊**Nan**), but it may originally
have been a similar formation deriving
from the common medieval given name
Annis, a vernacular form of ◊**Agnes**.
Nowadays it is an independent name,
and was especially popular in America
between about 1920 and 1960.

Variants: **Nancie**, **Nanci**.
Short forms: **Nan**, **Nance**.

Nanda ♀

In origin a short form of Italian *Ferdi-
nanda* or Spanish *Hernanda*, which are
the vernacular feminine equivalents of
◊**Ferdinand**. It is now in occasional use
in the English-speaking world as an
independent first name, perhaps in part
as an elaboration of ◊**Nan** by association with names such as ◊**Glenda** and
◊**Linda**.

Nanette ♀

Elaboration of ◊**Nan**, with the addition
of the French feminine diminutive
suffix *-ette*.

Naoise ♂

Traditional Irish Gaelic name, pronounced '*nee*-sha'. This was borne by
one of the best-known characters in all
Irish legend, the lover of Deirdre, with
whom he eloped, even though she was
betrothed to Conchobhar, king of Ulster.
Conchobhar hounded the lovers
throughout Ireland and Scotland, eventually offering Naoise promises of par-
don and security. But they were false
promises, and on his return to Ulster
Naoise was murdered.

Naomh ♀

Traditional Irish Gaelic name,
pronounced '*neev*', meaning 'holy'
or 'saint', not to be confused with
◊**Niamh**.

Naomi ♀

Biblical name (meaning 'pleasantness'
in Hebrew), borne by the wise mother-
in-law of Ruth. The name has long been
regarded as typically Jewish, but it

occurs occasionally from the 17th century and has recently begun to come into more general use.

Narelle ♀

Australian: of uncertain origin. It has been in use since the 19th century and seems to represent an elaboration of an unidentified word or name from an Aboriginal language. *Narellan* is a town in eastern New South Wales, south-west of Sydney; the names may be connected, but if so the details are unclear. As a given name this became widely popular in the 1940s; it is still in fairly frequent use.

Nat ♂

Short form of ◊**Nathan** and ◊**Nathaniel**.

Natalie ♀

French form of ◊**Natalya**, adopted from Russian in the early 20th century, probably, like ◊**Nadine**, under the influence of Diaghilev's Ballet Russe, which was established in Paris in 1909. The name is now very common in France and in the English-speaking world, where it was borne by the actress Natalie Wood (1938–82). She was born Natasha Gurdin, in San Francisco. Her father was of Russian descent, her mother of French extraction.
Variant: **Nathalie**.

Natalya ♀

Russian: from the Late Latin name *Natália*, a derivative of Latin *natális (diēs)* 'birthday', especially Christ's birthday, i.e. Christmas (compare ◊**Noël**). St Natalia was a Christian inhabitant of Nicomedia who is said to have given succour to the martyrs, including her husband Adrian, who suffered there in persecutions under Diocletian in 303. She is regarded as a Christian saint, although she was not herself martyred.

Natasha ♀

Russian: pet form of ◊**Natalya**, now widely adopted as an independent name in the English-speaking world and elsewhere. Like *Noëlle* and ◊**Noël**, it is sometimes given to girls born on or about Christmas Day.

Nathalie ♀

Variant spelling of ◊**Natalie**. The *th* is a mere elaboration in the French spelling and has not yet had any effect on the pronunciation.

Nathan ♂

Biblical name, meaning 'he (God) has given' in Hebrew (compare ◊**Nathaniel**). This was the name of a prophet who had the courage to reproach King David for arranging the death in battle of Uriah the Hittite in order to get possession of the latter's wife Bathsheba (2 Samuel 12:1–15). It was also the name of one of David's own sons. In modern times this name has often been taken as a short form of ◊**Nathaniel** or of ◊**Jonathan**.

Nathaniel ♂

English form of a New Testament name, which is derived from the Greek form of a Hebrew name meaning 'God has given' (compare ◊**Nathan**, which is sometimes taken as a short form of this name). It was borne by one of the less prominent of Christ's apostles (John 1:45; 21:2), who in fact is probably identical with ◊**Bartholomew**. The spelling used in the Authorized Version of the New Testament is **Nathanael**, but this has never been common as a given name in the English-speaking world.

Neal ♂

Variant spelling of ◊**Neil**.
Variant: **Neale**.

Ned ♂

Short form of ◊**Edward**, originating in the misdivision of phrases such as *mine Ed* (compare ◊**Nan**). It was common in the Middle Ages and up to the 18th century, but in the 19th was almost entirely superseded in the role of short form by ◊**Ted**. It is now, however, enjoying a modest revival.

Neil ♂

Anglicized form of the enduringly popular Gaelic name **Niall**. Its derivation is disputed, and it may mean

'cloud', 'passionate', or perhaps 'champion'. It was adopted by the Scandinavians in the form *Njal* and soon became very popular among them. From the Middle Ages onwards, this name was found mainly in Ireland, the Highlands of Scotland, and the English-Scottish Border region. However, in the 20th century it has spread to enjoy great popularity in all parts of the English-speaking world.
Variants: **Neal(e)**. See also ◊**Nigel**.

Nell ♀
Medieval short form of ◊**Eleanor**, ◊**Ellen**, and ◊**Helen**. For the initial *N*-, compare ◊**Nan** and ◊**Ned**. It was the name by which Charles II's mistress Eleanor Gwyn (1650–87) was universally known to her contemporaries, and at about that time it also became established as an independent name.
Pet forms: **Nellie**, **Nelly**.

Nelson ♂
Transferred use of the surname, which originated in the Middle Ages as either a patronymic from ◊**Neil** or a metronymic from ◊**Nell**. Use as a given name probably began as a tribute to the British admiral Lord Nelson (1758–1805), the victor of the Battle of Trafalgar; see also ◊**Horatio**. It is, however, now much more common in the United States than in Britain, and in the 1930s became associated with the American film actor and singer Nelson Eddy (1901–67), remembered particularly for his romantic roles with Jeanette MacDonald.

Nena ♀
Variant spelling of ◊**Nina**.

Nerida ♀
Apparently an elaborated form of ◊**Nerys**, probably influenced by ◊**Phillida**, a variant of ◊**Phyllis**. Alternatively it may derive from Greek *Nērēis* 'sea sprite' (see ◊**Nerissa**).

Nerissa ♀
Of Shakespearian origin. It is the name of a minor character in *The Merchant of Venice*, Portia's waiting woman, who marries Gratiano. The name seems to be a Latinate elaboration of Greek *nērēis* 'sea sprite'.

Neroli ♀
From the name of the fragrant oil, which was named after the Italian princess Anne Marie de la Tremoïlle of Neroli, who is said to have discovered it.

Nerys ♀
Welsh: of uncertain derivation, perhaps intended to be from Welsh *nêr* 'lord', with the suffix *-ys* by analogy with other girls' names such as ◊**Dilys** and ◊**Gladys**. This was not used as a given name in the Middle Ages, and dates only from the recent Welsh cultural revival; this has been accompanied by a spate of modern coinages of Welsh names, enabling Welsh parents to give their children names reflecting their national identity.

Nessa ♀
Traditional Irish Gaelic name, also found in the form ◊**Ness**, of unknown origin. It is borne by a character in *Táin Bó Cuailgne* (the Cattle Raid of Cooley), the mother of Conchobhar. This name is also found as a short form of *Agnessa*, a Latinate form of ◊**Agnes**, and in modern use as a short form of ◊**Vanessa**.
Pet form: **Nessie**.

Nesta ♀
Welsh: Latinized version of **Nest**, a Welsh pet form of ◊**Agnes**. Nesta was the name of the grandmother of the 12th-century chronicler Giraldus Cambrensis ('Gerald the Welshman').

Nestor ♂
Name born in classical legend by one of the leaders of the Greeks at Troy, the aged but still vigorous king of Pylos. It may represent a derivative of Greek *nostos* 'homecoming'.

Netta ♀
Apparently a Latinate variant of ◊**Nettie**, though in Gaelic-speaking areas of Scotland it is more probably a feminine form of ◊**Neil**.

Nettie ♀

Pet form derived from various girls' names ending in the syllable -nette, for example ◊**Annette** and ◊**Jeannette**, with the diminutive suffix -ie. It had a brief vogue in the late 19th and early 20th centuries.

Neve ♀

Anglicized spelling of the Irish Gaelic name ◊**Niamh**.

Neville ♂

Transferred use of the surname, in origin a Norman baronial name from any of several places in Normandy called *Néville* or *Neuville* 'new settlement'. First used as a given name in the 16th century, and with increasing regularity from the second half of the 19th, it is now so firmly established as a given name that it has lost touch with its origin as a surname.

Newton ♂

Mainly U.S.: transferred use of the surname, in origin a local name from any of the very numerous places so called from Old English *nēowe* 'new' + *tūn* 'enclosure', 'settlement'. This is said to be the commonest of all English place names. The most famous bearer of the surname is probably Sir Isaac Newton (1642–1727), the English scientist.
Short form: **Newt**.

Ngaio ♀

New Zealand name, pronounced '*nye*-oh': apparently from the Maori word *ngaio* which, among other things, means 'clever'. *Ngai* is also a prefix meaning 'tribe' or 'clan'; the given name may have originated as a tribal name.

Ngaire ♀

New Zealand (Maori) name, pronounced '*nye*-ree': of unknown origin. It is usually Anglicized as ◊**Nyree**. See also ◊**Ngaio**.

Nia ♀

Welsh form of the Irish name ◊**Niamh**.

Niall ♂

Original Irish and Scottish Gaelic spelling of ◊**Neil**. It has been strongly revived among non-Gaelic speakers in the 20th century.

Niamh ♀

Irish Gaelic name, pronounced '*nee*-uv', from a vocabulary word meaning 'brightness' or 'beauty'. It was borne in Irish mythology by the daughter of the sea god, who fell in love with the youthful Oisín, son of Finn mac Cumhaill (Finn MacCool), and carried him off over the sea to the land of perpetual youth, *Tír na nÓg*, where there is no sadness, no ageing, and no death. It is now a very popular given name in Ireland.

Nichelle ♀

Modern coinage, an altered form of ◊**Michelle** influenced by ◊**Nicole**.

Nichol ♂

Variant of ◊**Nicol**.
Variant: **Nicholl**.

Nicholas ♂

English form of the post-classical Greek personal name *Nikolaos*, derived from *nikē* 'victory' + *laos* 'people'. The spelling with -*ch*- first occurred as early as the 12th century, and became firmly established at the time of the Reformation, although *Nicolas* is still occasionally found. St Nicholas was a 4th-century bishop of Myra in Lycia, about whom virtually nothing factual is known, although a vast body of legend grew up around him, and he became the patron saint of Greece and of Russia, as well as of children, sailors, merchants, and pawnbrokers. His feast-day is 6 December, and among the many roles which legend has assigned to him is that of bringer of Christmas presents, in the guise of 'Santa Claus' (an alteration of the Dutch form of his name, *Sinterklaas*).
Variants: **Nicolas**, **Nickolas**.
Short form: **Nick**.
Pet form: **Nicky**.

Nicholl ♂

Variant spelling of ◊**Nichol**.

Nick ♂
Short form of ◊**Nicholas**.
Variant: **Nik**.

Nickie ♀
Variant of the girl's name ◊**Nicky**.
Variant: **Nicki**.

Nickolas ♂
Variant spelling of ◊**Nicholas**, influenced by the short form ◊**Nick**.

Nicky ♂, ♀
Pet form of ◊**Nicholas** and of ◊**Nicola**.
Variants: **Nickie**, **Nicki**, **Nikki** (♀).

Nico ♂, ♀
Modern short form of both ◊**Nicholas**
and ◊**Nicola**.

Nicol ♂
Common medieval vernacular form of
◊**Nicholas**, current until a relatively late
period in Scotland, and now being revived in more general use. Modern use
as a given name may owe something to
the character Bailie Nicol Jarvie in Sir
Walter Scott's novel *Rob Roy*.
Variants: **Nicoll**, **Nichol(l)**.

Nicola ♀
Latinate feminine form of ◊**Nicholas**.
Pet forms: **Nicky**, **Nickie**, **Nicki**, **Nikki**.

Nicole ♀
French feminine form of ◊**Nicholas**, now
increasingly common in the English-
speaking world.

Nicolette ♀
French diminutive form of ◊**Nicole**, now
also used as an independent given name
in the English-speaking world.

Nicoll ♂
Variant spelling of ◊**Nicol**.

Nigel ♂
Anglicized form of the medieval name
Nigellus, a Latinized version (ostensibly
representing a diminutive of Latin *niger*
'black') of the vernacular *Ni(h)el*, i.e.
◊**Neil**. Although it is frequently found in
medieval records, this form was probably not used in everyday life before its
revival by antiquarians such as Sir Walter Scott in the 19th century.

Nigella ♀
Latinate feminine form of ◊**Nigel**.
Adoption as a given name may also have
been encouraged by the fact that this is
an alternative name (from its black seed)
for the flower known as 'love-
in-a-mist'.

Nik ♂
Modern variant spelling of ◊**Nick**.

Nikita ♀
Originally a Russian boy's name, from
Greek *Anikētos* 'unconquered, unconquerable' (from *a-* 'not' + *nikān* 'to
conquer'). This was the name of an early
pope (*c*.152–160); he was a Syrian by
descent and is particularly honoured in
the Eastern Church. In recent years,
however, the name has begun to be used
in the English-speaking world as a girl's
name, perhaps being taken as an elaboration of ◊**Nikki** with the feminine
diminutive suffix *-ita*.

Nikki ♀
Pet form of ◊**Nicola**, now sometimes
used as an independent given name.

Nile ♀
Apparently from the name of the river in
Africa. This seems, like many of the
major rivers of the world, to have been
originally named with a word meaning
simply 'river'. As a given name, it is
often used among American Blacks.
Variant: **Niles**.

Nina ♀
Russian name (originally a short form of
names such as *Antonina*), now commonly also used in the English-speaking
world.
Variant: **Nena**.

Ninette ♀
French diminutive form of ◊**Nina**. Like
◊**Nadine**, this was one of the names
brought to the English-speaking world
from Russian via French in the early
20th century.

Ninian ♂
Scottish and Irish: of uncertain origin.
This was the name of a 5th-century

British saint who was responsible for evangelizing the northern Britons and the Picts. His name first appears in the Latinized form *Ninianus* in the 8th century; this appears to be identical to the *Nynnyaw* recorded in the *Mabinogi*. The given name was used in his honour until at least the 16th century in Scotland and has recently been revived. It is also recorded in Yorkshire during the 16th–18th centuries.

Nirvana ♀
From the Sanskrit word (meaning 'extinction') used in Buddhism and Hinduism to refer to the desirable ultimate state of absorption into the ground of all being. For its use as a modern first name, cf. ◊**Dharma**, ◊**Karma**, and ◊**Samsara**.

Nita ♀
Short form of various names that end in these syllables, as for example *Anita* and *Juanita*.

Noah ♂
English form of the name of the biblical character whose family was the only one saved from the great Flood ordained by God to destroy mankind because of its wickedness. The origin of the name is far from certain; in the Bible it is implied that it means 'rest' (Genesis 5:29, 'and he called his name Noah, saying, This same shall comfort us concerning our work and the toil of our hands, because of the ground which the Lord hath cursed'). One tradition indeed explains it as derived from the Hebrew root meaning 'to comfort' (see ◊**Nahum**) with the final consonant dropped.

Noam ♂
Modern Jewish name, from a Hebrew vocabulary word meaning 'delight', 'joy', 'pleasantness' (compare ◊**Naomi**, which is from the same Hebrew root). Its most famous bearer is the American linguist Noam Chomsky (b. 1928).

Noble ♂
Mainly U.S.: name derived from the modern English adjective (via Old

French from Latin *nobilis*). The idea behind it may have been to hint at highborn origin or to suggest qualities of character. In part there may be some influence from the surname, which arose in the Middle Ages as a descriptive nickname in the first sense.

Noël ♂, ♀
From Old French *noel*, *nael* 'Christmas', from Latin *natālis diēs (Domini)* 'birthday (of the Lord)'. The meaning is still relatively transparent, partly because the term occurs as a synonym for 'Christmas' in the refrain of well-known carols. The name is often given to children born at Christmas time.
Variants: **Noel**; **Noëlle**, **Noelle** (feminine forms).

Nola ♀
Anglicized short form of the Gaelic name ◊**Fionnuala** (see also ◊**Nuala**). It is now also used as a feminine form of ◊**Nolan**.

Nolan ♂
Transferred use of the Irish surname, Gaelic *Ó Nualláin* 'descendant of Nuallán'. The latter is an ancient Gaelic personal name, originally a byname representing a diminutive of *nuall* 'chariot-fighter', 'champion'.

Nolene ♀
Mainly Australian: name created as a feminine form of ◊**Nolan**.
Variant: **Noleen**.

Noll ♂
Pet form of ◊**Oliver**, frequent in the Middle Ages and occasionally revived in modern times. The initial consonant seems to derive from the misdivision of a vocative phrase; compare ◊**Ned** and ◊**Nan**.

Nona ♀
From the feminine form of the Latin ordinal *nonus* 'ninth', sometimes used as a given name in Victorian times for the ninth-born child in a family if it was a girl, or even for the ninth-born girl. At the present day, when few people have nine children, let alone nine daughters,

it has passed into more general, if only occasional, use.

Nonie ♀

Pet form of ◊**Ione** or of ◊**Nora**, also used to a limited extent as an independent given name.

Nora ♀

Short form of names such as *Leonora* and *Honora*. *Nora* (Gaelic *Nóra*) was at one time regarded as a peculiarly Irish name; as such, it may be a derivative of ◊**Fionnuala**, due to confusion of *l* and *r* (compare ◊**Molly** from ◊**Màire**). However, it is more probably an ancient borrowing into Gaelic of Latin *Honora*. *Variant*: **Norah**.

Norbert ♂

From an Old French name of Germanic (Frankish) origin, from *nord* 'north' + *berht* 'bright', 'famous'. The best-known bearer of this name was an 11th-century saint who founded an order of monks, known as Norbertians (also called Premonstratensians from their first home at Premontré near Laon). *Norbert* was one of several names of Germanic origin that were revived in Britain in the late 19th century, but it is now rather more common in North America than in Britain.

Noreen ♀

Anglicized form of the Irish Gaelic name **Nóirín**, a diminutive of *Nóra* (see ◊**Nora**). *Variants*: **Norene**, **Norine**.

Norma ♀

Apparently invented by Felice Romani in his libretto for Bellini's opera of this name (first performed in 1832). It is identical in form with Latin *norma* 'rule', 'standard', but there is no evidence that this word was the actual source of the name. In recent times, it has come to be taken in England and the Scottish Highlands as a feminine equivalent of ◊**Norman**. An influence on the popularity of the compound *Norma-Jean* has been the film star Marilyn

Monroe (1926–62), originally named Norma-Jean Baker.

Norman ♂

Of Germanic origin, from *nord* 'north' + *man* 'man', i.e. 'Norseman'. This name was in use in England before the Conquest, and was reinforced by its use among the Norman invaders themselves. The Normans were the inhabitants of Normandy in northern France, whose name is a reference to the Vikings who took control of the region in the 9th century. In the 11th and 12th centuries they achieved remarkable conquests, including not only Britain but also Sicily, southern Italy, and Antioch.

Norris ♂

Transferred use of the surname, which is derived from Norman French *norreis* (in which the stem represents the Germanic element *nord* 'north'), originally a local designation for someone who had migrated from the north.

Norton ♂

Transferred use of the surname, in origin a local name from any of the numerous places so called from Old English *norð* 'north' + *tūn* 'enclosure', 'settlement'.

Nuala ♀

Irish: short form of the Gaelic name ◊**Fionnuala**. It is now in general use as an independent given name.

Nye ♂

Pet form of the Welsh name ◊**Aneirin**, representing the middle syllable of that name as commonly pronounced. The name is particularly associated with the Welsh Labour statesman Aneurin Bevan (1897–1960).

Nyree ♀

New Zealand: Anglicized spelling of a Maori name usually transcribed as ◊**Ngaire**. It is relatively common in New Zealand and has been taken up to some extent in Britain due to the fame of the New Zealand-born actress Nyree Dawn Porter (b. 1940).

OBADIAH OBERON OCTAVIA OCTAVIUS O
DETTE ODILE OFRA OISÍN OLGA OLIVE OLI
VER OLIVIA OLLIE OLWEN OMAR ONORA
OONA OPAL OPALINE OPHELIA OPHRAH
OPRAH ORPAH ORALIE ORAN OREN ORSO
N ORVILLE OSBERT OSCAR OSSIAN OSWAL

Obadiah ♂

From a biblical name meaning 'servant of God' in Hebrew (compare Arabic *Abdullah*, which has the same meaning). This was the name of a prophet who gave his name to one of the shorter books of the Bible, and of two other minor biblical characters: a porter in the temple (Nehemiah 12:25), and the man who introduced King Ahab to the prophet Elijah (1 Kings 18).

Oberon ♂

Variant spelling of ◊**Auberon**.

Octavia ♀

Of Latin origin, representing a feminine form of ◊**Octavius**.

Octavius ♂

From the Roman family name, derived from Latin *octāvus* 'eighth'. The name is recorded from the 16th century and was fairly frequently given to the eighth child (or eighth son), particularly in large Victorian families. It is much less common these days, when families rarely extend to eight children, but is occasionally selected for reasons of family tradition or for some other reason without regard to its original meaning.

Odette ♀

French feminine diminutive form of the Old French male name *Oda*, which is of Germanic origin (from a word meaning 'prosperity', 'fortune', or 'riches'; see ◊**Otto**). Although the original boy's name has dropped out of use, this feminine derivative has survived.

Odile ♀

French: from the medieval Germanic name *Odila*, a derivative of *od* meaning 'prosperity', 'wealth' (see ◊**Otto**). This was the name of an 8th-century saint who founded a Benedictine convent at what is now Odilienburg in Alsace. She is the patron saint of Alsace.

Ofra ♀

Variant spelling of ◊**Ophrah**.

Oisín ♂

Gaelic name, pronounced '*oh*-sheen', from a diminutive of *os* 'stag'. See ◊**Ossian**.

Olga ♀

Russian name of Scandinavian origin, originally derived from the Old Norse adjective *heilagr* 'prosperous', 'successful'. It was imported by the Scandinavian settlers who founded the first Russian state in the 9th century. St Olga of Kiev (d. 969) was a Varangian noblewoman who was baptized at Byzantium in about 957 and set about converting her people. The name was introduced to the English-speaking world in the late 19th century, but retains a distinctively Russian flavour.

Olive ♀

From the medieval French form of the Late Latin name *Oliva*, which was borne by two obscure early saints. It is derived from the Latin name for the olive tree, and was no doubt adopted at first because of the associations of the olive tree with peaceful productivity and fruitfulness; the olive branch has been a symbol of peace since biblical times. The usual medieval English form is *Oliff(e)* See also ◊**Olivia**.

Oliver ♂

From a French name, *Olivier*, recorded as the name of one of Charlemagne's paladins (retainers), the close companion in arms of Roland in the *Chanson de Roland*. Whereas Roland is headstrong and rash, Oliver is thoughtful and cautious. Ostensibly this name derives from Late Latin *olivārius* 'olive tree' (compare ◊**Olive**), but Charlemagne's other paladins all bear solidly Germanic names, so it is more probably an altered form of a Germanic name, perhaps distantly connected with Old Norse *Óleifr* 'ancestral relic'.

Pet forms: **Ollie**, ◊**Noll**.

Olivia ♀

Latinate name, first used by Shakespeare for the rich heiress wooed by the duke in *Twelfth Night* (1599). Shakespeare may have taken it as a feminine form of ◊**Oliver** or he may have derived it from Latin *oliva* 'olive'. In the 1970s it came to be associated with the Australian pop singer and actress Olivia Newton-John (b. 1948).

Ollie ♂

Pet form of ◊**Oliver**, associated particularly with the comic film actor Oliver Hardy (1892–1957), the rotund partner of Stan Laurel.

Olwen ♀

Welsh: from *ôl* 'footprint', 'track' + *(g)wen* 'white', 'fair', 'blessed', 'holy'. A character of this name in Welsh legend had the magical property of causing flowers to spring up behind her wherever she went.

Omar ♂

Biblical name (apparently meaning 'talkative' in Hebrew) borne by a character mentioned in a genealogy (Genesis 36:11). It has been occasionally used from Puritan times down to the present day in America. More often, however, it is of Arabic origin, as in the case of the film actor and international bridge player Omar Sharif (b. 1926 in Egypt).

Onora ♀

Anglicized form of the Irish Gaelic name *Onóra*, which is from Latin ◊**Honora**. It is the source of the popular shortened form ◊**Nora**.

Oona ♀

Irish: Anglicized form of the Gaelic name *Úna* (see ◊**Una**).

Variant: **Oonagh**.

Opal ♀

One of the rarer girls' names created in the late 19th century from vocabulary words for gemstones. This English word is ultimately derived (via Latin and Greek) from an Indian language (compare Sanskrit *upala* 'precious stone').

Opaline ♀

Comparatively recent coinage: an elaboration of ◊**Opal** with the addition of *-ine*, a productive suffix of girls' names (originally a French diminutive suffix).

Ophelia ♀

The name of a character in Shakespeare's *Hamlet*, the beautiful daughter of Polonius; she loves Hamlet, and eventually goes mad and drowns herself. In spite of the ill omen of this literary association, the name has enjoyed moderate popularity since the 19th century. It was first used by the Italian pastoral poet Jacopo Sannazzaro (1458–1530), who presumably intended it as a feminine form of the Greek name *Ōphelos* 'help'. Shakespeare seems to have borrowed the name from Sannazzaro, without considering whether it was an appropriate name for a play set in medieval Denmark.

Ophrah ♀, ♂

Hebrew name meaning 'fawn'. In the Old Testament it is borne by a man (1 Chronicles 4:14), but it is now more commonly used as a girl's name.

Variants: **Ophra**, **Ofra**.

Oprah ♀

Of uncertain origin: presumably a variant of either ◊**Ophrah** or ◊**Orpah**. It was made famous by the American television personality Oprah Winfrey.

Orpah ♀

Biblical: name borne by the sister-in-law of Ruth, who unlike Ruth did not accompany their mother-in-law Naomi on her return from Moab to Bethlehem. It seems to be derived from a Hebrew word meaning 'hind', 'female deer'.

Oralie ♀

Of uncertain origin, possibly an altered form of French *Aurélie* (see ◊**Aurelia**). *Variant*: **Oralee**.

Oran ♂

Irish: Anglicized form of Gaelic *Odhrán*, originally a diminutive of *odhar* 'dun', 'sallow'. The name was borne by various early saints, notably a 6th-century abbot of Meath who accompanied Columba to Scotland and is said to have been buried alive by the latter as a foundation sacrifice.

Oren ♂

Biblical name, apparently meaning 'pine tree' in Hebrew, mentioned in a genealogy (1 Chronicles 2:25). This name is in use in the United States in a number of different spellings. In some cases it may be a variant of the Irish name ◊**Oran**. *Variants*: **Orren**, **Orin**, **Orrin**.

Orson ♂

From a Norman French nickname meaning 'bear-cub' (a diminutive of *ors* 'bear', Latin *ursus*). This was occasionally used as a given name in the Middle Ages, but in modern times it probably represents a transferred use of the surname derived from the medieval nickname. In the 20th century its most famous bearer has been the American actor and director Orson Welles (1915–85), who dropped his more prosaic first name, George, in favour of his middle name before embarking on a career in films.

Orville ♂

Though in appearance a surname of Norman baronial origin, this name was in fact invented (with the intention of evoking such associations) by the nov-

elist Fanny Burney for the hero, Lord Orville, of her novel *Evelina* (1778).

Osbert ♂

From an Old English personal name derived from *ōs* 'god' + *beorht* 'bright', 'famous'. It is not now common, but earlier in the 20th century it enjoyed a modest vogue in Britain, being borne for example by the cartoonist Osbert Lancaster and the writer Osbert Sitwell.

Oscar ♂

Old Irish name, apparently from Gaelic *os* 'deer' + *cara* 'friend'. This is borne in the Fenian sagas by a grandson of Finn mac Cumhaill (Finn MacCool). It was resuscitated by the antiquarian poet James Macpherson (1736–96), author of the Ossian poems. It is now also a characteristically Scandinavian name; it was introduced there because Napoleon, an admirer of the works of Macpherson, imposed the name on his godson Oscar Bernadotte, who became King Oscar I of Sweden in 1844 (see also ◊**Malvina**). In more recent times it has been associated particularly with the Irish writer and wit Oscar Wilde (1854–1900), and with the annual awards for achievement in the film industry made by the American Academy of Motion Picture Arts and Sciences.

Ossian ♂

Anglicized form of the Gaelic name ◊**Oisín**. In Irish mythology this name was borne most famously by the son of the hero Finn mac Cumhaill (Finn McCool), who was carried off by Niamh to Tír nan nÓg, the land of perpetual youth. It was resuscitated in 1760 by James Macpherson (1736–96) as the name of the supposed author of some ancient Gaelic poetry which Macpherson claimed to have translated. In fact he probably made it up.

Oswald ♂

From an Old English personal name, derived from *ōs* 'god' + *weald* 'rule'. This was the name of two English saints. The first was a 7th-century king of Northumbria, who was killed in battle in 641.

He was a Christian, a convert of St Aidan's, and his opponent, Penda, was a heathen, so his death was counted as a martyrdom by the Christian Church. The second St Oswald was a 10th-century bishop of Worcester and archbishop of York, of Danish parentage, who effected reforms in the English Church. The name was well established in northern England from the 15th century, particularly in parishes where the church was dedicated to St. Oswald. It enjoyed a modest revival in the 19th century as part of the vogue for pre-Conquest English names.

Otis ♂

Now mainly U.S.: transferred use of the surname, in origin a patronymic derived from the genitive case of the medieval given name *Ote* or *Ode* (of Norman, and ultimately Germanic, origin; compare ◊**Odette**). In northern England the medieval given name survived into the 19th century. It came to be used as a given name in America in honour of the Revolutionary hero James Otis (1725–83); in modern times it has been bestowed in honour of the American soul singer Otis Redding (1941–67).

Otto ♂

Originally a short form of any of the various Germanic compound personal names containing the element *od*, *ot* 'prosperity', 'wealth' (compare the corresponding Old English *ēad* in names such as ◊**Edward** and ◊**Edwin**). St Otto of Bamberg (d. 1139) was a missionary to the Pomeranians. Otto the Great (912–73) is generally regarded as the founder of the Holy Roman Empire, and the name has been borne by several members of German and Austrian royal houses.

Ottoline ♀

French diminutive of *Ottilie*, a variant of ◊**Odile**. The name acquired some currency in the English-speaking world in the early 20th century, partly due to the influence of the literary hostess Lady Ottoline Morrell (1873–1938).

Owen ♂

Very common Welsh name, of uncertain origin. It may have derived in the sub-Roman period from the Latin name *Eugenius* (see ◊**Eugene**). Alternatively, it may represent an Old Celtic name meaning 'born of Esos'. *Esos* or *Aesos* was a god with a cult in Gaul. It is also used as an Anglicized form of Scottish and Irish Gaelic ◊**Eóghan**, which is probably ultimately a cognate of the Welsh name.

PACEY PADDY PÁDRAIG PAIGE PALMER PA
MELA PANDORA PANSY PARIS PARKER PA
RRY PAT PATIENCE PATRICIA PATRICE PAT
RICK PATSY PATTY PAUL PAULA PAULETTE
PAULINE PAYTON PEADAR PEARCE PEARL
PEG PEGEEN PEGGY PELHAM PEN PENELOP

Pacey ♂

Transferred use of the surname, in origin a Norman baronial name from any of the places in northern France called *Passy* (Latin *Pacciācum*, a derivative of the Gallo-Roman personal name *Paccius*). Use as a first name may have been influenced by the rhyming ◊**Stacey**, ◊**Tracy**, ◊**Lacey**, and ◊**Macy**.

Paddy ♂

Pet form of ◊**Patrick**. The formation in -*y* is in origin characteristic of Lowland Scots, and this pet form seems to have arisen in Ulster in the 17th century. Since the 19th century it has come to function in English as a generic nickname for an Irishman.

Pádraig ♂

Irish Gaelic form of ◊**Patrick**.

Paige ♀

Used regularly in North America, but seldom elsewhere. It is evidently a transferred use of the surname *Paige*, a less common variant of *Page*, originally an occupational name given to someone who served as a page to a great lord. It is not clear why this should have been taken up in the 20th century as a girl's name. The American film actress Janis Paige (born in 1920 under the name Donna Mae Jaden) may have something to do with it. There are a number of actresses and singers with the surname *Page*, but they are unlikely to have directly influenced the choice of the given name in this spelling.
Variant: **Page**.

Palmer ♂

Transferred use of the surname, which originally denoted someone who had made a pilgrimage to the Holy Land. Such pilgrims generally brought back a palm branch as proof that they had actually made the journey.

Pamela ♀

Invented by the Elizabethan pastoral poet Sir Philip Sidney (1554–86), in whose verse it is stressed on the second syllable. There is no clue to the sources that influenced Sidney in this coinage. It was later taken up by Samuel Richardson for the name of the heroine of his novel *Pamela* (1740). In Henry Fielding's *Joseph Andrews* (1742), which started out as a parody of *Pamela*, Fielding comments that the name is 'very strange'.
Variant: **Pamella** (a modern spelling).

Pandora ♀

Name borne in classical mythology by the first woman on earth, created by the fire god Hephaistos as a scourge for men in general, in revenge for Prometheus' act of stealing fire on behalf of mankind. Pandora was given as a wife to Prometheus' foolish brother Epimetheus, along with a box which she was forbidden to open. Being endowed with great curiosity, she nevertheless did open it, and unleashed every type of hardship and suffering on the world, Hope alone being left inside the box. The name itself is ironically derived from the Greek words *pan* 'all', 'every' + *dōron* 'gift'.

Pansy ♀

19th-century coinage, from word denoting the garden flower, which is named from Old French *pensee* 'thought'. This was never particularly popular, and is seldom chosen at all now that the word *pansy* has acquired a derogatory slang sense denoting an effeminate man.

Paris ♂, ♀
As a male name in occasional use from the Middle Ages on, this was taken from Greek legend. Paris was the son of Priam who carried off Helen from Sparta to Troy and so caused the Trojan War; his name is of uncertain, probably non-Greek, derivation. Its more frequent use as a modern first name for boys and especially girls seems to represent an adoption of the name of the French capital (derived from the name of a Gaulish tribe, known in Latinized form as the *Parisii*, who once lived on the site where the city came to be built).

Parker ♂
Transferred use of the common surname, in origin an occupational name for a gamekeeper employed in a medieval game park.

Parry ♂
Transferred use of the surname, originally a Welsh patronymic meaning 'son (Welsh *ap*) of Harry'. Use as a first name may have been influenced by the recent popularity of Perry, and the rhyming ◊**Barry** and ◊**Larry**.

Pat ♂, ♀
Short form of both ◊**Patrick** and ◊**Patricia**.
Pet forms. **Patty, Pattie, Patti** (♀); ◊**Patsy**.

Patience ♀
From the vocabulary word denoting one of the Seven Christian Virtues. This name was a favourite with the Puritans, by whom it was sometimes used as a male name. It survived better than many similar names, and is now again coming back into use. The vocabulary word is derived from Latin *pati* 'to suffer', and was associated by the early Christians with those who endured persecution and misfortune without complaint or loss of faith.

Patricia ♀
From Latin *Patricia*, feminine form of

Patricius; see ◊**Patrick**.
Short forms: **Pat, Tricia, Trisha**.
Pet forms: **Patty, Pattie, Patti**.

Patrice ♂, ♀
Medieval French form of both the male and female Latin names *Patricius* (see ◊**Patrick**) and ◊**Patricia**. In modern French it is used only as a boy's name, but in the English-speaking world it is used occasionally also for girls, apparently under the influence of names such as *Bernice*.

Patrick ♂
Name of the apostle and patron saint of Ireland (c.389–461), Gaelic *Pádraig*. He was a Christian Briton and a Roman citizen, who as a young man was captured and enslaved by raiders from Ireland. He escaped and went to Gaul before returning home to Britain. In about 419 he felt a call to do missionary work in Ireland. He studied for twelve years at Auxerre, and in 432 returned to Ireland. For the rest of his life it is difficult to distinguish fact from fiction. He apparently went to the court of the high kings at Tara and made some converts there, then travelled around Ireland making further converts until about 445, when he established his archiepiscopal see at Armagh. By the time of his death almost the whole of Ireland is said to have been converted to Christianity. He is also credited with codifying the laws of Ireland. In his Latin autobiography, as well as in later tradition, his name appears as *Patricius* 'patrician' (i.e. belonging to the Roman senatorial or noble class), but this may actually represent a Latinized form of some lost Celtic (British) name.
Short form: ◊**Pat**.
Pet forms: ◊**Paddy**, ◊**Patsy**.

Patsy ♀, ♂
Pet form of ◊**Patricia** or ◊**Patrick**. It is generally a girl's name; as a boy's name it is almost completely restricted to Irish communities. Its popularity does not seem to have been seriously affected by its use in derogatory senses in the

general vocabulary, in America meaning 'a dupe' and in Australia 'a homosexual'.

Patty ♀
Pet form of ◊**Patricia**.
Variants: **Pattie**, **Patti**.

Paul ♂
From Latin *Paulus*, a Roman family name, originally a nickname meaning 'small', used in the post-classical period as a given name. Pre-eminently this is the name of the saint who is generally regarded, with St Peter, as co-founder of the Christian Church. Born in Tarsus, and originally named *Saul*, he was both a Roman citizen and a Jew, and at first found employment as a minor official persecuting Christians. He was converted to Christianity by a vision of Christ while on the road to Damascus, and thereafter undertook extensive missionary journeys, converting people, especially Gentiles, to Christianity all over the eastern Mediterranean. His preaching aroused considerable official hostility, and eventually he was beheaded at Rome in about AD 65. He is the author of the fourteen epistles to churches and individuals which form part of the New Testament.

Paula ♀
Latin feminine form of ◊**Paul**, borne by various minor early saints and martyrs.

Paulette ♀
French diminutive feminine form of ◊**Paul**. It is widely used in the English-speaking world, where, however, it is a more recent importation than ◊**Pauline**.

Pauline ♀
French form of the Latin name *Paulīna* (feminine of *Paulīnus*, a derivative of the family name *Paulus* 'small') that has long been common also in the English-speaking world, where it is now established as the most common feminine equivalent of ◊**Paul**.

Payton ♂
Transferred use of the surname, in origin a local name from *Peyton* in Sussex, probably named in Old English as 'Pæga's settlement'. *Payton Place* was the collective name of a novel by Mazo de la Roche, which was the basis for an American television soap opera in the 1950s.
Variant: **Peyton**.

Peadar ♂
Irish Gaelic form of ◊**Peter**.

Pearce ♂
Variant of ◊**Pierce**. It normally represents a transferred use of the English surname derived from the given name in the Middle Ages. It has been a popular name among Irish nationalists since the rising of 1916, led by the writer and educationist Patrick Henry Pearce; he was executed by the British and is regarded as a martyr to the nationalist cause.
Irish Gaelic forms: **Perais**, **Piaras**.

Pearl ♀
One of the group of names coined in the 19th century from words for precious and semi-precious stones. It has a longer history as a Jewish name, representing an Anglicized form of Yiddish *Perle* (see also ◊**Peninnah**).

Peg ♀
Pet form of ◊**Margaret**, a variant of ◊**Meg**. The reason for the alternation of *M*- and *P*-, which occurs also in *Molly/Polly*, is not known; it has been ascribed to Celtic influence, but this particular alternation does not correspond to any of the usual mutational patterns in Celtic languages.

Pegeen ♀
Anglicized form of Irish Gaelic *Peigín*, a diminutive of *Peig*, the Gaelic form of ◊**Peg**.

Peggy ♀
Pet form of ◊**Margaret**; see ◊**Peg**.
Variants: **Peggie**, **Peggi**.

Pelham ♂
Transferred use of the surname, in origin a local name from a place in Hertfordshire, so called from the Old English personal name *Pēo(t)la* + *hām* 'homestead'. From 1715 a family bearing

this surname held the dukedom of Newcastle.

Pen ♀

Short form of ◊**Penelope**, and sometimes also of ◊**Peninnah**.

Penelope ♀

Name borne in Greek mythology by the wife of Odysseus who sat patiently awaiting his return for twenty years, meanwhile, as a supposed widow, fending off by persuasion and guile a pressing horde of suitors for her hand in marriage. Her name would seem to derive from Greek *pēnelops* 'duck', and play is made with this word in the *Odyssey*. However, this may obscure a more complex origin, now no longer recoverable.
Short form: **Pen**.
Pet form: **Penny**.

Peninnah ♀

Jewish traditional name, meaning 'coral' in Hebrew. It was borne in the Bible by the co-wife (with Hannah) of Elkanah, the father of Samuel. In modern Hebrew it means 'pearl' and has become a popular name, often being substituted for Yiddish *Perle* and English ◊**Pearl**.
Variants: **Peninna**, **Penina**.

Penn ♂

Mainly U.S.: transferred use of the surname, for the most part originally a local name from any of various places named with the British element *pen* 'hill', which was adopted into Old English. In other cases it may have referred to someone who lived near a sheep pen (Old English *penn*). The given name is sometimes chosen in honour of the founder of Pennsylvania, the Quaker William Penn (1644–1718), who was born in London into a family of Gloucestershire origin.

Penny ♀

Pet form of ◊**Penelope**, now sometimes also used as an independent given name.

Perce ♂

Variant of ◊**Pierce** or informal short form of ◊**Percy**.

Percival ♂

From Old French versions of the Arthurian legend, where the name is spelled *Perceval*. According to Chrétien de Troyes (12th century) and Wolfram von Eschenbach (*c.* 1170–1220), Perceval (German *Parzifal*) was the perfectly pure and innocent knight who alone could succeed in the quest for the Holy Grail (a cup or bowl with supernatural powers, which in medieval legend was identified with the chalice that had received Christ's blood at the Crucifixion). Later versions of the Grail legend assign this role to Sir Galahad. The name *Perceval* probably represents a drastic remodelling of the Celtic name *Peredur*, as if from Old French *perce(r)* 'pierce' + *val* 'valley'. This may well have been influenced by ◊**Percy**, which was similarly analysed as a compound of *perce(r)* 'pierce' + *haie* 'hedge'.

Percy ♂

Originally a transferred use of a famous surname, but long established as a given name. In medieval times it was often used as a pet form of ◊**Piers**, and now often as a pet form of ◊**Percival**. The surname originated as a Norman baronial name, borne by a family who had held a fief in Normandy called *Perci* (from Late Latin *Persiācum*, composed of the Gallo-Roman personal name *Persius* and the local suffix *-ācum*). As a given name it was taken up in the early 18th century in the Seymour family, which had intermarried with the Percy family. The poet Percy Bysshe Shelley (1792–1822) was also distantly connected with this family, and it was partly due to his influence that the given name became more widespread. It is at present out of fashion.

Perdita ♀

A Shakespearian coinage, borne by a character in *The Winter's Tale* (1610). The feminine form of Latin *perditus* 'lost', it has a clear reference to the events of the play, and this is explicitly commented on in the text. The name is now more closely associated in some

people's minds with a (canine) character in Dodie Smith's *One Hundred and One Dalmatians* (1956), made into a film by Walt Disney.
Pet form: **Perdie**.

Peregrine ♂

From Latin *Peregrīnus* 'foreigner', 'stranger', a name borne by various early Christian saints, perhaps referring to the belief that men and women are merely sojourners upon the earth, their true home being in heaven. In modern times the name is rare, borne mostly by Roman Catholics, who choose it in honour of those saints.

Perry ♂

Pet form of ◊**Peregrine**, or transferred use of the surname *Perry*, in origin a local name for someone who lived by a pear tree (Old English *pirige*). In modern times, it has been borne by the American singer Perry Como (b. 1912), whose name was originally Nick Perido.

Perse ♂

Variant of ◊**Pierce**.

Persis ♀

Of New Testament origin, from Greek *Persis*, originally an ethnic name meaning 'Persian woman'. This name is borne by a woman mentioned fleetingly by St Paul—'the beloved Persis, which laboured much in the Lord' (Romans 16:12)—and was taken up from there at the time of the Reformation.

Pet ♀

Short form of ◊**Petula**, in part influenced by the common affectionate term of address 'pet', derived from the vocabulary word for a tame animal kept for companionship.

Peta ♀

Modern feminine form of ◊**Peter**, not used before the 1930s.

Petal ♀

From the vocabulary word for the part of a flower, also used as a term of endearment.

Pete ♂

Short form of ◊**Peter**.

Peter ♂

English form of the name of the best-known of all Christ's apostles, traditionally regarded as the founder of the Christian Church. The name derives, via Latin, from Greek *petros* 'stone', 'rock'. This is used as a translation of the Aramaic byname *Cephas*, given to the apostle Simon son of Jona, to distinguish him from another of the same name (Simon Zelotes). 'When Jesus beheld him, he said, Thou art Simon the son of Jona: thou shalt be called Cephas, which is by interpretation, A stone' (John 1:42). According to Matthew 16:17–18, Christ says more explicitly, 'Blessed art thou, Simon Bar-jona . . . thou art Peter, and upon this rock I will build my church'.
Short form: **Pete**.

Petra ♀

Feminine form of ◊**Peter**, representing a hypothetical Latin name *Petra*; *petra* is in fact the regular Late Latin word for 'stone' (Greek *petra*), of which *petrus* is a byform.

Petronel ♀

From Latin *Petronilla*, originally a feminine diminutive of the Roman family name *Petrōnius* (of uncertain derivation). The name *Petronilla* was borne by a 1st-century martyr, and early in the Christian era came to be connected with ◊**Peter**, so that in many legends surrounding her she is described as a companion or even the daughter of St Peter.

Petula ♀

Of uncertain origin, not used before the 20th century. It is possibly a Christian coinage intended to mean 'supplicant', 'postulant', from Late Latin *petulāre* 'to ask', or there may be some connection with the flower name *petunia*. Alternatively, it may be an elaboration of the vocabulary word *pet* used as a term of endearment, with the suffix *-ula* abstracted from names such as *Ursula*.
Short form: **Pet**.

Peyton ♂
Transferred use of the surname, a variant of ◊**Payton**.

Phelim ♂
See ◊**Felim**.

Phil ♂, ♀
Short form of ◊**Philip**, ◊**Phyllis**, or of any of the various other names (male and female) beginning with the syllable *Phil-*.

Philip ♂
From the Greek name *Philippos*, meaning 'lover of horses', from *philein* 'to love' + *hippos* 'horse'. This was popular in the classical period and since. It was the name of the father of Alexander the Great. It was also the name of one of Christ's apostles, of a deacon ordained by the apostles after the death of Christ, and of several other early saints.
Short forms: **Phil**, **Pip**.

Philippa ♀
Latin feminine form of ◊**Philip**. In England during the Middle Ages the vernacular name *Philip* was borne by women as well as men, but female bearers were distinguished in Latin records by this form. It was not, however, used as a regular given name until the 19th century.

Phillida ♀
Variant of ◊**Phyllis**, derived from the genitive case (Greek *Phyllidos*, Latin *Phyllidis*) with the addition of the Latin feminine ending *-a*.
Variant: **Phyllida**.

Phillip ♂
Variant spelling of ◊**Philip**, in part a reflection of the surname, which is usually spelled *Phillips*.

Philomena ♀
From the name of an obscure saint (probably of the 3rd century) with a local cult in Italy. In 1527 the bones of a young woman were discovered under the church altar at San Severino near Ancona, together with a Latin inscription declaring them to be the body of St Filomena. Her name seems to be a feminine form of Latin *Philomenus*, Greek *Philomenēs*, from *philein* 'to love' + *menos* 'strength'. The name became popular in the 19th century, as a result of the supposed discovery in 1802 of the relics of another St Philomena in the catacombs at Rome. All the excitement, however, resulted from the misinterpretation of the Latin inscription *Filumena pax tecum* 'peace be with you, beloved' (from Greek *philoumena* 'beloved').

Phineas ♂
Biblical name, borne by two minor characters. One was a grandson of Aaron, who preserved the purity of the race of Israel and deflected God's wrath by killing an Israelite who had taken a Midianite woman to wife (Numbers 25:6–15); the other, a son of the priest Eli, was killed in combat with the Philistines over the Ark of the Covenant (1 Samuel 1:3; 4:6–11). The name is spelled *Phinehas* in the Authorized Version, and has been taken to mean 'serpent's mouth' (i.e. 'oracle') in Hebrew, but this is an incorrect popular etymology. It is in fact derived from the Egyptian name *Panḥsj*, originally a byname meaning 'the Nubian' and used as a personal name in Ancient Egypt. *Phineas* was popular among the Puritans in the 17th century, and has been occasionally used since, especially in America.

Phoebe ♀
Pronounced '*fee*-bee': Latin form of the name of a Greek deity, *Phoibē* (from *phoibos* 'bright'), partly identified with Artemis, goddess of the moon and of hunting, sister of the sun god Apollo, who was also known as *Phoibos* (Latin *Phoebus*).

Phoenix ♂
Recent coinage as a given name, from the name of the mythological bird (Latin *phoenix*, Greek *phoinix*), which is said to live for an immensely long period and then, after being dead and consumed by

fire, to rise again from the ashes of its corpse. The town that became the state capital of Arizona was so named because traces of ancient indigenous dwellings were seen in the area, and the new settlement was thus taken to represent a fresh cycle of habitation on the site.

Phyllicia ♀
Elaborated form of ◊Phyllis, influenced by ◊Felicia.
Variant: **Phylicia**.

Phyllida ♀
Variant spelling of ◊Phillida.

Phyllis ♀
Name of a minor character in Greek mythology who killed herself for love and was transformed into an almond tree; the Greek word *phyllis* means 'foliage', so clearly her name doomed her from the start.

Piaras ♂
Irish Gaelic name, derived in the Middle Ages from Anglo-Norman ◊Piers. Piaras Feiritéar (1600–53) was a Kerry chieftain and poet. In the 20th century *Piaras* has been used as a Gaelic form of ◊Pearce.

Pierce ♀
English and Irish: variant of ◊Piers, in use in Ireland from the time of the Norman Conquest up to the present day. In many cases it may represent a transferred use of the English surname derived from the given name in the Middle Ages.

Piers ♂
Regular medieval vernacular form of ◊Peter (from the Old French nominative case, as against the oblique *Pier*, modern *Pierre*). In the form *Pierce* it survived into the 18th century, although in part this may be a transferred use of the surname derived from the medieval given name. *Piers* was revived in the mid-20th century, perhaps partly under the influence of William Langland's great rambling medieval poem *Piers Plowman* (1367–86), in which the character of Piers symbolizes the virtues of hard work, honesty, and fairness.

Pip ♂
Contracted short form of ◊Philip, best known as the name of the main character in Charles Dickens's *Great Expectations* (1861), whose full name was Philip Pirrip.

Pippa ♀
Contracted pet form of ◊Philippa, now quite commonly used as an independent given name. It was popularized in the 19th century by Browning's narrative poem *Pippa Passes* (1841), in which the heroine is a child worker in an Italian silk mill, whose innocent admiration of 'great' people is ironically juxtaposed with their sordid lives. The name is presumably supposed to be Italian, but is not in fact used in Italy.

Pitt ♂
Transferred use of the surname, which was originally given to someone who lived near to a hollow in the ground or a claypit. Use as a given name probably originated in honour of the British statesman William Pitt the Younger (1759–1806), who did much to undermine French power in Europe.

Polly ♀
Variant of ◊Molly, now established as an independent given name. The reason for the interchange of *M-* and *P-* is not clear; compare ◊Peg.
Short form: **Poll**.

Poppy ♀
From the word denoting the flower, Old English *popæg* (from Latin *papāver*). It has been used as a given name since the latter years of the 19th century, and reached a peak of popularity in the 1920s.

Porter ♂
Transferred use of the surname, in origin an occupational name, either for someone who worked as a carrier of goods (Old French *porteour*, from a derivative of Latin *portāre* 'to carry') or else for a gatekeeper (Old French *portier*, from a derivative of Latin *porta* 'door', 'gate').

Portia ♀

This is the name of two characters in the works of Shakespeare. The most celebrated of them is an heiress in *The Merchant of Venice* who, disguised as a man, shows herself to be a brilliant advocate and delivers a stirring speech on the quality of mercy. It is also the name of the wife of Brutus in *Julius Caesar*. The historical Brutus's wife was called *Porcia*, feminine form of the Roman family name *Porcius*, which is apparently a derivative of Latin *porcus* 'pig'.
Variant: **Porsha**.

Posy ♀

Pet form (originally a nursery version) of ◊**Josephine**. It has also been associated with the vocabulary word *posy* 'bunch of flowers' (originally a collection of verses, from *poesy* 'poetry'). It is occasionally used as an independent given name, fitting into the series of names associated with flowers that arose in the 19th century.

Potter ♂

Transferred use of the surname, in origin an occupational name for someone who made and sold pots (an agent derivative of *pot*, Old English *pott*). In the Middle Ages the term denoted workers in metal (who made pots and pans) as well as those using earthenware and clay.

Preston ♂

Transferred use of the surname, in origin a local name from any of the numerous places in England named with Old English *prēost* 'priest' + *tūn* 'enclosure', 'settlement'.

Primrose ♀

One of the several girls' names taken from words for flowers in the late 19th century. The word is from Latin *prima rosa* 'first rose', although it does not in fact have any connection with the rose family.

Prince ♂

Originally a nickname from the royal title, Old French *prince* (Latin *princeps*).

This word was introduced to Britain by the Normans. In the United States *Prince* is common as a Black name.

Priscilla ♀

Of New Testament origin: from a post-classical Latin personal name, a feminine diminutive of the Roman family name *Priscus* 'ancient'. *Priscilla* was the name of a woman with whom St Paul stayed at Corinth (Acts 18:3), referred to elsewhere as *Prisca*. The name was used among the Puritans in the later 16th century and again enjoyed a vogue in the 19th century.
Pet form: **Prissy**.

Pru ♀

Short form of ◊**Prudence** and ◊**Prunella**.
Variant: **Prue**.

Proinnsias ♂

Irish Gaelic form of ◊**Francis**.

Prudence ♀

Originally a medieval form of the Latin name *Prūdentia*, a feminine form of *Prūdentius*, from *prūdens* 'provident'. The Blessed Prudentia was a 15th-century abbess who founded a new convent at Como in Italy. Later, among the Puritans in 17th-century England, *Prudence* was associated with the vocabulary word for the quality name.
Short forms: **Prue**, **Pru**.

Prunella ♀

Latinate name, probably one of the names coined in the 19th century from vocabulary words for plants and flowers, in this case from a diminutive derived from Late Latin *pruna* 'plum'. The name has enjoyed a minor vogue in the latter part of the 20th century, being borne by two well-known English actresses, Prunella Scales and Prunella Gee.
Short forms: **Prue**, **Pru**.

Pryderi ♂

Welsh, pronounced 'prid-*er*-ee': traditional name, meaning 'caring for' (later 'anxiety'). It is borne in the *Mabinogi* by Pryderi, son of Pwyll, who makes several appearances in the narrative.

Psyche ♀

Pronounced 'sigh-kee'; from the Greek word *psykhē*, meaning both 'butterfly' and 'soul' or 'spirit'. Use as a given name may derive in part from the nymph in classical mythology beloved by Cupid; in other cases it has been chosen by parents interested in exploring the potential of the human spirit.

QUEENIE QUENTIN QUINCY QUINN QUIN
TIN QUINTON QUINTUS QUEENIE QUENT
IN QUINCY QUINN QUINTIN QUINTON Q
UINTUS QUEENIE QUENTIN QUINCY QUI
NN QUINTIN QUINTON QUINTUS QUEEN
IE QUENTIN QUINCY QUINN QUINTIN QU

Queenie ♀

Pet form from the affectionate nickname *Queen*, with the addition of the
diminutive suffix *-ie*. In the Victorian
era it was sometimes used as an allusive
pet form for ◊**Victoria**. The vocabulary
word *queen* goes back to Old English
cwēn, akin to *cwene* 'woman', with a
fanciful respelling.

Quentin ♂

From the Old French form of the Latin
name *Quintīnus*, a derivative of the
given name ◊**Quintus**. The name was
borne by a 3rd-century saint who
worked as a missionary in Gaul.
Variants: **Quintin**, **Quinton**.

Quincy ♂

Mainly U.S.: transferred use of the
English surname, in origin a Norman
baronial name borne by a family that
held lands at *Cuinchy* in Pas-de-Calais,
Normandy. The place name is derived
from the Gallo-Roman personal name
◊**Quintus**. This was the surname of a
prominent New England family in the
colonial era. Josiah Quincy (1744–75)
was a lawyer and Revolutionary patriot,
a close friend of John Adams (1735–1826)
who became second president of the
United States (1797–1801). The latter's
son, John Quincy Adams (1767–1848),
also served as president (1825–9). He
may have received his middle name in
honour of his father's friend Josiah
Quincy, or it may have been taken from
the township of Quincy, Massachusetts,
where he was born and where the Adams
family had their seat.
Variant: **Quincey**.

Quinn ♂

Transferred use of the Irish surname,
Gaelic *Ó Cuinn* 'descendant of Conn'.
The latter is from a word meaning
'leader' or 'chief'. It may also sometimes
be used as a short form of ◊**Quincy** or
◊**Quintin**.

Quintin ♂

Variant of ◊**Quentin**.

Quinton ♂

Variant of ◊**Quentin**, influenced by the
surname so spelled. The surname is a
local name from any of several places
named with Old English *cwēn* 'queen' +
tūn 'enclosure', 'settlement'.

Quintus ♂

An old Roman given name meaning
'fifth'. It has been used in the English-
speaking world, mainly in the 19th
century, for the fifth-born son or fifth-
born child in a family (compare ◊**Sextus**,
◊**Septimus**, ◊**Octavius**, and ◊**Nona**).

RABBIE RACHAEL RACHEL RACHELLE RAE R
AELENE RAFE RAFFERTY RAGHNALL RAINB
OW RAINE RALPH RAMSAY RAN RANALD
RANDA RANDALL RANDOLF RANDY RAN
UL RAQUEL RASTUS RAVEN RAVENNA RA
Y RAYMOND RAYNER READ REANNA REA

Rabbie ♂

Scottish: pet form of ◊**Robert**, from the short form *Rab*, *Rob*. It is now often associated with the poet Robert Burns (1759–96).

Rachael ♀

Variant of ◊**Rachel**, influenced by ◊**Michael**.

Rachel ♀

Biblical name (meaning 'ewe' in Hebrew), borne by the beloved wife of Jacob and mother (after long barrenness) of Joseph (Genesis 28–35) and of Benjamin, at whose birth she died. In the Middle Ages and later this was regarded as a characteristically Jewish name, but it is now also widely used among Gentiles.

Rachelle ♀

Elaborated form of ◊**Rachel**, as if from French, but actually a recent coinage in English.

Rae ♀

Mainly Australian: probably originally a short form of ◊**Rachel**, but now generally taken as a feminine form of ◊**Ray** or ◊**Raymond**, or simply a derivative of *ray* meaning 'sunbeam'. In some cases it may represent a transferred use of the Scottish surname *Rae*, originally either a short form of *MacRae* (from a Gaelic personal name meaning 'son of grace') or a nickname from the roebuck. It is often used in combinations such as *Rae Ellen* and *Mary Rae*.

Raelene ♀

Australian: fanciful coinage of recent origin, from ◊**Rae** + the productive feminine suffix *-lene*.

Rafe ♂

Spelling representation of the traditional pronunciation of the name ◊**Ralph**, a pronunciation now largely restricted to the upper classes in England.

Rafferty ♂, ♀

Transferred use of the Irish surname. The Gaelic form of this is *Ó Rabhartaigh* or *Ó Robhartaigh*, meaning 'descendant of *Robhartach*'. *Robhartach* is an old Irish personal name meaning 'wielder of prosperity'. The surname has recently come to be used fairly regularly in the United States as a given name for boys and less frequently also for girls.

Raghnall ♂

Irish Gaelic borrowing of the Old Norse name *Rögnvaldr*, derived from *regin* 'advice', 'decision' + *valdr* 'ruler'. The usual Anglicized form is ◊**Ranald**.

Rainbow ♀

From the vocabulary word (from Old English *regn* 'rain' + *boga* 'bow', 'arch'). This is one of the names taken from the world of nature in the 1960s under the influence of the 'flower-power' movement. It has not proved enduringly popular.

Raine ♀

Of modern origin and uncertain derivation. It is possibly a respelling of the French vocabulary word *reine* 'queen' (compare ◊**Regina**), or a transferred use of the surname *Raine* or *Rayne*. The surname is derived from a medieval given name, a short form of various Germanic compound names derived from *ra(g)in* 'advice', 'decision'. In modern times, this given name is borne by the Countess Spencer, daughter of the romantic novelist Barbara Cartland (1901–2000) and stepmother of the Princess of Wales (1961–97).

Ralph ♂

From a Norman French name, *Raulf*, a contracted form of the Germanic personal name *Radulf*, derived from *rād* 'counsel' + *wulf* 'wolf'. The spelling with *-ph* is due to classical influence in the 18th century.

Variants: **Ralf**, ◊**Rafe**.

Ramsay ♂

Transferred use of the Scottish surname, in origin a local name imported to Scotland from *Ramsey* in Huntingdonshire (so called from Old English *hramsa* 'wild garlic' + *ēg* 'island'). In the 12th century David, brother of King Alexander I of Scotland, was brought up at the English court, and acquired the earldoms of Huntingdon and Northampton. When he succeeded his brother as king, he took many of his retainers and associates with him to Scotland, and some of them took their surnames with them from places in eastern England. This explains why some famous Scottish surnames, such as *Ramsay*, *Lindsay*, *Graham*, etc., are derived from place names in that part of England. Some of these surnames have in turn gone on to be used as given names.

Variant: **Ramsey**.

Ran ♂

Short form of the various names beginning with this syllable, as, for example, ◊**Randolf**, ◊**Ranald**, and ◊**Ranulf**.

Ranald ♂

Scottish: Anglicized form of the Gaelic name ◊**Raghnall**.

Randa ♀

Modern coinage, probably a shortened form of ◊**Miranda**. See also ◊**Randy**.

Randall ♂

From a medieval vernacular form of ◊**Randolf**. This was in common use as a given name up to the 17th century and gave rise to a surname. In modern use the given name is often a transferred use of this surname.

Variants: **Randal**, **Randel(l)**, **Randle**.

Randolf ♂

From a Norman given name, Old Norse *Rannulfr*, derived from *rand* 'rim', 'shield' (or *hrafn* 'raven') + *úlfr* 'wolf'.

Variant: **Randolph**.

Randy ♂, ♀

Mainly North American and Australian: as a boy's name this originated as a pet form of ◊**Randall**, ◊**Randolf**, or ◊**Andrew**. As a girl's name it may have originated either as a transferred use of the boy's name or else as a pet form of ◊**Miranda** (compare ◊**Randa**). It is now fairly commonly used as an independent name, mainly by men, in spite of the unfortunate connotations of the slang term *randy* 'lustful'.

Variants: **Randie**, **Randi** (♀).

Ranulf ♂

Scottish and northern English: from an Old Norse personal name, *Reginulfr*, derived from *regin* 'advice', 'decision' + *úlfr* 'wolf'. This was introduced into Scotland and northern England by Scandinavian settlers in the early Middle Ages.

Raquel ♀

Spanish form of ◊**Rachel**, brought to public attention by the fame and good looks of the film actress Raquel Welch (b. 1940 as Raquel Tejada, in Chicago). Her father was Bolivian, her mother of English stock.

Variant: **Raquelle**.

Rastus ♂

Of New Testament origin, where it is a shortened form of the Latin name *Erastus* (Greek *Erastos*, from *erān* 'to love'). This was the name of the treasurer of Corinth converted to Christianity by St Paul (Romans 16:23). In the early 20th century *Rastus* came to be regarded as a typically Black name, for reasons which are unclear.

Raven ♂, ♀

From the word denoting the bird (Old English *hræfn*), which has strikingly black plumage. It is in occasional use as a given name for both boys (incidentally paralleling the Old Norse byname *Hrafn*) and girls (falling into a set with other given names derived from birds, such as ◊**Dove** and ◊**Teal**).

Ravenna ♀

Apparently from the name of the city in north-east Italy (compare ◊**Siena** and ◊**Venetia** for other names derived from the names of Italian cities). The place name is probably of Etruscan origin. Use as a given name may in part also represent an elaborated or more clearly feminine form of ◊**Raven**.

Ray ♂

Short form of ◊**Raymond**, now often used as an independent given name. In some instances it may represent a transferred use of the surname *Ray*, which for the most part originated as a nickname, from Old French *rei*, *roi* 'king' (cf. ◊**Roy** and ◊**Leroy**).

Raymond ♂

From an Old French name, *Raimund*, of Germanic origin, from *ragin* 'advice', 'decision' + *mund* 'protector'. This was adopted by the Normans and introduced by them into England. Subsequently it dropped out of use, but was revived in the middle of the 19th century, together with several other given names of Old English and Norman origin.
Short form: ◊**Ray**.

Rayner ♂

From a Norman personal name of Old French origin (*Rainer*), derived from a Germanic name composed of the elements *ragin* 'advice', 'decision' + *heri*, *hari* 'army'. This survived in use as an English given name at least until the end of the 15th century. In modern use it may also be a transferred use of the surname.

Read ♂

Transferred use of the English surname, which for the most part originated as a nickname for someone with red hair or a ruddy complexion (from Old English *rēad* 'red'; cf. ◊**Reid**). In other cases, it may have arisen as a local name, from Old English *hrēod* 'reeds' or *rēod* 'cleared land'.

Reanna ♀

Modern coinage, apparently an altered form of the Welsh name ◊**Rhiannon** influenced by the spelling of ◊**Deanna**.
Variant: **Reanne**.

Rearden ♂

Variant of ◊**Riordan**.

Reba ♀

Modern coinage, apparently derived from the first and last syllables of ◊**Rebecca**.

Rebecca ♀

Biblical, from the Latin form of the Hebrew name *Rebekah*, borne by the wife of Isaac, who was the mother of Esau and Jacob (Genesis 24–27). The Hebrew root occurs in the Bible only in the vocabulary word *marbek* 'cattle stall', and its connection with the name is doubtful. In any case, Rebecca was Aramean, and the name probably has a source in Aramaic. It has always been common as a Jewish name; in England and elsewhere it began to be used also by Christians at the time of the Reformation, when Old Testament names became popular. It was very common among the Puritans in the 17th century, and has enjoyed a tremendous vogue in England in the latter part of the 20th century, among people of many different creeds.
Short forms: **Becca**, **Beck**.
Pet form: **Becky**.

Redmond ♂

Irish: apparently an Anglicized form of the Gaelic name *Réamann*, itself a form of ◊**Raymond**. An alternative explanation derives it from an Old English personal name derived from *ræd* 'counsel' + *mund* 'protector'.

Reenie ♀

Respelling of ◊**Renée**, representing an Anglicized pronunciation of the name. It may also occasionally be a pet form of various names ending in the syllable -*reen*, such as ◊**Doreen** and ◊**Maureen**.

Rees ♂

Anglicized spelling of the Welsh name ◊**Rhys**, in some cases representing a transferred use of the surname so spelled, which is derived from the Welsh given name.
Variants: **Rees**, **Reece**.

Reg ♂

Short form of ◊**Reginald**, often preferred by bearers of that name for use in almost all situations, but rarely actually bestowed as a baptismal name.

Regan ♀

Apparently of Shakespearian origin. This is the name of one of the three daughters in *King Lear* (1605), a most unattractive character, who flatters her father into giving her half his kingdom and then turns him out into a raging storm at night. It is not known where Shakespeare got the name; he presumably believed it to be of Celtic origin. It can be identified with the Irish Gaelic word *ríogan* 'queen' (pronounced '*ree-gan*'). Modern use has been reinforced by the Irish surname *Re(a)gan* (Gaelic Ó *Riagáin*).

Reggie ♂

Pet form of ◊**Reg**, common in the 19th and early 20th centuries, but now less so.

Regina ♀

From the Latin vocabulary word meaning 'queen'. It was occasionally used as a given name among the early Christians; a St Regina, probably of the 3rd century, was venerated as a virgin martyr at Autun from an early date. In modern use it is normally borne by Roman Catholics in allusion to the epithet *Regina Coeli* 'Queen of Heaven', a cult title of the Virgin Mary since the 8th century.

Reginald ♂

Of Norman origin, derived from *Regi-naldus*, a Latinized form of ◊**Reynold** influenced by Latin *regina* 'queen'. The full form is now regarded as very formal, and bearers generally shorten it to ◊**Reg** in ordinary usage.

Reid ♂

Transferred use of Scottish and Northern English surname, in origin as a nickname for someone with red hair or a ruddy complexion (from Old English *read* 'red'; cf. ◊**Read**).

Reine ♀

French vernacular form of Latin *regina* 'queen', probably arising for the most part as an affectionate nickname, but also perhaps with reference to the Virgin Mary, one of whose titles is 'Queen of Heaven'.

Reith ♂

Transferred use of the Scottish surname, pronounced '*reeth*'. This is of uncertain origin: it may be a reduced form of *McReath*, from Gaelic *Mac Raith*, or a patronymic from the old personal name *Rath* meaning 'grace' or 'prosperity'. Use as a given name has probably been influenced by the more common ◊**Reid**; also by Lord Reith (1889–1971), the austere first director-general of the BBC (1927–38).

Rena ♀

Of recent origin, either an altered form of ◊**Renée**, or else a variant spelling of ◊**Rina**.

Renée ♀

French: from the Late Latin name *Renata*, feminine of *Renatus* 'reborn', used by early Christians as a baptismal name celebrating spiritual rebirth in Christ. The name is also used in the English-speaking world, often without the accent and in a highly Anglicized pronunciation (cf. ◊**Reenie**).

Reuben ♂

Biblical name (said to mean 'behold, a son' in Hebrew), borne by one of the twelve sons of Jacob, and so the name of one of the twelve tribes of Israel. Genesis

29:32 explains it as follows: 'and Leah conceived, and bare a son, and she called his name Reuben: for she said, Surely the Lord hath looked upon my affliction: now therefore my husband will love me'. In Genesis 30:14–15, Reuben is depicted as a devoted son to his mother, but he incurred his father's wrath for seducing his concubine Bilhah and on his deathbed Jacob, rather than blessing him, cursed Reuben because of this incident (Genesis 49:4). Despite this, the name has enjoyed steady popularity as a Jewish name. Among Christians (chiefly Nonconformists) it came into use after the Reformation and survived into the 20th century, but is now out of fashion, at least in England.

Rex ♂
From the Latin vocabulary word meaning 'king'. This was not used as a personal name in Latin of the classical or Christian periods, and its adoption as a given name seems to have been a 19th-century innovation. Its popularity was increased by the fame of the British actor Rex Harrison (1908–90), who was christened Reginald Carey.

Rexanne ♀
Altered form of ◊**Roxane** or feminine equivalent of ◊**Rex**.

Reynard ♂
From an Old French name of Germanic (Frankish) origin, derived from *ragin* 'advice', 'decision' + *hard* 'hardy', 'brave', 'strong'. In French, *renard* has become the generic term for a fox, as a result of the popularity of medieval beast tales featuring *Re(y)nard le goupil* 'Reynard the Fox'. The name was adopted by the Normans and introduced by them to Britain.

Reynold ♂
From an Old French name, *Reinald*, *Reynaud*, of Germanic (Frankish) origin, derived from *ragin* 'advice', 'decision' + *wald* 'ruler'. This was adopted by the Normans and introduced by them into England. In modern use, the given name sometimes represents a transferred use

of the surname derived from the Norman personal name.
Variant: ◊**Reginald**. See also ◊**Ronald**.

Rhea ♀
The name borne, according to Roman tradition, by the mother (Rhea Silvia) of Romulus and Remus, who grew up to be the founders of the city of Rome. It was also a title of the goddess Cybele, introduced to Rome from Phrygia. Its meaning is unknown. It is comparatively rarely used as a given name in the modern world.

Rheanna ♀
Altered form of the Welsh name ◊**Rhiannon**, influenced by the spelling of ◊**Deanna**.

Rhett ♂
Transferred use of a surname well established in South Carolina, an Anglicization of the Dutch surname *de Raedt* (from Middle Dutch *raet* 'advice'). This was brought to North America in 1694 by William Rhett (1666–1723). Robert Barnwell Rhett (1800–76) was a South Carolina congressman and senator, a noted secessionist. The name was used by Margaret Mitchell in *Gone with the Wind* (1936) for the character of the black sheep and charmer Rhett Butler. Like some of the other unusual names in that novel, it has attained a modest currency.

Rhetta ♀
Name coined as a feminine form of ◊**Rhett**.

Rhiannon ♀
Welsh: name borne in Celtic mythology by a minor deity associated with the moon, and in the *Mabinogi* by a daughter of Hyfeidd the Old. It is probably derived from the Old Celtic title *Rigantona* 'great queen'; it was not used as a given name before the 20th century.

Rhoda ♀
From the post-classical Greek name *Rhoda*, derived either from *rhodon* 'rose', or as an ethnic name meaning 'woman from Rhodes' (Greek *Rhodos*).

In the New Testament Rhoda was a servant in the house of Mary the mother of John, where Peter went after his release from prison by an angel (Acts 12:13). In the Scottish Highlands *Rhoda* is used as a feminine form of ◊**Roderick**.

Rhodri ♂

Welsh: from an Old Welsh personal name derived from *rhod* 'wheel' + *rhi* 'ruler', borne by a 9th-century Welsh king.
Variant: **Rhodrhi**.

Rhona ♀

Of uncertain derivation, apparently originating in Scotland sometime around 1870. The spelling *Rona* is also found, and it is probable that the name was devised as a feminine form of ◊**Ronald**. It has also been suggested that it may be associated with the Hebridean island name *Rona* (cf. ◊**Ailsa**, ◊**Iona**, ◊**Isla**). In either case the spelling would then have been altered by association with ◊**Rhoda**.

Rhonda ♀

Modern coinage, a blend of ◊**Rhoda** and ◊**Rhona**. It is now often taken to be a Welsh name derived from *rhon* 'pike', 'lance' (as in ◊**Rhonwen**) + *-da* 'good', as in ◊**Glenda**. The name is associated particularly with the red-haired American film actress Rhonda Fleming (b. 1922).

Rhonwen ♀

Welsh: traditional name derived either from *rhon* 'lance' + *(g)wen* 'white', 'fair', 'blessed', 'holy', or from *rhawn* 'hair' + *(g)wen*. It was used by medieval Welsh poets as a form of ◊**Rowena**, regarded as the progenitrix of the English nation, and is now fairly common in Wales.

Rhydderch ♂

Welsh: traditional name, pronounced '*hrith*-erkh', originally a byname meaning 'reddish-brown'. This was a relatively common name in the Middle Ages and in Tudor times, when it gave rise to the surname *Prothero(e)* (Welsh *ap Rhydderch* 'son of Rhydderch'). It has

recently been revived by parents proudly conscious of their Welsh roots and culture. See also ◊**Roderick**.

Rhys ♂

Welsh: traditional name meaning 'ardour'. The name was borne in the early Middle Ages by various rulers in south-west Wales, such as Rhys ap Tewdur (d. 1093) and Rhys ap Gruffudd (1132–97). See also ◊**Rees**.

Ria ♀

Short form of ◊**Maria**, of German origin but now also used occasionally in the English-speaking world.

Rian ♂

Irish: see ◊**Ryan**.

Rianna ♀

Modern name, an altered and more clearly feminine form of Welsh ◊**Rhiannon** or a feminine equivalent of Irish ◊**Ryan**.

Ricarda ♀

Latinate feminine form of ◊**Richard**.

Rich ♂

Short form of ◊**Richard**. There was a medieval given name *Rich(e)*, but it is connected only indirectly with the modern form. It represents a short form of several medieval names, including not only *Richard* but also other, rarer names of Old French (Germanic) origin with the same first element, as, for example, *Rich(i)er* 'power army' and *Richaud* 'power rule'.

Richard ♂

One of the most enduringly successful of the Old French personal names introduced into Britain by the Normans. It is of Germanic (Frankish) origin, derived from *rīc* 'power' + *hard* 'hardy', 'brave', 'strong'. It has enjoyed continuous popularity in England from the Conquest to the present day, influenced by the fact that it was borne by three kings of England, in particular Richard I (1157–99). He was king for only ten years (1189–99), most of which he spent in warfare abroad, taking part in the Third

Crusade and costing the people of England considerable sums in taxes. Nevertheless, he achieved the status of a folk hero, and was never in England long enough to disappoint popular faith in his goodness and justice. He was also Duke of Aquitaine and Normandy and Count of Anjou, fiefs which he held at a time of maximum English expansion in France. His exploits as a leader of the Third Crusade earned him the nickname 'Coeur de Lion' or 'Lionheart' and a permanent place in popular imagination, in which he was even more firmly enshrined by Sir Walter Scott's novel *Ivanhoe* (1820).

Short forms: **Rick**, ◊**Dick**, ◊**Rich**.
Pet forms: **Ricky**, **Rickie**; **Dicky**, **Dickie**; ◊**Richie**.

Richelle ♀
Modern feminine form of ◊**Richard**, derived from the first syllable of that name + *-elle*, feminine diminutive suffix of French origin. It may also have been influenced by ◊**Rachelle** and ◊**Rochelle**.

Richie ♂
Pet form of ◊**Richard**. The suffix *-ie* was originally characteristic of Scotland and northern England, but the name is now found elsewhere. In some cases it represents a transferred use of the surname derived from the Scottish pet name. *Variant*: **Ritchie** (probably also a transferred use of the surname spelled thus).

Rick ♂
Short form of ◊**Richard**.

Ricky ♂
Pet form of ◊**Richard**, also used independently as a girl's name.
Variants: **Rickie**; **Ricki**, **Rikki** (♀).

Ridley ♂
Transferred use of the surname, in origin a local name from any of various places so named. Those in Essex and Kent are from Old English *hrēod* 'reeds' + *lēah* 'wood' or 'clearing'. The two in Cheshire and Northumberland are from *rydde* 'cleared land' + *lēah*. The given name may have been chosen in some cases by

ardent Protestants in honour of Bishop Nicholas Ridley (?1500–55), burnt at the stake for his Protestantism under Mary Tudor.

Rikki ♀
Variant spelling of the girl's name *Ricky*.

Riley ♂
In some cases a transferred use of the English surname, a local name from a place named with Old English *ryge* 'rye' + *lēah* 'clearing', 'meadow'. There is one such place in Devon and another in Lancashire. In other cases it probably represents a respelling of the Irish surname *Reilly*, which is from an old Irish personal name, *Raghallach*, of unknown origin.

Rina ♀
Short form of ◊**Katerina** and ◊**Carina** or Anglicized form of Gaelic ◊**Rionach**.

Rionach ♀
Irish: traditional Gaelic name meaning 'royal' or 'queenly', sometimes found in the Latinized form ◊**Regina**. It is also spelled **Ríoghnach** and sometimes Anglicized as **Rinach**.

Riordan ♂
Irish: Anglicized form of the Gaelic name **Ríordán**, earlier *Ríoghbhardán*, from *ríogh* 'king' + *bardán*, a diminutive of *bard* 'poet'. Modern use of the given name is influenced by the surname *O'Riordan*, derived from the Gaelic personal name.
Variant: **Rearden**.

Rita ♀
Originally a short form of *Margarita*, the Spanish form of ◊**Margaret**, but now commonly used as an independent given name. It is associated particularly with the American film star Rita Hayworth (1918–87).

Ritchie ♂
Variant spelling of ◊**Richie**.

Ritzy ♀
Modern coinage, apparently from the colloquial term meaning 'luxurious', 'elegant'. This word derives from the

chain of luxury hotels founded in the
19th century by the Swiss entrepreneur
César Ritz.

River ♂
From the vocabulary word (Anglo-
Norman *river(e)*). This is one of the
names taken from the world of nature in
the 1960s under 'hippy' influence, and it
has not been enduringly popular. Use as
a given name may have been influenced
by the surname *Rivers*, in origin a
Norman baronial name from various
places in northern France called
Rivières.

Rob ♂
Short form of ◊**Robert**.

Robbie ♂
Pet form of ◊**Robert**.

Robert ♂
One of the many French names of
Germanic origin that were introduced
into Britain by the Normans, derived
from the nearly synonymous elements
hrod 'fame' + *berht* 'bright', 'famous'. It
had a native Old English predecessor of
similar form (*Hreodbeorht*), which was
supplanted by the Norman name. It was
the name of two dukes of Normandy in
the 11th century: the father of William
the Conqueror (sometimes identified
with the legendary Robert the Devil),
and his eldest son. It was borne by three
kings of Scotland, notably Robert the
Bruce (1274–1329), who freed Scotland
from English domination. The altered
short form *Bob* is very common, but
Hob and *Dob*, which were common in
the Middle Ages and gave rise to surnames, are extinct. See also ◊**Rupert**.
Short forms: **Bob**, **Rob**. Scottish **Rob**, **Rab**.
Pet forms: **Bobby**, **Robbie**, ◊**Robin**. Scottish
Robbie, **Rabbie**.

Roberta ♀
Latinate feminine form of ◊**Robert**.

Robin ♂, ♀
Originally a pet form of ◊**Robert**, from
the short form ◊**Rob** + the diminutive
suffix -*in* (of Old French origin), but now
nearly always used as an independent

name. In recent years it has been increasingly used as a girl's name, partly
under the influence of the vocabulary
word denoting the bird.
Variant: **Robyn** (♀).

Rochelle ♀
Of uncertain origin, probably a feminine
diminutive form of the French boy's
name *Roch* (from Germanic *hrok* 'rest'),
borne by a 14th-century saint, patron of
the sick. This girl's name is little used in
France but common in North America.
It may in part represent a respelling of
◊**Rachelle**.

Rocky ♂
Mainly U.S.: of recent origin, originally a
nickname for a tough individual. The
name came to public notice through the
American heavyweight boxing champion Rocky Marciano (1923–69). He was
of Italian extraction, and Anglicized his
original name, *Rocco* (akin to French
Roch; see ◊**Rochelle**), into a form that
seems particularly appropriate for a
fighter. It was later taken up in a series
of films as the name of a boxer played
by the muscular actor Sylvester
Stallone, and it has also been adopted as
a nickname among devotees of body-
building.

Rod ♂
Short form of ◊**Roderick** and ◊**Rodney**.
Pet form: **Roddy**.

Roda ♀
Variant spelling of ◊**Rhoda**.

Roderick ♂
Of Germanic origin, from *hrōd* 'fame' +
rīc 'power'. This name was introduced
into England, in slightly different forms,
first by Scandinavian settlers in the
Danelaw and later by the Normans.
However, it did not survive beyond the
Middle English period. It owes its modern use to a poem by Sir Walter Scott,
The Vision of Don Roderick (1811),
where it is an Anglicized form of the
related Spanish name *Rodrigo*, borne by
the last Visigothic king of Spain, whose
vision is the subject of the poem. It is

now also very commonly used as an Anglicized form of two unrelated Celtic names: Scottish Gaelic ◊**Ruairidh** and Welsh ◊**Rhydderch**.

Rodge ♂
Informal short form of ◊**Roger**.

Rodger ♂
Variant spelling of ◊**Roger**, in part from the surname derived from the given name in the Middle Ages.

Rodney ♂
Originally a transferred use of the surname, but in independent use as a given name since the 18th century, when it was bestowed in honour of Admiral Lord Rodney (1719–92), who soundly defeated the French navy in 1759–60. The surname probably derives ultimately from a place name, but the location and etymology of this are uncertain. Stoke Rodney in Somerset is probably named from the surname: the manor was held by one Richard de *Rodene* in the early 14th century.

Roger ♂
From an Old French personal name, *Rog(i)er*, of Germanic (Frankish) origin, from *hrōd* 'fame' + *gār, gēr* 'spear'. This was adopted by the Normans and introduced by them to Britain, replacing the native Old English form *Hrōðgār*. Roger, Count of Sicily (*c.* 1031–1101), son of Tancred, recovered Sicily from the Arabs. His son, also called Roger, ruled Sicily as king, presiding over a court noted for its splendour and patronage of the arts.
Variant: **Rodger**.

Róisín ♀
Irish Gaelic name, pronounced '*roe-sheen*': pet form of *Rós*, the Gaelic form of ◊**Rose**.
Variant: **Rosheen** (Anglicized spelling).

Roland ♂
From an Old French personal name of Germanic (Frankish) origin, from *hrōd* 'fame' + *land* 'land', 'territory'. This was adopted by the Normans and introduced by them to Britain. In Old French lit-

erature, it is borne by a legendary Frankish hero, a vassal of Charlemagne, whose exploits are told in the *Chanson de Roland*. The subject of the poem is Roland's death at the Battle of Roncesvalles in the Pyrenees in 778, while protecting the rearguard of the Frankish army on its retreat from Spain. Roland is depicted in literature and legend as headstrong and impulsive. His devoted friendship with the prudent Oliver is also legendary.
Variant: **Rowland**.
Pet forms: **Roly**, **Rowley**.

Rolf ♂
Contracted version of an old Germanic personal name derived from *hrōd* 'fame' + *wulf* 'wolf'. This is found in Old Norse as *Hrólfr*. As an English given name, it represents in part the survival of a form imported by the Normans, in part a much more recent (19th-century) importation of the modern German name. See also ◊**Rudolf**.

Rollo ♂
Latinized form of *Roul*, the Old French version of ◊**Rolf**. This form appears regularly in Latin documents of the Middle Ages, but does not seem to have been used in everyday vernacular contexts. It is the form by which the first Duke of Normandy (*c.*860–932) is generally known. He was a Viking who, with his followers, settled at the mouth of the Seine and raided Paris, Chartres, and elsewhere. By the treaty of St Clair he received the duchy of Normandy from Charles III, on condition that he should receive Christian baptism. Use of this name in English families in modern times seems to be a consciously archaistic revival.

Roly ♂
Pet form of ◊**Roland**. See also ◊**Rowley**.

Ron ♂
Short form of ◊**Ronald**.
Pet form: **Ronnie**.

Rona ♀
Variant spelling of ◊**Rhona**.

Ronald ♂

From the Old Norse personal name *Rögnvaldr* (see ◊**Ranald**). This name was regularly used in the Middle Ages in northern England and Scotland, where Scandinavian influence was strong. It is now widespread throughout the English-speaking world.
Short form: **Ron**.
Pet form: **Ronnie**.

Ronan ♂

Irish: from Gaelic *Rónán*, a diminutive from *rón* 'seal' (the animal). The name is recorded as being borne by various early Celtic saints, but there has been much confusion in the transmission of their names and most of them are also reliably named as *Ruadhán* (see ◊**Rowan**). The most famous is a 5th-century Irish saint who was consecrated as a bishop by St Patrick and subsequently worked as a missionary in Cornwall and Brittany.

Ronnie ♂, ♀

Pet form of ◊**Ronald**, or sometimes of ◊**Veronica**.

Roo ♂, ♀

Modern informal short form of names such as ◊**Rupert** and ◊**Ruth**. In A.A. Milne's *Winnie the Pooh*, Roo is the name of the irrepressible child of Kanga, whose name therefore represents the second element of the word *kangaroo*.

Rory ♂

Anglicized form of the Gaelic name *Ruaidhrí*, *Ruarí* (Irish) or *Ruairidh*, *Ruaraidh* (Scottish). In Scotland this is further Anglicized to ◊**Roderick**.

Ros ♀

Short form of ◊**Rosalind** and ◊**Rosamund**.

Rosa ♀

Latinate form of ◊**Rose**.

Rosaleen ♀

Variant of ◊**Rosalyn**, influenced by the suffix *-een* (in origin the Irish Gaelic diminutive *-ín*). 'Dark Rosaleen' was the title of a poem by James Clarence Mangan (1803–49), based on the Gaelic poem *Róisín Dubh*; in it the name is used as a figurative allusion to the Irish nation.

Rosalie ♀

French form of the Latin name *Rosalia* (a derivative of *rosa* 'rose'), introduced to the English-speaking world in the latter part of the 19th century. St Rosalia was a 12th-century Sicilian virgin, and is the patron of Palermo.

Rosalind ♀

From an Old French personal name of Germanic (Frankish) origin, from *hros* 'horse' + *lind* 'weak', 'tender', 'soft'. It was adopted by the Normans and introduced by them to Britain. In the Middle Ages it was reanalysed by folk etymology as if from Latin *rosa linda* 'lovely rose'. Its popularity as a given name owes much to its use by Edmund Spenser for the character of a shepherdess in his pastoral poetry, and by Shakespeare as the name of the heroine in *As You Like It* (1599).

Rosaline ♀

Originally a variant of ◊**Rosalind**; cf. ◊**Rosalyn** and ◊**Rosaleen**. It is the name of a minor character in Shakespeare's *Love's Labour's Lost* and is used for another, who does not appear but is merely mentioned, in *Romeo and Juliet*.

Rosalyn ♀

Altered form of ◊**Rosalind**. *Rosalin* was a common medieval form, since the letters *d* and *t* were often added or dropped capriciously at the end of words after *n*. The name has been further influenced by the productive suffix *-lyn* (see ◊**Lynn**).
Variants: **Rosalynn(e)**.

Rosamund ♀

From an Old French personal name of Germanic (Frankish) origin, from *hros* 'horse' + *mund* 'protection'. This was adopted by the Normans and introduced by them to Britain. In the later Middle Ages it was reanalysed by folk etymology as if from Latin *rosa munda* 'pure rose' or *rosa mundi* 'rose of the world', titles given to the Virgin Mary. The spelling **Rosamond** has been common since the Middle Ages, when scribes used *o* for *u*, to distinguish it from *n* and *m*, all of which consisted of very similar downstrokes of the pen. 'Fair Rosamond' (Rosamond Clifford) was a legendary beauty who lived at Woodstock in Oxfordshire in the 12th century. She is said to have been the mistress of King Henry II, and to have been murdered by the queen, Eleanor of Aquitaine, in 1176.

Rosanne ♀

From a combination of the names ◊**Rose** and ◊**Anne**, possibly influenced by ◊**Roxane**. The form **Rosanna** is recorded in Yorkshire in the 18th century.
Variants: **Roseanne**, **Rosanna**; **Rosannagh** (a fanciful respelling).

Roscoe ♂

Transferred use of the surname, in origin a local name from a place in northern England named with Old Norse *rá* 'roe deer' + *skógr* 'wood', 'copse'.

Rose ♀

Ostensibly from the vocabulary word denoting the flower (Latin *rosa*). However, the name was in use throughout the Middle Ages, long before any of the other girls' names derived from flowers, which are generally of 19th-century origin. In part it may refer to the flower as a symbol of the Virgin Mary, but it seems more likely that it also has a Germanic origin, probably as a short form of various girls' names based on *hros* 'horse' or *hrōd* 'fame'. The Latinate form *Rohesia* is commonly found in documents of the Middle Ages. As well as being a name in its own right, it is currently used as a short form of ◊**Rosemary** and, less often (because of their different pronunciation), of other names beginning *Ros-*, such as ◊**Rosalind** and ◊**Rosamund**.
Pet form: **Rosie**.

Roselle ♀

Modern coinage, a combination of the given name ◊**Rose** with the productive suffix *-elle* (originally a French feminine diminutive suffix).

Rosemary ♀

19th-century coinage, from the name of the herb (which is from Latin *ros marīnus* 'sea dew'). It is often also assumed to be a combination of the names ◊**Rose** and ◊**Mary**.
Variant: **Rosemarie**.
Pet form: **Rosie**.

Rosetta ♀

Italian pet form of ◊**Rosa**, sometimes also used in the English-speaking world.

Rosheen ♀

Irish: Anglicized form of ◊**Róisín**.

Rosie ♀

Pet form of ◊**Rose** and ◊**Rosemary**. It was first used in the 1860s and is now well established as an independent given name, particularly in the United States.

Ross ♂

Either an adoption of the Gaelic topographic term *ros* 'headland' (cf. ◊**Glen**, ◊**Kyle**) or a transferred use of the Scottish surname, which is borne by a large and ancient family whose members have played a major role in Scottish history.

Rowan ♂, ♀

As a boy's name this is a transferred use of the surname, which is of Irish origin, being an Anglicized form of the Gaelic byname *Ruadhán* 'little red one'. It was borne by a 6th-century saint who founded the monastery of Lothra. As a girl's name it seems to be from the vocabulary word (of Scandinavian origin) denoting the tree, an attractive sight with its clusters of bright red berries.

Rowena ♀

Latinized form of a Saxon name of uncertain form and derivation. It is perhaps from Germanic *hrōd* 'fame' + *wynn* 'joy'. It first occurs in the Latin chronicles of Geoffrey of Monmouth (12th century) as the name of a daughter of the Saxon invader Hengist, and was taken up by Sir Walter Scott as the name of a Saxon woman, Lady Rowena of Hargottstanstede, who marries the eponymous hero of his novel *Ivanhoe* (1819).

Rowland ♂

Variant of ◊**Roland**, or a transferred use of the surname derived from that given name in the Middle Ages.

Rowley ♂

Variant of ◊**Roly**, or transferred use of the surname, a local name from any of the various places in England named with Old English *rūh* 'rough', 'overgrown' + *lēah* 'wood', 'clearing'.

Roxane ♀

From Latin *Roxana*, Greek *Roxanē*, recorded as the name of the wife of Alexander the Great. She was the daughter of Oxyartes the Bactrian, and her name is presumably of Persian origin; it is said to mean 'dawn'. In English literature it is the name of the heroine of a novel by Defoe (1724), a beautiful adventuress who, deserted by her husband, enjoys a glittering career as a courtesan, but eventually dies in a state of penitence, having been thrown into prison for debt. *Variants*: **Roxanne**, **Roxanna**.

Roxy ♀

Pet form of ◊**Roxane**, influenced also by the British colloquial term meaning 'flashy', 'glamorous'. This word derives from the chain of cinemas founded by the U.S. entrepreneur Samuel L. Rothafel ('red apple'), who was known by the nickname *Roxy*.

Roy ♂

Originally a Scottish name, representing an Anglicized spelling of the Gaelic nickname *Ruadh* 'red'. It has since spread to other parts of the English-speaking world, where it is often reanalysed as Old French *roy* 'king' (cf. ◊**Leroy**).

Royce ♂

Transferred use of the surname, in origin a derivative of the vernacular form of the medieval female name *Rohesia* (see ◊**Rose**). As a modern first name it may in part be taken as a short form of ◊**Royston**.

Royle ♂

Transferred use of the surname, in origin a local name from a place in Lancashire,

so called from Old English *ryge* 'rye' + *hyll* 'hill'. It may have become popular as a given name because of association with the vocabulary word *royal* (cf. ◊**Noble** and ◊**King**).

Royston ♂

Transferred use of the surname, in origin a local name from a place in Hertfordshire, known in the Middle Ages as the 'settlement of Royce'. The latter is an obsolete variant of ◊**Rose**, from its Germanic form. Royston is now widely used as a given name especially among West Indians, although the reasons for its popularity in that community are not known.

Roz ♀

Variant spelling of ◊**Ros**, with the final consonant altered to represent the voiced sound of the names from which it derives.

Rozanne ♀

Variant of ◊**Rosanne** or *Roxanne* (see ◊**Roxane**).

Ruairidh ♂

Scottish Gaelic name, pronounced 'rue-er-ee', meaning 'red-haired' or 'fiery'. *Anglicized form*: **Rory**.

Rube ♂, ♀

Informal short form of ◊**Reuben** and ◊**Ruby**.

Ruben ♂

Variant spelling of ◊**Reuben**.

Ruby ♀

From the vocabulary word for the gemstone (Latin *rubīnus*, from *rubeus* 'red'). The name was chiefly common in the late 19th century and up to the middle of the 20th. It is now out of fashion.

Rudolf ♂

From a Latinized version, *Rudolphus*, of the Germanic name *Hrōdwulf* (see ◊**Rolf**). It was introduced to the English-speaking world from Germany in the 19th century. *Rudolf* was a hereditary name among the Habsburgs, the Holy Roman Emperors and rulers of Austria, from the Emperor Rudolf I (1218–91) to

the Archduke Rudolf, Crown Prince of Austria-Hungary, who died in mysterious circumstances at his country house at Meyerling in 1889. Rudolf Rassendyll was the central character of Anthony Hope's adventure stories *The Prisoner of Zenda* (1894) and *Rupert of Hentzau* (1898), in which he is an English gentleman who bears a great physical resemblance to the King of Ruritania, to whom he is distantly related. He successfully impersonates the king for reasons of state. In the 20th century the popularity of this name was further enhanced by the American silent-film actor Rudolph Valentino (1895–1926), born in Italy as Rodolpho di Valentina d'Antonguolla. It is at present out of fashion.
Variant: **Rudolph**.

Rudy ♂
Pet form of ◊**Rudolf**.

Rufus ♂
From a Latin nickname meaning 'red (-haired)', sometimes used in medieval documents as a translation of various surnames with the same sense. It began to be used as a given name in the 17th century.

Rupert ♂
Low German form of ◊**Robert**, first brought to England by Prince Rupert of the Rhine (1618–92), a dashing military leader who came to help his uncle, Charles I, in the Civil War.

Russ ♂
Short form of ◊**Russell**, now also used as an independent given name. In some cases it may represent a transferred use of the surname *Russ*, from Old French *rous* 'red'.

Russell ♂
Transferred use of the common surname, originally from the Old French nickname *Rousel* 'little red one' (a

diminutive of *rous* 'red', from Latin *russus*). Use as a given name may have been inspired by the philosopher Bertrand Russell (1872–1970), who was noted for his liberal agnostic views and his passionate championship of causes such as pacifism (in the First World War), free love, and nuclear disarmament. He was the grandson of the Victorian statesman Lord John Russell (1792–1878).

Rusty ♂, ♀
Nickname for someone with reddish-brown hair, a derivative of modern English *rust* (Old English *rust*).

Ruth ♀
Biblical name (of uncertain derivation) of a Moabite woman who left her own people to remain with her mother-in-law Naomi, and afterwards became the wife of Boaz and an ancestress of David. Her story is told in the book of the Bible that bears her name. It was popular among the Puritans, partly because of its association with the English vocabulary word *ruth* meaning 'compassion'. It has always been popular as a Jewish name, but is now also widespread among people of many different cultures and creeds.
Pet form: **Ruthi**.

Ryan ♂, ♀
From the Irish surname, Gaelic *Ó Riain* 'descendant of Rian'. The latter is an ancient Gaelic personal name of uncertain origin, probably a derivative of *rí* 'king'. *Ryan* is associated with the film actor Ryan O'Neal (b. 1941). It is also now well established in North America as a girl's name.

Ryanne ♀
Modern name, coined as a feminine equivalent or more obviously feminine form of ◊**Ryan**.

SABINA SABRINA SACHEVERELL SADHBH S
AD E SAGE ST JOHN SAFFRON SAL SALLY SA
LO E SAM SAMANTHA SAMMY SAMSAR
A SA SON SAMUEL SANDFORD SANDRA S
ANDY SANFORD SAOIRSE SAPPHIRE SAPP
H RA SARAH SARITA SASHA SASKIA SA

Sabina ♀

From the Latin name *Sabīna* 'Sabine woman'. The Sabines were an ancient Italic race whose territory was early taken over by the Romans. According to tradition, the Romans made a raid on the Sabines and carried off a number of their women, but when the Sabines came for revenge the women succeeded in making peace between the two groups. The name *Sabina* was borne by three minor early Christian saints, in particular a Roman maiden martyred in about 127.

Sabrina ♀

From the name of a character in Celtic legend, who supposedly gave her name to the River Severn. In fact this is one of the most ancient of all British river names, and its true origins are obscure. Legend, as preserved by Geoffrey of Monmouth, had it that Sabrina was the illegitimate daughter of a Welsh king called Locrine, and was drowned in the river on the orders of the king's wife Gwendolen. The river name is found in the form *Sabrina* in the Latin writings of Tacitus, Gildas, and Bede. Geoffrey of Monmouth comments that in Welsh the name is *Habren* (modern Welsh *Hafren*). The name of the legendary character is almost certainly derived from that of the river, rather than vice versa.

Sacheverell ♂

Pronounced 'sash-*ev*-er-ell': transferred use of the surname, apparently originally a baronial name of Norman origin (from an unidentified place in Normandy believed to have been called *Saute-Chevreuil*, meaning 'roebuck leap'). It was made familiar as a given name by the writer Sacheverell Sitwell (1897–1985), who was named in honour of his ancestor William Sacheverell (1638–91), a minor Whig statesman. *Pet form*: **Sachie**.

Sadhbh ♀

Traditional Irish Gaelic name, pronounced '*syve*', from an obsolete Irish word meaning 'sweet'. In Irish legend, Sadhbh, daughter of Conn Cétchathach (Conn of the Hundred Battles), was considered 'the best woman in Ireland who ever lay with a man'. It was a common girl's name during the Middle Ages and has recently been revived. It is sometimes Anglicized as ◊**Sally**.

Sadie ♀

Originally a pet form of ◊**Sarah**, but now generally considered as an independent name. The exact formation is not clear: probably a nursery form.

Sage ♀, ♂

Apparently from the name of the herb (Middle English *sauge*, via Old French from Latin *salvia*), cf. ◊**Sorrel** and ◊**Bay**. In part it may also have been taken from the vocabulary word meaning 'wise' (from Latin *sapius*).

St John ♂

Name expressing devotion to St John, generally pronounced '*sin*-jen'; it has been in use in the English-speaking world, mainly among Roman Catholics, from the last two decades of the 19th century up to the present day.

Saffron ♀

From the name of the precious spice, noted for its vivid yellow colour. The word is from Old French *safran*, ultimately of Arabic origin: the plant was introduced to Europe from the East in the early Middle Ages. As a given name it is most often given to babies born with strikingly golden hair.

Sal ♀
Short form of ◊**Sally**.

Sally ♀
In origin a pet form of ◊**Sarah**, but in the 20th century normally considered as an independent name. It is frequently used as the first element in combinations such as *Sally-Anne* and *Sally-Jane*. In Ireland it sometimes represents an Anglicization of ◊**Sadhbh**.
Short form: **Sal**.

Salome ♀
Greek form of an unrecorded Aramaic name, akin to the Hebrew word *shalom* 'peace'. It was common at the time of Christ, and was borne by one of the women who were at his tomb and witnessed the Resurrection (Mark 16: 1–8). This would normally have led to its common use as a Christian name, and it is indeed found as such in medieval times. However, according to the Jewish historian Josephus, it was also the name of King Herod's stepdaughter, the daughter of Queen Herodias. In the Bible, a daughter of Herodias, generally identified as this Salome, danced for Herod and so pleased him that he offered to give her anything she wanted. Prompted by her mother, she asked for (and got) the head of John the Baptist, who was in one of Herod's prisons (Mark 6:17–28). This story so gripped medieval imagination that the name Salome became more or less taboo until the end of the 19th century, when Oscar Wilde wrote a play about her and some unconventional souls began to choose the name for their daughters.

Sam ♂, ♀
Short form of ◊**Samuel** (or less frequently of ◊**Samson**), and of ◊**Samantha**.

Samantha ♀
Of problematic and much debated origin. It arose in the southern states of America in the 18th century, possibly as a combination of *Sam* (from ◊**Samuel**) + a newly coined feminine suffix *-antha* (perhaps suggested by ◊**Anthea**).

Sammy ♀, ♂
Pet form of *Samantha*, or much less frequently of ◊**Samuel** or ◊**Samson**.
Variants: **Sammie**, **Sammi** (♀).

Samsara ♀
From the Sanskrit word (meaning 'passing through') used in Hinduism and Buddhism to refer to the cycle of birth, death, and rebirth. It has sometimes been chosen as a given name by parents with an interest in Oriental spirituality.

Samson ♂
Biblical name (Hebrew *Shimshon*, probably derived from *shemesh* 'sun'), borne by a Jewish champion and judge famous for his prodigious strength. He was betrayed by his mistress, Delilah, and enslaved and blinded by the Philistines; nevertheless, he was able to bring the pillars of the temple of the Philistines crashing down in a final suicidal act of strength (Judges 13–16). This famous story provided the theme for Milton's poetic drama *Samson Agonistes* (1671), which is modelled on ancient Greek tragedy. In the Middle Ages the popularity of the given name was increased in Celtic areas by the fame of a 6th-century Celtic saint who bore it, probably as a classicized form of some ancient Celtic name. He was a Welsh monk who did missionary work in Cornwall and afterwards established a monastery at Dol in Brittany.
Variant: **Sampson** (usually a transferred use of the surname, derived from the given name in the Middle Ages).

Samuel ♂
Biblical name (Hebrew *Shemuel*), possibly meaning 'He (God) has hearkened' (presumably to the prayers of a mother for a son). It may also be understood as a contracted form of Hebrew *sha'ulme'el* meaning 'asked of God'. In the case of

Samuel the son of Hannah, this would be more in keeping with his mother's statement 'Because I have asked him of the Lord' (1 Samuel 1:20). Living in the 11th century BC, Samuel was a Hebrew judge and prophet of the greatest historical importance, who established the Hebrew monarchy, anointing as King both Saul and, later, David. In the Authorized Version two books of the Old Testament are named after him, although in Roman Catholic and Orthodox versions of the Bible they are known as the first and second Book of Kings. The story of Samuel being called by God while still a child serving in the house of Eli the priest (1 Samuel 3) is of great vividness and has moved countless generations. In England and America the name was particularly popular among the 16th-century Puritans and among Nonconformists from the 17th to the 19th century.

Sandford ♂
Mainly U.S.: transferred use of the surname (see ◊**Sanford**).

Sandra ♀
Short form of *Alessandra*, the Italian form of ◊**Alexandra**. A major influence in establishing this as a common given name in the English-speaking world was George Meredith's novel *Sandra Belloni* (1886), originally published as *Emilia in England* (1864); the heroine, Emilia Sandra Belloni, is a beautiful, passionate young singer.

Sandy ♂, ♀
Pet form, originally Scottish, of ◊**Alexander** and ◊**Alexandra**, now sometimes used as an independent given name. It is also used as a nickname for someone with a crop of 'sandy' (light reddish-brown) hair.
Variant: **Sandie** (♀).

Sanford ♂
Mainly U.S.: transferred use of the surname, in origin a local name from any of numerous places in England called *Sandford*, from Old English *sand* 'sand' + *ford* 'ford'. Use as a given name

honours Peleg Sanford, an early governor (1680–3) of Rhode Island.
Variant: **Sandford**.

Saoirse ♀
Irish Gaelic name, pronounced '*seer-sha*': a modern coinage from the vocabulary word meaning 'freedom'.

Sapphire ♀
From the word for the gemstone (via Old French and Latin from Greek *sappheiros*, probably ultimately of Semitic origin). The Greek term seems to have originally denoted lapis lazuli, but was later transferred to the transparent blue stone. As a given name this is typically bestowed on a girl with deep blue eyes.

Sappho ♀
Name occasionally given in honour of the Greek lyric poet Sappho, who lived in the 6th century BC. Nothing is known about her life beyond what can be deduced from her poetry, which is fragmentary and may or may not be autobiographical, and the origin of her name is quite obscure. Her verse is noted for its Lesbian passion; the name is now sometimes chosen by feminists in token of their liberation.

Sara ♀
Variant of ◊**Sarah**. This is the form used in the Greek of the New Testament (Hebrews 11:11).

Sarah ♀
Biblical name, borne by the wife of Abraham and mother of Isaac. According to the Book of Genesis, she was originally called *Sarai* (possibly meaning 'contentious' in Hebrew), but had her name changed by God to the more auspicious *Sarah* 'princess' in token of a greater blessing (Genesis 17:15, 'And God said unto Abraham, As for Sarai thy wife, thou shalt not call her name Sarai, but Sarah shall her name be').
Variants: **Sara**, ◊**Zara**.
Pet forms: ◊**Sally**, ◊**Sadie**.

Sarita ♀
Spanish diminutive form of ◊**Sara**, now also sometimes used as an independent

first name in the English-speaking world.

Sasha ♂, ♀

English spelling of a Russian pet form of ◊**Alexander** and ◊**Alexandra**. It has been used in the English-speaking world as an independent name, introduced in the 20th century via France. Use as a girl's name in the English-speaking world is encouraged by the characteristically feminine *-a* ending.

Saskia ♀

Dutch: of uncertain derivation. The name has been in use since the Middle Ages, and was borne, for example, by the wife of the artist Rembrandt. It may be derived from Germanic *sachs* 'Saxon'.

Satin ♀

From the vocabulary word denoting the sleek and luxurious fabric. It reached English from French in the 14th century, and comes from Arabic *zaitūni*, a derivative of the place name *Tsingtung*, in southern China, from which the fabric was at first exported to the West.

Saul ♂

Biblical name (from a Hebrew word meaning 'asked for' or 'prayed for'), borne by one of the first kings of Israel. It was also the name of St Paul before his conversion to Christianity (Acts 9:4). It enjoyed some popularity among the Puritans, but is now once again mainly a Jewish name.

Saundra ♀

Scottish variant of ◊**Sandra**, reflecting the same development in pronunciation as is shown by surnames such as *Saunders* and *Saunderson*, originally from short forms of ◊**Alexander**.

Savannah ♀

Mainly U.S.: apparently from the name of cities in Georgia and South Carolina. Both are on the Savannah River, ostensibly named with the word for a treeless plain (derived via Spanish from a native South American word). However, the river name may be an adaptation of some other name existing prior to European settlement. The given name may be taken directly from the vocabulary word, more under the influence of its sound than its meaning. In this case, it could be regarded as no more than a fanciful elaboration of ◊**Anna** or ◊**Hannah**.
Variant: **Savanna**.

Sawney ♂

Scottish variant of ◊**Sandy**, resulting from a pronunciation which is also reflected in the surname *Saunders*. The name declined in popularity after the 18th century, no doubt adversely affected by the use of *Sawney* as a vocabulary word for a simpleton.

Scarlett ♀

Name popularized by the central character in the novel *Gone With the Wind* (1936) by Margaret Mitchell, later made into a famous film. The characters in the novel bear a variety of unusual given names, which had a remarkable influence on naming practices throughout the English-speaking world in the 20th century. According to the novel, the name of the central character was Katie Scarlett O'Hara (the middle name representing her grandmother's maiden surname), but she was always known as Scarlett. The surname *Scarlett* is in origin an occupational name for a dyer or for a seller of rich, bright fabrics, from Old French *escarlate* 'scarlet cloth' (Late Latin *scarlāta*, of uncertain, probably Semitic, derivation).
Variant: **Scarlet**.

Scott ♂

Although this was in use as a personal name both before and after the Norman Conquest, modern use in most cases almost certainly represents a transferred use of the surname. This originated as a byname for someone from Scotland or, within Scotland itself, for a member of the Gaelic-speaking people who originally came from Ireland. The given name is now often chosen by parents conscious of their Scottish ancestry and heritage, but it is also used more widely.

Séamas ♂
Modern Irish Gaelic form of ◊**James**, pronounced '*shay*-mus'.

Séamus ♂
Earlier Irish Gaelic form of ◊**James**; cf. ◊**Séamas**. This is also used without the accent as a partially Anglicized form of the name.

Seán ♂
Irish Gaelic form of ◊**John**, pronounced '*shawn*'. It was derived in the early Middle Ages from Anglo-Norman *Jehan*. The name has always been common in Ireland, but is now also being increasingly chosen (usually without the accent) by parents who have no Irish connections. One influence on its popularity has been the actor Sean Connery (born 1930), of James Bond fame.

Seanan ♂
Traditional Irish Gaelic name, pronounced '*shan*-nan', from a diminutive of the vocabulary word *sean* 'old', 'venerable'.
Variant: **Senan**.

Sebastian ♂
From Latin *Sebastiānus*, the name of a 3rd-century saint, a Roman soldier martyred by the arrows of his fellow officers. His sufferings were a favourite subject for medieval artists. The name means 'man from Sebastē', a city in Asia Minor so called from Greek *sebastos* 'august', 'venerable', used as a translation of the Latin imperial title *Augustus*.
Short forms: **Seb**.

Selena ♀
Variant of ◊**Selina**.

Selima ♀
Of uncertain origin. Its first known occurrence is in a poem by Thomas Gray (1716–71), recording the death of Horace Walpole's cat Selima, 'drowned in a tub of gold fishes'. The metre shows that the name was stressed on the first syllable, but there is no clue as to its derivation. Gray (or Walpole) was possibly influenced by the Arabic name *Selim* 'peace'.

Selina ♀
Of uncertain origin. It is first found in the 17th century, and it may be an altered form of *Selena* (Greek *Selēnē*), the name of a goddess of the moon, or of *Celina* (Latin *Caelīna*), a derivative of ◊**Celia**. The name suddenly became more popular in Britain in the 1980s, partly perhaps due to the television personality Selina Scott.

Selma ♀
Of uncertain origin, probably a contracted form of ◊**Selima**. It has also been occasionally used in Germany and Scandinavia, probably because it occurs as the name of Ossian's castle in Macpherson's ballads.

Selwyn ♂
Transferred use of the surname, which is of disputed origin. There was a given name *Selewyn* in use in the Middle Ages, which probably represents a survival of an unrecorded Old English name derived from *sēle* 'prosperity' or *sele* 'hall' + *wine* 'friend'. Alternatively, the surname may be Norman, derived from *Seluein*, an Old French form of the Latin name *Silvānus* (from *silva* 'wood'; cf. ◊**Silas**).
Variant: **Selwin**.

Senga ♀
Scottish: common in the north-east of Scotland, this name is popularly supposed to represent ◊**Agnes** spelled backwards (which it undeniably does). However, it is more likely to have originated from the Gaelic vocabulary word *seang* 'slender'.

Seònaid ♀
Scottish Gaelic form of ◊**Janet**, pronounced '*shaw*-natch'.
Variants: **Shona** (Anglicized), **Seona** (semi-Anglicized).

Septimus ♂
From a Late Latin name derived from Latin *septimus* 'seventh'. It was fairly commonly used in large Victorian families for the seventh son or a male seventh child, but is now rare.

Seraphina ♀
Latinate derivative of Hebrew *seraphim* 'burning ones', the name of an order of angels (Isaiah 6:2). It was borne by a rather shadowy saint who was martyred at the beginning of the 5th century in Italy, Spain, or Armenia.
Variant: **Serafina**.

Serena ♀
From a Latin name, representing the feminine form of the adjective *serēnus* 'calm', 'serene'. It was borne by an early Christian saint, about whom little is known. In her biography she is described as wife of the Emperor Domitian (AD 51–96), but there is no mention of her in any of the historical sources that deal with this period. In recent years the name has been made famous by the American tennis player Serena Williams.

Seth ♂
Biblical name (from a Hebrew word meaning 'appointed', 'placed'), borne by the third son of Adam, who was born after the murder of Abel (Genesis 4:25, 'And Adam knew his wife again; and she bare a son, and called his name Seth: For God, said she, hath appointed me another seed instead of Abel, whom Cain slew'). It is recorded in England from the 1400s and was popular among the Puritans (particularly for children born after the death of an elder sibling). By the 20th century it had become rare. It was used for the darkly passionate rural character Seth Starkadder in Stella Gibbons's satirical novel *Cold Comfort Farm* (1932).

Seumas ♂
Scottish Gaelic form of ◊**James**, pronounced '*shee*-mas'; it is also an older Irish Gaelic form (cf. ◊**Séamas**).

Seumus ♂
Older Irish Gaelic form of ◊**James** (see ◊**Séamas**).

Sextus ♂
Traditional Latin given name, meaning 'sixth'. It was taken up in England during the Victorian period, often for a

sixth son or a sixth child, but it is now little used.

Seymour ♂
Transferred use of the surname, originally a Norman baronial name from *Saint-Maur* in Normandy. This place was so called from the dedication of its church to St *Maurus* (cf. ◊**Maurice**).

Shae ♀
Modern variant of the girl's name ◊**Shea**.

Shalene ♀
Modern variant of ◊**Charlene**.

Shamus ♂
Anglicized spelling of Irish Gaelic ◊**Séamus**, occasionally used in Ireland, but now rare.

Shan ♀
Short form of ◊**Shantelle**.

Shana ♀
Modern coinage, apparently an altered and more obviously feminine form of ◊**Siân**.

Shanae ♀
Modern name, most often borne by Blacks in the United States. It seems to represent an elaboration of ◊**Shana** by association with names such as ◊**Fae** and ◊**Gae**.

Shandy ♀
Modern coinage, apparently from the term for the drink (earlier *shandigaff*, of uncertain origin); cf. ◊**Brandy** and ◊**Sherry**. It may also have arisen as a combination of names such as ◊**Shanelle** and ◊**Shantelle** with ◊**Mandy**.

Shane ♂, ♀
Anglicized form of Irish Gaelic ◊**Seán**, representing a Northern Irish pronunciation of the name. In recent years it has also been used as a girl's name.

Shanee ♀
Anglicized form of Welsh *Siani* (see ◊**Siân**).

Shanelle ♀
Recent coinage, apparently a respelled elaboration of ◊**Chanel**.

Shania ♀

Recent coinage, an elaborated form of
◊**Shana**, recently popularized by the
singer Shania Twain. It is pronounced
with the stress on the *i*, as in the
traditional pronunciation of ◊**Maria**.

Shanna ♀

Recent coinage, apparently an altered,
more obviously feminine form of
◊**Shannon**.

Shannagh ♀

Variant of ◊**Shannah** or a transferred use
of the Irish surname *Shannagh*, Gaelic
Ó Seanaigh 'descendant of Seanach'.
The latter is a Gaelic personal name
derived from *sean* 'old', 'wise'.

Shannah ♀

Variant of ◊**Shanna** or a short form of
Shoshannah, the Hebrew form of
◊**Susanna**.

Shannon ♀, ♂

From the name of a river in Ireland. It is
not clear why it has become so popular
as a given name, but cf. ◊**Clodagh**. In part
it may also be a transferred use of the
Irish surname, Gaelic *Ó Seanáin*
'descendant of Seanán'. The latter is a
diminutive of *Seán*. Shannon is not
found as a traditional given name in
Ireland itself.

Shantelle ♀

Recent coinage, apparently a respelled
elaboration of ◊**Chantal**.

Shari ♀

Anglicized spelling of *Sári*, the Hungarian form of ◊**Sarah**.

Sharissa ♀

Modern name, most often borne by
Blacks in the United States. It is probably an elaborated form of ◊**Sharon**
influenced by names such as ◊**Clarissa**
and ◊**Nerissa**.

Sharlene ♀

Variant spelling of ◊**Charlene**.

Sharman ♂, ♀

As a boy's name this represents a transferred use of the surname, a variant of

◊**Sherman**. As a girl's name it is an
altered form of ◊**Charmaine**.

Sharon ♀

20th-century coinage, from a biblical
place name. The derivation is from the
phrase 'I am the rose of Sharon, and the
lily of the valleys' (Song of Solomon 2:1).
The plant name 'rose of Sharon' is used
for a shrub of the genus *Hypericum*,
with yellow flowers, and for a species of
hibiscus, with purple flowers. *Rosa-
sharn* (Rose of Sharon) is the name of one
of the characters in John Steinbeck's
novel *The Grapes of Wrath* (1936).
Variant: **Sharron**.

Sharona ♀

Latinate elaborated form of ◊**Sharon**,
now quite often used in the English-
speaking world.

Sharonda ♀

Elaboration of ◊**Sharon**, with the suffix
-*da* abstracted from names such as
◊**Glenda** and ◊**Linda**.

Sharron ♀

Variant spelling of ◊**Sharon**.

Shaughan ♂

Variant spelling of ◊**Shaun**, probably
influenced by ◊**Vaughan**.
Variant: **Shaughn**.

Shaun ♂, ♀

Anglicized spelling of Irish Gaelic
◊**Seán**. In Canada it is also found as a
girl's name.

Shauna ♀

Name invented as a feminine form of
◊**Shaun**.

Shaw ♂

Transferred use of the surname, in origin
a local name meaning 'wood', 'copse'
(Old English *sceaga*, Old Norse *skógr*).

Shawn ♂, ♀

Anglicized spelling of Irish Gaelic
◊**Seán**, used mainly in North America. In
Canada it is also found as a girl's name.

Shawna ♀

Recently coined feminine form of
◊**Shawn**.

Shay ♀
Variant spelling of ◊**Shea** as a girl's name.
Variant: **Shaye**.

Shayla ♀
Recent coinage, apparently a variant of
◊**Sheila**.

Shayna ♀
Modern name, either taken from a Yid-
dish name derived from German
Schön(e) 'beautiful', or else a variant of
◊**Sheena**.

Shea ♂, ♀
Transferred use of the Irish surname,
Gaelic *O Séaghdha* 'descendant of
Séaghdha'. The latter is a traditional
name of uncertain derivation,
perhaps meaning 'hawk-like', i.e. 'fine',
'goodly'.
Variants: **Shay**, **Shaye**, **Shae** (♀).

Sheela ♀
Variant spelling of ◊**Sheila**.
Variants: **Sheelah**, **Sheelagh**.

Sheena ♀
Anglicized spelling of **Sìne** (Scottish) or
Síne (Irish), the Gaelic equivalents of
◊**Jane**.

Sheila ♀
Anglicized spelling of *Síle*, the Irish
Gaelic form of ◊**Cecily**. This name has
become so common and widespread that
it is hardly felt to be Irish any longer. In
Australia since the 19th century it has
been a slang generic term for any
woman.
Variants: **Sheela**, **Sheelah**, **She(e)lagh**.

Shelagh ♀
Variant of ◊**Sheila**. The final consonants
in the written form seem to have been
added to give a Gaelic feel to the name.
There is no etymological justification
for them.
Variant: **Sheelagh**.

Shelby ♀, ♂
Mainly U.S.: transferred use of the surname (now more common in America
than Britain). This has the form of a
northern English local name, but no
place bearing it has been identified. The
chief inspiration for its use as a given
name seems to be Isaac Shelby (1750–
1826), Revolutionary commander and
first governor of Kentucky.

Sheldon ♂
Transferred use of the surname, which
originated as a local name from any of
the various places so called. Examples
occur in Derbyshire, Devon, and the
West Midlands. The place name has a
variety of different origins.

Shell ♀
Generally, this is a shortened form of
◊**Michelle**, respelled by association
with the vocabulary word. In some
cases it may be a shortened form of
◊**Shelley**.

Shelley ♀, occasionally ♂
Transferred use of the surname, the
most famous bearer of which was the
English Romantic poet Percy Bysshe
Shelley (1792–1822). The surname is in
origin a local name from one of the
various places (in Essex, Suffolk, and
Yorkshire) named in Old English as the
'wood (or clearing) on (or near) a slope (or
ledge)'. The name is now used almost
exclusively for girls, in part perhaps as
a result of association with ◊**Shirley** (the
actress Shelley Winters was born in
1922 as Shirley Schrift), and in part due
to the characteristically feminine
ending -*(e)y*.

Sheree ♀
Respelled form of ◊**Cherie**.

Sheridan ♂, ♀
Transferred use of the surname made
famous by the Irish playwright Richard
Brinsley Sheridan (1751–1816). The surname is from Gaelic *Ó Sirideáin* 'descendant of Sirideán'. The latter is a
personal name of uncertain origin,
possibly connected with *sirim* 'to seek'.
This is now occasionally also used as a
girl's name. In the United States the
inspiration is probably the Unionist
commander General Philip Henry
Sheridan (1831–88).

Sherman ♂
Transferred use of the surname, which is an occupational name for someone who trimmed the nap of woollen cloth after it had been woven, from Old English *scēara* 'shears' + *mann* 'man'. In the United States it is sometimes bestowed in honour of the Civil War general William Tecumseh Sherman (1820–71).

Sherry ♀
Probably in origin a respelled form of ◊**Cherie**, but now associated with the fortified wine, earlier *sherry wine*, so named from the port of *Jérez* in southern Spain.
Variants: **Sherrie**, **Sherri**.

Sheryl ♀
Variant of ◊**Cheryl**.

Shevaun ♀
Anglicized form of Irish Gaelic ◊**Siobhán**.

Shilla ♀
Modern coinage, apparently an altered form of ◊**Sheila**.

Shireen ♀
Variant of ◊**Shirin**, by association with the productive suffix *-een*, abstracted from names such as ◊**Maureen** and ◊**Doreen**.

Shirin ♀
Muslim name of Persian or Arabic origin, now beginning to be used quite widely in the English-speaking world.
Variants: **Shirrin**, **Shireen**.

Shirley ♀, formerly ♂
Transferred use of the surname, in origin a local name from any of the various places (in the West Midlands, Derbyshire, Hampshire, and Surrey) named in Old English from *scīr* 'county', 'shire' or *scīr* 'bright' + *lēah* 'wood', 'clearing'. It was given by Charlotte Brontë to the heroine of her novel *Shirley* (1849). According to the novel, her parents had selected the name in prospect of a male child and used it regardless. *Shirley* had earlier been used as a boy's name (Charlotte Brontë refers to it as a 'masculine

cognomen'), but this literary influence fixed it firmly as a girl's name. It was strongly reinforced during the 1930s and 1940s by the popularity of the child film star Shirley Temple (b. 1928).

Sholto ♂
Scottish: apparently an Anglicized form of a Gaelic name, *Sìoltach*, originally a byname meaning 'sower', i.e. 'fruitful' or 'seed-bearing'. This name is traditional in the Douglas family.

Shona ♀
Scottish: Anglicized form of Gaelic *Seonag* or *Seònaid*, Gaelic versions of ◊**Joan** and ◊**Janet** respectively. In America it is pronounced identically with ◊**Shauna**, and may be used as a variant spelling of that name. It has also become popular as a Black name, probably in part because it is spelled the same as the name of a central African people. Compare ◊**Zula** for a similar formation.

Shula ♀
As a Jewish name this is a short form of ◊**Shulamit**. It has been adopted by non-Jews in the English-speaking world as an independent given name. Its popularity has been increased by its use as the name of a character in 'The Archers', the long-running radio soap opera.

Shulamit ♀
Hebrew name meaning 'peacefulness', a derivative of *shalom* 'peace'. The name occurs as a personification in the Song of Solomon (6:13): 'Return, return, O Shulamite; return, return, that we may look upon thee'. It is a popular modern Hebrew name.
Variants: **Shulamith**, **Shulamite**.

Shaz ♀
Modern informal pet form of ◊**Sharon**.
Variant: **Shazza**.

Siân ♀
Welsh form of ◊**Jane**, derived from Anglo-Norman form *Jeanne*. In the English-speaking world it is sometimes used without the accent.
Pet form: **Siani**.

Sibyl ♀

Variant spelling of ◊**Sybil**. Even in classical times there was confusion between the two vowels in this word.
Variants: **Sibylla** (Latinate); **Sibilla**; **Sibella** (by association with the Italian feminine diminutive suffix *-ella*).

Sidney ♂, occasionally ♀

Transferred use of the surname, which is usually said to be a Norman baronial name from *Saint-Denis* in France. However, at least in the case of the family of the poet and soldier Sir Philip Sidney (1554–86), it appears to have a more humble origin, being derived from lands in Surrey named as the 'wide meadow' (Old English *sīdan* 'wide' (dative case) + *ēg* 'island in a river', 'riverside meadow'). The popularity of the boy's name increased considerably in the 19th century, probably due to Sidney Carton, hero of Dickens's novel *A Tale of Two Cities* (1859). As a girl's name it is perhaps in part a contracted form of ◊**Sidony**, and coincidentally represents an altered form of ◊**Sindy**, but this use is quite rare.
Variant: **Sydney**.
Short form: **Sid**.

Sidony ♀

From Latin *Sidōnia*, feminine of *Sidōnius*, in origin an ethnic name meaning 'man from Sidon' (the city in Phoenicia). This came to be associated with the Greek word *sindon* 'winding sheet'. Two saints called Sidonius are venerated in the Catholic Church: Sidonius Apollinaris, a 4th-century bishop of Clermont, and a 7th-century Irish monk who was the first abbot of the monastery of Saint-Saëns (which is named with a much altered form of his name). *Sidonius* was not used as a given name in the later Middle Ages, but the feminine form was comparatively popular and has continued in occasional use ever since.
Variant: **Sidonie**.

Siena ♀

Apparently from the name of the city in central Italy (cf. ◊**Ravenna** and

◊**Venetia**). The place name is derived from that of a Gaulish tribe who once occupied the area, recorded in Latin sources as the *Senōnes*. Use as a given name may in part also have been inspired by the name ◊**Sierra**.
Variant: **Sienna**.

Sierra ♀

Mainly U.S.: apparently from the Spanish vocabulary word denoting a mountain range (from Latin *serra* 'saw', referring to the saw-toothed appearance). The reasons for its adoption and popularity are not clear, but this was among the top one hundred girls' names in the United States in 1989. Compare ◊**Savannah**.

Sigrid ♀

From an Old Norse female personal name derived from *sigr* 'victory' + *fríðr* 'fair', 'beautiful'.

Silas ♂

Of New Testament origin: Greek name, a short form of *Silouanus* (Latin *Silvānus*, a derivative of *silva* 'wood'). This name was borne by a companion of St Paul, who is also mentioned in the Bible in the full form of his name. The Eastern Church recognizes two separate saints, Silas and Silvanus, but honours both on the same day (20 July).

Síle ♀

Irish Gaelic form of ◊**Cecily**, pronounced '*shee*-la', derived in the early Middle Ages from the Anglo-Norman form *Cecile*.
Anglicized forms: ◊**Sheila**, **Sheela(h)**, **She(e)lagh**, **Shayla**, **Shilla**.

Silver ♀, ♂

From the name of the precious metal (Old English *siolfor*). It is sometimes given to babies born with very fair hair. It is also occasionally used as a pet form of the names ◊**Silvestra** and ◊**Silvester**.

Silvester ♂

From a Latin name, meaning 'of the woods'. It was borne by various early saints, most notably by the first pope to

govern a Church free from persecution (314–35). His feast is on 31 December, and in various parts of Europe the New Year is celebrated under his name. The name has been continuously, if modestly, used from the Middle Ages to the present day.
Variant: **Sylvester**.

Silvestra ♀
Latin feminine form of ◊**Silvester**.

Silvia ♀
From Roman legend. Rhea *Silvia* was, according to Roman tradition, the mother of the twins Romulus and Remus, who founded Rome. Her name probably represents a reworking, by association with Latin *silva* 'wood', of some pre-Roman form. It was borne by a 6th-century saint, mother of Gregory the Great, and has always been relatively popular in Italy. Shakespeare used it as a typically Italian name in *Two Gentlemen of Verona*. It is now well established as an independent name in the English-speaking world.
Variant: **Sylvia**.

Sim ♂
Short form of ◊**Simon**, now rare, but more common in the Middle Ages, when it gave rise to the surnames *Simms* and *Simpson*.

Simeon ♂
Biblical name, from a Hebrew word meaning 'hearkening'. It is borne by several Old and New Testament characters, rendered in the Authorized Version variously as *Shimeon*, *Simeon*, and ◊**Simon**. In the New Testament, it is the spelling used for the man who blessed the infant Christ (Luke 2:25).

Simmie ♂
Pet form of ◊**Simon**, used mainly in Scotland.

Simon ♂
Usual English form of ◊**Simeon**, borne in the New Testament by various characters: two apostles, a brother of Jesus, a Pharisee, a leper, a tanner, a sorcerer (who offered money for the gifts of the Holy Ghost, giving rise to the term *simony*), and the man who carried Jesus's cross to the Crucifixion.

Simone ♀
French feminine form of ◊**Simon**, now also quite commonly used in the English-speaking world.

Sinclair ♂
Transferred use of the Scottish surname, in origin a Norman baronial name borne by a family that held a manor in northern France called *Saint-Clair*, probably Saint-Clair-sur-Elle in La Manche. It is an extremely common Scottish surname: the Norman family received the earldoms of Caithness and Orkney. They merged with the Norse- and Gaelic-speaking inhabitants of their domains to form one of the most powerful of the Scottish Highland families. The name of the novelist Sinclair Lewis (1885–1951) may have had some influence on the choice of this as a 20th-century given name.

Sinda ♀
Variant of ◊**Sindy**.

Sindy ♀
Variant spelling of ◊**Cindy** that came into use in about 1950 and is most common in America.

Síne ♀
Irish Gaelic form of ◊**Jane**, pronounced '*shee*-na', derived from Anglo-Norman *Jeanne*.
Variant: **Sheena** (Anglicized).

Sinéad ♀
Irish Gaelic form of ◊**Janet**, pronounced 'shin-*aid*', derived from the French form *Jeannette*. In the English-speaking world it is usually written without the accent, as in the case of the actress Sinead Cusack (b. 1948).

Siobhán ♀
Irish Gaelic form of ◊**Joan**, pronounced 'shiv-*awn*' or '*shoo*-an', derived from the Anglo-Norman form *Jehanne*. It became widely known in the English-speaking world, written without the accent,

through the actress Siobhan McKenna (1923–86).
Variants: **Shevaun**, **Chevonne** (Anglicized).

Siôn ♂
Welsh form of ◊**John**, derived from Anglo-Norman *Jean*.

Sioned ♀
Welsh form of ◊**Janet**.

Sissy ♀
Pet form of ◊**Cicely** that came into use about 1890 but largely disappeared again after about 1920. In recent years it has undergone something of a revival.
Variants: **Sissey**, **Sissie**.

Skipper ♂
Originally a nickname from the vocabulary word *skipper* 'boss' (originally denoting a ship's captain, from Middle Dutch *schipper*), or else representing an agent derivative of *skip* 'to leap or bound' (probably of Scandinavian origin). It is now sometimes used as an independent given name in the United States.
Short forms: **Skip**, **Skipp**.

Sky ♀, ♂
From the vocabulary word (from Old Norse *ský* 'cloud'). This was one of the names taken from the world of nature (cf. ◊**Rainbow**, ◊**Leaf**, ◊**River**) during the 1960s under the influence of the hippy and flower-power movements. It continues to enjoy a modest popularity.

Skye ♀
Elaborated spelling of ◊**Sky**, influenced by the name of the island of *Skye* in the Hebrides, which is of Gaelic origin. Compare ◊**Ailsa**, ◊**Isla**, and ◊**Rona** for similar derivations.

Slaney ♂, ♀
Transferred use of the Irish surname. The Gaelic form of this is *Ó Sláine*, meaning 'descendant of *Sláne*'. *Sláine* is an old Irish personal name derived from *slán* 'challenge', 'defiance'. The surname has recently come to be used fairly regularly in the United States as a given

name for boys and less frequently also for girls.

Slater ♂
Transferred use of the surname, in origin an occupational name for a builder who specialized in fixing slates on roofs.

Sloan ♂
Transferred use of the Irish surname. The Gaelic form of this is *Ó Sluaghhadáin*, meaning 'descendant of *Sluaghadhán*'. *Sluaghadhán* is an old Irish personal name representing a diminutive of *sluaghadh* 'expedition', 'raid'. The surname has recently come to be used fairly regularly as a given name in the United States.

Sloane ♀
In origin a variant of **Sloan**. It is associated with *Sloane Square* in west London, where a particular kind of fashionable young, upper-class women (known colloquially as 'Sloane Rangers') tend to have their flats.

Sly ♂, ♀
Mainly U.S.: recent coinage. The reasons for its adoption as a given name are not clear. In the case of the American actor Sylvester Stallone, it is used as a contracted pet form of his given name. As a girl's name it may have originated as a pet form of ◊**Selina**. The fact that it coincides in form with the vocabulary word *sly* meaning 'cunning' or 'devious' does not seem to have inhibited its current use as a given name.

Sofia ♀
Variant spelling of ◊**Sophia**.

Sofie ♀
Variant spelling of ◊**Sophie**.

Solomon ♂
Biblical name (Hebrew *Shlomo*, derived from *shalom* 'peace'), borne by one of the great kings of Israel, son of David and Bathsheba, who was legendary for his wisdom (2 Samuel 12–24; 1 Kings 1–11; 2 Chronicles 1–9). The books of Proverbs and Ecclesiastes were ascribed to him, and the Song of Solomon, otherwise

known as the Song of Songs, bears his name. It has been sporadically used among Gentiles since the Middle Ages, but is still mainly a Jewish name.

Somerled ♂

Scottish (Highland): from the Old Norse personal name *Sumarliðr*, probably originally a byname meaning 'summer traveller'. This was the name of the founder of the powerful and widespread Clan Macdonald, Lords of the Isles from the 12th to the 15th century, and it is still occasionally bestowed on members of clan Macdonald and its septs.
Variants: **Summerlad** (altered by folk etymology); **Somhairle** (Gaelic form, also used in Ireland; Anglicized as **Sorley**).

Sondra ♀

Of recent origin, apparently an altered form of ◊**Sandra**.

Sonia ♀

Variant spelling of ◊**Sonya**.

Sonny ♂

Originally a nickname, from a pet form of the word *son* used as an affectionate term of address, but now sometimes used as a first name in its own right. In communities of Italian origin, it is sometimes used as an English equivalent of *Sandro*. See Italian supplement.

Sonya ♀

Russian pet form of *Sofya* (see ◊**Sophia**), popular as a given name in its own right in Britain and elsewhere since the 1920s.

Soo ♀

Recent coinage, a fanciful variant spelling of ◊**Sue**.

Sophia ♀

From the Greek word meaning 'wisdom'. The Eastern cult of St Sophia arose as a result of misinterpretation of the phrase *Hagia Sophia* 'holy wisdom' as if it meant 'St Sophia'. The name became popular in England in the 17th and 18th centuries. The heroine of Fielding's novel *Tom Jones* (1749) is called Sophia Weston. In recent years, its popularity has been further increased by the fame of

the Italian film actress Sophia Loren (b. 1934).
Variant: **Sofia**.

Sophie ♀

French form of ◊**Sophia**. In the English-speaking world, where it has been popular since the 18th century, it is often taken as a pet form of that name.
Variants: **Sofie**, **Sophy**.

Sorcha ♀

Irish and Scottish Gaelic name, pronounced 'sorr-kha'. It is derived from a Celtic word meaning 'brightness'. In Ireland it has long been considered a Gaelic form of ◊**Sarah**, and Anglicized as *Sarah* and *Sally*, but this is based on no more than a slight phonetic similarity.

Sorley ♂

Scottish (Highland) and Irish: Anglicized form of the Gaelic name *Somhairle* (pronounced 'sorr-lee'). See ◊**Somerled**.

Sorrel ♀

From the vocabulary word for the plant (Old French *surele*, apparently a derivative of *sur* 'sour' (of Germanic origin), alluding to the acid taste of its leaves).
Variants: **Sorrell**, **Sorell**, **Sorel**.

Spencer ♂

Transferred use of the surname, in origin an occupational name for a 'dispenser' of supplies in a manor house. This is the name of a great English noble family, traditionally supposed to be descended from someone who performed this function in the royal household. Its popularity as a given name was influenced in the mid-20th century by the American film actor Spencer Tracy (1900–67).

Spike ♂

Normally a nickname, but occasionally used as a given name in recent years, due to the influence of the bandleader Spike Jones (1911–65) and the comedian Spike Milligan (b. 1918). As a nickname it usually refers to an unruly tuft or 'spike' of hair.

Sprite ♀

Modern coinage, from the vocabulary word denoting a small supernatural creature, mischievous yet benevolent (from Old French *esprit*, Latin *spiritus* 'spirit', 'incorporeal being').

Stacey ♀, ♂

Of uncertain derivation, probably a transferred use of the surname, itself derived in the Middle Ages from a diminutive of *Stace*, a short form of ◊**Eustace**. It is not clear why this name should have become so common in the 1970s and 1980s as a girl's name (less commonly a boy's name).

Variants: **Stacy**, **Stacie**, **Staci**.

Stafford ♂

Transferred use of the surname, in origin a local name from any of various places so called from Old English *stæð* 'landing place' + *ford* 'ford', most notably the county town of Staffordshire. This was the surname of the family that held the dukedom of Buckingham in the 15th and 16th centuries.

Stamford ♂

Transferred use of the surname, in origin a variant of ◊**Stanford**. Use as a given name may in part have been influenced by the city of Stamford in Connecticut (established in 1642) and by Sir Thomas Stamford Raffles (1781–1826), British founder of Singapore.

Stan ♂

Short form of ◊**Stanley**.

Standish ♂

Transferred use of an English surname, in origin a local name from a place in Lancashire named with the Old English elements *stān* 'stone' + *edisc* 'pasture'. This was borne most famously by Miles Standish (?1584–1656), soldier, military leader, and law-enforcement officer of the Pilgrim Fathers, the subject of a historically inaccurate poem by Longfellow.

Stanford ♂

Transferred use of the surname, in origin a local name from the very numerous places named with the Old English elements *stān* 'stone' + *ford* 'ford'. Use as a given name may have been influenced by the prestigious Californian university named after Senator Leland Stanford, on whose land it was built. It may also in some cases have been adopted as an alternative elaboration of ◊**Stan**.

Stanislas ♂

Latinized form of an old Slavonic personal name composed of the elements *stan* 'government' + *slav* 'glory', used in Irish as an Anglicized form of the Gaelic name ◊**Anéislis**.

Stanley ♂

Transferred use of the surname, in origin a local name from any of numerous places (in Derbys., Durham, Gloucs., Staffs., Wilts., and Yorks.) so called from Old English *stān* 'stone' + *lēah* 'wood', 'clearing'. This is well established as a given name, and has been widely used as such since the 1880s. It had been in occasional use earlier. Its popularity seems to have stemmed at least in part from the fame of the explorer Sir Henry Morton Stanley (1841–1904), who was born in Wales as John Rowlands but later took the name of his adoptive father, a New Orleans cotton dealer.

Short form: **Stan**.

Star ♀

Modern name, a vernacular equivalent of ◊**Stella**.

Variant: **Starr**.

Steel ♂

From the name of the hard and durable metal (Middle English *steel*, from Old English *stȳle*), in part a transferred use of the surname derived from this word as a nickname or occupational name.

Variant: **Steele**.

Steff ♀

Short form of ◊**Stephanie**.
Pet forms: **Steffie**, **Steffy**.

Steffany ♀

Respelled form of ◊**Stephanie**.

Stella ♀

From Latin *stella* 'star'. This was not used as a given name before the 16th century, when Sir Philip Sidney seems to have been the first to use it (as a name deliberately far removed from the prosaic range of everyday names) in the sonnets addressed by Astrophel to his lady, Stella. *Stella Maris* 'star of the sea' was, however, established long before that as a byname of the Virgin Mary, and may have had some influence on the choice of the word as a name.

Steph ♀

Short form of ◊**Stephanie**.

Stephan ♂

Variant of ◊**Stephen**, preserving the vowels of the Greek name.

Stephanie ♀

From French *Stéphanie*, vernacular form of Latin *Stephania*, a variant of *Stephana*, which was in use among early Christians as a feminine form of *Stephanus* (see ◊**Stephen**).
Variant: **Steffany**.
Short form: **Steff**.
Pet forms: **Steffie**, **Steffy**, **Stevie**.

Stephen ♂

Usual English spelling of the name of the first Christian martyr (Acts 6–7), whose feast is accordingly celebrated next after Christ's own (26 December). His name is derived from the Greek word *stephanos* 'garland', 'crown'.
Variants: **Steven**, **Stephan**.
Short form: **Steve**.
Pet form: **Stevie**.

Sterling ♂

Transferred use of the surname, a variant of ◊**Stirling**. As a given name, however, it is likely to have been chosen because of its association with the vocabulary word occurring in such phrases as 'sterling qualities' and 'sterling worth'. This is derived from the Middle English word *sterrling* 'little star': some Norman coins had a little star on them. A 20th-century influence on the name has been the

American film actor Sterling Hayden (1916–86).

Steve ♂

Short form of ◊**Stephen** and ◊**Steven**, associated with the American film star Steve McQueen (1930–80), noted for his 'tough-guy' roles.

Steven ♂

Variant of ◊**Stephen**, reflecting the normal pronunciation of the name in the English-speaking world.

Stevie ♂, ♀

Pet form of ◊**Stephen** and of ◊**Stephanie**. A well-known female bearer was the poet Stevie Smith (1902–71), whose baptismal name was Florence Margaret Smith.

Stewart ♂

Variant of ◊**Stuart**, less common as a given name, although more common as a surname.

Stirling ♂

Transferred use of the surname, in origin a local name from the town in Scotland. The place name is of uncertain derivation, perhaps from Old Welsh *ystre Velyn* 'dwelling of Melyn'.

Stone ♂

Probably for the most part a transferred use of the surname, which originally denoted someone who lived near a large boulder or outcrop. In other cases it may derive directly from the vocabulary word (Old English *stān*), and be chosen as representing qualities of strength and endurance.

Storm ♀

Apparently a 20th-century coinage, although it may have been in use slightly earlier. The name is presumably derived from the vocabulary word, adopted by admirers of *Sturm und Drang*.

Stuart ♂

From the French version of the surname *Stewart*. This form was introduced to Scotland in the 16th century by Mary Stuart, Queen of Scots, who was brought up in France. The surname originated as

an occupational or status name for someone who served as a *steward* in a manor or royal household. The Scottish royal family of this name are traditionally supposed to be descended from a family who were hereditary stewards in Brittany before the Conquest. Use as a given name originated in Scotland, but is now widespread throughout the English-speaking world.
Variant: **Stewart**.
Short forms: **Stu**, **Stew**.

Sue ♀
Short form of ◊**Susan** and, less commonly, of ◊**Susanna** and ◊**Suzanne**.
Variants: **Su**, **Soo**.

Sukie ♀
Pet form of ◊**Susan**, very common in the 18th century, but now rare.
Variant: **Sukey**.

Summer ♀
Mainly U.S.: from the vocabulary word for the season (Old English *sumor*), used in modern times as a given name because of its pleasant associations. Nevertheless, the name ◊**Autumn** is now more common.

Summerlad ♂
Scottish: variant spelling of ◊**Somerled**, being taken by folk etymology as derived from the words *summer* and *lad*.

Sunny ♀
From the vocabulary word used to describe someone with a bright and cheerful personality (a derivative of *sun*, referring to the light and warmth provided by that heavenly body). Compare ◊**Sonny**.

Susan ♀
English vernacular form of ◊**Susanna**, always the most common of this group of names. A 20th-century influence has been the American film star Susan Hayward (1918–75).
Variant: **Suzan**.
Short form: **Sue**, **Su**, **Soo**.
Pet forms: **Susie**, **Suzie**, **Suzy**, **Sukie**, **Sukey**.

Susanna ♀
New Testament form (Luke 8:3) of the Hebrew name *Shoshana* (from *shoshan* 'lily', which in modern Hebrew also means 'rose').
Variant: **Susana**.

Susannah ♀
Variant of ◊**Susanna**. This is the form of the name used in the Old Testament. The tale of Susannah, wife of Joachim, and the elders who falsely accused her of adultery, is to be found in the apocryphal book that bears her name, and was popular in the Middle Ages and later.
Variant: **Suzanna**.

Susie ♀
Pet form of ◊**Susan** and, less commonly, of ◊**Susanna(h)** and ◊**Suzanne**.
Variants: **Suzie**, **Suzy**.

Suzanne ♀
French form of ◊**Susanna**, now also used in the English-speaking world.

Suzette ♀
French pet form of ◊**Suzanne**, now also used in the English-speaking world.

Suzie ♀
Variant spelling of ◊**Susie**.
Variant: **Suzy**.

Swift ♂
Probably from the name of the bird, so called because of its rapid, darting flight (Old English *swift*, referring to a sweeping motion). In part it may represent a transferred use of the surname, in origin usually a nickname for a fast runner. As an Irish surname it represents an Anglicized form of Gaelic *Ó Fuada* 'descendant of *Fuada*', a personal name derived from *fuad* 'haste'.

Sybil ♀
From the name (Greek *Sibylla* or *Sybilla*, with confusion over the vowels from an early period) of a class of ancient prophetesses inspired by Apollo. According to medieval theology, they were pagans denied the knowledge of Christ but blessed by God with some insight into things to come and accordingly

admitted to heaven. It was thus regarded as a respectable name to be borne by Christians.

Variants: **Sybilla** (Latinate), **Sybille** (from French). See also ◊**Sibyl**.

Sydney ♂, occasionally ♀
Variant spelling of ◊**Sidney**. It was a medieval practice to write *y* for *i*, for greater clarity since *i* was easily confused with other letters.

Sylphide ♀
From the vocabulary word referring to one of the invisible spirits supposed to populate the air (from French, a derivative of *sylpha*, a Latinate term apparently coined by Paracelsus).

Sylvester ♂
Variant spelling of ◊**Silvester**.

Sylvestra ♀
Variant spelling of ◊**Silvestra**.

Sylvia ♀
Variant spelling of ◊**Silvia**. It is now rather more common than the plain form.

Sylvie ♀
French form of ◊**Silvia**, now also used in the English-speaking world.

TABITHA TACEY TACITA TAD TADHG TALB
OT TALFRYN TALIA TALIESIN TALITHA TAL
ULLA TALYA TAM TAMARA TAMMY TAMS
IN TANIA TANNER TANSY TANYA TARA T
ARE TARLACH TARQUIN TARRA TASHA T
ATHNA TAWNY TAYLOR TEAGUE TEAL TE

Tabitha ♀

Aramaic name, meaning 'doe' or 'roe', borne in the New Testament by a woman who was restored to life by St Peter (Acts 9:36–41). In the biblical account this form of the name is given together with its Greek equivalent, ◊**Dorcas**. It was one of the names much favoured by Puritans and Disssenters from the 16th to the 19th centuries, and is still occasionally used.

Pet form: **Tabby** (obsolete).

Tacey ♀

As a medieval given name this is derived from the Latin imperative *tace* 'be silent', regarded as a suitable admonition to women. As a modern name, it is a pet form of ◊**Tacita** or perhaps derived from ◊**Tracy**.

Tacita ♀

From Latin *Tacita*, feminine form of the Roman family name *Tacitus*, originally a byname meaning 'silent'.

Tad ♂

Normally an Anglicized form of Gaelic ◊**Tadhg**, but sometimes a short form of ◊**Thaddeus**. It is fairly commonly used as an independent given name, especially in America.

Tadhg ♂

Irish and Scottish Gaelic traditional name, pronounced '*teig*'. It was originally a byname meaning 'poet' or 'philosopher'. This was a very common given name in Ireland throughout the Middle Ages.

Anglicized forms: **Tad**, **Teague**, **Teigue**.

Talbot ♂

Transferred use of the surname. This is of much debated origin, but seems most likely to be from a Norman French personal name of Germanic origin, composed of the elements *tal* 'to destroy' + *bod* 'message', 'tidings'. This is the surname of an ancient Irish family of Norman origin, who have held the earldoms of Shrewsbury and Waterford since the 15th century. The old word *talbot*, denoting a kind of hunting dog, is from the surname.

Talfryn ♂

Welsh: modern given name, originally a local name, from Welsh *tal* 'high', 'end of' + a mutated form of *bryn* 'hill'.

Talia ♀

Variant spelling of ◊**Talya** and ◊**Thalia**.

Taliesin ♂

Welsh, pronounced 'tal-*yes*-in': from *tâl* 'brow' + *iesin* 'shining'. This was the name of a legendary 6th-century Welsh poet, and has been revived in recent times.

Talitha ♀

Of New Testament origin: from an Aramaic word meaning 'little girl'. Jesus raised a child from the dead with the words 'Talitha cumi; which is, being interpreted, Damsel, I say unto thee, arise' (Mark 5:41).

Talulla ♀

Irish: Anglicized form of the Gaelic name *Tuilelaith*, pronounced '*til*-a-la', derived from words meaning 'abundance' and 'lady' or 'princess'. This name was borne by at least two Irish saints of the 8th and 9th centuries. The spelling **Tallulah** was made famous by the American actress Tallulah Bankhead

(1903–68), who inherited the name from her grandmother.

Talya ♀
Shortened form of ◊Natalya.
Variant: **Talia** (see also ◊**Thalia**).

Tam ♂
Scottish short form of ◊**Thomas**.

Tamara ♀
Russian: probably derived from the Hebrew name *Tamar*, from a vocabulary word meaning 'date palm', with the addition of the feminine suffix *-a*. The name Tamar is borne in the Bible by two female characters: the daughter-in-law of Judah, who is involved in a somewhat seamy story of sexual intrigue (Genesis 38), and a daughter of King David (2 Samuel 13), the full sister of Absalom, who is raped by her half-brother Amnon, for which Absalom kills him. It is rather surprising, therefore, that it should have given rise to such a popular given name. However, Absalom himself later has a daughter named Tamar, who is referred to as 'a woman of a fair countenance' (2 Samuel 14:27), and the name may derive its popularity from this reference. The name is now also used in the English-speaking world.

Tammy ♀
Pet form of ◊**Tamara** and ◊**Tamsin**.

Tamsin ♀
Contracted form of Latinate *Thomasina*, a feminine form of ◊**Thomas**. This was relatively common throughout Britain in the Middle Ages, but confined to Cornwall immediately before its recent revival.

Tania ♀
Variant spelling of ◊**Tanya**.

Tanner ♂
Transferred use of the common surname, in origin an occupational name for someone who treated animal skins to form leather (via Old English and Old French from a Late Latin word apparently derived from a Celtic name for the oak, whose bark was used in the process).

Tansy ♀
From the vocabulary word for the flower (Old French *tanesie*, derived from Greek *athanasia* 'immortal'). It has enjoyed some popularity as a given name in the 20th century.

Tanya ♀
Russian pet form of ◊**Tatiana**, now quite commonly used as an independent given name in the English-speaking world.
Variant: **Tania**.

Tara ♀
From the name (meaning 'hill') of a place in Meath, seat of the high kings of Ireland. It has been used as a girl's name in America since around 1940, probably as a result of the success of the film *Gone with the Wind*, in which the estate of this name has great emotional significance. In Britain it was not much used before the 1960s. Its popularity then was influenced by the character Tara King in the television series *The Avengers*.
Variant: **Tarra**.

Taree ♀
Occasionally used as a given name in Australia. It appears to represent an elaboration of ◊**Tara**, influenced by the name of a place in New South Wales. The place name probably derives from an Aboriginal word for a type of fig tree found in the area.

Tárlach ♂
Irish Gaelic name, pronounced '*tor-lakh*': a modern shortened form of the traditional name *Toirdhealbhach*, apparently originally a byname meaning 'instigator', from *toirdhealbh* 'prompting'. It was the name of a high king of Ireland who died in 1156. The notion that this is a derivative of *Þorr*, the name of the Norse god of thunder, is probably no more than folk etymology.

Tarquin ♂
The name borne by two early kings of Rome, Tarquinius Priscus 'the Old' (616–578 BC) and Tarquinius Superbus 'the Proud' (534–510 BC). It is of

uncertain, probably Etruscan, origin; many of the most ancient Roman institutions and the vocabulary associated with them, as well as many Roman family names, were borrowed from the Etruscans. The name is now occasionally used in the English-speaking world.

Tarra ♀
Variant of ◊Tara.

Tasha ♀
Shortened form of ◊Natasha.

Tatiana ♀
Russian: of early Christian origin. This was the name of various early saints honoured particularly in the Eastern Church. In origin it is a feminine form of Latin *Tatiānus*, a derivative of *Tatius*, a Roman family name of obscure origin. Titus Tatius was, according to tradition, a king of the Sabines who later shared with Romulus the rule over a united population of Sabines and Latins. The name is now also used in the English-speaking world, though not so commonly as the pet form ◊Tanya.

Tawny ♀
From the vocabulary word denoting a light brown hair colour (Anglo-Norman *tauné*, Old French *tané* 'tanned'). This is probably a modern name created on the lines of examples such as ◊Ginger and ◊Sandy. However, it may also be a transferred use of the surname *Tawney*, which is a Norman baronial name from one of two places in Normandy: *Saint-Aubin-du-Thenney* or *Saint-Jean-du-Thenney*.
Variant: **Tawney**.

Taylor ♂, ♀
Transferred use of the surname, in origin an occupational name for a tailor (Anglo-Norman *taillour*, a derivative of *taillier* 'to cut', Late Latin *tāleāre*). Use as a given name was influenced by the U.S. president Zachary Taylor (1784–1850), hero of the Mexican War. It is now well established as a girl's name in North America; it was one of the top hundred girls' names bestowed in 1989. This may have been inspired by the film actress Elizabeth Taylor (b. 1932).

Teague ♂
Irish: Anglicized form of Gaelic ◊Tadhg.
Variant: **Teigue**.

Teal ♀
One of the girls' names taken from birds in the past couple of decades. The teal is a kind of small duck; its name is attested in English since the 14th century and is probably connected with Middle Low German *tēlink*, Middle Dutch *tēling*.
Variant: **Teale**.

Teàrlach ♂
Scottish Gaelic, pronounced 'tcharlakh': a modern shortened form of the ancient Gaelic name *Toirdhealbhach*; see ◊Tárlach.

Ted ♂
Short form of ◊Edward.
Pet form: **Teddy**.

Teddy ♂, ♀
Now generally used as a pet form of ◊Edward, although it was originally used of ◊Theodore. Teddy bears were so named from the American president Theodore Roosevelt (1858–1919). Occasionally it is also used as a girl's name, in part as a pet form of ◊Edwina.

Tegwen ♀
Welsh: modern coinage from *teg* 'lovely' + *(g)wen*, feminine form of *gwyn* 'white', 'fair', 'blessed', 'holy'.

Teigue ♂
Irish: Anglicized form of Gaelic ◊Tadhg.

Tel ♂
Altered short form of ◊Terry or ◊Terence, of recent origin. For the substitution of *-l* for *-r*, cf. ◊Hal.

Teleri ♀
Welsh: extension of the name ◊Eleri, with the addition of the honorific prefix *ty-* 'your'. Teleri, daughter of Peul, is mentioned in the *Mabinogi*.

Tempe ♀
Pronounced 'tem-pee': from the name of a valley in eastern Greece, situated

between Mount Olympus and Mount Ossa. In classical times it was regarded as the home of the Muses. The place name may be derived from Greek *temnein* 'to cut', referring to a valley carved between mountains.

Tempest ♂, ♀

Transferred use of the surname, which most probably originated as a nickname for someone with a stormy temperament, from the Middle English and Old French vocabulary word *tempeste*, from Latin *tempestās*. This was used in Yorkshire as a given name from the 1570s onwards, almost always in families with some connection with the Tempest family of Broughton Hall. In the 20th century the name has sometimes been adopted independently from the vocabulary word, especially as a female name, by admirers of powerful emotions.

Terence ♂

From the Latin name *Terentius*, which is of uncertain origin. It was borne by the Roman playwright Marcus Terentius Afer (who was a former slave, and took his name from his master, Publius Terentius Lucanus), and later by various minor early Christian saints. As a modern given name it is a 'learned' back-formation from the supposed pet form ◊**Terry**. It has become common in Ireland through being used as an Anglicized form of the Gaelic name *Toirdhealbhach* (see ◊**Tárlach**).
Variants: **Terrance**, **Terrence**.
Short form: **Tel**. See also ◊**Terry**.

Teresa ♀

Italian and Spanish form of ◊**Theresa**. In the English-speaking world the name is often chosen in this spelling by Roman Catholics, with particular reference to the Spanish saint, Teresa of Ávila (Teresa Cepeda de Ahumada, 1515–82).

Terrance ♂

The most common U.S. spelling of ◊**Terence**.

Terrell ♂

Transferred use of the surname, a variant of ◊**Tyrrell**.

Terrence ♂

Variant spelling of ◊**Terence**.

Terri ♀

Mid 20th-century coinage, originating either as a pet form of ◊**Theresa** or as a feminine spelling of ◊**Terry**. It is now well established as an independent given name, particularly in North America.

Terry ♂

As a medieval given name this is a Norman form of the French name *Thierri*, from Germanic *Theodoric*, from *þeud* 'people', 'race' + *rīc* 'power', 'ruler'. This was adopted by the Normans and introduced by them to Britain. In modern English use it seems at first to have been a transferred use of the surname derived from the medieval given name, and later to have been taken as a pet form of ◊**Terence**.
Short form: **Tel**.

Terryl ♀

Modern coinage, apparently an elaboration of ◊**Terri** with the suffix -*yl* seen in names such as ◊**Cheryl**.

Tess ♀

Short form of ◊**Tessa**.

Tessa ♀

Now generally considered to be a pet form of ◊**Theresa**, although often used independently. However, the formation is not clear, and it may be of distinct origin. Literary contexts of the late 19th century show that the name was thought of as Italian, although it is in fact unknown in Italy.
Short form: **Tess**.

Tessie ♀

Pet form of ◊**Tessa**.
Variant: **Tessy**.

Tetty ♀

Pet form of ◊**Elizabeth**, common in the 18th century (when it was used, for example, by Samuel Johnson's wife) but now rare or obsolete.

Variant: **Tettie**.

Tex ♂

Mainly U.S.: in origin a nickname for someone from *Texas*. The name of the state derives from an Indian tribal name, meaning 'friends', recorded as early as 1541 in the form *Teyas* and subsequently transmitted through Spanish sources.

Thaddeus ♂

Latin form of a New Testament name, the byname used to refer to one of Christ's lesser-known apostles, whose given name was *Lebbaeus* (Matthew 10:3). It is of uncertain origin, possibly derived via Aramaic from the Greek name *Theodōros* 'gift of God' or *Theodotos* 'given by God'.

Short forms: **Thad**, ◊**Tad**.

Thalia ♀

Name borne in classical mythology by the Muse of comedy; it is derived from Greek *thallein* 'to flourish', and has occasionally been chosen in recent years by parents in the English-speaking world in search of novelty.

Variant: **Talia** (see also ◊**Talya**).

Thea ♀

Shortened form of ◊**Dorothea**.

Thecla ♀

Contracted form of the Greek name *Theokleia*, derived from *theos* 'God' + *kleia* 'glory'. The name was borne by a 1st-century saint (the first female martyr), who was particularly popular in the Middle Ages because of the lurid details of her suffering recorded in the apocryphal 'Acts of Paul and Thecla'.

Theda ♀

Latinate short form of the various ancient Germanic female personal names derived from *þeud* 'people', 'race'. It enjoyed a brief popularity in the United States from about 1915 to 1925, due to the popularity of the silent-film actress Theda Bara (1890–1955), the original 'vamp'. Her original name was Theodosia Goodman.

Thelma ♀

First used by the novelist Marie Corelli for the heroine of her novel *Thelma* (1887). She was supposed to be Norwegian, but it is not a traditional Scandinavian name. Greek *thelēma* (neuter) means 'wish' or '(act of) will', and the name could perhaps be interpreted as a contracted form of this.

Theo ♂

Short form of ◊**Theodore** and, less commonly, of ◊**Theobald**.

Theobald ♂

From an Old French name of Germanic (Frankish) origin, derived from *þeud* 'people', 'race' + *bald* 'bold', 'brave'. The first element was altered under the influence of Greek *theos* 'god'. This name was adopted by the Normans and introduced by them to Britain.

Short form: **Theo**.

Theodora ♀

Feminine form of ◊**Theodore**, borne most notably by a 9th-century empress of Byzantium, the wife of Theophilus the Iconoclast. It has frequently been used as an English given name. It means 'gift of God'; the elements are the same as those of ◊**Dorothea**, but in reverse order.

Theodore ♂

From the French form of the Greek name *Theodōros*, derived from *theos* 'god' + *dōron* 'gift'. The name was popular among early Christians and was borne by several saints.

Short forms: **Theo**, **Ted**.

Pet form: **Teddy**.

Theodosia ♀

Greek name derived from *theos* 'god' + *dōsis* 'giving'. It was borne by several early saints venerated in the Eastern Church, and is only very occasionally used in the English-speaking world today.

Thera ♀
Of uncertain derivation: it could represent a shortened form of ◊**Theresa**, or be derived from the name of the Greek island of *Thēra*.

Theresa ♀
Of problematic origin. The name seems to have been first used in Spain and Portugal, and, according to tradition, was the name of the wife of St Paulinus of Nola, who spent most of his life in Spain; she was said to have originated (and to have derived her name) from the Greek island of *Thēra*. However, this story is neither factually nor etymologically confirmed.
Variants: **Teresa**, **Treeza**.
Pet forms: ◊**Terri**, ◊**Tessa**.

Thessaly ♀
From the name of the region in eastern central Greece. The place name is of ancient Illyrian origin and uncertain meaning.

Thirzah ♀
Variant of ◊**Tirzah**.
Variant: **Thirza**.

Thos ♂
Written abbreviation of ◊**Thomas**.

Thomas ♂
New Testament name, borne by one of Christ's twelve apostles, referred to as 'Thomas, called Didymus' (John 11:16; 20:24). *Didymos* is the Greek word for 'twin', and the name is the Greek form of an Aramaic byname meaning 'twin'. The given name has always been popular throughout Christendom, in part because St Thomas's doubts have made him seem a very human character.
Short forms: **Tom**. Scottish: **Tam**.
Pet form: **Tommy**.

Thorn ♂
Short form of ◊**Thornton** or transferred use of the surname (originally denoting someone who lived near a large thorn bush), or direct adoption of the vocabulary word because of its association with natural hardiness.

Thornton ♂
Transferred use of the surname, in origin a local name from the very numerous places named with Old English *þorn* 'thornbush' + *tūn* 'enclosure', 'settlement'. The given name is associated with the U.S. writer Thornton Wilder (1897–1975).

Tia ♀
Recent coinage, apparently originating as a short form of the various given names ending in *-tia*, as for example ◊**Laetitia** and ◊**Lucretia**.

Tiana ♀
Recent coinage, apparently an elaborated form of ◊**Tia** or a shortened form of ◊**Christiana**.

Tiara ♀
Recent coinage, apparently from the vocabulary word for a woman's jewelled headdress (via Latin, from Greek *tiara(s)*, originally denoting a kind of conical cap worn by the ancient Persians). Compare ◊**Tierra**.

Tiernan ♂
Transferred use of the Irish surname, Gaelic Ó *Tíghearnáin* 'descendant of Tighearnán'. The latter is a diminutive of *tighearna* 'lord'.

Tierney ♂, ♀
Transferred use of the Irish surname, Gaelic Ó *Tíghearnaigh* 'descendant of Tighearnach'. The latter is a derivative of *tighearna* 'lord'. Tighearnach was the name of a 6th-century saint who served as abbot of Clones and later as bishop of Clogher. This is now well established in North America as a girl's name, at least in part due to the influence of the film actress Gene Tierney (1920–91).

Tierra ♀
Recent coinage, of uncertain derivation, ostensibly from Spanish *tierra* 'land', 'earth' (Latin *terra*), but cf. ◊**Tiara**.

Tiffany ♀
Usual medieval English form of the Greek name *Theophania* 'Epiphany',

from *theos* 'god' + *phainein* 'to appear'. This was once a relatively common name, given particularly to girls born on the feast of the Epiphany (6 January), and it gave rise to an English surname. As a given name, it fell into disuse until revived in the 20th century under the influence of the famous New York jewellers, Tiffany's, and the film, starring Audrey Hepburn, *Breakfast at Tiffany's* (1961). In America this is a very popular Black girl's name.

Tilda ♀
Shortened form of ◊**Matilda**.

Tilly ♀
Pet form of ◊**Matilda**, much used from the Middle Ages to the late 19th century, when it also came to be used as an independent given name. It is rare in either use nowadays.
Variant: **Tillie**.

Tim ♂
Short form of ◊**Timothy**, also used in Ireland as an Anglicized form of ◊**Tadhg**.
Pet form: **Timmy** (normally used only for young boys).

Timothy ♂
English form of the Greek name *Timotheos*, from *timē* 'honour' + *theos* 'god'. This was the name of a companion of St Paul; according to tradition, he was stoned to death for denouncing the worship of Diana. It was not used in England before the Reformation.
Short form: **Tim**.
Pet form: **Timmy**.

Tina ♀
Shortened form of ◊**Christina** and other girls' names ending in -*tina*; now often used as an independent given name.

Tirion ♀
Welsh: modern given name, from the vocabulary word meaning 'kind', 'gentle'.

Tirzah ♀
Biblical name, meaning 'pleasantness' or 'delight' in Hebrew, borne by a minor character mentioned in a genealogy

(Numbers 26:33). It is also a biblical place name.
Variants: **Tirza**, **Thirzah**, **Thirza**.

Tisha ♀
In origin a respelling of a reduced form of ◊**Laetitia** or ◊**Patricia**. It is now fairly commonly used as an independent given name.

Tita ♀
Either a short form of names ending in these two syllables, as for example *Martita*, or a feminine form of ◊**Titus**.

Titty ♀
Pet form of ◊**Laetitia**, which has now become obsolete because of its unfortunate coincidence in form with the slang word for a female breast.

Titus ♂
From an old Roman given name, of unknown ultimate origin. It was borne by a companion of St Paul who became the first bishop of Crete, and also by the Roman emperor who destroyed Jerusalem in AD 70. It has never been very common in the English-speaking world, but is recorded steadily in some families from the 17th century onwards.

Tobias ♂
Biblical name: Greek form of Hebrew *Tobiah* 'God is good'. This name is borne by several characters in the Bible (appearing in the Authorized Version also as *Tobijah*), but in the Middle Ages it was principally associated with the tale of 'Tobias and the Angel'. According to the Book of Tobit in the Apocrypha, Tobias, the son of Tobit, a rich and righteous Jew of Nineveh, was lucky enough to acquire the services of the archangel Raphael as a travelling companion on a journey to Ecbatana. He returned wealthy, married, and with a cure for his father's blindness. A historical St Tobias was martyred (*c*.315) at Sebaste in Armenia, together with Carterius, Styriacus, Eudoxius, Agapius, and five others.

Toby ♂
English vernacular form of ◊**Tobias**.

Todd ♂
Transferred use of the surname, which was originally a nickname from an English dialect word meaning 'fox'.

Tom ♂
Short form of ◊**Thomas**, in use since the Middle Ages, and recorded as an independent name since the 18th century.

Tommy ♂
Pet form of ◊**Thomas**.

Tone ♂
Transferred use of the English surname, which originated as a local name for someone who lived in the main settlement of a village (Middle English *tone*, from Old English *tūn*) rather than an outlying dwelling. As an Irish first name it is used in honour of Theobald Wolfe Tone, leader of a rebellion against English rule in 1798. This name is also used as an informal pet form of ◊**Anthony**; cf. ◊**Tony**.

Toni ♀
Feminine form of ◊**Tony**, in part used as a pet form of ◊**Antonia** but more commonly as an independent given name.

Tonia ♀
Shortened form of ◊**Antonia**, now quite widely used as an independent given name.

Tony ♂, occasionally ♀
Shortened form of ◊**Anthony**, now sometimes used as an independent given name.

Tonya ♀
Variant of ◊**Tonia**.

Topaz ♀
One of the rarer examples of the class of modern girl's names taken from vocabulary words denoting gemstones. The topaz gets its name via French and Latin from Greek; it is probably ultimately of Oriental origin. In the Middle Ages this was sometimes used as a boy's name, being taken as a form of ◊**Tobias**.

Torquil ♂
Scottish: Anglicized form of the trad-itional Gaelic name *Torcall*, originally a borrowing of the Old Norse personal name Þorketill, composed of the name of the god Þorr + *ketill* '(sacrificial) cauldron'.

Tory ♀
Pet form of ◊**Victoria**.

Tottie ♀
Pet form of ◊**Charlotte**, a rhyming variant of ◊**Lottie**. The name was most common in the 18th and 19th centuries, like ◊**Tetty**.
Variant: **Totty**.

Tracy ♀, formerly ♂
Transferred use of the surname, in origin a Norman baronial name from places in France called *Tracy*, from the Gallo-Roman personal name *Thracius* + the local suffix -*ācum*. In former times, *Tracy* was occasionally used as a boy's name, as were the surnames of other English noble families. Later, it was also used as a girl's name, generally being taken as a pet form of ◊**Theresa**. In recent years, it has become an immensely popular girl's name. A strong influence was the character of Tracy Lord, played by Grace Kelly in the film *High Society* (1956).
Variants: **Tracey**, **Tracie** (♀).

Trahaearn ♂
Welsh: traditional name composed of the intensive prefix *tra*- + *haearn* 'iron'.

Travis ♂
Transferred use of the surname, in origin a Norman French occupational name (from *traverser* 'to cross') for someone who collected a toll from users of a bridge or a particular stretch of road. It is now regularly used as a given name, especially in America and Australia.

Traynor ♂
Transferred use of the Irish surname, Gaelic *Mac Thréinfhir* 'son of *Thréin-fear*', a byname meaning 'champion' (from *tréan* 'strong' + *fear* 'man').

Treena ♀
Variant spelling of ◊**Trina**.

Treasa ♀
Traditional Irish Gaelic name, said to be from *tréan* 'strength', 'intensity'. It is now more often used as the Irish equivalent of **Teresa**.

Treeza ♀
Modern contracted spelling of ◊**Theresa** or Anglicization of Irish ◊**Treasa**.

Trefor ♂
Welsh variant of ◊**Trevor**.

Tremaine ♂
Transferred use of the Cornish surname, in origin a local name from any of several places named with Cornish *tre* 'homestead', 'settlement' + *men* 'stone'.

Trent ♂
Especially U.S.: from the name of the river that flows through the British Midlands (cf. ◊**Clyde**), or a transferred use of the surname derived from it. The river name is of British origin: it may be composed of elements meaning 'through', 'across' and 'travel', 'journey', or it may mean 'traveller' or 'trespasser', a reference to frequent flooding. The given name may also in some cases be used as a short form of ◊**Trenton**.

Trenton ♂
Mainly U.S.: from the name of the city in New Jersey, the site of a decisive defeat of the British (1776) by Washington during the American Revolution. The city was founded in the late 17th century by a group of English Quakers under the leadership of a certain William Trent. It was originally *Trent's Town*, reduced within half a century to *Trenton*.

Trevelyan ♂
Transferred use of the Cornish surname, in origin a local name from a place mentioned in the Domesday Book as *Trevelien*, i.e. 'homestead or settlement (Cornish *tref*) of Elian'. The latter is an ancient Celtic personal name of obscure origin (cf. ◊**Elvis**).

Trevor ♂
Transferred use of the Welsh surname, in origin a local name from any of the very many places in Wales called *Trefor*, from *tref* 'settlement' + *fôr*, mutated form of *mawr* 'large'. In the mid-20th century it enjoyed considerable popularity in the English-speaking world among people with no connection with Wales, for example the actor Trevor Howard (1916–88), who was born in Kent.
Variant: **Trefor**.
Short form: **Trev**.

Trey ♂
U.S.: apparently from the vocabulary word *trey*, denoting the three in a suit of playing cards (from Old French *treis*, Latin *trēs*). It may sometimes be given to a third son, but often it is regarded as no more than a variant of ◊**Troy**.

Tricia ♀
Shortened form of ◊**Patricia**.
Variant: **Trisha**.

Trina ♀
Shortened form of ◊**Katrina**.
Variant: **Treena**.

Triona ♀
Shortened form of ◊**Catriona**.

Trisha ♀
Variant spelling of ◊**Tricia**.

Trista ♀
Name invented as a feminine form of ◊**Tristan**.

Tristan ♂
From Celtic legend, the name borne by a hero of medieval romance. There are many different versions of the immensely popular tragic story of Tristan and his love for Isolde. Generally, they agree that Tristan was an envoy sent by King Mark of Cornwall to bring back his bride, the Irish princess Isolde. Unfortunately, Tristan and Isolde fall in love with each other, having accidentally drunk the love potion intended for King Mark's wedding night. Tristan eventually leaves Cornwall to fight for King Howel of Brittany. Wounded in battle, he sends for Isolde. She arrives too late, and dies of grief beside his bier. The

name *Tristan* is of unknown derivation, though it may be connected with Pictish *Drostan*; it has been altered from an irrecoverable original as a result of transmission through Old French sources that insisted on associating it with Latin *tristis* 'sad', a reference to the young knight's tragic fate.
Variant: **Trystan** (mainly Welsh).

Tristram ♂
Variant of ◊**Tristan**. Both forms of the name occur in medieval and later versions of the legend. In Laurence Sterne's comic novel *Tristram Shandy* (1759–67), the name is bestowed on the narrator through a misunderstanding and is regarded by his father as a great misfortune. Since the name originally intended for him was *Trismegistus*, the degree of misfortune may be taken as somewhat exaggerated.
Variants: **Tristam**, **Trystram**.

Trixie ♀
Pet name derived from ◊**Beatrix**.
Variant: **Trixi**.

Troy ♂, ♀
Probably originally a transferred use of the surname, which is derived from *Troyes* in France. Nowadays, however, the given name is principally associated with the ancient city of Troy in Asia Minor, whose fate has been a central topic in epic poetry from Homer onwards. The story tells how Troy was sacked by the Greeks after a siege of ten years; according to classical legend, a few Trojan survivors got away to found Rome (and, according to medieval legend, another group founded Britain).

Trudi ♀
German (especially Swiss) pet form of the various girls' names ending in -trud(e), from Germanic *þrūþ* 'strength'.
Variants: **Trudie**, **Trudy**.

Truman ♂
Mainly U.S.: transferred use of the surname, in origin a nickname from Old English *trēowe* 'true', 'trusty' + *mann* 'man'. Use as a given name was boosted by the fame of Harry S. Truman (1884–1972), president of the United States (1945–52), although it was in occasional use before he became president.
Variant: **Trueman**.

Trystan ♂
Variant (mainly Welsh) of ◊**Tristan**.

Tucker ♂
Transferred use of the surname, in origin an occupational name for a fuller (from Old English *tūcian* 'to torment').

Tudor ♂
Welsh: traditional name derived from the Old Celtic form *Teutorix*, composed of elements meaning 'people' or 'tribe' and 'ruler' or 'king'. It has often been described as a Welsh form of ◊**Theodore**, but there is in fact no connection between them. Rather, the Welsh name is ultimately akin to the Germanic name *Theodoric* (see ◊**Terry**).
Variants: **Tudyr** (an earlier spelling); **Tudor** (an Anglicized spelling).

Turlough ♂
Irish: Anglicized form of Gaelic *Toirdhealbhach* (see ◊**Tárlach**).

Turner ♂
Transferred use of the surname, in origin an occupational name for someone who made articles of wood, bone, or metal by turning them on a lathe. Among Blacks in the United States it is sometimes used as a given name in honour of Nat Turner, a slave who in 1831 led an insurrection against local landowners before being captured and executed.

Ty ♂
Mainly U.S.: short form of ◊**Tyler** and ◊**Tyrone**.

Tybalt ♂
The usual medieval form of ◊**Theobald**, rarely used nowadays. It occurs in Shakespeare's *Romeo and Juliet* as the name of a brash young man who is killed in a brawl.

Tyler ♂
Mainly North American: transferred use of the surname, in origin an

occupational name for a tiler (an agent derivative of Old English *tigele* 'tile', from Latin *tēgula* 'covering'). John Tyler (1790–1862) was the tenth president of the United States.

Tyrone ♂

Mainly U.S.: from the name of a county in Northern Ireland and a city in Pennsylvania. Its use as a given name seems to be due to the influence of the two film actors (father and son) called Tyrone Power, especially the younger one (1913–58).

Tyrrell ♂

Mainly U.S.: transferred use of the surname, which is common in Ireland, but of uncertain derivation. It may have originated as a nickname for a stubborn person, from Old French *tirel*, used of an animal which pulls on the reins, a derivative of *tirer* 'to pull'.
Variant: **Tyrell**.

Tyson ♂

Mainly U.S.: transferred use of the surname, which is of dual origin. In part it is a metronymic from the medieval woman's given name *Dye*, pet form of *Dionysia*, and in part it is a nickname for a hot-tempered person, from Old French *tison* 'firebrand'. As a given name it is often taken as an expanded form or patronymic from ◊**Ty**.

UILLEAM UISDEAN ULICK ULTAN ULYSSES
UN UNIT URIAH URIEL URIEN URSULA U
ILLEAM U DEAN ULICK ULTAN ULYSSES U
NA UNITY URIAH URIEL URIEN URSULA UI
LLEAM U DEAN ULICK ULTAN ULYSSES UN
A UNITY URIAH URIEL URIEN URSULA UILL

Uilleam ♂

Scottish Gaelic form of ◊**William**.

Uisdean ♂

Scottish Gaelic: traditional name, originally a borrowing of the Old Norse personal name *Eysteinn*, which is from *ei, ey* 'always', 'for ever' + *steinn* 'stone'.

Ulick ♂

Irish: Anglicized form of Gaelic *Uilleac* or *Uilleag*. This name probably derives from Old Norse *Hugleikr*, from *hugr* 'heart', 'mind', 'spirit' + *leikr* 'play', 'sport'. Alternatively, it may be a diminutive derived from a short form of *Uilleam*, a Gaelic form of ◊**William** (cf. ◊**Liam**).

Ultan ♂

Irish: Anglicized form of the Gaelic name *Ultán*, a diminutive form of the ethnic name *Ultach* 'Ulsterman'.

Ulysses ♂

Latin form of the Greek name *Odysseus*, borne by the famous wanderer of Homer's *Odyssey*. The name is of uncertain derivation (it was associated by the Greeks themselves with the verb *odyssesthai* 'to hate'). Moreover, it is not clear why the Latin form should be so altered; mediation through Etruscan has been one suggestion. As an English given name it has occasionally been used in England from the 16th century and more commonly in America in the 19th and 20th centuries (like other names of classical origin such as ◊**Homer** and ◊**Virgil**). It was the name of the 18th president of the United States, Ulysses S. Grant (1822–85). It has also been used in Ireland as a classicizing form of ◊**Ulick**.

Una ♀

Anglicized form of Irish Gaelic *Úna*, a traditional name of uncertain derivation. It is identical in form with the vocabulary word *úna* 'hunger', 'famine', but is more likely to be derived from *uan* 'lamb'. In Irish legend Úna is the mother of the hero Conn Cétchathach (Conn of the Hundred Battles). It was also the name of the beloved of the 17th-century poet Tomás Láidir Costello: banned by her parents from seeing him, Úna fell into a decline and died, leaving him to mourn her in his verse. The Anglicized form of the name is sometimes taken to be from the feminine of Latin *unus* 'one'. It is the name used by Spenser for the lady of the Red Cross Knight in *The Faerie Queene*: he probably had Latin rather than Irish in mind, even though he worked in Ireland for a while.
Variants: **Oona, Oonagh**.

Unity ♀

From the vocabulary word for the quality (Latin *unitās*, a derivative of *unus* 'one'). It achieved some currency among the Puritans, but has been mainly used in Ireland as a kind of Anglicized extended form of ◊**Una**.

Uriah ♂

Biblical name (from Hebrew, meaning 'God is light'), borne by a Hittite warrior treacherously disposed of by King David after he had made Uriah's wife Bathsheba pregnant (2 Samuel 11). The Greek form *Urias* occurs in the New Testament (Matthew 1:6). The name was used occasionally from the 16th century onwards, but is now most closely associated with the character of the obsequious Uriah Heep in Dickens's

David Copperfield (1850) and has consequently undergone a sharp decline in popularity.

Uriel ♂

Biblical name derived from Hebrew *uri* 'light' + *el* 'God', and so a doublet of ◊**Uriah**. It is borne by two minor characters mentioned in genealogies (1 Chronicles 6:24; 2 Chronicles 13:2).

Urien ♂

Welsh: name borne by a character in the *Mabinogi*, Urien of Rheged. He is probably identical with the historical figure Urien who fought against the Northumbrians in the 6th century. The name is of uncertain origin: it may be derived from the Old Celtic elements *ōrbo* 'privileged' + *gen* 'birth'.

Ursula ♀

From the Latin name *Ursula*, a diminutive of *ursa* '(she-)bear'. This was the name of a 4th-century saint martyred at Cologne with a number of companions, traditionally said to have been eleven thousand, but more probably just eleven, the exaggeration being due to a misreading of a diacritic mark in an early manuscript. A more recent, secular influence has been the film actress Ursula Andress (b. 1936 in Switzerland).

VAL VALDA VALENE VALENTINE VALERIE V
ALETTA VALMAI VAN VANESSA VAUGHA
N VLMA VENESSA VENETIA VENUS VERA V
ERE VERENA VERGIL VERINA VERITY VERN
A VERNON VERONA VERONICA VESSA VES
TA VI VIC VICKY VICTOR VICTORIA VIENN

Val ♀, occasionally ♂
Short form of ◊**Valerie**, and sometimes also of ◊**Valentine**.

Valda ♀
20th-century coinage, an elaboration of the girl's name ◊**Val** with the suffix -*da*, extracted from names such as ◊**Glenda** and ◊**Linda**.

Valene ♀
20th-century coinage, an elaboration of the girl's name ◊**Val** with the productive feminine suffix -*ene*.

Valentine ♂, occasionally ♀
English form of the Latin name *Valentīnus*, a derivative of *valens* 'healthy', 'strong'. This was the name of a Roman martyr of the 3rd century, whose feast is celebrated on 14 February. This was the date of a pagan fertility festival marking the first stirrings of spring, which has survived in an attenuated form under the patronage of the saint.
Short form: **Val**.

Valerie ♀
From the French form of the Latin name *Valēria*, feminine of *Valērius*, an old Roman family name apparently derived from *valēre* 'to be healthy', 'be strong'. The name owes its popularity as a male name in France to the cult of a 3rd-century saint who was converted to Christianity by Martial of Limoges. The masculine form **Valery** is found occasionally in England in the 16th century, but by the 17th century had fallen into disuse.
Short form: **Val**.

Valetta ♀
20th-century coinage, an elaboration of

the girl's name ◊**Val** with the ending -*etta*, originally an Italian feminine diminutive suffix. *Valetta* or *Valletta* is (apparently coincidentally) the name of the capital of Malta.

Valmai ♀
Name used fairly regularly in Australia since the 1920s, with some currency to the present day. It is said to be of Welsh origin, meaning 'mayflower'. However, no Welsh word of appropriate meaning equating to the first element can be identified, and the letter *v* is not used in Welsh. It may have been inspired by the ancient Welsh boy's name *Gwalchmai* (from *gwalch* 'falcon' + *May* 'May'), but it seems more likely to be an elaboration of ◊**Val**.

Van ♂
Short form of ◊**Ivan** or ◊**Evan**, as in the case of the American film actor Van Heflin (1910–71), born Emmett Evan Heflin and the Irish folk singer Van Morrison (b. 1945).

Vanessa ♀
Name invented by Jonathan Swift (1667–1745) for his friend Esther Vanhomrigh. It seems to have been derived from the first syllable of her (Dutch) surname, with the addition of the suffix -*essa* (perhaps influenced by the first syllable of her given name). The name has been quite popular in the 20th century, being borne for example by the actress Vanessa Redgrave (b. 1937).
Short form: **Nessa**.

Vaughan ♂
Transferred use of the Welsh surname, in origin a nickname from the mutated form (*fychan* in Welsh orthography) of

the Welsh adjective *bychan* 'small'.
Variant: **Vaughn**.

Velma ♀
Of modern origin and uncertain derivation, possibly based on ◊**Selma** or ◊**Thelma**.

Venessa ♀
A modern altered form of ◊**Vanessa**.

Venetia ♀
Of uncertain origin, used occasionally since the late Middle Ages. In form the name coincides with that of the region of northern Italy.

Venus ♀
From the name borne in classical mythology by the goddess of love and feminine beauty (the Latin equivalent of Greek Aphrodite; her name is related to *venustas* 'beauty', 'delight'). In recent years the name has been made famous by the American tennis player Venus Williams.

Vera ♀
Russian name, meaning 'faith', introduced to Britain at the beginning of the 20th century. It coincides in form with the feminine form of the Latin adjective *vērus* 'true'.

Vere ♂
Transferred use of the surname, in origin a Norman baronial name, from any of the numerous places in northern France so called from Gaulish *ver(n)* 'alder'.

Verena ♀
Characteristically Swiss name, first borne by a 3rd-century saint who lived as a hermit near Zurich. She is said to have come originally from Thebes in Egypt, and the origin of her name is obscure. This name is now also used in the English-speaking world, where it is taken as an elaboration of ◊**Vera**.
Variant: **Verina**.

Vergil ♂
Variant spelling of ◊**Virgil**.

Verina ♀
Variant spelling of ◊**Verena**.

Verity ♀
From the archaic abstract noun meaning 'truth' (via Old French from Latin *vēritās*, a derivative of *vērus* 'true'; cf. ◊**Vera**). It was a popular Puritan name, and is still occasionally used in the English-speaking world.

Verna ♀
Name coined in the latter part of the 19th century, perhaps as a contracted form of ◊**Verena** or ◊**Verona**, or as a feminine form of ◊**Vernon**.

Vernon ♂
Transferred use of the surname, in origin a Norman baronial name from any of various places so called from Gaulish elements meaning 'place of alders' (cf. ◊**Vere**).
Short form: **Vern**.

Verona ♀
Of uncertain origin. It seems to have come into use towards the end of the 19th century, and may either represent a shortened form of ◊**Veronica** or be taken from the name of the Italian city. It became more widely known from Sinclair Lewis's novel *Babbitt* (1923), in which it is borne by the daughter of the eponymous hero.

Veronica ♀
Latin form of ◊**Berenice**, influenced from an early date by association with the Church Latin phrase *vera icon* 'true image', of which this form is an anagram. The legend of the saint who wiped Christ's face on the way to Calvary and found an image of his face imprinted on the towel seems to have been invented to account for this derivation.
Pet form: **Ronnie**.

Vessa ♀
Modern creation, a contracted form of ◊**Vanessa** or an assimilated form of ◊**Vesta**.

Vesta ♀
From the Latin name of the Roman goddess of the hearth, akin to the name of a Greek goddess with similar functions, *Hestia*, but of uncertain

derivation. It is only rarely used as a given name in the English-speaking world, but was borne as a stage name by the Victorian music-hall artiste Vesta Tilley (1864–1952). In some cases it may represent a simplified form of ◊**Silvestra**.

Vi ♀

Short form of ◊**Violet** or the girls' names ◊**Vivien** and ◊**Vivian**.

Vic ♂

Short form of ◊**Victor**.

Vicky ♀

Pet form of ◊**Victoria**.
Variants: **Vickie**, **Vicki**, **Vikki**.

Victor ♂

From a Late Latin personal name meaning 'conqueror'. This was popular among early Christians as a reference to Christ's victory over death and sin, and was borne by several saints. A 20th-century influence on the choice of the name has been the actor Victor Mature (b. 1915).
Short form: **Vic**.

Victoria ♀

Feminine form of the Latin name *Victōrius* (a derivative of ◊**Victor**), also perhaps a direct use of Latin *victōria* 'victory'. It was little known in England until the accession in 1837 of Queen Victoria (1819–1901), who got it from her German mother, Mary Louise Victoria of Saxe-Coburg. It did not begin to be a popular name among commoners in Britain until the 1940s, reaching a peak in the 1970s.
Pet forms: **Vicky**, **Vickie**, **Vicki**, **Vikki**.

Vienna ♀

From the name of the capital of Austria (so called from the river on which it stands, thought to have derived its name from the Celtic element *vindo* 'white'). Modern adoption as a female first name follows the pattern of other female-sounding city names such as ◊**Verona**, ◊**Sienna**, ◊**Ravenna**, and ◊**Paris**.

Vikki ♀

Respelled form of ◊**Vicky**.

Vince ♂

Short form of ◊**Vincent**, in use at least from the 17th century, and probably earlier, since it has given rise to a surname.

Vincent ♂

From the Old French form of the Latin name *Vincens* 'conquering' (genitive *Vincentis*). This name was borne by various early saints particularly associated with France, most notably the 5th-century St Vincent of Lérins.
Short form: **Vince**.

Viola ♀

From Latin *viōla* 'violet'. The name is relatively common in Italy and was used by Shakespeare in *Twelfth Night*, where most of the characters have Italianate names. Its modern use in English has been influenced by the vocabulary word denoting the somewhat larger flower (a single-coloured pansy).

Violet ♀

From the name of the flower (Old French *violette*, Late Latin *violetta*, a diminutive of *viōla*). This was one of the earliest flower names to become popular in Britain, being used as early as 1700 and becoming well established in the 19th century, although it is now somewhat out of favour.
Short form: **Vi**.

Viona ♀

Apparently an altered form of ◊**Fiona**, resulting from a blend with ◊**Viola** or ◊**Violet**.

Virgil ♂

Mainly U.S.: usual English form of the name of the most celebrated of Roman poets, Publius Vergilius Maro (70–19 BC). The correct Latin spelling is *Vergilius*, but it was early altered to *Virgilius* by association with *virgo* 'maiden' or *virga* 'stick'. Today the name is almost always given with direct reference to the poet, but medieval instances may have been intended to honour instead a 6th-century bishop of Arles or an 8th-century Irish monk who evangelized

Carinthia and became archbishop of Salzburg, both of whom also bore the name. In the case of the later saint, it was a classicized form of the Gaelic name *Fearghal* (see ◊**Fergal**).
Variant: **Vergil**.

Virginia ♀

From the feminine form of Latin *Virginius* (more correctly *Verginius*; cf. ◊**Virgil**), a Roman family name. It was borne by a Roman maiden killed, according to legend, by her own father to spare her the attentions of an importunate suitor. It was not used as a given name in the Middle Ages. It was bestowed on the first American child of English parentage, born at Roanoke in August 1587, and has since become very popular. Both child and province were named in honour of Elizabeth I, the 'Virgin Queen'. Among modern influences on the choice of the name has been the actress Virginia McKenna (b. 1931). *Pet form*: **Ginny**. See also ◊**Ginger**.

Vita ♀

19th-century coinage, either directly from Latin *vita* 'life', or else as a feminine form of the male name *Vitus*. It has been borne most notably by the English writer Vita Sackville-West (1892–1962), in whose case it was a pet form of the given name *Victoria*.

Viv ♀, ♂

Short form of ◊**Vivian** and ◊**Vivien**.

Vivi ♀

Pet form of the girls' names ◊**Vivien** and ◊**Vivian**.

Vivian ♂, occasionally ♀

From an Old French form of the Latin name *Viviānus* (probably a derivative of *vivus* 'alive'). The name was borne by a 5th-century bishop of Saintes in western France, remembered for protecting his people during the invasion of the Visigoths.
Variants: **Vivien**, **Vyvyan**.
Short forms: **Viv**; **Vi**, **Vivi** (♀).

Vivien ♀, formerly ♂

Originally a boy's name, generally taken as a variant of ◊**Vivian**. This spelling was quite common in Old French. It owes its popularity as a girl's name in the English-speaking world to Tennyson's *Merlin and Vivien* (1859). This name, from Arthurian legend, may represent an altered form of a Celtic name (perhaps akin to the Irish Gaelic name *Béibhinn* 'white lady', pronounced 'bee-*veen*'). The actress Vivien Leigh (1913–67) was christened *Vivian*.
Short forms: **Vi**, **Viv**, **Vivi**.

Vivienne ♀

French feminine form of ◊**Vivien**, popular also in the English-speaking world as an unambiguously female form of the name.

Voirrey ♀

Manx form of ◊**Mary**, representing the vocative form (cf. Irish *Mhuire*).

Vyvyan ♂

Fanciful respelling of the boy's name ◊**Vivian**.

WADE WALDO WALKER WALLACE WALLY
WALTER WANDA WARD WARNER WARRE
N WARWICK WASHINGTON WAT WATKIN
WAYNE WEBSTER WENDA WENDELL WEN
DY WENTWORTH WESLEY WESTON WHILT
IERMA WHITLEY WHITNEY WILBERFORCE

Wade ♂

Transferred use of the surname, in origin
either a local name from the medieval
vocabulary word *wade* 'ford' (old English
(ge)wæd), or else from a medieval given
name representing a survival of Old
English *Wada*, a derivative of *wadan* 'to
go', borne, according to legend, by a great
sea-giant.

Waldo ♂

From a Latinate short form of various
old Germanic personal names derived
from *wald* 'rule'. This gave rise in the
Middle Ages to a surname, borne notably by Peter Waldo, a 12th-century
merchant of Lyons, who founded a
reformist sect known as the Walden-
sians, which in the 16th century took
part in the Reformation movement. In
America the name is particularly associated with the poet and essayist Ralph
Waldo Emerson (1803–82), whose father
was a Lutheran clergyman.

Walker ♂

Transferred use of the surname, in origin
an occupational name for a fuller, Old
English *wealcere*, a derivative of *weal-
can* 'to walk', 'to tread'; the fulling
process involved treading cloth in vats of
lye.

Wallace ♂

Transferred use of the surname, in origin
an ethnic byname from Old French
waleis 'foreign', used by the Normans to
denote members of various Celtic races
in areas where they were in the minor-
ity: Welshmen in the Welsh marches,
Bretons in East Anglia, and surviving
Britons in the Strathclyde region. The
given name seems to have been first
used in Scotland, being bestowed in
honour of the Scottish patriot William
Wallace (?1272–1305).

Wally ♂

Pet form of ◊**Walter** or, less commonly,
of ◊**Wallace**. It has dropped almost completely out of fashion, especially since
the advent in the 20th century of the
slang term *wally*, denoting a stupid or
incompetent person.

Walter ♂

From an Old French personal name of
Germanic (Frankish) origin, derived
from *wald* 'rule' + *heri, hari* 'army'. This
was adopted by the Normans and introduced by them to England, superseding
the native Old English form, *Wealdhere*.
It was a very popular name in medieval
England, normally pronounced 'Water'.
Short forms: **Wat, Walt**.

Wanda ♀

Of uncertain origin. Attempts have been
made to derive it from various Germanic
and Slavonic roots. It was certainly in
use in Poland in the 19th century, and is
found in Polish folk tales as the name of
a princess. The derivation may well be
from the ethnic term *Wend* (see ◊**Wendell**). The name was introduced to the
English-speaking world by Ouida (Marie
Louise de la Ramée), who used it for the
heroine of her novel *Wanda* (1883).

Ward ♂

Transferred use of the surname, originally an occupational name from Old
English *weard* 'guardian', 'watchman'.

Warner ♂

Transferred use of the surname, which
is from a medieval personal name

introduced to Britain by the Normans. It is of Germanic origin, from *war(in)* 'guard' + *heri, hari* 'army'.

Warren ♂

Transferred use of the surname, which is of Norman origin, a coalescence of two different surnames, one derived from a Germanic personal name based on the element *war(in)* 'guard' and the other from a place in Normandy called *La Varenne* 'the game park'. The Norman personal name survived at least into the 17th century in Yorkshire, where it was particularly associated with the Scargill family. In America this name has sometimes been chosen in honour of General Joseph Warren, the first hero of the American Revolution, who was killed at Bunker Hill (1775). Among modern influences on the choice of the name has been the film actor Warren Beatty (b. 1937).

Warwick ♂

Transferred use of the surname, in origin a local name from the city in the West Midlands. The place name is probably from Old English *wær, wer* 'weir', 'dam' + *wīc* 'dairy farm'.

Washington ♂

Especially U.S.: transferred use of the surname of the first president of the United States, George Washington (1732–99), whose family came originally from Northamptonshire in England. They had been established in Virginia since 1656. The surname in this case is derived from the village of Washington in Co. Durham (now Tyne and Wear), so called from Old English *Wassingtūn* 'settlement associated with Wassa'.

Wat ♂

The usual medieval short form of ◊**Walter**, now occasionally revived.

Watkin ♂

Either a revival of the medieval given name (a pet form of ◊**Walter** (see ◊**Wat**), with the diminutive suffix *-kin*), or a transferred use of the surname derived from it.

Wayne ♂

Transferred use of the surname, in origin an occupational name for a carter or cartwright, from Old English *wægen* 'cart', 'waggon'. It was adopted as a given name in the second half of the 20th century, mainly as a result of the popularity of the American film actor John Wayne (1907–82), who was born Marion Michael Morrison; his screen name was chosen in honour of the American Revolutionary general Anthony Wayne (1745–96).

Webster ♂

Transferred use of the surname, in origin an occupational name for a weaver, Old English *webbestre* (a derivative of *webb* 'web'). The *-estre* suffix was originally feminine, but by the Middle English period the gender distinction had been lost. Use as a given name in America no doubt owes something to the politician and orator Daniel Webster (1782–1852) and the lexicographer Noah Webster (1758–1843).

Wenda ♀

Recent coinage, an altered form of ◊**Wendy** (cf. *Jenna* from *Jenny*). There has probably also been some influence by ◊**Wanda**. In the early Middle Ages a female name of this form was in occasional use on the Continent as a short form of various female names containing as their first element the ethnic name of the Wends (cf. ◊**Wendell**).

Wendell ♂

Especially U.S.: from the surname derived in the Middle Ages from the Continental Germanic personal name *Wendel*, in origin an ethnic name for a *Wend*, a member of the Slavonic people living in the area between the Elbe and the Oder, who were overrun by Germanic migrants in the 12th century. It has been adopted as a given name as a result of the fame of the American writer Oliver Wendell Holmes (1809–94) and his jurist son, also Oliver Wendell Holmes (1841–1935), members of a leading New England family.

Wendy ♀

Invented by J. M. Barrie for the 'little mother' in his play *Peter Pan* (1904). He took it from the nickname *Fwendy-Wendy* (i.e. 'friend') used for him by a child acquaintance, Margaret Henley. It achieved great popularity in its short lifespan, but is now out of fashion. *Variant*: **Wendi**.

Wentworth ♂

Transferred use of the surname, in origin a local name from places in Cambridgeshire and South Yorkshire. These were named with Old English *winter* 'winter' and *worð* 'enclosure'; the reference was to settlements that were inhabited only in winter, the inhabitants taking their flocks to other pastures in summer. In Australia it probably came into use as a given name in honour of D'Arcy Wentworth (?1762–1827), who was born in Ireland and played an important role in the early days of the Botany Bay settlement, and his son William Wentworth (1790–1872), an explorer and politician known as 'the Australian patriot' because of his advocacy of self-government.

Wesley ♂

From the surname of the founder of the Methodist Church, John Wesley (1703–91), and his brother Charles (1707–88), who was also influential in the movement. Their family must have come originally from one or other of the various places in England called *Westley*, the 'western wood, clearing, or meadow'. The given name was at first confined to members of the Methodist Church, but is now widely used without reference to its religious connotations. *Short form*: **Wes**.

Weston ♂

Transferred use of the surname, in origin a local name from any of the very many places in England named in Old English as 'the western enclosure', from *west* 'west' + *tūn* 'enclosure', 'settlement'.

Whiltierna ♀

Irish: Anglicized form of the Gaelic name *Faoiltiarna*, derived from *faol* 'wolf' + *tighearna* 'lord'.

Whitley ♀

Mainly U.S.: transferred use of the surname, a local name from any of various places in England named with Old English *hwīt* 'white' + *lēah* 'wood', 'clearing'. Use as a girl's name may have been influenced by the adoption of ◊**Whitney** for the same purpose.

Whitney ♀, ♂

Mainly North American: transferred use of the surname, in origin a local name from any of various places in England named with the Middle English phrase *atten whiten ey* 'by the white island'. In the 1980s its popularity as a girl's name was increased by the fame of the American singer Whitney Houston.

Wilberforce ♂

Transferred use of the surname, in origin a local name from *Wilberfoss* in North Yorkshire, so called from the Old English female personal name *Wilburg* (see ◊**Wilbur**) + Old English *foss* 'ditch' (Latin *fossa*). It was taken up as a given name in honour of the anti-slavery campaigner William Wilberforce (1759–1833). It is now sometimes taken as an extended form of *Wilbur*.

Wilbur ♂

Mainly North American: transferred use of a comparatively rare surname, which is probably derived from a medieval female given name composed of Old English *will* 'will', 'desire' + *burh* 'fortress'.

Wilfrid ♂

From an Old English personal name, derived from *wil* 'will', 'desire' + *frīð* 'peace'. This was borne by two Anglo-Saxon saints: there is some doubt about the exact form of the name of the more famous, who played a leading role at the Council of Whitby (664); it may have been *Walfrid*, 'stranger peace'. Wilfrid the Younger was an 8th-century bishop of York. The name enjoyed some popularity in Yorkshire (often in the form

Wilfrey) in the 16th and 17th centuries. It was revived more widely in the 19th century, and enjoyed great popularity then and in the first part of the 20th century.
Variant: **Wilfred**.
Short form: **Wilf**.

Wilhelmina ♀

Feminine version of *Wilhelm*, the German form of ◊**William**, formed with the Latinate suffix *-ina*. This name was introduced to the English-speaking world from Germany in the 19th century. It is now very rarely used.
Pet forms: **Minnie**.

Will ♂

Short form of ◊**William**, in use since the early Middle Ages, when it was occasionally used also for various other given names of Germanic origin containing the first element *wil* 'will', 'desire'.

Willa ♀

Name recently coined as a feminine form of ◊**William**, by appending the characteristically feminine ending *-a* to the short form ◊**Will**.

Willard ♂

Especially U.S.: transferred use of the surname, which is probably derived from the Old English personal name *Wilheard*, from *wil* 'will', 'desire' + *heard* 'hardy', 'brave', 'strong'.

William ♂

Probably the most successful of all the Old French names of Germanic origin that were introduced to England by the Normans. It is derived from Germanic *wil* 'will', 'desire' + *helm* 'helmet', 'protection'. The fact that it was borne by the Conqueror himself does not seem to have inhibited its favour with the 'conquered' population: in the first century after the Conquest it was the commonest male name of all, and not only among the Normans. In the later Middle Ages it was overtaken by ◊**John**, but continued to run second to that name until the 20th century, when the picture became more fragmented.

Short forms: **Will**, ◊**Bill**.
Pet forms: **Willy**, **Willie**, **Billy**.

Willis ♂

Transferred use of the surname, which is a derivative of ◊**William**.

Willoughby ♂

Transferred use of the surname, in origin a local name from any of various places in northern England so called from Old English *welig* 'willow' + Old Norse *býr* 'settlement'.

Willow ♀

From the name of the tree (Old English *welig*), noted for its grace and the pliancy of its wood.

Willy ♂

Pet form of ◊**William**.

Wilma ♀

Contracted form of ◊**Wilhelmina**, which has retained rather more currency (especially in America) than the full form of the name.

Wilmer ♂

From an Old English personal name, derived from *wil* 'will', 'desire' + *mær* 'famous'. This died out in the Middle Ages, but gave rise to a surname before it did so. The modern given name is probably a transferred use of that surname, perhaps adopted in particular as a masculine form of ◊**Wilma**.

Wilmette ♀

Especially U.S.: a recent coinage, elaborated from ◊**Wilma** by means of the productive ending *-ette* (originally a French feminine diminutive suffix).

Wilmot ♂, ♀

Transferred use of the surname, which is derived from a medieval pet form (with the Old French diminutive suffix *-ot*) of ◊**William**.

Wilson ♂

Transferred use of the surname, in origin a patronymic from ◊**Will**. Use as a given name in the United States was inspired by President (Thomas) Woodrow Wilson

(1856–1924); cf. the similar adoption as a given name of ◊**Woodrow**.

Win ♀
Short form of ◊**Winifred**.

Windsor ♂
Transferred use of the surname, which is derived from a place in Berkshire, originally named in Old English as *Windels-ōra* 'landing place with a windlass'. It is the site of a castle that is in regular use as a residence of the royal family. Use as a given name dates from the mid-19th century and was reinforced by its adoption in 1917 as the surname of the British royal family (from their residence at Windsor). It was felt necessary to replace the German name *Wettin*, which had been introduced by Queen Victoria's husband Albert, in deference to anti-German feeling during the First World War.

Winifred ♀
Anglicized form of the Welsh female personal name *Gwenfrewi*, derived from *gwen* 'white', 'fair', 'blessed', 'holy' + *frewi* 'reconciliation'. This was borne by a 7th-century Welsh saint around whom a large body of legends grew up. The form of the name has been altered by association with Old English *wynn* 'joy' + *friŏ* 'peace'.
Short form: **Win**.
Pet form: **Winnie**.

Winnie ♀
Pet form of ◊**Winifred** and of ◊**Winston**.

Winona ♀
Mainly North American: from a Sioux girl's name, said to be reserved normally for a first-born daughter.

Winston ♂
Although there was an Old English personal name, *Wynnstan*, from *wynn* 'joy' + *stān* 'stone', which would have had this form if it had survived, the modern given name is a transferred use of the surname, a local name from *Winston* in Gloucestershire. Use as a given name originated in the Churchill family: the first Winston Churchill

(b. 1620) was baptized with the surname of his mother's family. The name has continued in the family ever since, and has been widely adopted in honour of the statesman Winston Spencer Churchill (1874–1965).

Winthrop ♂
Especially U.S.: from the surname of a leading American pioneering family. John Winthrop (1588–1649) was governor of Massachusetts Bay Colony from 1629, and played a major role in shaping the political institutions of New England. His son (1606–76) and grandson (1638–1707), who bore the same name, were also colonial governors. Their family probably came originally from one of the places in England called *Winthorpe* (named in Old English as the 'village of Wynna').

Winton ♂
Transferred use of the surname, in origin a local name from any of the various places so called. One in Cumbria gets its name from Old English *winn* 'pasture' + *tūn* 'enclosure', 'settlement'; another in the same county is from *wiŏig* 'willow' + *tūn*; the one in North Yorkshire is from the Old English personal name *Wina* + *tūn*.

Wolf ♂
From the name of the animal (Old English *wolf*), in part a transferred use of the surname which originated as a nickname from this word, or an adoption of a German short form of any of the various compound names (such as *Wolfgang* and *Wolfram*) with this first element.

Wolfe ♂
Transferred use of the surname (see ◊**Wolf**), sometimes used as a first name in honour of the Irish rebel Theobald Wolfe Tone (see ◊**Tone**) or the English General James Wolfe (1727–59), who died at the Battle of Quebec.

Woodrow ♂
Transferred use of the surname, in origin a local name for someone who lived in a

row of houses by a wood. Use as a given name was inspired by the American president (Thomas) Woodrow Wilson (1856–1924).

Woody ♂

Mainly U.S.: pet form of ◊**Woodrow**, or in some cases perhaps a nickname bestowed because of some imagined similarity to the cartoon character Woody Woodpecker. It has been borne by the American folk singer Woody (Woodrow Wilson) Guthrie (1912–67) and the 1940s band leader Woody (Woodrow Charles) Herman (1913–87). The American humorist Woody Allen was born Allen Stewart Konigsberg in 1935.

Worth ♂

Transferred use of the surname, in origin a local name from any of the very numerous places named with the Old English word *worð* 'enclosure' (used especially of a subsidiary settlement dependent on a main village). Use as a given name has probably been inspired in part by the modern English vocabulary word referring to high personal merit (Old English *weorth*).

Wyatt ♂

Transferred use of the surname, derived from a medieval given name representing a Norman French alteration of the Old English personal name *Wīgheard*,

from *wīg* 'war' + *heard* 'hardy', 'brave', 'strong'.

Wyn ♂

Welsh: originally a byname from the Welsh vocabulary word *(g)wyn* 'white', 'fair', 'blessed', 'holy'. The name is found in this form from the early Middle Ages. It is at present extremely popular in Wales.

Wyndham ♂

Transferred use of the surname, which is derived from a contracted form of the name of *Wymondham* in Norfolk, originally named in Old English as the 'homestead of Wigmund'. John Wyndham was the pseudonym of the British science-fiction writer John Wyndham Parkes Lucas Beynon Harris (1903–63), creator of the Midwich cuckoos.

Wynne ♂, ♀

Probably a transferred use of the surname, which is derived from the Old and Middle English personal name *Wine*. *Variant*: **Wynn**. See also ◊**Wyn** and ◊**Win**.

Wystan ♂

From an Old English personal name derived from *wīg* 'battle' + *stān* 'stone'. St Wistan was a 9th-century prince of Mercia, murdered by his nephew Bertulf. The modern given name is rare, being best known as that of the poet Wystan Hugh Auden (1907–73).

XANDER XANTHE XAVIER XAVIERA XENA XENIA XANDER XANTHE XAVIER XAVIER A XENIA XENIA XANDER XANTHE XAVIER XAVIERA XENA XENIA XANDER XANTHE X AVIER XAVIERA XENA XENIA XANDER XANTHE XAVIER XAVIERA XENA XENIA X

Xander ♂

Shortened form of ◊**Alexander**. It is pronounced, like other names beginning with *X-*, as though spelled with *Z-*.

Xanthe ♀

From the feminine form of the Greek adjective *xanthos* 'yellow', 'bright'. The name was borne by various minor figures in classical mythology and is occasionally chosen by parents in search of an unusual given name for a daughter.

Xavier ♂

From the surname of the Spanish soldier–saint Francis Xavier (1506–52), one of the founding members of the Society of Jesus (the Jesuits). He was born on the ancestral estate at Xavier (now Javier) in Navarre, which in the early Middle Ages was an independent Basque kingdom. *Xavier* probably represents a Hispanicized form of the Basque place name *Etcheberria* 'the new house'. (Spanish *x* was pronounced in the Middle Ages as 'sh', now as 'h'.) The given name is used almost exclusively by Roman Catholics.

Xaviera ♀

Name created as a feminine form of ◊**Xavier**.

Xena ♀

Apparently from Greek *xena* (feminine form) 'stranger', 'foreigner' (cf. ◊**Xenia**). It has recently become familiar because of the popularity of the television show featuring Xena, the warrior princess.

Xenia ♀

Comparatively rare given name, coined from the Greek vocabulary word *xenia* 'hospitality', a derivative of *xenos* 'stranger', 'foreigner'.

YARROW YASMIN YNYR YOLA YOLANDE Y
ORATH YORICK YORK YSANNE YSEULT YU
AN YVETTE YVONNE YARROW YASMI
N YNYR YOLA YOLANDE YORATH YORICK
YORI YSANNE YSEULT YUAN YVES YVETTE
YVONNE YARROW YASMIN YNYR YOLA Y

Yarrow ♀
From the name of a plant, *Achillea millefolium* (Middle English *yarrowe*, from Old English *gearwe*) used in traditional medicine.

Yasmin ♀
Variant of ◊**Jasmine**, representing a 'learned' re-creation of the Persian form.

Ynyr ♂
Welsh, pronounced '*inn-eer*': traditional name of uncertain derivation, probably from the Latin name *Honōrius* (a derivative of *honor* 'renown'). There is a passing reference in the *Mabinogi* to 'the battle between the two Ynyrs'.

Yola ♀
Shortened form of *Yolanda* (see ◊**Yolande**).

Yolande ♀
Of uncertain origin. It is found in Old French in this form, and may be ultimately of Germanic origin, but if so it has been altered beyond recognition. It is also sometimes identified with the name of St *Jolenta* (d. 1298), daughter of the king of Hungary.
Variant: **Yolanda** (Latinate).

Yorath ♂
Anglicized form of the Welsh personal name ◊**Iorwerth** or, in some cases, a transferred use of the surname derived from it.

Yorick ♂
The name of the (defunct) court jester in Shakespeare's *Hamlet*. This is a respelling of *Jorck*, a Danish form of ◊**George**.

York ♂
Transferred use of the surname, which originated as a local name from the city in north-eastern England. The place name was originally *Eburacon*, a derivative of a Welsh word meaning 'yew'. The Anglo-Saxon settlers changed this to Old English *Eoforwīc* 'boar farm', which in Old Norse became *Iorvík* or *Iork*. There has probably also been some influence from ◊**Yorick**.

Ysanne ♀
Pronounced '*iz-ann*'; recent coinage, a blend of the first syllable of ◊**Yseult** + the given name *Anne*.

Yseult ♀
Medieval French form of ◊**Isolde**, still occasionally used as a given name in the English-speaking world.

Yuan ♂
Manx form of ◊**John**.

Yves ♂
French: from a Germanic personal name representing a short form of various compound names containing the element *iv* 'yew'. The final *-s* is the mark of the Old French nominative case. The name was introduced to Britain from France at the time of the Norman Conquest, and again in the 20th century. See also ◊**Ivo**.

Yvette ♀
French feminine diminutive form of ◊**Yves**, now also used in the English-speaking world.

Yvonne ♀
French feminine diminutive form of ◊**Yves** (or simply a feminine form based on the Old French oblique case *Yvon*; cf. ◊**Ivon**) now also widely used in the English-speaking world.

ZACHARY ZACK ZANE ZANNA ZARA ZAYLI
E ZEB ZEBEDEE ZEBULUN ZED ZEKE ZELAH Z
ELDA ELMA ZENA ZENITH ZEPH ZEPHYRI
NE ZITA ZILLAH ZINA ZINNIA ZIPPORAH
ZITA ZOE ZOLA ZULA ZACK ZANE ZANNA
ZARA ZAYLIE ZEB ZEBEDEE ZEBULUN ZED Z

Zachary ♂

English vernacular form of the New Testament Greek name *Zacharias*, a form of Hebrew *Zechariah* 'God has remembered'. This was the name of the father of John the Baptist, who underwent a temporary period of dumbness for his lack of faith (Luke 1), and of a more obscure figure, Zacharias son of Barachias, who was slain 'between the temple and the altar' (Matthew 23:35; Luke 11:51). Like many biblical names, it is now out of fashion, although in the United States it is familiar as the name of a 19th-century president, Zachary Taylor.

Zack ♂

Mainly North American: short form of ◊**Zachary**.

Zane ♂

Transferred use of a surname of uncertain origin. It came to prominence as the given name of the American writer Zane Grey (1875–1939), a descendant of the Ebenezer Zane who founded *Zaneville* in Ohio.

Zanna ♀

Modern coinage, apparently a shortened form of *Suzanna*.

Zara ♀

Of uncertain origin. It is sometimes said to be of Arabic origin, from *zahr* 'flower', but is more probably a respelled form of ◊**Sara**. It was given by Princess Anne and Mark Philips to their second child (b. 1981), which aroused considerable comment at the time as it was a departure from the traditional patterns of royal nomenclature.

Zaylie ♀

Of uncertain origin, perhaps a respelling of the rare French name *Zélie*, an altered form of *Célie*, the French version of ◊**Celia**.

Zeb ♂

Especially U.S.: short form of ◊**Zebedee** and ◊**Zebulun**.

Zebedee ♂

Name borne in the New Testament by the father of the apostles James and John, who was with his sons mending fishing nets when they were called by Christ (Matthew 4:21; Mark 1:20). This is from a Greek form of the Hebrew name that appears in the Old Testament as *Zebadiah* or *Zabdi* 'gift of Jehovah'.

Zebulun ♂

Biblical name, borne by the sixth son of Leah and Jacob. The name may mean 'exaltation', although Leah derives it from another meaning of the Hebrew root *zabal*, namely 'to dwell': 'now will my husband dwell with me, because I have born him six sons' (Genesis 30:20). It appears in the New Testament (Matthew 4:13) in the form *Zabulon*.
Variant: **Zebulon**.

Zed ♂

Especially U.S.: short form of the much rarer full name **Zedekiah**. This name, meaning 'justice of Yahweh' in Hebrew, is borne in the Bible by three separate characters.

Zeke ♂

Especially U.S.: shortened form of ◊**Ezekiel**.

Zelah ♀

Biblical name (meaning 'side' in Hebrew), borne by one of the fourteen cities of the tribe of Benjamin (Joshua 18:28). It is far from clear why it should have come to be used, albeit rarely, as a girl's given name in the English-speaking world. It may simply be a variant of ◊**Zillah** under the influence of the place name. However, for evidence that biblical place names did yield English given names, cf. ◊**Ebenezer**.

Zelda ♀

Modern name of uncertain origin, possibly a short form of ◊**Griselda**. It came to prominence in the 1920s as the name of the wife of the American writer F. Scott Fitzgerald (1896–1940).

Zelma ♀

Modern coinage, an altered form of ◊**Selma**.

Zena ♀

Of uncertain origin, probably a variant spelling of ◊**Zina**.

Zenith ♀

From the vocabulary word referring to the highest point in the heavens, directly above the observer, and figuratively also to the greatest development of perfection. The word came into English in the Middle Ages, via French and Spanish, from Arabic *samt* 'way', 'path' (taken from the phrase *samt ar-rās* 'overhead path'). This has sometimes been used as a first name by parents who wish their daughter to 'reach the heights'.

Zeph ♂

Especially U.S.: short form of the much rarer full name **Zephaniah**. This name, meaning 'hidden by God' in Hebrew, was borne by one of the minor biblical prophets, author of the book of the Bible that bears his name.

Zephyrine ♀

From French *Zéphyrine*, an elaborated name derived from Latin *Zephyrus*, Greek *Zephyros* 'west wind'. St Zephyrinus was pope 199–217, but there is no equivalent female saint, so it is

rather surprising that this name should have survived only in a female form.

Zeta ♀

Of uncertain origin, probably a variant spelling of ◊**Zita**. It also coincides in form with the name of the letter of the Greek alphabet equivalent to English *z* (but not the last letter of the Greek alphabet).

Zillah ♀

Biblical name (from a Hebrew word meaning 'shade'), borne by one of the two wives of Lamech (Genesis 4:19). The name was taken up in the first place by the Puritans, and again by fundamentalist Christian groups in the 19th century, partly because Zillah is only the third woman to be mentioned by name in the Bible, and her name was therefore prominent to readers of the Book of Genesis.

Zina ♀

Russian short form of **Zinaida** (from Greek *Zēnais*, a derivative of the name of the god *Zeus*), the name of an obscure saint venerated in the Eastern Church. It is also a Russian short form of the rarer given name *Zinovia* (from Greek *Zēnobia*, a compound of *Zeus* + *bios* 'life'). Its adoption as a given name in the English-speaking world probably owes something to its resemblance to the popular girl's name ◊**Tina**.

Zinnia ♀

From the name of a genus of plants with brightly coloured flowers, originally native to Mexico and now widely cultivated. The botanical name is derived from the surname of the German botanist J.G. Zinn (1727–59).

Zipporah ♀

Jewish: common feminine form of the rare Hebrew boy's name *Zippor*, from Hebrew *zippor* 'bird'. The girl's name is borne in the Bible by the wife of Moses (Exodus 18:2–4).

Zita ♀

From the name of a 13th-century saint from Lucca in Tuscany, who led an uneventful life as a domestic servant; she was canonized in 1696, and is regarded as the patroness of domestic servants. Her name was probably a nickname from the medieval Tuscan dialect word *zit(t)a* 'girl', although efforts have been made to link it with Greek *zētein* 'to seek'.

Zoë ♀

From a Greek name meaning 'life'. This was already in use in Rome towards the end of the classical period (at first as an affectionate nickname), and was popular with the early Christians, who bestowed it with reference to their hopes of eternal life. It was borne by martyrs of the 2nd and 3rd centuries, but was taken up as an English given name only in the 19th century.
Variant: **Zoe**.

Zola ♀

Apparently a late 20th-century creation, formed from the first syllable of ◊**Zoë** with the ending *-la*, common in girls' names. It coincides in form with the surname of the French novelist Émile Zola (1840–1902), who was of Italian descent, but it is unlikely that he had any influence on the popularity of the name.

Zula ♀

Modern coinage derived from the tribal name of the Zulus. The Zulu people of Southern Africa formed a powerful warrior nation under their leader Chaka in the 19th century, and controlled an extensive empire. In 1838, under the leadership of their ruler Dingaan, they ambushed and slaughtered a group of some five hundred Boers. Not surprisingly, this given name is chosen mainly by Black people proud of their African origins.

Appendices

FRENCH NAMES

A

Achille ♂ From Greek *Achilleus*, hero of Homer's Iliad, also the name of one or two minor saints.

Adam ♂ Biblical. See main dictionary.

Adélaïde ♀ Germanic. See ◊**Adelaide** in main dictionary, ◊**Adelheid** in German supplement.

Adelard ♂ Germanic: 'noble hardy'.

Adèle ♀ Short form of ADÉLAÏDE.

Adeline ♀ Pet form of ADÈLE.

Adolphe ♂ Germanic. See ◊**Adolf** in German supplement.

Adrien ♂ From Latin. See ◊**Adrian** in main dictionary. *Feminine form*: **Adrienne**.

Agathe ♀ From Greek. See ◊**Agatha** in main dictionary.

Agnès ♀ From Greek. See ◊**Agnes** in main dictionary.

Aimée ♀ 'Beloved'; see English ◊**Amy** in main dictionary.

Alain ♂ Breton. See ◊**Alan** in main dictionary.

Albert ♂ Germanic. See ◊**Albert** in main dictionary, ◊**Albrecht** in German supplement.

Alette ♀ Pet form of ADÈLE.

Alexandre ♂ From Greek. See ◊**Alexander** in main dictionary.

Alfred ♂ From English. See main dictionary.

Alice ♀ See main dictionary.

Aline ♀ Reduced form of ADELINE.

Alison ♀ See main dictionary.

Alphonse ♂ From Spanish ◊**Alfonso** (see Spanish supplement). *Feminine pet form*: **Alphonsine**.

Ambroise ♂ See ◊**Ambrose** in main dictionary. *Also* **Ambrois**, **Ambroix**.

Amédée ♂ From Late Latin *Amadeus* 'love God', translating German *Gottlieb*; a royal name in the house of Savoy.

Amélie ♂ From Latin. See ◊**Amelia** in main dictionary.

Anatole ♂ From Greek *Anatolē* 'sunrise'.

André ♂ New Testament. See ◊**Andrew** in main dictionary. *Feminine form*: **Andrée**.

Ange ♀ From Latin *Angela* 'angel'; see ◊**Angela** in main dictionary.

Angeline ♀ Feminine derivative of Greek *Angelos* 'messenger (of God)'.

Angélique ♀ From Latin *Angelica* 'of the angels'; see ◊**Angela** in main dictionary.

Anne ♀ Biblical. See main dictionary.

Annette ♀ Pet form of ANNE.

Antoine ♂ From Latin. See ◊**Anthony** in main dictionary.

Antoinette ♀ Feminine pet form of ANTOINE.

Apollinaire ♂ From Italian *Apollinare*, name of an early martyr.

Apolline ♀ From Greek *Apollōneia*, name of a 3rd-century martyr.

Arianne ♀ See ◊**Ariadne** in main dictionary.

Aristide ♂ From Greek *Aristides* 'best', name of a 5th-century BC Athenian statesman noted for his incorruptibility; also the name of an early Christian apologist.

Arlette ♀ Of Germanic origin. See main dictionary.

Armand ♂ From Germanic. See ◊**Hermann** in German supplement.

Arnaud ♂ Germanic. See ◊**Arnold** in main dictionary.

Arthur ♂ Celtic. See main dictionary.

Athanase ♂ From Greek *Athanasios* 'immortal'.

Aubry ♂ Germanic. See ◊**Aubrey** in main dictionary.

Auguste ♂ From Latin. See ◊**Augustus** in main dictionary.

Augustine ♂ See main dictionary.

Aurèle ♂ From Latin *Aurēlius*, name of the philosopher-emperor Marcus Aurelius (121–180 AD). *Feminine form*: **Aurèle**.

Aurore ♀ From Latin. See ◊**Aurora** in main dictionary.

B

Baptiste ♂ Religious name commemorating John the Baptist; often in the combination **Jean-Baptiste**.

Barbara ♀ Greek: 'foreign woman'. See main dictionary.

Barnabé ♂ New Testament. See ◊**Barnabas** in main dictionary.

Barthélemy ♂ New Testament. See ◊**Bartholomew** in main dictionary.

Bastien ♂ Reduced form of SÉBASTIEN.

Baudouin ♂ Germanic. See ◊**Baldwin** in main dictionary.

Béatrice ♀ From Latin. See ◊**Beatrix** in main dictionary.

Benoît ♂ From Latin. See ◊**Benedict** in main dictionary.

Bérénice ♀ From Greek. See ◊**Berenice** in main dictionary.

Bernadette ♀ Feminine of BERNARD. See main dictionary.

Bernard ♂ Germanic. See main dictionary.

Bernice ♀ Contracted form of BÉRÉNICE.

Berthe ♀ Germanic. See ◊**Bertha** in main dictionary.

Bertrand ♂ Germanic. See main dictionary.

Blaise ♂ From Latin. See main dictionary.

Blanche ♀ Literally 'white', i.e. 'pure'; also a nickname meaning 'blonde'. See main dictionary.

Brigitte ♀ From Irish *Brighid*, name of a patron saint of Ireland (English ◊**Bridget**; see main dictionary), or from the Swedish derivative *Birgit*, name of the patron saint of Sweden. *Also* **Brigette**.

C

Camille ♂, ♀ From Latin. See ◊**Camilla** in main dictionary.

Caroline ♀ Feminine derivative of Latin *Carolus*. See ◊**Charles** in main dictionary.

Catherine ♀ From Greek. See ◊**Katherine** in main dictionary.

Cécile ♀ From Latin. See ◊**Cecilia** in main dictionary.

Céleste ♀ From Latin *Caelestis* 'heavenly'. *Pet form*: **Célestine**.

Céline ♀ From Latin *Caelīna*, derivative of *Caelia*; see ◊**Celia** in main dictionary.

Césaire ♂ From the Late Latin personal name *Caesarius*, name of a 6th-century saint, a bishop of Arles.

César ♂ From Latin. See ◊**Caesar** in main dictionary.

Chantal ♀ After Ste Jean-Françoise, baronne de Chantal (1572–1641), co-founder of the Order of Visitation. See main dictionary.

Charisse ♀ From Greek *kharis* 'grace'. See ◊**Charis** in main dictionary.

Charles ♂ Germanic. See main dictionary.

Charmaine ♀ See main dictionary.

Charlotte ♀ Feminine pet form of CHARLES. See main dictionary. *Also*: **Charlette**.

Christine ♀ See main dictionary.

Christophe ♂ From Greek. See ◊**Christopher** in main dictionary.

Claire ♀ From Latin. See ◊**Clare** in main dictionary.

Claude ♂, ♀ From Latin. See ◊**Claude** in main dictionary.

Claudette ♀ Feminine pet form of CLAUDE.

Claudine ♀ Feminine pet form of CLAUDE.

Clément ♂ From Late Latin. See ◊**Clement** in main dictionary.

Clémentine ♀ Feminine pet form of CLÉMENT.

Clothilde ♀ Germanic: 'famous battle'; name of the queen of the Franks (474–545) who was chiefly responsible for their conversion to Christianity.

Clovis ♂ Germanic: 'fame war'; equivalent of German ◊**Ludwig**. Clovis (*c*.466–511) was the founder of the medieval Frankish kingdom, a precursor of modern France.

Colette ♀ Short form of NICOLETTE. *Also*: **Collette**.

Colombe ♂, ♀ From Late Latin *Columba* 'dove', representing Irish Gaelic ◊**Calum** (see main dictionary).

Constance ♀ From Late Latin. See main dictionary.

Constant ♂ From Late Latin. See main dictionary.

Constantin ♂ From Late Latin. See ◊**Constantine** in main dictionary.

Corinne ♀ from Greek. See main dictionary.

Cyrille ♂ From Greek. See ◊**Cyril** in main dictionary.

D

Damien ♂ From Greek. See ◊**Damian** in main dictionary.

Daniel ♂ Biblical. See main dictionary. *Feminine forms*: **Danièle**, **Danielle**.

David ♂ Biblical. See main dictionary.

Delphine ♀ From Latin. See main dictionary.

Denis ♂ From Greek; name of a patron saint of Paris. See ◊**Dennis** in main dictionary. *Feminine form*: **Denise**.

Desirée ♀ From Latin *Dēsīderāta* 'longed for'. *Masculine form*: **Desiré**.

Diane ♀ From Latin. See ◊**Diana** in main dictionary.

Didier ♂ From Late Latin *Dēsīderius*, derivative of *dēsīderium* 'longing'. Compare ◊**Desiderio** in Spanish supplement.

Dion ♂ See main dictionary.

Dominique ♂, ♀ From Late Latin. See ◊**Dominic** and ◊**Dominique** in main dictionary.

Donatien ♂ From Late Latin *Dōnātiānus*, a derivative of *Dōnātus* 'given (by God)'.

E

Edgar ♂ From English. See main dictionary.

Edmond ♂ From English. See ◊**Edmund** in main dictionary.

Édouard ♂ From English. See ◊**Edward** in main dictionary.

Eléonore ♀ From Old Provençal. See ◊**Eleanor** in main dictionary.

Éliane ♀ From Late Latin *Aeliānus*, probably a derivative of Greek *hēlios* 'sun'.

Elisabeth ♀ New Testament. See ◊**Elizabeth** in main dictionary.

Élise ♀ Short form of ELISABETH.

Éloise ♀ Name of the wife of the 12th-century Parisian philosopher Pierre Abélard. The story of their love is famous: after they married secretly, Éloise's uncle had Pierre castrated; he became a monk and she a nun, but they continued to write to each other and were eventually buried side by side. *Also* **Héloïse**.

Émilie ♀ From Latin. See ◊**Emily** in main dictionary. *Masculine form*: **Émile**.

Émilien ♂ From the Latin family name *Aemiliānus*, a derivative of *Aemilius* (see ◊**Emily** in main dictionary).

Eric ♂ Norman. See main dictionary.

Ernest ♂ Germanic. See main dictionary.

Esmé ♂ From Latin *Aestimātus* 'esteemed', 'highly valued'. *Feminine form*: **Esmée**.

Étienne ♂ From Greek. See ◊**Stephen** in main dictionary.

Eugène ♂ From Greek. See ◊**Eugene** in main dictionary. *Feminine form*: **Eugénie**.

Euphémie ♀ From Latin. See ◊**Euphemia** in main dictionary.

Eustache ♂ From Late Greek. See ◊**Eustace** in main dictionary.

Eve ♀ Biblical. See main dictionary.

Eveline ♀ Pet form of EVE, or French form of English ◊**Evelyn** (see main dictionary).

Evette ♀ Pet form of EVE. See also YVETTE.

F

Fabien ♂ From Latin. See ◊**Fabian** in main dictionary. *Feminine form*: **Fabienne**.

Fabrice ♂ From the Latin family name *Fabricius*. Caius Fabricius Luscinus (d. 250 BC) was a Roman statesman noted for his incorruptibility.

Félix ♂ From Latin ◊**Felix** in main dictionary.

Ferdinand ♂ From Spanish. See main dictionary. *Also* **Fernand**.

Flavien ♂ From Latin *Flāviānus*, a derivative of *Flāvius* 'yellow-haired'.

Florence ♀ From Latin. See main dictionary. *Masculine form*: **Florent**.

François ♂ Medieval name meaning 'French'. See ◊**Francis** in main dictionary. Its popularity in France has been greatly influenced by Italian *Francesco* and the fame of St Francis of Assisi. *Feminine form*: **Françoise**.

Francine ♀ Pet form of FRANÇOISE.

Frédéric ♂ From German. See ◊**Friedrich** in German supplement and ◊**Frederick** in main dictionary. *Feminine form*: **Frédérique**.

G

Gabriel ♂ Biblical. See main dictionary. *Feminine forms*: **Gabrièle**, **Gabrielle**. *Feminine pet form*: **Gaby**.

Gaétan ♂ From Italian ◊**Gaetano** (see Italian supplement).

Gaspard ♂ Name of one of the three Magi. See ◊**Caspar** in main dictionary.

Gaston ♂ Of uncertain origin; a traditional name in aristocratic families of Languedoc.

Gaut(h)ier ♂ Germanic. See ◊**Walter** in main dictionary.

Geneviève ♀ Name of the patron saint of Paris. See main dictionary.

Geoffroi ♂ Germanic. See ◊**Geoffrey** in main dictionary.

Georges ♂ From Greek. See ◊**George** in main dictionary.

Georgette, Georgine ♀ Feminine pet forms of GEORGES.

Gérard ♂ Germanic. See ◊**Gerard** in main dictionary.

Géraud ♂ Germanic. See ◊**Gerald** in main dictionary.

Germaine ♀ French, meaning 'sibling'. See main dictionary. *Masculine form*: **Germain**.

Gervais ♂ Origin uncertain. See ◊**Gervaise** in main dictionary.

Ghislaine ♀ Old French: oblique case of GISELLE, in a spelling that suggests Dutch or Flemish influence.

Gigi ♀ Pet form of GISELLE.

Gilbert ♂ Germanic. See main dictionary.

Gilles ♂ From Latin *Aegidus*, Old French *Gide*. See ◊**Giles** in main dictionary.

Ginette ♀ Pet form of ◊**Gina** (see Italian supplement and main dictionary).

Giselle ♀ From Germanic. See ◊**Gisela** in German supplement. *Also*: **Gisele**.

Gratien ♂ Derivative of Latin *grātus* 'pleasing'. St Gratian was the first bishop of Tours.

Grégoire ♂ From Late Greek. See ◊**Gregory** in main dictionary.

Guillaume ♂ Germanic. See ◊**William** in main dictionary.

Gustave ♂ From Scandinavian *Gustaf*, from the tribal name *Gautr* + *stafr* 'staff'.

Guy ♂ Germanic. See main dictionary.

H

Hector ♂ Classical. See main dictionary.

Hélène ♀ From Greek. See ◊**Helen** in main dictionary.

Héloïse ♀ Variant of ÉLOISE.

Henri ♂ Germanic. See ◊**Henry** in main dictionary.

Henriette ♀ Feminine pet form of HENRI.

Herbert ♂ Germanic. See main dictionary.

Hercule ♂ From Latin *Hercules*, name of a mythological hero noted for his great physical strength.

Hervé ♂ Originally Breton. See ◊**Harvey** in main dictionary.

Hilaire ♂ From Latin. See ◊**Hilary** in main dictionary.

Hippolyte ♂ From Greek *Hippolytos* 'horse free'; name of several early saints.

Honore ♀ From Latin *Honōria*, derivative of *honor* 'honour'.

Honoré ♂ From Late Latin *Honōrātus* 'honoured'.

Honorine ♀ From Late Latin *Honōrīna*, a derivative of *Honōria*. See HONORE. *Pet form*: **Norine**.

Hortense ♀ From Latin. See main dictionary.

Hubert ♂ See main dictionary.

Hugues ♂ See ◊**Hugh** in main dictionary.

Huguette ♀ Feminine pet form of HUGUES. *Also*: **Huette**.

I

Ignace ♂ From Latin. See ◊**Ignatius** in main dictionary.

Irène ♀ From Greek. See ◊**Irene** in main dictionary.

Iréné ♂ From Latin *Irēnaeus*, from Greek *Eirēnaios* 'peaceable'. St Iréné (*c*.125–202), a Church Father, was an early bishop of Lyons.

Isabel ♀ From Spanish. See main dictionary. *Also*: **Isabelle**.

Isaïe ♂ Biblical. See ◊**Isaiah** in main dictionary.

Isidore ♂ From Greek *Isidōros* 'gift of Isis'. See main dictionary.

J

Jacqueline ♀ Feminine pet form of JACQUES. See main dictionary.

Jacques ♂ From Latin *Jacobus*. See ◊**James** and ◊**Jacob** in main dictionary.

Jean ♂ From New Testament Greek *Iōannēs*. See ◊**John** in main dictionary.

Jeanette ♀ Pet form of JEANNE. *Also*: **Jeannette**.

Jeanne ♀ Feminine form of JEAN.

Jeannine ♀ Pet form of JEANNE.

Jérôme ♂ From New Testament Greek *Hieronymos*. See ◊**Jerome** in main dictionary.

Joachim ♂ Biblical. See main dictionary. *Also*: **Joaquin**.

Joël ♂ Biblical. See ◊**Joel** in main dictionary. *Feminine form*: **Joëlle**.

Joseph ♂ Biblical. See main dictionary.

Joséphine ♀ Feminine pet form of JOSEPH.

Josette ♀ Pet form of JOSÉPHINE.

Julie ♀ From Latin. See ◊**Julia** in main dictionary.

Jules ♂ From Latin ◊**Julius** (see main dictionary).

Julien ♀ From Late Latin *Juliānus*. See ◊**Julian** in main dictionary. *Feminine form*: **Julienne**.

Juliette ♀ Pet form of JULIE.

Justin ♂ From Latin. See main dictionary. *Feminine form*: **Justine**.

L

Lambert ♂ Germanic. See main dictionary.

Laure ♀ From Latin. See ◊**Laura** in main dictionary. *Pet form*: **Laurette**.

Laurence ♀ Feminine form of LAURENT.

Laurent ♂ From Latin. See ◊**Laurence** in main dictionary.

Léon ♂ From Late Latin. See ◊**Leo** in main dictionary. *Feminine form*: **Léonne**.

Léonard ♂ Germanic. See ◊**Leonard** in main dictionary.

Léonce ♂ From Italian ◊**Leonzio** (see Italian supplement).

Léonie ♀ From Latin. See main dictionary.

Léonore ♀ Short form of ELÉONORE. See ◊**Leonora** in main dictionary.

Liane ♀ Short form of ÉLIANE. *Also:* **Lianne**.

Lisette ♀ Pet form of *Lise*, itself a shortened form of ELISABETH.

Louis ♂ Of Germanic origin; name of sixteen kings of France before the Revolution. See main dictionary. *Feminine form:* **Louise**.

Luc ♂ From New Testament Greek. See ◊**Luke** in main dictionary.

Lucie ♀ From Latin. See ◊**Lucy** in main dictionary. This has now largely replaced the older French form **Luce**.

Lucien ♂ From Latin *Luciānus*, a derivative of the Roman given name *Lucius*, which is probably derived from *lux* 'light'.

Lucille ♀ From Latin. See main dictionary.

M

Madeleine ♀ New Testament. See main dictionary.

Marc ♂ From Latin. See ◊**Mark** in main dictionary.

Marcel ♂ From Latin *Marcellus*, a diminutive of ◊**Marcus** (see main dictionary). It owes its popularity in France to a 3rd-century missionary of this name, martyred at Bourges. *Feminine form:* **Marcelle**.

Marcellin ♂ From Latin *Marcellīnus*, a double diminutive of *Marcus*.

Margot ♀ Pet form of MARGUERITE.

Marguerite ♀ From Greek. See ◊**Margaret** and ◊**Marguerite** in main dictionary.

Marianne ♀ Blend of MARIE and ANNE, used as the name of the female figure symbolizing the French Republic.

Marie ♀ From Latin. See ◊**Maria** and ◊**Mary** in main dictionary.

Marie-Ange ♀ French equivalent of Spanish *Maria de los Angeles* 'Mary of the angels'.

Marie-France ♀ Name coined in the 19th century as invoking the protection of the Virgin Mary as the special guardian of France.

Marielle ♀ Pet form of MARIE.

Marthe ♀ New Testament. See ◊**Martha** in main dictionary.

Martin ♂ From Latin. See main dictionary. *Feminine form:* **Martine**.

Mathilde ♀ Germanic. See ◊**Matilda** in main dictionary. *Also:* **Matilde**.

Mathieu ♂ New Testament. See ◊**Matthew** in main dictionary.

Maurice ♂ From Late Latin. See main dictionary.

Maxime ♂ From Latin *maximus* 'greatest'.

Mélanie ♀ From Greek. See ◊**Melanie** in main dictionary.

Michel ♂ Biblical. See English ◊**Michael** in main dictionary. *Feminine forms:* **Michèle**, **Michelle**.

Micheline ♀ Pet form of MICHÈLE.

Mirabelle ♀ French coinage from Latin *mīrābilis* 'wonderful'. See main dictionary.

Mireille ♀ From Provençal *Mireio*. See main dictionary.

Monique ♀ From Latin. See ◊**Monica** in main dictionary.

Moïse ♂ Biblical. See ◊**Moses** in main dictionary.

N

Nadia ♀ From Russian. See main dictionary.

Nadine ♀ French elaboration of NADIA. See main dictionary.

Narcisse ♂ From Greek *Narkissos*. See ◊**Narciso** in Spanish supplement.

Natalie ♀ From Russian. See main dictionary. *Also:* **Nathalie**.

Nazaire ♂ From the Late Latin Christian name *Nazarius* 'of Nazareth'.

Nicolas ♂ From Late Greek. See ◊**Nicholas** in main dictionary.

Nicole ♀ Feminine form of NICHOLAS.

Nicolette ♀ Pet form of NICOLE.

Nina ♀ From Russian. See main dictionary.

Ninette ♀ Pet form of NINA. See main dictionary.

Ninon ♀ Pet form of ANNE or NINA.

Noë ♂ Biblical. See ◊**Noah** in main dictionary.

Noël ♂ From Latin *natālis (diēs)* 'birthday' (i.e. the birthday of Christ, i.e. Christmas). See main dictionary. *Feminine forms:* **Noëlle**, **Noelle**.

Norine ♀ Pet form of HONORINE.

O

Odette ♀ French feminine pet form of the Germanic male name *Oda*. See main dictionary.

Odile ♀ Germanic. See main dictionary.

Olivier ♂ Germanic. See ◊**Oliver** in main dictionary.

Olympe ♀ From Greek *Olympia* 'woman of Olympus' (home of the gods).

Ottilie ♀ French derivative of the medieval Germanic given name *Odila* (see ◊**Odile** in main dictionary).

Ottoline ♀ Pet form of OTTILIE. See main dictionary.

P

Pascal ♂ From Late Latin *Paschālis* 'relating to Easter' *Also*: **Paschal**. *Feminine form*: **Pascale**.

Patrice ♂, ♀ See ◊**Patrick** and ◊**Patricia** in main dictionary.

Paul ♂ From Latin. See main dictionary.

Paulette ♀ Feminine pet form of PAUL.

Pauline ♀ Feminine pet form of PAUL.

Philippe ♂ From Greek. See ◊**Philip** in main dictionary.

Pierre ♂ From New Testament Greek. See ◊**Peter** in main dictionary.

Pierette ♀ Feminine pet form of PIERRE.

Prosper ♂ From Latin *Prosperus* 'fortunate', 'prosperous'.

Q

Quentin ♂ From Latin. See main dictionary.

R

Rachel ♀ Biblical. See main dictionary. *Also*: **Rachelle**.

Raoul ♂ Germanic. See ◊**Ralph** in main dictionary. *Also*: **Raul**.

Rainier ♂ Germanic. See ◊**Rayner** in main dictionary.

Raphael ♂ Biblical: name of an archangel.

Raymond ♂ Germanic. See main dictionary.

Régine ♀ From Latin. See ◊**Regina** in main dictionary.

Régis ♂ Given in honour of St Jean-François Régis (d. 1640) of Narbonne, who strove to reform prostitutes.

Reine ♀ From the French word corresponding to Latin *rēgina* 'queen'. Compare RÉGINE.

Rémy ♂ From Latin *Rēmigius*, a derivative of *rēmex* 'oarsman'; name of a 6th-century bishop of Rheims who converted and baptized Clovis, king of the Franks. *Also*: **Rémi**.

René ♂ From Late Latin *Renātus* 'reborn', a popular name among early Christians celebrating spiritual rebirth in Christ. *Feminine form*: **Renée**.

Reynaud ♂ Germanic. See ◊**Reynold** in main dictionary.

Richard ♂ Germanic. See main dictionary.

Robert ♂ Germanic. See main dictionary.

Roch ♂ From Italian ◊**Rocco** (see Italian supplement).

Rodolphe ♂ Germanic. See ◊**Rudolf** in main dictionary and German supplement.

Roger ♂ Germanic. See main dictionary.

Roland ♂ Germanic. See main dictionary. *Also*: **Rolland**.

Romain ♂ From the Late Latin personal name *Rōmānus* 'Roman'. *Feminine form*: **Romaine**.

Rosalie ♀ From Latin *Rosālia*. See main dictionary.

Rosaire ♀ Roman Catholic name meaning 'rosary'. See ◊**Rosario** in Spanish supplement.

Rose ♀ See main dictionary.

Roxane ♀ From Greek. See main dictionary. *Also*: **Roxanne**.

S

Sabine ♀ From Latin. See ◊**Sabina** in main dictionary.

Sacha ♂ From Russian. See ◊**Sasha** in Russian supplement.

Salomé ♀ From Greek. See ◊**Salome** in main dictionary.

Samuel ♂ Biblical. See main dictionary.

Sébastien ♂ From Latin. See ◊**Sebastian** in main dictionary.

Serge ♂ From Latin *Sargius*. See ◊**Sergei** in Russian supplement.

Simon ♂ Biblical. See main dictionary. *Feminine form*: **Simone**.

Solange ♀ From the Late Latin name *Sollemnia*, a derivative of *sollemnis* 'solemn'. St Solange was a 9th-century martyr of Bourges.

Sophie ♀ From Greek. See main dictionary.

Stéphane ♂ Learned variant of ÉTIENNE.

Stéphanie ♀ From Latin. See ◊**Stephanie** in main dictionary.

Suzanne ♀ Biblical. See ◊**Susanna** and ◊**Susan** in main dictionary. *Also*: **Susanne**.

Suzette ♀ Pet form of SUZANNE.

Sylvain ♂ From Italian ◊**Silvano** (see Italian supplement).

Sylvie ♀ From Latin. See ◊**Silvia** in main dictionary.

T

Théodore ♂ From Greek. See ◊**Theodore** in main dictionary.

Thérèse ♀ From Spanish. See ◊**Theresa** in main dictionary.

Thibault ♂ From Germanic. See ◊**Theobald** in main dictionary.

Thierry ♂ From Germanic *Theodoric* 'people ruler'. Compare English ◊**Terry** in main dictionary.

Thomas ♂ New Testament. See main dictionary.

Timothée ♂ From New Testament Greek. See ◊**Timothy** in main dictionary.

Toussaint ♂ Chosen by parents who wish to invoke the blessing and protection of 'all the saints' (*tous les saints*); often given to a boy born on the feast of All Saints.

Tristan ♂ Celtic. See main dictionary.

V

Valentin ♂ From Latin. See ◊**Valentine** in main dictionary.

Valère ♂ From Latin *Valērius*, which is probably a derivative of *valēre* 'to be healthy'. There are several early saints of this name who have connections with France, in particular a Roman missionary martyred at Soissons in 287. It has now largely been superseded by VALÉRY.

Valérie ♀ From Latin *Valēria*. See ◊**Valerie** in main dictionary.

Valéry ♂ Masculine form of VALÉRIE, which has absorbed an older name of Germanic origin meaning 'foreign power'.

Véronique ♀ From Latin. See ◊**Veronica** in main dictionary.

Victoire ♀ French form of English ◊**Victoria**. See main dictionary. *Pet form*: **Victorine**.

Victor ♂ From Late Latin. See main dictionary.

Vincent ♂ From Latin. See main dictionary.

Violette ♀ From the name of the flower and the colour. See ◊**Violet** in main dictionary.

Virginie ♀ From Latin. See ◊**Virginia** in main dictionary.

Vivien ♂ From Latin. See main dictionary.

Vivienne ♀ Feminine form of VIVIEN.

X

Xavier ♂ See main dictionary.

Y

Yolande ♀ Of uncertain origin. See main dictionary.

Yves ♂ From a short form of a Germanic compound name containing the element *iv-* 'yew'. St Yve was an 11th-century bishop of Chartres. *Also*: **Yvon**.

Yvette ♀ Feminine pet form of YVES.

Yvonne ♀ Feminine derivative of YVES. See main dictionary.

APPENDIX 2:

GERMAN NAMES

A

Achim ♂ Short form of JOACHIM. *Also*: **Akim**.

Adalbert ♂ Germanic: older form of ALBRECHT. *Also*: **Adalbrecht, Adelbrecht**.

Adam ♂ Biblical, name of the first man. See main dictionary.

Adelheid ♀ Germanic: 'noble kind'. See ◊**Adelaide** in main dictionary.

Adeltraud ♀ Germanic: 'noble strength'. See ◊**Audrey** in main dictionary.

Adolf ♂ Germanic: *Adelwolf* 'noble wolf', = Old English *Æthelwolf*.

Aegidus ♂ Latin, from Greek. See ◊**Giles** in main dictionary. *Also*: **Ägid**.

Albrecht ♂ Germanic: *Adalbrecht* 'noble bright'. See ◊**Albert** in main dictionary.

Alexander ♂ Greek: 'defender of men'. See main dictionary.

Alexia ♀ Feminine of ALEXIS.

Alexis ♂ Greek: 'defender'. See main dictionary.

Alfred ♂ From English. See main dictionary.

Alke ♀ North German form of ADELHEID.

Alois ♂ = Latin *Aloysius*, probably from Germanic *Alwisi* 'all wise'.

Alois(i)a ♀ Feminine of ALOIS.

Andrea ♀ Feminine of ANDREAS.

Andreas ♂ From Latin and Greek. See ◊**Andrew** in main dictionary.

Angelika ♀ From Greek. See ◊**Angelica** in main dictionary.

Anke ♀ North German pet form of ANNA.

Anna ♀ Biblical. See ◊**Anne** in main dictionary.

Anneliese ♀ Blend of ANNA and ELISABETH.

Anton ♂ From Latin. See ◊**Anthony** in main dictionary.

Armin ♂ Latin *Arminius*, name of a Germanic military leader who defeated the Romans in AD 9.

Arnold ♂ Germanic: *Arnhold* 'eagle splendid', alteration of older *Arnwald* 'eagle power'. See ◊**Arnold** in main dictionary. *Also*: **Arno**.

Arnulf ♂ Germanic: 'eagle wolf'.

August ♂ From Latin. See ◊**Augustus** in main dictionary.

Augustin ♂ From Latin. See ◊**Augustine** in main dictionary.

B

Baldur ♂ From Old Norse *Baldr*, name of a god, son of Odin.

Balthasar ♂ Name of one of the three Magi. See main dictionary.

Balzer ♂ Vernacular form of BALTHASAR.

Barbara ♀ Greek. See main dictionary.

Bartholomäus ♂ New Testament. See ◊**Bartholomew** in main dictionary.

Beat ♂ Swiss: from Latin *Beātus* 'blessed', name of the apostle of Switzerland; pronounced as two syllables.

Beate ♀ Feminine of BEAT.

Beatrix ♀ Latin: 'fortunate'. See ◊**Beatrix** in main dictionary.

Benjamin ♂ Biblical. See main dictionary.

Benno ♂ Pet form of BERNHARD, later associated with Latin *Benedictus* (see ◊**Benedict** in main dictionary).

Bernhard ♂ Germanic: 'bear staunch'. See ◊**Bernard** in main dictionary. *Also*: **Bernd**.

Berta ♀ Germanic: 'bright' or 'famous'. See ◊**Bertha** in main dictionary.

Berthold ♂ Germanic: 'bright and splendid'; alteration of earlier *Bertwald*, 'bright power'.

Bettina ♀ Pet form of ELISABETH.

Birgit(ta) ♀ Variant of BRIGITTA.

Bodo ♂ Germanic: 'messenger'.

Brigitta ♀ From Irish *Brighid*. See ◊**Bridget** in main dictionary.

Brünhild(e) ♀ Germanic: 'armour battle', name of a Valkyrie.

Bruno ♂ Germanic: 'the brown one' (i.e. a bear).

C

Cäcilie, -lia ♀ From Latin *Caecilia*, patron saint of music. See ◊**Cecily** in main dictionary.

Cajetan ♂ See KAJETAN.

Carsten ♂ North German form of CHRISTIAN.

Carl ♂ See KARL.

Charlotte ♀ Feminine of KARL; see main dictionary. Sophie Charlotte was the name of the wife of Friedrich I of Prussia.

Christa ♀ Pet form of CHRISTIANE.

Christian ♂ 'Believer in Christ'. See main dictionary.

Christiane ♀ Feminine of CHRISTIAN.

Christoph ♂ See KRISTOF.

Clara ♀ Latin: 'bright, famous'. See ◊**Clare** in main dictionary.

Claudia ♀ From the Latin family name *Claudius*. See ◊**Claudia** in main dictionary.

Claus ♂ See KLAUS.

Conrad ♂ See KONRAD.

Constantin ♂ See KONSTANTIN.

Constanze ♀ See KONSTANZE.

Corinna ♀ Latin, from Greek: 'maiden'; name of Ovid's beloved.

Cornelia ♀ Feminine of CORNELIUS.

Cornelius ♂ Latin, a Roman family name.

Cosima ♀ Feminine of COSIMO.

Cosimo ♂ From Greek *kosmios* 'orderly; well-formed'.

D

Dagmar ♀ See main dictionary.

Daniel ♂ Biblical: 'God is my judge'. See main dictionary.

Detlev ♂ North German: 'inheritance of the people'. The standard German form *Dietleib* is rarer. *Also*: **Detlef**.

Dieter ♂ Germanic: *Diotheri* 'army of the people'.

Dietlind(e) ♀ Germanic: 'tender for the people'.

Dietmar ♂ Germanic: 'famous among the people'.

Dietrich ♂ Germanic: 'ruler of the people'. See ◊**Derek** in main dictionary.

Dietwald ♂ Germanic: 'people power'.

E

Ebba ♀ Germanic: short form of various names formed with *eber* 'boar'.

Ebbo ♂ Germanic: short form of various names formed with *eber* 'boar'.

Eberhard ♂ Germanic: 'boar staunch'.

Eck(e)hard ♂ Germanic: 'sword staunch'.

Edda ♀ Pet form of any of several old German names beginning with *Ed-*. The Elder

and Younger *Eddas* are also the name of two
influential Old Icelandic books of Norse
myths and poems.

Edeltraud ♀ Germanic: 'noble strength'.

Egmont, Egmunt ♂ Germanic: 'sword
protector'.

Egon ♂ Short form of various Germanic
names formed with *Egin-* or *Egil-* 'sword'.

Ehrenfried ♂ Germanic: 'eagle peace' or
'honour peace'.

Ehrenreich ♂ 17th-century coinage: 'rich
in honour'.

Ehrentraud ♀ Germanic: 'eagle strength' or
'honour strength'.

Eleanore ♀ From French or English. See
◊**Eleanor** in main dictionary.

Elfriede ♀ Germanic: 'noble peace', but
compare English ◊**Elfreda** in main dictionary.

Elisabeth ♀ Biblical. See main dictionary at
◊**Elizabeth**.

Elke ♀ North German: reduced pet form of
ADELHEID.

Ella ♀ Short form of ELISABETH, Germanic
names beginning with *El-*, or GABRIELLA.

Elmar ♂ Germanic: 'sword fame'.

Else ♀ Pet form of ELISABETH.

Emil ♂ German form of French ◊**Émile** (see
French supplement).

Emma ♀ See main dictionary.

Emmerich ♂ Germanic: from earlier
Heimerich 'ruler of the homeland'.

Engelbert, -brecht ♂ Germanic: 'angel
bright'.

Erhard ♂ Germanic: 'staunch in honour'.

Erich ♂ Nordic: 'sole ruler'. See ◊**Eric** in
main dictionary.

Ermengard ♀ Germanic: 'protector of all'.
Also: **Ermgard, Irmgard**.

Ermenhild(e) ♀ Germanic: 'total fight'.
Also: **Irmhild(e)**.

Ermentraud, -trud ♀ Germanic: 'total
strength'.

Erna ♀ Pet form of ERNESTA.

Ernesta ♀ Feminine of ERNST.

Ernst ♂ Germanic: 'serious business', 'fight
to the death'.

Erwin ♂ Germanic: 'friend of honour'.

Etta ♀ Pet form abstracted from HENRIETTA,
etc.

Eugen ♂ From Greek *Eugenios* 'well-born'.
See ◊**Eugene** in main dictionary.

Eva ♀ Biblical. See ◊**Eve** in main dictionary.

Ewald ♂ Germanic: *Ewawalt* 'power of
law'.

Eward ♂ Germanic: *Ewawart* 'guardian of
the law'. *Also*: **Ewart**.

F

Ferdinand ♂ Traditional name among the
Habsburgs, of Visigothic (Spanish) origin:
see main dictionary.

Florian ♂ From Latin *Floriānus* 'flowery'.
St Florian is the patron saint of Upper
Austria and of Poland.

Folker ♂ See VOLKER.

Frank ♂ Byname meaning 'free', 'trustworthy', or 'Frankish'. See main dictionary.

Franz ♂ German form of Italian ◊**Francesco**.
See Italian supplement, and see ◊**Francis** in
main dictionary.

Franziska ♀ Feminine form of FRANZ.

Frederik ♂ North German form of
FRIEDRICH.

Frederika ♀ Feminine form of FREDERIK.

Friede ♀ Short form of names beginning
with *Fried* 'peace'. *Also*: **Frieda**.

Friedemann ♂ Germanic: 'man of peace'.

Friederike ♀ Feminine form of FRIEDRICH.

Friedhelm ♂ Germanic: 'helmet of peace'.

Friedrich ♂ Germanic: 'peace ruler'; a royal
and imperial name from an early date. *Also*:
Friederich.

Fritz ♂ Pet form of FRIEDRICH.

Fürchtegott ♂ Protestant name meaning
'fear God', intended as a translation of
Greek *Timotheos*; see ◊**Timothy** in main
dictionary.

G

Gabriel ♂ Biblical: Hebrew, 'man of God'.
See main dictionary.

Gabriele, -ela, -elle ♀ Feminine of
GABRIEL.

Gebhard ♂ Germanic: 'staunch gift'.

Georg ♂ From Greek *Geōrgos* 'farmer'. See
◊**George** in main dictionary.

Gerd ♂ Reduced form of GERHARD.

Gerde, -da ♀ Reduced form of GERTRUD.

Gerhard ♂ Germanic: 'spear staunch'. See
◊**Gerard** in main dictionary.

Gerlach ♂ Germanic: 'spear game'.

Gerlind(e) ♀ Germanic: 'spear tender'.

Gernot ♂ Germanic: 'spear need'.

Gert ♂ North German reduced form of
GERHARD. *Also*: **Geert**.

Gertrud, -traud ♀ Germanic: 'spear
strength'. See ◊**Gertrude** in main dictionary.

The German name is much more widely used.

Gertrun ♀ Germanic: 'spear rune or magic'.

Gisela ♀ Germanic: 'pledge' or 'scion', = French ◊**Giselle** (see main dictionary).

Gottfried ♂ Germanic: 'God peace'. See ◊**Godfrey** in main dictionary.

Gotthard ♂ Germanic: 'God staunch'.

Gotthold ♂ Protestant coinage: 'God splendid'; variant by folk etymology of the older Germanic name GOTTWALD.

Gottlieb ♂ Protestant coinage: 'love God'; translation of Greek *Theophilos*; Late Latin equivalent *Amadeus*.

Gottlob ♂ Protestant coinage: 'praise God'.

Götz ♂ Reduced form of GOTTFRIED.

Grete ♀ Short form of MARGARETE.

Gretch ♀ Pet form of GRETE.

Gudrun ♀ Nordic: 'God rune' or 'God magic'.

Gunther ♂ Germanic: 'battle army', name of a tragic hero in the Nibelungenlied and in Wagner's Ring cycle. *Also*: **Gunter**, **Günt(h)er**.

H

Hagen ♂ **1** Germanic: 'stockade or enclosure'. **2** altered form of Nordic *Håkon* 'son of the high one'.

Hanne, Hanna ♀ Pet form of JOHANNA.

Hannelore ♀ Blend of HANNE and ELEANORE.

Hans ♂ Pet form of JOHANNES. *South German double diminutive*: **Hansel**.

Harald ♂ Germanic: from earlier *Harwald* 'army power'. See ◊**Harold** in main dictionary.

Hartmann ♂ Germanic: 'staunch man'.

Hartmut ♂ Germanic: 'staunch spirit'.

Hartwig ♂ Germanic: 'staunch in battle'.

Hedda ♀ Nordic pet form of HEDWIG.

Hedwig ♀ Germanic: 'battle strife'.

Heidi ♀ Southern German pet form of ADELHEID.

Heike ♀ North German feminine pet form of HEINRICH.

Heimo ♂ Pet form of any of various old Germanic names formed with *Heim* 'home'.

Heinrich ♂ Germanic: 'home ruler'. See ◊**Henry** in main dictionary.

Heinz ♂ Pet form of HEINRICH.

Helga ♀ Nordic: 'prosperous' or 'holy'.

Helge ♂ Nordic: 'prosperous' or 'holy'.

Helger ♂ Germanic: 'holy spear' or 'prosperous spear'.

Helma, Helme ♀ Feminine of names ending in *-helm*, e.g. FRIEDHELM, WILHELM.

Helmine, Helmina ♀ Short form of WILHELMINA.

Helmut ♂ Germanic: 'sound mind'.

Henk ♂ North German reduced form of HEINRICH.

Herbert ♂ Germanic: 'army bright'. See ◊**Herbert** in main dictionary.

Hermann ♂ Germanic: 'army man'.

Hermine ♀ 19th-century coinage as a feminine form of HERMANN.

Hertha ♀ From a misreading of Latin *Nertha*, name of a fertility goddess mentioned by Tacitus.

Hilde, Hilda ♀ Short form of Germanic names formed with *hilde* 'battle'.

Hildebrand ♂ Germanic: 'flaming sword of battle'.

Hildebrecht, -bert ♂ Germanic: 'battle bright'.

Hildegard ♀ Germanic: 'battle protector'.

Hildegund(e) ♀ Germanic: 'battle strife'.

Holger ♂ Nordic: from earlier *Holmger* 'island spear'.

Horst ♂ Saxon: altered form of *Horsa* 'horse'.

Hu(g)bert ♂ Germanic: 'bright spirit'. See ◊**Hubert** in main dictionary.

Hugo ♂ Germanic: 'bright spirit'. See ◊**Hugo** in main dictionary.

I

Ignaz ♂ Vernacular form of Latin ◊**Ignatius** (see main dictionary).

Ilsa, Ilse ♀ Pet form of ELISABETH.

Immanuel ♂ Biblical: Hebrew, 'God is with us'. See ◊**Emmanuel** in main dictionary.

Inge, Inga ♀ Pet form of INGEBORG or INGETRAUD.

Ingeborg ♀ Nordic: 'stronghold of Ing' (an ancient Germanic god).

Ingemar ♂ Nordic: 'Ing's fame'.

Ingetraud ♀ Blend of INGEBORG and names ending in *-traud*, such as ADELTRAUD.

Ingrid ♀ Nordic: 'Ing the beautiful'.

Irene ♀ Greek: 'peace'. See ◊**Irene** in main dictionary.

Iris ♀ Greek: 'rainbow'. See main dictionary.

Irma ♀ Short form of any of the feminine names formed with *Irmen-* 'totality', 'everything', 'all'. See also ERMEN-.

Irmengard ♀ Variant of ERMENGARD. *Also*: **Irmgard, Irmingard**.

Irmentrud, -traud ♀ Variant of ERMEN-TRUD.

Irwin ♂ Variant of ERWIN.

Isolde ♀ See main dictionary.

J

Jakob ♂ Biblical: Hebrew, 'supplanter'. See ◊**Jacob** and ◊**James** in main dictionary.

Jan ♂ North German and Slavic reduced form of JOHANNES.

Jeremias ♂ Biblical: Hebrew, 'appointed by God'. See ◊**Jeremy** in main dictionary.

Joachim ♂ Biblical: Hebrew, 'established by God'.

Johann ♂ Vernacular form of JOHANNES.

Jo(h)anna ♀ Feminine form of JOHANNES.

Johannes ♂ Latin, from Hebrew, 'God is gracious'. See ◊**John** in main dictionary.

Jolanda ♀ German form of French and English ◊**Yolande** (see main dictionary).

Jonas ♂ Biblical: 'dove'. See ◊**Jonah** in main dictionary.

Jonathan ♂ Biblical. See main dictionary.

Jordan ♂ Crusader name. See main dictionary.

Josef ♂ From Hebrew *Yosef* 'God shall add (a son)'. See ◊**Joseph** in main dictionary.

Josefa ♀ Feminine form of JOSEF.

Judith ♀ Biblical: Hebrew, 'Jewish woman'. See main dictionary.

Jürgen ♂ North German form of GEORG.

Jutta ♀ Pet form of JUDITH.

K

Kai ♂ Nordic: of uncertain origin.

Kajetan ♂ From Latin *Caietanus* 'man from Caieta'. St Caietano or Gaetano was a 16th-century Neapolitan religious reformer. Sometimes adopted by Roman Catholics in honour of Cardinal Gaetano, opponent of Martin Luther.

Kamil ♂ From Latin *Camillus*, of unknown origin. St Camillus (1550–1614) was the founder of an order of monks who nursed the sick.

Kamilla ♀ Feminine form of KAMIL. See ◊**Camilla** in main dictionary.

Karl ♂ Germanic: 'man', an ancient royal and imperial name. See ◊**Charles** in main dictionary.

Karsten ♂ North German form of CHRISTIAN.

Kaspar ♂ Name of one of the three magi. See ◊**Caspar** in main dictionary.

Katharina ♀ From Greek. See ◊**Katherine** in main dictionary.

Käthe ♀ Pet form of KATHARINA.

Katja ♀ Pet form of KATHARINA.

Klara ♀ See CLARA.

Klaus ♂ Pet form of NIKOLAUS.

Klemens ♂ From Latin. See ◊**Clement** in main dictionary.

Konrad ♂ Germanic: 'bold counsel'. See ◊**Conrad** in main dictionary.

Konstantin ♂ From Late Latin *Constantīnus*, name of the first Christian Roman emperor (?288–337).

Konstanze ♀ From Latin *Constantia*. See ◊**Constance** in main dictionary.

Kriemhild(e) ♀ Germanic: 'battle mask'.

Kristof ♂ From Greek *Christophoros* 'bearer of Christ'. See ◊**Christopher** in main dictionary.

Kurt ♂ Pet form of KONRAD.

L

Ladislaus ♂ Latinized form of the Slavic name *Vladislav* 'rule of glory'.

Laurenz ♂ From Latin *Laurentius*. See ◊**Laurence** in main dictionary.

Leberecht ♂ Protestant name: 'live right'.

Lena, Leni ♀ Reduced forms of MAGDALENA.

Lenz ♂ Reduced form of LAURENZ.

Leo ♂ Latin: 'lion'. See main dictionary.

Leonhard ♂ Blend of Latin *Leo(n)-* and Germanic *hard* 'tough', 'staunch'.

Leonore, -nora ♀ Reduced form of ELEANORE.

Lienhard ♂ South German variant of LEONHARD.

Liese ♀ Pet form of ELISABETH.

Li(e)selotte ♀ Blend of LIESE and LOTTE.

Lili ♀ Pet form of ELISABETH. *Also*: **Lilli**.

Lisa ♀ Pet form of ELISABETH.

Lorenz ♂ Variant of LAURENZ.

Lothar ♂ Germanic 'fame army'; a Frankish royal name.

Lotte ♀ Reduced form of CHARLOTTE.

Ludwig ♂ Germanic: 'fame warrior'; an ancient royal and imperial name, = French ◊**Louis** (see French supplement and main dictionary).

Luither ♂ Germanic: 'army of the people'; the root of the surname *Luther*.

Lukas ♂ Greek. See ◊**Luke** in main dictionary.

M

Magda ♀ Short form of MAGDALENA.

Magdalena ♀ Latin, from Aramaic. See ◊**Madeleine** in main dictionary.

Manfred, -fried ♂ Germanic: 'peace among men'.

Margaret(h)e, -a ♀ Latin and Greek: 'pearl'. See ◊**Margaret** in main dictionary.

Maria ♀ New Testament; Greek and Latin derivative of Aramaic *Miriam*. See ◊**Mary** in main dictionary.

Marian ♂ From Latin *Mariānus*, a derivative of MARIUS. In the Christian era it has found favour as a name for devotees of the Virgin Mary (see MARIA).

Marianne ♀ Blend of MARIA and ANNA.

Marius ♂ Latin. See main dictionary.

Markus ♂ Latin. See ◊**Marcus** in main dictionary.

Marlene ♀ Blend of MARIA and MAGDALENA.

Mart(h)a, Mart(h)e ♀ Aramaic. See ◊**Martha** in main dictionary.

Martin ♂ From Latin. See ◊**Martin** in main dictionary.

Mathilde ♀ Germanic: 'might in battle'.

Matthäus ♂ From Latin *Matthaeus*; variant of MATTHIAS.

Matthias ♂ New Testament. See ◊**Matthew** in main dictionary.

Max ♂ Short form of MAXIMILIAN.

Maximilian ♂ From Latin. See main dictionary.

Maxine ♀ Feminine form of MAX.

Mechthild(e) ♀ Variant of MATHILDE.

Meinhard ♂ Germanic: 'staunch in ability'.

Meinrad ♂ Germanic: 'ability in counsel'.

Melchior ♂ Name of one of the three magi. See main dictionary.

Mercedes ♀ Spanish. See main dictionary.

Michael ♂ Biblical: Hebrew, 'Who is like God?' See main dictionary.

Mirjam ♀ Biblical. See ◊**Miriam** in main dictionary.

Mitzi ♀ South German pet form of MARIA.

Monika ♀ See ◊**Monica** in main dictionary.

Moritz ♂ From Latin. See ◊**Maurice** in main dictionary.

N

Nathan ♂ Biblical: Hebrew, 'God-given'. See main dictionary.

Nepomuk ♂ Czech: 'from Pomuk', byname of St John Nepomuk (1350–93), patron saint of Bohemia.

Nikolaus ♂ Greek. See ◊**Nicholas** in main dictionary.

Norbert ♂ Germanic: 'north bright'.

O

Olaf ♂ Nordic: 'heir of the ancestors'.

Olof ♂ North German reduced form of OT(T)WOLF, influenced by OLAF.

Oskar ♂ See ◊**Oscar** in main dictionary.

Oswald ♂ See main dictionary.

Oswin ♂ Germanic: 'God friend'.

Ot(t)mar ♂ Germanic: 'prosperity fame'. *Also*: **Ottomar**.

Otto ♂ Short form of any of the Germanic male names formed with *ot*- 'prosperity'; a royal and imperial name from an early date.

Ottokar ♂ Germanic: 'prosperity watchful'; as *Odovacar*, name of the king of the Goths who controlled Italy 476–93.

Ot(t)wolf ♂ Germanic: 'prosperity wolf'.

P

Paul ♂ See main dictionary.

Paula ♀ Feminine of PAUL.

Paulus ♂ Latin form of PAUL.

Peter ♂ See main dictionary.

Petra ♀ Feminine of PETER.

Petrus ♂ Latin form of PETER.

Philipp ♂ See ◊**Philip** in main dictionary.

Pia ♀ Latin: 'pious'. See Italian supplement.

R

Radegund(e) ♀ Germanic: 'counsel for battle'.

Rafael ♂ German spelling of *Raphael*, name of one of the archangels.

Raimund ♂ Germanic: 'counsel protector'. See ◊**Raymond** in main dictionary.

Rainer ♂ Variant of REINER.

Randolf, Randulf ♂ Germanic: 'shield wolf'.

Reimund ♂ Variant of RAIMUND.

Reineke ♂ North German pet form of any of the Germanic male names formed with *Rein* 'counsel'.

Reiner ♂ Germanic: from earlier *Reinher* 'counsel army'.

Reinhard ♂ Germanic: 'counsel staunch'.

Reinhold ♂ Germanic: ostensibly 'counsel splendid', but actually a variant of earlier REINWALD.

Reinmar ♂ Germanic: 'counsel famous'.

Reinwald ♂ Germanic: 'counsel power'.

Renata ♀ Latin: 'reborn'. See main dictionary.

Resi ♀ Pet form of THERESE.

Ria ♀ Pet form of MARIA.

Richard ♂ Germanic: 'power staunch'. See ◊**Richard** in main dictionary.

Rike ♀ Pet form of ULRIKE or FRIEDERIKE.

Robert ♂ Germanic: 'fame bright'. See ◊**Robert** in main dictionary.

Rosa ♀ Latin: 'rose'. See main dictionary.

Rosamunde ♀ Germanic: 'fame protector'.

Röschen ♀ Pet form of ROSA, ROSEMARIE, or ROSAMUNDE.

Rosemarie ♀ Blend of ROSA and MARIA.

Rudi ♂ Pet form of RUDOLF.

Rüdiger ♂ Germanic: 'fame spear'. This is the name of a hero in the Nibelungenlied. See ◊**Roger** in main dictionary.

Rudolf ♂ Germanic: 'fame wolf'.

Rupert ♂ North German variant of ROBERT. See ◊**Rupert** in main dictionary.

Ruprecht ♂ Variant of RUPERT.

S

Sebastian ♂ See main dictionary.

Siegfried ♂ Germanic: 'victory peace'.

Sieghard ♂ Germanic: 'victory staunch'.

Sieghild(e) ♀ Germanic: 'victory battle'.

Sieglind(e) ♀ Germanic: 'victory tender'.

Siegmund ♂ Germanic: 'victory wolf'.

Siegrun ♀ Germanic: 'victory rune' or 'victory magic'. *Also*: **Sigrun**.

Siegward ♂ Germanic: 'victory protector'.

Sig(g)i ♂, ♀ Pet form of SIEGFRIED, SIEGMUND, SIEGLINDE, SIGRID, etc.

Sigismund ♂ Variant of SIEGMUND.

Sigiswald ♂ Variant of SIEGWALD.

Sigrid ♀ Nordic: 'victory beauty'.

Sigurd ♂ Nordic form of SIEGWARD.

Silke ♀ North German pet form of CÄCILIE.

Simon ♂ See main dictionary.

Simone ♀ Feminine of SIMON.

Sissy ♀ South German pet form of ELISABETH.

Sofie, Sofia ♀ From Greek. See ◊**Sophia** in main dictionary.

Stefan ♂ From Greek. See ◊**Stephen** in main dictionary.

Stefanie ♀ Feminine of STEFAN.

Steffen ♂ North German form of STEFAN.

Steffi ♀ Pet form of STEFANIE.

Stoffel ♂ Pet form of KRISTOF.

Susann(a) ♀ From Hebrew. See ◊**Susan** in main dictionary.

Susi ♀ Pet form of SUSANN(A).

T

Teres(i)a ♀ Variant of THERES(I)A.

Theda ♀ Latinate pet form of any of several names formed with *diet-* 'people', e.g. DIETLINDE.

Theodor ♂ From Greek. See ◊**Theodore** in main dictionary.

Theres(i)a, Therese ♀ Name traditionally associated with the Habsburg family. See ◊**Theresa** in main dictionary.

Thomas ♂ See main dictionary.

Timo ♂ Pet form of obsolete *Timotheus*, Latin form of Greek *Timotheos* 'honour God'. See ◊**Timothy** in main dictionary.

Traude, Traute ♀ Pet forms of GERTRAUD, WALTRAUD, etc.

Traugott ♂ Protestant name: 'trust in God'.

Trude, Trudi ♀ Pet forms of GERTRUD.

U

Udo ♂ Germanic: 'prosperity'.

Ulf ♂ Nordic: 'wolf'.

Ulla ♀ Pet form of ULRIKE.

Ulrich ♂ Germanic: 'prosperity power'.

Ulrike, -a ♀ Feminine form of ULRICH.

Urban ♂ From Latin *Urbānus* 'city dweller'.

Urs ♂ Swiss: masculine equivalent of URSULA.

Ursula ♀ See main dictionary.

Uschi ♀ Pet form of URSULA.

Ute ♀ From earlier *Uda*, Germanic name meaning 'heritage'; name of the mother of Kriemhild in the Nibelungenlied.

Utz ♂ Pet form of ULRICH.

Uwe ♂ North German: from a Nordic name meaning either 'blade' or 'awe'.

V

Veit ♂ From Germanic *Wido* (see ◊**Guy** in main dictionary), but confused with Latin *Vītus* (from *Vīta* 'life'), name of an early child martyr in Sicily.

Veronika ♀ From Latin. See ◊**Veronica** in main dictionary.

Viktor ♂ From Latin. See ◊**Victor** in main dictionary.

Viktoria ♀ From Latin. See ◊**Victoria** in main dictionary.

Vinzenz ♂ From Latin. See ◊**Vincent** in main dictionary.

Volkard ♂ Variant of VOLKHARD.

Volker ♂ Germanic: from earlier *Volkher* 'people army'.

Volkhard ♂ Germanic: 'people staunch'.

Volkmar ♂ Germanic: 'people famous'.

Vroni ♀ Pet form of VERONIKA.

W

Walburg(a) ♀ Germanic: 'rule stronghold'.

Waldemar ♂ Germanic: 'rule famous'.

Walt(h)er ♂ Germanic: 'rule of the army'.

Waltraud ♀ Germanic: 'rule of strength'.

Wendel ♂ Germanic: from the folk name 'Vandal'.

Wendelin ♀ Feminine form of WENDEL.

Wenzel ♂ German equivalent of *Wenceslaus*, of Slavic origin, meaning 'greater glory'.

Wern(h)er ♂ Germanic: 'Warin's army'.

Wert(h)er ♂ Perhaps 'worthy army'; name of the hero of a novel by Goethe.

Wieland ♂ Name of the king of the elves in Germanic legend.

Wilfried ♂ Germanic: 'peace of the will'.

Wilhelm ♂ Germanic: 'helmet of the will'; an ancient royal name. See ◊**William** in main dictionary.

Wilhelmina ♀ Feminine form of WILHELM.

Willi ♂ Pet form of WILHELM.

Willibald ♂ Germanic: 'will brave'.

Willibrand ♂ Germanic: 'flaming sword of the will'.

Wilma ♀ Reduced form of WILHELMINA.

Wim ♂ Reduced form of WILHELM.

Winfried ♂ Germanic: 'friend of peace'.

Winfriede ♀ Feminine form of WINFRIED.

Wolf ♂ Short form of names formed with *Wolf* 'wolf', especially WOLFGANG.

Wolfgang ♂ Germanic: 'track of the wolf'.

Wolfger ♂ Germanic: 'wolf spear'.

Wolfram ♂ Germanic: 'wolf raven'.

X

Xaver ♂ Roman Catholic name. See ◊**Xavier** in main dictionary.

Xaveria ♀ Feminine form of XAVER.

Z

Ziska, Zissi ♀ Pet forms of FRANZISKA.

APPENDIX 3:

ITALIAN NAMES

A

Abbondio ♂ From Late Latin *Abundius*, from *abundans* 'abundant'; name of a 5th-century bishop of Como.

Achilleo ♂ From Greek *Achilleus*, hero of Homer's Iliad, also the name of one or two minor saints.

Adamo ♂ Biblical. See ◊**Adam** in main dictionary.

Addolorata ♀ From a title of the Virgin Mary, *Madonna Addolorata* 'Our Lady of Sorrows'.

Adriano ♂ From Latin. See ◊**Adrian** in main dictionary. *Feminine form*: **Adriana**.

Agata ♀ From Greek. See ◊**Agatha** in main dictionary.

Agnese ♀ From Greek. See ◊**Agnes** in main dictionary.

Agostino ♂ From Latin. See ◊**Augustine** in main dictionary.

Alba ♀ From the feminine form of Latin *albus* 'white' or from Germanic *alb* 'elf'.

Alberto ♂ Germanic. See ◊**Albert** in main dictionary and ◊**Albrecht** in German supplement.

Aldo ♂ Germanic, ultimately from *adal* 'noble'.

Alessandro ♂ From Greek. See ◊**Alexander** in main dictionary. *Feminine form*: **Alessandra**.

Alessio ♂ From Latin. See ◊**Alexis** in main dictionary. *Feminine form*: **Alessia**.

Alfio ♂ Sicilian name of uncertain origin, borne in honour of a saint martyred in 251.

Alfredo ♂ From English. See ◊**Alfred** in main dictionary.

Allegra ♀ From feminine form of *allegro* 'gay', 'happy'. See main dictionary.

Amato ♂ From the Latin name *Amātus* 'beloved'.

Ambrogio ♂ From Late Greek. See ◊**Ambrose** in main dictionary.

Amedeo ♂ From the medieval Latin name *Amadeus* 'love God'; a traditional name in the royal house of Savoy.

Amerigo ♂ An early byform of ENRICO, sometimes used among Italian Americans in honour of the explorer Amerigo Vespucci, after whom the continent of America was named.

Amilcare ♂ From the name of the Carthaginian general Hamilcar Barca, father of Hannibal. The name is Phoenician and means 'friend of the god Melkar'.

Anacleto ♂ From Greek *Anaklētos* 'invoked'.

Anastasio ♂ From Greek *Anastasios*, a derivative of *anastasis* 'resurrection'. *Feminine form*: **Anastasia**.

Andrea ♂ From Greek. See ◊**Andrew** in main dictionary.

Angelo ♂ From Greek *Angelos* 'messenger (of God)'.

Angela ♀ From Latin. See main dictionary.

Aniceto ♂ From Greek *Anikētos* 'unconquered' or 'unconquerable'.

Aniello ♂ From Latin *Agnellus* 'little lamb', name of one of the patron saints of Naples. *Feminine form*: **Aniella**.

Anna ♀ New Testament. See ◊**Anne** in main dictionary.

Annibale ♂ Bestowed in honour of the Carthaginian general Hannibal (247–182 BC), who led an army from Spain into Italy and wreaked havoc on the Romans for 15 years before eventually being defeated by Scipio in 202 BC. The name is Phoenician and means 'grace or favour of the god Baal'.

Annunziata ♀ Religious name commemorating the Annunciation to the Virgin Mary of the forthcoming birth of Christ.

Anselmo ♂ Germanic, = 'divinity helmet'. St Anselm of Piedmont was archbishop of Canterbury in the late 11th and early 12th centuries.

Antonio ♂ From Latin. See ◊**Anthony** in main dictionary. *Feminine form*: **Antonia**.

Antioco ♂ From Greek *Antiochos* 'to hold out against', bestowed in honour of a saint martyred in Sardinia in *c*.110.

Apollinare ♂ Derivative of *Apollo*, the Greek sun god. The name is characteristic of Romagna, especially Ravenna. St Apollinaris was a 1st-century bishop martyred under Vespasian.

Arduino ♂ Italian form of Germanic *Hartwin* 'staunch friend'.

Arianna ♀ From Classical mythology. See ◊**Ariadne** in main dictionary.

Arnaldo ♂ Germanic. See ◊**Arnold** in main dictionary.

Arturo ♂ Celtic. See ◊**Arthur** in main dictionary.

Assunta ♀ Marian name, from a title of the Virgin Mary, *Maria Assunta*, referring to her assumption into heaven.

Attilio ♂ From the Latin family name *Attilius*, of Etruscan origin.

Augusto ♂ From Latin. See ◊**Augustus** in main dictionary.

Aurelio ♂ From Latin *Aurēlius*, name of the philosopher-emperor Marcus Aurelius (121–180 AD).

B

Baldassare ♂ See ◊**Balthasar** in main dictionary.

Battista ♂ Religious name commemorating John the Baptist.

Bartolom(m)eo ♂ From Greek. See ◊**Bartholomew** in main dictionary.

Beatrice ♀ Italian form of ◊**Beatrix**. See main dictionary.

Bella ♀ Short form of ISABELLA.

Benedetto ♂ From Latin. See ◊**Benedict** in main dictionary. *Feminine form*: **Benedetta**.

Benigno ♂ From Late Latin *Benignus* 'kind', a name borne by several early saints.

Benvenuto ♂ Literally 'welcome', from a medieval given name.

Berenice ♀ From Greek. See main dictionary.

Bernadetta ♀ Feminine pet form of ◊**Bernard** (see main dictionary).

Bernardo ♂ Germanic. See ◊**Bernard** in main dictionary.

Bianca ♀ 'White' (i.e. pure). See ◊**Blanche** in main dictionary.

Biag(g)io ♂ Italian form of French ◊**Blaise**. See main dictionary.

Bona ♀ Feminine form of the Late Latin name *Bonus* 'good'. A traditional name in the royal house of Savoy.

Bonaventura ♂ Medieval vernacular personal name, meaning 'good fortune'.

Bonifacio ♂ From the Late Latin name *Bonifatius* 'good fate'. Borne by several early saints.

Bonito ♂ From the Latin personal name *Bonitus*, a derivative of *bonitas* 'goodness'. *Feminine form*: **Bonita**.

Brizio ♂ From *Brictius*, an ancient name probably of Gaulish origin. It is the name of a patron saint of Umbria. The name is also a short form of FABRIZIO.

Brigida ♀ From Irish *Brighid*, name of one of the patron saints of Ireland (English ◊**Bridget**; see main dictionary) or from its Swedish derivative *Birgit*, name of the patron saint of Sweden.

Bruno ♂ Germanic. See main dictionary.

C

Callisto ♂ From Greek *kallistos* 'best', 'most fair'.

Calogero ♂ Southern Italian, especially Sicilian, name, from Greek elements meaning 'good old age'. St Calogerus the Anchorite (d. *c*.486) lived near Grigenti in Sicily.

Camillo ♂ From the Roman family name *Camillus. Feminine form*: **Camilla**.

Carlo ♂ Italian form of Latin *Carolus*. See ◊**Charles** in main dictionary. *Feminine form*: **Carla**.

Carlotta ♀ Italian form of ◊**Charlotte** (see main dictionary).

Carmela ♀ Italian form of ◊**Carmel** (see main dictionary).

Carolina ♀ Feminine pet form of CARLO.

Caterina ♀ From Greek. See ◊**Katherine** in main dictionary.

Cecilia ♀ From Latin. See main dictionary.

Celia ♀ From Latin. See main dictionary.

Celso ♂ From the Latin family name *Celsus* 'tall', originally a nickname.

Cesare ♂ From *Caesar*, name of the first imperial Roman family. See ◊**Caesar** in main dictionary.

Chiara ♀ From Latin. See ◊**Clare** in main dictionary. The name was borne by several saints, notably Santa Chiara di Assisi, an associate of Francis of Assisi and founder of the order of nuns known as the Poor Clares.

Cinzia ♀ From Greek. See ◊**Cynthia** in main dictionary.

Cipriano ♂ From Latin *Cypriānos* 'person from Cyprus'.

Ciro ♂ From Greek. See ◊**Cyrus** in main dictionary.

Clara ♀ From Latin. See main dictionary.

Claudio ♂ From Latin. See ◊**Claude** in main dictionary. *Feminine form*: **Claudia**.

Clelia ♀ From Latin *Cloelia*, name of a semi-mythological heroine of early Roman history.

Clemente ♂ From Latin. See ◊**Clement** in main dictionary.

Concetta ♀ Marian name referring to a title of the Virgin Mary, *Maria Concetta*, alluding to the Immaculate Conception.

Corrado ♂ Italian form of English ◊**Conrad** (see main dictionary).

Cosmo ♂ From Greek. See main dictionary. *Also*: **Cosimo**. *Feminine form*: ◊**Cosima** (see main dictionary).

Cristina ♀ From Latin. See ◊**Christina** in main dictionary.

Cristoforo ♂ From Greek. See ◊**Christopher** in main dictionary.

D

Dalmazio ♂ From the Late Latin personal name *Dalmatius*, 'person from Dalmatia'.

Damiano ♂ From Greek. See ◊**Damian** in main dictionary.

Daniele ♂ Biblical. See ◊**Daniel** in main dictionary.

Dante ♂ Medieval personal name representing a contracted form of *Durante* 'steadfast'. Nowadays it is bestowed in honour of the poet Dante Alighieri (1265–1321).

Dario ♂ From Greek. See ◊**Darius** in main dictionary. *Feminine form*: **Daria**.

Demetrio ♂ From Greek *Dēmētrios*, equivalent of Russian ◊**Dmitri**. See Russian supplement.

Desiderio ♂ Italian form of Latin *Dēsīderius*. See ◊**Didier** in French supplement.

Domenico ♂ From Late Latin. See ◊**Dominic** in main dictionary.

Domitilla ♀ Feminine pet form of the Roman family name *Domitius*, borne by a 2nd-century saint who was a member of Roman imperial family.

Donatella ♀ Feminine pet form of DONATO.

Donato ♂ From Latin *Donātus* 'given (by God)'.

E

Edmondo ♂ From English. See ◊**Edmund** in main dictionary.

Edoardo ♂ From English. See ◊**Edward** in main dictionary.

Efisio ♂ Sardinian name, borne in honour of a martyr allegedly put to death in 303 at Cagliari. The name is from Latin *Ephesius*, denoting someone from the Greek city of Ephesus.

Egidio ♂ From Greek. See ◊**Giles** in main dictionary.

Eleonora ♀ From Old French. See ◊**Eleanor** in main dictionary.

Elena ♀ From Greek. See ◊**Helen** in main dictionary.

Elettra ♀ From Greek *ēlektōr* 'brilliant'. The name of a heroine in classical mythology (in English **Electra**) who, with her brother Orestes, avenges the murder of her father Agamemnon by her mother and stepfather.

Eliana ♀ From Late Latin. See ◊**Éliane** in French supplement.

Eligio ♂ From Latin *Eligius* 'chosen'.

Elisabetta ♀ New Testament. See ◊**Elizabeth** in main dictionary.

Eliseo ♂ Italian form of the biblical name *Elisha*.

Elmo ♂ Originally probably Germanic, from *helm* 'helmet', 'protection'. Later used as a pet form of ◊**Erasmus** (see main dictionary).

Emanuele ♂ Biblical. See ◊**Emmanuel** in main dictionary.

Emilio ♂ From the Latin family name *Aemilius*. *Feminine form*: **Emilia**.

Ennio ♂ From the Latin family name *Ennius*.

Enrico ♂ Italian form of German ◊**Heinrich** (see German supplement) and English ◊**Henry** (see main dictionary).

Enzo ♂ Probably originated as a short form of given names such as LORENZO or VICENZO, or perhaps an Italianized version of German ◊**Heinz** (see German supplement).

Ercole ♂ Italian derivative of *Hercules*, Latin name of the Greek hero *Hēraklēs*, who was noted for his exceptional physical strength. The name is common in Emilia.

Ermanno ♂ Italian form of German ◊**Hermann**. See German supplement.

Ermete ♂ From Greek *Hermēs*, name of the Greek messenger god. This was borne as a personal name by several early Christians. In modern use found mainly in Tuscany and Emilia.

Ernesto ♂ Germanic. See ◊**Ernest** in main dictionary.

Ettore ♂ From Greek. See ◊**Hector** in main dictionary.

Eufemia ♀ From Greek. See ◊**Euphemia** in main dictionary.

Eugenio ♂ From Greek. See ◊**Eugene** in main dictionary. *Feminine form*: **Eugenia**.

Eusebio ♂ From Late Greek *Eusebios* 'pious', 'reverent'.

Eustachio ♂ From Late Greek. See ◊**Eustace** in main dictionary.

Eva ♀ Biblical. See ◊**Eve** in main dictionary.

Evaristo ♂ From the Late Greek personal name *Euarestos* 'well pleasing'.

Ezio ♂ From the Late Latin personal name *Aetius*, a conflation of the Roman family name *Aetius* with *Aëtios*, a Late Greek name derived from *a(i)etos* 'eagle'.

Ezzo ♂ Possibly Germanic, from *adal* 'noble'.

F

Fabiano ♂ From Late Latin. See ◊**Fabian** in main dictionary.

Fabio ♂ From the Roman family name *Fabius*. *Feminine form*: **Fabia**.

Fabiola ♀ Feminine pet form of FABIO.

Fabrizio ♂ From the Latin family name *Fabricius*. Caius Fabricius Luscinus (d. 250 BC) was a Roman statesman noted for his incorruptibility.

Fedele ♂ Italian form of Spanish *Fidel*. See Spanish supplement.

Federico ♂ Germanic. See ◊**Frederick** in main dictionary.

Felice ♂ 'Lucky'. See ◊**Felix** in main dictionary.

Feliciano ♂ From Latin *Felicius*, a derivative of ◊**Felix** (see main dictionary).

Fel{i'}cita ♀ From Latin. See ◊**Felicity** in main dictionary.

Ferdinando ♂ From Spanish. See ◊**Ferdinand** in main dictionary.

Ferruccio ♂ From a medieval pet form of the byname *Ferro* 'iron'.

Fiamma ♀ Recent coinage meaning 'flame' or 'fire'.

Fiametta ♀ Pet form of FIAMMA.

Filiberto ♂ Germanic, meaning 'very bright'. A traditional name in the royal house of Savoy.

Filippo ♂ From Greek. See ◊**Philip** in main dictionary.

Fiorella ♀ Recent coinage, a pet form from *fiore* 'flower'.

Fiorenzo ♂ From Latin *Flōrentius*, a derivative of *flōrens* 'blossoming'.

Firmino ♂ Italian form of French *Firmin*. See French supplement.

Flavia ♀ From Latin. See main dictionary.

Fortunato ♂ From Late Latin *fortūnātus* 'fortunate'. *Feminine form*: **Fortunata**.

Francesco ♂ Originally a vocabulary word meaning 'French' or 'Frenchman', from Late Latin *Franciscus*. See ◊**Francis** in main dictionary. Choice much influenced by St Francis of Assisi. *Feminine form*: ◊**Francesca** (see main dictionary).

Franco ♂ Contracted form of FRANCESCO. *Feminine form*: **Franca**.

Fulgenzio ♂ From the Latin name *Fulgentius*, a derivative of *fulgens* 'shining'.

Fulvia ♀ From Latin. See main dictionary.

G

Gabriele ♂ Biblical. See ◊**Gabriel** in main dictionary. *Feminine form*: **Gabriella** (see main dictionary).

Gaetano ♂ From Latin *Caietānus* 'person from Caetia', a town in Latium (now *Gaeta*); the name was borne by a Neapolitan saint and religious reformer (c.1480–1547).

Gaspare ♂ See ◊**Caspar** in main dictionary.

Gavino ♂ Sardinian, probably from Late Latin *Gabīnus* 'person from Gabium', a city in Latium. St Gabinus was martyred at Torres in Sardinia c.130.

Gemma ♀ From a medieval Italian nickname meaning 'jewel'. See main dictionary.

Gennaro ♂ From Latin *Januārius* 'January' (from *Janus*, god of beginnings). This was borne by several saints, including a bishop of Benevento beheaded at Pozzuoli in 304, the patron saint of Naples.

Genoveffa ♀ From French ◊**Geneviève**, name of the patron saint of Paris. See main dictionary. *Also*: **Ginevra**.

Gerardo ♂ Germanic. See ◊**Gerard** in main dictionary.

Gervasio ♂ Norman. See ◊**Gervaise** in main dictionary.

Gesualdo ♂ From a medieval personal name of Germanic origin, probably meaning 'pledge ruler'. It has been influenced in form by association with *Gesù* 'Jesus'.

Giacomo ♂ New Testament. See ◊**James** in main dictionary.

Giambattista ♂ Contracted form of *Giovanni Battista* 'John the Baptist'.

Gianmaria ♂ Contracted form of GIOVANNI and MARIA.

Giampaolo ♂ Contracted form of GIOVANNI and PAOLO.

Gianni ♂ Contracted form of GIOVANNI. *Feminine form*: **Gianna**.

Gilda ♀ Germanic. Feminine short form of names containing the element *gild* 'sacrifice'.

Gino ♂ Short form of any of the many given names ending in *-gino*, e.g. *Giorgino*, pet form of GIORGIO, and *Luigino*, pet form of LUIGI. *Feminine form*: **Gina**.

Giordano ♂ Biblical, name of the river Jordan. See ◊**Jordan** in main dictionary.

Giorgio ♂ From Greek. See ◊**George** in main dictionary.

Giosuè ♂ Biblical. See ◊**Joshua** in main dictionary.

Giovanni ♀ From Latin. See ◊**John** in main dictionary. *Feminine form*: **Giovanna**.

Giraldo ♂ Germanic. See ◊**Gerald** in main dictionary.

Girolamo ♂ Biblical. See ◊**Jerome** in main dictionary.

Giulio ♂ From Latin. See ◊**Julius** in main dictionary. *Feminine form*: **Giulia**.

Giuseppe ♂ Biblical. See ◊**Joseph** in main dictionary.

Giuseppina ♀ Feminine pet form of GIUSEPPE.

Gofredo ♂ Germanic. See ◊**Geoffrey** in main dictionary.

Grazia ♀ From Latin. See ◊**Grace** in main dictionary.

Graziano ♂ From the Latin name *Grātiānus*, a derivative of *grātus* 'pleasing', 'lovely'.

Graziella ♀ Pet form of GRAZIA.

Gregorio ♂ From Greek. See ◊**Gregory** in main dictionary.

Gualtiero ♂ Germanic. See ◊**Walter** in main dictionary.

Guglielmo ♂ Germanic. See ◊**William** in main dictionary.

Guido ♂ From Old French. See ◊**Guy** in main dictionary.

I

Ignazio ♂ From Latin. See ◊**Ignatius** in main dictionary.

Ilario ♂ From Latin. See ◊**Hilary** in main dictionary.

Imelda ♀ Germanic name meaning 'whole battle'.

Immacolata ♀ Marian name meaning 'without taint', referring to the doctrine of the Immaculate Conception.

Innocenzo ♂ From Late Latin *Innocentius*, from *innocens* 'harmless', 'non-violent', name of several saints and popes.

Ippolito ♂ From the Greek name *Hippolytos* 'horse free', borne by several early saints.

Isabella ♀ Italian form of Spanish ◊**Isabel** (see main dictionary).

Italo ♂ From Latin *Italus*, in mythology the name of the father of Romulus and Remus, founders of Rome. *Feminine form*: **Itala**.

L

Laura ♀ From Latin; name of Petrarch's beloved. See main dictionary. *Masculine form*: **Lauro**.

Leandro ♂ From Greek. See ◊**Leander** in main dictionary.

Leone ♂ From Late Latin. See ◊**Leo** in main dictionary.

Leonardo ♂ Germanic. See ◊**Leonard** in main dictionary.

Leonzio ♂ From the Late Latin personal name *Leontius*, a derivative of *Leo* 'lion'.

Leopoldo ♂ Germanic. See ◊**Leopold** in main dictionary.

Letizia ♀ From Latin. See ◊**Lettice** in main dictionary.

Lia ♀ See main dictionary.

Lodovico ♂ Learned form of LUIGI (see ◊**Ludovic** in main dictionary).

Loredana ♀ Invented by Luciano Zoccoli for the heroine of his novel *L'amore di Loredana* (1908).

Lorenzo ♂ From Latin. See ◊**Laurence** in main dictionary.

Luca ♂ From Greek. See ◊**Luke** in main dictionary.

Lucia ♀ From Latin. See main dictionary.

Luciano ♂ From Latin. See LUCIEN in French supplement. *Feminine form*: **Luciana**.

Lucio ♂ From *Lucius*, a Roman personal name probably derived from *lux* 'light'.

Luigi ♂ Germanic. See ◊**Louis** in main dictionary.

M

Macario ♂ From Greek *makarios* 'blessed'.

Maddalena ♀ New Testament. See ◊**Madeleine** in main dictionary.

Manfredo ♂ Germanic name, borne by a 13th-century king of Sicily; see ◊**Manfred** in main dictionary.

Manlio ♂ From *Manlius*, name of a Roman family famous for its republican virtues.

Marcello ♂ From the Latin name *Marcellus*. See ◊**Marcel** in main dictionary. *Feminine form*: **Marcella**.

Marcellino ♂ Pet form of MARCELLO. *Feminine form*: **Marcellina**.

Marco ♂ From Latin. See ◊**Mark** in main dictionary.

Margherita ♀ From Greek. See ◊**Margaret** in main dictionary.

Maria ♀ New Testament. See ◊**Mary** in main dictionary.

Mariano ♂ From Latin; a derivative of ◊**Marius** (see main dictionary). *Feminine form*: **Mariana**.

Marina ♀ From Latin. See main dictionary.

Mario ♂ From the Roman family name ◊**Marius** (see main dictionary), but in modern times generally taken as a masculine equivalent of MARIA.

Marisa ♀ Elaboration of MARIAN. See main dictionary.

Marta ♀ New Testament. See ◊**Martha** in main dictionary.

Martino ♂ From Latin. See ◊**Martin** in main dictionary. *Feminine form*: ◊**Martina** (see main dictionary).

Massimo ♂ From Latin *maximus* 'greatest'.

Matteo ♂ From Hebrew. See ◊**Matthew** in main dictionary. *Also*: **Mattia**.

Maurizio ♂ From Late Latin. See ◊**Maurice** in main dictionary.

Mauro ♂ From Latin *Maurus* 'Moor', i.e. 'swarthy', borne by one of the earliest followers of St Benedict. *Feminine form* **Maura**.

Melchiorre ♂ Name of one of the three Magi. See ◊**Melchior** in main dictionary.

Michele ♂ Biblical. See ◊**Michael** in main dictionary.

Michelangelo ♂ From MICHELE and *angelo* 'angel', famous as the name of the Florentine painter, sculptor, and architect Michelangelo Buonarotti (1475–1564).

Mirella ♀ Italian form of French ◊**Mireille** (see main dictionary).

Modesto ♂ From the Late Latin personal name *Modestus* 'restrained'. *Feminine form*: **Modesta**.

N

Narciso ♂ From Greek. See Spanish supplement.

Natanaele ♂ New Testament. See ◊**Nathaniel** in main dictionary.

Nazario ♂ From the Late Latin name *Nazarius* 'of Nazareth'.

Nero ♂ Tuscan name, a short form of RANIERO.

Nestore ♂ From the Greek personal name *Nestōr*. In Homer's *Iliad* Nestor, King of Pylos, is one of the leaders of the Greeks at Troy. The name was borne by several early Christian martyrs.

Nic(c)olò ♂ From Greek. See ◊**Nicholas** in main dictionary. *Also:* **Nicola**.

Noemi ♀ Biblical. See ◊**Naomi** in main dictionary.

Norma ♀ See main dictionary.

Nunzia ♀ Short form of ANNUNZIATA. *Masculine form:* **Nunzio**.

O

Orazio ♂ Italian form of Latin *Horatio*, English ◊**Horace** (see main dictionary).

Orlando ♂ Germanic. See ◊**Roland** in main dictionary.

Ornella ♀ Name of a character in Gabriele d'Annunzio's *Figlia de Iorio* (1904), probably taken from the Tuscan dialect word *ornello* 'flowering ash tree'.

Ornetta ♀ Altered form of ORNELLA.

Ottavio ♀ From the Latin personal name ◊**Octavius** (see main dictionary). *Feminine form:* **Ottavia**.

P

Palmiro ♂ From the vocabulary word *palmiere* 'pilgrim' (specifically, one who had brought back a palm from the Holy Land).

Pancrazio ♂ From Greek *pankratios* 'all-powerful'. Borne by a 1st-century saint stoned to death in Sicily.

Paolo ♂ From Latin. See ◊**Paul** in main dictionary. *Feminine form:* **Paola**.

Pasquale ♂ From Late Latin *Paschālis* 'relating to Easter'.

Patrizio ♂ Italian form of English and Irish ◊**Patrick** (see main dictionary), name of the apostle and patron saint of Ireland. *Feminine form:* **Patrizia**.

Pellegrino ♂ From Latin. See ◊**Peregrine** in main dictionary.

Pietro ♂ From Greek. See ◊**Peter** in main dictionary. *Also:* **Piero**. *Feminine form:* **Piera**.

Pia ♀ From the feminine form of Latin *pius* 'pious'. *Masculine form:* **Pio**.

Pierluigi ♂ Compound name from *Piero* (see PIETRO) and LUIGI.

Placido ♂ From the Late Latin name *Placidus* 'untroubled'.

Pompeo ♂ From the Roman family name *Pompeius*.

Porfirio ♂ From the Greek name *Porphyrios* 'purple'.

Primo ♂ From the Late Latin name *Prīmus* 'first'.

Prudenzio ♂ From Late Latin *Prūdentius* 'prudent'.

R

Rachele ♀ Biblical. See ◊**Rachel** in main dictionary.

Raffaele ♂ Italian form of *Raphael*, name of one of the archangels. *Also:* **Raffaello**. *Feminine form:* **Raffaella**.

Raimondo ♂ Germanic. See ◊**Raymond** in main dictionary. *Feminine form:* **Raimonda**.

Raniero ♂ Germanic. See ◊**Rayner** in main dictionary.

Raul ♂ From Norman French. See ◊**Ralph** in main dictionary.

Remigio ♂ From the Latin name *Rēmigius* 'oarsman'. See ◊**Rémy** in French supplement.

Renato ♂ From the Late Latin name *Renātus* 'reborn', popular among early Christians as a name celebrating spiritual rebirth in Christ. *Feminine form:* **Renata**.

Riccardo ♂ Germanic. See ◊**Richard** in main dictionary.

Rinaldo ♂ Germanic. See ◊**Reynold** in main dictionary.

Roberto ♂ Germanic. See ◊**Robert** in main dictionary.

Rocco ♂ Germanic, derived from *hrok* 'rest'; name of a 14th-century French saint who tended plague victims in northern Italy.

Rodolfo ♂ Italian form of ◊**Rudolf** (see main dictionary).

Romano ♂ From the Late Latin personal name *Rōmānus* 'Roman'.

Romeo ♂ Medieval religious name meaning 'pilgrim to Rome', from Latin *Rōma* 'Rome'.

Romilda ♀ Germanic, meaning 'fame battle'.

Romolo ♂ From the Latin name *Rōmulus*, borne by the legendary founder of Rome.

Rosa ♀ Italian form of English ◊**Rose** (see main dictionary).

Rosalba ♀ From Latin: 'white rose'.

Rosalia ♀ From Latin. See ◊**Rosalie** in main dictionary.

Rosangela ♀ Compound name from ROSA and ANGELA.

Ruf(f)ino ♂ From Latin *Rufīnus*, a derivative of *Rufus* 'red-haired'.

Ruggiero ♂ Germanic. See ◊**Roger** in main dictionary.

S

Salvatore ♂ Religious name borne in honour of Christ the Saviour: from Late Latin *salvātor* 'saviour'.

Sandro ♂ Short form of ALESSANDRO.

Sansone ♂ Biblical. See ◊**Samson** in main dictionary.

Saturnino ♂ Derivative of Latin *Saturnus*, name of the Roman god of agriculture and vegetation.

Saverio ♂ Italian form of Spanish ◊**Xavier** (see main dictionary).

Sebastiano ♂ From Latin. See ◊**Sebastian** in main dictionary.

Serafino ♂ Masculine form of ◊**Seraphina** (see main dictionary).

Sergio ♂ From Latin, = Russian *Sergei*. See Russian supplement.

Sesto ♂ From Latin. See ◊**Sextus** in main dictionary.

Severiano ♂ From Latin *Sevēriānus*, a derivative of *Sevērus*. See SEVERO.

Severino ♂ From the Latin family name *Sevērīnus*, a derivative of *Sevērus*. See SEVERO.

Severo ♂ From the Roman family name *Sevērus* 'stern', 'severe'.

Silvano ♂ From Latin *Silvānus*, from *silva* 'wood'. *Feminine form*: **Silvana**.

Silvestro ♂ From Latin. See ◊**Silvester** in main dictionary.

Silvia ♀ Ancient Latin name, which was also the name of the mother of Gregory the Great. See main dictionary. *Masculine form*: **Silvio**.

Stefano ♂ From Greek. See ◊**Stephen** in main dictionary.

Stefania ♀ Feminine of STEFANO. See ◊**Stephanie** in main dictionary.

T

Taddeo ♂ New Testament. See ◊**Thaddeus** in main dictionary.

Tammaro ♂ Germanic, meaning 'thought fame'. St Tammarus was a priest from Africa who landed in southern Italy in the 5th century, after being cast adrift by the Arian Vandals.

Tancredo ♂ Germanic, 'thought counsel'.

Teodoro ♂ From Greek. See ◊**Theodore** in main dictionary. *Feminine form*: **Teodora**.

Teodosio ♂ From Greek *Theodosios* 'god giving'.

Teresa ♀ See main dictionary.

Timoteo ♂ From Greek. See ◊**Timothy** in main dictionary.

Tiziano ♂ From Latin *Titiānus*, a derivative of ◊**Titus** (see main dictionary); bestowed in honour of the medieval painter Tiziano Vecellio (1490–1576), known in English as Titian.

Tommaso ♂ New Testament. See ◊**Thomas** in main dictionary.

Tullio ♂ From the Roman family name *Tullius*, borne by the orator Marcus Tullius Cicero (106–43 BC).

U

Ugo ♂ Italian form of English ◊**Hugh** (see main dictionary).

Ulisse ♂ Italian form of ◊**Ulysses** (see main dictionary).

Umberto ♂ Germanic. See ◊**Humbert** in main dictionary. The former Italian royal family is descended from the Blessed Umberto of Savoy (1136–88).

V

Valentino ♂ From Latin. See ◊**Valentine** in main dictionary. *Feminine form*: **Valentina**.

Vasco ♂ From Spanish. See Spanish supplement.

Vincenzo ♂ Italian form of ◊**Vincent** (see main dictionary). *Also*: **Vincente**.

Virgilio ♂ From Latin. See ◊**Virgil** in main dictionary.

Viola ♀ From Latin. See main dictionary.

Violetta ♀ From Late Latin. See ◊**Violet** in main dictionary.

Virginia ♀ From Latin. See main dictionary.

Vitale ♂ From Latin *vītālis* 'lively', 'life-affirming'. There are more than a dozen early saints bearing this name.

Vittore ♂ From Late Latin. See ◊**Victor** in main dictionary.

Vittoria ♀ From Latin. See ◊**Victoria** in main dictionary.

Vittorio ♂ From Latin *Victōrius*, a derivative of *Victor* 'conqueror'.

Z

Zita ♀ See main dictionary.

SPANISH NAMES

Note: Many Spanish names, especially girls' names, are derived from terms used in various aspects of the cult of the Virgin Mary. This has the somewhat bizarre result that many common female names, e.g. *Pilar* and *Rosario*, have masculine grammatical gender.

A

Adán ♂ Biblical. See ◊**Adam** in main dictionary.

Adolfo ♂ Germanic. See ◊**Adolf** in German supplement.

Adrián ♂ From Latin. See ◊**Adrian** in main dictionary. *Feminine form*: **Adriána**.

Águeda ♀ From Greek. See ◊**Agatha** in main dictionary.

Agustín ♂ From Latin. See ◊**Augustine** in main dictionary. *Feminine form*: **Agustína**.

Aitor ♂ Basque: name of the legendary founder of the Basque people.

Alberto ♂ Germanic. See ◊**Albert** in main dictionary, ◊**Albrecht** in German supplement.

Alejandro ♂ From Greek. See ◊**Alexander** in main dictionary. *Feminine form*: **Alejandra**.

Alejo ♂ From Latin. See ◊**Alexis** in main dictionary.

Alfonso ♂ Visigothic: probably meaning 'noble ready'; a traditional royal name. *Also*: **Alonso**.

Alfredo ♂ From English. See ◊**Alfred** in main dictionary.

Alicia ♀ Spanish form of ◊**Alice** (see main dictionary).

Alonso ♂ Variant of ALFONSO. *Also*: **Alonzo**.

Álvaro ♂ Visigothic name, probably meaning 'all wise'.

Amado ♂ From the Latin name *Amātus* 'beloved'. See ◊**Amato** in Italian supplement.

Amador ♂ From Latin *Amātor* 'lover'.

Amancio ♂ From Latin *Amantius* 'loving'.

Ambrosio ♂ From Late Greek. See ◊**Ambrose** in main dictionary.

Amparo ♀ Marian name meaning 'protection', with reference to the role of the Virgin Mary in protecting Christians.

Ana ♀ From Hebrew. See ◊**Anne** in main dictionary.

Andrés ♂ From New Testament Greek. See ◊**Andrew** in main dictionary. *Feminine form*: **Andrea**.

Ángel ♂ From Greek *Angelos* 'messenger (of God)'.

Ángela ♀ From Latin. See ◊**Angela** in main dictionary.

Ángeles ♀ Marian name honouring *Nuestra Señora de los Ángeles* 'Our Lady of the Angels'.

Angustias ♀ Marian name honouring *Nuestra Señora de las Angustias*, from *angustias* 'sufferings'.

Aniceto ♂ From Greek *Anikētos* 'unconquered' or 'unconquerable'.

Antonio ♂ From Latin. See ◊**Anthony** in main dictionary. *Feminine form*: **Antonia**.

Anunciación ♀ Marian name commemorating the Annunciation to the Virgin Mary of the forthcoming birth of Christ. *Also*: **Anunciata**.

Aquiles ♂ From Greek *Achilleus*, name of the hero of Homer's *Iliad*, also the name of one or two minor saints.

Arantxa ♀ Pet form of the Basque name *Aránzazu*, derived from a place name meaning 'thorn bush'.

Armando ♂ Germanic. See ◊**Hermann** in German supplement.

Arnaldo ♂ Germanic. See ◊**Arnold** in main dictionary.

Arsenio ♂ From Greek *Arsenios* 'virile'.

Arturo ♂ Celtic. See ◊**Arthur** in main dictionary.

Asunción ♀ Marian name commemorating the assumption of the Virgin Mary into heaven.

Augusto ♂ From Latin. See ◊**Augustus** in main dictionary.

Aurelio ♂ From Latin. See Italian supplement.

Azucena ♀ Marian name meaning 'madonna lily' (from Arabic *as-susana*). Adopted as a personal name because the flower is used as a symbol of the Virgin Mary.

B

Baltasar ♂ See ◊**Balthasar** in main dictionary.

Barbara ♀ Greek: 'foreign woman'. See main dictionary.

Bartolomé ♂ New Testament. See ◊**Bartholomew** in main dictionary.

Bautista ♂ Religious name commemorating John the Baptist.

Beatriz ♀ From Latin. See ◊**Beatrix** in main dictionary.

Begoña ♀ Marian name honouring *Nuestra Señora de Begoña*, the Virgin Mary as patron saint of Bilbao.

Belén ♀ Religious name, Spanish form of *Bethlehem*.

Beltrán ♂ Germanic. See ◊**Bertram** in main dictionary. *Also*: **Bertran**.

Benigno ♂ From Late Latin *Benignus* 'kind'.

Benito ♂ From Latin. See ◊**Benedict** in main dictionary. *Feminine form*: **Benita**.

Bernabé ♂ New Testament. See ◊**Barnabas** in main dictionary.

Bernardo ♂ Germanic. See ◊**Bernard** in main dictionary. *Feminine form*: **Bernarda**.

Berta ♀ Germanic. See ◊**Bertha** in main dictionary.

Blanca ♀ 'White' (i.e. pure). See ◊**Blanche** in main dictionary.

Blas ♂ From Latin. See ◊**Blaise** in main dictionary.

Brígida ♀ From Irish *Brighid*, name of one of the patron saints of Ireland (English ◊**Bridget**; see main dictionary), or from the Swedish derivative *Birgit*, name of the patron saint of Sweden.

Bruno ♂ Germanic. See main dictionary.

C

Camilo ♂ From the Roman family name *Camillus*. *Feminine form*: **Camila**.

Candelaria ♀ Marian name, referring to Candlemas, the festival commemorating the purification of the Virgin Mary and the presentation of Christ in the temple.

Carlos ♂ Spanish form of Latin *Carolus*. See ◊**Charles** in main dictionary. *Feminine form*: **Carlota**.

Carmel ♀ Marian name honouring *Nuestra Señora de Carmel* 'Our Lady of Carmel'. Carmel is a mountain in the Holy Land populated from an early date by Christian hermits, who were later organized into the Carmelite order of monks. *Also*: **Carmela**.

Carmen ♀ Alteration of CARMEL under the influence of the word *carmen* 'song'.

Catalina ♀ From Greek. See ◊**Katherine** in main dictionary.

Cayetano ♂ From Italian ◊**Gaetano**. See Italian supplement.

Cayo ♂ From the Latin personal name *Caius*.

Cecilia ♀ From Latin. See main dictionary. *Masculine form*: **Cecilio**.

Celso ♂ From the Latin family name *Celsus*, 'tall', originally a nickname.

Cesar ♂ From the Latin family name *Caesar*. See ◊**Caesar** in main dictionary.

Clara ♀ From Latin. See ◊**Clare** in main dictionary.

Claudio ♂ From Latin. See ◊**Claude** in main dictionary. *Feminine form*: **Claudia**.

Clemente ♂ From Latin. See ◊**Clement** in main dictionary.

Concepción ♀ Marian name commemorating the Immaculate Conception of the Virgin Mary.

Conchita ♀ Pet form of CONCEPCÍON.

Conseja ♀ Marian name honouring *Nuestra Señora del Buen Consejo* 'Our Lady of Good Counsel'.

Consuelo ♀ Marian name honouring *Nuestra Señora del Consuelo* 'Our Lady of Solace'.

Corazón ♀ Religious name meaning 'heart', referring to the Sacred Heart of Jesus.

Cristina ♀ From Latin. See ◊**Christina** in main dictionary.

Cristobál ♂ From Greek. See ◊**Christopher** in main dictionary.

Cugat ♂ Catalan, a name of Carthaginian origin (Latin *Cucuphas*) and unknown derivation.

D

Damaso ♂ From Greek *damān* 'tame', 'subdue', borne in honour of a 4th-century pope.

Damián ♂ From Greek. See ◊**Damian** in main dictionary.

Daniel ♂ Biblical. See main dictionary. *Feminine form*: **Daniela**.

David ♂ Biblical. See main dictionary.

Delfina ♀ From Latin. See ◊**Delphine** in main dictionary.

Demetrio ♂ From Greek *Dēmētrios*, equivalent of Russian ◊**Dmitri**. See Russian supplement.

Desiderio ♂ Spanish form of Latin *Desiderius* 'longing'. See ◊**Didier** in French supplement.

Diana ♀ From Latin. See main dictionary.

Diego ♂ Origin uncertain; perhaps from SANTIAGO (literally 'Saint James') or from a

native Iberian name found in Latin as
Didacus.

Dolores ♀ Marian name honouring *Nuestra Señora de los Dolores* 'Our Lady of Sorrows'.

Domingo ♂ From Late Latin. See ◊**Dominic** in main dictionary. *Feminine form*: **Dominga**.

Donato ♂ From Latin *Dōnātus* 'given (by God)'.

E

Edmundo ♂ From English. See ◊**Edmund** in main dictionary.

Eduardo ♂ From English. See ◊**Edward** in main dictionary.

Efraín ♂ Spanish form of the biblical name ◊**Ephraim** (see main dictionary).

Eladio ♂ From Late Greek *Helladios* 'from Greece'.

Elena ♀ From Greek. See ◊**Helen** in main dictionary.

Eliseo ♂ Spanish form of the biblical name *Elisha*.

Elodia ♀ Visigothic name meaning 'foreign wealth'.

Eloy ♂ From Latin *Eligius* 'chosen'.

Elvira ♀ Visigothic, probably meaning 'foreign true'.

Emilio ♂ From the Latin family name *Aemilius*. *Feminine form*: **Emilia**.

Encarnación ♀ Religious name commemorating the festival of the Incarnation, celebrated on Christmas Day.

Enrique ♂ From German ◊**Heinrich** (see German supplement) or English ◊**Henry** (see main dictionary). *Feminine form*: **Enriqueta**.

Ernesto ♂ From German ◊**Ernst** (see German supplement) or English ◊**Ernest** (see main dictionary).

Esperanza ♀ From Late Latin *Sperantia* 'hope'.

Estéban ♂ From Greek. See ◊**Stephen** in main dictionary. *Feminine form*: **Estefanía**.

Estrella ♀ From Latin. See ◊**Stella** in main dictionary.

Eufemia ♀ From Greek. See ◊**Euphemia** in main dictionary.

Eugenio ♂ From Greek. See ◊**Eugene** in main dictionary. *Feminine form*: **Eugenia**.

Eulalia ♀ From Late Greek, 'fine speaking'. *Also*: **Olalla**.

Eusebio ♂ From the Late Greek name *Eusebios* 'pious', 'reverent'.

Eustaquio ♂ From Late Greek. See ◊**Eustace** in main dictionary.

Eva ♀ Latinate form of the biblical name represented by English ◊**Eve** (see main dictionary).

Evaristo ♂ From Late Greek *Euarestos* 'well pleasing'.

Evita ♀ Pet form of EVA.

F

Fabián ♂ From Late Latin. See ◊**Fabian** in main dictionary.

Fabio ♂ From Latin *Fabius*, name of a Roman family whose members were prominent in republican Rome.

Fabricio ♂ From Latin. See ◊**Fabrizio** in Italian supplement.

Federico ♂ From German ◊**Friedrich** (see German supplement) or English ◊**Frederick** (see main dictionary).

Feliciano ♂ From Latin *Felicius*, derivative of ◊**Felix** 'happy' (see main dictionary).

Felicidad ♀ From Latin. See ◊**Felicity** in main dictionary.

Felipe ♂ From Greek. See ◊**Philip** in main dictionary.

Fernando ♂ A modern form of the old Spanish name ◊**Ferdinand** (see main dictionary), which is a hereditary royal name. *Also*: **Hernando, Fernán, Hernán**.

Fidel ♂ From Late Latin *fidēlis* 'faithful'.

Florencio ♂ From Latin *Flōrentius*, a derivative of *flōrens* 'blossoming'.

Fortunato ♂ From Late Latin *fortūnātus* 'fortunate'. *Feminine form*: **Fortunata**.

Francisco ♂ Spanish form of Italian *Francesco*. See ◊**Francis** in main dictionary. *Feminine form*: **Francisca**.

Fulgencio ♂ From the Latin name *Fulgentius*, a derivative of *fulgens* 'shining'.

G

Gabriel ♂ Biblical. See main dictionary. *Feminine form*: **Gabriela**.

Gaspar ♂ See ◊**Caspar** in main dictionary.

Gerardo ♂ Germanic. See ◊**Gerard** in main dictionary.

German ♂ From the Late Latin name *Germanus* 'brother', sometimes used with the meaning 'brother in God'.

Gervasio ♂ Norman. See ◊**Gervaise** in main dictionary.

Godofredo ♂ Germanic. See ◊**Geoffrey** in main dictionary.

Gil ♂ From Latin *Aegidus*. See ◊**Gilles** in French supplement and English ◊**Giles** in main dictionary.

Gilberto ♂ Germanic. See ◊**Gilbert** in main dictionary.

Gloria ♀ From Latin. See main dictionary.

Gonzalo ♂ Visigothic, 'battle ready'.

Gracia ♀ From Latin. See ◊**Grace** in main dictionary.

Graciano ♂ From Latin *Grātiānus*. See ◊**Gratien** in French supplement.

Graciela ♀ Pet form of GRACIA.

Gregorio ♂ From Greek. See ◊**Gregory** in main dictionary.

Guadalupe ♀ Marian name from a place in Cáceres, the site of a convent with a famous image of the Virgin; named in Arabic as 'river of the wolf'.

Gualtiero ♂ Germanic. See ◊**Walter** in main dictionary.

Guillermo ♂ From German *Wilhelm* or English ◊**William** (see main dictionary).

Gumersindo ♂ Visigothic, 'path of man'.

Gustavo ♂ From Scandinavian *Gustaf*. See ◊**Gustave** in French supplement.

H

Hermenegildo ♂ Visigothic, 'whole sacrifice'. *Also*: **Ermengildo**.

Hilario ♂ From Latin. See ◊**Hilary** in main dictionary.

Hipolito ♂ From Greek. See ◊**Hippolyte** in French supplement.

Hugo ♂ See main dictionary.

Humberto ♂ See ◊**Humbert** in main dictionary and ◊**Umberto** in former Italian supplement.

I

Ignacio ♂ From Latin. See ◊**Ignatius** in main dictionary.

Imelda ♀ Visigothic, 'whole battle'.

Indalecio ♂ Latin *Indalētius*, of unknown origin.

Inés ♀ From Greek. See ◊**Agnes** in main dictionary.

Inmaculada ♀ Marian name meaning 'without taint', referring to the doctrine of the Immaculate Conception.

Inocencio ♂ From Late Latin *Innocentius*, a derivative of *innocens* 'innocent'; name of several early saints.

Isabel ♀ Of Spanish origin: a much altered version of ◊**Elizabeth** (see main dictionary).

Isidro ♂ From Greek. See ◊**Isidore** in main dictionary. *Also*: **Isidoro**.

J

Jacinto ♂ From Greek *Hyakinthos* 'hyacinth', the name of several early saints. See also the English girl's name ◊**Hyacinth** in main dictionary.

Jaime ♂ Spanish form of ◊**James** (see main dictionary).

Javier ♂ Another spelling in Spanish of ◊**Xavier** (see main dictionary).

Jerónimo ♂ From Greek. See ◊**Jerome** in main dictionary.

Jesús ♂ Religious name bestowed as a token of Christian faith. *Jesus* 'saviour' is an Aramaic form of the earlier Hebrew name ◊**Joshua** (see main dictionary).

Joaquin ♂ Biblical. See ◊**Joachim** in main dictionary.

Jorge ♂ From Greek. See ◊**George** in main dictionary.

José ♂ Biblical. See ◊**Joseph** in main dictionary. *Feminine form*: **Josefa**.

Juan ♂ New Testament. See ◊**John** in main dictionary. *Feminine form*: **Juana**.

Juanita ♀ Feminine pet form of JUAN.

Julián ♂ From Late Latin. See ◊**Julian** in main dictionary.

Julio ♂ From Latin. See ◊**Julius** in main dictionary. *Feminine form*: **Julia**.

L

Laura ♀ From Latin. See main dictionary.

Leocadio ♀ Latinate derivative of Greek *leukas*, 'bright', 'clear'. St Leocadia was a virgin martyr of Toledo. *Feminine form*: **Leocadia**.

León ♂ From Late Latin. See ◊**Leo** in main dictionary.

Leonardo ♂ Germanic. See ◊**Leonard** in main dictionary.

Leoncio ♂ Spanish form of Italian ◊**Leonzio**. See Italian supplement.

Leopoldo ♂ Germanic. See ◊**Leopold** in main dictionary.

Leticia ♀ From the Latin personal name *Laetitia*; see ◊**Lettice** in main dictionary.

Lola ♀ Nursery form of DOLORES.

Lope ♂ From the Late Latin name *Lupus* 'wolf'.

Lorena ♀ Spanish equivalent of ◊**Lauren** (see main dictionary).

Lorenzo ♂ From Latin. See ◊**Laurence** in main dictionary.

Lourdes ♀ Religious name, from the place in southern France where a young girl had visions of the Virgin Mary in 1858. *Also*: **Lurdes**.

Lucía ♀ From Latin. See ◊**Lucy** in main dictionary.

Luciano ♂ From Latin *Luciānus*, a derivative of the Roman personal name *Lucius*, itself probably derived from *lux* 'light'. *Feminine form*: **Luciana**.

Luis ♂ Germanic. See ◊**Louis** in main dictionary. *Feminine form*: **Luisa**.

Luz ♀ Marian name honouring *Nuestra Señora de la Luz* 'Our Lady of Light'.

M

Magdalena ♀ New Testament. See ◊**Madeleine** in main dictionary.

Manuel ♂ Spanish form of ◊**Emmanuel** (see main dictionary). *Feminine form*: **Manuela**.

Marcelo ♂ From Latin *Marcellus*. See ◊**Marcel** in main dictionary. *Feminine form*: **Marcela**.

Marcelino ♂ From Latin *Marcellīnus*, a double diminutive of *Marcus*. *Feminine form*: **Marcelina**.

Marco ♂ From Latin. See ◊**Mark** in main dictionary. *Also*: **Marcos**.

Margarita ♀ From Greek. See ◊**Margaret** in main dictionary.

María ♀ Biblical. See ◊**Maria** and ◊**Mary** in main dictionary. Also used as a male name in combinations such as **José María**. *Masculine form*: **Mario**.

Mariano ♂ From the Roman family name *Marianus*, ultimately from *Mars*, the Roman god of war. *Feminine form*: **Mariana**.

Maribel ♀ Contracted short form of *María Isabel*.

Marisol ♀ Compound name from MARÍA and SOL.

Marta ♀ New Testament. See ◊**Martha** in main dictionary.

Martín ♂ From Latin. See ◊**Martin** in main dictionary. *Feminine form*: **Martina**.

Mateo ♂ New Testament. See ◊**Matthew** in main dictionary.

Matilde ♀ Germanic. See ◊**Matilda** in main dictionary.

Mauricio ♂ From Late Latin. See ◊**Maurice** in main dictionary.

Mauro ♂ See Italian supplement. *Feminine form*: **Maura**.

Máximo ♂ From Latin *maximus* 'greatest', = Russian ◊**Maxim** (see Russian supplement).

Mercedes ♀ Marian name honouring *Nuestra Señora de las Mercedes* 'Our Lady of Mercies'.

Miguel ♂ Biblical. See ◊**Michael** in main dictionary.

Milagros ♀ Marian name honouring *Nuestra Señora de los Milagros* 'Our Lady of Miracles'.

Modesto ♂ From the Late Latin name *Modestus* 'restrained'. *Feminine form*: **Modesta**.

Montserrat ♀ Marian name from a Catalan title of the Virgin Mary, *Nuestra Señora del Montserrat*, referring to the Benedictine monastery on Mt Montserrat near Barcelona.

N

Narciso ♂ From Greek *Narkissos*. In classical mythology Narcissus was a beautiful youth who fell in love with his own reflection in a pool of water and remained staring at himself until he faded away and turned into a flower. It was also the name of the first bishop of Jerusalem (d. 195) and various other early Christians.

Natividad ♀ Religious name meaning 'nativity', referring to the festival of the Nativity of the Virgin Mary, celebrated on 5 September.

Nicanor ♂ From Late Greek *Nikanēr* 'victory man'.

Nicasio ♂ From Late Greek *Nikasios* 'victorious'.

Nicolás ♂ From Greek. See ◊**Nicholas** in main dictionary. *Also*: **Nicolao**.

Nieves ♀ Marian name honouring *Nuestra Señora de las Nieves* 'Our Lady of the Snows'.

O

Octavio ♂ From Latin. See ◊**Octavius** in main dictionary.

Ofelia ♀ See ◊**Ophelia** in main dictionary.

Onofre ♂ From an Egyptian saint's name, said to mean 'he who opens the good'.

Oscar ♂ From Gaelic. See main dictionary.

Osvaldo ♂ From English. See ◊**Oswald** in main dictionary.

P

Pablo ♂ From Latin. See ◊**Paul** in main dictionary.

Paco ♂ Pet form of FRANCISCO.

Paloma ♀ From Latin *palumba* 'dove'.

Pascual ♂ From Late Latin *Paschālis* 'relating to Easter', = French *Pascal*. See French supplement. *Feminine form*: **Pascuala**.

Patricio ♂ Spanish form of English and Irish ◊**Patrick** (see main dictionary). *Feminine form*: **Patricia**.

Paulino ♂ Pet form of *Paulus*. See PABLO. *Feminine form*: **Paulina**.

Paz ♀ Marian name honouring *Nuestra Señora de la Paz* 'Our Lady of Peace'.

Pedro ♂ From Greek. See ◊**Peter** in main dictionary.

Pepe ♂ Pet form of JOSÉ.

Piedad ♀ Religious name meaning 'piety', from Latin *pietās*.

Pilar ♀ Marian name honouring *Nuestra Señora del Pilar* 'Our Lady of the Pillar', referring to an alleged appearance of the Virgin standing on a pillar to St James the Greater at Saragossa.

Pio ♂ From Latin *pius*, 'pious', 'respectful'.

Placido ♂ From Late Latin *Placidus* 'untroubled'.

Presentación ♀ Religious name referring to the feast of the Presentation, commemorating the presentation of the Virgin Mary in the temple at Jerusalem after the birth of Christ; celebrated on 21 November.

Primo ♂ From the Late Latin name *Primus* 'first'.

Prudencio ♂ From Late Latin *Prūdentius* 'prudent'.

Purificación ♀ Marian name, bestowed in honour of the feast of the Purification, in which the infant Jesus was presented to God at the temple and his mother was purged of the uncleanliness associated with childbirth.

R

Rafael ♂ Biblical; Spanish form of *Raphael*, name of one of the archangels. *Feminine form*: **Rafaela**.

Raimundo ♂ Germanic. See ◊**Raymond** in main dictionary. *Feminine form*: **Raimunda**.

Rainerio ♂ Germanic. See ◊**Rayner** in main dictionary.

Ramiro ♂ Visigothic: probably composed of elements meaning 'advice famous'.

Ramón ♂ Germanic; variant of RAIMUNDO. See ◊**Raymond** in main dictionary. *Feminine form*: **Ramona**.

Raúl ♂ Germanic. See ◊**Ralph** in main dictionary.

Raquel ♀ See main dictionary.

Reinaldo ♂ Germanic. See ◊**Reynold** in main dictionary.

Remedios ♀ Marian name honouring *Nuestra Señora de los Remedios* 'Our Lady of Remedies', with reference to her promise to relieve the sufferings of those who pray to her.

Renato ♂ From Late Latin *Renātus* 'reborn', = French ◊**René**. See French supplement. *Feminine form*: **Renata**.

Ricardo ♂ Germanic. See ◊**Richard** in main dictionary.

Rigoberto ♂ From a Germanic name composed of the elements *ric* 'power' + *berht* 'bright', 'shining', 'famous'.

Roberto ♂ Germanic. See ◊**Robert** in main dictionary.

Rocío ♀ Marian name honouring *Nuestra Señora de la Rocío* 'Our Lady of the Dew'. Dew is associated in Roman Catholic hagiography with tears shed by the Virgin Mary for the wickedness of the world.

Rodolfo ♂ Spanish form of ◊**Rudolf** (see main dictionary).

Rodrigo ♂ Visigothic: 'fame power'. It was the name of the last king of the Visigoths, defeated by the Moors in 711.

Rogerio ♂ Germanic. See ◊**Roger** in main dictionary. *Also*: **Rogelio**.

Roldán ♂ Germanic. See ◊**Roland** in main dictionary.

Román ♂ From Late Latin *Rōmānus* 'Roman'.

Rosario ♀ Marian name honouring *Nuestra Señora del Rosario* 'Our Lady of the Rosary'.

Roque ♂ From Germanic. See ◊**Rocco** in Italian supplement.

Rosa ♀ Spanish form of English ◊**Rose** (see main dictionary).

Rosendo ♂ Visigothic: 'fame path'.

Rufino ♂ From Latin *Rufīnus*, a derivative of *Rufus* 'red-haired'.

S

Sabina ♀ From Latin. See main dictionary. *Masculine form*: **Sabino**.

Salvador ♂ Religious name borne in honour of Christ the Saviour: from Late Latin *salvātor* 'saviour'.

Sancho ♂ Of uncertain origin, perhaps from Latin *sanctus* 'holy'. It will always be associated with Sancho Panza, Don Quixote's companion.

Santiago ♂ Literally 'St James': *Iago* is an obsolete Spanish form of the Biblical name *Jacobus* (see ◊**Jacob** and ◊**James** in main dictionary). The disciple St James the Greater, brother of John the Baptist, is the patron saint of Spain.

Santos ♂ Religious name meaning 'Saints', a name chosen to invoke the protection of all the saints for a son.

Sebastián ♂ From Latin. See ◊**Sebastian** in main dictionary.

Sergio ♂ From Latin *Sergius*. See ◊**Sergei** in Russian supplement.

Seve ♂ Pet form of SEVERIANO and SEVERINO.

Severiano ♂ From Latin *Sevēriānus*, a derivative of *Sevērus*. See SEVERO.

Severino ♂ From Latin *Sevērīnus*, a derivative of *Sevērus*. See SEVERO.

Severo ♂ From the Roman family name *Sevērus* 'stern', 'severe'.

Silvestre ♂ From Latin. See ◊**Silvester** in main dictionary.

Silvia ♀ Ancient Latin name; also the name of the mother of Gregory the Great. See main dictionary. *Masculine form*: **Silvio**.

Simón ♂ New Testament. See ◊**Simon** in main dictionary.

Socorro ♀ Marian name honouring *Nuestra Señora del Socorro* 'Our Lady of Perpetual Succour'.

Sofía ♀ From Greek. See ◊**Sophia** in main dictionary.

Soledad ♀ Marian name honouring *Nuestra Señora de Soledad* 'Our Lady of Solitude'.

Susana ♀ From Hebrew. See ◊**Susanna** in main dictionary.

T

Tadeo ♂ New Testament. See ◊**Thaddeus** in main dictionary.

Teodoro ♂ From Greek. See ◊**Theodore** in main dictionary. *Feminine form*: **Teodora**.

Teodosio ♂ From Greek *Theodosios* 'god giving'.

Teresa ♀ See ◊**Theresa** in main dictionary.

Timoteo ♂ From New Testament Greek. See ◊**Timothy** in main dictionary.

Tito ♂ From Latin. See ◊**Titus** in main dictionary.

Tomás ♂ New Testament. See ◊**Thomas** in main dictionary.

Toribio ♂ From Latin *Turibius*, probably a Latinized form of an indigenous Iberian name.

Trinidad ♀ Religious name meaning 'trinity'.

U

Ulises ♂ Spanish form of ◊**Ulysses** (see main dictionary).

V

Valentín ♂ From Latin. See ◊**Valentine** in main dictionary. *Feminine form*: **Valentina**.

Vasco ♂ Contracted form of the medieval Spanish personal name *Velasco* or *Belasco*, from which is derived the surname *Velásquez*. The modern name has the same form as the Spanish adjective *vasco* 'Basque'.

Vicente ♂ From Latin. See ◊**Vincent** in main dictionary.

Victor ♂ From Late Latin. See main dictionary.

Victoria ♀ From Latin. See main dictionary.

Violeta ♀ From Late Latin. See ◊**Violet** in main dictionary.

Virgilio ♂ From Latin. See ◊**Virgil** in main dictionary.

X

Xavier ♂ See main dictionary.

APPENDIX 5:

RUSSIAN NAMES

A

Afanasi ♂ From Greek *Athanasios* 'immortal'.

Agafya ♀ From Greek *Agapia* 'Christian love'.

Agrafena ♀ From Latin *Agrippīna*, from an old Roman family name of uncertain (probably Etruscan) origin.

Akilina ♂ From Latin *Aquilīna* 'eagle-like'.

Akim ♂ From Hebrew: 'established by God'. See ◊**Joachim** in main dictionary.

Aleksandr ♂ From Greek: 'defender of men'. See ◊**Alexander** in main dictionary.

Aleksandra ♀ Feminine of ALEKSANDR.

Aleksei ♂ From Greek: 'defender'. See ◊**Alexis** in main dictionary.

Anastasia ♀ From Greek: 'resurrection'.

Anatoli ♂ From Greek: 'sunrise'.

Andrei ♂ From Greek *Andreas* 'manly'. See ◊**Andrew** in main dictionary.

Anfisa ♀ From Greek *Anthousa* 'flowery'.

Anisim ♂ From Greek *Onēsimos* 'useful'.

Anna ♀ From Hebrew: 'God has favoured me'. See ◊**Anne** in main dictionary.

Anton ♂ From Latin *Antōnius*. See ◊**Anthony** in main dictionary.

Arkadi ♂ From Greek *Arkadios* 'man from Arcadia'.

Arkhip ♂ From Greek *Arkhippos* 'ruler of horses'.

Arseni ♂ From Greek *Arsēnios* 'virile'.

Artemi ♂ From Late Greek *Artemios* 'devotee of Artemis'.

Avdotya ♀ From Greek *Eudokia* 'seemly'.

B

Boris ♂ Probably from a Tartar nickname meaning 'small'. Saints Boris and Gleb were sons of Prince Vladimir, first Christian ruler of Kiev in the 10th century.

D

Darya ♀ Greek, from a feminine form of a Persian royal name apparently meaning 'good ruler'.

Demid ♂ From Greek *Diomēdēs* 'counsel of Zeus'.

Demyan ♂ From Greek *Damianos*. See ◊**Damian** in main dictionary.

Dmitri ♂ From Greek *Dēmētrios* 'devotee of Demeter'.

F

Fedot ♂ From Greek *Theodotos* 'given by God'.

Ferapont ♂ From Greek *Therapōn* 'servant', 'worshipper'.

Filat ♂ Short form of *Feofilakt*, from Greek *Theophylaktos* 'protected by God'.

Firs ♂ From Greek *Thyrsos* 'staff of Dionysos'.

Foka ♂ From Greek *Phōcas*, denoting someone from the ancient city of Phocaea in Asia Minor. The stress is on the second syllable.

Foma ♂ Aramaic 'twin'. See ◊**Thomas** in main dictionary. The stress is on the second syllable.

Fyodr ♂ From Greek *Theodōros* 'gift of God'. See ◊**Theodore** in main dictionary.

G

Galina ♀ Probably from Greek *galēnē* 'calm'.

Gennadi ♂ Probably from a short form of Greek names such as *Diogenēs* 'born of Zeus' and *Hermogenēs* 'born of Hermes'.

Gerasim ♂ From Greek *Gerasimos*, meaning either 'old man' or 'honoured'.

Gleb ♂ From Old Norse *Gudleifr* 'god life'. Saints Boris and Gleb were sons of Prince Vladimir, first Christian ruler of Kiev in the 10th century.

Grigori ♂ From Greek *Grēgorios* 'watchful'. See ◊**Gregory** in main dictionary.

I

Ignati ♂ From Latin ◊**Ignatius**. See main dictionary.

Igor ♂ From Old Norse *Yherr* 'yew-bow warrior'. See ◊**Ivor** in main dictionary.

Illarion ♂ From Greek *Hilarion* 'cheerful'.

Ilya ♂ From Greek *Elias*, the name used in the New Testament for the prophet *Elijah* 'Yahweh is God'.

Innokenti ♂ From Latin *Innocentius* 'innocent'.

Ipati ♂ From Greek *Hypatios* 'highest'.

Ira ♀ Pet form of IRINA.

Irina ♀ From Greek *Eirēnē* 'peace'. See ◊**Irene** in main dictionary.

Ivan ♂ From Hebrew: 'God is gracious'. See ◊**John** in main dictionary.

K

Kapiton ♂ From Latin *Capito* 'big-headed'. This was the name of a missionary who preached in Crimea and south Russia in the 4th century.

Karp ♂ From Greek *Karpos* 'fruit'. This was the name of an early Christian mentioned in St Paul's epistle to Timothy.

Katya ♀ Pet form of YEKATERINA.

Kirill ♂ From Greek *Kyrillos* 'of the Lord'; name of the saint who brought Christianity to Russia in the 9th century. See ◊**Cyril** in main dictionary.

Klara ♀ From Latin *Clara* 'famous'. See ◊**Clare** in main dictionary.

Klavdia ♀ From the feminine of the Latin family name *Claudius*, literally 'lame'. See ◊**Claudia** in main dictionary.

Kliment ♂ From Latin *Clēmens* 'merciful'. See ◊**Clement** in main dictionary.

Kolya ♂ Pet form of NIKOLAI.

Kondrati ♂ From Latin *Quadrātus* 'square', i.e. 'stout'. This was the name of the writer of the first known apologia for Christianity, addressed to the emperor Hadrian.

Konstantin ♂ From Latin *Constantīnus*, 'steadfast', the name of the first Christian Roman emperor (?288–337).

L

Lara ♀ Pet form of LARISSA.

Larissa ♀ From Greek, of uncertain meaning (perhaps from the name of a town in Thessaly). This was the name of an early Christian martyr venerated in the Eastern Church.

Lavrenti ♂ From Latin *Laurentius* 'man from Laurentum' (a town in Latium). See ◊**Laurence** in main dictionary.

Lena ♀ Pet form of YELENA.

Leonid ♂ From Greek *Leōnidas*, the name of a Spartan hero who was named after his grandfather *Leōn* 'lion'. Later the name was borne by two early saints venerated in the Eastern Church.

Leonti ♂ From Greek *Leonteios* 'lion-like'.

Lev ♂ From the Russian vocabulary word meaning 'lion'; vernacular equivalent of ◊**Leo**.

Lyuba ♀ Pet form of LYUBOV.

Lyubov ♀ From the Russian vocabulary word meaning 'love'; vernacular equivalent of AGAFYA.

Lyuda ♀ Pet form of LYUDMILA.

Lyudmila ♀ Slavonic: 'grace of the people'. This was the name of the grandmother of St Wenceslas of Bohemia.

M

Makari ♂ From Greek *Makarios* 'blessed'.

Maksim ♂ From Latin *Maximus* 'greatest'.

Marina ♀ Latin: 'of the sea'. See main dictionary.

Marta ♀ From Aramaic: 'lady'. See ◊**Martha** in main dictionary.

Marya ♀ From Hebrew. See ◊**Maria** and ◊**Mary** in main dictionary.

Masha ♀ Pet form of MARYA.

Matrona ♀ Latin: 'lady'.

Matvei ♂ From Hebrew: 'gift of God'. See ◊**Matthew** in main dictionary.

Mavra ♀ From Latin *Maura* 'swarthy'.

Mefodi ♂ From Greek *Methodios* 'fellow traveller'. This was the name of the 9th-century evangelist who first translated the Bible into Slavonic.

Mikhail ♂ From Hebrew: 'who is like God?'. See ◊**Michael** in main dictionary.

Misha ♂ Pet form of MIKHAIL.

Mitrofan ♂ From Greek *Mētrophanēs* 'appearance of the Mother' (i.e. Mary, Mother of God).

Mitya ♂ Pet form of DMITRI.

Modest ♂ From Latin *Modestus* 'unassuming'.

N

Nadezhda ♀ The Russian vocabulary word 'hope'.

Nadya ♀ Pet form of NADEZHDA.

Natalya ♀ Latin: 'associated with birth', i.e. the birth of Christ at Christmas or the concept of Christian rebirth.

Natasha ♀ Pet form of NATALYA.

Nikifor ♂ From Greek *Nikēphoros* 'bringer of victory'.

Nikita ♂ From Greek *Anikētos* 'unconquered'.

Nikolai ♂ From Greek *Nikolaos* 'victory people'. See ◊**Nicholas** in main dictionary.

Nina ♀ In origin a short form of *Antonina*, but now usually used as an independent name.

O

Oleg ♂ From Old Norse *Helgi* 'prosperous'. This was the name of a Scandinavian leader who established the city of Kiev.

Olga ♀ Feminine of OLEG.

Osip ♂ From Hebrew: 'God shall add'. See ◊**Joseph** in main dictionary.

P

Pavel ♂ Latin: 'small'. See ◊**Paul** in main dictionary.

Pelageya ♀ From Greek *Pelagia* 'of the ocean'.

Petya ♀ Pet form of PYOTR.

Pimen ♂ From Greek *Poimēn* 'shepherd'.

Praskovya ♀ From Greek *Paraskeuē* 'Friday', literally 'preparation' (i.e. Friday as the day of preparation for Easter).

rokhor ♂ From Greek *Prokhōros* 'leader in the dance'.

Prokopi ♂ From Greek *Prokopios* 'successful'.

Pyotr ♂ From Greek *Petros* 'rock'. See ◊**Peter** in main dictionary.

R

Raisa ♀ Slavonic: 'paradise'.

Rodion ♂ From Greek: short form of *Hērodion* 'devotee of Hera'.

Roman ♂ From Latin *Rōmānus* 'Roman'. This was the baptismal name of St Boris.

Rurik ♂ From Old Norse *Hrodrik* 'fame rule'. See ◊**Roderick** in main dictionary. This was the name of a Scandinavian leader who established the city of Novgorod in the 9th century.

S

Sasha ♂ Pet form of ALEKSANDR.

Semyon ♂ From Hebrew: 'hearkening'. See ◊**Simon** in main dictionary.

Serafima ♀ From Hebrew: 'angel of flame'.

Serezha ♂ Pet form of SERGEI.

Sergei ♂ From Latin *Sergius*, an old Roman family name of uncertain origin. St Sergei of Radonezh (1314–92) is one of the most popular of all Russian saints.

Sevastyan ♂ From Greek *Sebastianos* 'man from Sebasta', = English ◊**Sebastian**.

Slava ♂, ♀ Short form of many Slavonic names containing the element *slav* 'glory'.

Sofya ♀ From Greek *Sophia* 'wisdom'. See ◊**Sophie** in main dictionary.

Sonya ♀ Pet form of SOFYA.

Spiridion ♂ From Late Greek, from Latin: 'little soul'.

Stepan ♂ From Greek *Stephanos* 'crown'. See ◊**Stephen** in main dictionary.

Sveta ♀ Pet form of SVETLANA.

Svetlana ♀ Slavonic: 'light'.

T

Tamara ♀ From Hebrew: 'date palm'. See main dictionary.

Tanya ♀ Pet form of TATYANA.

Taras ♂ From Greek *Tarasios* 'man from Tarentum' (a town in southern Italy).

Tatyana ♀ From Latin: from an old Roman family name of uncertain (apparently Sabine) origin.

Tikhon ♂ From Greek *Tychōn* 'hitting the mark'.

Timofei ♂ From Greek *Timotheos* 'honour God'. See ◊**Timothy** in main dictionary.

Trofim ♂ From Greek *Trophimos* 'nutricious', 'fruitful'.

V

Vadim ♂ Of uncertain origin, perhaps a contracted form of VLADIMIR.

Valentin ♂ From Latin *Valentīnus* 'flourishing'.

Valentina ♀ Feminine of VALENTIN.

Valeri ♂ From Latin *Valērius* 'healthy'.

Vanya ♂ Pet form of IVAN.

Varvara ♀ From Greek *Barbara* 'foreign woman'. See ◊**Barbara** in main dictionary. *Pet form*: **Varya**.

Vasili ♂ From Greek *Basilios* 'royal'. See ◊**Basil** in main dictionary.

Vera ♀ Slavonic: 'faith'. See main dictionary.

Viktor ♂ From Latin *Victor* 'conqueror'. See ◊**Victor** in main dictionary.

Vissarion ♂ From Greek *Bessarion*, of uncertain origin.

Vitali ♂ From Latin *Vitālis* 'lively'.

Vladimir ♂ Slavonic: 'power great'. This was the name of the ruler of Kiev who brought Russia into the Christian Church.

Volodya ♂ Pet form of VLADIMIR.

Vsevolod ♂ Slavonic: 'all power', coined as a vernacular equivalent of Greek *Pankratios*.

Vyacheslav ♂ Slavonic: 'more glory'. The Czech and Polish version of this name is familiar in the Latinized form *Wenceslas*.

Y

Yakov ♂ From Hebrew: 'supplanter'. See ◊**Jacob** in main dictionary.

Yefim ♂ From Greek *Euphēmios* 'well-spoken', 'using words of good omen'.

Yefrem ♂ From Hebrew *Ephraim* 'fruitful'.

Yekaterina ♀ From Greek *Aikaterinē*. See ◊**Katherine** in main dictionary.

Yelena ♀ From Greek *Hēlēnē*. See ◊**Helen** in main dictionary.

Yelisaveta ♀ From Hebrew: 'God is my oath'. See ◊**Elizabeth** in main dictionary.

Yermolai ♂ From Greek *Hermolaos* 'people of Hermes'.

Yevgeni ♂ From Greek *Eugenios* 'well-born'. See ◊**Eugene** in main dictionary.

Yevgenia ♀ Feminine of YEVGENI.

Yura ♂ Pet form of YURI.

Yuri ♂ From Greek *Georgios* 'of a farmer'. See ◊**George** in main dictionary.

Z

Zina ♀ Pet form of ZINAIDA.
Zinaida ♀ From Greek *Zēnais* 'descended from Zeus'.
Zinovia ♀ From Greek *Zēnobia* 'life of Zeus'.

APPENDIX 6:

ARABIC NAMES

Note: The names in this supplement, though of Arabic origin, have spread throughout the Muslim world. There are many local variations.

A

ʿAbbās ♂ 'Austere'. Abbās ibn ʿAbd-al-Mualib (*c.*566–652) was the Prophet's uncle and ancestor of the Abbasid caliphs, who ruled the Islamic world between 750 and 1258.
ʿAbd-al-ʿAi ♂ 'Servant of the Giver' (i.e. Allāh).
ʿAbd-al-ʿAzīz ♂ 'Servant of the Mighty' (i.e. Allāh).
ʿAbd-al-Fattāḥ ♂ 'Servant of the Opener' (i.e. Allāh as opener of the gates of wealth).
ʿAbd-al-Hādi ♂ 'Servant of the Guider' (i.e. Allāh).
ʿAbd-al-Ḥakīm ♂ 'Servant of the Wise' (i.e. Allāh).
ʿAbd-al-Ḥalīm ♂ 'Servant of the Patient' (i.e. Allāh).
ʿAbd-al-Ḥamīd ♂ 'Servant of the Praiseworthy' (i.e. Allāh).
ʿAbd-al-Jawād ♂ 'Servant of the Magnanimous' (i.e. Allāh).
ʿAbd-al-Karīm ♂ 'Servant of the Generous' (i.e. Allāh).
ʿAbd-Allāh ♂ 'Servant of Allāh'. This was the name of the Prophet's father, who, however, died before Muḥammad was born.
ʿAbd-al-Laṭīf ♂ 'Servant of the Kind' (i.e. Allāh).
ʿAbd-al-Malik ♂ 'Servant of the King' (i.e. Allāh).
ʿAbd-al-Muʿi ♂ 'Servant of the Giver' (i.e. Allāh).
ʿAbd-al-Qādir ♂ 'Servant of the Capable' (i.e. Allāh).

ʿAbd-al-Raḥīm, ʿAbder-Rahīm ♂ 'Servant of the Compassionate' (i.e. Allāh).
ʿAbd-al-Raḥmān, ʿAbder-Rahmān ♂ 'Servant of the Merciful' (i.e. Allāh).
ʿAbd-al-Rāziq, ʿAbd-al-Razzāq, ʿAbder-Razzāʾ ♂ 'Servant of the Provider' (i.e. Allāh).
ʿAbd-al-Salām, ʿAbdes-Salām ♂ 'Servant of the Peaceable' (i.e. Allāh).
ʿAbd-al-Wahhāb ♂ 'Servant of the Giver' (i.e. Allāh).
ʿAbid ♂ 'Worshipper'.
ʿAbīr ♀ 'Fragrance'.
ʿAbla ♀ 'Woman with a full figure'.
ʿĀdil ♂ 'Just', 'fair'.
ʿAdnān ♂ Origin uncertain: possibly meaning 'settler'. The ʿAdnāniyūn were Arabs living in the north part of the Arabian Peninsula.
ʿAfāf ♀ 'Chastity', 'decorum'.
Aḥlām ♀ 'Dream', 'vision of perfection'.
Ahmad ♂ 'Highly commendable'.
ʿĀʾisha ♀ 'Alive', 'thriving'; name of Muḥammad's third and favourite wife.
ʿAlāʾ ♂ 'Excellence', 'supremacy'.
ʿAli ♂ 'Sublime'; name of a cousin of the Prophet, who married his daughter Fāṭima and in 656 became the fourth rightly guided caliph. His sons Ḥasan and Ḥusayn are regarded by Shiites as Muḥammad's true successors. *Feminine form*: ʿAliyya.
Amal ♀, ♂ 'Hope', 'expectation'.
Amāni ♀ 'Desires', 'aspirations'.
Amīn ♂ 'Honest', 'trustworthy'.
Amīna ♀ 'Peaceful', 'secure'; name of the Prophet's mother.
Amīr ♂ 'Prince', 'ruler'. *Feminine form*: Amīra.
ʿĀmir ♂ 'Prosperous'.
Amjad, Amgad ♂ 'Glorious'.
ʿAmmār ♂ 'Long-lived'; name of one of the earliest converts to Islam, renowned for his piety despite much persecution.
Anwar ♂ 'Clear', 'bright'.
Asʿad ♂ 'Happy', 'fortunate', 'lucky'.
Ashraf ♂ 'Honourable', 'distinguished'.
ʿĀsim ♂ 'Protector', 'guardian'.
Asmāʾ ♀ 'Prestige'; name of a woman who helped Muḥammad and her father, Abu-Bakr, to escape from Mecca in 622, when their opponents were planning to murder them.
ʿĀṭif ♂ 'Compassionate', 'sympathetic'.
ʿAwāṭif ♀ 'Affections', 'tender feelings'.
ʿAyda ♀ 'Benefit', 'advantage'.

ᴍan ♂ 'Blessed', 'prosperous'; name of ᴍuḥammad's nurse.

Azīz ♂ 'Invincible' or 'cherished'. *Feminine form*: **'Azīza**.

'Azza ♀ Probably from a word meaning 'pride' or 'power'.

B

Badr ♂, ♀ 'Full moon'. See also ʙᴜᴅᴜʀ.

Baha' ♂ 'Splendour', 'glory'.

Bahīja, Bahīga ♀ 'Joyous', 'delightful'.

Bahiyya ♀ 'Beautiful', 'radiant'.

Bahjat, Bahgat ♂ 'Joy', 'delight'.

Bakr ♂ 'Young camel'. Abu-Bakr al-Ṣiddīq (573–634) was the Prophet's successor and the first rightly guided caliph (632–4).

Bāsim ♂ 'Smiling'.

Basma ♀ 'A smile'.

Budūr ♀ Plural of *badr* 'full moon', from *badara* 'to come up unexpectedly', 'take by surprise'. *Badr-al-Budūr* is a complimentary expression meaning roughly 'beauty of beauties'.

Buthayna, Busayna ♀ Diminutive of *bathua* 'flat fertile land'.

D

Dawūd ♂ Biblical. See ◊**David** in main dictionary.

Dīma ♀ 'Torrential rain'. The word has positive connotations in Arabic.

Ḍiyā' ♂ 'Brightness'.

Du'a' ♀ 'Prayer'.

Ḍuḥa ♀ 'Morning'.

F

Fādi ♂ 'Redeemer', 'saviour'; an attribute of Jesus Christ. *Feminine form*: **Fadia**.

Fāḍil ♂ 'Virtuous', 'generous', 'distinguished'. *Also*: **Fadle**.

Faḍīla ♀ 'Moral excellence', 'virtue'.

Fahd ♂ 'Panther' or 'leopard'; name of the king of Saudi Arabia from 1982.

Fahīm ♂ 'Person of profound understanding'.

Fakhr-al-Dīn, Fakhr-ud-Dīn ♂ 'Glory of religion'.

Fakhri ♂ 'Meritorious', 'glorious'. *Feminine form*: **Fakhriyya**.

Faraj ♂ 'Remedy (for worries or grief)'.

Farīd ♂ 'Unique', 'unrivalled'. *Feminine form*: **Farīda** *(also meaning 'gem')*.

Farūq ♂ Literally 'distinguisher', i.e. one who can distinguish right from wrong and truth from falsehood. *Al-Farūq* was a byname of 'Umar ibn-al-Khaāb, second rightly guided caliph (634–44), known for his uncompromising execution of justice.

Fatḥi ♂ Probably from *fatih* 'releaser' or 'conqueror'. *Feminine form*: **Fatḥiyya**.

Fāṭima ♀ 'Abstainer (from forbidden things)', i.e. chaste; also 'weaner', i.e. one who cares for her children. This was the name of the Prophet's favourite daughter, wife of 'Ali ibn-Abi-Ṭālib, fourth rightly guided caliph, and mother of ʜᴀsᴀɴ and ʜᴜsᴀʏɴ.

Fawzi ♂ From *fawz* 'triumph', 'victory', 'accomplishment'. *Feminine form*: **Fawziyya**.

Fāyiz ♂ 'Victor', 'winner'. *Feminine form*: **Fayza**.

Fayrūz ♀ 'Turquoise' (the precious stone); of Persian origin.

Fayṣal, Feiṣal ♂ 'Judge', literally 'separator' (i.e. between right and wrong).

Fiḍḍa, Fiẓẓa ♀ 'Silver'.

Fihr ♂ Ancient name of uncertain origin, apparently from a word denoting a type of stone pestle used for pounding the ingredients of medicines.

Fikri ♂ 'Intellectual', 'meditative'. *Feminine form*: **Fikriyya**.

Firdos ♂ 'Paradise'.

Firoz ♂ 'Victorious' or 'successful'.

Fu'ād ♂ 'Heart'.

G

Ghāda ♀ 'Graceful young woman'.

Ghadīr ♀ 'Brook', 'stream'.

Ghālib ♂ 'Conqueror', 'victor'.

Ghassān ♂ 'Prime of youth'.

Ghayth ♂ 'Rain'; a word with favourable connotations in a desert climate.

Ghufrān ♀ 'Forgiveness'.

H

Ḥabīb ♂ 'Beloved'. *Feminine form*: **Ḥabība**.

Hādi ♂ **1** 'Guide', 'leader' (in particular, a spiritual guide or leader). **2** 'calm', 'quiet', 'peaceable'. *Feminine form*: **Hadya**.

Hadīl ♀ 'Cooing of doves'.

Ḥāfiẓ ♂ 'Custodian', 'guardian'. *Al-Ḥāfiẓ* was an honorific term denoting someone who knew the Qur'an by heart. *Feminine form*: Ḥafẓa.

Haidar ♂ 'Lion'. *Haidar Allāh* 'Lion of Allāh' was an epithet of 'Ali, son-in-law of the Prophet Muḥammad and fourth rightly guided caliph.

Hājar, Hāgar ♀ Ancient name of uncertain origin. Hājar was the Egyptian concubine of ɪʙʀāʜīᴍ (Abraham), mother of Ismā'īl (Ishmael), from whom Arabs believe they are descended.

Ḥakīm ♂ 'Wise', 'judicious'.

Hāla ♀ Ancient name meaning 'halo (around the moon)'.

Ḥamdi ♂ 'Pertaining to praise and gratitude' (in particular for Allāh's favours).

Ḥāmid ♂ 'Thankful', 'praising' (i.e. praising Allāh).

Ḥamza ♂ Ancient name, probably meaning 'steadfast'.

Hanā' ♀ 'Bliss', 'happiness', 'well-being'.

Ḥanān ♀ 'Tenderness', 'affection'.

Hāni ♂ 'Happy'. *Feminine form*: **Haniyya**.

Ḥārith ♂ 'Provider', 'breadwinner'. *Al-Ḥārith* is also an epithet of the lion.

Hārūn ♂ Biblical. See ◊**Aaron** in main dictionary; the name of a famous caliph, Hārūn al-Rashīd (*c*.764–809).

Ḥasan ♂ 'Good', 'beautiful'. Shiites regard Ḥasan and his brother ʜᴜsᴀʏɴ as the legitimate successors of Muḥammad.

Hāshim ♂ Literally 'crusher', i.e one who breaks bread; a byname of the great-grandfather of the Prophet, who provided food at the Ka'ba temple. Muslims are sometimes referred to as 'Hashemites' because they are regarded as the descendants of Hāshim.

Ḥāsim ♂ 'Decisive'. The ability to make a swift and decisive distinction between right and wrong is a quality greatly prized among Muslims.

Ḥātim ♂ 'Decisive', 'determined'. Ḥātim ibn-'Abd-Allāh (d. 605) was famous for his generosity.

Hayfā' ♀ 'Slender', 'delicate'.

Haytham ♂ 'Young eagle'.

Hiba ♀ 'Gift', 'grant'.

Ḥikmat ♂, ♀ 'Wisdom'.

Hind ♀ Ancient name of unknown origin. It was borne by one of the Prophet's wives, renowned for her beauty.

Hishām ♂ Literally 'crushing' but with the transferred meaning 'having a generous nature', by association with the crushing and distribution of bread. See ʜāsʜɪᴍ.

Huda ♀ 'Right guidance'.

Ḥusayn ♂ Diminutive of *asan* 'good', 'beautiful', 'exquisite'. Al-Ḥusayn (*c*.626–680) was the grandson of the Prophet, whose supporters emerged after his death as the Shiite party.

Ḥusām ♂ 'Sword'.

Ḥusni ♂ 'Excellence'.

I

Ibrāhīm ♂ Arabic form of ◊**Abraham** (see main dictionary), the biblical patriarch and father of Ismā'īl and Isāq (Ishmael and Isaac), founding fathers of the Arabic and Jewish peoples respectively.

Ibtisām ♀ 'Smiling'.

Idrīs ♂ Name of a man mentioned twice in the Qur'an, described as 'a true man, a prophet' and 'of the righteous'. It was also the name of the founder of the first Shiite dynasty (788–974).

Ihāb ♂, ♀ 'Gift'.

Iḥsān ♂, ♀ 'Charity', 'benefaction'.

Imām ♂ 'Leader'. For Sunnis this can denote any pious Muslim who leads prayers in a mosque, but for Shiites it refers specifically to the descendants of 'Ali and Fāṭima, whom they regard as the only true successors of Muḥammad.

Imān ♀ 'Faith', 'belief'.

In'ām ♀ 'Benefaction', 'bestowal'.

'Iṣām ♂ 'Strap' (implying protection), 'pledge', 'security'. *'Iṣām al-Dīn* is a title meaning 'protector of religion'.

Ismā'īl ♂ Name of the son of ɪʙʀāʜīᴍ (Abraham) by Hājar, his Egyptian concubine. Arabs believe that they are descended from Ismā'īl, while the Jews are descended from Isaac, the son of Abraham by Sarah. The Ismaili sect of Shiites believe that on the death of the imam Ja'far al-Ṣidīq in 765 the Divine Spirit passed to his son Ismā'īl rather than to his other son Mūsa.

'Iṣmat ♂, ♀ 'Sinlessness' or 'infallibility'.

Isrā' ♀ 'Night journey', with reference to the story of Muḥammad's night journey to Jerusalem, which recounts how he visited the mosque and the temple and met Jesus and Moses before returning to Mecca the same night.

I'tidāl ♀ 'Temperance', 'moderation'.

'Izz-al-Dīn, 'Izz-ed-Dīn ♂ 'Power (or glory) of religion'.

J

Jābir, Gābir ♂ 'Comforter', 'restorer', 'one who assists in time of need'.

abr, Gabr ♂ 'Consolation', 'assistance in time of need'.

Ja'far, Ga'far ♂ 'Small river', 'stream'. Ja'far ibn-Abi-Ṭālib (d. 629) died heroically at the Battle of Mota (629), holding aloft the Muslim banner proclaiming 'Paradise!'

Jalāl, Galāl ♂ 'Greatness', 'glory'.

Jalīla, Galīla ♀ 'Honourable', 'exalted'.

Jamāl, Gamāl ♂, in some places also ♀ 'Good looks', 'beauty'.

Jamīl, Gamīl ♂ 'Handsome', 'graceful'. *Feminine form*: **Jamīla**.

Jāthibiyya, Gāzbiyya ♀ 'Attractiveness', 'charm'.

Jawāhir, Gawāhir ♀ 'Jewels'.

Jawdat, Gawdat ♂ 'Goodness', 'excellence'.

Jinān ♂, ♀ 'Garden', 'paradise'.

Jūda, Gūda ♂ 'Goodness', 'excellence'.

K

Kamāl ♂ 'Perfection'.

Kāmil ♂ 'Perfect'.

Karam ♂, ♀ 'Generosity', 'magnanimity'.

Karīm ♂ 'Noble', 'generous'. *Feminine form*: **Karīma**.

Khadīja, Khadīga ♀ Ancient name, originally a byname meaning 'premature child'. Khadīja bint-Khuwaylid (d. 619) was the Prophet's first wife and mother of all his children.

Khālid ♂ 'Undying', 'eternal'. Khālid ibn-al-Walīd (d. 642) was the military strategist principally responsible for the spread of Islam by force in its early days.

Khalifa ♂ 'Caliph', literally 'successor'.

Khalīl ♂ 'Bosom friend'.

Khayrat ♂ 'Good deed'.

Khayri ♂ 'Charitable', 'benevolent'. *Feminine form*: **Khayriyya**.

L

Lamyā' ♀ 'Possessing brown lips'.

Lawāḥiz ♀ 'Shy glances'.

Layla ♀ 'Wine' or 'intoxication'; name of the beloved of the poet Qays ibn-al-Mulawwa (d. 688).

Līna ♀ From a word denoting a type of palm tree.

Lubna ♀ 'Storax', a tree with a sweet honey-like sap, used for making incense and perfume and still popular in most Arab countries.

Lujayn ♀ 'Silver'.

M

Madīa ♀ 'Praise', 'commendation'.

Maha ♀ 'Wild cow'. Wild cows are admired for their large, beautiful eyes.

Mahāsin ♀ 'Charms', 'good qualities'.

Māhir ♂ 'Skilful', 'proficient'.

Mahmūd ♂ 'Praiseworthy', 'commendable'.

Majdi, Magdi ♂ 'Praiseworthy'. *Feminine form*: **Magda**.

Mājid ♂ 'Glorious', 'illustrious'. *Feminine form*: **Mājida**.

Makram ♂ 'Generous', 'noble', 'magnanimous'.

Malak ♀ 'Angel'.

Mamdūḥ ♂ 'Praised', 'commended'.

Ma'mūn ♂ 'Reliable', 'trustworthy'.

Manāl ♂, ♀ 'Attainment' or 'acquisition'.

Manār ♂, ♀ 'Lighthouse', 'beacon'.

Manṣūr ♂ 'Victorious', 'triumphant'.

Marwa ♀ From a word denoting both a fragrant plant and a type of shiny pebble.

Maryam ♀ Biblical. See ◊**Miriam** and ◊**Mary** in main dictionary.

Mas'ūd ♂ 'Lucky'.

Maysa ♀ Perhaps from *mayyas* 'to walk with a graceful, proud gait'.

Māzin ♂ Of uncertain origin; possibly from *muzn* 'rain clouds'.

Midhat ♂ 'Commendation', 'eulogy'.

Mubārak ♂ 'Blessed', 'fortunate'.

Muhammad ♂ 'Praiseworthy', 'possessing fine qualities'. An extremely common Muslim name, bestowed in honour of Muḥammad ibn-'Abd-Allāh ibn-'Abd-al-Muṭṭalib (570–632) of Mecca, the Prophet of Islam.

Muhayya ♀ 'Face', 'countenance' (i.e. beautiful face).

Muḥsin ♂ 'Charitable', 'beneficent'. *Feminine form*: **Muḥsina**.

Mujtaba ♂ 'Chosen', a byname of the Prophet Muḥammad.

Mukhtār ♂ 'Preferred'.

Muna ♀ 'Hope' or 'object of desire'.

Mun'im ♂ 'Benefactor', 'donor'.

Munīr ♂ 'Luminous', 'bright', 'shining'. *Feminine form*: **Munīra**.

Mus'ad ♂ 'Lucky', 'favoured by fortune'.

Muṣtafa ♂ 'pure' or 'chosen'. *Al-Muṣtafa* 'the Chosen One' is an epithet of Muḥammad. For Arabic-speaking Christians it is an epithet of St Paul. Muṣtafa Kamāl (1881–1938) was the founder of modern Turkey (president from 1922), known in Turkish as *Ataürk* 'father of the Turks'.

Mu'taṣim ♂ 'Adhering to (God)' or 'seeking refuge in (God)'.

Mu'tazz ♂ 'Proud', 'powerful'.

N

Nabīl ♂ 'Noble', 'high-born', 'honourable'. *Feminine form*: **Nabīla**.

Nada ♀ 'Morning dew'; also 'generosity'.

Nadīm ♂ 'Drinking companion', 'confidant'.

Nādir ♂ 'Rare', 'precious'. *Feminine form*: **Nād(i)ra**.

Nadiyya ♀ 'Moist with dew'; in a hot, dry climate, morning dew is highly valued. There has been some influence from the Russian and Croatian name ◊**Nadia** (see main dictionary).

Nāhida ♀ From a word denoting a young girl with swelling breasts.

Nahla ♀ 'Drink of water', 'thirst-quenching draught'.

Nā'il ♂ 'One who attains his desires', 'winner'. *Feminine form*: **Nā'ila**.

Na'īm ♂ 'Contented', 'tranquil', 'happy'. *Feminine form*: **Na'īma**.

Najāḥ, Nagāḥ ♀ 'Success', 'progress'.

Najāt, Nagāt ♀ 'Salvation', 'redemption'.

Nāji, Nāgi ♂ 'Saved', 'rescued'.

Najīb, Nagīb ♂ 'Noble', 'well-born', 'distinguished', 'high-minded'. *Feminine forms*: **Najība, Nagība**.

Najlā', Naglā' ♀ 'Having large and beautiful eyes'.

Najwa, Nagwa ♀ 'Intimate confidential conversation'.

Nāṣir ♂ 'Helper', 'supporter'.

Naṣr ♂ 'Victory', 'triumph'.

Nasrīn ♀ **1** From Persian: 'wild rose'. **2** Arabic: denoting the constellation the Eagle and the Lyre.

Nawāl ♀ 'Gift', 'benefit'.

Nibāl ♀ 'Arrows'.

Nihād ♀ Of uncertain origin; perhaps from a word meaning both 'high ground' and 'female breasts'.

Nihāl ♀ 'Those whose thirst is quenched'.

Ni'mat ♀ 'Boon', 'favour', 'blessing'.

Nizār ♂ Of uncertain origin; possibly from a word meaning 'little one'.

Nuha ♀ From *nuha* 'mind', 'intellect'.

Nūr ♀, ♂ 'Light'.

Nura ♀ Of uncertain origin, perhaps a variant of NŪR, although there is also an Arabic word *nura* meaning 'feature', 'characteristic'.

Q

Qāsim ♂ 'One who divides or distributes (money or food)'.

Quṣay ♂ Ancient name of uncertain origin; perhaps from a word meaning 'distant', 'remote'. Quṣay ibn-Fihr (*fl.* 420) of the Quraish tribe was the great-great-great grandfather of the Prophet.

R

Rabāb ♀ From a word denoting a stringed musical instrument resembling the fiddle.

Ra'd ♂ 'Thunder'.

Raḍwa ♀ Name of a district of Mecca, the birthplace of the Prophet.

Raḍwān ♂ 'Pleasure', 'contentment'.

Ra'fat ♂ 'Mercy', 'compassion'.

Rafīq ♂ Meaning either 'comrade', 'friend' or 'kind', 'gentle'.

Raghīd ♂ 'Carefree', 'enjoyable'. *Feminine form*: **Raghda**.

Rajā', Ragā' ♀ 'Hope', 'anticipation'.

Rajab, Ragab ♂ Seventh month of the Muslim calendar.

Rājya, Rāgya ♀ 'Hopeful'.

Ramaḍān ♂ Ninth month in the Muslim calendar, 'the hot month'. During Ramadan Muslims fast from dawn until sunset.

Rana ♀ 'Beautiful object'.

Randa ♀ From a word denoting a sweet-smelling tree that grows in the desert.

Ranya ♀ 'Looking or gazing at (the beloved)'.

Rashād ♂ 'Good sense' or 'good guidance' (especially in religious matters).

Rāshid, Rashīd ♂ 'Rightly guided'. *Feminine form*: **Rāshida**.

Ra'ūf ♂ 'Merciful', 'compassionate'.

Rāwiya ♀ 'Narrator', 'reciter', 'transmitter' (especially of classical Arabic poetry).

Riaz ♂ 'Meadows', 'gardens'; in some countries denoting meadows where horses were broken in.

Riḍa ♂, ♀ 'Contentment', 'approval' (by Allāh).

Rīm ♀ 'White antelope'.

Ruqayya ♀ 'Ascent', 'progress', or 'spell', 'charm'; the name of one of Muḥammad's daughters.

ashdi ♂ 'Sensible conduct', 'emotional maturity'.

S

Ṣabāḥ ♀ 'Morning'.

Ṣābir, Ṣabri ♂ 'Patient', 'persevering'. *Feminine form*: **Ṣabriyya**.

Saʻd ♂ 'Good luck', 'fortune'. Saʻd ibn-Abi-Waqqās was a cousin of the Prophet, who led the Muslims to victory in the Battle of Qadisiyya (637). In 639 he founded Kufa, the holy city of Shiites.

Ṣafāʼ ♀, ♂ 'Purity', 'sincerity'.

Safdar ♂ 'One who breaks ranks', suggesting an impetuous but brave soldier.

Ṣafiyya ♀ 'Confidante', 'bosom friend'.

Ṣafwat ♂ 'Choicest', 'best'.

Saḥar ♀ 'Early morning', 'dawn'.

Saʻīd ♂ 'Happy', 'lucky'.

Ṣakhr ♂ 'Solid rock'.

Ṣalāḥ ♂ 'Goodness', 'righteousness'. *Salah-ud-Din* (Saladdin) means 'righteousness of religion'.

Salāma ♂ 'Safety', 'well-being'.

Ṣāliḥ ♂ 'Virtuous', 'devout'. *Feminine form*: **Ṣālḥa**.

Salīm, Sālim ♂ 'Safe', 'unharmed'. *Feminine form*: **Salma**.

Salwa ♀ 'Consolation', 'solace'.

Sāmi ♂ 'Elevated', 'sublime'. *Feminine form*: **Samya**.

Samīḥ ♂ 'Tolerant', 'magnanimous'. *Feminine form*: **Samīha**.

Samīr ♂ 'Companion in night talk'. *Feminine forms*: **Samar, Samīra**.

Sanāʼ ♀ 'Brilliance', 'radiance'.

Saniyya ♀ 'Brilliant', 'radiant', 'resplendent'.

Sāra ♀ Biblical. See ◊**Sarah** in main dictionary.

Sarāb ♀ 'Mirage'.

Sawsan ♀ 'Lily of the valley'.

Sayyid ♂ 'Master', 'lord'.

Shaʻbān ♂ Eighth month of the Muslim calender.

Shabbir ♂ Biblical, name of a son of Aaron.

Shādi, Shādya ♀ 'Singer'.

Shafīq ♂ 'Compassionate'. *Feminine form*: **Shafīqa**.

Shahīra ♀ 'Famous'.

Shakīl ♂ 'Handsome'.

Shākir ♂ 'Thankful', 'grateful'.

Shamīm ♀, ♂ 'Fragrance', 'perfume'.

Sharīf ♂ 'Eminent', 'honourable'. *Feminine form*: **Sharifa**.

Shatha ♀ 'Fragrance', 'perfume'.

Shukri ♂ 'Giving thanks'. *Feminine form*: **Shukriyya**.

Sihām ♀ 'Arrows'.

Suʻād ♀ Of unknown origin.

Suha ♀ 'Star'.

Suhād, Suhair ♀ 'Sleeplessness'.

Suhayl ♂ Arabic name of the bright star Canopus

Suleimān, Sulaymān ♂ Biblical. See ◊**Solomon** in main dictionary.

Sultan ♂ 'Ruler', 'king', 'emperor'. *Feminine form*: **Sultana**.

Surayya ♀ Variant of THURAYYA.

T

Taghrīd ♀ 'Bird song'.

Ṭāha ♂ From the Arabic letters *ta* and *ha*, the opening letters of the twentieth sura in the Qurʼan.

Ṭāhir ♂ 'Pure', 'virtuous'.

Taḥiyya ♀ 'Greeting', 'salutation'.

Ṭalāl ♂ 'Dew' or 'fine rain'.

Tāmir ♂ 'Rich in dates'.

Taqi ♂ 'Piety', 'fear of God'. Muḥammad Taqi (811–??5) was the ninth Shiite imam.

Ṭāriq ♂ 'One who knocks at the door at night', 'nocturnal visitor'; also 'morning star'.

Ṭarūb ♀ 'Enraptured'.

Tawfīq ♂ 'Good fortune', 'prosperity'.

Thanāʼ ♀ 'Praise', 'commendation'.

Thheiba ♀ 'Gold bar'.

Thurayya, Surayya ♀ 'The Pleiades'.

U

ʻUmar, Omar 'Flourishing'. ʻUmar ibn-al-Khaṭṭāb was the second rightly guided caliph (634–44), a man noted for his justice, administrative ability, and the simplicity of his lifestyle.

ʻUmayma ♀ 'Little mother'.

ʻUm-Kalthūm ♀ 'Mother of one with plump cheeks'; name of one of the Prophet's daughters.

ʼUmniya ♀ 'Wish', 'desire'.

ʻUthmān, ʻUsmān ♂ 'Bustard' (the bird). ʻUthmān ibn-ʻAffān was the third rightly guided caliph (644–56), noted for his generosity and loyalty.

W

Wafā' ♀ 'Loyalty', 'fidelity'.

Wahīb ♂ 'Donor', 'generous giver'. *Feminine form*: **Wahība**.

Wā'il ♂ 'One who reverts' (i.e. to Allāh).

Wajīh ♂ 'Distinguished', 'notable'.

Walīd ♂ 'Newborn baby'. Al-Walīd ibn-'Abd-al-Malik (d. 715) was the Umayyad caliph (705–15) whose armies conquered Spain and attempted to capture Constantinople.

Wasīm ♂ 'Handsome', 'good-looking'.

Widād ♀ 'Affection', 'friendship'.

Y

Yahya ♂ Biblical. See ◊**John** in main dictionary.

Ya'qūb ♂ Biblical. See ◊**Jacob** in main dictionary.

Yasīn ♂ From the Arabic letters *ya* and *si*, the opening letters of the thirty-sixth sura of the Qur'an.

Yāsir, Yusri ♂ 'Rich', 'well-off'. *Feminine form*: **Yusriyya**.

Yasmīn ♀ 'Jasmine'.

Yūnis ♂ Biblical. See ◊**Jonah** in main dictionary.

Yusra ♀ 'Prosperity', 'affluence', 'good fortune'.

Yūsuf ♂ Biblical. See ◊**Joseph** in main dictionary.

Z

Zāhir ♂ 'Shining', 'radiant'.

Zahra ♀ 'Shining', also 'flower'.

Zaynab, Zeinab ♀ From the name a beautiful, sweet-smelling plant. This was the name of the Prophet's daughter, two of his wives, and his granddaughter. The latter brought Islam to Egypt.

Zakariyya ♂ Biblical. See ◊**Zachary** in main dictionary.

Zaki ♂ 'Pure', 'virtuous'. *Feminine form*: **Zakiyya**.

Zamir ♂ 'Thought'.

Zayd ♂ Ancient name, possibly meaning 'increase'. It was borne by one of Muḥammad's earliest converts and loyalist supporters.

Ziyād ♂ 'Growth'.

Zubaida ♀ 'Marigold'.

Zuhayr ♂ Diminutive of *zahr* 'flowers'.

Zulēkha ♀ Biblical: name of Potiphar's wife, who conceived a passion for Joseph.

APPENDIX 7:

INDIAN NAMES

Note The names in this supplement are borne mainly by Hindus; also in some cases by Jains, Buddhists, Parsees, and Sikhs. India has a large population of Muslims, who bear names that are mostly of Arabic origin. For an explanation of Muslim names of Arabic origin, see Appendix 6. Muslim names of Persian and other origin are included here.

A

Ajit ♂ Sanskrit: 'invincible'.

Amitabh ♂ Sanskrit: 'of unmeasured splendour', one of the five aspects of Buddha in Mahayana Buddhism.

Amrit ♂, ♀ Sanskrit: 'immortal', 'ambrosia', a byname of Shiva and Vishnu.

Anand ♂ Sanskrit: 'happiness', 'bliss-consciousness', a byname of Shiva; also a Buddhist and Jain divine attribute. *Feminine form*: **Ananda**.

Anil ♂ Sanskrit: 'air', 'wind', one of the commonest names of the wind god Vayu, charioteer of Indra. *Feminine form*: **Anila**.

Anuradha ♀ Sanskrit: probably meaning 'stream of oblations', the name of one of the 28 asterisms at the heart of Hindu astrology.

Arjun ♂ Sanskrit: 'white' (the colour of dawn, lightning, milk, and silver), the name of the noblest of the five Pandava princes in the Mahabharata, who received Krishna's divine oration called the *Bhagavad Gita*.

Arun ♂ Sanskrit: 'reddish-brown', the colour of dawn, gold, and rubies, and personification of the dawn, the charioteer of the sun. *Feminine form*: **Aruna**.

Arvind ♂ Sanskrit: 'lotus'.

Asha ♀ Sanskrit: 'hope'.

Ashish ♂ Probably Sanskrit: 'prayer' or 'blessing'.

Ashok ♂ Sanskrit: 'not causing or feeling sorrow', the name of a common Indian tree. Emperor Asoka ruled *c.*269–232 BC over most of the subcontinent, from Afghanistan to Sri Lanka; he converted to Buddhism after a particularly bloody military campaign, and marked this by erecting thousands of inscribed pillars.

B

abar ♂ Muslim name, from Turkish: 'lion', the byname of Zahir ud-Din Muhammad (c.1482–1530), first of the Mogul rulers in India.

Bala ♂, ♀ Sanskrit: 'young', often used in compound epithets of Krishna.

Baldev ♂ Sanskrit: 'god of strength', name of the elder brother of Krishna, described as wine-loving and irascible. The name is especially favoured by Sikhs.

Balu ♂ Pet form of BALA.

Bano ♀ Muslim name, from Persian: 'lady', 'princess', 'bride'.

Bharat ♂ Sanskrit: 'being maintained', an epithet of Agni, the god of fire; also the name of a legendary emperor, ancestor of both the warring parties in the Mahabharata, and of Rama's loyal younger brother and regent in the Ramayana. Bharat was adopted as the official name of India at independence. *Feminine form*: **Bharati**.

Bhaskar ♂ Sanskrit: 'bright light', denoting the sun; also the name of ancient India's most famous mathematician and astrologer.

Bibi ♀ Muslim name, from Persian: 'lady of the house'.

Bishen ♂ North Indian variant of VISHNU, especially common among Sikhs.

C

Chandan ♂ Sanskrit: 'sandalwood', with reference especially to the paste made from sandalwood, used in Hindu ceremonies to anoint images of deities and to make an auspicious mark on the forehead of participants.

Chandra ♂, ♀ Sanskrit: 'moon'. Though the moon is always regarded as a male deity in Hinduism, it is also popular as a female name.

Chandrakant ♂ Sanskrit: 'moonstone', also 'white water-lily', literally 'beloved of the moon'.

Chandrakanta ♀ The feminine form of CHANDRAKANT, regarded as the wife of the moon and therefore used to denote night.

D

Damayanti ♀ Sanskrit: 'subduing (men)', i.e. by beauty or personality. In Classical legend Damayanti is the name of a beautiful princess who is courted by Prince Nala, and by her intelligence distinguishes him from his rival suitors, four gods masquerading as him.

Damodar ♂ Sanskrit: 'having a rope round his belly', an epithet of Krishna based on the legend in which, as a child, he stole butter and broke pots of milk and curds in his foster-mother's house. She tied him to a large vessel by means of a rope round his waist to prevent him getting up to more mischief. *Feminine form*: **Damodari**.

Dayaram ♂ Sanskrit: 'compassionate as Rama'.

Deb ♂ Variant of DEV.

Deo ♂ Variant of DEV.

Dev ♂ Sanskrit: 'god', often referring in particular to Indra; also a term of address for kings, equivalent to 'Your Majesty'.

Devdan ♂ Sanskrit: 'gift of the gods'.

Devdas ♂ Sanskrit: 'servant of the gods'.

Devi ♀ Feminine form of DEV; referring especially to the wife of Shiva.

Dilip ♂ Of uncertain etymology, probably Sanskrit: 'protector of Delhi', the name of various legendary kings.

Dinesh ♂ Sanskrit: 'lord of the day' (i.e. the sun).

Dipak ♂ Sanskrit: 'little lamp' or 'like a lamp'; an epithet of Kama, the god of love.

Durga ♀ Sanskrit: 'inaccessible', an epithet of the wife of Shiva, because of her propensity for prolonged meditation. Durga represents her terrifying form, reflecting her anger when disturbed.

G

Ganesh ♂ Sanskrit: 'lord of the hosts', a title of the god Shiva and the name of his eldest son, who has the head of an elephant and the body of a short fat imp with a huge belly.

Gauri ♀ Sanskrit: 'white', a byname of Shiva's previously dark-skinned wife who, after being teased by Shiva, acquired a brilliant white complexion through meditation in the Himalayas.

Gautam ♂ Sanskrit: 'descendant of GOTAM', a name of the historical Buddha and of a major Jain saint, therefore especially favoured by Buddhists and Jains.

Gita ♀ Sanskrit: literally 'song', probably in the sense 'one whose praises are sung'.

Gobind ♂ Variant of GOVIND, the name of one of the ten Sikh gurus, therefore especially popular among Sikhs.

Gopal ♂ Sanskrit: 'cowherd', also used to mean 'king', the earth being regarded fancifully as the milch-cow of kings. It is a byname of Krishna in the Mahabharata and among his cult worshippers.

Gotam ♂ Sanskrit: 'the best ox', name of an ancient Hindu sage. In Indian literature cattle are a symbol of wealth. The name was borne by the chief disciple of Mahavira, hence is popular among Jains.

Govind ♂ Sanskrit: 'cow finder', originally an epithet of the god Indra, but now most strongly associated with Krishna.

Gowri ♀ Variant of GAURI.

Gulzar ♂ Muslim name, from Persian: 'rose garden'.

H

Hari ♂ Sanskrit: denoting a colour variously interpreted as brown, yellow, or green, and used particularly to describe the horses of Indra. It is also used as a noun with various meanings ('lion', 'sun', 'monkey', or 'wind') and is especially a byname of Vishnu or Krishna.

Harinder ♂ Compound of HARI and INDRA, favoured especially by Sikhs as suggesting the warrior attributes of the two great gods.

Harish ♂ Sanskrit: 'lord of the monkeys', used since medieval times as a byname of Vishnu.

I

Inderjit ♂, ♀ Sanskrit: 'conqueror of Indra', name of the son of the demon king Ravana in the Ramayana. Because of its martial connotations it is popular among Sikhs.

Inderpal ♂ Sanskrit: 'protector of Indra' or perhaps 'Indra's bodyguard', popular among Sikhs because of its martial connotations.

Indira ♀ Sanskrit: a byname of Lakshmi, the wife of Vishnu. It is said to mean 'beauty' or 'splendour'.

Indra ♂ Etymology uncertain; probably from a Sanskrit compound meaning 'possessing drops (of rain)'. Indra is the name of the god of the sky and lord of the rain, who conquers the demons of darkness by using his thunderbolt. Indra is now found mainly in compound names such as INDERJIT and JASWINDER.

J

Jagannath ♂ Sanskrit: 'lord of the world', a byname of Vishnu, and especially the name of his image in the great temple of Puri.

Jagdish ♂ Sanskrit: 'ruler of the world', applied to the gods Brahma, Vishnu, and Shiva.

Jagjit ♂ Sanskrit: 'conqueror of the world', a popular name among Sikhs.

Jahangir ♂ Muslim name, from Persian: 'holder of the world'. It was the regnal name of the Mogul emperor Nur ud-Din Muhammad (1569–1627).

Jai ♂ Variant of JAY.

Jamshed ♂ Name borne chiefly by Parsis and Muslims. Jamshed was a legendary king of ancient Persia, the founder of Persepolis.

Janaki ♀ Sanskrit: meaning uncertain. It is an epithet of Sita, daughter of King Janaka and the wife of Rama.

Janmuhammad ♂ Muslim name, from Persian: 'breath (i.e. life) of Muhammad'.

Jaswinder ♀ Sikh name, from Sanskrit: 'Indra of the thunderbolt'.

Javed ♂ Muslim name, from Persian: 'eternal'.

Jay ♂ Sanskrit: 'victory'.

Jaya ♀ Feminine form of JAY; an epithet of Durga, the wife of Shiva. Also the name of a Buddhist goddess.

Jayakrishna ♂ Sanskrit: 'victorious Krishna'.

Jayant ♂ Sanskrit: 'victorious', name of the son of Indra.

Jayanti ♀ Feminine form of JAYANT; an epithet of Durga, the wife of Shiva; also the name of Indra's daughter.

Jayashankar ♂ Sanskrit: 'victorious Shiva'.

Jayashree ♀ Sanskrit: a byname of the goddess Lakshmi, wife of Vishnu, meaning 'goddess of victory'.

Jaywant ♂ Sanskrit: 'possessing victory', a popular name among Sikhs because of its martial connotations.

Jitender, Jitinder ♂ Variants of JITENDRA, especially common among Sikhs.

Jitendra ♂ Sanskrit: 'having conquered Indra' (i.e. so powerful as to have conquered even the god Indra), or a misunderstanding of Sanskrit *jitendriya* 'having one's senses under control', a central aim of yoga and meditation.

Jyoti ♀ Sanskrit: 'light', often used as a symbol of heaven, intelligence, and liberation.

K

Kailash ♂, ♀ Sanskrit: the name of a mountain in the Himalayas, the site of

Shiva's paradise and abode of Kubera, the god of wealth.

Kalidas ♂ Sanskrit: 'servant of Kali' (literally 'the black one', name of Shiva's wife in her fierce form).

Kalpana ♀ Sanskrit: 'fantasy' or 'ornament'.

Kalyan ♂ Sanskrit: 'beautiful' or 'auspicious'. *Feminine form*: **Kalyani**.

Kamal ♂ **1** Sanskrit: 'pink', also a name for the lotus. **2** Muslim name: see Arabic supplement.

Kamala ♀ Feminine form of KAMAL 1; a byname of the goddess Lakshmi, wife of Vishnu.

Kannan ♂ South Indian variant of KRISHNA.

Kanta ♀ Sanskrit: 'desired', 'beautiful'.

Kanti ♀ Sanskrit: 'beauty', especially with reference to the shining beauty of the moon or a lovely woman.

Kapil ♂ Sanskrit: probably meaning 'monkey-coloured' or 'reddish brown'; the name of an ancient Hindu sage.

Karan ♂ Sanskrit: 'ear', name of a mighty warrior king of Anga (Bengal) in the Mahabharata. He is the son of Surya the sun god, and (unbeknownst to them) the half-brother of the Pandava princes, against whom he fights.

Kasi ♂ Sanskrit: 'shining'; a name of Varanasi (Benares), most sacred Hindu city on the Ganges.

Kausalya ♀ Sanskrit: 'belonging to the Kosala people'; the name of the grandmother of both sets of princes who fight in the Mahabharata war; also the name of the mother of Rama in the Ramayana.

Khurshid ♂ Muslim name, from Persian: 'sun'.

Khwaja ♂ Muslim name, from Persian: 'master'.

Kiran ♂ Sanskrit: 'ray of light', especially denoting 'sunbeam' or 'moonbeam'.

Kishen ♂ North Indian variant of KRISHNA.

Kishore ♂ Sanskrit: 'colt' or 'young boy'. *Feminine form*: **Kishori** (*'filly'*).

Kistna ♂ Central Indian variant of KRISHNA.

Krishna ♂ Sanskrit: literally 'black', 'dark'; the name of a legendary hero, later elevated to divinity and usually regarded as an incarnation of Vishnu.

Kumar ♂ Sanskrit: 'boy', 'son', or 'prince'; a byname of the beautiful youth Skanda, son of Shiva. *Feminine form*: **Kumari** (*'daughter', 'princess'*: an epithet of Shiva's wife).

L

Lakshman ♂ Sanskrit: 'having auspicious marks', name of the half-brother and faithful companion of Rama in the Ramayana, regarded as a partial incarnation of Vishnu.

Lakshmi ♀ Sanskrit: 'sign', 'lucky omen', name of the goddess of beauty, good fortune, and wealth, wife of Vishnu.

Lal ♂ **1** Sanskrit: a term of endearment, 'darling boy'. **2** Prakrit: 'king'.

Lalita ♀ Sanskrit: 'playful', 'amorous'; name of one of the cowherdesses who were the amorous playmates of the adolescent Krishna.

Lata ♀ Sanskrit: 'tendril' or 'creeper', often used in metaphors describing the slender curvature of eyebrows, arms, hair, swords, lightning, and women's bodies.

Laxman ♂ Modern variant of LAKSHMAN.

Leela ♀ Sanskrit: 'play', 'amorous sport'.

Liaqat ♂ Muslim name, from Persian: 'dignity', 'merit', 'ability', 'good judgement'.

Lila ♀ Variant of LEELA.

M

Madhav ♂ Sanskrit: a byname of Krishna, meaning 'descendant of MADHU'. *Feminine form*: **Madhavi** (a byname of the goddess Lakshmi).

Madhu ♀ Sanskrit: 'sweet', 'honey'; also 'springtime'; name of a legendary king, one of whose descendants was the god Krishna.

Madhukar ♂ Sanskrit: 'honey-maker', i.e. 'bee'.

Madhur ♀ Sanskrit: 'sweet'.

Mahavir ♂ Sanskrit: 'great hero'; the name of the founder of Jainism.

Mahendra ♂ Sanskrit: 'great Indra', a byname of Vishnu in the Ramayana and of Shiva in Tantric texts; also the name of Emperor Asoka's brother, the first great Buddhist missionary.

Mahesh ♂ Sanskrit: 'great ruler', a byname of Shiva; also the name of a Buddhist deity.

Mahinder ♂ North Indian variant of MAHENDRA.

Malati ♀ Sanskrit name of the jasmine plant, whose flowers open in the evening.

Mani ♂, occasionally ♀ Sanskrit: 'jewel'; also used to denote the phallus. The name carries magical or mystical connotations. It is often used as a short form of **Subrahmanya**, son of Shiva and brother of Ganesh.

Meena ♀ Sanskrit: 'fish', 'Pisces'; name of the daughter of the goddess of the dawn, and of the wife of the ancient sage Kasyapa. Often a short form of **Meenakshi** ('having eyes shaped like a fish'), the name of a princess of Madurai, now its patron goddess and commonly identified with Durga, the wife of Shiva.

Mehjibin ♀ Muslim name, from Persian: 'with temples like the moon', suggesting a woman with a beautiful face.

Mirza ♂ Muslim name, from Persian: 'prince', an honorific title introduced into the subcontinent by the Moguls.

Mohan ♂ Sanskrit: 'enchanting', a byname of Shiva and of one of the five arrows of Kama, the god of love. It is also an epithet of Krishna, who beguiles the cowherdesses and enchants his devotees. *Feminine form*: **Mohana**.

Mohinder ♂ North Indian variant of MAHENDRA.

Mohini ♀ Sanskrit: 'enchanting woman', a name of Vishnu, from the myth in which he disguises himself as a beautiful woman in order to distract Shiva from a dangerously deep meditation.

Mukesh ♂ Sanskrit: of uncertain origin, probably from an epithet of Shiva, 'conqueror of the wild boar demon Muka'.

Murali ♂ Sanskrit: 'flute', with reference to various compound epithets of Krishna, especially **Muralidhara** 'bearer of the flute'.

N

Nagendra ♂ Sanskrit: 'mighty serpent' or 'mighty elephant' (literally 'a (veritable) Indra among serpents/elephants').

Nanda ♂ Sanskrit: 'joy', 'son'; name of the foster-father of Krishna, also a byname of Vishnu. In Buddhist texts it is the name of the step-brother of Buddha. Associated with prodigious wealth as the name of a historical dynasty of kings.

Narain ♂ North Indian variant of NARAYAN.

Narayan ♂ Sanskrit: literally 'path of man', i.e. 'son of man'; a byname of Brahma, god of creation, and of Vishnu.

Narendra ♂ Sanskrit: 'an Indra among men', i.e. 'mighty man', 'king'; also 'doctor', associated with cures and charms against snake-bite.

Naresh ♂ Sanskrit: 'ruler of men'.

Narottam ♂ Sanskrit: 'best of men'; popular especially among Jains.

Nataraj ♂ Sanskrit: 'lord of the dance', a byname of Shiva.

Naveed ♂ Muslim name, from Persian: 'glad tidings' or 'wedding invitation'.

Niaz ♂ Muslim name, from Persian: 'prayer', 'gift', or 'offering'.

P

Padma ♂, ♀ Sanskrit: 'lotus', symbolizing the *cakras* or centres of psychic energy in the human body; the female name is a byname of the goddess Lakshmi.

Padmavati ♀ Sanskrit: 'full of lotuses' or 'lotus-like'.

Padmini ♀ Sanskrit: 'full of lotuses' or 'lotus pond'.

Parvaiz ♂ Muslim name, from Persian: 'victorious' or 'fortunate'.

Parvati ♀ Sanskrit: 'daughter of the mountain', a byname of Shiva's wife.

Parvin ♀ Muslim name, from Persian, denoting the Pleiades.

Pitambar ♂ Sanskrit: 'wearing yellow garments', an epithet of Vishnu or Krishna. Yellow (saffron) clothes are traditionally worn by Hindus for worship and for pilgrimage.

Prabhakar ♂ Sanskrit: 'light maker', a byname of Shiva. In medieval times, the name of a Hindu philosopher.

Prabhu ♂ Sanskrit: 'mighty', 'king'; an epithet of Surya, the sun god, and of Agni, god of fire.

Prabodh ♂ Sanskrit: 'awakening', also 'the blooming of flowers'; frequently used in religious and philosophical texts as a metaphor for the awakening of consciousness.

Pradeep ♂ Sanskrit: 'light', 'lantern', 'glory'.

Prakash ♂ Sanskrit: 'light', 'famous'.

Pramod ♂ Sanskrit: 'joy', 'pleasure'.

Pran ♂ Sanskrit: 'breath', 'life-force'.

Prasad ♂ Sanskrit: 'brightness'; also 'the grace of God', denoting especially the offerings made to a deity and then distributed to the worshippers.

Pratap ♂ Sanskrit: 'heat', also 'splendour', 'majesty', 'power', applied to kings and warriors.

Pratibha ♀ Sanskrit: 'light', 'image', also 'intelligence', 'audacity', 'imagination'.

Pravin ♂ Sanskrit: 'skilful'.

Prem ♂ Sanskrit: 'love', 'affection'. *Feminine form*: **Prema**.

Premlata ♀ Sanskrit: denoting a kind of small creeping plant, sometimes used as a metaphor for love.

Priya ♀ Sanskrit: 'beloved'.

Purnima ♀ Sanskrit: 'day (or night) of the full moon'.

urushottam ♂ Sanskrit: 'highest of beings', a byname of Vishnu or Krishna. It is the term for a deified teacher in the Jain religion, hence a popular name among Jains.

R

Radha ♀ Sanskrit: 'success'; the name of the favourite consort of Krishna.

Raghav ♂ Sanskrit: 'descendant of Raghu', an epithet of Rama.

Raghu ♂ Sanskrit: 'swift', name of an ancestor of Rama.

Raj ♂ Sanskrit: 'king', applied to various gods, for example Varuna, Aditya, Indra, and Yama. It is a name of Yudhisthira, the eldest Pandava prince in the Mahabharata.

Rajani ♀ Sanskrit: 'the dark one', 'night'; a byname of Durga, the wife of Shiva.

Rajanikant ♂ Sanskrit: 'beloved of the night', an epithet of the moon.

Rajendra ♂ Sanskrit: 'an Indra among kings', hence 'mighty king', 'emperor'.

Rajesh ♂ Sanskrit: 'ruler of kings', 'emperor'.

Rajiv ♂ Sanskrit: 'striped', the name of a species of fish and of the blue lotus.

Rajkumar ♂ Sanskrit: 'king's son', 'prince'. *Feminine form*: **Rajkumari**.

Rajni ♀ Either a contracted form of RAJANI or from a Sanskrit word meaning 'queen'.

Rajnish ♂ Sanskrit: 'ruler of the night', i.e. the moon.

Raju ♂ Variant of RAJA or abbreviation of any of various compound names with *Raja*- as first element.

Rakesh ♂ Sanskrit: 'ruler of the day of the full-moon', a byname of Shiva.

Ram ♂ North Indian variant of RAMA.

Rama ♂ Sanskrit: 'pleasing'. Three famous bearers of the name are known: **Parasurama** 'Rama of the axe', the sixth incarnation of Vishnu; **Balarama** 'the strong Rama', elder brother of Krishna and eighth incarnation of Vishnu; and above all **Ramachandra**, seventh incarnation of Vishnu, whose story is told in the Ramayana.

Ramakrishna ♂ Compound name from RAMA and KRISHNA.

Ramesh ♂ Sanskrit: from 'rest', 'repose', 'night', a byname of Lakshmi + 'lord', hence meaning 'lord of Lakshmi', a byname of Vishnu.

Rameshwar ♂ Sanskrit: synonymous with RAMESH; or RAMA + 'lord', i.e. 'lord Rama'.

Ramgopal ♂ Compound name from RAM and GOPAL, synonymous with RAMA-KRISHNA, *gopal* being originally an epithet of Krishna.

Ramnarayan ♂ Compound name from RAM and NARAYAN.

Ramnath ♂ Sanskrit: 'Lord Rama'.

Ramu ♂ Variant of RAM or RAMA, or pet form of any of the many compound names formed with *Ram*- or *Rama*-.

Ranjit ♂ Sanskrit: 'coloured', 'painted', also meaning 'charmed' or 'delighted'. This name was borne by Ranjit Singh (1780–1839), founder of the Sikh kingdom in the Punjab.

Ratan ♂ Prakrit: 'jewel'.

Rati ♀ Sanskrit: 'repose', 'pleasure', especially 'sexual pleasure', hence often personified as the wife of Kama, god of love.

Ratilal ♂ Prakrit: 'lord of pleasure', an epithet of Kama, the god of love.

Ravi ♂ Sanskrit: 'sun', name of the sun god.

Ravindra ♂ Sanskrit: 'mightiest of suns' (literally 'an Indra among suns').

Rohan ♂ Sanskrit: 'ascending', also used to mean 'healing' or 'medicine'.

Roshan ♂, ♀ Muslim name, from Persian: 'shining', 'splendid'. It is used in Urdu to mean 'famous'.

Roshanara ♀ Muslim name, from Persian: 'light of the assembly', suggesting a woman whose beauty attracts everyone.

Rukmini ♀ Sanskrit: 'adorned with gold'; name of a character in the Mahabharata who becomes the secret lover of Krishna.

Rupchand ♂ Sanskrit: 'as beautiful as the moon'.

Rupinder ♀ Sanskrit: 'superlatively beautiful'; literally 'an Indra of beauty'. The name is especially popular among Sikhs.

S

Sachdev ♂ Sanskrit: 'truth of god', i.e. 'of impeccable honesty'.

Samant ♂ Sanskrit: 'universal', 'whole'.

Sandhya ♀ Sanskrit: 'junction' or 'twilight', used to denote the rituals performed three times daily by the twice-born Hindu castes; personified in the Epics and Puranas as a daughter of the god Brahma.

Sanjay ♂ Sanskrit: 'triumphant'; name of the main narrator of the daily battles in the Mahabharata.

Sanjeev ♂ Sanskrit: 'reviving'.

Sankar ♂ Variant of SHANKAR.

Sarala ♀ Sanskrit: 'straight', 'honest'; also denotes the pine tree.

Saraswati ♀ Sanskrit: 'having or possessing waters'; the name of a river (sometimes identified with the Indus) deified as a goddess; also the name of Brahma's wife, goddess of education, arts, and sciences.

Sardar ♂ Mainly Muslim, from Persian: 'head man', 'nobleman'. It was adopted as an honorific title by the Sikhs. *Also*: **Sirdar**.

Sarfraz ♂ Muslim name, from Persian: 'holding one's head up high'.

Saroja ♀ Sanskrit: 'born in a lake', also 'lotus'.

Sarojini ♀ Sanskrit: 'having lotuses', 'lotus-pond'.

Satish ♂ Sanskrit: 'lord of Sati' (reality, truth; a byname of the goddess Durga).

Savitri ♀ Sanskrit: 'belonging to Savitr' (the sun god); the name of the main prayer in Hindu ceremonies, personified as the wife or daughter of the sun or of Brahma. In legend, she is the faithful wife who rescues her husband from Yama (Death, king of the underworld).

Sekar ♂ Sanskrit: 'peak', 'crest', also 'the best'. Common as an abbreviated form of compound names such as **Chandrasekhar** 'moon-crested', an epithet of the god Shiva.

Seth ♂ Of uncertain origin, possibly from Sanskrit *setu* 'bridge' or *sveta* 'white'.

Shah ♂ Muslim name, from Persian: 'king', 'emperor'. The name is especially associated with Sufi mystics.

Shahjahan ♂ Muslim name, from Persian: 'king of the world', name of the Mogul emperor (1592–1666) for whom the Taj Mahal in Agra was built.

Shahnawaz ♂ Muslim name, from Persian: 'cherisher of kings'.

Shahnaz ♀ Muslim name, from Persian: 'glory of kings'.

Shahzad ♂ Muslim name, from Persian: 'prince'.

Shakti ♀ Sanskrit: 'power', in particular the power of a deity, personified as his wife; especially a byname of Shiva's wife.

Shakuntala ♀ Sanskrit: the name of the heroine of a drama by Kalidasa. Her name is said to derive from the name of a type of bird, because she was abandoned in a forest soon after birth and reared by birds. She was the beloved of King Dushyanta, and their son Bharat was the founder of a race of kings.

Shamshad ♂, ♀ Muslim name, from Persian: 'box tree'. It suggests a woman who is tall, slender, and graceful.

Shankar ♂ Sanskrit: 'conferrer of welfare', a euphemistic epithet of the god Rudra

(Shiva). It is the name of one of the most famous Hindu philosophers (8th–9th century AD).

Shanta ♀ Sanskrit: 'calmed', referring especially to spiritual calmness acquired through yoga or meditation.

Shanti ♀ Sanskrit: 'tranquillity', usually associated with yoga or meditation.

Sharada ♀ Sanskrit: 'autumnal', 'mature'; a byname of Durga, wife of Shiva.

Sharma ♂ Sanskrit: 'protection', 'refuge'; later 'joy' or 'comfort'; traditionally a name favoured by Brahmins (priests).

Sharmila ♀ Hindi: 'modest', from Sanskrit, 'protection', an epithet of Draupadi, shared wife of the Pandava princes in the Maha-bharata, from the episode in which her sari miraculously grows longer and continues to cover her body, although it is being un-wound and pulled off her by a shameless Kaurava prince.

Shashi ♂ Sanskrit: literally 'having a hare', an epithet of the moon (the visible features of the moon being interpreted as resembling a hare). It is often found as the first element in compound names such as **Shashikant** 'beloved of the moon' and **Sashichand** 'the hare-marked moon'.

Sheela ♀ Sanskrit: 'good character', 'piety'; in Buddhism one of the six perfections to be striven for.

Sher ♂ Muslim name, from Persian: 'lion'; Sher Shah (1486–1545) was Mogul emperor from 1540 to 1545.

Shirin ♀ Muslim name, from Persian: 'sweet', 'charming'; name of the daughter of the Byzantine emperor Maurice (c. 539–602), celebrated in Persian and Turkish romances as the beloved of the lowly Farhad, whose royal rival Khusrao deceitfully brings about his death.

Shiva ♂ Sanskrit: 'benign', 'auspicious'; originally a euphemistic epithet of the terrifying god of destruction, Rudra. Shiva is one of the most important of the Hindu gods, associated in particular with asceti-cism, generative power, and the dance of cosmic destruction.

Shobha ♀ Sanskrit: 'brilliance', 'beauty'.

Shobhana ♀ Sanskrit: 'brilliant', 'beauti-ful'.

Shripati ♂ Sanskrit: 'husband of Sri, god-dess of fortune' or 'lord of fortune'; a byname of Vishnu or Krishna.

Shyam ♂ Sanskrit: 'black', 'dark', 'beauti-ful', a byname of Krishna.

Shyama ♀ Feminine form of SHYAM, also meaning 'night'; a byname of Durga, the wife of Shiva. It is also the name of a Jain goddess.

Siddhartha ♂ Sanskrit: 'one who has accomplished his goal'; an epithet of the Buddha.

Sita ♀ Sanskrit: 'furrow', personified as the goddess of agriculture and the harvest; the name of the wife of Rama, identified with the goddess Lakshmi, and a symbol of all the wifely virtues: purity, tenderness, and fidelity.

Sitaram ♂ Compound name from SITA and RAMA, meaning 'Rama whose wife was Sita', also denoting godhead as the union of male and female.

Sneh ♀ Sanskrit: 'viscous', 'oil', also 'affection' or 'tenderness'.

Sri ♀ Sanskrit: 'light', 'beauty', 'prosperity', also 'rank', 'power', 'royal majesty', a byname of the goddesses Lakshmi and Saraswati. Also widely used as an honorific title.

Sridhar ♂ Sanskrit: 'bearing or possessing Sri (the goddess Lakshmi)', an epithet of the god Vishnu.

Srikant ♂ Sanskrit: **1** 'having a beautiful throat', an epithet of Shiva, from the myth in which he saves the universe by swallowing the poison that threatens to engulf it, his throat turning blue in the process. **2** 'the beloved of Sri', an epithet of Vishnu.

Srinivas ♂ Sanskrit: 'the abode of the goddess Sri', an epithet of Vishnu.

Sriram ♂ Sanskrit: 'Lord Rama'; also used as a salutation by Rama devotees.

Subhash ♂ Sanskrit: literally '(of) good speech', hence 'eloquent'.

Sudhir ♂ Sanskrit: literally 'good firmness', hence 'wise', 'resolute'.

Sujata ♀ Sanskrit: 'of noble birth' or 'of an excellent nature'.

Suman ♂ Sanskrit: 'well-disposed', 'cheerful'; also 'wise'.

Sumanjit ♂ Sanskrit: 'the conqueror of the demon Sumana'.

Sumantra ♂ Sanskrit: '(giver of) good advice'; an archetypal name for a minister in Classical and later texts.

Sumati ♀ Sanskrit: 'good mind', also denoting 'benevolence' or 'prayer'; originally a masculine name but now exclusively feminine. In legend, it is the name of the wife of King Sagara, who bore 60,000 sons.

Sundar, Sunder ♂ Sanskrit: 'beautiful'; often the first element in compound names such as **Sundararaja** and **Sunder Ram**.

Sunil ♂ Sanskrit: 'very dark blue'; also said to denote the pomegranate tree or the flax plant.

Sunita ♀ Sanskrit: **1** probably meaning 'of good conduct'. **2** 'giving good guidance, righteous'. Originally a masculine name, now exclusively feminine.

Suniti ♀ Sanskrit: 'of good conduct'; the name of the mother of the pole star Dhruva.

Suresh ♂ Sanskrit: 'ruler of the gods', sometimes the name of a distinct god, but more commonly an epithet of Indra, Shiva, or Vishnu.

Surendra, Surinder ♂ Sanskrit: 'the mightiest of gods', an epithet of various gods, but especially of Indra. The form **Surinder** is especially common among Sikhs.

Surjit ♂ Sanskrit: 'one who has conquered the gods'.

Surya ♂ Sanskrit: 'sun', the name of the sun god in his physical form, ruler of the sky, said to be the father of the twins Yama and Yami, primal man and woman.

Sushil ♂ Sanskrit: 'well-disposed' or 'good-tempered'.

Sushila ♀ Feminine form of SUSHIL; the name of a wife of Krishna, or a female attendant of Krishna's mistress Radha.

Swapan ♂ Sanskrit: 'sleep', 'dream'.

Swaran ♂ Sanskrit: 'beautiful in colour', 'golden'.

T

Tara ♂ Sanskrit: **1** probably meaning 'carrying', 'saviour', an epithet of Rudra, and of Vishnu. **2** 'shining'.

Tara ♀ Sanskrit: 'star' or 'asterism', a byname of Durga especially in her meditative and magical guise; also the name of the wife of Brhaspati, preceptor of the gods, and mother of Buddha (the Indian equivalent of the god Mercury); in Mahayana Buddhism, the name of the wife of Buddha, and of a Buddhist goddess; in Jain texts, the name of a female deity.

Tarun ♂ Sanskrit: 'young', 'tender', used especially of the newly risen sun and of young plants; also 'tenderness of feelings' or 'affection'.

Tulsi ♂ Sanskrit: denoting the holy basil plant, regarded as sacred to Vishnu, and personified as a goddess.

U

Uma ♀ Sanskrit: denoting the flax plant or turmeric; the name of a goddess who mediates between Brahma and the other gods, identified with the goddess Vac, the personification of speech; also a byname of Parvati, wife of Shiva.

Umashankar ♂ Sanskrit: compound name meaning either 'Shankar whose wife is Uma', (i.e. Shiva), or 'Uma and Shankar', referring to the godhead as the union of male and female.

Usha ♀ Sanskrit: 'dawn', personified as the daughter of heaven, the sister of the solar gods and of night, the wife of the god Rudra; said to be very beautiful, the friend of men, the bringer of wealth, and always young although she makes men grow old.

Uttam ♂ Sanskrit: 'highest', 'furthest', 'last', 'best'.

V

Vasant ♂ Sanskrit: denoting the spring season, often personified and regarded as the friend or attendant of Kama, the god of love. *Feminine form*: **Vasanta**.

Vasu ♂ Sanskrit: 'bright', 'beneficent', 'excellent', an epithet of various gods, including Indra, Agni, and Vishnu; also the name of one of the seven great ancient sages, authors of the Rig-Veda; often used as an abbreviation of Vasudeva, a name of Vishnu and of the father of Krishna.

Venkat ♂ Sanskrit: the name of a sacred peak near Madras, dedicated to the god Vishnu, and a major Hindu pilgrimage centre.

Vijay ♂ Sanskrit: 'victory', also 'booty'; an epithet of Arjuna. *Feminine form*: **Vijaya** (a byname of Durga, wife of Shiva).

Vijayalakshmi ♀ Sanskrit: a particular form of Lakshmi regarded as the goddess of victory.

Vijayashree ♀ Another name for VIJAYA-LAKSHMI.

Vikram ♂ Sanskrit: 'stride', 'pace', also 'heroism' or 'strength'; a byname of Vishnu, probably derived from his earlier epithet *trivikrama* 'thrice stepping', from the myth in which he encompasses the three worlds in three steps (an exploit repeated in his incarnation as Vamana, the dwarf); also the name of a historical king of Ujjain, said to have driven the Scythian invaders out of India, and possibly the founder of the Vikrama era, which began in 58 BC.

Vimal ♂ Sanskrit: 'stainless', 'pure', a name especially frequent in Buddhist literature. *Feminine form*: **Vimala** (the name of various minor goddesses, and occasionally a byname of Durga, Shiva's wife).

Vinay ♂ Sanskrit: originally meaning 'leading asunder', but later usually 'guidance', 'training' or 'education', sometimes personified as a son of Kriya (religious ritual) or of Lajja (modesty); a key term in Buddhist texts, meaning 'conduct appropriate to monks', the title of one of the three main sections of the Buddhist canon.

Vinayak ♂ Sanskrit: 'one who leads asunder', originally the name of a class of demons that cause despondency, failure, and madness, and are loosely connected with Rudra, god of destruction; later, a name of the elephant-headed god Ganesh, son of Shiva.

Vinod ♂ Sanskrit: 'driving away', hence 'diversion', 'sport', or 'pleasure'.

Vishnu ♂ Sanskrit: the name of a secondary god in the Rig-Veda, who joins Indra in slaying the demon Vrtra and drinking the divine Soma juice. Vishnu is a personification of the sun, striding the heavens in three paces. In the Epics, Vishnu becomes a supreme god and Shiva's rival. Myths of his incarnations proliferate, now usually limited to ten, including Rama of the Ramayana, Krishna, Buddha, and Kalki (who is yet to come). Of these only Rama and Krishna receive full worship as Vishnu.

Vishwanath ♂ Sanskrit: 'lord of all', a byname of Shiva.

Y

Yadav ♂ Sanskrit: 'descendant of Yadu', an epithet of Krishna.

Yashpal ♂ Sanskrit: 'protector of splendour'.

Z

Zaibunissa ♀ Muslim name, from Persian: 'woman of beauty'; the name of the eldest child (1673–1702) of the Mogul emperor Aurangzeb.

Zarina ♀ Muslim name, from Persian: 'golden'.

CHINESE NAMES

Note: Personal names in Chinese culture are very different from their English counterparts. They consist of one or two characters. In theory they can be freely chosen from the 60,000 or so characters which make up the Chinese lexicon, but in practice this is not the case, as some characters are more often chosen as names, and certain characters are more commonly associated with one or the other of the sexes. Names are often descriptive, for example *Dong*, a male name meaning 'winter', chosen partly for ornamental reasons, but often also indicating a connection with that season. A name may also represent qualities which the giver of the name, typically the grandparents or an elder in the family, hopes the bearer of the name will develop, for example *Fuhua* 'fortune', 'flourishing'. Female names of this sort often relate to beauty, flowers, fragrances, kindness, or intelligence, while male names often tend to the traditional male virtues of strength, benevolence, sharpness, uprightness, and honesty.

A

Ai ♀ 'Loving'.
Aiguo ♂ 'Love country', i.e. 'patriotic'.

B

Bai ♂ 'White'. Li Bai (701–762) was a famous Tang poet. This name is also pronounced 'Bo'.
Baozhai ♀ 'Precious hairpin'.
Bingwen ♂ 'Bright and cultivated'.
Biyu ♀ 'Jasper', a reddish-brown semiprecious stone, a type of quartz.
Bo ♂ 'Waves'. See also BAI.
Bohai ♂ 'Elder brother sea'. *Bo* is used to refer to the eldest of a group of brothers.
Bojing ♂ 'Win admiration'.
Bolin ♂ 'Elder brother rain'. For the interpretation of *Bo* see BOHAI. *Lin* denotes a continuous downpour of rain lasting several days.
Boqin ♂ 'Win respect'.

C

Changchang ♀ 'Flourishing'. The reduplication of *Chang* makes the name more intimate and familiar.

Changming ♂ 'Forever bright'.
Changpu ♂ 'Forever simple'.
Changying ♀ 'Flourishing and lustrous'.
Chao ♂ 'Surpassing'.
Chaoxiang ♂ 'Expecting fortune'.
Cheng ♂ 'Accomplished'.
Chenglei ♂ 'Become great'.
Chenguang ♀ 'Morning light'.
Chongan ♂ 'Second brother peace'. For the interpretation of *Chong* see CHONGLIN.
Chonglin ♂ 'Second brother unicorn'. *Chong* refers to the second brother in a family, while *lin* denotes a mythical beast similar to a unicorn.
Chongkun ♂ 'Second brother Kunlun mountain'. For the interpretation of *Chong* see CHONGLIN. *Kun* is short for *Kunlun*, the name of a mountain range extending across Qinghai, Tibet and Xinjiang.
Chuntao ♀ 'Spring peach'.
Chuanli ♂ 'Transmitting propriety'.
Chunhua ♀ 'Spring flower' or 'spring flourishing'.
Cuifen ♀ 'Emerald fragrance'.

D

Da ♂ 'Attainment'.
Daiyu ♀ 'Black jade'. See HUIDAI.
Dandan ♀ 'Cinnabar' or 'cinnabar red'. Cinnabar is associated with loyalty and sincerity. The reduplication of *Dan* makes it more intimate and familiar.
Delun ♂ 'Virtuous order'.
Deming ♂ 'Virtue bright'.
Dingxiang ♂ 'Stability and fortune'.
Dong ♂ **1** 'East'. **2** 'Winter'.
Donghai ♂ 'Eastern sea'.
Dongmei ♀ 'Winter plum'.
Duyi ♂ 'Independent wholeness'.

E

Ehuang ♀ 'Beauty August'. In Chinese mythology this is the name of the twin sister of Nuying; see NUYING.
Enlai ♂ 'Favour coming'. This was the given name of Premier Zhou Enlai (1899–1976).

F

Fa ♂ 'Setting off'.
Fang 1 ♂ 'Upright and honest'. **2** ♀ 'Fragrance'.
Fenfang ♀ 'Fragrant and aromatic'.

Feng ♂ **1**'Sharp blade'. **2**'Wind'.
Fengge ♂ 'Phoenix pavilion'.
Fu ♂ 'Wealthy'.
Fuhua ♂ 'Fortune flourishing'.

G

Gang ♂ 'Strength'.
Geming ♂ 'Revolution', a popular name after the founding of the People's Republic of China in 1949.
Gen ♂ 'Root'.
Guang ♂ 'Light'.
Guangli ♂ 'Making propriety bright'.
Gui ♂ 'Honoured' or 'noble'.
Guiren ♂ 'Valuing benevolence'.
Guoliang ♂ 'May the country be kind'.
Guowei ♂ 'State preserving' or perhaps 'May the state be preserved'.
Guozhi ♂ 'The state is ordered' or 'May the state be ordered'.

H

Hai ♂ 'Sea'.
He ♂ 'River'; specifically, the Yellow River.
Heng ♂ 'Eternal'.
Hong 1 ♂ 'red', the auspicious colour of weddings, also of the Communist party. **2** ♂ 'Wild swan'. **3** ♂ 'Great'.
Honghui ♂ 'Great splendour'.
Hongqi ♂ 'Red flag'.
Hualing ♀ 'Flourishing fu-ling'. Fu-ling (*Poris cocos*) is a herb used in Chinese medicine.
Huan ♀, ♂ 'Happiness'.
Hui ♂ 'Splendour'.
Huian ♂ 'Kind peace'.
Huidai ♀ 'Wise blacking'. Dai is a dark pigment, which was used by women in times past to paint their eyebrows.
Huifang ♀ 'Kind and fragrant'.
Huifen ♀ 'Wise fragrance'.
Huiliang ♀ 'Kind and good'.
Huiling ♀ 'Wise jade tinkling'. See LING.
Huiqing ♀ 'Kind and affectionate'.
Huizhong ♀ 'Wise loyalty'.
Huojin ♂ 'Fire metal'.

J

Jia ♀ 'Beautiful'.
Jian ♂ 'Healthy'.
Jiang ♂ 'River'; specifically the Yangtze.
Jianguo ♂ 'Building the country'; a common patriotic name in mainland China.

Jianjun ♂ 'Building the army'.
Jianyu ♂ 'Building the universe'.
Jiao ♀ 'Lovely' or 'dainty'.
Jiayi ♀ 'Household fitting' !
Jiaying ♀ 'Household flourishing'.
Jie ♀ 'Cleanliness'.
Jing 1 ♂ 'Capital'; used for a man born in the capital city. **2** ♀ 'Stillness'. **3** ♀ 'Luxuriance'.
Jingfei ♀ 'Still fragrance'.
Jingguo ♂ 'Administering the state'.
Jinghua ♀ 'Situation splendid'.
Jinhai ♂ 'Golden sea'.
Jinjing ♂ 'Gold mirror'.
Ju ♀ 'Chrysanthemum'.
Juan ♀ 'Graciousness'.
Junjie ♂ 'Handsome and outstanding'.

K

Kang ♂ 'Wellbeing'.

L

Lan ♀ 'Orchid'.
Lanfen ♀ 'Orchid fragrance'.
Lanying ♀ 'Indigo lustrousness'.
Lei ♂ 'Thunder'.
Li 1 ♂ 'Profit' or 'sharp'. **2** ♀, ♂ 'Upright'.
Liang ♂ 'Bright'.
Lifen ♀ 'Beautiful fragrance'.
Lihua ♀ **1**'Beautiful and flourishing'. **2**'Beautiful China'.
Lijuan ♀ 'Beautiful and graceful'.
Liling ♀ 'Beautiful jade tinkle'. See LING 2.
Lin ♀ 'Beautiful jade'. See LING 2.
Ling 1 ♀, ♂ 'understanding' and 'compassion'. **2** ♀ 'Tinkle', in particular the tinkling sound of pieces of jade hanging in the wind. For the significance of jade in Chinese culture, see also YU.
Liqin ♀ 'Beautiful zither'.
Liqiu ♀ 'Beautiful autumn'.
Liu ♀, ♂ 'Flowing'.
Liwei ♂ 'Profit and greatness'.
Longwei ♂ 'Dragon greatness'.
Luli ♀ 'Dewy jasmine'.

M

Mei ♀ 'Plum'. One of the three so-called 'friends of winter' (*dong sanyou*): plum (*mei*), pine (*song*), and bamboo (*zhu*), which stay green throughout the winter. It is also a symbol of endurance.
Meifen ♀ 'Plum fragrance'.

Meifeng ♀ 'Beautiful wind'.

Meihui ♀ 'Beautiful wisdom'.

Meili ♀ 'Beautiful'.

Meilin ♀ 'Plum jade'.

Meirong ♀ 'Beautiful countenance'.

Meixiang ♀ 'Plum fragrance'.

Meixiu ♀ 'Beautiful grace'.

Mengyao ♂ Meng is the surname of the Chinese philosopher Mencius (372–289 BC), founder of the idealist wing of Confucianism, holding that man's nature is inherently good. Yao is the name of a mythical sage emperor. This name is one of aspiration, implying the wish: 'May the child be as wise and good as Mencius and Yao.'

Mingli ♂ 'Bright propriety' or 'making propriety bright'.

Mingxia ♀ 'Bright glow'. Xia is the rosy glow seen through the clouds at dawn and dusk.

Mingyu ♀ 'Bright jade'. See YU.

Mingzhu ♀ 'Bright pearl'.

Minsheng ♂ 'Voice of the people'.

Minzhe ♂ 'Sensitive and wise'.

N

Nianzu ♂ 'Thinking of ancestors'.

Ning ♀ 'Tranquillity'.

Ninghong ♀ 'Tranquil red'; or conceivably 'rather be red'. See HONG.

Niu ♀ 'Girl'.

Nuo ♀ 'Graceful'.

Nuying ♀ 'Female flower'. In Chinese mythology this is the name of the twin sister of EHUANG, daughters of the mythical sage king Yao, and both were wives to Yao's successor in wise kingship, Shun.

P

Peijing ♀ 'Admiring luxuriance'.

Peizhi ♀ 'Admiring iris'. See XIAOZHI.

Peng ♂ 'Roc', a legendary bird. This is the given name of the Chinese premier Li Peng (b. 1928).

Pengfei ♂ 'Flight of the roc'. See PENG.

Ping ♂ 'Stable'.

Q

Qi 1 ♂ 'Wondrous'; 'enlightenment'. **2** ♀ 'Fine jade'.

Qianfan ♂ 'Thousand sails'.

Qiang 1 ♀ 'Rose'. **2** ♂ 'Strong'.

Qiao ♀ 'Skilful'.

Qiaohui ♀ 'Skilful and wise'.

Qiaolian ♀ 'Skilful always'.

Qing ♀ 'Dark blue'.

Qingge ♀ 'Clear pavilion'.

Qingling ♀ 'Celebration of understanding'.

Qingshan ♂ 'Celebrating goodness'.

Qingsheng ♂ 'Celebrating birth'.

Qingzhao ♀ 'Clear understanding' or 'clear illumination'. This was the given name of China's greatest woman poet, Li Qingzhao (1084–c.1151).

Qiqiang ♂ 'Enlightenment and strength'.

Qiu ♀,♂ 'Autumn'; given to a child born in that season.

Qiuyue ♀ 'Autumn moon'.

Quan ♂ 'Spring' (of water) as in 'hot spring'.

R

Renshu ♂ 'Benevolent forbearance'.

Renxiang ♀ 'Benevolent fragrance'.

Rong ♀,♂ 'Martial'. This is the name of Zhang Rong (Jung Chang; b. 1952), author of *Wild Swans*. Before 1949, it was almost exclusively a male name.

Rou ♀ 'Gentle' or 'mild'.

Ru ♂ 'Scholar', specifically a Confucian scholar.

Ruiling ♀ 'Auspicious jade tinkling'. See LING 2.

Ruolan ♀ 'Like an orchid'.

Ruomei ♀ 'Like a plum'. See MEI.

S

Shan 1 ♂ 'Mountain'. A symbol of greatness, achievement, and longevity. See SHOUSHAN. **2** ♀ 'Elegant bearing'.

Shanyuan ♂ 'Mountain source'.

Shaoqing ♀ 'Young blue'.

Shen ♂ **1** 'Cautious'. **2** 'Deep'.

Shi ♂ 'Horizontal front bar on a cart or carriage'. This was the given name of Su Shi, literary giant of the Song dynasty (1037–1101).

Shihong ♀ 'The world is red' or conceivably 'Let the world be red'.

Shining ♂ 'World at peace' or 'let the world be at peace'.

Shirong ♂ 'Scholarly honour'.

Shoushan ♂ 'Longevity mountain'. There are at least six Chinese mountains with this name. Two lie in Fujian province, another in Hubei province, a fourth in Shanxi province, a fifth in Zhejiang province, and a sixth in Jilin province.

Shu ♀ 'Fair'.

Shuang ♀ **1** 'Bright' or 'clear'. **2** 'Frank' or 'open-hearted'.

Shuchun ♀ 'Fair purity'.

Shun ♀ 'Smooth'.

Shunyuan ♂ 'Follow to the source'.

Siyu ♂ 'Thinking of the world'.

Song ♀ 'Pine tree'. See MEI.

Suyin ♀ 'Plain or unadorned sound', a classical expression referring to news, as in news of a person. This is the given name of the 20th-century writer Han Suyin, author of *A many-splendoured Thing* and *My house has two doors*.

T

Tao ♂ 'Great waves'.

Tengfei ♂ 'Soaring high'.

Ting ♀ 'Graceful'.

Tingguang ♂ 'Courtyard bright'. See YAOTING.

Tingfeng ♂ 'Thunderbolt peak' (perhaps a place name).

Tingzhe ♂ 'May the court be wise'.

W

Wei ♂ 'Impressive might'.

Wei ♂ 'Greatness'.

Weici ♀ 'Preserving love'. *Ci* 'love' is used of motherly love in particular.

Weimin ♂ 'Bring greatness to the people'.

Weisheng ♂ 'Greatness is born'.

Weiyuan ♂ 'Preserving depth'.

Weizhe ♂ 'Great sage' or 'greatness and sagacity'.

Wen ♀ 'Refinement'.

Wencheng ♂ 'Refinement accomplished'.

Wenling ♀ 'Refined jade tinkling'; see LING 2.

Wenqian ♀ 'Refined madder'. Madder is a type of herb whose red roots are used in the making of dyes.

Wenyan ♂ 'Refined, virtuous, and talented'.

Wuzhou ♂ 'Five continents'.

X

Xia ♀ 'Rosy clouds'. See MINGXIA.

Xiang 1 ♂ 'Circling in the air'. **2** ♀ 'Fragrant'.

Xianliang ♂ 'Worthy brightness'. Personal name of Zhang Xianliang (b. 1936), author of *Half of Man is Woman*.

Xiaobo ♂ 'Little wrestler'.

Xiaodan ♀, ♂ 'Little dawn'.

Xiaofan ♀ 'Little ordinary'.

Xiaofan ♀ 'Dawn ordinary'.

Xiaohui ♀ 'Little wisdom'.

Xiaojian ♀, ♂ 'Little healthy'.

Xiaojing ♀ 'Morning luxuriance'.

Xiaoli ♀ 'Morning jasmine'.

Xiaolian ♀ 'Little lotus'.

Xiaoling ♀ 'Morning tinkle'. See LING.

Xiaoqing ♀ 'Little blue'.

Xiaosheng ♀, ♂ 'Little birth'.

Xiaotong ♀ 'Morning redness'. See HONG.

Xiaosi ♂ 'Filial thoughts'.

Xiaowen ♀ 'Morning cloud colouring'.

Xiaozhi ♀ 'Little iris.' Zhi denotes an iris, a symbol of noble character, true friendship, or beautiful surroundings. It is also a fungus with a purplish stalk, which will keep for a long time and indicates long life and prosperity.

Xifeng ♀ 'Western phoenix'.

Xin ♂ 'New'.

Xing ♂ 'Arising'.

Xingjuan ♀ 'Propagating grace'.

Xiu ♀ 'Grace'.

Xiu ♂ 'Cultivated'.

Xiulan ♀ 'Graceful orchid'.

Xiurong ♀ 'Elegant countenance'.

Xiuying ♀ 'Graceful flower'.

Xue ♂ 'Studious'.

Xue ♀ 'Snow', symbol of whiteness, purity, and beauty in a woman.

Xueman ♀ 'Snowy grace'. See XUE.

Xueqin ♂ 'Snow-white celery'. This is the given name of China's greatest novelist, Cao Xueqin (1715–1764), author of *The Dream of Red Mansions*.

Xueyou ♂ 'Studious and friendly'.

Y

Ya ♀ 'Grace'.

Yan ♀ 'Swallow'.

Yan ♀ 'Gorgeous'.

Yang ♂ 'Model' or 'pattern'.

Yanlin ♂; also ♀ 'Swallow forest'. *Yan* 'swallow' is also an old word for Beijing, so the name may also mean 'Beijing forest', denoting a person born in Beijing.

Yanmei ♀ 'Swallow plum' or 'Beijing plum'. See YANLIN and MEI.

Yanyu ♀ 'Swallow jade' or 'Beijing jade'. See YANLIN for 'swallow' and YU for 'jade'.

Yaochuan ♂ 'Honouring the river'. *Chuan* is sometimes a shortened form of *Sichuan* (a province of west central China).

Yaoting ♂ 'Honouring the courtyard', courtyard perhaps implying 'family'.

Yaozu ♂ 'Honouring the ancestors'.

Ye ♂ 'Bright'.

Yi ♂ 'Firm and resolute'.

Ying ♀ **1** 'Clever'; a word which originally meant 'grain husk'. **2** 'Eagle'.

Yingjie ♂ 'Heroic and brave'.

Yingpei ♂ 'Should admire'.

Yingtai ♀ 'Flower terrace'.

Yong ♂ 'Brave'.

Yongliang ♂ 'Forever bright'.

Yongnian ♂ 'Eternal years'.

Yongrui ♂ 'Forever lucky'.

Yongzheng ♂ 'Forever upright'.

You ♂ 'Friend'.

Yu ♀ **1** 'Jade'. Jade is a symbol of purity, longevity, or immortality, also of feminine beauty. **2** 'Rain'.

Yuan ♀ 'Shining peace'.

Yuanjun ♂ 'Master of Yuan river'. The Yuan is a river in Hunan, provincial birthplace of Chairman Mao.

Yubi ♀ 'Jade emerald'.

Yue ♀ 'Moon'.

Yuming ♀ 'Jade brightness'. For the significance of jade, see YU.

Yun ♀ 'Cloud'.

Yunxu ♂ 'Cloudy emptiness'.

Yunru ♀ 'Charming seeming'.

Yusheng ♀, ♂ 'Jade birth'. See also LIN.

Z

Zedong ♂ 'East of the marsh'. This was the given name of Chairman Mao Zedong (1893–1976).

Zemin ♂ 'Favour to the people'. This is the given name of the president of China since 1993, Jiang Zemin.

Zengguang ♂ 'Increasing brightness'.

Zhaohui ♀ 'Clear wisdom'.

Zhen ♂ 'Shake' or 'greatly astonished'.

Zhengsheng ♂ 'May the government rise'.

Zhengzhong ♂ 'Upright and loyal'.

Zhenzhen ♀ 'Precious'. The reduplication of *Zhen* makes it more intimate and familiar.

Zhilan ♀ 'Iris orchid'. See XIAOZHI for the significance of *zhi* 'iris'.

Zhiqiang ♂ 'The will is strong' or 'may your will be strong'.

Zhong ♂ 'Loyal' or 'steadfast'.

Zhu ♀ 'Bamboo'. See MEI.

Zian ♂ 'Self peace'.

Zihao ♂ 'Son heroic'.

Zixin ♂ 'Self confidence'.

Zongmeng ♂ 'Take Mencius as a model'. See also MENGYAO.

Zongying ♀ 'Taking heroes as a model' or conceivably 'taking flowers as a model,' as *ying* denotes either flowers or heroes.

APPENDIX 9:

JAPANESE NAMES

Note: Most Japanese personal names are written using combinations of one, two, or three Chinese characters. In English transcription, many names may have dozens of possible meanings, because several different Japanese characters can have the same pronunciation. Also, a single character can have more than one pronunciation and meaning. Often, characters are used phonetically to 'spell' a name, with no regard to meaning, and puns are common. Only the one or two most common meanings can be given here. From the mid-20th century onwards, female names tended to have the suffix *-ko* ('child'). Recently, that suffix has begun to disappear again, as people mimic the naming habits of popular entertainers. Female names of western origin are becoming popular, usually written in the *kana* syllabary instead of Chinese characters.

A

Aika ♀ 'Love song'.

Aiko ♀ 'Loving or beloved child'.

Akemi ♀ 'Bright beauty'.

Aki ♂, ♀ 'Autumn'; 'bright'; also short for any name beginning with *Aki*-.

Akihiko ♂ 'Bright or shining prince'.

Akihiro ♂ 'Shining abroad'; 'bright scholar'.

Akiko ♀ 'Bright child'; 'child [born in] autumn'.

Akio ♂ 'Bright man'.

Akira ♂, ♀ 'Clear'; 'bright'; 'dawn'.

Anna ♀ Japanese adoption of the English name. See main dictionary.

Arisu ♀ Japanese version of the English name ◊**Alice**.

Asami ♀ 'Morning beauty'.

Atsuko ♀ 'Warm child'; 'industrious child'.
Atsushi ♂ 'Cordial'; 'industrious'.
Ayako ♀ 'Literary or scholarly child'.
Ayumi ♀ 'Stroll'.
Azumi ♀ 'Safe residence'.

B

Bunko ♀ 'Literary or scholarly child'.

C

Chiasa ♀ 'One thousand mornings'.
Chie ♀ 'Wisdom'; 'thousand blessings'.
Chieko ♀ 'Wise child'; 'thousand blessings child'.
Chiharu ♀ 'One thousand springs'.
Chisato ♂ 'Sagacious'.

D

Daisuke ♂ 'Great helper'.

E

Eiji ♂ 'Splendid ruler'; 'excellent second [son]'.
Eiko ♀ 'Splendid child'; 'long-lived child'.
Emi ♀ 'Smile'.
Emiko ♀ 'Smiling child'.
Eri ♀ 'Blessed prize'.
Erika ♀ Japanese version of the English name ◊**Erica**. See main dictionary. This name is usually written in *kana*, although it is sometimes also written with characters meaning 'blessed prize increasing'.
Etsuko ♀ 'Joyful child'.

F

Fuji ♀ 'Wisteria'. Resemblance to the name of Mount Fuji is mostly coincidental, but in some cases both meanings could be intended.
Fumiko ♀ 'Child of treasured beauty'; 'literary or scholarly child'.
Fumio ♂ 'Literary or scholarly man'.

H

Hanako ♀ 'Flower child'.
Hajime ♂ 'Beginning'.
Haruki ♀ 'Springtime tree'.
Haruko ♀ 'Springtime child'.
Harumi ♀ 'Springtime beauty'.
Haruo ♂ 'Springtime man'.

Hideaki ♂ 'Splendid brightness'; 'shining excellence'.
Hideki ♂ 'Splendid opportunity'. The most famous bearer was Tōjō Hideki (1884–1948), prime minister during the Second World War.
Hideko ♀ 'Splendid child'.
Hideo ♂ 'Splendid man'.
Hiro ♂, ♀ 'Widespread'; 'broad'; also short for any name beginning with *hiro*.
Hiroaki ♂ 'Widespread brightness'.
Hiroki ♂ 'Abundant joy'; 'abundant strength'.
Hiroko ♀ 'Generous child'; 'prosperous child'.
Hiromi ♂, ♀ 'Wide-seeing'; 'widespread beauty'.
Hiroshi ♂ 'Abundant'; 'widespread'.
Hiroyuki ♂ 'Widespread happiness'.
Hisako ♀ 'Long-lived child'.
Hisao ♂ 'Long-lived man'.
Hisashi ♂ 'Long-lived'.
Hitomi ♀ 'Pupil' (of the eye), given to girls with especially beautiful eyes.
Hitoshi ♂ 'Level'; 'even [tempered]'.

I

Ichirō ♂ 'First son'.
Isamu ♂ 'Courageous'; 'warrior'.
Isao ♂ 'Merit'; 'honour'.
Iwao ♂ 'Stone man'.

J

Jirō ♂ 'Second son'.
Jun ♂, ♀ 'Obedient'; as a female case, possibly referring to the English name ◊**June** (see main dictionary).
Jun'ichi ♂ 'Obedience first'; 'purity first'.
Junko ♀ 'Obedient child'; 'pure child'.

K

Kaori ♀ 'Fragrance'.
Kaoru ♀ 'Fragrance'.
Katsumi ♀ 'Victorious beauty'.
Kayo ♀ 'Beautiful generation'; 'increasing generation'.
Kazue ♀ 'First blessing'; 'harmonious branch'.
Kazuhiko ♂ 'Harmonious prince'; 'first prince'.
Kazuhiro ♂ 'Harmony widespread'.
Kazuko ♀ 'Harmonious child'.
Kazumi ♀ 'Harmonious beauty'.

Kazuo ♂ 'Harmonious man'.

Kei ♀ 'Respectful'; also possibly a Japanese version of the English name ◊**Kay** (see main dictionary).

Keiichi ♂ 'Respectful first [son]'.

Keiji ♂ 'Respectful second [son]'.

Keiko ♀ 'Blessed child'; 'respectful child'.

Ken'ichi ♂ 'First builder'; 'govern first'.

Kenji ♂ 'Intelligent ruler'.

Kiku ♀ 'Chrysanthemum'.

Kimi ♀ Short for any name beginning with *Kimi-*.

Kimiko ♀ 'Ruling child'; 'dear child'; 'beautiful history child'.

Kiyoko ♀ 'Pure child'.

Kiyomi ♀ 'Pure beauty'.

Kiyoshi ♂ 'Pure'; 'saintly'. A famous bearer is the actor Atsumi Kiyoshi, but the name was popular before he became well known.

Kōichi ♂ 'Widespread first [son]'; 'shining first [son]'.

Kōji ♂ 'Filial ruler'; 'happy second [son]'.

Kumiko ♀ 'Long-lived, beautiful child'.

Kunio ♂ 'Countryman'.

Kyōko ♀ 'Child of the capital city'.

M

Madoka ♂, ♀ 'Tranquil'.

Maiko ♀ 'Dancing child'.

Maki ♀ 'True record'; 'true tree'.

Makoto ♂ 'True'.

Mamoru ♂ 'Protect'.

Mana ♀ 'True'.

Manabu ♂ 'Studious'.

Mari ♀ Japanese version of the English name ◊**Mary**. See main dictionary.

Maria ♀ Japanese version of the European name ◊**Maria**. See main dictionary, also Spanish and Italian supplements.

Mariko ♀ 'True reason child'.

Masa ♂, ♀ Short for any name beginning with *Masa-*.

Masaaki ♂ 'Correct brightness'.

Masahiko ♂ 'Correct prince'.

Masahiro ♂ 'Govern widely'.

Masaki ♂ 'Elegant tree'; 'correct record'.

Masako ♀ 'Governing child'; 'correct child'. The most famous bearer of the name was Hōjō Masako (1157–1225), wife of the Shōgun Minamoto Yoritomo, who ruled Japan from behind the scenes after her husband's death.

Masami ♀ 'Elegant beauty'; 'correct beauty'.

Masanori ♂ 'Correct principles'; 'prosperous government'.

Masao ♂ 'Correct man'.

Masaru ♂ 'Victorious'; 'intelligent'.

Masashi ♂ 'Correct'; 'splendid official'.

Masato ♂ 'Elegant man'; 'correct man'.

Masayoshi ♂ 'Govern righteously'; 'shining goodness'.

Masayuki ♂ 'Correct happiness'.

Masumi ♀ 'True purity'; 'increasing beauty'.

Mayumi ♀ 'True intent beauty'; 'true bow' (as in archery).

Megumi ♀ 'Blessing'.

Michi ♂, ♀ 'Pathway'.

Michiko ♀ 'Child on the [correct] path'; 'thousand beauties child'.

Michio ♂ 'Man on the [correct] path'.

Midori ♀ 'Verdant'.

Mieko ♀ 'Beautiful blessing child'.

Miho ♀ 'Beautiful bay'. The Miho pine grove in Shimizu City is famous for its view of Mount Fuji.

Mika ♀ 'Beautiful fragrance'.

Miki ♀ 'Three trees'; 'beautiful tree'.

Mikio ♂ 'Tree trunk man'; implying one who will have many descendants.

Minori ♂, ♀ 'Beautiful harbor'; 'village of beautiful fields'.

Minoru ♂ 'Ear of grain'; 'fruitful'.

Mitsuko ♀ 'Shining child'; 'child full [of blessings]'.

Mitsuo ♂ 'Shining man'; 'third male [son]'.

Mitsuru ♂ 'Full'; 'growing'.

Miwa ♀ 'Three rings'; 'beautiful harmony'. Mount Miwa is a sacred hill in Nara Prefecture.

Miyoko ♀ 'Beautiful generation child'; 'child [of the] third generation'.

Miyuki ♀ 'Happiness'; 'beautiful happiness'.

Momo ♀ 'Peach'.

Momoe ♀ 'Hundred blessings'; 'hundred rivers'; popularized in the 1970s as the name of the singer Yamaguchi Momoe.

N

Nana ♀ 'Seven'; often given to girls born on the seventh day of the seventh month.

Nao ♂, ♀ 'Honest'; also short for any name beginning with *Nao-*.

Naoki ♀ 'Honest tree'; 'honest joy'.

Naoko ♀ 'Honest child'.

Natsuko ♀ 'Summer child'.

Natsumi ♀ 'Summer beauty'.

Noboru ♂ 'Climb'; 'ascend'; 'virtuous'.
Nobuko ♀ 'Faithful child'.
Nobuo ♂ 'Faithful man'.
Nobuyuki ♂ 'Faithful happiness'.
Nori ♂, ♀ Short for any name beginning with *Nori-*.
Noriko ♀ 'Child of principles'.
Norio ♂ 'Man of principles'.

O

Osamu ♂ 'Ruler'.

R

Reiko ♀ 'Courteous child'; 'beautiful child'.
Rie ♀ 'Valued blessing'.
Rika ♀ 'Valued fragrance'.
Rina ♀ Japanese version of the English name ◊**Lena**. See main dictionary.
Risa ♀ Japanese version of the English name ◊**Lisa**. See main dictionary.
Ryōko ♀ 'Good child'.

S

Saburō ♂ 'Third son'.
Sachiko ♀ 'Happy child'.
Sadao ♂ 'Decisive man'.
Sakiko ♀ 'Earlier child' (given in the hope of more children), 'blossoming child'.
Sara ♀ Japanese version of the English name ◊**Sara(h)**. See main dictionary.
Sari ♀ Japanese version of the English name ◊**Sally**. See main dictionary.
Satoru ♂ 'Enlightened'; from the Japanese word for *nirvana*.
Satoshi ♂ 'Wise'; 'quick-witted'; 'clear [thinking]'.
Seiichi ♂ 'Admonishing first [son]'; 'pure first [son]'.
Seiji ♂ 'Admonishing second [son]'; 'pure second [son]'.
Setsuko ♀ 'Temperate child'.
Shig ♂, ♀ Short for any name beginning with *Shige-*.
Shigeko ♀ 'Luxuriant child'.
Shigeo ♂ 'Luxuriant man'.
Shigeru ♂ 'Luxuriant'; 'excellent'.
Shin'ichi ♂ 'Faithful first [son]'.
Shinji ♂ 'Faithful second [son]'.
Shiori ♀ 'Bookmark'; 'guide'.
Shirō ♂ 'Fourth son'.
Shizuko ♀ 'Quiet child'.
Shōichi ♂ 'Prosperous first [son]'; 'correct first [son]'.

Shōji ♂ 'Shining second [son]'; 'correct second [son]'.
Shūichi ♂ 'Governing first [son]'; 'excellent first [son]'.
Shūji ♂ 'Governing second [son]'; 'excellent second [son]'.
Sumiko ♀ 'Clear [thinking] child'; 'pure child'.
Susumu ♂ 'Progressing'.

T

Tadao ♂ 'Loyal man'.
Tadashi ♂ 'Correct'; 'loyal'; 'righteous'.
Takahiro ♂ 'Abundantly filial'; 'widespread nobility'.
Takako ♀ 'Filial child'; 'noble child'; 'high child'.
Takao ♂ 'Filial man'; 'noble man'; 'high man'.
Takashi ♂ 'Praiseworthy'; 'filial official'.
Takayuki ♂ 'Noble'; 'filial happiness'.
Takeo ♂ 'Warrior'.
Takeshi ♂ 'Warrior'; 'fierce'.
Tamotsu ♂ 'Protect'; 'complete'.
Tarō ♂ 'Great son'; name given only to a first son.
Tatsuo ♂ 'Dragon man'; the dragon is believed to be wise and long-lived.
Tatsuya ♂ 'Become dragon' [and possess its virtues].
Teruko ♀ 'Shining child'.
Teruo ♂ 'Shining man'.
Tetsuo ♂ 'Clear [thinking] man'; 'iron man'.
Tetsuya ♂ 'Clear evening'; 'become iron'.
Tomiko ♀ 'Treasured child'; 'treasured beauty child'.
Tomio ♂ 'Treasured man'.
Tomoko ♀ 'Friendly child'; 'wise child'.
Tōru ♂ 'Wayfarer'; 'penetrating [mind]'.
Toshi ♂, ♀ 'Alert': not usually used by itself, but often as a short form for names beginning with *Toshi-*.
Toshiaki ♂ 'Ripe brightness'; 'alert and bright'.
Toshiko ♀ 'Alert child'; 'valued child'; 'child of [many] years'.
Toshio ♂ 'Alert man'; 'valued man'; 'man of genius'.
Toshiyuki ♂ 'Alert and happy'.
Tsuneo ♂ 'Common man'.
Tsutomu ♂ 'Worker'.
Tsuyoshi ♂ 'Strong'.

Y

Yasuhiro ♂ 'Abundant honesty'; 'widespread peace'.

Yasuko ♀ 'Honest child'; 'peaceful child'.

Yasuo ♂ 'Honest man'; 'peaceful man'.

Yasushi ♂ 'Honest'; 'peaceful'.

Yayoi ♀ 'Spring'; from a traditional name for the third lunar month, corresponding approximately to April. This is also the name of a district in Tokyo where important prehistoric archaeological artifacts from the period c. 300 BC–AD 300 were first discovered.

Yōichi ♂ 'Masculine first [son]'.

Yōko ♀ 'Positive child'; 'ocean child'.

Yoshi ♂, ♀ 'Good'; also short for any name beginning with Yoshi-.

Yoshiaki ♂ 'Righteous glory'; 'shining luck'.

Yoshie ♀ 'Fragrant branch'; 'good bay'.

Yoshihiro ♂ 'Widespread goodness'.

Yoshikazu ♂ 'Righteous first [son]'; 'good and harmonious'.

Yoshiko ♀ 'Good child'; 'fragrant child'; 'noble child'.

Yoshinori ♂ 'Noble virtue'; 'righteous principles'.

Yoshio ♂ 'Good man'.

Yoshito ♂ 'Good man'; 'lucky man'.

Yoshiyuki ♂ 'Righteous happiness'.

Yūichi ♂ 'Courageous first [son]'; 'friendly first [son]'.

Yūji ♂ 'Second male'; 'courageous second [son]'.

Yuka ♀ 'Fragrant'; 'friendly blossom'.

Yuki ♂, ♀ 'Happiness'; 'snow'; also short for any name beginning with Yuki-.

Yukiko ♀ 'Happy child'.

Yukio ♂ 'Happy man'.

Yūko ♀ 'Helpful or superior child'.

Yumi ♀ 'Bow' (as in archery); 'helpful beauty'; also short for any name beginning with Yumi-.

Yumiko ♀ 'Helpful, beautiful child'.

Yūna ♀ Possibly a Japanese version of the Irish name ◊**Una**. See main dictionary.

Yuri ♀ 'Lily'.

Yuriko ♀ 'Prized child'; 'lily child'.

Yutaka ♂ 'Abundant'; 'prosperous'.